The Myth of the JEWISH RACE

The Myth of the JEWISH RACE

Revised Edition

RAPHAEL PATAI
and
JENNIFER PATAI

WAYNE STATE UNIVERSITY PRESS DETROIT 1989

93 92 91 90 89   5 4 3 2 1

Manufactured in the United States of America.

Library of Congress Cataloging-in-Publication Data
Patai, Raphael, 1910–
   The myth of the Jewish race.

   Includes index.
   1. Jews. I. Patai, Jennifer, 1942–   . II. Title.
GN547.P37 1989   305.8'924   88–27721
ISBN 0–8143–1948–3 (alk. paper)
ISBN 0–8143–1949–1 (pbk. : alk. paper)

ACKNOWLEDGMENT
   Columbia University Press for the statistical table on
page 48 from *A Social and Religious History of the Jews* by
Salo W. Baron. Copyright © 1967 by Columbia University
Press. Used by permission.

   For photographs numbers 1 to 24, 26 to 31, 33 to 51, 57
to 69, 73 to 81, and 100 the authors are indebted to El Al
Israel Airlines. All individuals shown on these pictures are
or were El Al employees.
   Pictures numbers 32a to c, 53a to c, 72a to c, 82a to 86c,
88a to 98c were taken by the late Dr. Erich Brauer of the
Hebrew University, Jerusalem, in the late 1930's and early
1940's in Jerusalem. They were kindly put at our disposal
by the Israel Ethnographic Society.
   Pictures numbers 70, 71, 99, and 101 are published here
by courtesy of the Zionist Archives and Library, New York.
   Pictures numbers 25a to c, 52a to b, and 87a to c were
taken by R. Patai.

To Benjamin and Jessica

Contents

Preface to the Revised Edition

W E WELCOME THE initiative of Wayne State University Press to publish a revised edition of this book, which has been out of print for several years. The first edition, published in 1975 by Scribner's, was enthusiastically received by a wide public, pronounced an important contribution by many reviewers, and earned the prestigious Anisfield-Wolf Award given to the best book on race relations. Since its publication, two disparate developments took place that made it necessary to add a considerable amount of new material to the book. These additions are of two kinds:

1. Part II was supplemented by a chapter titled "The Latest Libel: The Jew as Racist," which discusses the attacks launched in the 1970's against Zionism and the State of Israel, accusing them, and by implication the Jews and Judaism in general, of racism. Although these attacks were politically inspired, their effect was more psychological than political: they made many non-Jews, and even some Jews and Israelis, take a negative view of Israel, Zionism, the Jewish religion, and the Jewish people as a whole. Thus, within a generation after the holocaust, in which six million Jews were exterminated for no other reason than their alleged membership in the "Jewish race," the Jews of Israel and of the Diaspora are again forced into a position where they must defend themselves against the old libel with a new twist: not only are they pronounced an evil race, as the Nazis taught, but a race that holds itself superior and practices racial discrimination against other races that it considers inferior. Since the 1975 United Nations resolution that equated Zionism with racism, the issue has been kept alive by annual Arab attempts to oust Israel from the United Nations, and by such crude efforts as those of the Iranian Embassy in Bra-

zil, which circulated in 1987 a reprint of the infamous nineteenth-century forgery known as the "Protocols of the Elders of Zion." We believed that in view of this new virulence of racist anti-Semitism the issue of the Jews as racists has a definite bearing on the subject of our book. Hence the addition of a chapter on this latest libel, presenting its extent and implications, which endow with added importance the dissemination of the basic thesis of our book—that the Jews are not a race, and hence, because of this fact alone (and there are many other weighty factors involved) cannot be racists.

2. Part III has been rewritten and greatly expanded by presenting an overview and the results of the very energetic research activity of the last dozen years in Jewish genetics. This is reflected in the number of the tables and of source references. The first edition contained 18 tables and listed 67 source references; the present edition contains 28 tables and 107 source references. The discussion in almost every chapter in this part has been expanded to take into account the newly available data, including studies dealing with the frequencies found among Jews and non-Jews of several alleles that have been published in the intervening twelve years. Similarly, the chapter "'Jewish' Diseases" includes an augmented discussion of these phenomena and presents new data on several diseases that have only recently become the subject of scholarly investigation. As a result of this rich new material Part III has increased from its length of 130 pages in the first edition to its present length of 211 pages. For all practical purposes, this part of the book is entirely new compared with the first edition.

Despite the much richer data basis in the present edition, we found no reason to change the conclusions we reached twelve years ago: the genetic data continue to harmonize with the data assembled in the historical-cultural parts of the book. Both types of data point to the occurrence of substantial modifications in the racial identity of the original biblical Children of Israel, which itself is still overshadowed by a great question mark. The Jewish sojourn in a constantly expanding global Diaspora for some two and a half millennia resulted in an increasing diversification that, by the outgoing Middle Ages, reached a stage at which the Jewish people, whatever their historical antecedents and the power of their cultural and religious traditions that sustained them, could no longer be considered members of a single race. In a word: to be a Jew has for long not been a question of genes, but of a mind-set.

Preface to the First Edition

PRIOR TO THE present volume only one book was available in English on the question of the Jewish "race": Dr. Maurice Fishberg's *The Jews: A Study in Race and Environment,* which was published jointly in 1911 by Charles Scribner's Sons of New York and the Walter Scott Publishing Company of London.[1] In the sixty-three years that have elapsed since, the physical anthropology of the Jews has been the subject of numerous studies reported in journal articles. More importantly, methods and approaches of the new science of genetics, developed since World War I, have been applied to the Jews, and a considerable number of surveys, comparing Jewish and non-Jewish groups with respect to various serological and other genetic features, have been carried out and reported in scholarly literature. These developments have brought about a new understanding of the genetic relationship between the Jews and their non-Jewish neighbors. A re-examination of the question of the Jewish "race" thus seemed to be called for.

Another development that has taken place in the two generations since Fishberg published his book has been the intensification of the study of Jewish history. As a result of the work of modern Jewish historians, we know much more today about the history of the Jews in general and in individual countries in particular than we did before World War I. A part of this deeper and broader knowledge stems from the amassing of numerous case histories and details concerning proselytism, intermarriage, slavery, concubinage, and the like, all of which contribute to our knowledge of non-Jewish genetic influences on the Jews.

A third factor which lends special poignancy to a discussion of the problem of whether or not the Jews constitute a race consists of the great

1

historical events that have taken place in Jewish life in the last generation. During the years of World War II some 6 million Jews were slaughtered by the Germans and their satellites, who claimed that the Jews were an inferior and evil race which must be exterminated for the benefit of the Aryan master race. In 1948, the State of Israel was founded and has since absorbed close to 2 million Jewish immigrants from the four corners of the earth. This "in-gathering of the exiles" brought together in Israel numerous Jewish ethnic groups which so obviously and unmistakably belonged to different "races" that their very juxtaposition in one small country seemed to relegate the view that the Jews constitute a single human race to the realm of myth. At the same time, the very presence in Israel of numerous disparate Jewish ethnic groups has produced serious cultural clashes bearing many of the hallmarks of "racial" friction, or at least perceived as such by those directly involved in them. It would be tragic indeed if the Jews, after having been reduced to almost one-half their number by the Nazi racist madness, now encountered the specter of racism within their own ranks in Israel.

The holocaust and the establishment of Israel—events of unparalleled magnitude in Jewish history—point up the importance of the racial question for the Jews in the recent past and at present. It is hoped that this book will contribute in some measure to a proper understanding of what the intra-Jewish ethnic differences in Israel and elsewhere actually are: the results of physical, cultural, and psychical influences absorbed by the Jews in all countries of the Diaspora, and hence not permanent, immutable traits but features which can be molded and changed, albeit not without difficulties and patient, painstaking, and sustained effort.

This work attempts to approach the question of the Jewish race from every angle which might contribute to its understanding. After a brief review of the several (often diametrically opposed) views held on the issue by past scholars, the first chapters present historical data bearing on the basic question of Jewish-Gentile race mixture in the course of more than three thousand years of documented Hebrew-Jewish history. These chapters consider, in particular, the extent and probable effects on the Jews as a genetic entity of Jewish proselytism, Jewish-Gentile intermarriage, concubinage, other forms of extramarital sexual intercourse, and slavery. Although the available information on these subjects leaves much to be desired, the volume of data is still considerable.

The racial identity of any human group has not only a physical but also a psychological dimension. The question of whether or not the Jews constitute a race psychologically has occasioned much discussion. In fact, in the racist writings of the nineteenth century and the Nazi era, in which the racial specificity of the Jews was taken for granted, much more attention was devoted to the psychological aspects of the Jewish "race" than to the physical. For this reason, as well as for several others, it seemed necessary to discuss the question of whether or not there exists such a thing as a "Jewish mind," different from the Gentile mind and typical of Jews everywhere. However, the complexity of the issues involved meant that this could be given only a rather sketchy treatment here.

The biological-genetic part which concludes the book aims to present all the available serological, medical, and anthropometric data that bear on the topic. It examines both the degree of variation in measurable genetic features among different Jewish groups or communities, and the similarities and differences of these same features between Jews and non-Jews in various places. Ultimately, these genetic and serological data supply the concrete evidence as to the present-day "racial" composition of Jewish communities all over the world. The fact that the two types of data—the historical and the genetic—collected and interpreted independently, yielded results which confirm each other, gave no small measure of satisfaction to both authors.

In conclusion, the authors wish to express their thanks to all the institutions and individuals who helped them in producing this book, and in particular to:

Miss Annette Bruhwiler, director of the library of Fairleigh Dickinson University at Rutherford, New Jersey, and her staff; Mr. Leonard S. Gold, chief of the Jewish Division, New York Public Library; Mlle Madeleine Neige, chief of the Service Hébraïque of the Bibliothèque Nationale of Paris; the staff of the libraries of the Hebrew University of Jerusalem, the Tel Aviv University, and Yale University; and to Professor William H. Wing for his help in mathematical analysis of the genetic data and a critical review of the entire genetic part. Special thanks are also due to the Lucius N. Littauer Foundation of New York and its president, Mr. Harry Starr, for a generous grant which enabled the authors to devote the requisite time to research in the libraries of three continents and to the writing of this book.

Note on the Illustrations

FOR OBVIOUS REASONS, the photographs printed in the picture section (following p. 262) are not a true representative sample of all the physical types found among the Jews around the globe. Thus, it so happens that none of them shows a person with red hair, although a certain percentage of Ashkenazi Jews (i.e., European Jews outside the Mediterranean area) do, in fact, have red or reddish hair color. The pictures taken by the late Dr. Erich Brauer did not carry a notation as to hair and eye color; hence no such identification could be included in their captions. However, since almost all the Brauer photographs have Middle Eastern Jews as subjects, it can be taken for granted that their hair and eye colors range from dark brown to black. Despite these limitations, the sixteen-page picture supplement should prove useful in illustrating the marked variety of Jewish physical types which is discussed in some detail in the text.

Introduction

"Jew: a person of the Hebrew race."
—Oxford English Dictionary

T HE SYSTEMATIC EXTERMINATION of 6 million Jews by Nazi Germany and its satellites was the culmination of the notion that the Jews were a race, with distinct inherited physical and mental characteristics, alien to the Gentile population in whose midst they lived, and overtly or secretly inimical to it. Modern European racial anti-Semitism, which in the years of World War II led to the largest genocide ever perpetrated, is a special subvariety of a generic phenomenon known as "racism," which was characterized by Ashley Montagu as "a malfunctioning of the mind which endangers human relations, a disease due to the infection of the mind by false ideas concerning the status of other groups of human beings." [1] In more restrained terms, S. L. Washburn in his presidential address to the American Anthropological Association stressed that "racism is based on a profound misunderstanding of culture, of learning, and of the biology of the human species." [2] The intrinsic connection between racism and racial anti-Semitism makes it necessary that we introduce our study of the problem of the Jewish "race" by a brief discussion of the origin and phenomenology of racism in general and of racial anti-Semitism in particular.

RACISM AND SLAVERY

The race concept itself, which underlies the disease of racism, is of relatively recent origin. Only in the nineteenth century did the idea gain currency that mankind was divided into numerous groups, each with a complement of physical and mental traits which were genetically determined and which set it apart from other such groups. Among several European peoples

5

this popular concept of race became bound up with the conviction that the ingroup constituted the superior or "master" race of mankind, and that the greater the "racial" differences between it and a given outgroup, the more inferior the outgroup was. Racial superiority, moreover, was somehow identified with the notion of the "purity" of the blood—itself a heritage from past ages. In the Nazi German ideology, the blood of the outgroups or the inferior races was considered "impure," and as such capable of defiling the blood of the master race.

The most frightening thing about racism was, and is, that once its virus lodges in the mind it dims perception to the degree of making all persons appear not primarily as individual human beings but as members of a race. If an individual is perceived as belonging to a different race, he is stereotyped as an alien, almost like a creature from another galaxy in modern science fiction, and as such an enemy whose capture, enslavement, immobilization, or murder lies in "our" interest. To the diseased racist mind there is, therefore, no such thing as mankind; there are only disparate races which, whenever they encounter one another, are destined to enter into a deadly struggle whose foreordained outcome is the victory of the master race.

The pages of history are full of unspeakable atrocities committed by members of one human group against another solely as a result of apparent physical differences. Such differences, to be sure, have not been the only basis for man's inhumanity to man. Differences in religion, language, and politics also provided the impetus and the justification for the persecution or even annihilation of weaker groups. But in these cases, the members of a persecuted group at least had a chance to save their lives by adopting the faith, the speech, or the views of their enemies, to dissimulate or assimilate. No such escape existed for groups which were hounded because they differed in physical features, because they were perceived as "racially" different. In a racial conflict situation it did not matter much whether the physical differences were real or imagined. An individual or a group *believed* to be physically alien was marked as expendable and doomed.

Like many another phenomenon in human history which reached full fruition in modern times, racism was adumbrated, albeit not too clearly, in earlier periods. Millennia ago, in the Ancient Near East, each group was considered descended from separate single ancestors whose inclinations, talents, and other characteristics they were supposed to have inherited—a concept not identical with, but unmistakably akin to, the racial idea. Traces of this view have been preserved in the Bible, and especially in the early chapters of Genesis. Just as all the Children of Israel were considered the descendants of Jacob (who was also named Israel), all the Edomites those of Esau (also called Edom), and so forth, so "all such as handle the harp and pipe" were held to be the sons of Jubal, and all those who were "forgers of

6

every cutting instrument of brass and iron" were regarded as the sons of Tubal-cain.[3]

Approaching the issue from different premises, Aristotle came close to a racist view when he elaborated the idea that there existed mental and physical differences between those who "are by nature free" and those who "are by nature slaves": "The intention of nature therefore is to make the bodies also of freemen and of slaves different—the latter strong for necessary service, the former erect and unserviceable for such occupations but serviceable for a life of citizenship. . . ." [4] Since the Greek freemen came of one genetic stock and the Greek slaves of another, the differences Aristotle postulated between the physical and mental traits of the free Greeks and their slaves do lend themselves to a racial interpretation.

Speeding ahead through the centuries we find that Masudi (Abu 'l-Ḥasan 'Alī ibn Ḥusayn al-Mas'ūdī), the early medieval Arab traveler, geographer, and historian, made some observations on the physical and mental characteristics of the Negroes. Quoting Galen, the second-century Greek physician, and the ninth-century Arab philosopher Ya'qūb b. Isḥāq al-Kindī, Masudi asserted that the Negroes were characterized by the weakness of their brains, which resulted in a weakness of intellect, levity, excitability, and emotionalism. This opinion was criticized by Ibn Khaldūn (1332–1406), the greatest Arab historian, who explained that while indeed "the Negroes are in general characterized by levity, excitability and great emotionalism, . . . are eager to dance whenever they hear a melody," and "are everywhere described as stupid," these traits were due to the hot zone of the earth in which they lived.[5] Here we have a prefiguration of the two competing hypotheses developed in the nineteenth century to explain apparent racial differences: the genetic and the environmental theories.

Throughout the Middle Ages Negroes remained on the periphery of European consciousness, more objects of curiosity than subjects of either scholarly or popular consideration. This situation changed in the middle of the fifteenth century, when the Portuguese embarked on the African slave trade in earnest, a move facilitated—indeed, officially sanctioned—by Pope Nicholas V's issuance of a decree approving the subjugation of the infidels to Christians. After the discovery of America, a papal bull issued by Alexander VI in 1493 encouraged the Spanish to subdue the natives of the newly discovered lands and bring them to the Catholic faith. Thereafter, the subjugation, exploitation, and enslavement of the natives of Africa and the New World was justified by two authorities: the most admired Greek philosopher, Aristotle, and the Catholic Church.

By the seventeenth century, slavery was a thoroughly entrenched institution in Europe as well as in America. The attacks upon it on moral, humanistic, religious, or any other grounds were still to come. Although the discovery of the far corners of the globe, and hence of the most remote variants of mankind, proceeded apace, all savants (with one or two notable exceptions) still believed in the biblical story of Adam and Eve as the original progenitors of the entire human family. Whatever apparent disparities among various human groups came to the attention of Europeans were explained—as Ibn Khaldūn had postulated—as having resulted from long sojourn in widely differing climates. Leibniz, the great German mathematician and philosopher, summed up the prevalent view at the end of the seventeenth century: ". . . there is no reason why all men who inhabit the earth should not be of the same race, which has been altered by different climates. . . ." [6]

However, by the turn of the century new views started to emerge. In the early eighteenth century, the idea began to spread that humanity comprised several genetically unconnected racial groups. The newly discovered strange inhabitants of the Pacific and other areas created an increasing interest in the variability of mankind, which now proved greater than ever before envisaged. In the meantime the African slave trade, with the active participation of the Arabs as middlemen, assumed large proportions. By 1776 there were more than half a million slaves in the thirteen American colonies; before the slave shipments were discontinued in the nineteenth century, close to 15 million Negroes had been imported from Africa to the New World. [7]

From the middle of the eighteenth century, numerous weighty voices were raised against the theory of innate racial differences which had become the tacit assumption underlying and justifying slavery. The great scholarly forerunners and protagonists of the Enlightenment, Montesquieu, Buffon, and Rousseau in France, Herder, Blumenbach, and the two Humboldts in Germany, as well as others, all went on record in opposition to the idea that mankind was divided into races which differed from one another in origin. [8] The libertarian principles which came to the fore in the French Revolution also led in a direction hostile to slavery.

Even this impressive chorus of scholarly, philosophical, and political opinion, however, could not silence those whose economic interests lay with slavery. They reiterated their conviction that the races from which the slaves were recruited were inferior, and, misreading or misinterpreting the opinions of the savants, argued that racial differences being what they were it was proper and just, as well as rightful, to purchase and keep slaves. Thus, where Buffon spoke of the various "races" of mankind, using the term as a convenient designation of the populations of given localities while describing them in quasi-zoological terms, he was popularly misinterpreted as teaching that there existed an actual natural separation of the "races" of man. [9] Racists were most inclined to attribute—as Masudi did in the tenth and eleventh century—specific characteristics of the Negro slaves to their racial origin.

They spoke of the racial basis for the benightedness and indolence of the slaves, using characteristics which developed in response to the condition of slavery itself to justify an institution which was enormously lucrative for the masters.

Nevertheless, it was inevitable that once slavery became a subject of controversy it was only a question of time before it was abolished. The slaves were liberated in England in 1833, in Sweden in 1846, in France and Denmark in 1848, in Holland in 1860, and in the United States in 1865. At present, while de facto slavery still exists in the Arabian Peninsula, the institution is outlawed all over the earth. The abolition of slavery, however, remained a far cry from the disappearance of racism, against which the fight still has to be carried on in many countries. How deeply the racialist disease was embedded in the minds of millions of Europeans even in the middle of the present century was demonstrated by the fate of the Jews in Germany and her satellites during World War II.

RACISM AND ANTI-SEMITISM

When the French Revolution made religious liberty something of a new dogma in European thought, it became outmoded to base one's dislike of the Jews on their religious separatism; the new scholarly vogue of making a racial distinction among peoples was seized upon to justify anti-Jewish feelings. This changeover from the traditional medieval religious anti-Semitism to modern racial anti-Semitism was facilitated by the development in the first half of the nineteenth century of the scholarly distinction between "Semitic" and "Aryan" peoples. Originally, the differentiation between the two was a linguistic one; it was in this sense that the terms were first used in the late eighteenth century. Soon, however, the designations acquired a racial connotation, which resulted in numerous scholarly essays attempting psychological characterizations of the two "races." One of the first to draw a character picture of the "Semites" was Christian Lassen (1800–1876), a professor at Bonn, who in 1844 made the pronouncement:

> History proves that the Semites do not possess the harmonious proportion of all psychical forces which distinguishes the Indo-Germanics. The Semite is ruled by temper and with it by passion, by the distinct personality with an energetic will and sharp intellect; he is altogether unable to divorce the relationship between the world and man from the relationship of the world to his own ego; he cannot place thought in pure objectivity before the spirit. . . .[10]

Within a decade of the appearance of Lassen's first volume, the French writer and diplomat comte de Gobineau (1816–1882) published his *Essai sur l'inégalité des races humaines* (*Essay on the Inequality of the Human Races*), which was to have a profound influence on the concept of race and on racism in the latter half of the nineteenth century. Gobineau held that the white race was superior to the yellow and black races in intellectual and spiritual quality, and that the Aryans were the élite of the white race.[11] His theory, which implied but never made explicit that the non-Aryan Jewish "race" was inferior to the noble Aryan race, became one of the foundation stones of Nazi doctrine.

Another Frenchman who had an important share in the development of European racism was the historian and Oriental scholar Ernest Renan (1823–1892). In his 1856 volume of essays, *Etudes d'histoire religieuse (Studies of Religious History)*, Renan characterized the "Semites" as "an incomplete race," as having "never had any comprehension of civilization in the sense which we attribute to the term," lacking public-spiritedness and personal courage, being selfish, intolerant (as a result of their monotheism), and as possessed of a morality altogether different from "ours." In comparison, "to the Indo-European race belonged almost all the great military, political, and intellectual movements of the history of the world."[12] Although Renan, like Gobineau, did not express himself negatively about the Jews, his "racial" view of history was utilized by the anti-Semites, who applied to the Jews everything he said about the Semites, claiming as their authority this man of great scholarly reputation, the head of the Collège de France.

Side by side with the scholarly works, which were not anti-Semitic in themselves but served as the basis for anti-Semitic theories and pronouncements, there appeared a veritable flood of anti-Semitic pamphlets, attacking the Jews for something the very existence of which had been unsuspected by the world until a few decades earlier: their being members of the "Semitic race." This was an entirely new twist in the centuries-old game of Jew baiting.

From early antiquity the Jews had been persecuted because their religion was different from that of the majority populations among whom fate placed them. They were subjected to the most inhuman treatment in those countries where, in addition, they also appeared physically, that is, "racially," alien. When Muslims mistreated Jews who lived in their midst, when Christian Spaniards persecuted them, the mere act of conversion to the ruling religion was sufficient to stay persecution. Only where the idea of the "purity of the blood" was influential, as in Christian Spain, did the conversion of Jews to the ruling religion not eliminate objections to intermarriage with them. With a few insignificant exceptions, the concept of the Jews as a separate racial entity was notably absent all over the Mediterranean area.

It was different in the more northerly parts of Christian Europe. Here, Jewish religious, linguistic, and cultural differences were enhanced by an aura of physical difference whose perception remained part of the image of the Jew even after the passage of centuries had gradually obliterated or at least greatly diminished it. As a consequence, after religious differences ceased to be a crucial issue, persecution of Jews continued because of a new

10

pseudo-religious belief in their racial otherness. To be sure, there was no dearth in "scholarly" underpinnings for this popularly held view. Most famous among these was a book entitled *The Foundations of the Nineteenth Century*, written by the renegade Englishman Houston Stewart Chamberlain (1855–1927), who had married the daughter of Richard Wagner and was influenced by the anti-Semitism of his famous father-in-law. The Chamberlain doctrine was that race rules history. All history, he taught, was a conflict between the Aryans and the Semites; the former were the noblemen of humanity, the latter an inferior human species to which Chamberlain gave the scholarly sounding name *Homo Syriacus*. A typical subdivision of this Syrian Man was the *Homo Judaicus*, described by Chamberlain as possessed of evil and dangerous intellectual, moral, and religious qualities. In the nineteenth century the Semites were still plotting for world supremacy. Chamberlain solved the problem presented by the Jewish origin of Christianity by claiming that Jesus was not a Jew and by attributing to the new blood of Germanism a revivifying influence on Christianity. Chamberlain's opus was first published in 1899, and went through several editions within a few years. Its influence on the racial theories of the Nazis was considerable.[13]

The theories developed by Nazi scholars to "prove" the "racial inferiority" of the Jews make frightening reading even today, more than a generation after they were written. During the years of World War II, they served as justification for the extermination of 6 million Jews by the Germans and their followers among the Poles, Austrians, Hungarians, and other nations allied with or subjected to the Third Reich.[14] During those six years, the number of Jews slaughtered in the name of racism was greater than that of all Jewish victims claimed by religious persecution in all countries throughout the preceding three thousand years of Jewish history. For this reason alone, one feels that a detailed scrutiny of all the scientifically ascertainable facts pertaining to the problem of the Jewish "race" is long overdue.

PRE-RACIST ANTI-SEMITISM

As the foregoing, necessarily sketchy, remarks show, the Nazi genocide was the culmination of a racial anti-Semitism which arose on the European Continent following the spread of Enlightenment. Before that time, differences between Jews and Gentiles were perceived and conceptualized by the latter in religious terms. As for the Jews, they, it is true, always considered themselves, if not a race, at least a greatly enlarged family, in the sense of maintaining a belief in the descent of all Jews from "Abraham our father." In the first century A.D., Josephus Flavius, the Jewish historian, identified himself at the beginning of his great book on *The Jewish War* with these words: "I, Josephus, son of Matthias, a Hebrew by race. . . ." Eighteen centuries later, Benjamin Disraeli continued to consider himself a Jew by race, although he was converted to Christianity as a boy. "All is race, there is no other truth," was his maxim, and even while he served as the prime minister of England he never ceased championing the "Hebrew race" which, he held, had given the West its spiritual values. The essentially mythical nature of this Jewish belief in the Jewish race will be amply demonstrated in our chapters dealing with Jewish proselytism, intermarriage, and related subjects. It is also shown by the fact that in every age the Gentile converts came to be considered true children of Abraham. This grafting of Gentile branches on the Jewish family tree was not a matter of pious fiction; it was considered an actual incorporation into the Jewish people and therefore in some ways more profoundly meaningful than mere genetic descent.

This religio-racial view was not paralleled on the Gentile side until the eighteenth century in Christian Europe and the twentieth in the Muslim world. The followers of the two daughter religions of Judaism had throughout conceived of the fundamental difference between Gentile and Jew as a matter of religion. The Jew was hated and despised because he refused to accept Muḥammad as his prophet or Christ as his saviour. Once the ruling religious powers succeeded in overcoming this Jewish obstinacy—whether by suasion or force did not make much difference—the major objection to the Jew was eliminated and he became a member of the dominant religious community.

If the conversion took place individually, soon many of the New Muslims or New Christians managed to intermarry with members of the majority; if it was a group affair, as in Majorca in 1391 or in several Persian cities in the seventeenth century, the tendency developed on both sides to preserve the newly converted Jewish group as a separate endogamous entity. In either case, anti-Semitism having based itself on religious criteria, conversion signaled its end. In the House of Islam this remained the case almost down to the present time, when identification with the State of Israel rather than with the religion of Judaism has become the chief Jewish crime in Muslim eyes. In the Christian world, the spread of Enlightenment reduced the significance of religion as a criterion of group identification in general and as the mark of Cain on the Jewish forehead in particular. The churches, it is true, continued to labor for the saving of Jewish souls, with each denomination urging on them the acceptance of its particular version of Christianity. Because the hold of religion weakened on members of the Jewish community as a result of the Enlightenment, the number of Jews who did convert grew considerably in the nineteenth and early twentieth centuries. A consequence of the development of the new racial approach to Jewish otherness was, however, that it became much more difficult for the Jew to give up his old identity. A change in religion could be accomplished with the single act of conversion; a change of race, whether race was a genetic fact or merely a figment of the social imagination, took several generations at least, as the offspring of one

12

Jewish and three Gentile grandparents learned to their dismay in Nazi Germany. As the German and Hungarian anti-Semitic ditties put it many years before Hitler came to power:

> In the Jew the foul disgrace
> Is not religion but the race.[15]

However, in earlier periods too, anti-Semitism had not been completely tied to religion. Medieval anti-Semites repeatedly spoke of various physical characteristics in which the Jews were supposed to differ from Gentiles. Some of these were clearly mythical in character; others had some semblance of being based on observation.

To the first type belongs the well-known medieval allegation that the Jews had a characteristic strong body odor, the *foetor Iudaicus*. This odor, while physical and powerful, was believed to have its origin in the assumed association of the Jews with the Devil: it was the stench of Lucifer that exuded from the bodies of Jews. This being the case, the sacrament of baptism was widely believed to be sufficient not only to deodorize the Jews but also to replace their offensive smell with a sweet scent. Another such folkloristic feature of the Jewish body was a pair of horns. This popular belief may have been influenced by a mistranslation of the biblical story about Moses whose face "shone" when he descended from Mount Sinai: the Hebrew expression "shone" could also be translated (as in the Vulgate) as "grew horns" or "had horns"—hence the horns that adorn the head of the famous Moses of Michelangelo. More likely, the Jews' horns, like their odor, were a feature transferred by medieval folklore from the Devil onto the Jews.[16]

On a less fantastic note, but equally without foundation in fact, Arab folklore maintained that the arms of some Jews were so long that their hands touched their knees.[17] In Europe, some authors reported on the basis of "trustworthy" eyewitness accounts that all Jews were afflicted with disfiguring and loathsome bodily blemishes. Johann Jakob Schudt (1664–1722), a German polyhistor and Orientalist who devoted most of his work to studying the Jews, quotes the preacher Scriver, who in turn quotes a learned contemporary to the effect that

among several hundred of their [the Jews'] kind he had not encountered a single person without a blemish or other repulsive feature: for they are either pale and yellow or swarthy; they have in general big heads, big mouths, everted lips, protruding eyes and bristle-like eyelashes, large ears, crooked feet, hands that hang below their knees, and big shapeless warts, or are otherwise asymmetrical and malproportioned in their limbs.[18]

These views could not help but influence some of the Jews themselves, especially those who converted to Christianity. Thus one converted Jew argued that the Jews were the ugliest people on earth while the French were good-looking. The contrary argument was voiced by Jewish apologists.

Looking at such statements from the vantage point of our familiarity with the laws of heredity, they impress us as being based on racial views. The physical characteristics enumerated by Schudt and others are traits which we know are determined by heredity; therefore it seems to us that the meaning of statements such as "the hands of the Jews hang below their knees" can be nothing else but that excessive arm length is a Jewish racial feature, and that, in general, the Jews are a race characterized by the hereditary traits listed. This impression, however, is not necessarily true. The medieval mind—and Schudt's credulous and totally uncritical assertions must be classified as manifestations of a medieval mentality—unaware of the laws and processes of heredity, did not identify the sum total of the physical features of a human group with the concept of race. Firmly convinced of the reality of the Devil, the medieval mentality could easily believe that the Jews were allied with him and that this Jewish spiritual blemish was inevitably correlated with telltale signs of physical deformity. The physical difference of the Jew was not considered a manifestation of racial, but of religious difference. Once the Jew joined the ranks of the ruling religion, both his spiritual and his physical deformities were believed to disappear.

RACE AS A GENETIC CONCEPT

As we have just seen, men have ever since antiquity been conscious of differences in physical appearance among various groups of human beings. The most obvious of these physical differences, such as color of skin and hair, texture of hair, and shape of nose, have traditionally been used as a means of separating people into "races." In other words, "races were regarded as types." [19] Depending on the number of traits used in their classification, anthropologists have divided mankind into a mere three races ("white," "yellow," and "black"), or dozens. This tendency has survived even among leading anthropologists well into the middle of the present century. Carleton S. Coon, for example, a foremost "splitter" of human races (as opposed to a "lumper"), has divided the "white" people of Europe alone into ten major races, each containing several subtypes. [20]

Since the advent of modern genetics in the early twentieth century, it has been realized that physical features are but the final product of the interaction of units of genetic material called *genes*. These reside in the body's cells and direct them to form, for example, the pigment which determines the color of the skin. Each person, it was found, has two *alleles*, or "copies," of every gene, one inherited from the father and one from the mother. The copies may be either identical or different; in either case, their combined effect determines the manner in which heredity becomes visible in the physical traits of the individual. The sum total of these visible traits is called the *phenotype*.

14

Certain genes, for example those making for dark pigment, are more common in some races than others. Once this was clearly recognized and understood, anthropologists and geneticists began discussing "races" in terms of genes rather than phenotypically. Thus Dunn and Dobzhansky define a race as a population which differs from others in the incidence of certain genes.[21] It so happens that this type of definition lends itself to far greater "splitting" than do the traditional classifications based on the external physical features, and the larger the number of racial units arrived at, the more difficult it is to utilize the race concept for general comparative purposes. The population geneticists Cavalli-Sforza and Bodmer pointed out that most human populations show sufficient local variation so that almost every town or city would have to be considered a separate race if the Dunn and Dobzhansky definition were not further qualified.[22]

In order to make the genetic definition of race useful, it must therefore be augmented by an indication of the *amount* of difference required for any two groups to be considered as belonging to, or constituting, two different races. For this purpose, various statistical measures of "genetic distance" between two populations have been devised, in which the differences in the gene frequencies of several genes are combined. If the figure thus obtained is high, it indicates a considerable "genetic distance" between the two populations compared: they can be considered as belonging to two widely different races. If it is low, it indicates that the two populations studied are racially near each other. Thus one can translate into quantitative terms the relative genetic differences between any two populations. In addition, of course, the distribution of individual genes in various populations can be examined. Recurring patterns may supply clues as to the relationships of various populations. For example, if the frequencies of several genes are more similar in populations A and B than in A and C, or in B and C, then it makes sense to conclude that populations A and B are more closely related to each other than either one of them is to population C. Utilizing this approach, the frequency (or incidence) of several genes in Jewish and non-Jewish populations will be compared in a number of chapters, and a statistical treatment applied to allow a more objective determination of whether or not different Jewish populations are sufficiently similar to one another in their gene frequencies, and sufficiently different from the non-Jews in whose midst they live, to warrant calling the Jews a race. In addition, we will look at the incidence of certain diseases which are either more or less common in Jews than in non-Jews, or are found only in certain groups of Jews, and will consider what evidence—if any—these data furnish on the question of the Jewish race.

It is important to realize that racial classifications have to take into account the historical processes to which every human group was subject: the number of persons involved in the early history of the group (as a clue to the

15

possible effects of genetic drift), the migrations which resulted in transplantation of a group or parts of it to different places, and the possibilities of interbreeding with other groups. Since the evolution of races is due also to mutation and selection, these factors, too, must be considered. In brief, raciation (i.e., the evolution of races) is a function of cultural and historical factors as much as of genetic factors.

These considerations lead to one more important conclusion. The genetic composition of human groups is fluid, and any classification of races based on a study of their genetic features is valid only for the particular time of the study. Nonetheless, the fact that races are not static groups is no reason for discarding the race concept entirely or for denying it any usefulness. The fact remains that a study of present-day human populations can give valuable clues to their history, their migrations, and their interbreeding with other groups. When dealing with the historical period (which in the case of the Jews covers the last three thousand years), the biological evidence can be supplemented by recorded historical data; for the much longer prehistoric past the biological evidence may be all we have.

One by-product of the preoccupation with race and interbreeding between races is the erroneous assumption, already referred to, that at some time in the past there existed "pure races" which later became "less pure" because of migration and interbreeding. What is meant by "pure" is never clearly defined. If by "pure" we mean uniform, then it is unlikely that pure races of man ever existed. Even in domesticated animals, whose breeding nowadays is scientifically controlled for the purpose of producing homogeneous stocks, the resulting strain or race may be fairly uniform in some selected features, such as gait in trotting horses, or coat color or conformation in dogs, but it will maintain its diversity in other, less emphasized traits. As far as man is concerned, there is little evidence to support the view that earlier populations were substantially less variable than many modern ones. In fact, "the only sense in which the notion of pure races seems to have any reality is that some populations have been more isolated than others and that gene exchange with other populations has been relatively small at least in the recent past." [23] "Reproductive isolation," that is, the absence of interbreeding between one group and others because of geographical and/or social barriers, can, over a period of time, lead to genetic differences, especially if the isolated population is small (see chapter IX). This, however, does not mean that the isolated population is necessarily more "pure" than another population which practices extensive interbreeding with other groups.

It is most doubtful whether, in the course of their three thousand years of history, the Jews ever lived in sufficient reproductive isolation to develop distinctive genetic features. On the contrary, all the available evidence indicates that throughout their history the Jews continually received an inflow of genes from neighboring populations as a result of proselytism, intermarriage, rape, the birth of illegitimate children fathered by Gentiles, and so on. A discussion of these historical processes forms the first part of this book.

RACE AND CULTURE

Ever since his emergence from the subhuman level, man has lived not only in a natural but also in a cultural environment. Beginning with the New Stone Age, when man mastered techniques of food production, and continuing thereafter at an ever-increasing rate, culture has been interposed between the human organism and the natural environment.[24] This new factor has had a profound influence on the racial evolution of man. As a culture carrier man has become subjected to the impact of new processes of selection, social and cultural, which supplemented the old natural selection. New causes of mutation appeared, and new possibilities for the spread of advantageous traits produced by mutation. Migration increased to formerly undreamed of dimensions. Huge regions of the globe, previously uninhabitable because of climatic conditions, became the home of human communities. This, in turn, set new processes of physical and mental adaptation in motion. Wherever he lived, man became molded by a combination of pressures exerted upon his genetic equipment by both the natural and the socio-cultural environment. The fact that the latter was the product of human activity in no way prevented it from impressing its stamp on every individual who grew up in it.

This being the case, although it is methodologically sound to discuss the races of man in purely biological terms, it is impossible in practice to disregard those historical factors which left their mark upon the members of each human group. When applied to the problem of the Jewish race, this means that the physical features that characterize the Jews in their numerous and widely dispersed communities are everywhere accompanied by cultural features. When the impression "Jew" registers on the mind of an observer, the features on which the identification is based are, in fact, more often cultural than physical. The observer himself remains, as a rule, unaware of this fact, and considers all characteristics as "racial" features. In numerous instances even serious students of the Jewish "race" fail to distinguish between the two types of traits and list together genetically determined characteristics and culturally acquired features, such as behavioral traits or traditional manners, customs, even fashions. Carl Vogt, the nineteenth-century pioneer anthropologist, included "short beard" and "small shrewd eyes" among the chief characteristics of Ashkenazi Jews, and "long hair and beard" as well as "black eyes of a melancholy expression" among those of the Sephardim.[25] Similarly, Maurice Fishberg, the most outstanding early student of the Jewish "race," in describing the Sephardi hair color, eye color and shape, complexion, and the like, adds: "They are medium-sized, slender,

17

narrow-shouldered, but graceful people, with a somewhat melancholy and thoughtful expression. Only very rarely is to be seen a Spanish Jew displaying a servile or cringing attitude in the presence of superiors, as is often to be seen among German and Polish Jews.'' [26]

Because culturally acquired traits, such as gracefulness, facial expression, behavior patterns, and so on, not to mention the length to which hair and beard are allowed to grow, are not inherited, they have no place in a study of racial differences if races are defined in exclusively genetic terms. On the other hand, as indicated above, cultural traits are often important elements of the mental picture which allows us to identify different human groups at a glance. An Indian Sikh may be identified instantly by his turban and beard style; and an American southerner or a Yorkshire man by his accent; examples of this kind are of course numerous.

The issue is further complicated by the fact that it is often difficult to separate actual physical features from culturally superimposed traits. Some married couples, it has been observed, tend to converge in appearance after living together for many years. Most of us would agree that such resemblances are due to the acquisition of similar expression and mannerisms over years of close association. A related phenomenon is the passing on of patterns of behavior from one generation to the next, until they eventually may come to be considered ''innate'' features of the population; this is why the Scots ''are'' thrifty, the Irish loquacious, the Chinese industrious, the Sephardi Jews melancholy. These stereotyped characterizations have an element of truth in them. What we must realize is that they refer to culturally imposed features which do not properly belong in a *genetic* characterization of races. However, since the Jews perhaps more than any other people have in many ages and places been identified by, and described by, precisely such culturally determined traits rather than by purely physical features, and since racial anti-Semitism has most often sought to justify itself by alleged Jewish personality traits and behavioral features, the discussion of this subject must form part of our study of the problem of the Jewish ''race.''

PART ONE

Historical

CHAPTER I

Four Views on
the Jewish "Race"

R ARELY HAS THERE been a subject on which so many scholars
have expressed so many different views as that of the Jewish "race."
Discounting the rantings of such racists as Dühring, Chamberlain, Gobineau, Fritsch, and Vacher de Lapouge in the nineteenth century, and their
latter-day disciples among the Nazi pseudo-scientists,[1] legitimate scholarship has taken several mutually contradictory positions on the question.
These can be subsumed under the following major headings:

1. Jews constitute one single race.
2. Jews comprise two distinct races or racial types.
3. Jews comprise three races or racial types.
4. Jews are not a separate racial group at all.

Some scientists, hesitating to commit themselves clearly on the question,
substitute for the term "race" such expressions as "racial specificity"
("*Eigenart*"), and then discuss group differences between the Jews and the
Germans on this basis.[2] We shall not consider those racial scientists who
resort to such subterfuges, but confine ourselves to a sampling of those
scholars who unequivocally embrace one of the aforementioned four views.

1. JEWS CONSTITUTE ONE SINGLE RACE

One of the earliest anthropologists to propound the view that the Jews
constitute a single race and to support it with a theory on the historical im-
mutability of the Jewish racial character was Johann Friedrich Blumenbach
(1752–1840). This German pioneer of physical anthropology published in

1775 his treatise *De generis humani varietate nativa,* in which he stated that "the Jewish race presents the most notorious and least deceptive" example of typical physiognomy, "which can easily be recognized everywhere by their eyes alone, which breathe of the East." Twenty years later, in a new edition of his treatise, Blumenbach explained that ". . . the nation of Jews . . . under every climate remains the same as far as the fundamental configuration of face goes, [and is] remarkable for a racial character [that is] almost universal, which can be distinguished at the first glance even by those little skilled in physiognomy, although it is difficult to limit and express [it] by words."

This view is the more remarkable since Blumenbach's general position on the feasibility of classifying mankind into disparate subgroups was decidedly negative. Only a few pages before this statement he noted that "one variety of mankind does so sensibly pass into the other that you cannot mark out the limits between them. Very arbitrary indeed both in number and definition have been the varieties of mankind accepted by eminent men." [3] It would almost seem that when it came to the Jews, the famed father of modern physical anthropology allowed himself to be influenced by considerations other than scholarly observation.

By the middle of the nineteenth century, the notion of the "permanence" of the Jewish race or racial type found many adherents. An American savant, Dr. Josiah Clark Nott, expressed the idea even more emphatically than Blumenbach. Nott lived in Mobile, Alabama, where he happened to know a respected Jewish citizen whose physiognomy reminded him of a colossal Chaldaean head from the days of Sennacherib, and he marveled that "still, after 2,500 years, so indelible is the [Jewish] type, every resident of Mobile will recognize in this Chaldaean effigy the facsimile portrait of one of their city's most prominent citizens. . . ." And he went on to say: "Jewish features meet one in almost every country under the sun . . . well-marked Israelitish features are never beheld out of that race . . . in obedience to an organic law of animal life, they have preserved, unchanged, the same features which the Almighty stamped on the first Hebrew pairs created." In brief, the Jewish type has come down ". . . from Mesopotamia to Mobile for at least 5,500 years, unaltered. . . ." [4]

Let us refrain from commenting on Dr. Nott's shaky chronology, and pass on to an early French representative of this school of thought. Paul Broca, writing in 1859–60 in the *Journal de Physiologie de l'Homme et des Animaux,* stated that "the Jewish race, scattered for more than eighteen centuries in the most different climates, is everywhere the same now as it was in Egypt at the time of the Pharaohs." [5] At the same time, Broca recognized and repeatedly emphasized that as a result of group and individual conversions of Gentiles to Judaism, a fair Jewish type came into existence, especially in Germany and Slavic lands. Despite this insight (of which more will

22

be said later in connection with the notion that there are two Jewish racial types), the view that the Jews are all of one racial type persisted among both German and French scholars.

In an article written in 1872, the well-known naturalist Friedrich Anton Heller von Hellwald combined his assertion that the Jews form a distinct race with a sharp condemnation of the Jews.[6] In 1876, the French anthropologist Paul Topinard used the Jews as an example to illustrate his "law of the permanence of types": ". . . from heredity emanates the law of the permanence of types, which shows the identity between the ancient Egyptian type of five or six thousand years ago, as represented on ancient monuments, and the Fellahs who still inhabit the banks of the Nile; the identity of the Jewish types of the same period and of the present. . . ." And again, after stressing that there is no proof of change of type due to "external circumstances": "Wherever one encounters either Arabs or Jews, their type is the same as the one we find in the Egyptian monuments. . . ." [7]

In 1881, the German ethnographer and geographer Richard Andree, who devoted one of his books to the ethnography of the Jews, had this to say about the "permanence" of the Jewish racial type:

> . . . no other racial type can be traced back through millennia with the same certainty as precisely that of the Jews, and no other has shown such a constancy of forms, none has resisted time and the influences of environment, as has the Jewish type. . . . One only has to glance at Egyptian and Assyrian monuments on which Jews of a few thousand years ago are depicted with masterly sureness in order to become convinced of the unchangeability of the Jewish type, and one will be stimulated to making comparisons, since one will think that one sees there the portraits of Jews who to this day walk in our midst in flesh and blood.

A few pages later, in apparent contradiction to this theory of Jewish racial unchangeability, Andree embarks upon a discussion of two distinct types that he and several of his predecessors found among the Jews:

> One is the finer and nobler, with a fine nose, black, shining eyes, graceful extremities; this type predominates among the Sephardim or Spanish Jews. The other is the less noble, mostly with a big mouth, thick nose, deep nose and mouth wrinkles, and often curly hair. . . . This type predominates among the Ashkenazim or German-Polish Jews. Both types occur side by side and are constant.[8]

The notion of the "permanence" or "indelibility" of the Jewish racial type through thousands of years was explained by Joseph Jacobs, a British Jewish scholar, by positing the existence of a mysterious "superior prepotency of the Jewish blood," through which the Jewish cast of features and expression were transmitted from generation to generation, even in the offspring of mixed Jewish-Gentile marriages.[9] Before the end of the nineteenth century, similar ideas were expressed by Georg Buschan.[10] Several decades later, the idea of Jewish racial prepotency was embraced by Madison Grant, who said flatly: "The cross between any of the three European races and a Jew is a Jew"; and by Eugen Fischer, renowned German anthropologist and early exponent of the "Nordic" idea, who spoke of the predominance of the Jewish "West Asian-Oriental" racial characteristics in the offspring of Jewish-Gentile interbreeding.[11]

The conviction that there is a typical and uniform Jewish physiognomy, despite the wide geographical dispersion of the Jews, persisted from the nineteenth into the twentieth century. In a study prepared in the 1890's and published in 1903, A. D. Elkind, an early Russian anthropologist, embraced it,[12] as did a Polish colleague of his, I. M. Judt, whose book on *The Jews as a Race* was published in the same year in a German translation.

Judt reaches the following conclusions:

> 1. The Jews did not succumb to racial mixture with the native populations, either through conversion or through intermarriage. . . . 2. The Jews as a physical race are a product of an amalgamation that took place, not in Europe, but in the remote times of primary wanderings and political independence. The Hebrew branch of the Semites absorbed various racial components which caused a marked deviation among the Jews from their originally Semitic type. The contemporary Jews, as a physical race, are related to the Alpine-Himalayan rather than to the Mediterranean race.[13]

Judt's views were re-echoed and elaborated by Ignaz Zollschan, an Austrian Jewish anthropologist whose book, *Das Rassenproblem (The Race Problem)*, was published in no less than four editions from 1909 to 1920, and remained influential for quite a while thereafter. The following quotations, taken from the last edition, sum up Zollschan's views:

> I can fully confirm the assertion that the main features of the Jewish type reappear with the same clarity in every geographical longitude and latitude. . . . He who has attained the ability to recognize the anthropological type beneath the social one will no longer be misled by apparel, style of beard, external forms, or an artificially inculcated lively or cool temperament. Similarly, he who can disregard the various national costumes will be extremely surprised when he recognizes completely identical types among Persian Jews and Moroccan Jews, when he recognizes in the synagogues of old-established Arab Jews in, say, Cairo or Beirut, not only exactly the same faces as in East Europe, but also the same chaotic variety of Andree's "fine" and "plump" types, long, medium and broad heads, light and dark pigmentation, the same contrast between red hair and blue eyes on the one hand and the deepest black on the other. I saw the same alternation in the old Jewish streets of Haifa, among the Sephardi Jews of Constantinople, Corfu, Amsterdam, in the ghetto of Venice, among the Jews of Rome, as among the Russian and Rumanian Jewish immigrants in America, and among our familiar Hungarian, Bohemian, and German Jews. The observation that identical types recur in the remotest zones is a fascinating one, and the fact that even such important indices as hair and eye color are identical proves Judt's conclusions concerning the racial homogeneity of all major parts of the Jewish people. . . .

24

The present-day Jews, therefore, constitute a type which is uniform to a high degree, irrespective of the geographical terrain and the racial characteristics of the natives.[14]

Zollschan's position, therefore, is that while in every local Jewish population there is a great variety of types, the total range of these types is identical in every place, and that this proves the racial homogeneity of the Jews.

2. JEWS COMPRISE TWO DISTINCT RACES

The second view, that the Jews comprise two distinct races or racial types, originated in the early or middle nineteenth century among Jewish historians and scholars. As Carl Vogt observed,

almost all Jewish scholars are unanimous concerning the age-old origin of the two types that are present in Jewry; some of them even attribute it to that "mixed multitude" which, according to the biblical story, left Egypt together with the Jews, and undertook with them the dangerous passage through the Red Sea. . . . Thus it appears that the differences which mark the Jews stem from original racial characteristics rather than changes that came about as a result of changes in locality. . . .[15]

Vogt himself finds that

especially in the North, in Russia and Poland, Germany and Bohemia, one finds a Jewish race with often red hair, short beard, somewhat upturned short nose, small, grey, shrewd eyes, and a more compressed body build, with a round face and mostly wide cheekbones, which has many similarities with several Slavic races, especially of the North. In the Orient, on the other hand, and around the Mediterranean, as well as from there into Portugal and Holland, we find that Semitic race with long black hair and beard, large, almond-shaped black eyes with a melancholy expression, elongated faces, high noses, in brief, that type which we find again in Rembrandt's portraits. Finally, in Africa, along the Red Sea in Abyssinia we find a Jewish nation that . . . seems not to be distinguishable at all from the other peoples of the country.[16]

Leaving aside the Abyssinian Jews, whom Vogt himself considers a special case (as do practically all subsequent students of the Jewish race problem), we have here the fully developed notion of a racially bifurcate Jewry. Almost simultaneously with Vogt, several French anthropologists made the same observation and discussed its explanation repeatedly at meetings of the Anthropological Society of Paris. One of the first to report on the phenomenon was Gustave Lagneau, who on May 16, 1861, described the Jews as being "generally noted for the black color of their hair, their beard, their long eyelashes, their thick, protruding and well-arched eyebrows; for their dark, large and lively eyes; for their yellowish skin, and for their strongly aquiline nose, narrow at its base, the bones being square, hollow at the top and arched at the bottom." However, Lagneau added, "in our east-

25

ern provinces [i.e., eastern France] numerous inhabitants professing Judaism are blond or red and exhibit entirely different anthropological characteristics from those of the other Jews. Of these blond Israelites, generally called German Jews, some seem to be the result of the crossing of the German and Slavic races with the ancient Jews; while others appear to be but people of the German and Slavic races who adopted Judaism about the ninth century. . . ." In the discussion that followed Lagneau's report, Paul Broca explained that this modification of the Jewish type must be attributed to the conversion in Poland and southern Russia in the ninth century of certain Slavic elements with whom the Jews intermarried. This is the ancestry of the blond Jews in Poland and Germany. Broca was followed by M. Boudin, who opined that the Jews fall into two racial groups, that of the southern or Portuguese Jews, among whom there were no blonds, and that of the northern or German Jews, among whom there were many with blue eyes and blond hair. At the same meeting, Pruner-Bey referred to several instances of conversions of non-Jews to Judaism and concluded that "these data can sufficiently explain the lack of homogeneity of the Jewish race in Europe." [17]

Four years later, on October 19, 1865, the Société d'Anthropologie returned to the problem of the Jewish race, and on this occasion M. Boudin quoted Prichard's observations (of whom more below) on the blond and blue-eyed Jews in England, adding that he himself had seen such Jews in Germany: in both countries this must be the result of race mixture.[18]

In 1867 the Austrian physician Augustin Weisbach began anthropometric measurements, but it was not until 1878 that he published his results. Having measured nineteen male Jews (eleven from Galicia, five from Hungary, and three from Moldova), he concluded that

the [European] Jews have a small stature, have mostly straight, but often also curly, hair, of predominantly dark, not rarely also red, color, usually grey and light brown eyes, and a lively pulse. They have a large, mesocephalic (more often dolicho- than brachycephalic) * head, which is narrow at its base; a long face which is moderately wide between the cheeks, very narrow at the top, and narrow between the corners of the lower jaw, with a moderately high forehead. . . . The nose starts out very narrow at its root, is in general very big and of considerable length and height, but at the same time very narrow. The mouth and ears are of medium size.

While these generalizations were made by Weisbach on the basis of his own measurements, he also remarks that, in general, "there are doubtless two cephalic types among the European Jews, one dolichocephalic, with a narrow, long face, a similar, on the whole big, nose, and thin lips; and a brachycephalic, with a broad face, low, broad, small nose and thick lips." [19]

---

* Mesocephalic; medium-headed; dolichocephalic; long-headed; brachycephalic; broadheaded. Cf. Ch. VII. Morphological Traits.

The same conclusions were reached by Józef Majer and Izydor Kopernicki, who in 1876 published their measurements of 316 Galician Jews. Adding the results of measurements of sixty-seven Jews in the Minsk Guberniya carried out by W. Dybowski, Ludwig Stieda, the German anthropologist, came to the conclusion in 1883 that among the East European Jews there is a brachycephalic and a dolichocephalic type, the former predominating.[20] A year earlier, an "inaugural dissertation" written by Bernhard Blechmann recapitulated the same argument, and in 1885 Kollman and Kahnt reiterated it on the basis of skeletal material from the thirteenth and fourteenth centuries found in the Jewish cemetery of Basle.[21]

On the basis of cephalic measurements of 120 Russian Jews and 20 Karaites, Constantin Ikow distinguished between a brachycephalic "Russian Jewish race" and a dolichocephalic "Mediterranean Jewish race." He concluded that the former must definitely be excluded from the Semitic race, while the latter is Semitic and belongs to the same race as the Arabs. In Western Europe, Ikow found, the two types were intermixed.[22]

In 1887 the French anthropologist Abel Hovelacque and the French physician Georges Hervé went on record to the effect that there are two Jewish racial types: one, characterized by

a long head; dark, abundant, and often wavy hair; large and lively eyes; aquiline and fine nose resulting in a very accentuated profile; rather narrow lips; oval face; small stature. One meets this type among the Jews of all countries, not only in Europe but also among some of those who are established in Persia, Bokhara, and so on. One should not confuse with this very remarkable type of a fine race, a much heavier type which one encounters quite frequently among the German Jews and which is characterized by a round head, curly hair, large nose, thick lips, features without any delicacy. This type has nothing in common with the true type of Asiatic origin. The latter is dolichocephalic or sub-dolichocephalic. Cephalic indices of 82 or more are found in Russia and Galicia (85.5 according to Majer and Kopernicki), showing that we are dealing here with individuals converted to Judaism and not with Jews by race. . . . The true Syrian head, absolutely comparable to the veritable Jewish head, has the definitely elongated form. . . ."[23]

In 1891 John Beddoe in England distinguished between the "two curiously discriminated Jewish types . . . the Sephardim, who have usually the rather small oval (i.e. dolichocephalic) true Semitic type of head," and "the Ashkenazim, who are mostly of the broad-headed type."[24]

The same basic distinction between a brachycephalic and a dolichocephalic Jewish type continued to crop up all over Europe from the 1880's on, although its adherents were far from unanimous as to the terminology to be employed in describing the two Jewish races. Friedrich Maurer, for instance, called them "Turanian" and "Semitic," respectively; Joseph Deniker, "Assyrian" and Arab."[25]

In 1901 the French psychologist Maurice Muret published his book *L'Esprit juif,* in which chapter II is devoted to "The Israelite Race." In it the author states that

> today the Israelite race presents us with two very different aspects: the Ashkenazim and the Sephardim. These are, in effect, two very distinct types. In the north of Russia and in Poland, in Germany, in Bohemia, one encounters a Jewish tribe with generally red hair, short beard, broad nose, grey, small, shrewd eyes, and stocky body. These are the Ashkenazim or Polish Jews or German Jews, or *Tedeschi,* thus named in contrast to the *Spagnuoli* or Sephardim, or Jews of Portugal and Spain. The latter are encountered in the Orient and in the Mediterranean Basin, principally in the Iberian Peninsula, from where they spread into The Netherlands. The Sephardim are thought to have conserved the ancient Jewish type much more purely than their brothers dispersed among the Central and Eastern Europeans. They are generally of a tall stature, occasionally beautiful. Their shoulders are narrow, the head well set, the face slightly prognathous. The nose is strong but narrow, often curved. The mouth is big, the hair abundant, and most frequently dark brown, occasionally red, very rarely blond. The eyes are brown, more rarely grey, very rarely blue. . . .[26]

A few years later S. Weissenberg, one of the most persevering early students of the physical anthropology of the Jews, joined the chorus of those who distinguished two races among the Jews. He went on record as stating that there was a Sephardi, dolichocephalic, Jewish race, and an Ashkenazi, brachcephalic one; the latter, he said, was very different from the true Semitic race as manifested, for example, by the Arabs.[27]

But the search for the identification of the two Jewish races or types continued. In 1922, F. Wagenseil and M. W. Hauschild found that the *"Ostjuden"* (Eastern Jews, i.e., Ashkenazim) were predominantly Amenoid in physical type, while the *"Südjuden"* (Southern Jews, i.e., Sephardim) were predominantly Oriental.[28]

The same view was accepted by the anthropologist Hans F. K. Günther, one of the exponents of the "Nordic" idea. After discussing the subject in an appendix to his 1922 *Rassenkunde des deutschen Volkes (The Racial Study of the German People),* Gunther developed it fully in his *Rassenkunde des jüdischen Volkes (Racial Study of the Jewish People).* Following some rather complex racial characterizations of the two Jewish groups, Günther explains that "the Jewish racial amalgam" possesses a relatively greater uniformity than the racial amalgams of several other peoples.[29]

Günther's dichotomy (East Jewry, South Jewry), together with the idea that each of the two groups comprises a characteristic "racial amalgam," was duplicated in the influential German textbook of human genetics by Erwin Baur, Eugen Fischer, and Fritz Lenz. In the second edition (1923) of this book, Eugen Fischer explains:

> The differences among the Jews of Europe have their explanation in mixture with those peoples among whom they dwell. The South Jews received masses of

Mediterranean blood, the East Jews—Alpine and Mongolid blood. . . . What we see is racial mixture . . . one cannot speak of a Jewish race any more as of a Germanic race, but that, naturally, both the Jews and the Germans represent each a special racial mixture. One can, thus, very well speak of the racial characteristics and races of the Jews and of the Germanic peoples, and sharply and clearly distinguish between the two.[30]

Sigmund Feist in his 1925 *Stammeskunde der Juden* (*The Racial Study of the Jews*) reached the conclusion that one type found among almost all Jewish groups is that characteristic of "the Semitic race"; while the other, also everywhere present, is "the so-called Hittite type." [31]

The Jewish anthropologist, Y. D. Brutzkus reiterated the same idea in a pamphlet published in Paris in 1937,[32] and again in a study he contributed to an American encyclopedic handbook on the Jews. He terms his two Jewish types "Western Asiatic" and "Semitic-Oriental." [33]

In the early 1940's, Carleton S. Coon likewise maintained that the Sephardim form one race and the Ashkenazim another. As to the former, "there can be no reasonable doubt that the Sephardim form a single population in the racial sense, despite their geographical discontinuity," and that they "preserve with reasonable fidelity the racial character of their Palestinian ancestors. They are Mediterraneans, metrically of a central or generalized Mediterranean position, except that they have unusually narrow lateral dimensions of the face, including the distance between the eyes."

The Ashkenazim, according to Coon, "differ slightly in racial content from country to country . . . but these differences are not great. They are regional differences within a population which has its own racial identity. The Jewish groups differ much less from each other regionally than they do from Gentile populations." While there are individuals among the Ashkenazim who are Nordic, Alpine, Dinaric, and so on, these are in the minority, and

the bulk of the Ashkenazim show both a blending and a re-combination of Palestinian Mediterranean features with those of the populations among whom their ancestors have, for over two millenniums, lived on European soil. . . . It is the blending of Nordic and Alpine with eastern Mediterranean elements which gives the [Ashkenazi] Jews their characteristic physical features. . . . These are the combination of a relatively wide head and narrow face, with a slanting axis to the ears; a narrow lower jaw; a narrow interocular distance; and a considerable nose length, with convexity of profile and tip depression.

As for the Oriental Jews (of Yemen, Iraq, Iran, the Caucasus, Turkestan, etc.), according to Coon, "most of them have preserved a purely Mediterranean and apparently largely Palestinian racial character."

In sum, while the Jews are not a race like the Nordic or Alpine races, they are a "population; i.e., a group of people as united biologically as is the average intermarrying social or geographical unit found among white peoples; they have racial peculiarities which serve to differentiate the majority of them anthropometrically from their non-Jewish compatriots and neighbors." The retention of their "religious and ethnic solidarity has served to preserve, in solution, their Palestinian racial heritage and to permit its identification." [34]

3. JEWS COMPRISE THREE RACES

A third group of anthropologists found not two, but three racial components among the Jews. This view was broached in 1891 by Mme Clémence Royer, at a meeting of the Paris Anthropological Society. She suggested that, in addition to the by then well-known Northern and Mediterranean Jewish types, there was a third Jewish type, that of North Africa, which resulted from "a mixture of primitive Jewish colonies from Egypt and Carthage with indigenous Coptic, Berber, and Phoenician elements, and later with Latin and Greek colonists, and still later with Arabs, Turks, and Moors. Also, the African Jewish type is more clearly Semitic than the others, and it approaches the Arab type, but with the inferior traits of races thoroughly mixed with very diverse elements." [35] In the following year, Felix von Luschan, a leader in early German anthropology, concluded that the modern Jews comprise three distinct races: 1. Aryan Amorites, 2. Real Semites, and 3. Descendants of the ancient Hittites, with the last having the greatest incidence. [36]

Three "large ethnic complexes" (i.e., racial types) were discerned among both the biblical and the modern Jews by Fritz Kahn, a German-Jewish author. The former, he said, comprised: "1. The Jacob-tribes, descendants of the Babylonian Terahides and Abrahamides, who came from Egypt; 2. The Israel-tribes who came from Arabia and were anthropologically Bedouins; and 3. The Canaanites who represented an older cultural layer of Arabian Semites and were mixed with Babylonian, Egyptian and Hittite culture carriers." The modern Jews are "primarily the descendants of the Terahides who came from Babylonia, of the Abrahamides who settled in Canaan, and of the Jacobites who had been in Egypt," that is, of group 1. As if this were not confusing enough, Kahn adds that while there are physical differences between the Ashkenazim who absorbed Slavic-Mongolic influences, and the Sephardim who are an older, "more original" Jewish type, nevertheless "the Jews are a race, not in the strict zoological sense . . . but in that broader and higher sense given the term by cultural history and linguistic usage. . . . The Jews in their totality, despite all the variety of types and all historical intermingling, constitute as much an anthropologically-culturologically determined unity as any other community of blood and culture of the Western World." [37] If any sense can be read into the last two sentences, it is that the Jews are not a race but a people sharing a common cultural heritage.

Three racial types ("*Stammtypen*") are discerned among the Jews also by Arthur Ruppin, who calls them Babylonian, Sephardi, and Ashkenazi. The Babylonian received a stronger influence from the "Oriental (Bedouin)" race; the Sephardi—from the "Occidental (Philistine)" race; the Ashkenazi—from the "Southwest Asian (Alpine)" race. We may mention that of these three races, to whose influence Ruppin attributes the existence of the three Jewish "racial types," only one, the Alpine, is known to anthropology. The "Bedouin" and "Philistine" races are Ruppin's ad hoc creations, hence their influence on the Jews must be considered, to say the least, questionable. As to the modern Jews, Ruppin maintains that, following their exile from Palestine, the Jews in the Diaspora absorbed much non-Jewish blood, but mainly from peoples which belonged racially to one of the same three races mentioned above. As a result, most present-day Jews remained racially similar to their Palestinian ancestors. In addition to these three "racial types," there are Jewish "special types" (e.g., the Yemenite, Caucasian, and Bokharan Jews), as well as Jewish "foreign types," born of interbreeding with Negro slaves, and Mongoloid and North European peoples.[38]

The idea of three Jewish races surfaced again in 1939 in the writings of Jan Czekanowski, a Polish anthropologist, who distinguished the following three "anthropological formations" (his term for race):

1. That of the Sephardim, the Jews of the Mediterranean Basin and the Near East, who preserved the original Jewish anthropological formation. They are characterized by "a strong plurality of the Oriental component and with it a strong minority of the Mediterranean component; the Armenoid is a stronger admixture than the Alpine, the Nordic is quite insignificant. Only in Syria the Nordic admixture may surpass the Alpine."

2. That of the Ashkenazim, a "typically Central European mixed formation whose peculiarity is due to the presence of an Oriental admixture. . . . The strongest ingredient is either the Nordic or the Alpine . . . these Jews have absorbed the most European blood in Central Europe. . . ."

3. That of the Caucasian and Armenian Jews. These have an Oriental admixture, but their bulk comes from the Armenoid race element, which supplies a strong majority. "This formation is the result of a strong influence on the part of the Caucasian population upon the original Jews from the neighboring Orient." [39]

4. JEWS ARE NOT A SEPARATE RACIAL GROUP

The view that the Jews are not a race but exhibit different physical characteristics in each country or world area they inhabit began to take shape with the early observation that the skin color of Jews varied from place to place. Since skin color was regarded by early students of the human races as one of the most basic racial characteristics, this implied that the Jews did not form a uniform racial group.

One of the first to propound this idea was the French traveler François-

Maximilien Misson (1650–1722), who made an extensive tour of several European countries in 1688, and published his observations in 1691. He has the following to say about the Jews:

> 'Tis also a vulgar Error that the *Jews* are all black; for this is only true of the *Portuguese Jews,* who, marrying always among one another, beget Children like themselves, and consequently the Swarthiness of their Complexion is entail'd upon their whole Race, even in the Northern Regions. But the *Jews* who are originally of *Germany,* those, for Example, I have seen at *Prague,* are not blacker than the rest of their Countrymen.[40]

Misson's argument was incorporated without any change by Georges Louis Leclerc comte de Buffon (1707–1788) into his *magnum opus* the *Natural History,* which was published from 1749 on in several dozens of volumes.[41] Among the numerous reverberations of Misson's and Buffon's theory let us mention one only, which appears in the *Essay on the Causes of the Variety of Complexion and Figure in the Human Species* by an early president of Princeton University, Samuel Stanhope Smith (1750–1819). As an illustration of the effect of climate on skin color, Smith takes a page out of Buffon's *Natural History* and refers to the Jews. "But no example," he says,

> can carry with it greater authority on this subject than that of the Jews. Descended from one stock, prohibited by their most sacred intitutions from intermarrying with strangers, and yet widely dispersed into every region on the globe, this one people is marked with the peculiar characteristics of every climate. In Britain and Germany they are fair, brown in France and in Turkey, swarthy in Portugal and Spain, olive in Syria and Chaldea, tawny or coppercolored in Arabia and Egypt.[42]

James Cowles Prichard, a contemporary English ethnologist and physician, also adumbrated the idea that the Jews assimilated in physical character to the nations among which they had lived for a long time.[43]

From the second half of the nineteenth century on, the number of scholars taking the position that the Jews are not a race and that they exhibit physical similarity to the non-Jews among whom they live increased so considerably that our presentation of this argument must become even more selective. The view received important support from the anthropometric studies carried out in 1874–75 at the initiative of Rudolf Virchow, the great German pathologist and anthropologist. The large-scale survey covered over 10 million schoolchildren, almost 7 million in Germany and the rest in Switzerland, Austria, and Belgium. The features studied were skin, hair, and eye color. Among the children, over 75,000 were Jewish. The results of the study were highly significant both in what they showed and in what they failed to show. For instance, it was found that of all the children studied, 42.97 per cent had blue eyes; of the Jewish children, only 18.65 per cent had blue eyes. No less than 72.18 per cent of all the children had blond hair;

of the Jewish children, 32.71 per cent.[44] Subsequent studies carried out in Austria, Hungary, Bulgaria, and Palestine yielded similar results. Studies of adult Jews indicated that growing up did not mean growing dark, and fair eyes were found in more than half of the adult Jews in Galicia, Ruthenia, Rumania, Hungary, and Baden, Germany; the hair color was fair in the same countries in 12.80 to 20.03 per cent of the Jews.[45] In other words, despite the statistically significant differences, the eye and hair color of the Jews showed a definite correlation with that of the Gentiles in each country. Although these results were by no means conclusive, they strengthened the argument of those who denied racial identity to the Jews.

Without referring to (and probably unaware of) these large-scale surveys carried out under German auspices, Ernest Renan went on record in 1883 affirming that "the result of my experience is that there is no unique Jewish type, but that there are several which are absolutely irreducible the one to the other." [46] And a few years later Friedrich Ratzel, a leading early German anthropologist, asserted categorically:

> In the [Jewish] race itself alterations went on under the influence of variation in national environments. They [the Jews] have by the most various roads adjusted themselves to the cultured races of Europe, but have undoubtedly brought with them very various racial elements. The contrast between the German and Polish Jews and their Portuguese kinsmen may certainly be traced to the influence of the surrounding peoples; and intermixture, opposed though it be by sundry laws and usages, has surely effected much. . . .[47]

Carl Hahn, in his 1892 report of his Caucasian journey, quotes Anisinow, a Caucasian Jew, to the effect that the Jews and the Tats (one of the indigenous non-Jewish peoples of the Caucasus) can be told apart only by the fact that the Jews wear sidelocks. The Jewish type, adds Hahn, has changed here greatly as a result of intermingling with Gentiles.[48]

Just prior to the end of the century, William Z. Ripley, a Harvard economist and sociologist, author of the classic *Races of Europe,* discussed the Jews on the basis of 2,500 measurements which were available to him at the time. Referring to similar opinions by Renan and Lombroso, Ripley came to the conclusion that the Jews were not a race: "They have unconsciously taken on to a large extent the physical traits of the people among whom their lot has been thrown. In Algiers they remained long-headed like their neighbors . . . in Piedmont, Austria, or Russia . . . they became in time assimilated to the type of these neighbors as well." In explanation of this phenomenon, Ripley refers to wholesale conversions of Gentiles to the Jewish faith, such as those of the Khazars and the Falashas, and to the frequent infusion of Christian blood "through clandestine or irregular marriages." [49]

Maurice Fishberg, a pioneer student of Jewish physical anthropology, while emphatically denying the existence of a Jewish race or races, recognizes two major and several minor Jewish "types." His two major ones are "the Sephardi type of Jews" and "the Ashkenazi type of Jews." The former

conforms most to the ideal Jewish type, and anthropologically corresponds to the "Mediterranean" race of Ripley, or the *"race Ibero-Insulaire"* of Deniker. They have generally black or brown hair, occasionally red and rarely blonde; large black or brown eyes, seldom grey and rarely blue. In addition to their dark complexion, they are short of stature and either dolichocephalic or mesocephalic. The face is oval, the forehead receding, the eyes almond-shaped with the outer extremity very pointed, while the dark eyebrows are very bushy at the inner end, where they tend to unite over the root of the nose. . . . Their long, narrow heads often have prognathous faces, the upper and lower jaws protruding forward. The nose is generally narrow, prominent, often convex, but only rarely of the kind popularly considered "Jewish." Many of them have a rather large mouth with thick lips, especially the underlip. They are medium-sized, slender, narrow-shouldered, but graceful people, with a somewhat melancholy and thoughtful expression . . . this type of Jews is . . . met with [not only] among those who can trace their ancestry back to Spain and Portugal. Many of the Russian, Polish, German and English Jews are of this type. [On the other hand] many Sephardim look like the Spanish among whom they have lived for many centuries; others remind one of the Moors. . . . The Sephardim of today in various European countries have taken on many somatological traits of the races and peoples among whom they live. . . .

The Ashkenazi type, according to Fishberg, is brunette, with 30 per cent blond and 50 per cent blue eyes. The Ashkenazim

are brachycephalic, and in the Caucasus even hyperbrachycephalic. They correspond on the whole to the "Alpine" race of Ripley. Their face is round, with prominent cheekbones, and the nose medium-sized, broad, with fleshy wings, often narrow and depressed at the root, appearing generally somewhat pear-shaped. . . . The chin is heavy, the mouth large, and the lips thick, all of which give a rather heavy expression to the countenance. What has been said about the diversity of type of the Spanish [i.e., Sephardi] Jews applies with more emphasis to the German, Polish and Russian follower of Judaism [i.e., the Ashkenazim] who are even less uniform physically.

Among these European Jews, says Fishberg, we encounter the Sephardi type, as well as the following five other types:
The Slavonic, which is most prominent, with

usually grey or beer-colored eyes, deeply set in the sockets, a very broad face, prominent cheek-bones, and an abundant beard. They are of medium height and brachycephalic. In fact many of these Jews are hardly to be distinguished from their Slavonic neighbors. . . . It is also a striking fact that anthropologically they conform to certain ethnic types encountered in this region of Europe, which Deniker called *race orientale,* and *race vistulienne.* . . .

The Turanian type, "encountered very often among the Jews in South Russia and Austrian Galicia, Bukovina and Rumania . . . is slightly above the median height," with "a short square face with very prominent cheek-bones with some depression immediately below. The nose is short and thick, with a deep indentation at the root; it is straight, never hooked, often re-troussé or snub. . . ."

The North European or Teutonic type is also "often found among the Russian, Polish, German and English Jews. They have the usual character-istics of North Europeans: they are tall, or above the medium height, often dolichocephalic, have blonde hair and blue eyes; the face is narrow and oval in shape, the nose delicate, narrow, long and straight, rarely aquiline, and the lips of medium size. . . ."

The Mongoloid type, which Fishberg calls "the most curious," is

> often seen in Russia, Poland and Germany, especially among women and children. . . . Their chief characteristics are long, smooth, black hair, which is very thick. . . . The most distinguishing trait, however, is the Mongolian eye, which is placed obliquely, or slanting . . . it has the appearance of a triangle. In general, the face of these people is square or lozenge-shaped, and the nose small, short, slightly depressed at its upper half, while broad at its lower half.

Weissenberg, says Fishberg, found "slanty eyes" among 13 per cent of the adult male Jews in Europe, but he found the epicanthic fold only among children.

The Negroid type is met with among the Jews of Eastern Europe, "who have not come in contact with Negroes for centuries." The skin of this type "is very dark, the hair black and woolley, the head long with a prominent occiput. The face is prognathous, the two jaws are projecting in the form of a muzzle. The lips are large, thick and upturned, and the nose flat, broad, and the wings upturned so that the nostrils can be seen in profile."

After disposing of these "main types of Jews in Europe," Fishberg goes on to describe the physical types found among the Jews of Asia and Africa. But here, in contrast to his procedure in dealing with the European Jews, he does not describe a type and then state in which countries it is found, but takes the individual countries as his point of departure—Yemen, Bokhara, Persia, and so on. He goes along with the view of Burchard and Weissen-berg that the Yemenite Jews "are racially Arabs who have adopted Ju-daism." The Persian Jews "differ physically very little from the rest of the population of Persia." As for the Jews of the Caucasus, and especially of Daghestan, "it is impossible to distinguish them from the Tats, Lesghians, and Circassians among whom they live." On the so-called white Jews of India, Fishberg quotes Emil Schmidt, a German traveler and ethnographer, who described them in 1892 and 1894 as belonging to either of the two types termed by Fishberg Ashkenazim and Sephardim, respectively. The "black Jews" of India range from fair to dark in skin color, but their major-ity "are hardly to be distinguished from the native Hindus living on the Malabar coast." The Chinese Jews "can easily pass as Chinamen." The

Jews in North Africa "are of distinctly African appearance." The Tunisian Jews have a cephalic index of 77.56, "thus corresponding to the type of head among the Mohammedans of that region of Africa. The author [Fishberg] was unable to distinguish a Jew from a Mohammedan while passing along the streets of Algiers, Constantine, and Tunis." The Berber Jews or Daggatuns of the oases of the Sahara, says Fishberg, are described by late nineteenth-century observers as "physically . . . hardly to be distinguished from their Mohammedan neighbors, excepting by the color of their skin which is said to be somewhat fairer." In the oasis of Mzab in Southern Algeria the Jews can hardly be distinguished from the non-Jews. The Jews in northern Morocco who live among the Riff Berbers are physically "decidedly of the Berber race, having blond hair and blue eyes." The Falashas are "physically akin to other Abyssinians." [50]

In 1914 Karl Kautsky, the German Socialist, published a small book entitled *Rasse and Judentum* (*Race and Jewry*) in which, relying heavily on Fishberg, he explained:

> The Jews of the present day are not a pure race, either geographically or chronologically . . . even if the Jews had originally constituted a pure race, they could not have maintained their purity, owing to the impossibility of preventing a mingling with foreign elements . . . the Jews of each region present many physical characteristics in common with the non-Jewish population of the same region. This may, perhaps, be an effect of like natural conditions on both Jews and non-Jews. But it is just as plausible to assume that it may be the result of sexual contact between Jews and non-Jews.[51]

In 1921 Felix von Luschan, modifying his earlier views, went on record against the "uniform origin of the Jews" and against the argument that the Jews represent an absolutely pure race—a view which at the time was embraced by "Jewish colleagues with special energy." Luschan reminded the scholarly gathering he was addressing that he himself

> had emphasized again and again ever since 1892 that essentially the Jews emerged from a mixture of the non-Semitic Hittites (and their relatives) with Semitic nomads for whom Abraham is the eponymous hero. To these two main elements was added an influx, never interrupted for thousands of years, of the actual neighbors of the Jews, which led, in several localities, to an almost total displacement of the old somatic elements. Thus the Jews in Yemen are in reality Yemenites, the Abyssinian Jews are somatically almost pure Abyssinians, the Jews in China almost pure Chinese, and the Italian Jews almost pure Italians.[52]

New insight into the racial position of the Jews was expressed with force and clarity by Franz Boas, who is generally considered the father of modern American anthropology. In a paper first published in 1923, Boas stated:

> Even in antiquity, while the Jews still formed an independent state, they represented a thorough mixture of divergent racial types . . . three elements (the Armenian type of Asia Minor, the Arab type of the Arabian Peninsula, and

the Kurdish type of Asia Minor) were represented in the ancient Jews. . . .
Even in antiquity, therefore, we cannot speak of a Jewish race as distinct from
other races in Asia Minor. . . . What we ordinarily designate as a Jewish type
is, as a matter of fact, simply an Oriental type.

The dispersion of the Jews all over the world has tended to increase considerably the intermixture. A comparison of the Jews of North Africa with those of
Western Europe and those of Russia, not to speak of those of Southern Asia,
shows very clearly that in every single instance we have a marked assimilation
between the Jews and the people among whom they live. . . . The Jews of
North Africa are, in their essential traits, North Africans. The Jews of Europe
are in their essential traits Europeans, and the black Jews of the East are in their
essential traits members of a dark-pigmented race.

The assimilation of the Jews by the people among whom they live is much
more far-reaching than a hasty observation might suggest. In stature as well as
in head form and in other features there is a decided parallelism between the
bodily form of the Jews and that of the people among whom they live.[53]

In the same year in which Boas made these observations, another American anthropologist, Roland B. Dixon, remarked in his *Racial History
of Man* that in North Africa, among both Jews and non-Jews one finds a
predominance of dolichocephaly, which becomes more pronounced as one
proceeds from the west toward Egypt, and that "in Germany, the lower
proportion of brachycelphalic factors of the Jews in Cologne and
Frankfort-on-Main, as compared with Baden, was the same as the Gentile
German population." [54]

Just one year later, Eugène Pittard, a French anthropologist, flatly denied
the existence of a Jewish race: "No Jewish race, in the zoological sense of
the word, exists. . . . There is no more a Christian race than a Musulman
race. And neither is there any such thing as a Jewish race." [55]

Earnest A. Hooton expressed the identical idea in 1926: "To refer to the
'Jewish race' is to differentiate race on the basis of religion." [56] And Julian
S. Huxley and A. C. Haddon reiterated practically the same argument in
1936:

The ancient Jews were formed as the result of crossing between several groups
of markedly distinct type. Later there has always been a certain amount of
crossing between the Jews and the non-Jewish inhabitants of the countries where
they have dwelt. . . . The result is that the Jews of different areas are not genetically equivalent, and that in each country the Jewish population overlaps
with the non-Jewish in every conceivable character.[57]

In 1939 two American anthropologists reached the same conclusion.
Louis L. Snyder stated: "The Jews, like other peoples, reflect the physical
type among which they live. . . ." [58]

And in a similar vein, the Harvard anthropologist Carl C. Seltzer came
to the conclusion, in a paper devoted to the racial status of the Jews, that

in the anthropological meaning of the word "race," it can be said with conviction that the Jewish people, taken as a whole, show no preponderance, nor con-

sistency, nor exclusiveness of physical features which allow them to be classified as a unified racial group. They are a conglomerate mixture of many races in disparate proportions bound together by common religion, familial, and historical traditions, but showing in many instances varying amounts of physical distinctiveness. We can no more classify the Jews into a race than we can say that there is an American race. . . . [59]

Typical of the lack of agreement that prevailed as late as 1942 is the fact that in the same volume in which Coon developed his views on the preservation of their Palestinian racial heritage by the Jews, another anthropologist, Melville Jacobs, propounded a diametrically opposing view. According to Jacobs, "there is no evidence for the existence of a distinctive Jewish blood or 'race,' nor has there ever been a group of family lines of Jews that could be called a 'race.' The Jewish leader who speaks about 'our race' is talking unadulterated nonsense . . . linguistically and biologically the Jewish people have often changed into forms indistinguishable from the Gentile people around them." [60]

Ellsworth Huntington considers the Jews a "kith," that is, "a group of people relatively homogeneous in language and culture, and freely intermarrying with one another," and claims that "to call them [the Jews] a race like the Nordic or Mediterranean races would be comparable to listing the English or French in the same way. Biologically they are about as uniform as is the average intermarrying social and geographical unit among other white peoples. . . ." The Jews nevertheless "stand out so distinctly" because "the process of selection depends upon mentality far more than upon the external physical traits on which races are based." In a later passage Huntington speaks of the " 'racial' diversity and outward physical resemblances [of the Jews] to the gentiles among whom they live," in spite of which, "there is reason to think that the Jews tend to preserve a preponderance of certain innate temperamental aptitudes and capacities." [61]

As early as 1923, Alfred Kroeber, one of the most influential American anthropologists, had expressed the view that the Jews were not a race. In 1948, he reiterated this with greater emphasis:

The Jews everywhere considerably approximate the local gentile type. In Algiers they tend to resemble Mediterraneans, in Turkey Armenoids, in northern Germany Nordics. There has evidently been more mixture across the religious caste line through the generations than either side likes to admit. To put it differently, normally a part of any Jewish population is physically indistinguishable, by measures or by observation, from the Christians or the Mohammedans of the same area. The part that is differentiable appears to be so through hereditary persistence of either Armenoid or Oriental-Mediterranean traits. . . . There is certainly no single crude physical trait that is a safe index of Jewishness. [62]

Let us close this list with a quotation from Ashley Montagu, who expressed the same idea in the following way:

The fact is that there is not now nor was there ever a Jewish race . . . the Jewish religion is not a mark of any race whatsoever since any member of any race may belong to it. As for people who are identified with "the" Jews, they are drawn from probably more heterogeneous sources than any other identifiable people in the world. The ethnic ingredients entering into the formation of the group called Jews have not undergone mixture in a common melting pot, but remain very various. Clearly, then, the Jews are not anything approaching a homogeneous, biological entity, nor are they a race or an ethnic group.[63]

CHAPTER II

An Excursus
into Statistics

INTRODUCTORY REMARKS

W ERE THE DATA available, we would proceed directly at this
point to a statistical presentation of the non-Jewish contribution
to the Jewish gene pool from the days of Abraham (seventeenth century
B.C.) to the twentieth century. Since, however, such statistics are no-
toriously lacking, we will have to be satisfied instead with whatever estimates can be made of the extent of Jewish-Gentile interbreeding. Even this
more modest goal cannot be reached easily or with any degree of reliability.
In fact, there seems to be only a rather cumbersome and indirect way in
which one can get even the roughest idea of the relative weight of non-
Jewish genes in the racial composition of the Jews. This roundabout route
can be mapped out as follows:

First, we shall have to try to estimate the size of the various Jewish communities dispersed in the midst of many different host peoples. The importance of this figure becomes evident if we consider that the smaller the size
of a Jewish community, the greater the genetic significance for it of every
single child born as the result of Jewish-Gentile interbreeding and brought
up as a member of that community. Second, we shall have to concentrate
on the question of the frequency of such interbreedings. What information,
we must ask, exists on the various circumstances which led to interbreeding?
As we shall see, there were individual and group conversions of non-Jews;
there were slavery and concubinage; there were Jewish prostitutes; and there
was forced intercourse. In addition, in recent times there has also been intermarriage with neither of the partners adopting the religion of the other. The

40

children of converts were, of course, brought up as Jews. As to those born as the issue of the various forms of Jewish-Gentile interbreeding, it is extremely difficult to estimate how often they were brought up as Jews. In the great majority of cases, events which led to Jewish-Gentile interbreeding remained unnoticed and unrecorded. Traces of them were preserved only if they were accompanied by something unusual, such as a major scandal, litigation, public punishment, or forced renunciation. The pages of Jewish history contain numerous accounts of such occurrences, but the nature of the records is such that one cannot total them up and on this basis calculate the percentage of non-Jewish genes added in any given generation to the Jewish gene pool. Nevertheless, we shall have to try to pull together all the available data and consider the combined effect of all this on the Jewish gene pool. The results will, of course, be very tentative; but they should, at least, give us some idea about the Gentile contribution to the genetic make-up of the Jewish people at the present time.

Before embarking on our quest for data, let us illustrate the cumulative effects of even the most limited interbreeding if practiced over several generations. Let us assume that there was a Jewish community somewhere in the Rhineland which in the year A.D. 800 numbered 100 souls, and that it maintained the same number until A.D. 1600. If, in this community, one case of interbreeding occurred once every ten years, then, after 100 years there were in it 95 per cent Jewish and 5 per cent Gentile genes; after 200 years, the ratio was 90.5 to 9.5; after 400 years, 82 to 18; and after 800 years, 67.1 to 32.9. In other words, after 800 years about one-third of the genes of the community would be of Gentile origin. If one case of interbreeding occurred, not once every ten years, but once every five years, then, after 100 years the ratio was 90.5 to 9.5; after 200 years, 82 to 18; after 400, 67.1 to 32.9; and after 800, 45 to 55. In this case, after 800 years only 45 per cent of the genes of the community would still be of Jewish origin.

With this purely hypothetical example in mind, we shall try in this chapter to put together sample estimates of the size of Jewish communities from about the eleventh to the seventeenth centuries. These seven centuries were the period in which the Jews spread all over Europe. They were also the times of the worst persecutions of Jews in many countries, including massacres, expulsions, and forced conversions. They were times of great upheaval and of great scattering for the Jews, throughout which they nevertheless managed to hold their own demographically, so that whenever massacres or pestilences decimated their numbers, in two or three generations they again attained their former numerical strength. They were, finally, the times in which much of the genetic basis for today's "racial" configuration of the Jews was laid down.

BENJAMIN OF TUDELA

In the middle of the twelfth century, a Jew of Tudela, Spain, driven by a quite unusual curiosity about his brethren dispersed in the three continents of the Old World, set out on a long and perilous voyage which took him as far east as Iraq and Egypt before he returned home in about 1173. Wherever he went he set down the number of the Jews as best he could ascertain it, as well as other details about them; the record of his trip, the famous itinerary of Benjamin of Tudela, is one of the first and most valuable sources of Jewish demography and ethnography. However, Benjamin's figures are of very uneven reliability. Generally speaking, the farther away he got from his home base, the larger his figures become and the less reliable they must be judged. Close to home in neighboring Italy, for example, he gives realistic figures which are almost without exception quite small, and which must be judged relatively accurate. When he notes that there were 20 Jews in Pisa, one can assume that this was the actual figure given by his hosts during his visit to the city. Moreover, the appearance of an inquisitive foreigner must have created sufficient interest in the small Jewish community for all the adult males to wish to see, meet, and greet him, and thus give him a chance to have the figure confirmed by several informants, or perhaps to make a personal count of the families. When, on the other hand, he states that there were 40,000 Jews in Baghdad, we cannot but ascribe much less reliance to such a large figure, which must have been given him by one or more of the local leaders who would be inclined to exaggerate in order to impress the Western visitor. Needless to say, in such a large community a visitor would have no opportunity to make a personal count of families or persons involved.

The rapid increase of Benjamin's figures with the growth of his mileage can be illustrated by referring to a few of the countries he covered. His figures for the number of Jews in French and Italian cities range from 2 Jews in Genoa to 600 in Salerno. In Greece the numbers become somewhat higher, but are still realistic; they range from 30 Jews in Aphilon (Achelous) to 2,000 in Thebes. In Palestine, too, his figures are modest, ranging from 1 Jew in Lod (Lydda) to 300 in Ramleh. It is to the east of Palestine that his figures become suspiciously high for the countries he actually visited, and nothing less than fantastic for those lands of which he reports on the basis of hearsay. He did visit (in addition to France, Italy, Sicily, and Greece) Syria, Palestine, Iraq, the Persian Gulf, and Egypt. His figures for Iraq typically range in the thousands and tens of thousands (from 2,000 in Rahbah to 40,000 in Baghdad). For Persia and Arabia, which he did not visit, he gives the Jewish populations in the tens and hundreds of thousands (e.g., Samarkand 50,000 Jews; Ghaznah 80,000; Tilmas in the oasis of Teyma, in Arabia, 100,000; in the district of which Tanai is the principal city, between

Teyma and Khaybar, 300,000). Evidently these figures have no realistic value whatsoever.[1]

For some reason, Baghdad provoked other observers, too, to gross exaggerations. Thus, according to the famous Arab geographer Yaqut (1179–1229), in the early thirteenth century "the Jews had 6,000 streets in the west of Baghdad and 4,000 streets on the east side, within a perimeter of nearly 20 miles." The total population of Baghdad in the early tenth century was given at the time as 2 million, which is quite surprising considering that Angevin England in the twelfth century seems to have had a total population of no more than 1.5 million.[2]

MEDIEVAL SPAIN

In medieval Spain the number of Jews in general was on the increase until the expulsion of 1492. In 1079, there were 60 Jewish households in Barcelona. In 1266, in Jerez de la Frontera there were 102 Jewish house owners, or about 120 to 150 Jewish families. In 1290, there were 50 Jewish families in Avila, 55 in Segovia, and 350 in Toledo. In 1388, there were 20 Jewish families in the hamlet of Valdeolivas in the district of Cuenca. Baer estimates that by the end of the thirteenth century there were 3,600 Jewish families in Castile, the same number in Aragon, and 400 in Navarre, or a total of some 40,000 Jews in the three kingdoms. Baron, on the other hand, estimates that in 1300 their number was over 150,000, and that by 1490 this number had increased to about 250,000. In the same two centuries, the number of the Jews of Portugal increased from about 40,000 to 80,000. However, we must not imagine that this increase took place evenly in all places and throughout the period in question. For instance, the largest Jewish community of Navarre, that of the city of Tudela, was reduced from some 500 families before 1300 to 270 in 1366, and to 90 in 1391. In 1348–49, and again in 1369–70, the Black Death struck Spain, and its result, combined with that of anti-Jewish riots, was a reduction of the Jewish population of Sargossa, the new capital of Aragon, to one-fifth of its former size. Before the 1492 expulsion, only 2,000 Jews lived in the city.[3]

ENGLAND

In medieval England the total number of the Jews seems to have gradually increased from about 4,000 in 1194 to 8–10,000 in 1290. The largest community was that of London, with about 2,000 to 2,500 Jews just before 1290. In Oxford, in the twelfth to thirteenth centuries, there were about 200 Jews; in Canterbury in 1240–70, 69 Jewish men and 5 women. Bristol in 1250–90 counted 53 Jews (probably only adult males). The rest, some 7,000, were dispersed in about 200 settlements, yielding an average of 35 persons per locality.[4]

The Jews were expelled from England in 1290 and readmitted in 1656. A century and a half later (early nineteenth century) their number had reached only 8,000, equaling the minimum estimate for 1290. Of these, 6,000 were concentrated in London.

FRANCE

In the eleventh to fifteenth centuries the size of the Jewish communities in France, as in the rest of Christian Europe, was in most cases surprisingly small. At Chalons, only two Jewish families are mentioned. In several communities it was impossible to assemble a *minyan*—the ten adult males required for communal prayer. This led to the development of the custom of placing a Torah scroll into the hands of a boy-child, and thus counting him as the tenth if only nine men were present—a practice condemned twice by Rashi (1040–1105), the sage of Troyes. Since in those days the local lords did not look with favor upon Jewish meetings, the community would assemble in secret, in a cellar or graveyard, which again indicates its small size.[5]

Even the largest Jewish communities in the period discussed—those of Aix, Avignon, Arles, Gascony, and Narbonne—numbered no more than up to 1,000 persons or 200 families. In many other places, such as Carpentras, Dijon, Mayence, Tarascon, Toulouse, there were 10 to 100 Jewish families. In Paris in 1292 there were only 86 Jewish households comprising the surprisingly low number of 124 persons; by 1296–97, the number of Jewish households had decreased to 82. In eleventh-century Troyes, at the very time when Rashi, the greatest Jewish commentator of all times, headed his famous school in the city, there were only 100 Jews. In 1391, there were 9 families in Folcalquier; Reillance had 7 families, and Viens 2.[6] Since hundreds of French Jewish communities are mentioned in rabbinic sources, and it has been estimated that at the final expulsion of the Jews from France in 1394 some 100,000 Jews may have been affected, the average French Jewish community could not have numbered more than 200 persons, if that many.

ITALY

The situation was not much different in Italy: a few communities with a thousand or more Jews, and several dozen, if not a few hundred, small communities with not more than 100 persons each. Thus, in the 1160's there were 1,500 Jewish families in Palermo (Sicily); 600 in Salerno; 500 each in Naples and Otranto; 300 each in Taranto and Capua; and 200 each in Messina (Sicily), Benevento, Malfi, and Trani. In many other places the numbers were much smaller. In Lucca, Tuscany, there were 40 Jewish families; in Pisa and Amalfi 20 each; and so on. By the fifteenth and sixteenth centuries, the size of the Jewish communities in Italy had increased markedly in some places while remaining small in others. Thus, in 1381 there were 33 Jewish families in Perugia. In the fifteenth century Palermo and Syracuse had 5,000 Jews. All in all, the expulsion of 1492 affected some 50,000 Sicilian Jews. In the same century there were another 50,000 Jews in the Neapolitan provinces, while in 1429 there were 638 Jewish taxpayers in Lanciano, or approximately 3,000 Jews. Trapani in 1439 had 240 Jewish tax-paying households; in 1492, 336.[7]

A few Italian Jewish communities exhibited phenomenal growth, due primarily to their ability to attract immigrants from other parts of the country or from abroad. Rome was one of them. In 1526–27, 285 Jewish families or 1,500 persons lived in Rome out of a total population of 55,000. By 1555, their number had grown to 3,000; by 1592, to 3,500 in a total population of 97,000; and by 1655, to 4,500, of whom, however, 1,600 perished in the pestilence of 1656. Nevertheless, the Roman Jewish community almost quadrupled in the course of the seventeenth century, and continued to grow in the eighteenth despite the conversion of 2,430 Roman Jews to Christianity between 1634 and 1790. In 1688 Misson estimated their number at 6–7,000. Venice experienced a similar growth. Jews began to settle in 1509; in the early sixteenth century, the city numbered only a few hundred Jews. By 1552, they had increased to 902 (in a total population of 158,067); by 1586, to 1,694; by 1632, to 2,414 (while epidemics had reduced the total population to 98,244); and by 1655, allegedly to 4,870 (the total population meanwhile recovered its 1552 strength and numbered 158,722).[8]

Other Italian cities and duchies, too, attracted large numbers of Jews in the sixteenth and seventeenth centuries. Among them were Padua, Mantua, Leghorn, Turin, Lugo, Ferrara, Pisa, and Pesaro.[9] That Jews did not hesitate to settle in cities in which there was no Jewish community is shown by such instances as that of Turin, where the 1428–29 census recorded only 4 Jewish families and the subsequent 1431 census 11. The records also show that occasionally a few Jews sought and obtained permission to reside in a city temporarily, for a few years, as happened in 1550 in Genoa. While no historical records are extant as to the number of Jewish settlements in Italy in the Middle Ages, Baron estimates that the total number of Jews in Italy in 1300 was 50,000 and in 1490, 120,000.[10] Deducting the known figures of the large Jewish communities from this total, one is led to estimate that on the average not more than 100–200 Jews resided in each of the 100–200 smaller Jewish settlements of Italy.

GERMANY

The figures were comparable in the German lands. A few cities had a relatively large concentration of Jews, while many more Jews lived in extremely small groups in hundreds of towns, hamlets, and other localities. Moreover, the number of Jews in the large communities was subject to rapid fluctuations. In Mainz in 1096 there were at most 1,300 Jews; in Magdeburg and Merseburg, about 1,000 each. In the whole of Germany prior to the First Crusade their number could not have exceeded 20,000. Nuremberg in 1298 had about 1,000 Jews; in 1338, the city census showed 2,006 Jews; in 1349, the number dwindled to 1,000; and in 1449, it was further reduced to about 750. The isolation of the Jews in fourteenth-century Germany is illustrated by figures such as those for Wismar, in which in 1311 there were only 6 Jewish families. Erfurt in 1389 had 76 families of Jewish taxpayers and an additional 26 indigent Jewish families, giving a total of 102 families or about 750 persons, counting more than 7 persons per household. In 1438, when the Jews were exiled from Augsburg, more than 300 were forced to depart. The number of Jews in Germany remained small in the fifteenth century. Baron estimates that in 1438 the 16 largest German Jewish communities had a total of some 15–18,000 persons, or an average of 1,000 per community.[11]

In evaluating these figures one must not forget that most medieval cities were very small—at least when measured by modern standards. In the fifteenth century only twenty-one German cities boasted a population of over 10,000. Thus, in the largest cities the Jews constituted a sizable minority approximating up to 10 per cent of the total population. In most places, however, during the fifteenth and sixteenth centuries we find only a few isolated Jewish families. Memmingen and its environs in 1541 had 40 Jewish families scattered in eleven localities; Koblenz in 1512, 2 Jewish families; Boppard in 1518, 3, and in 1547, 34. In Berlin in 1564 there were 10 Jewish families, and in Stendal in the same year, 9. In 1571 there were 25 Jewish men and 78 women and children in Frankfort on the Oder. On the other hand, in Würzburg in 1556 there were allegedly 300 Jews, and in Hotzenplotz (Osoblaha) in 1616, 135 Jewish families. Some Jewish communities remained small throughout the seventeenth century, others experienced considerable growth: Hanau from 1612 to 1700 had only 10 Jewish families; Friedberg in Upper Hesse had 16 Jewish taxpayers in 1536 and 107 in 1609.[12]

The fluctuation in size of Jewish communities is well illustrated by Frankfort on the Main. In 1417–39 only 2 to 6 Jewish families lived in this city. By 1463 their number had grown to 110 persons. By 1496 they were reduced to 14 households; by 1520 they again increased to 250 persons. In 1536 the number was roughly the same—56 families. The city had 900 Jews in 1569; in 1600, 2,200. Ten years later the number was reduced to about one-half—197 families. But by 1613 they had again more than doubled—454 families. In 1618 they were reduced to 370 households or 1,998 persons. The year 1624 showed a slight increase: 409 households with 2,209 persons. In 1639 the figures were again down to 285 households with 1,539 persons; and in 1648, they numbered 329 households with 1,777 persons.[13]

As in Spain, wars, pestilence, and expulsion were among the chief causes of these fluctuations on the downward side. Thus Glogau, Silesia, had 600 Jews in 1625; by 1631 the war and pestilence had reduced their number to 200. Factors making for increase were the issuance of residence permits by the authorities, and the ever-present high rates of natural increase among the Jews. Occasionally, Jews from remote parts of the world were admitted to residence. In the late sixteenth century the Elector Johann of Trèves, wishing to extend commerce with the East, gave residence licenses to Jewish merchants from Egypt and Syria, for example. This, incidentally, is one of the cases where historical documentation is available for Ashkenazi-Oriental Jewish interbreeding in Central Europe.[14]

HUNGARY

The largest Jewish community in Hungary in the late fifteenth and early sixteenth century was that of Buda, with 3,000 persons. Five additional communities, Pozsony (Pressburg), Nagyszombat, Székesfehérvár, Györ, and Esztergom, comprised 800 persons each; six others had 500 each, and seven 200 each. The total number of Jews in these 19 largest communities was 11,400. In other, smaller communities scattered over villages on the domains of feudal lords, there may have been about the same number of Jews. Thus the total number can be estimated at 20,000 to 22,000. After their conquest of central Hungary (1526), the Turks deported many Jews to Turkey; in 1547 only 100 Jewish taxpayers, representing 500–600 persons, remained in Buda. During the Turkish occupation, the number of Jews in Buda seems to have remained unchanged: in 1686, after the defeat of the Turks, there were 25 Jewish houses or 500–600 persons in the city.[15]

BOHEMIA

In Prague, the Jewish community lost three-quarters of its members in the pestilence of 1473; in the 1546 census of the city, 1,000 Jews are listed; and a not quite reliable census carried out in 1638 showed 7,815 Jews, which number, however, was again reduced to half by the pestilence of the following year.[16]

POLAND, LITHUANIA, RUSSIA

The number of Jews in East Europe remained very small until the end of the Middle Ages. It has been estimated that in 1300 there were only 5,000 Jews in all Poland and Lithuania, and that by 1490 their number had reached 30,000. The sixteenth century saw a considerable increase of the Jewish communities in East Europe, so much so that it is estimated that in the catastrophic decade of 1648–58 no less than 250,000 (and according to other estimates 500,000) Jews perished as a result of the Cossack uprisings and the plague.

However, even after the intellectual and numerical center of Jewry had moved to East Europe, its numbers still remained relatively small. In 1648, just before the Chmielnicki massacres, there were Jewish communities in 115 localities in the districts of Volhynia, Podolia, Kiev, and Bratslav, with a total of 51,000 Jews, which averages out at 444 Jews per community. The overwhelming majority of the Jews lived in communities with fewer than 500 persons: in Masovia, 93.5 per cent of all Jews lived in such relatively small groups; in Great Poland, 91.7 per cent; in the Ukraine, 85 per cent; in Lesser (or Little) Poland, 76.5 per cent; and in Lvov, 61.7 per cent. As late as the end of the eighteenth century, there were only 3,532 Jews in Warsaw (constituting a mere 4.5 per cent of the total population), while only 11 Jews (or 5.7 per cent of the total) lived in Lodz. The number of Jews in the Kingdom of Poland (including Lithuania) is estimated at about 300,000; not more than another 100,000 Jews were found at the time in all the rest of Europe. The phenomenal increase of Polish Jewry began around the middle of the nineteenth century, bringing the number of Jews in the two cities mentioned to 219,141 in Warsaw by 1897, and to 166,628 in Lodz by 1910. By 1930 there were some 6 million Jews in Poland and European Russia alone.[17]

SUM TOTALS

In summing up the Jewish population of Europe in 1300 and in 1490, Baron gives the following table of figures which, he cautions, are of a "wholly tentative character":

COUNTRY	1300		1490	
	JEWS	TOTAL POP.	JEWS	TOTAL POP.
France (incl. Avignon)	100,000	14,000,000	20,000	20,000,000
Holy Roman Empire (incl. Switzerland and the Low Countries)	100,000	12,000,000	80,000	12,000,000
Italy	50,000	11,000,000	120,000	12,000,000
Spain (Castile, Aragon, and Navarre)	150,000	5,500,000	250,000	7,000,000
Portugal	40,000	600,000	80,000	1,000,000
Poland-Lithuania	5,000	500,000	30,000	1,000,000
Hungary	5,000	400,000	20,000	800,000
Total in Christian Europe	450,000	44,000,000	600,000	53,800,000

SOURCE: Salo W. Baron, *A Social and Religious History of the Jews*, New York: Columbia University Press, and Philadelphia: The Jewish Publication Society of America, vol. xii, p. 25.

It might be mentioned in passing that earlier students of Jewish statistics and demography gave lower estimates for the number of the Jews in the Middle Ages. According to Ruppin, there were in 1300 only 300,000, and in 1500 only 500,000 Ashkenazi Jews, and he gives the number of Sephardi and Oriental Jews as 1.7 million and 1 million respectively.[18]

CONCLUSION

In summarizing this data, two points are particularly important. One is the proportion of Jews to Gentiles; the other, the average size of the Jewish communities in which most Jews lived. Throughout the period in question, the Jews in Europe generally constituted about 1 per cent of the total population. Since in modern times European (Ashkenazi) Jews have accounted for some four-fifths of the world Jewish population, their racial antecedents are more significant for the problem of the Jewish "race" at present than those of the Sephardi and Oriental (Middle Eastern) divisions of Jewry. If, then, we consider only the Ashkenazi Jews, we find that in 1300 they numbered about 260,000 in the midst of 37.9 million Gentiles, or about 0.7 per cent of the total population; while in 1490 they numbered 270,000 among 50 million Gentiles, or 0.54 per cent of the total. The vulnerability of such a small minority to the genetic influence of a 150 to 190 times larger majority requires no elaboration.

To this overall numerical relationship between Jews and Gentiles must be added the effect of the small size of most Jewish communities. As we have seen, medieval historical records show extremely small numbers for the Jewish contingents in almost every one of the thousands of localities in which Jews lived all over the European Continent. In search of a livelihood, individual Jews or single Jewish families would settle in many a town or village in which no other Jews lived. In other places, no more than 4 or 5 Jewish families would constitute the Jewish community. In medieval England the great majority of the Jews lived in small communities of 35 persons each on the average. The figures for France show a similar picture. In many parts of Europe this general pattern continued down to the nineteenth century, despite the phenomenal growth of a few central Jewish communities, usually in capital cities. In Hungary, for instance, in the village of Pata where the father of one and the grandfather of the other author of this book lived as a child in the 1880's, there were only 5 Jewish families in a village of some 2,000. The problem of how to assemble a *minyan* for communal prayer, which preoccupied Rashi in eleventh-century France, was acute in nineteenth-century Pata: on Friday evenings and Saturday mornings a *minyan* could be assembled only if at least 5 adult Jews came over from the neighboring village of Szücsi, which also lacked the number for an independent *minyan*.

In the fervently religious atmosphere of the Jewish communities of medi-

49

eval Europe outside the Mediterranean area, voluntary interbreeding with Gentiles was rarely initiated by Jews. However, forcible violations of Jewish women by Gentiles were more frequent, especially in localities where the few Jews could offer no resistance to even a small group of Gentile hooligans, and where there was no Jewish ghetto with walls and gates to protect them. The frequent recurrence of such incidents was the reason for rabbinical injunctions against settling in localities where no other Jews lived. The very presence of small and scattered splinter groups of outlandish Jews, differing in religion and mores, language and mannerisms, appearance, customs, and occupations, disliked at best and hated at worst, brought about the sexual violation of Jewish women among several other types of abuses.

It appears that the hypothetical example with which we opened this chapter is not so far-fetched after all. Whether violations and impregnations of Jewish women in a given locality actually occurred once in 5 or 10 years on the average we have, of course, no way of knowing. But there can be no doubt that the situation, the circumstances, the folk mores being what they were in the Middle Ages all over Europe, forcible interbreeding between Gentile males and Jewish females did occur quite frequently. It is here that we must seek a primary explanation for the often striking genetic and phenotypic similarity between Ashkenazi Jews and the Gentiles of the countries in which they have lived during and since the Middle Ages. Several specific aspects of this issue will be considered in subsequent chapters.

CHAPTER III

Proselytism

"Abraham was the first proselyte"
—B. Sukka 49b

Proselytism, the conversion of Gentiles to Judaism and their incorporation into the Jewish community, is a phenomenon which has accompanied the Jewish people throughout its long history,[1] and which, among its other results, has had far-reaching genetic consequences for the Jewish community.

EXTENT AND EVALUATION

The documentary evidence concerning proselytism, although available from biblical times down to the present, is sporadic and gives no total picture of the phenomenon in any age. It is in the nature of historical records that they either pertain to the lives and doings of important figures or else describe great group actions and events. The lives and works of simple folk have always passed unnoticed. If a bishop, count, merchant prince, officer, scholar, or author converted to Judaism, there was a chance that the event would leave its traces in some records. Even in such cases the embarrassment of the ruling church which the proselyte deserted, and the possibility of vengeful persecution of the community whose ranks he joined, often resulted in a conspiracy of silence. If the convert was one of the common people, the fateful step taken in embracing Judaism would remain unrecorded, except in those cases in which the convert subsequently suffered a martyr's death, and his name was listed in a communal martyrology along with born Jews who shared the same fate.

In every age and place, there must have been many times more converts to Judaism that those whose names have come down to us. How many times

51

more is difficult to guess. But considering the numerical relationship between outstanding people and the common folk, and the fact that it was the
common folk for whom Judaism held more attraction, it does not seem far-
fetched to assume that for every known proselyte there may have been a
hundred or more whose conversion left no traces in the annals.

While the historical evidence is thus tantalizingly unsatisfactory, it nevertheless appears that the early centuries of Jewish dispersion before the
triumph of Christianity were especially propitious for Jewish proselytizing.
After examining all the extant Greco-Roman sources, the German historian
Emil Schürer came to the conclusion that "the Jewish propaganda in Hellenistic-Roman times must have been a very lively one." He emphasizes that in
the Diaspora, *"Israel felt itself the teacher of the world of nations,"* and
that

> the *success* of these endeavors was a very considerable one. By all the indica-
> tions which we have it can be assumed that, in Hellenistic-Roman times, the
> number of those who joined the Jewish communities . . . participated in the
> Jewish synagogue service, and observed the Jewish law, sometimes completely,
> was very great.

Schürer finds that

> *almost everywhere in the Diaspora the Jewish communities were joined by a fol-
> lowing of "God-fearing" pagans* who adopted the Jewish (i.e., monotheistic
> and aniconic) manner of worshipping God, frequented the Jewish synagogues,
> but as to the observances of the ritual law confined themselves to certain main
> points, and were, consequently, not at all counted as part of the Jewish commu-
> nites.

Of those Gentiles who completed their conversion by baptism and circumcision and thus became full members of the Jewish community, Schürer
remarks that while we do not know how large was their number, "in the
early period of the Jewish propaganda it was presumably very great, since
the enormous spread of Judaism can scarcely be explained by the natural
increase of the people alone." [2]

There is general scholarly agreement that the large number of Jews
found in the Roman Empire in the first century A.D. cannot be attributed
to natural increase alone, but was to a great extent due to proselytism.[3]
Sociologists and historians estimate that at the time of the destruction of
Judaea by Titus (A.D. 70), the actual number of Jews reached about 4.5
million, constituting 8 to 10 per cent of the total population of the Roman
Empire; and the latter was shown by a census carried out in the year of
Augustus' death (A.D. 14) to have been 54 million.[4] Soon thereafter the
number of the Jews declined and remained fluctuating between 1 and 2
million until the end of the eighteenth century, when it began its rapid
increase. It reached 4.5 million again by 1840, and peaked at 16.5 million
by 1940, just prior to the Nazi genocide.

In the High Middle Ages Jewish proselytism again intensified, and at least one historian has estimated that in Muslim lands the conversion of slaves alone doubled the number of the Jews.[5] Since in this period many slaves were practically coerced by their Jewish masters into accepting Judaism, it is understandable that the attitude of some contemporary rabbis to proselytism was negative or skeptical. Another factor making for such a negative view was that in both the Muslim countries and Christian Europe proselytizing entailed grave dangers, not only for those directly involved in the conversion of a Gentile but also for the entire community. For this reason many leaders discouraged proselytism, except in the case of New Christians or New Muslims, that is, former Jews or people of Jewish ancestry who wished to return to Judaism.[6] Some would-be proselytes traveled from one country to another in futile search for a rabbi willing to accept them into the Covenant of Abraham. It is remarkable, to say the least, that despite such difficulties and obstacles the number of proselytes was so great, even in countries and periods in which the Jews were despised and persecuted and where Gentiles who converted to Judaism courted death at the stake.

Those who persisted in their desire and joined the Jewish community were considered—in most ages by most rabbis—full Jews, children of "Abraham our father" and, more than that, precious jewels in the crown of Israel. We shall have repeated occasion to return to this later in this chapter. But as an introduction let us quote here two different attitudes toward proselytes. The first is that of Maimonides, writing to a scholarly proselyte, Obadiah by name, who lived in Palestine. Maimonides addresses Obadiah as "Master and teacher, the enlightened and understanding Obadiah, the righteous proselyte," and says in the course of his lengthy responsum:

> Anyone who becomes a proselyte is a pupil of our father Abraham and all of them are members of his household . . . hence you may say the prayer "Our God, and the God of our fathers," for Abraham, peace be upon him, is your father . . . for since you have entered beneath the wings of the Divine Presence and attached yourself to Him, there is no difference between us and you . . . in any matter. . . . You may certainly recite the blessings, "Who has chosen us; who has given us; who has caused us to inherit; and who has separated us." For the Creator has chosen you and has separated you from the nations, and has given you the Torah, since the Torah was given both to us and to the proselytes. . . . And do not belittle your lineage: if we trace ourselves back to Abraham, Isaac, and Jacob, you trace yourself to Him by whose word the world came into being.[7]

Baḥya ben Asher ben Halawa (d. 1340), while he cannot be compared in breadth of knowledge and vision with Maimonides, was one of the most distinguished biblical exegetes of Spain. In his book of religious and moralistic teachings, *Kad HaQemaḥ* (*Jar of Flour*), Baḥya displays a decidedly ambivalent attitude toward proselytes. On the one hand he says that the reason for the Talmudic rule that a would-be proselyte must be told about the penalties he would incur were he to disobey the commandments is "to discourage him from converting, since there is no advantage at all in proselytes" and "their joining the Jewish community does not turn out well, nor, in most cases, is their offspring worthy. . . ." But after adducing biblical examples in support of this negative view, Bahya goes on to say that the difficulties proselytes cause to Israel stem from the fact that they are more pious than the born Israelites and shed an unfavorable light on the latters' lack of complete devotion to God. This positive and, in fact, glowing, view of the proselytes' piety is illustrated by Bahya with numerous Talmudic quotations, all of which speak in praise of proselytes. Bahya concludes his discourse on proselytes with the expression of the messianic hope that ultimately all the nations of the world will convert to Judaism.[8]

The story of proselytism as it unfolded in one country after another will be outlined beyond the Middle Ages and even into the nineteenth century. It is, however, not our intention to discuss the phenomenon of conversion to Judaism in modern times, although the process is continuing at present in those countries in which Jews live as free and equal citizens. In the United States there are now about 2,000 conversions annually; this influx of Gentile blood into the Jewish gene pool is bound to have the long-range effect of gradually obliterating whatever genetic difference still exists between Jews and Gentiles in those countries where conversion is common. For our purposes, proselytism in past periods is the important factor because its result decisively contributed to the Jewish gene pool in recent times.

IN BIBLICAL TIMES

In early biblical times the process of joining the Israelite people was not a religious one but rather one of ethnic or geographical adhesion: foreigners settled among the Israelites and became absorbed by them. In this process the adoption of Yahwism was incidental. Accordingly, the Hebrew term "gēr," later to assume the meaning of proselyte, designated in biblical usage a foreigner who lived in another country among another people. The Hebrews themselves were gērīm in Egypt. After the Hebrew tribes settled in Canaan, non-Israelites who came to live among them were called gērīm. Since in those early days the god or gods of a people were considered the divine rulers and possessors of the land inhabited by their worshippers, a resident alien was expected to observe the laws of the Hebrew religion: "If a stranger (gēr) sojourn with you . . . and will offer an offering made by fire, of a sweet savor unto Yahweh, as ye do so he shall do . . . there shall be one statute both for you and for the stranger that sojourneth with you . . . as ye are so shall the stranger be before Yahweh. . . ."[9]

It seems that it was left up to the gēr whether or not to submit to circumcision. If he did, he was allowed to offer up a Passover sacrifice, and became "as one that is born in the land. . . . One law shall be to him that is homeborn and unto the stranger that sojourneth among you." The admonition that the stranger must be treated with the same consideration as the homeborn is coupled in Leviticus with the express commandment, "and thou shalt love him as thyself, for ye were strangers in the land of Egypt." [10]

Except for the Ammonites and Moabites against whom the Israelites bore a historical grudge, all other strangers were allowed to join the Israelite people and intermarry with them. There was no question of conversion as a precondition of such intermarriage, although circumcision seems to have been a requirement for males in accordance with the old Hebrew tribal tradition. [11] In the early Israelite period (twelfth to eighth centuries B.C.), therefore, there was no such thing as a religious conversion in itself, but aliens were welcome to settle in the land and to become genetically as well as culturally assimilated to the Israelites. Since religion was a predominant part of the total way of life, a stranger who settled in the country would inevitably adopt the religious customs of Israel anyway.

In their early nomadic period a large number of varied population elements joined the Israelites and were absorbed by them. After their settlement in Canaan, both the peaceful and the warlike contacts between the Israelites and the old inhabitants of the country often resulted in assimilation. While these indigenous ethnic groups were reduced to a servile status (which, of course, did not prevent mixture with the Israelites), other ethnic elements joined them as free settlers whose equal status was never questioned. Thus the Kenites, a subdivision of the Midianites, were incorporated into southern Judah where they had several cities, while some of them moved up north as far as the neighborhood of Kedesh in Galilee where they supported the Israelites against the Canaanites. A group of Kenite extraction was the Rechabites, whose pious conduct—they practiced nomadism and abstention from wine as religious observances—was held up by Jeremiah as an example. A neighbor of the Kenites in the Negev was the tribe of Yerachmeel, which had Hurrian connections and was of non-Hebrew origin but later became affiliated with Judah. [12]

With the Kenizzites we are on less certain ground, but it seems that they were among the pre-Israelitish inhabitants of Canaan spread over the Negev and Edom, and that after the Israelite conquest they were absorbed partly by the Edomites and partly by the tribe of Judah. The latter portion embraced the clans of Caleb and Othniel. [13] As these brief references show, the tribe of Judah had absorbed a large number of foreign ethnic groups before it rose to pre-eminence among the Israelite tribes under David.

Biblical sources contain numerous references to "fearers of Yahweh" (Hebrew: $yir^{\circ}\bar{e}$-$Yahweh$). These references, most of which are found in the Book of Psalms, indicate that there were, in later biblical times and espe-

55

cially in the post-Exilic period, Gentiles who worshipped the God of Israel, without however converting fully to the religion of Israel. Some scholars consider them semi-converts, some see in them full converts.[14]

In one of the Psalms, the psalmist addresses three groups of people one after the other and exhorts them to "trust in Yahweh": Israel, the House of Aaron, and "Ye that fear Yahweh." The same three groups appear elsewhere, too, which certainly gives the impression that the "fearers of Yahweh" were a distinct category of people. Also, the prophet Malachi in the early post-Exilic period speaks of "those that feared Yahweh." [15] There can be little doubt that some of these, or their descendants, ultimately converted fully to Judaism and merged in the Jewish people.

After the subjugation of the northern Hebrew kingdom, Israel, by the Assyrians, a major part of the population was carried off into captivity in Assyria. In their place Shalmaneser, king of Assyria, settled ethnic elements from various parts of his empire. When some of these newcomers were mauled and killed by lions, they concluded that "the god of the land" was wroth with them because they did not worship him. Informed of the problem, the king of Assyria sent back one of the Israelite priests to teach them "how they should fear Yahweh," that is, how to worship the god of the land in which they now lived. This move resulted in the development of a two-faceted religion: on the one hand, the new settlers in Samaria continued to worship the gods of their old home countries; but on the other, "they feared Yahweh" and adopted the Israelite manner of serving him by offering him sacrifices "in the houses of the high places." [16]

After the return of the Judaite exiles to Jerusalem, these non-Jewish inhabitants of Samaria came to the leaders of the returnees and offered to join them in rebuilding the Temple, "for we seek your God as ye do; and we do sacrifice unto Him since the days of Esarhaddon king of Assyria who brought us hither." Ezra rejected them at the time, but a few years later those non-Jews who converted wholeheartedly to Judaism were accepted and became part of the Jewish community. Among them were

> gate keepers, singers, the Nethinim, and all they had separated themselves from the peoples of the lands unto the law of God, their wives, their sons, and their daughters . . . they cleaved to their brethren [i.e., to the Jews] and entered into a curse and into an oath to walk in God's law which was given by Moses the servant of God, and to observe and do all the commandments of Yahweh. . . .[17]

Here we have the first detailed account of a conversion ritual: it comprised an oath of obedience to the law of Yahweh, and a self-imprecation in case of noncompliance.

The sources indicate that the concept of conversion to the teachings of Judaism without any national or ethnic connotation developed in the early decades of the Babylonian Exile. The possibility of a religious conversion for political reasons is taken for granted in the Book of Esther, which was written some time after the fourth century B.C. In it we are informed that "many from among the peoples of the land became Jews (*mityahadim*) for the fear of the Jews was fallen upon them." [18]

THE SECOND COMMONWEALTH AND HELLENISM

In the latter days of the Second Jewish Commonwealth, the biblical prohibition against admitting Ammonites and Moabites was reinterpreted so as to refer only to intermarrying with them, not to accepting them as proselytes. About 100 B.C. the apocryphal Book of Judith mentions the conversion of Achior the Ammonite, who had himself circumcised and joined the House of Israel. The point that this conversion contravened a biblical prohibition does not arise. Later, the rabbis went further and permitted Jewish men to marry Ammonite and Moabite women. By the end of the first century A.D., male Ammonite and Moabite converts were admitted to marriage with Jewish women. [19]

On the rare occasions when Jews were able to impose their will on members of other nations, they sometimes used their power to force a subjected population group to convert to Judaism. Thus the Hasmonean ruler and high priest John Hyrcanus (r. 135–104 B.C.) forced the Edomites to accept Jewish religion and submit to circumcision. Within two generations, the descendants of the converted Idumaeans considered themselves completely Jewish, although the Jewish aristocracy refused to acknowledge their equality. However, the Deuteronomic law was on their side: it provided that the grandchildren of converted Edomites and Egyptians "may enter into the assembly of Yahweh," that is, count as full Jews. Hyrcanus' son and successor Aristobulus conquered part of the land of the Ituraeans—a Syrian-Arab people—and forced them to be circumcised and accept Judaism. [20]

Whenever Aristobulus' successor, Alexander Jannaeus, conquered a city he demanded that the inhabitants accept Judaism. If they demurred, their city was destroyed. [21]

After Alexander the Great conquered Palestine (332 B.C.), the Jewish people were brought in contact with Hellenism, and subsequently with Greece's heir and the mistress of the Hellenistic world, imperial Rome. While the peoples of the Greco-Roman world in general were at first repelled by Judaism, whose doctrines, let alone practices, they simply could not understand, gradually a number of factors developed which made many of them susceptible to Jewish influences. Among these were the successful Jewish efforts to present Judaism in a form acceptable to Greeks and Romans by emphasizing the superiority of their monotheistic faith and stressing its ethical-spiritual essence. Apart from this, the Roman world in general became attracted at the time to the religions of the East, which led to the penetration of various Oriental cults into the western Mediterranean.[22] Of the numerous Greek and Roman authors whose comments attest to the spread of Judaism in the Hellenistic world, one of the earliest is Strabo (c. 64 B.C.–A.D. 19), who remarks: "It is not easy to find any place in the habitable world that has not yet received this nation and in which it has not made its power felt." [23]

Contact with the Greco-Roman world had two effects on the Jews: one was the ready acceptance by many, especially members of the aristocracy, of the Hellenistic way of life. The second was the resurgence of the conviction that it was the duty of the Jews to serve as teachers to the world in matters religious, ethical, and spiritual, in accordance with the old prophetic idea of Israel as the light to the nations. The concrete result of these factors was seen in numerous conversions or half-conversions to Judaism among the Romans. As a rule, the would-be converts went through a number of stages which constituted a pattern that has been followed down to modern times in many places among proselytes coming to Judaism from the most varied religious backgrounds. The process would usually start with an interest in the Jewish concept of God: the lofty, universal, ethical monotheism which is the core of Judaism opened new religious horizons to people brought up in Greco-Roman traditions. Once belief in the One God was implanted, it followed that at least the most important demands put by Him to man must be fulfilled. This led to the observance of some of the basic Jewish religious laws, such as the Sabbath rest, the abstention from eating pork and other forbidden food, and attendance at synagogue services on the Sabbath and holy days. The third and last step was the total acceptance of the "yoke of the law," signified by a formal conversion which consisted of baptism for both men and women, as well as circumcision for men. There were, of course, always many pagans who took only the first step, and not all of those who observed some of the Jewish laws decided to accept full conversion. In Roman times—as well as later—there were thus many who stopped at various stages of "Judaizing" without becoming full proselytes.

The historical sources convey the impression that throughout the Roman Empire large numbers of Gentiles became *iudaisantes* or half-proselytes. These "Judaizers" believed in the One God, attended services in the synagogues, and observed some parts of the Jewish ritual, but did not complete their conversion by baptism and circumcision. They were also known as "those who honor God" and "those who fear God."

By the middle of the first century A.D. such "God fearers" were found in all parts of the world in which there were Jewish communities. When Paul visited the synagogue in Antioch in Pisidia, exhorting the people assembled for the Sabbath service, he addressed them as "Men of Israel and ye that fear God" and as "Children of the stock of Abraham, and whosoever among you feareth God." In Derbe and Lystra in Lycaonia, Asia Minor, Paul circumcised a certain Timotheus who was the son of a Greek father and a Jewish mother. In the city of Thyatira near the Aegean coast of Asia Minor, Paul met a Gentile woman named Lydia who "worshipped God," and baptized her and her household. Such "fearers of God" are often referred to in the Acts of the Apostles as being attached to the Jewish communities in Palestine, Antioch, Thessalonica, Athens, Corinth, and elsewhere. These *metuentes,* although merely half-proselytes, were nevertheless considered part of the community of Israel, and were often led to full conversion. Once a man submitted to circumcision, he was considered a full proselyte and was expected to carry the full weight of "the yoke of the law." [24]

In the western part of the Roman Empire the Judaizers seem to have been equally numerous, as we learn from the Hellenistic Jewish philosopher Philo of Alexandria (*c.* 20 B.C.–*c.* A.D. 40) and the inimical comments of contemporary Roman authors. Philo, in accord with his older contemporary Strabo, asserts that "Not only the Jews but also all the other people who care for righteousness adopt them [the Jewish laws]. . . . The Jewish Law attracts and links together" all the peoples of the east and the west.[25] Numerous Roman authors make similar assertions in the first and second centuries A.D.

The Roman philosopher and statesman Seneca is quoted by St. Augustine to the effect that "the customs of this criminal nation [i.e., the Jews] prevail to such an extent that they already have adherents in every country, and thus the defeated gave laws to their victors" and attracted them, and especially the Romans, to their religion. The Roman converts to Judaism aroused the ire of the great Roman historian Tacitus, who asserts that "the worst rascals among the other peoples, renouncing their ancestral religions . . . kept sending tributes and contributions to Jerusalem," and that those who convert to the religion of the Jews follow their practices, "and the earliest lesson they receive is to despise the gods, to disown their country, and to regard their parents, children and brothers as of little account. . . ." Elsewhere Tacitus mentions that 4,000 of those "tainted with the [Egyptian and Jewish] superstition" were exiled from Rome to the island of Sardinia. If this statement is correct, the number of Judaizers in Rome must have been considerable indeed. Actual cases of conversion are cited by the later Roman historian Dio Cassius, who says that the emperor Domitian had his relative Flavius Clemens executed and many others punished either by death or loss of property because "they followed the false path of Jewish customs." After the assassination of Domitian, Romans were so often accused of following the Jewish way of life that the emperor Nerva issued a decree prohibiting the lodging of such complaints.[26]

In the early second century A.D. Juvenal published the satires in which he pilloried the conditions in Rome. Some of the sharpest of his barbs were directed against those Romans who were attracted to Judaism and obeyed certain Jewish laws, such as eating no pork, observing the Sabbath, worshipping only the heavenly God, circumcising their sons, and studying the Torah of the Jews. These and many more similar statements made by such anti-Jewish authors as Horace, Persius, Suetonius, and Plutarch constitute cumulative evidence to the great impact Jewish proselytism made on the Roman world.

Among the many members of the Roman nobility who became half-proselytes were those who formed the circle of Epaphroditus, the patron and supporter of the Jewish historian Josephus Flavius (c. A.D. 38–100).[27] Josephus refers repeatedly to the numerous proselytes who in his days flocked to the synagogue. Many of the rich offerings pouring into the Temple of Jerusalem from all over the world, says Josephus, came from the "fearers of God." In Antioch (Syria), "the Jews constantly attracted great multitudes of Hellenes to their synagogue services and made them in a sense a part of their own group." In Damascus, almost the entire female part of the population was attracted to Judaism. These converts were often recruited from among the women of the nobility. The royal family of the kingdom of Adiabene (on the upper reaches of the Euphrates River, on the frontier between the Roman and the Parthian empires), motivated by religious, political, and economic considerations, converted to Judaism in the first century A.D., had a palace in Jerusalem, and donated golden vessels to the Temple. Some of its members fought on the Jewish side in the Roman-Jewish war, others were buried in Jerusalem. Josephus also emphasizes that many Hellenes accepted the Jewish law, and that there was no city, either among the Hellenes or the barbarians, nor any other single place or nation, where the observance of the Sabbath, the fasting, the lighting of candles, and many Jewish dietary laws had not penetrated.[28]

In the early second century A.D. there were so many converts to Judaism among the Romans that the emissaries of Alexandria in Rome felt constrained to complain to Trajan that "his senate was full of Jews." In any case, under Roman law it was not illegal to convert to Judaism as long as the proselyte did not demonstrate his refusal to worship the Roman gods; only if he did, was he accused of apostasy. Although Hadrian issued a decree prohibiting circumcision, the rite was again allowed for Jews, but not for converts, by Antoninus Pius. Nevertheless, conversions continued, especially in places remote from the center of the empire, such as Petra in Idumaea, in Transjordan, as well as beyond the Roman borders, in fourth-century Mehoza, Babylonia, for example. It was not until Christianity became the official religion in A.D. 391 that conversion to Judaism was outlawed in Rome.[29]

A study of the entire spectrum of historical material available for the Hellenistic period leads Baron to the conclusion that

> the farther away from Palestine a country was situated, the less pure racially and ethnically its Jewish settlers were. . . . A large section of Syrian Jewry, and probably a still larger section of the Jewries of Asia Minor, the East Mediterranean islands, and the Balkans, must have consisted of former proselytes and their descendants. The same is true of the Jews in Italy, Carthage, and Armenia. . . .[30]

THE TALMUDIC PERIOD: PALESTINE AND BABYLONIA

The Hellenistic-Roman references to proselytism are paralleled and amplified by the Talmudic data, which cover the first to fifth centuries. The Talmudic sources deal in great detail with the requirements for the admission of Gentiles to Judaism, the ritual of the conversion itself, the status of the convert in Jewish law, his rights and duties, and the question of whom he was allowed to marry. Talmudic law carefully distinguishes among various types of proselytes, the most important of whom was the *gēr toshav* (Hebrew: "resident alien"), a person who has rejected idolatry but has not yet been converted; the "fearer of heaven" (Hebrew: *y'rē shamayim*), heir to the biblical "fearer of Yahweh," who had accepted Jewish monotheism and observed some Jewish rites; and the full proselyte. In addition to the legal material, the Talmudic sources contain numerous legends about proselytes in biblical times, much information about individuals who were proselytes or descendants of proselytes, and many opinions, most of them favorable, about converts. All in all we must conclude from the frequency of references to these subjects that proselytes and proselytism were an integral part of Jewish life in the Talmudic period.[31]

From Talmudic times on, it became a part of Jewish ritual law that a full proselyte was allowed to marry an Israelite woman, and even the daughter of a *Kohen,* (i.e., a priest, considered a descendant of Aaron),[32] while a priest was allowed to marry the children of either male or female proselytes or of a proselyte couple.

Of special interest is the question of the motivation that prompted pagans to convert to Judaism. Some men were known to have converted for the sake of women they loved; and likewise, pagan women converted because they fell in love with Jewish men. Others became Jews because they were thus enabled to obtain high positions; others again were moved by dreams to do so. Because of the frequency of conversions prompted by worldly motivations, the rabbis insisted on examining would-be proselytes very carefully even in times of great hardship, such as the Hadrianic era in which conversion meant joining an oppressed and persecuted people. The proselyte was asked: "What has made you want to be converted? Do you not know that these days Israel is afflicted, oppressed, despised, and preyed upon, and sufferings are come upon them [the Jews]?'' If the candidate thereupon answered: ''I know, and although I am not worthy, I wish to convert,'' he was accepted immediately.[33]

Some teachers considered proselytism of such paramount importance that they found in it the divine purpose of the dispersion of Israel. Both Rabbi Johanan and Rabbi Eleazar in the third century A.D. taught: ''It was only for one purpose that the Holy One, blessed by He, exiled Israel among the nations: so that proselytes be joined to them.'' Once the conversion was accomplished, the proselyte was considered one of the progeny of Abraham and a party to the covenant God made with Israel on Mount Sinai.[34]

The available data are far from conclusive as to the actual extent of proselytism in the Talmudic period. In the Roman Empire, the prohibitive laws as well as the derision and antipathy provoked by Jewish customs and behavior must have deterred many who were attracted to the teachings of Judaism. On the other hand, conversion to Judaism carried with it certain economic advantages (such as the complex contacts of the Diaspora, the solidarity of the Jewish people, the protection and financial help extended by its communal organization), which by far outweighed the minor disadvantages connected with Jewishness.[35] Beyond the Roman boundaries conditions were more favorable for proselytism. In Babylonia, home of the most important Jewish community of the period, the number of proselytes seems to have been considerable. The third-century Babylonian teacher Rabba ben Abuha was approached by entire groups of pagans in Mehoza who wanted to convert to Judaism, which he did not make at all easy for them.[36]

In discussing Babylonian Jewry in the early Talmudic period, the historian Jacob Neusner comes to the conclusion that ''either by natural increase or by conversion, the descendants of the early Jewish captives increased in number, and by the time of the conversion of the Adiabenian royal family [i.e., the first century A.D.] . . . they must have formed a significant part of the population of northern Mesopotamia.'' [37]

IN PRE-ISLAMIC ARABIA AND NORTH AFRICA

Arabia

The dispersion of the Jews to the east and west was paralleled by their movement into Arabia and North Africa. In 25–24 B.C., when 500 Jewish soldiers of Herod accompanied Aelius Gallus on his ill-fated expedition to southern Arabia, they encountered a Jewish settlement in Ḥijr on their way to the south.[38]

Following the destruction of the Second Jewish Commonwealth by the

Romans in A.D. 70, Jews began to move into Arab-controlled lands, first in the Syrian Desert and Arabia Petraea, located between the two major remaining Jewish centers of Babylonia and Egypt, and subsequently into more southerly parts of the peninsula, mainly along and near its west coast. Wherever Jews settled they attracted converts from among the pagan Arabs. After the Persian occupation of the island of Yotabe in the Gulf of Aqaba in 473, Jewish merchants engaged in the Red Sea trade established a colony there which enjoyed a semi-autonomous status until 535.[39]

In the southwestern corner of the peninsula, after the ruling House of Ḥimyar (roughly the area of modern Yemen and western South Yemen) had re-established the independence of its country in the late fourth century A.D., it proceeded to make Judaism the official religion. The Jewish King Abū Kariba Asʻad mounted a military expedition in support of the Jews of Medina, who were at the time embroiled in a struggle against one of the Christian kings of northern Arabia. According to a Muslim legend, King Abū Kariba Asʻad converted to Judaism after his encounter with the rabbis of Yathrib, took two of them back to Ḥimyar, and demanded that all his people convert to Judaism. First there was resistance, but after an ordeal had justified the king's demand and confirmed the truth of Jewish religion, all the Ḥimyarites converted to Judaism. Such conversions as a result of a trial by ordeal were not unusual in Arabia. It has been argued that the Ḥimyarite conversion took place, not because of political motivations, but because Judaism was attractive to the mentality and thinking of the people. In any case, in the fifth and sixth centuries Judaism flourished in Ḥimyar; and in inscriptions dating from those centuries Jewish religious terms, such as "Raḥmān" ("the Merciful," a divine epithet), "the God of Israel," and "the Lord of Judah" occur.[40]

The Ḥimyarite Jewish dynasty continued in power until King Yūsuf Ashʻar Dhū Nuwās (r. c. 518–525) was finally defeated by Christian Ethiopian invaders. This signaled the beginning of the decline of Ḥimyarite Jewry. Under Ethiopian rule many Jews converted to Christianity. One Jewish leader, however, organized an uprising and succeeded in regaining for a while the throne of his ancestors. The rule of this king, Sayf Dhū Yazan, was soon terminated by the Persian conquest of the country. When the Muslims conquered Ḥimyar in the last days of the Prophet Muḥammad, several princes of the state converted to Islam.[41]

Arab chroniclers tell of the large number of Jews among the Bedouins of southern Arabia, such as the tribes of Ḥārith ibn Kaʻb (usually called Balḥārith) in the Najrān area, the Ghassān, Judhām, Beni Kināna, and Beni Kinda. Most of these had converted to Judaism in the days of Dhū Nuwās. Ibn al-Kalbī suggests that the Hamdān, a large Arab tribe of the Yemen group, may have accepted Judaism at the same time. The tradition that Jewish villagers of Yemen were descendants of converts or slaves, in contrast to the Jews of the capital city of San'a who are true descendants of Abraham, was preserved in San'a until the second half of the nineteenth century.[42]

In general, Jews held dominant positions in several places in the Hijaz and the Nejd. Occasionally it happened that the Jewish masters of an area, territory, or oasis demanded conversion to Judaism as a precondition to giving permission to newcomers wishing to settle there. This is known to have occurred in Teyma (some 200 miles north of Medina), in Kheybar (halfway between Teyma and Medina), and elsewhere. In Juwwaniyya, north of Medina, Jews, or Arab converts to Judaism, held two castles, Ṣirār and Riyān. Arab sources say that the Beni Qayla (the name under which the Aws and Khazraj tribes were known in pre-Islamic times) were so strongly influenced by the Jews that part of them converted to Judaism.[43]

In Yathrib (Medina) itself, the majority of the population prior to Muḥammad's appearance was Jewish, Jewish clans controlled the city, and their cultural and economic power was such that the newly arrived Arab settlers converted and were soon absorbed by the Jewish community. The very name Medina, which Muḥammad accepted in place of the name Yathrib, was given to the city by the Jews.[44]

The sources mention repeatedly that there were more than twenty Jewish tribes in Yathrib-Medina and its surroundings, and that Arab tribes lived in their midst. Several South Arabian tribes, probably converts to Judaism, had settled in the city in the fourth and fifth centuries, some of them even earlier. At the time of Muḥammad's appearance in Medina (622), many Arabs in the city stood under the protection of Jews. Several splinter groups of the Bali tribe lived in Medina. The bulk of this tribe, however, lived in the oasis of Teyma and had converted to Judaism in order to receive permission from the Jewish overlords of the fort of Teyma to settle in the oasis.[45]

This is but one example of the numerous occurrences which led pagan Arab tribes in the *Jahiliyya* (the pre-Islamic period of pagan "ignorance") to convert to Judaism. Thus, there can be little doubt that the vigorous Jewish tribes of Arabia in the days of Muḥammad, who possibly constituted the majority of the settled population, were in large part of native Arab extraction. On the other side of the genetic ledger, Jewish genes may have entered the Arab gene pool as a result of the *jus primae noctis* exercised, according to an Arab legend, by the Jewish autocrat of Yathrib, which was said to have been the cause of Malik's revolt.[46]

Infant mortality rates among the Jews were much lower than among the Arabs, and for this reason Arab mothers would vow to bring up their children in the Jewish faith. Among the Arabs of Medina it was therefore customary for young mothers who had lost several of their infants to deliver children born to them subsequently into the hands of Jewish families to be brought up as Jews. When the Jewish Naḍīr tribe was expelled from Medina, great confusion spread among the Arabs whose children lived with families belonging to the tribe.

Another setting for Jewish proselytizing in the pre-Islamic period was supplied by the markets, which played a central role in Arab social life. Most important were the markets of Mecca during the pilgrimage, and of 'Ukaz near Ta'if south of Mecca. Jews and Christians used to come to these markets to trade with their neighbors and also to carry on religious propaganda.[47]

In all the places where they settled, the Jews constituted a culturally active population. They introduced and practiced advanced methods in irrigation and agriculture, in various arts and crafts, and in commerce and finance. Being heirs to an old religion, in possession of holy books, and with a great tradition of literacy and oral folklore, these Arabian Jews made an impression on their pagan Arab neighbors, many of whom consequently were attracted to Judaism. Conversions were numerous, as was intermarriage. By the time Muḥammad appeared on the scene, a considerable part of the peninsula's population was Jewish by religion, while genetically it was the offspring partly of Jewish emigrants from Palestine and partly of Arab proselytes. Thus, when Arab historians speak of "Jewish" tribes in Medina (they mention about twenty) who occupied some fifty-nine strongholds and controlled practically the entire fertile countryside, we have to understand the adjective "Jewish" in the religious, not the genetic, sense. Linguistically, and to a great extent culturally, these Arabian Jews were Arab.[48]

North Africa

North Africa, with its long and varied past, occupies a special place in the history of Jewish proselytism. To begin with, North Africa enters the historical stage as a result of colonization by the Phoenicians, the next-door northern neighbors of the Hebrews. Cultural connections between the Phoenicians and the Hebrews began in the tenth century B.C. at the latest. In the eighth century B.C., the Phoenicians embarked on their large-scale maritime colonization with the founding of trade posts in North Africa, Sicily, Sardinia, the Balearic Islands, and Spain. The most important of these colonies was Carthage, famous in history for menacing Rome until the Romans finally destroyed it in 146 B.C.

Under Roman rule many of the inhabitants of Carthage and of the other Phoenician colonies responded positively to Judaism. Among the Phoenicians circumcision was an old religious practice. The language spoken in the Phoenician motherland, as well as in her overseas colonies, was a Semitic tongue which bore close resemblance to the languages spoken by the Jews, Hebrew and Aramaic. After the loss of the independence of their mother city-states—Tyre and Sidon on the east Mediterranean coast and Carthage on the southwestern—the Phoenician and Punic peoples found themselves in a situation analogous to the Jewish Diaspora. Trading across seas and continents was as much the mainstay of their livelihood as it was that of the Jews. To this must be added the puzzling historical fact that the Phoenicians actually disappeared during the first centuries of the Christian era. On the basis of all this, an impressive number of historians reached the conclusion that the Phoenicians "quite naturally . . . adopted the patterns of belief and behavior developed by a related people [i.e., the Jews] through centuries of similar experience . . . swelled the ranks of Jewish converts . . . and disappeared within the new world factor, the Diaspora Jew." [49]

The history of the Jews in North Africa, according to the Jewish historian Josephus, began with the 30,000 Jews exiled to Carthage by Titus after he conquered Jerusalem (A.D. 70). From the second century A.D. there is historical documentation attesting to the conversion of Libyan, Carthaginian, and other North African natives to Judaism. Some of these became full proselytes, others merely observed part of the Jewish precepts and became "fearers of Heaven" such as we have already met. Since under the Roman emperors Septimius Severus and his son Marcus Aurelius Antoninus (nicknamed Caracalla) Judaism was a "licit" religion, while Christianity was not, many pagans who were attracted to Christianity converted to Judaism in order to be able to become secret Christians. The bitter denunciation of Judaism by Tertullian must be understood as stemming from the North African Christian theologian's ire over the success of Judaism in attracting such proselytes. [50]

Almost two centuries later, St. Augustine refers to the great number of converts to Judaism among the Christians of the Byzantine Province (Central Tunisia). The poet-bishop Commodianus, who was of North African origin and lived either in the third to fourth centuries or, according to others, in the fifth century, wrote several satirical poems against the Jews and the pagans who converted to Judaism. [51]

In the last century prior to the Arab invasion of North Africa, both Christianity and Judaism made considerable headway among the Berber tribes. One of the leading tribes among the Zenata group of the Berbers was the Jewish Jarāwa, headed by a woman chieftain or queen named Dahya al-Kāhina ("the Seeress"), who dealt a crushing defeat to the Muslim Arab general Ḥasan ibn Nu'mān in the late seventh century, only to be defeated in turn several years later by a coalition of Muslim Arab and Christian forces. Tradition has it that she was 125 or 127 years old when she was killed (perhaps a reminiscence of the 127 years of the life of Sarah), and that she had ruled the Berbers for thirty-five or sixty-five years. [52]

On the basis of admittedly scanty historical data, most scholars have formed the opinion that *most* of the Jews of North Africa are of Berber origin. Hirschberg, however, holds that only a relatively small number of

Berber proselytes were incorporated into the North African Jewish communities.[53] The problems involved are too technical to discuss here in detail, but our own impression is that the first view is correct. Particularly convincing is the argument that the presence of Jews (i.e., Jewish Berbers) deep in the Sahara and along its southern borders, attested to as early as the twelfth century, can be explained only on the basis of the conversion of sizable native Berber groups before the period in which these remote regions were reached by Islam.

UNDER ISLAM

In pre-Islamic times, as we have just seen, numerous proselytes were recruited to Judaism in both Arabia and North Africa. With the appearance of Islam this trend was suddenly checked. While Jewish proselytism was the result of suasion and precept or, at the most, of occasional political and economic pressure, Islam spread "the religion of Muḥammad with the sword," as the old Arabic saying puts it succinctly. Wherever the Muslim Arabs encountered pagan ethnic elements they allowed them a choice between conversion or death. The result of this policy was the rapid, although in many instances superficial, Islamization of the huge area conquered by the Arabs—from Morocco in the west to Central Asia and India in the east. Where the conquered people were not idolaters but adherents of one of the monotheistic religions possessing their own Scriptures (whence the Muslim Arabic term *ahl al-kitāb,* "people of the book"), the Muslims allowed them to retain their religion provided they submitted to the dominion of Islam. They were given the status of *dhimmīs,* protected, second-class subjects, who had to pay a special head-tax in exchange for grudging toleration. However, conversion from Islam to Judaism (or any other religion) was punished with the death penalty, as was conversion from Christianity in Christian Europe. In both realms, moreover, not only the convert but those instrumental in his conversion were liable to execution. Curiously enough, even in these circumstances conversions of Muslims to Judaism did take place. There are records of numerous cases in which Jewish proselytes were actually executed.[54]

When the Arabs established their empire and imposed their religion upon the subject peoples, the Jewish communities in the Near East and North Africa had been absorbing proselytes for centuries. While the actual number of proselytes cannot be estimated, there are solid grounds for assuming that they must have been considerable and that, as a result, the genetic structure of the Arabian, North African, and other Jewish communities on the eve of the Muslim conquests had largely approximated that of the non-Jewish local populations. The Arab expansion was accompanied by considerable voluntary or forced migrations of the Jews, which had further far-reaching

67

genetic consequences. Thus many of the Arabian Jews who refused to accept Islam were forced to settle in what was at the time the periphery of the Muslim domain. Muḥammad himself exiled many Medinese Jewish tribesmen who surrendered to him to Edrei in Transjordan. And the Caliph Omar, his successor, deported some surviving Jews from Kheybar and other places in Arabia to Jericho in Palestine and to the new Arab encampments in Iraq, particularly Kufa where a large Jewish community soon developed.[55]

Some Jewish proselytes in the Muslim domains were Christians or pagans who had converted to Judaism while they still lived in areas outside Muslim control and thereafter settled in Muslim lands. Others were slaves and concubines brought in from outside areas and bought by Jews or Muslims and Christians who lived in Muslim lands and converted to Judaism, defying danger. It is impossible to estimate their total number. However, the numerous responsa or rabbinical documents dealing with proselytes in Muslim lands show that conversions to Judaism must have been frequent.[56]

Apart from the responsa literature, the documents found in the Geniza (Hebrew: "hidden place") of the old synagogue of Fostat near Cairo are the most valuable sources for the medieval history of the Jews in the circum-Mediterranean area. These documents give the impression that most of the proselytes were Christians from Byzantium or Western Europe, who came to Muslim countries for reasons of safety. An Arabic name frequently assumed by the proselytes was Mubārak ("Blessed") or the feminine form Mubāraka. Another Arabic name often used by proselytes was Abu 'l-Khayr (lit. "Father of Goodness"). It appears that when the available supply of such common names was exhausted, the proselytes chose, or were given, less usual names, such as those of the proselytes Asher, Issachar, and Dan mentioned in a Geniza document.[57]

Although in general Muslim law prohibited conversion to any religion but Islam, Muslim authorities occasionally countenanced conversion by Christians to Judaism. An interesting example is supplied by the activities of a German nobleman and deacon called Bodo, who was attached to the court of Louis the Pious and became attracted to Judaism in 839. Bodo moved to Saragossa, had himself circumcised, took the name Eleazar, let his beard grow, and married a Jewish woman. In his zeal for his new religion, Bodo-Eleazar is said to have been instrumental in the promulgation by the Muslim authorities of an edict giving Christians the choice of converting either to Judaism or to Islam under the threat of death. Even Christians who were merely passing through the Muslim domain were subject to this law.[58]

Because of the danger involved in the conversion of a Muslim to Judaism, many Jewish leaders opposed all Jewish proselytizing among Muslims. Maimonides ruled that Jewish religious propaganda should be made among Christians, not Muslims.[59] On the other hand, one of the Geniza documents contains powerful imprecations against those who opposed Jewish missionary activities,[60] indicating a continuing desire to encourage proselytism.

Conversions of Muslims to Judaism occurred even in the most unlikely places. From a Geniza document we know of an elderly woman from an Egyptian village who began to observe the Sabbath and the Jewish holy days, and resolved to convert to Judaism. She left her village, went to the town of Aftīḥ in which there was a Jewish community, and requested its leaders to accept her as a proselyte. They felt that it was not in their competence to do so (they might have been afraid) and advised her to apply to the head of the Egyptian Jewish community.[61]

For reasons of security, Muslims who converted to Judaism had to leave their places of residence and settle in another country where they were not known and could appear as born Jews. These circumstances forced many proselytes to live on Jewish charity in strange cities. The poor proselytes received donations, including bread, wheat, and clothes, either from private donors or from the Jewish communities in whose lists of indigents they frequently appear. There were also wealthy proselytes, among them international merchants, whose names appear among those of the donors. As often happens, some of the proselytes were much more scrupulous in their religious observances than born Jews.[62]

One of the consequences of the need for utter secrecy was that in most cases the conversion of Muslims to Judaism left no traces in the historical documents. Still, Muntafil, an Arab poet of Granada, could write in a poem extolling the greatness of his patron, Samuel ben Joseph ibn Nagrela (993–1056), vizier of Granada and head of the city's Jewish community: "When I find myself near you and your people, I overtly profess the faith which prescribes the observance of the Sabbath. When I stay with my own people, I profess it secretly." [63]

Some traces of proselytism in Muslim countries were preserved in Jewish folklore. Folk tales current among Jews from Morocco, Syria, Iraq, and Afghanistan tell about conversions of Muslims.[64] While it would be difficult to establish whether or not these stories have a historical kernel, they show that the possibility of Muslims converting to Judaism was frequently envisaged by Jews in Muslim lands.

Within a few generations after their conversion, the non-Jewish origin of Arab proselytes was usually forgotten and their Jewish descent assumed as a matter of course. The most remarkable example of the survival of a Jewish community of largely proselyte—and forgotten—origin in a Muslim environment through thirteen centuries of harshly oppressive Muslim rule down to the present is that of the Yemenite Jews. The physical type of the Yemenite Jews, studied in recent decades, clearly indicates the influence of a pre-Islamic proselyte movement in the southwestern corner of the Arabian Peninsula. Yet despite their non-Jewish antecedents (of which they were unaware), and their isolation and persecution, the Yemenite Jews remained a flourishing branch on the tree of Jewry, and ultimately joined their brethren in faith in the Land of Israel, where in 1970 they numbered some 190,000.[65]

Apart from the Yemenite Jews, only a few more scattered remnants survived from the Jewish tribes of the Arabian Peninsula. Small Jewish contingents remained in Najrān and other small settlements in ʿAsīr in southwestern Saudi Arabia, and were encountered by St. John Philby in the 1930's. In Habban and several other towns in the Hadhramaut Valley, in what is today the People's Republic of Southern Yemen, a few hundred Jews survived until they too were brought to Israel. Jewish tombstones testify to the presence of Jews in Oman as late as the nineteenth century. In contrast to these examples of ethnic survival in relative isolation despite tremendous social pressure, most of the Jewish tribes of Arabia submitted to force and converted to Islam. Only legends, still current among the tribes, preserve the memory of the once powerful Jewish tribes of Arabia, and especially that of the "Yahūd Kheybar." [66]

In North Africa larger Jewish communities managed to hold their own, and even to grow and absorb Jewish exiles from Spain. In 1947, before the large-scale emigration of North African Jews to Israel began, there were about 623,000 Jews in the five African Arab countries (Morocco, Algeria, Tunisia, Libya, Egypt) bordering on the Mediterranean. By 1960, about 235,000 of these had migrated to Israel and 327,000 to other countries, mostly to France. Additional large Jewish contingents which came to Israel from Muslim countries are the Jews of Iraq (125,000), Iran, and Turkey (about 40,000 each). It has been estimated that by 1967 more than half of the Jewish population of Israel was of Sephardi and Oriental origin,[67] that is, had come from presently or formerly Muslim-ruled countries. The foregoing remarks should be helpful in evaluating the genetic meaning of such a mass influx of Middle Eastern Jews to Israel, while subsequent sections of this chapter will lay the foundation for an appreciation of the genetic background of the other, Ashkenazi, half of Israel's Jewish population.

THE KHAZARS

A celebrated case of proselyte movement that introduced Turkic, and to some extent Mongoloid, genes into Jewish communities in both East Europe and Asia is that of the Khazars.

The Khazars were a Turkic people from Central Asia with some Mongoloid admixture who originally practiced a primitive shamanism. They are described in early Arab sources as having a white complexion, blue eyes, and reddish hair. The Turkic affinities of the Khazars are borne out by modern anthropological studies.[68] Up to the end of the sixth century they wandered between the Volga and the Caucasus, but by the early seventh century they controlled a wide region north of the Caucasus extending roughly from the Black Sea and the Sea of Azov in the west to the southern reaches of the Ural Mountains in the east. Thereafter, until the middle of the tenth century, the Khazars fought intermittently the Byzantine Christians in the Crimea and the Muslim Arabs in the Caucasus, stopping the latter's northward thrust.

However, the contact between the Khazars and their Christian and Muslim neighbors was not solely warlike. Missionaries of both monotheistic religions were active in Khazaria and succeeded in making converts. By the early eighth century Jews, too, having been forced out by persecution from Christian Byzantium and the Iraqi Muslim caliphate, had settled in the country. After the conquest of Khiva to the east of the Caspian Sea by the Muslims (705–712), many of the Jews who had lived there moved northeast into Khazaria. Discussions among representatives of the three monotheistic religions, none of which enjoyed the official support of the pagan Khazar rulers, became frequent. About 740, so the story goes, after listening to such a discussion, the *khagan* (king) of Khazaria decided to adopt Judaism. While the historicity of this story is not proven, it recurs in both Arab and Jewish sources, and it is more than likely that some event of this kind led the Khazar khagans first to adopt a partial Judaism and then, a few decades later, to become actual converts.[69]

Together with the ruling family the court nobility, and soon a part of the population as well, adopted Judaism. Later in the eighth century King Obadiah more fully adopted the normative doctrines and rituals of biblical Judaism. The Talmudic development of the Jewish faith remained largely unknown in Khazaria. But in their own eyes, as well as in those of the Christians and Muslims, the Jewish Khazars were full Jews. After a period of gradual disintegration under the blows of Russian raiders from the tenth century on, in 965 the Russians invaded Khazaria, which forced the Khazars into an alliance with neighboring Muslim states. A diminished and weakened Khazar state continued to survive until its final downfall before the Mongol invasions of the thirteenth century.[70]

Of special interest for our present study is the fate of the Jewish Khazars after the subjugation and disintegration of their state. While the precise circumstances of this concluding chapter in the history of Khazaria are as yet unknown, it is assumed by all historians that those Jewish Khazars who survived the last fateful decades sought and found refuge in the bosom of Jewish communities in the Christian countries to the west, and especially in Russia and Poland, on the one hand, and in the Muslim countries to the east and the south, on the other. Some historians and anthropologists go so far as to consider the modern Jews of East Europe, and more particularly of Poland, the descendants of the medieval Khazars. Thus, Kutschera following Carl Vogt's description of the East European Jewish type explains it as due to their Khazar descent.[71] Others hold that the Khazar Jews had at least mingled with the East European Jews.[72] During the period of both Khazaria's heyday and its decline, Khazar Jews drifted westward and settled in Slavonic lands, contributing to the foundation of a Jewish community together with Jews whom they met there and who had come from German lands and the Balkans. Some Khazars went as far west as Hungary, where the Magyars learned the Khazar language and spoke it in addition to their own, at least until the middle of the tenth century. Still in the tenth century the Hungarian Duke Taksony is said to have invited the Khazars to settle in his domains, and in the eleventh or early twelfth century they built a town called Biela Viezha (or Sarkil, near Chernigov) in the territory controlled by Vladimir Monomach. By 1117 they had settled in Chernigov itself. At the time of the Mongol invasion larger numbers of Jewish Khazars moved into or toward Hungary, reinforcing in general the settlements of their coreligionists in Eastern Europe. The twelfth-century Byzantine historian John Cinnamus mentions a group of *Khalisioi* who were among the Hungarian allies of Dalmatia in the 1154 war and who observed Mosaic law. These *Khalisioi* are identified with the *Khwalisi,* and some derive their name from *ḥalūṣ* (Hebrew: "pioneer," "armed troops"). Another such ethnic element allied with the Hungarians were the *Khabaroi* (possibly derived from *ḥavēr* [Hebrew: "companion"]). Both the *Khwalisi* and the *Khabaroi* were, according to the Russian historian Tolstov, originally Jewish groups from Khiva-Khwarizm who had reached the Hungarian plain in the ninth and tenth centuries.[73]

Down to the present times East European (and in general Ashkenazi) Jewry contained a light-complexioned physical type which constituted quite a sizable minority among them. According to Ruppin, 10 to 15 per cent of the Ashkenazim and up to 5 per cent of the Sephardim and Oriental Jews were blond. He agrees with Fishberg and Günther in attributing the origin of the blond component among the Ashkenazi Jews to admixture with blond Slavs in Eastern Europe during the Middle Ages.[74] While this theory is acceptable, one should remember that the Khazars were described by several contemporary authors as having a pale complexion, blue eyes, and reddish hair. Red, as distinguished from blond, hair is found in a certain percentage of East European Jews, and this, as well as the more generalized light coloring, could be a heritage of the medieval Khazar infusion.

Even less is known about the influence of the Jewish Khazar settlers in Asiatic lands. For one thing, Russian proselytes from the Volga Basin and the Caucasus are reported to believe themselves to be descendants of the Khazars. The Komeks in the Caucasus trace their descent to Jews, and their Tat language, says Ben-Zvi, proves their kinship with the "Mountain Jews" of the Caucasus. The latter are the descendants of native Caucasian Jews and of Alan converts who settled in the Caucasus. The kings of the Alans, who were under Khazar domination in the eighth and ninth centuries and are the ancestors of the present-day Ossets, seem to have converted to Judaism about the same time as the Khazars. Karaite leaders have repeatedly argued that the Karaites were the descendants, not of Jews but of the Khazars.* In fact, explorers found that Karaites in Poland who had migrated in the fourteenth century from their native Crimea had definite Tartar and Khazar traits. For lack of data and of studies, we can only make the very tentative assumption that some Jewish Khazars must have fled to the south and joined their co-religionists in Iran and neighboring Muslim countries.[75]

EARLY MEDIEVAL CHRISTENDOM

In the Early Middle Ages the Roman Church and its ecclesiastic authorities in the Western countries were almost incessantly preoccupied with efforts to prevent the conversion of Christians to Judaism. Laws prohibiting such conversions were enacted and re-enacted by one Church Council after another, and often included warnings, directed to Christians, against their observance of the Sabbath rest, participation in Jewish festivals, sharing of meals with Jews, and other forms of Jewish-Christian conviviality. From 465 to the end of the eleventh century, more than forty Church Councils enacted legislation concerning the Jews, that is, once every sixteen years on the average. The fact that the Church felt constrained to reiterate these prohibitions and warnings with such frequency can lead to only one conclusion: there was something in the Jewish ritual and way of life, and undoubtedly also in the Jewish religious doctrine, which continued to attract Christians to the Jewish fold.

In some cases proselytism was spontaneously triggered by the mere fact of Jewish presence in a Christian community. Thus, according to Archbishop Julian, Duke Paul, the general of the armies of the Visigothic King Wamba (872–80), became a Judaizer. In other cases, individual Jews (but never the Jewish community as an organized group) exerted themselves to make proselytes. Occasionally, newly converted Jewish proselytes would compose missionary tracts or pamphlets to persuade their former co-religionists to follow their example. Bodo-Eleazar, the ninth-century ex-deacon of Louis the Pious whose political efforts to convert Christians to Judaism in Muslim Spain we referred to above, wrote polemical and missionary tracts directed to Christians. In the early eleventh century, another renowned convert from Christianity, Wecelin, who was a deacon in the household of Duke Conrad (a nephew of Emperor Conrad II), wrote a missionary pamphlet of which some fragments are extant. While these authors addressed themselves to Christians in Latin, Jewish authors wrote anti-

---

* The Karaites are members of a heretical sect which split off the main body of Judaism in the eighth century.

Christian treatises in Hebrew, with a twofold purpose in mind: to counteract Christian missionary work among the Jews by showing the Christian religion in an unfavorable light, and to supply ammunition to Jewish missionaries in their efforts to convert Christians to Judaism. A famous book of this type was the *Toldot Yeshu* (*History of Jesus*), the full text of which is preserved. Lengthy extracts from it are given in the anti-Jewish writings of Agobard, and his successor Amulo, both archbishops of Lyon, in the ninth century. Agobard for his part—as well as many other Christian polemicists, such as Fulbert of Chartres and Peter Damian—noted that it was often the ignorant Christian folk who were led astray by the Jewish argument and came to believe that Judaism was better than Christianity.[76]

Some Jews went so far in their missionary zeal as to employ whatever coercive measures were at their disposal. If the complaint voiced by Archbishop Amulo is indeed based on fact, some Jewish tax collectors first pressed hard the poor ignorant Christian peasants, and then promised them a reduction in their tax assessment if they converted to Judaism.[77] Jewish owners exerted similar pressure on their slaves, as we shall see in a later chapter.

It would, however, be erroneous to assume that only ignorant Christians were vulnerable to the enticements of Judaism. There is historical evidence to show that educated Christian priests of high rank also converted occasionally, although such cases were an embarrassment for the Christian Church and a source of potential danger—because of provocation to retaliation—for the Jews; hence both sides tended to keep silent about them. We have already heard of two deacons who not only converted to Judaism but became energetic missionaries for their newly won faith. In the latter part of the eleventh century Andreas, archbishop of Bari, fled to Egypt, converted to Judaism, and was followed by a number of his former flock. Toward the end of the same century John, a young Catholic priest of Norman extraction who was then living in Oppido near Bari, followed the example of Archbishop Andreas, converted to Judaism, took the name of Obadiah, and barely managed to escape death by fleeing to Muslim territory where he wrote an account of his conversion which, fortunately, is extant. Other proselytes suffered the death penalty; among them were Jacob bar Sullam in Mainz and another anonymous victim at Xanten, both of whom died a heroic death in 1096.[78]

On rare occasions we hear of feudal lords who instigated Judaizing movements. One such was Count Rainard (or Raymond) of Sens, who called himself a Jewish king and whose religious heterodoxy was reinforced by his political opposition to King Robert the Pious (996–1031) and to Archbishop Leotheric of Sens.[79]

As to the common folk, from whose ranks the great majority of the converts were recruited, their acts of conversion remained as unnoticed and unrecorded as their entire lives. We have no way of knowing how great was their number and what percentage of non-Jewish blood entered with them into the Jewish community. Those who became proselytes took good care to do so surreptitiously without alerting the authorities and, consequently, without leaving behind any traces. Many undoubtedly followed the route taken by Archbishop Andreas and the Norman priest John, and emigrated to a Muslim country where they could pretend to being born Jews; at the least, they probably moved to another town where they were unknown.[80]

While we can thus form no concrete idea of the extent of conversions, occasional clues indicate that they must have been quite frequent. Among the sources which are invaluable in this connection are the records of persecutions and the commemorative lists of their victims: both contain the names of many converts.

SPAIN AND PORTUGAL

In 1263 James I of Aragon issued a decree upholding the prohibition enacted in 1228 against the conversion of Muslims to Judaism and of Jews to Islam. This meant that, officially at least, the Jews were barred from all proselytizing. Nevertheless, they persisted in their efforts to win converts, and in 1312 large fines were imposed on the Jewish community of Tarragona because ten of its members allegedly helped in the conversion of two Germans in Toledo. Three years later, several Majorcan Jews were condemned and fined for having circumcised two Christians and for other unspecified crimes. In 1326, the property of two Tarragona Jews was confiscated because they had converted a French girl to Judaism; and in the following year, the entire community of Calataynd was condemned for its role in converting Christians and helping a baptized Jew to relapse. The prosecution of Jews for the crime of proselytizing was a welcome field of activity for the Inquisition. In 1489–90 the Aragonese branch of the Inquisition tried the leaders of the Jewish community of Huesca for having allegedly abetted the circumcision of Christians.[81]

About 1540 the influential Jewish family of Mendez, headed by Dona Gracia and Don Joseph Nasi, the duke of Naxos, was instrumental in rescuing many Marranos from Portugal. The refugees were helped to go to France, Germany, or Italy, and from there to the Balkan peninsula which was under Muslim Turkish rule and where the New Christians could openly profess their Judaism. In the same period, many New Christians went to North Africa or to Western Europe, to London, Bristol, and Antwerp. In all these places the majority of the resident Jews, especially those who themselves were of Sephardi descent, welcomed their returning brethren. Since the Marranos were forbidden to circumcise their male children, many of the returnees had to undergo the operation after they arrived in their new places of settlement and before they could join the local Jewish communities. On the other hand, despite the traditional Jewish law according to which children follow the religion of their mother, the New Christians were not required to prove that their mothers were Jewish. The tacit assumption seems to have been that Marrano men only married Marrano women and that the children of a Marrano father could be considered as being of Jewish descent on their mother's side too.[82]

Despite this clandestine exodus, many Marranos remained in Portugal. In 1630 they were again accused of converting Christians to Judaism in Lisbon, and especially Christian servants. Their persistent adherence to a faith that their ancestors had been forced to renounce formally more than a century and a half earlier led Juan Escobar de Corro, inquisitor of Llerena, to consider the Marranos genetically incapable of changing their character. "From the moment of its conception," wrote de Corro in 1628 or soon thereafter, "every fetus permanently carries with it the moral attributes—in the case of the Marranos, the moral depravity—of its parents." This was not a new idea in Portugal. Many of the fifteenth-century sermons preached on the occasion of autos-da-fé by inquisitors or other churchmen stressed the innate incorrigibility of most offspring of Jews.[83]

This favorite theory of the genetic predestination of character and faith was frequently vitiated not only by true Jewish conversions to Christianity but also by Christian proselytism to Judaism. Among the Christian Portuguese who converted to Judaism was Diego de Assumpçao (b. 1579) in Lisbon. This young Franciscan friar, who had only a few drops of Jewish blood in his veins, was attracted to Judaism, tried to escape to England or France, but was caught and imprisoned by the Inquisition for two years. When all the efforts of the most learned theologians to make him repent proved useless, he was burned at the stake in Lisbon in 1603. Since many of the Old Christians were connected through family relations with New Christians, we do not have to look far for the sources by which the Jewish religion reached these Portuguese Christians, several more of whom suffered the auto-da-fé for a faith with which they had no ancestral connection.[84]

A remarkable case was that of Luis Dias of the port of Setúbal, south of Lisbon. This half-illiterate Christian tailor came to believe that he was the Messiah, and gained the adherence and veneration of many New and Old Christians, many of whose sons he circumcised. He was arrested, released, arrested again, and burned in an auto-da-fé (the second in Portugal) in 1542 in Lisbon. Eighty-three of his followers, Old and New Christians, were executed with him. One remarkable Old Christian was a high government official, the Desembargador Gil Vaz Bugalho who, under the influence of "the Messiah of Setúbal" had converted to Judaism, translated parts of the Bible into the vernacular, and composed a handbook of Jewish religious practice for the New Christians. He was burned in an auto-da-fé in 1551.

76

Francisco Mendes, personal physician to the Infante Alphonso, escaped only by flight. Other members of the same circle were the physician Master Gabriel, who made many proselytes, and Gonçalo Eannes Bandorra of Trancoso, a popular mystic poet, both of whom were burned.[85]

At the university town of Coimbra lived Antonio Homem (b. 1564 at Coimbra), a professor of canon law and deacon of the Church. His mother, Isabel Nuñez de Almeida, belonged to an Old Christian family, but his father, Jorge Vaz Brandão, was a Marrano. Antonio was attracted to Judaism, and became the leading spirit of the Marrano group which flourished at Coimbra and included several distinguished scientists at the university. The group held regular services which were attended by as much as two dozen people. In 1619 Homem was betrayed, arrested, sent to Lisbon for trial and, after four and a half years of imprisonment, sentenced to death and execution by garroting at Lisbon in 1624. Several other members of the group, among them half-New Christians, were tried at the same time and sentenced to various punishments.[86]

Don Lope de Vera, the son of Fernando de Vera y Alarcón, a nobleman of pure Christian blood, from San Clemente (near Cuenca), was a child prodigy who at the age of fourteen became a student at the University of Salamanca. There, among other languages, he studied Hebrew, read the Bible, and through it was attracted to Judaism. In 1639 he was arrested at Valladolid, and informed the inquisitorial authorities that he wanted to become a full Jew. For years he was kept in prison in the midst of continuous attempts to make him change his mind. After five years, in 1644, when he was twenty-five years old, he was burned alive in an auto-da-fé in Valladolid.[87]

The Inquisition followed its victims to the New World. The Peruvian Francisco Maldonaldo de Silva, son of a New Christian father and an Old Christian mother, after having been brought up as a pious Christian and become a surgeon, studied the Bible, adopted Judaism, and circumcised himself in Santiago de Chile. In 1627, when he was thirty-four years old, he was incarcerated in Lima for Judaizing. For twelve years the Inquisition tried in vain to make him repent. Instead, he managed to convert several fellow inmates of the prison to Judaism. In 1639 he was burned alive in Lima together with another ten Judaizers.[88]

A younger contemporary was Rodrigo Mendez da Silva, a well-known historian and royal chronicler at the Spanish court. Arrested in 1659 for Judaizing, he was admitted to penance after prolonged torture. He managed to move to Venice where he took up residence in the ghetto and was circumcised.[89]

The same religious fervor which made the Catholics of Spain and Portugal relentlessly persecute the Jews and especially the Marranos expressed itself in the equally strong determination of many Jews, Marranos and Old

Christian proselytes, to die for their faith rather than pay even lip service to Christianity. Some of them literally courted death even after an almost fatal first encounter with the Inquisition. One of these was Antonio José da Silva, the outstanding Portuguese poet and satirist of the early eighteenth century. He was first arrested for Judaizing in 1726 when he was only twenty-one years old, and was so cruelly tortured that he was unable to sign his name and remained crippled throughout his life. He was pronounced penitent and released, but despite this ominous experience continued to practice Judaism while scoring success after success as a poet and playwright. His comedies were popularly known as the *"operas du Judeu."* Rearrested in 1737, he was testified against by his colored slave girl and, since he resisted all attempts to make him recant, two years later was publicly garroted and burned at Lisbon. His family was forced to attend his auto-da-fé which took place on the very day on which one of his operettas was performed in the Lisbon theater.[90]

The intensive intermingling of Jews and Christians left its traces not only among the Sephardi Jews but also among the present-day Christian population of the Iberian Peninsula. According to an anthropometric study carried out in the city of Valladolid, "15 per cent of the population still reveal typically Jewish features," and this situation is probably typical for most other Iberian regions as well.[91]

ITALY

Italy, which as we have seen was in antiquity the home of one of the earliest Jewish settlements on the European Continent, remained a country of Jewish concentration throughout the Middle Ages. In many of the medieval Italian cities the relationship between Jews and Christians was friendly, and Italian humanists not infrequently turned to Jews for help in connection with their biblical studies. Such interest was considered by Jewish scholars a first step which possibly might lead to conversion. Rabbi Isaiah ben Elijah di Trani the Younger, the thirteenth-century Italian rabbinic scholar, permitted teaching Christians the Prophets and the Hagiographa (but not the Pentateuch) because he felt "the Gentile will find there comforting predictions of Israel's ultimate salvation and authoritative answers to skeptics," as a result of which "he may possibly join the Law of Israel." This view was re-echoed in the opinion of the sixteenth-century scholar Franz Joel, who claimed that those who study the Hebrew language become Jews.

From time to time events took place which alerted the Italian authorities to the danger that lay in close contact with the Jews. On May 25, 1518, Pope Leo X addressed a rescript to the papal nuncio and the doge of Venice asking for the elimination of the "depraved and perfidious contagion of Jews living in the Venetian possessions." In 1571 twelve Catalan ladies were made to retract their Judaizing beliefs in a public ceremony held in front of the Naples cathedral. The following year a provincial synod meeting in Lanciano resolved "that Christians should not receive Jews or New Christians in their homes, eat in their homes, or serve them. . . ."

Some Italian principalities welcomed the arrival and settlement of Marranos who brought along good commercial connections with many parts of the world and, in many cases, capital as well. In 1593 Grand Duke Ferdinand II, in his *La Livornina,* addressed to foreign merchants and primarily to Marranos, declared: ". . . there shall be no inquisition, search, denunciation, or accusation against you or your families, even if in the past you lived, outside our Possessions, in the manner and under the name of Christians." While this was an overt departure from the generally pursued ecclesiastical policies, it was strictly observed by the Tuscan authorities.

The frequent prohibitions of Jewish-Christian intercourse, both social and sexual, issued by many Italian authorities throughout the Middle Ages are an eloquent testimony to the close relationship between members of the two faiths. A central concern in all these injunctions was to prevent Christians from becoming attracted to Judaism. This fear was so strong that occasionally Christians were warned not to make use of the services of Jewish doctors, although medicine was a famous Jewish specialization in the Mediterranean area in the Middle Ages and the Renaissance. As late as 1636 the papal congregation warned against consulting Jewish physicians: "The practice of medicine generates too much intercourse with both patients and other members of the household; intercourse leads to friendship, friendship to protection, and from the protection of Jews arises at least some scandal, even if there is no direct contamination" in religious convictions.[92]

FRANCE

We have mentioned French proselytes who joined Judaism in the early Middle Ages. In the twelfth century a French proselyte is stated by Moses ben Abraham of Pontoise, the French tosafist, to have had the habit of studying "Bible and Mishna day and night." In 1270 a respected French monk, who converted to Judaism and took the name of Abraham ben Abraham, fled from France to Germany but was caught and burned in Wiesenburg.

A Judaizing sect arose in connection with the Waldensian movement; its members called themselves *Passagii* (i.e., "Wanderers") or *Circumcisi* ("Circumcised Ones"). The main centers of this sect, which preached return to the Old Testament, were in the region of those cities which had considerable Jewish communities, such as Beziers, Carcassone, Albi, and Toulouse. In 1273 in Provence the monk Bertrand Delaroche was appointed "inquisitor against the heretics and the Judaizing Christians," and in 1276 the provincial council of Saumur-Brouges adopted a resolution to eliminate Jews from the countryside lest "they deceive the simple country people and induce them to share their errors." The following year French judges of heretics asked Pope Nicholas III what to do with those Christian converts to Judaism who had been in prison for more than a year but still refused to return to the Church. The pope's answer was that they should be delivered into the hands of the secular authorities to be burned at the stake. In 1299, Philip IV issued an order to the royal officials to cooperate with the inquisitors in apprehending Jews guilty of abetting Christian heresies. Such measures, however, do not seem to have been able to quench the Jewish missionary zeal, and in 1355 two Jews, Vivant and Menessier de Viergon, were tried in Paris for, among other crimes, having preached to Jews and Gentiles.[93]

From the mid-fourteenth century on, inquisitors widely used a handbook entitled *Practica inquisitionis hereticae pravitatis* written by Bernard Gui. A basic assumption of this handbook is that "the perfidious Jews attempt, when and wherever they can, secretly to pervert Christians and to attract them to the Jewish perfidy. They do it particularly in the case of those who had been Jews. . . ." The defendant, Gui says, must tell "whether he knew of any other Christian who had been Judaized, or any baptized person who had apostasized, or returned to Judaism. . . ." The penitent had to swear that he would "in no way knowingly receive or admit to my home, extend counsel, aid, or favors to either a Judaizing Christian who renounces the true Christian faith, or a convert reverting to Judaism. . . ."[94]

In the early seventeenth century, Nicholas Antoine (*b.* about 1602), a son of Roman Catholic peasants at Briey, Lorraine, and a student at a theological college, became attracted first to Protestantism and then to Judaism. His request for admission into the Jewish community was refused by the rabbis of Metz, Venice, and Padua. Disappointed, Antoine went to Switzerland, and became the pastor of Divonne, a village in the district of Gex. He continued to practice Judaism in secret, until his Jewish leanings became known and he was accused of heresy, taken to Geneva, and handed over to the Swiss Protestant equivalent of the Inquisition. There he openly declared himself a Jew, was tried, condemned, and, in 1632, executed by strangling.[95]

ENGLAND

In 1222 an Oxford deacon converted to Judaism, after which he married a Jewish woman. He was burned to death. Half a century later a Dominican friar, Robert of Reading, converted. He, too, died by burning. That these were not isolated occurrences is shown by the bull *Turbato corde* issued in 1286, in which Pope Honorius IV complains of the success of the Jewish mission among the Christians in England. Such conversions may have been a contributing factor in the decision taken by Edward I in 1290 to expel the Jews from England.[96] However, while the English could expel the Jews, they could not do the same to the Bible. Some readers of the "Old Testament" were impressed by the laws and warnings contained in it, and took to observing the will of God as expressed in them.

In the early seventeenth century a Judaizing sect sprang up in England under the leadership of John Traske. Its members observed the Sabbath and followed the rules of the Hebrew Scriptures. In 1618 the Star Chamber condemned Traske to savage punishment, which induced him to recant and publish a *Treatise of Liberation from Judaisme by John Traske, of late stumbling, now happily running again in the Race of Christianitie* (London, 1620). Some of the sectarians, however—including one Hamlet Jackson, a tailor who originally had aroused Traske's interest in the Old Testament— emigrated to Amsterdam where they formally joined the Jewish community.[97]

Events such as these alerted the English political leadership to the potential danger of religious influence which would emanate from the Jews were they to be readmitted to England. Their fears are highlighted in the debate that preceded the readmission of the Jews to England after they had been absent for two and a half centuries. When Manasse ben Israel, the Dutch Jewish leader, submitted his "Humble Address" to the English government asking permission for the Jews to settle in England (1655), those who opposed the approval of the petition argued that the admission of Jews would likely result in the emergence of Judaizing sects among Christian Englishmen. And when Cromwell admitted Jews to England, one of the conditions was that they would refrain from proselytizing. Similarly, when England declared war against Spain (1656), and the Spanish Marranos, who had settled in England in considerable numbers a few years earlier, had no choice but to admit that they were not really Spaniards but Spanish Jews, they were permitted by Cromwell to remain in England and continue with their businesses only after they undertook to refuse proselytes from among the Christians.[98]

The number of Jews who made use of the newly won permission to settle in England was surprisingly small. Even 150 years later, they did not exceed 8,000. However, their presence in the country contributed its share to the emergence of Anglo-Israelism. This movement began with the preachments of Richard Brothers, an English eccentric who claimed to be a scion of the House of David and who, in 1822, published a "Correct Account of the Invasion of England by the Saxons, Showing the English Nation to be Descendants of the Lost Ten Tribes." Throughout the nineteenth century several more leaders of the movement published books elaborating this basic theme, and in the early years of the twentieth the number of its adherents in England and the United States was estimated at 2 million. The identification

81

of the British (explained as derived from the Hebrew *"B'rit ish,"* which was ungrammatically taken to mean "man of the covenant") with the ten tribes of Israel did not interfere with the religious beliefs of the adherents of the movement: they remained members of the Church of England, and held themselves apart from the Jews, whom they considered the descendants of Judah cursed repeatedly by the biblical prophets. While Anglo-Israelism did not lead directly to proselytism, its intensive preoccupation with Old Testament prophecies and texts did create an atmosphere of heightened interest in biblical Hebrew religion which, occasionally at least, led individuals to Judaizing and ultimately to conversion.[99]

Even before Anglo-Israelism claimed the attention of many, Lord George Gordon, a younger son of the third duke of Gordon and member of Parliament, had himself circumcised (in 1787) either in Holland or in Birmingham where he lived for a while, and assumed the name of Israel ben Abraham. He scrupulously observed all the rules of Jewish religion, grew a long beard, and tried to convince Jews less observant than he to lead a truly pious life. He was tried for libel, and sent in 1788 to Newgate Prison in London, where he died five years later.[100]

SWEDEN

In Sweden, too, the Jews were feared as a potential source of Christian apostasy and as such were excluded from the country. In 1685, Charles XI ordered the governor-general of his capital, Stockholm, to see to it that no Jew be allowed to settle in any part of Sweden, "on account of the danger of the eventual influence of the Jewish religion on the pure evangelical faith." A few decades later, permission was granted to Jews to settle in Sweden (1718). In 1782 this permission was expanded: the Jews were allowed to settle anywhere in the country and to practice their religion freely, but at the same time were forbidden to establish schools for the propagation of their creed and to perform such ceremonies as might possibly cause disquietude in the minds of the Christian population. Despite these laws, contact between Jews and Christians grew and led to intermarriage. Consequently, in 1873 the authorities felt the need to issue an ordinance stipulating that children born to mixed Jewish-Christian couples must be brought up in the Lutheran faith.

Conversions, too, began to occur, exactly as Charles XI had feared. Again, as in other countries, the historical documentation is confined to a few cases involving important personages. One of these was a Swedish nobleman by the name of Graanboom, who decided to convert to Judaism in the mid-eighteenth century, when he was sixty-nine years old. He took his wife, his fourteen-year-old daughter, and twelve-year-old son (*b.* 1736) to Amsterdam—well known to us by now as a haven of refuge for Judaizers and would-be converts—and there the whole family underwent conversion. His son received the name Aaron Moses Isaac, was given a Yeshiva education, became head of a Yeshiva and one of the rabbis of the Amsterdam community. In 1797 he became rabbi of the newly founded liberal congregation Adath Jeshurun, in which position he served until his death in 1807 when he was succeeded by his son, Israel Graanboom.[101]

BOHEMIA

The Bohemian religious movement of the Hussites, which began in the fifteenth century, comprised diverse sectarian groups, among them some of outright Judaizers. In the sixteenth century, reports from various parts of Germany, and especially from the Austrian hereditary possessions where Hussite traditions were still very much alive, speak of the emergence of new sects which were following the Old Testament literally and were adopting such basic Jewish practices as circumcision and the observance of the Sabbath. There were rumors that many Christians had actually converted to Judaism and were helped by the Jews to emigrate to Turkey in order to escape the wrath of the Christian authorities.[102]

GERMANY

Once again history records only the conversions of those few proselytes in Germany who were exceptional among the many converts to Judaism because they were of high status in Gentile society prior to their conversion, or because they achieved renown after they had become Jewish. One way to such renown was to die a martyr's death. Martyrs, whether born Jews or proselytes, were often remembered by Jewish chroniclers and elegists.

From the eleventh to the thirteenth centuries, cases are known of proselytes who converted to Judaism with the intention of suffering martyrdom. During the massacres of the First Crusade in 1096, a proselyte triumphantly exclaimed before his martyrdom: "Hitherto you have scorned me!" In 1264 a proselyte named Abraham son of Abraham our father conducted a campaign for Judaism among the Christians, attacked and broke the symbols of Christianity, was imprisoned, tortured, and then burned at Augsburg. In Würzburg in the second half of the twelfth century the memory of a proselyte has been preserved not because of the way he died but because of what he did while he was alive. He made himself a copy of the Latin Pentateuch from "a rejected book belonging to priests," and subsequently mastered Hebrew sufficiently to be allowed by Rabbi Joel to act as a reader for the congregation.

Protestantism, which made the Bible more easily accessible to large numbers of Christian laymen, felt threatened by the attraction emanating from the pages of the Old Testament. In 1530 the diet of Augsburg officially execrated Protestant Judaizing. Eight years later Luther published his warning "Against the Sabbatarians," which contains a severe censure of the sect for emulating Jewish customs. It also attacks the Jews because, somewhere in Moravia, they preached to the Protestants about the sanctification of the Sabbath, and warns the Christians lest the Jews persuade them to undergo circumcision. Luther was especially worried about the influence of the rabbis on Christian Hebraists who occasionally translated biblical passages not in accordance with the Lutheran Bible translation. A few cases of individual conversions are briefly sketched below.

In the early seventeenth century, Conrad Victor, a professor of classical languages at the University of Marburg, became attracted to Judaism. In 1607, he left his wife and family and went to Salonica in Greece (at the time under Muslim Turkish rule), converted to Judaism, and took the name of Moses Prado.

In the early 1640's a Viennese Catholic shoemaker named Spaeth moved to Augsburg where he had his son Johann Peter (*b.* 1640) educated by Jesuits. Young Johann became attracted to Lutheranism, and was appointed a Lutheran pastor in Frankfort on the Main, but returned to Catholicism in 1683. Still dissatisfied, he went to Amsterdam, where he converted to Judaism and took the name Moses. He wrote books defending Judaism, attacked the unorthodox philosophy of Spinoza, and became known among the Jews of Amsterdam as Moses Germanus.

In the first half of the eighteenth century, a German Catholic monk converted to Judaism and became known as Israel ben Avraham Avinu, or *Yisrael Gēr* ("Israel Proselyte"). He, too, converted in Amsterdam, and afterwards wrote Jewish apologetics and attacks on Christianity. He established printing presses in several German cities, published some of the most important Jewish religious source books, and became a close friend of Rabbi David Fraenkel, who was the teacher of Moses Mendelssohn in Dessau. He married a Jewish woman, and their two sons, Abraham and Tobias, succeeded him in the printing business.[103]

HUNGARY

Little is known of the history of the Jews in the early centuries after the conquest of Hungary by the Magyar tribes (896). However, among the Bulgars, who lived in the south and southeast of Hungary in the ninth century, there were apparently Jews who either had come from the vicinity of the Volga River, or had originated from the Byzantine Empire. Some of these Bulgarian Jews, possibly of Khazar origin, engaged in proselytizing, as we learn from the reply sent by Pope Nicholas I (r. 858–67) to the Bulgarian Prince Michael Bogor in response to a series of 106 religious questions asked by the prince.

About 1096 a proselyte from France, fleeing from Crusaders' atrocities, arrived in Hungary with his two sons. The father, Abraham by name, devoted himself to biblical and Talmudic exegesis and to apologetics. One of his sons, known as Isaac Viscount, continued in his father's footsteps; the other, Joseph-Yehosaphia, was a liturgical poet. This family of proselytes did much to transplant Jewish intellectual life into Hungary.

As in other countries so in Hungary Jewish slave-owners insisted on converting their slaves to Judaism. One of those converted in this manner about 1215–18 was a slave girl owned by the Jew Salomon in Üregh, in the Neutra county. Subsequently she ran off to the palatine (or governor) and returned to her original religion. Soon, however, she became dissatisfied with the treatment accorded to her, and returned to Üregh to Isaac, her new Jewish master. The frequency of conversions to Judaism in this period can be seen from the fact that in 1234 young King Béla IV rendered a solemn oath to Jacob, bishop of Praeneste, that he would put to death every Christian who dared adopt the Jewish faith.

In the twelfth and thirteenth centuries, the relationship between the Jews and the Christians in Hungary was perhaps closer and more friendly than in any other country. Jews and Christians lived together in one and the same courtyard, house, and family. These conditions provoked the dissatisfaction of the Church, and the Council of Buda, held in 1279, lists the measures to be taken to put an end to them:

> Since it is very dangerous, and is in sharp contradiction to the holy canons, that the Jews, whom Christian love accepts and tolerates, should not be set apart from the Christians by certain signs and badges; that they should dwell or sojourn together with Christians in one family, or stay in their courtyards and houses; or that Christians should live together with them; therefore we decide by this decree . . . every Jew, man or woman, whenever he goes in or out of his house or home, or appears in public in any circumstances, should wear as a distinguishing badge a circle made of red cloth which must be sewn onto his chest on the left side of the outer garment which he wears normally on top of his other garb. . . . Those Christians who engage in commerce with Jews not wearing the red badge, or remain in familial or friendly relations with Jews, or live with them in one courtyard or house, are prohibited from entering the church. . . .[104]

In the early sixteenth century, a German Jewish traveler reports that while he was in Hungary he saw three *gērim* (Christians who had become Jews) begging and receiving generous donations from Jewish communities.

About 1686 a Hungarian Christian by the name of Haase, who was born in Nikolsburg, converted to Judaism in Amsterdam, took the name Moses ben Abraham Avinu, and married the daughter of one of the rabbis of the city. He became proficient in Hebrew and Yiddish, opened a printing shop in 1689, and printed several books in both languages. Moving about in Europe he opened printing and publishing houses in several German cities. His children—a son, Israel, and two daughters named Ella and Gella—assisted him in his shop as Hebrew typesetters. Gella wrote a Yiddish rhymed introduction to the prayer book *T'fila l'Moshe,* which she typeset in 1710.

The sixteenth century saw the foundation of the Sabbatarian sect in Transylvania. Its originator was a Székely-Hungarian nobleman, András Eössi, who in 1567, together with several other Transylvanian nobles, converted to the Unitarian faith, and a few years later founded the Sabbatarian sect. The doctrines of the sect were developed by Eössi together with his adopted son, Simon Péchi (who was the leading Transylvanian statesman of his age) and Miklós Bogáthy Fazekas. Péchi (b. *c.* 1565) prepared a Hungarian prayer book for the Sabbatarians, while Fazekas translated the Pslams into Hungarian. Péchi became chancellor of the state of Transylvania and his great reputation led to the conversion of some 20,000 Székelys to the Sabbatarian faith. In 1595 the diet of Fehérvár passed a decree against the Sabbatarians which was renewed in 1618 by Gábor Bethlen, the ruling prince of Transylvania. The sect nevertheless continued to spread among both peasantry and nobility. Sabbatarian preachers roamed the country and convinced many to adopt the faith, which demanded a strict observance of the Sabbath and adherence to the laws of the Pentateuch.

In 1635 the diet decreed loss of property or death for all Judaizers. This law resulted in the reconversion to Christianity of many Sabbatarians. Others emigrated to Turkey where they could openly practice Judaism. Several dozen families persevered in their new faith in Transylvania itself, and in 1869, after the emancipation of Hungarian Jews (1867), 105 Székely-Hungarian Sabbatarian peasants converted to Judaism in the Transylvanian village of Bözödujfalu. In 1874 they built a synagogue, and by 1920 their congregation consisted of fifty to eighty strictly Orthodox Jewish families of which thirty-two were of purely Sabbatarian descent. They wore Hungarian peasant clothes, but over their shirt they wore the four-fringed ritual "small *tallith,"* the so-called *arba^c kanfoth.* The faces of the men were framed by sidelocks and the women kept a scrupulously kosher kitchen.

About 1929 they rebuilt their synagogue and school. In 1941 a Hungarian scholar, George Balázs, visited them and found a thriving community of seventy members. They spoke Hungarian (although the village, as part of Transylvania, had been under Rumanian rule since the end of World War I), prayed in Hebrew, used the synagogue and the school, and inscribed their tombstones in Hebrew. During World War II the village was re-annexed by Hungary, and, in order to save themselves from the persecution and death which became the fate of most Hungarian Jews as a consequence of the Nazi laws, they returned to Christianity. This, it seems, was the end of Hungarian Sabbatarianism.[105]

POLAND

Jews came to Poland approximately from the tenth century on, mainly from the Ashkenazi west, from Byzantium in the south, and from Khazaria in the east. Within a few centuries Ashkenazi culture became dominant among them, replacing all other cultural influences. Their presence soon evoked the enmity of the Church, and as early as 1267 the Wroclaw (Breslau) Polish Church Council outlined an anti-Jewish policy aiming to isolate the Jews from the Christians. It expressed the fear, as the Church did elsewhere, that the Christian people of Poland, "newly grafted onto the Christian body," might "easily be misled by the superstitious and evil habits of the Jews that live among them." The same purpose of segregating Jews from Christians was enunciated, with various modifications, in several subsequent Church Councils.

As far as the secular authorities were concerned, their fear that the Jews could attract Christians to Judaism was temporarily overshadowed in the fourteenth century by the threat they saw in the Jews as economic competitors. The statute issued by Casimir the Great in favor of Little Poland in about 1347 contains a warning against "the aspirations of the perverse Jews which are aimed at depriving Christians not so much of their faith as of their riches and property. . . ." By the sixteenth century, however, the stereotype of the Jew intent on catching innocent Christian souls was firmly established. The Polish chronicler Martin Bielski writes about the events of 1539: "The Jews of that period seduced not a few Christians among us to the Jewish religion and circumcised them." In the same year a seventy-year-old Christian woman, Catherine Weigel, widow of a Cracow councilman, was accused of Judaizing, and after all efforts to persuade her to return to the Church proved in vain, was burned at the stake. This event set off a Judaizing scare and a hunt for proselytes all over Poland-Lithuania which continued into the year 1540.

Under Sigismund I, king of Poland, the Catholic clergy, deeply disturbed by the first successes of the Reformation in the country, saw in Judaism an ally of the spreading heresy and felt that the doctrine of "anti-Trinitarianism" in particular was a result of Jewish propaganda. At the same time the rumor spread that in several parts of Poland, and especially in the Cracow district, many Christians had converted to Judaism, had themselves circumcised, and fled to Lithuania or to Turkish-dominated Hungary and thence to Turkey itself. A renegade Jew from Turkey informed King Sigismund that he had seen whole trains of Poles in Moldavia who had converted

87

to Judaism and were on their way to Turkey. The king's reaction was both prompt and energetic. He had the leaders of the Jews in Cracow and Poznan arrested, and dispatched commissioners to Lithuania to apprehend the Judaizing Christians who had fled there (1539). After the Jews complained, the order was revoked and the arrested Jewish elders were set free against a payment of 20,000 ducats.

The danger of Judaizing continued to haunt Poland in the eighteenth century. In 1716 two Christian women, accused of having converted to Judaism, were subjected to questioning by the legal authorities in Dubno. Both were condemned to death and executed.

The story of Count Valentine Potocki (Pototzki), who converted to Judaism and was burned at the stake in Vilna in 1749, is so remarkable that it must be told in some detail. It appears that Potocki and his friend Zaremba went to Paris to study, made the acquaintance of an old Jew whom they found poring over a large tome of the Talmud when they entered his wine shop, and received instruction from him in Hebrew. Impressed by the teachings of the Old Testament, Potocki went to Amsterdam, converted there to Judaism, had himself circumcised, assumed the name Abraham ben Abraham, and after a brief stay in Germany returned to Poland. He lived for a while as a Jew among the Jews of Ilye (Vilna district), until he was denounced to the authorities and arrested. He turned a deaf ear to the entreaties of his mother and his friends to return to Christianity, and after a long imprisonment was burned alive in Vilna, on the second day of Shavu'ot, on May 24, 1749. Zaremba, who had returned to Poland before Potocki, married the daughter of a Polish nobleman, and a few years later went with his family to Amsterdam where he, his wife, and son all converted to Judaism, after which they settled in Palestine. A few weeks after the burning of Potocki, a seventy-year-old Jew, Menahem Man ben Arye Loeb of Visun, was tortured and executed in Vilna (July 3, 1749), and it has been assumed that it was this martyr who induced the two Polish noblemen to convert to Judaism.[106]

RUSSIA

Jews have lived in the southern parts of the area which today constitutes the U.S.S.R. since Roman times. From the ninth century on, Jews migrated into the Ukraine from Khazaria, Byzantium, and the Muslim domains. The first recorded Russian pogrom took place in 1113, when the Jewish quarter of Kiev was looted.

In 1470 a Jewish scholar named Zakharia arrived from Kiev in Novgorod, contacted several Greek Orthodox priests, and succeeded in winning them over to Judaism. Soon a sect of Judaizers developed, led by the priests Denis and Alexius. In 1479 they accompanied Ivan III to Moscow and were placed by him in two Moscow churches. As a result of their missionary activities, many Russians turned away from Christianity. Several of these Judaizers submitted themselves to circumcision. This sectarian movement penetrated even the highest circles. The daughter-in-law of Ivan III, Helena, and his chancellor, Fedor Kuritzin, joined the sect, as did, according to some sources, the metropolitan of Moscow, Zosima (in 1494). In 1487 Archbishop Gennadi of Novgorod launched an energetic and cruel campaign against the Judaizers. In 1504 the leaders of the sect were burned and many of its members were imprisoned either in jails or in monasteries.

Despite the persecutions, underground interest in Judaizing continued. In 1737 a retired Russian naval officer, Alexander Vosnitzyn, became acquainted with the teachings of Judaism, converted, and had himself circumcised. His wife denounced him to the authorities, and he was arrested and questioned. After a thorough investigation he was condemned to death and burned in Petrograd on July 15, 1738, as was the Jew Baruch Leibov under whose influence Vosnitzyn had embraced Judaism.

During the second half of the eighteenth century, sects of Judaizers and Sabbath observers emerged in several parts of Russia, including the Volga provinces and the northern Caucasus. Most prominent among these was the Molokan sect, which soon after its foundation split into two groups, one of which, the Molokan Sabbath Observers, moved toward closer association with the Jews.

In 1796 (or 1806) a sect of Sabbath observers (*Subbotniki*) arose in the Voronesh guberniya in Russia, as well as in the Saratov and Tula guberniyas. Among the Jewish customs adhered to by the sect were circumcision, voluntary marriage and divorce, the manner of burial, and prayer meetings. By 1817, in the Voronesh bishopric alone they numbered 1,500, and there were many others who were secret sectarians. The situation was similar in the bishoprics of Tura, Oryol, and Saratov. In Saratov the preacher Milyukhin won over whole villages to his faith. The Judaizing heresy spread in the country as well as the towns, among both peasants and merchants, and all efforts of the Church could not stem it.

In 1823 the Russian government took strong measures against the Subbotniki, whose numbers it estimated at 20,000. Their leaders were conscripted into the army; those unfit for army service were exiled to Siberia; the Jews who lived in the districts infected by the heresy were deported; and all sectarian activities, gatherings, customs, and so on, were strictly forbidden. The sect was to be called "Jew sect," so as to make it clear to all and sundry that its members were actually converts to Judaism. As a result of these measures whole villages were ruined, thousands of sectarians banished to Siberia or the Caucasus, and small children taken away from their parents to be brought up in Christianity.

The fear of proselytizing by the Jews, which produced this Russian reaction to the Subbotniki, also led to restrictive laws (1820) prohibiting Jews from having Christian servants. In 1821 the Jews were expelled from the villages of White Russia. By early 1827 some 20,000 Jews had been thrust out; many of these died of hunger, the cold, and diseases.

With the accession of Alexander II the position of the Judaizers improved, and in 1887 the government permitted them to observe their own marriage and burial customs. The manifesto of October 17, 1905, abolished all discrimination againt Judaizers and Sabbath observers, while emphasizing that they were not to be regarded as Jews.

One of the main divisions of the Judaizers were the *geri* ("proselytes"), who considered themselves Jews in every respect, and made a point of intermarrying with Jews. They sent their children to Yeshivot to study, and many of them settled in Palestine—in Metula, Y'sud haMa'ala, and so on—and became completely integrated with the Jewish population.[107]

CONCLUSION

Throughout the long history of the Jews, both in their own land and in the Diaspora, proselytes joined them individually and occasionally in groups. The available historical data do not give us a clear picture of this movement, but they suffice to allow the conclusion that cumulatively, in the course of three millennia, it must have had a considerable impact on the Jewish gene pool. Even were one to assume that the original Israelites of the biblical period constituted a "Hebrew race"—in itself a most improbable supposition—proselytism alone would have been sufficient to replace any ancient Hebrew racial unity with a marked Jewish physical diversity.

The historical record of proselytism tells only a very small part of its story, most of which is, and will forever remain, unknown. The striking physical similarity between the Jews and the non-Jews in every country in which the Jews settled not later than the end of the Middle Ages can serve to confirm that the non-Jewish genetic influence on the Jews must indeed have been considerable. The nature of these physical similarities will be dealt with in the latter part of this book. In the next chapter we turn to the question of Jewish-Gentile intermarriage, which went everywhere hand in hand with proselytism.

CHAPTER IV

Intermarriage
and Interbreeding

INTRODUCTORY REMARKS

THE PROCESS OF absorbing foreign genetic influences as a result of interbreeding has been part of the anthropological history of the Jews from earliest times to the present. Jewish-Gentile interbreeding has resulted from intermarriage, concubinage, extramarital relations, slavery, prostitution, rape, and possibly also the exercise of the *jus primae noctis.* In most places and most eras all contact that could result in sexual relations between Jews and Gentiles was strenuously opposed by those in positions of authority on either side. But again in most places and most eras, the practices continued despite warnings, bans, rules, laws, and the application of the most severe sanctions, including death by burning.[1]

One of the main difficulties for the historian trying to assess Jewish-Gentile intermarriage is that technically, from the Jewish religious point of view, only a marriage which is solemnized without either of the spouses having earlier converted to the religion of the other is considered intermarriage. If the non-Jewish partner converts to Judaism before the wedding, the union is a Jewish marriage between a Jew and a proselyte; if the Jewish partner embraces the religion of the other partner before the wedding, it is a case of conversion of a Jew to another religion, and the marriage that takes place thereafter is no longer of any concern to the Jewish community. Neither of these marriages will figure in any statistics dealing with Jewish-Gentile intermarriage. Genetically speaking, the question of whether or not one of the two partners to a marriage converts to the religion of the other obviously makes no difference at all, since the genetic make-up of the children born to

91

such mixed couples remains the same in both cases. What *is* genetically significant is the question of the community in which children live as they grow up: if Gentile, the mixed marriage remains without genetic effects on the Jewish community; if Jewish, the Gentile genes carried by them will become part of the Jewish gene pool.

It is therefore unnecessary, for our present purpose, to distinguish between mixed marriages in which the two spouses retain their original religions and those in which premarital conversion resolves their religious differences. Consequently, we shall treat both types of mixed marriages indiscriminately. The question of Jewish *versus* Gentile upbringing of the children born to mixed couples, on the other hand, is genetically of basic importance, and will have to occupy us repeatedly.

In general terms it can be stated at the outset that if the Jewish partner converts to the religion of the Gentile prior to the wedding, the children are invariably brought up as Gentiles; and conversely, if the Gentile spouse converts to Judaism before the marriage, the children are brought up as Jews. If no pre-nuptial conversion takes place, the spouses may or may not enter into an agreement as to the religion (or religions) in which they will bring up their children. The percentage of children born to such couples who are brought up as Jews varies, but in most cases it falls below 50 per cent. Thus, demographically, mixed marriages in which both partners retain their original religions usually represent a loss for the Jewish contingent, but genetically their effect is much less marked than that of marriages between Jews and proselytes.

The *halakha*—the Jewish traditional law based on the Bible—does not recognize mixed marriages; that is, a marriage between a Jewish male and a non-Jewish female, or a Jewish female and a non-Jewish male, is considered invalid, it does not exist legally. Such marriages are prohibited in biblical legislation which specifies that no connubium must be contracted with any member of the seven Canaanite nations: the Hittites, Girgashites, Amorites, Canaanites, Perizzites, Hivites, and Jebusites. This biblical prohibition forms the basis of the Talmudic law, which expands it so as to include all nations, and non-marital sexual intercourse as well. If a mixed marriage is contracted in contravention of the *halakha,* it is invalid and the Jewish spouse is considered legally unmarried. The same principle was subsequently incorporated into the medieval Jewish codes and the *Shulḥan 'Arukh,* which tradition-abiding Jews still regard as valid and binding.[2] Basically, the same principle is still upheld by the Rabbinate in the State of Israel, except that, if a Jew and a non-Jew marry in another country in accordance with the laws of that country, such a marriage cannot be challenged in Israel before a rabbinical court, inasmuch as these courts have jurisdiction only if both spouses are Jews. In practice this means that, throughout history, according to the *halakha,* a Jew could marry only a Jew or a proselyte.

IN BIBLICAL TIMES

However, law is one thing, practice frequently quite another. Despite the consistently maintained legal prohibition, mixed marriages between Jews and Gentiles were a frequent occurrence throughout the ages. In biblical times, whatever the law said, the actual practice was that a child was considered the descendant only of his father and his patrilineal ancestors, and not of his mother and his matrilineal forebears. This meant that the child of an Israelite father was considered an Israelite, irrespective of its mother's religion and ethnic background. In fact, the author of the Book of Genesis considered the identity of the mother so unimportant that he made mention only exceptionally of the names of the women married by the men of the Abrahamic family. Nevertheless we learn that, despite the prevailing ideal of close kin endogamy, both Abraham and Jacob had children with outsider women in addition to their endogamous wives: Abraham had Ishmael by his Egyptian handmaid-wife Hagar, and another six sons by an otherwise unidentified wife, Keturah, as well as additional offspring by unnamed "concubines." Abraham's son and heir, Isaac, had only one wife, his cousin Rebekah, and only two twin sons, Esau and Jacob. But even the strong-willed matriarch Rebekah could not prevent Esau from marrying Hittite Canaanite women who "were a bitterness of spirit unto Isaac and Rebekah." As for Jacob, Rebekah's stratagem succeeded in having him sent back to the old country, Paddan-Aram, where he duly married the two daughters of his mother's brother, Leah and Rachel.[3]

When we come to the twelve sons of Jacob, the wives of the only two of them who are named in Genesis were both aliens to the Abrahamic kin group: one was the daughter of Shua, a Canaanite, whom Judah married; the other Asenath, daughter of the Egyptian Poti-phera, priest of On (Heliopolis), whom Joseph married in Egypt.[4] No word is said about the wives of the other ten sons of Jacob, but we must conclude that, for lack of any other choice, they married either Canaanite women or, after their descent to Egypt, Egyptian women.

It would seem that in the patriarchal period, marriage between daughters of the Abrahamic family and foreign men was countenanced on condition that the foreigners first underwent circumcision. Although the sons of Jacob, in discussing the marriage of their sister Dinah and "Shechem, son of Hamor, the Hivite, prince of the land," put this condition "with guile," the custom must have actually existed, otherwise the people of Hamor would not have believed them.[5]

There is no express mention in the Bible of the marriage customs of the Children of Israel during their sojourn in Egypt, but there are some indications which make it likely that mixed marriages between them and members of other ethnic groups did, in fact, occur. One is that Moses married a Midianite woman and then a Cushite woman as well. The latter marriage provoked the censure of his older siblings Miriam and Aaron. Another case of intermarriage involved an Israelite woman of the tribe of Dan and an Egyptian man. It is also recorded that when the Children of Israel left Egypt, a "mixed multitude" went up with them. The presence of such alien population elements cannot be imagined without interbreeding. So it seems quite certain that the Israelite tribes which settled in Canaan in the thirteenth century B.C. contained, in addition to the original Aramaean stock of Abraham and his half-sister Sarah, also Amorite and Hittite, as well as Canaanite and Egyptian, racial elements.[6]

Once the struggle for the possession of Canaan began, the victorious Israelites spared the women, or at least the virgins, and the children of their vanquished foes. This means that these foreigners were absorbed into the Israelite tribes. When the Children of Israel had defeated the Midianites, we are told, Moses allowed them to "keep alive for themselves" all the Midianite "women children that have not known man by lying with him." The tally showed that these virgins numbered no less than 32,000, of whom Moses gave 32 to the Levites as "Yahweh's tribute." Deuteronomic legislation put the stamp of official approval on this procedure and provided that if an Israelite wished to marry "a woman of goodly form" from among those captured in battle, he could do so after he had allowed her to mourn her father and her mother for a full month. He also could take a female prisoner of war as a slave, in accordance with old customary law.[7]

After the Israelite settlement in Canaan, frequent contact with the native peoples of the country led to intermarriage on the one hand, and the promulgation of laws against it on the other. In Exodus Yahweh warns the Children of Israel: "Behold, I am driving out before thee the Amorite, and the Canaanite, and the Hittite, and the Perizzite, and the Hivite, and the Jebusite. Take heed to thyself lest thou . . . take of their daughters unto thy sons, and their daughters go astray after their gods and make thy sons go astray after their gods." In Deuteronomy the same law is repeated with the addition of the Girgashite as the seventh proscribed nation, and the prohibition of giving an Israelite daughter to their son in marriage. Elsewhere in Deuteronomy the Ammonites and Moabites are excluded from "entering into the Assembly of Yahweh" which, of course, includes the prohibition of intermarrying with them.[8]

However, it has to be understood that these laws represented an ideal that was rarely, if ever, translated into reality. Both royalty and common people did intermarry with non-Israelites. One famous example is provided by the story of Samson, who married a Philistine woman and cohabited with a Philistine harlot before falling in love with yet another Philistine woman, Delilah, who caused his downfall. Another is the story of Ruth, which is set in the days of the Judges (thirteenth to twelfth century B.C.). From it we learn that after a certain Elimelech from Bethlehem in Judah went to Moab in search of a livelihood, both his sons married Moabite women. More than that: when Ruth, the Moabite wife of one of Elimelech's sons, remained a childless widow and returned to Judah with her mother-in-law, a kinsman of her deceased husband, "a mighty man of valor" Boaz by name, "acquired her to be his wife to raise up the name of the dead upon his inheritance, that the name of the dead be not cut off from among his brethren," exactly as prescribed by Deuteronomic law which, evidently, was based on an old folk custom. Incidentally, the issue of the union between Ruth and Boaz was Obed, who begot Jesse, who begot David. Thus, at least two non-Israelite ancestresses figured in the genealogy of David: one was his great-grand-mother Ruth, the Moabite; the other, ten generations back, the Canaanite woman Tamar.[9]

While direct evidence for Israelite-Canaanite intermarriage is scanty, there is no dearth of circumstantial evidence. The very first chapter of the Book of Judges contains a detailed list of those peoples whom the Israelite tribes were not able to "drive out" or defeat, and "among" whom or "with" whom they consequently had to dwell. We are told that the tribe of Judah "could not drive out the inhabitants of the valley, because they had chariots of iron," nor could the Children of Dan dislodge the Amorites who dwelt in the valley adjoining Dan's hill country. Similarly, "the Children of Benjamin did not drive out the Jebusites that inhabited Jerusalem; but the Jebusites dwelt with the Children of Benjamin in Jerusalem unto this day." Again, "Manasseh did not drive out the inhabitants of Beth-Shean and its towns, nor Taanach and its towns, nor the inhabitants of Ibleam and its towns, nor the inhabitants of Megiddo and its towns; but the Canaanites were resolved to dwell in that land. And it came to pass, when Israel was waxen strong, that they put the Canaanites to task-work, but did in no wise drive them out." Likewise, the Canaanites remained dwelling in Gezer among the Children of Ephraim; in Kitron and Nahalol among the Children of Zebulun as tributaries; in Zidon, Ahlab, Achzib, Helbah, Aphik, and Rehov among the Children of Asher; in Beth-Shemesh and Beth-Anath as tributaries of Naphtali; in Harheres, Aijalon, and Shaalbim as tributaries of Joseph. This dry factual record, augmented elsewhere by similar statements, indicates clearly that the thirty-one Canaanite "kings" who were "smitten" by Joshua suffered, in several cases at least, only temporary defeat. Four cities—Taanach, Megiddo, Gezer, and Aphek (Aphik)—appear in Joshua's list as having been "smitten" and in the Judges' list as having remained independent of the Israelites. A fifth one, Hazor, is mentioned as an independent kingdom a few decades later, strong enough to subjugate the Israelites.[10]

The fact that the Israelites "dwelt among" the Canaanites and vice versa resulted very soon in the adoption by the former of the agricultural practices and religious customs of the latter. No sooner had Joshua died than the

Children of Israel began to serve the Baalim and the Astartes, that is, the gods of Canaan. In the Yahwist historiography of the author of the Book of Judges, the theological explanation of the political situation that obtained throughout the period of the Judges was that God allowed the Philistines, Canaanites, Zidonians, Hivites, Hittites, Amorites, Perizzites, and Jebusites to remain in the country in order to use these peoples as his instruments in punishing Israel for its idolatry. In the next breath, however, he reverts to reporting a fact: "And they [i.e., the Israelites] took their daughters to be their wives, and served their gods." [11]

We know too little about the racial identity of the Israelites and the nations enumerated above in this early period to be able to assess the racial significance of these intermarriages. There can, however, be little doubt that several nations were racially quite different from the Israelites. Thus the Philistines had come, in all probability, from the island of Crete ("Caphtor").[12] The Hivites, generally identified with the Hurrians, were a non-"Semitic" people whose original home seems to have been in eastern Anatolia. The Hittites had come from Central Anatolia where they had a powerful empire in the second millennium B.C. The Canaanites and Zidonians seem to have been of a racial stock similar to that of the Israelites. The racial identity of the Amorites, Perizzites, and Jebusites is unknown.

We cannot attempt here to track down the uncertainties of the racial history of the Israelites throughout the four centuries of the monarchic period (c. 1020–586 B.C.). In a small country such as biblical Israel, with non-Hebrew ethnic elements interspersed with the Hebrews and surrounding them on all sides within a few miles of their main urban population centers, and with lively commercial, cultural, and often also hostile contacts across the borders (all of which is amply attested in the books of Samuel and Kings), there can be no question but that interbreeding was an everyday occurrence. Occasionally, when the protagonists were people of consequence, the traces of such relations are preserved in the Bible. To mention only a few examples, all taken from the time of King David (c. 1000–960 B.C.): David had a Hittite officer in his army, Uriah, whose wife was an Israelite woman. Tyrian carpenters and masons lived for years in Jerusalem while they built a palace for David. David himself had numerous concubines, some of whom must have been alien slave girls. His servants, too, had such handmaids. Among his slaves were Moabites. After he smote Hadadezer, king of Zobah in Syria, he brought back thousands of prisoners of war. Part of his own army consisted of Cherethites and Pelethites who were, in all probability, foreign troops. He also had troops from the Philistine city of Gath. Among his servants there was a Cushite; and among the thirty "mighty men" of David, who seem to have been commanders of élite troops, there were several foreigners.[13] The commander of his camel corps was Obil the Ishmaelite. His flocks were under the control of Jaziz the Hagrite; the Hagrites were, like the Ishmaelites, nomadic, tent-dwelling tribes located east of Gilead in the Syrian Desert.[14] The presence of so many foreign men could not help but lead to interbreeding with the Israelite women.

Toward the end of this period, the mixed origin of the Judaites must have been common knowledge. The Prophet Ezekiel refers to it as to a well-known fact: ". . . the word of Yahweh came unto me, saying: 'Son of man, cause Jerusalem to know her abominations, and say: Thus says the Lord God unto Jerusalem: Thine origin and thy nativity is of the land of the Canaanite; thy father was the Amorite, and thy mother a Hittite.' "[15]

IN THE SECOND COMMONWEALTH

Nor did these conditions change until the very end of the Davidic dynasty in Jerusalem. Following the defeat of Judah by the Babylonians in 586, a new element was added to the ethnic groups with whom the Judaites intermarried or interbred: the Babylonians. We can gain a very rough idea of the extent of Jewish-Babylonian intermarriage in the half-century that elapsed between their arrival as exiles in Babylon and their first return to the land of Judah (538 B.C.) from the following considerations: The total number of Jews who returned from Babylonia was 42,360. They were accompanied by 7,337 male and female slaves, as well as 200 (or 250) male and female singers; all these were, evidently, non-Jews. Moreover, they were joined by 392 "Nethinim," a servile class of uncircumcised foreigners, probably the descendants of Canaanite peoples subjugated by Solomon, who functioned as Temple servants in the days of the First Temple. Along came also 652 (or 642) persons who "could not tell their fathers' houses, and their seed, whether they were of Israel." Less than a hundred years later, another 220 Nethinim came with the Jews who accompanied Ezra from Babylonia to Judah. In the detailed account of the struggle led by Ezra and Nehemiah against the mixed marriages between Jews and non-Jews, the Nethinim are not mentioned at all; hence it has been concluded that intermarriage with them was not forbidden, and that they were gradually absorbed into the Jewish population, probably among the Levites.[16]

In any case, one gains the impression that in the century and a half that elapsed from the beginning of the Babylonian Exile to the arrival of Ezra and Nehemiah in Jerusalem, neither the Babylonian Jewish community nor their brethren in Judah were too much concerned with religious scruples against exogamy, and that throughout their sojourn in Babylonia the Jews willingly accepted proselytes.

The situation in Judah prior to the arrival of Ezra and Nehemiah was definitely conducive to outgroup marriage. The newly returned community suffered, like all emigrant groups, from a shortage of women. The poor, unable to compete for the Jewish women against their wealthier brethren, were driven to exogamy by necessity. They turned to the nomadic tribes of the grazing lands of southern Judah, the Calebites, Jerachmeelites, and Kenites, who in the past had provided Judah with many male converts and now supplied the poorest with proselyte wives. Following the Babylonian tradition, these plebeian Jews considered a man or a woman who accepted Judaism as fully a member of the faith as a native Israelite. This is the viewpoint represented, as we have seen, by the Book of Ruth. The peasantry, who formed something like a middle class, was intensely chauvinistic and had neither the need nor the desire to intermarry with aliens. The aristocracy among the returnees, and in the first place the priestly families, too proud to marry below their caste, turned to the upper class of the neighboring peoples for wives. The Samaritans figured most prominently in this connection.[17]

This was the situation when Ezra appeared on the scene in 458 B.C. Together with Ezra, another 1,496 Israelite men, 38 Levites, and 220 Nethinim came from Babylonia to Judah. Fourteen years later Nehemiah, whom King Artaxerxes I (Longimanus) appointed *Tirshatha* or governor of Judah, arrived in Jerusalem. These two Jewish leaders found, to their utter dismay, that the Jewish returnees, including their princes, rulers, priests, and Levites, had been intermarrying for about three generations. Ezra prevailed upon the leaders of the Jews to help him put an end to this state of affairs. The separation procedures took three months, which indicates that many hundreds of couples must have been involved.[18]

The Book of Ezra ends with a long, but still only partial, list containing well over a hundred names of those priests, Levites, and Israelites who had married foreign women and now promised to divorce them. All these efforts, however, were of no avail and the struggle against intermarriage had to be continued by Nehemiah, who arrived in Jerusalem in 444 B.C. Curiously, the very last sentence in the Book of Ezra states that "some of them had wives by whom they had children," without giving any clue as to what happened to these children when their mothers were sent away by the fathers. We can, however, assume that in a patrilineal society the children would remain with their fathers and be brought up as Jews. This is at least hinted at in the Book of Nehemiah, which says with indignation that the children of these mixed marriages were unable to "speak in the Jews' language but spoke according to the language of each people" to which their mothers belonged. This fact is mentioned just before the drastic measures Nehemiah took to force the Jewish men to divorce their foreign wives are described: hence it seems probable that one of the purposes of these measures was to ensure that the children would be brought up as Jews.[19]

All the measures taken by Ezra and Nehemiah to force the Jews to divorce their foreign wives brought only temporary results, if any. Very soon after Nehemiah's return to the winter residence of the Persian court, the intermarriages again increased considerably and this—together with other factors which showed how conditions had deteriorated—motivated Nehemiah a few years later to return again to Jerusalem, where he preached against those priests, Levites, and Israelites who had married foreign wives. About the same time, the Prophet Malachi again had reason to reproach Judah with having "profaned the holiness of the Lord which He loveth and married the daughter of a strange god," which must be interpreted as a prophecy against exogamous marriages.[20] Historical evidence dating from the same period shows that marriages between Jews and Egyptians took place in the Jewish military colony of Elephantine in Upper Egypt.[21]

In the fourth century B.C., Finkelstein has emphasized, "mixed marriages between the Samaritans and the Judaites continued; and there were even marriages between Judaites and pagans." The leading members of the Jewish population in particular "continued to marry heathen women, almost until the end of the Second Commonwealth" (i.e., A.D. 70).[22]

The spread of Hellenism among the Jews of Palestine following its conquest by Alexander the Great (332 B.C.) brought them face to face not only with a new culture but also with a different race. Again, it was especially the Jewish nobility that turned to the Greeks for cultural guidance and for marriage partners. These mixed Jewish-Greek marriages were repeatedly execrated by the authors of apocryphal books in the second and first centuries B.C.[23]

IN TALMUDIC TIMES

It would be much too lengthy and technical to present in detail the rabbinic evidence concerning Jewish-Gentile interbreeding contained in the Mishna (completed c. A.D. 200), the Palestinian or Jerusalem Talmud (completed c. A.D. 425), the Babylonian Talmud (c. A.D. 500), and the very extensive Midrash literature (from about the second to the tenth century A.D.). Briefly, rabbinic legislation makes a clear-cut distinction between sexual relations with Gentiles and intermarriage with proselytes. The former is strictly forbidden in both its marital and extramarital varieties. If an Israelite was caught in flagrante with a Gentile woman, the "Zealous" were permitted to kill him on the spot, following the biblical example of Phinehas. If he committed the sin and was found guilty subsequently, he was flogged. In addition to the earthly punishment, a Jew who cohabited with a non-Jewish woman was believed to suffer after his death the fires of the Gehenna. A Talmudic tradition attributes the prohibition of intercourse with Gentile women to a Hasmonean legislation which would take it back to the second century B.C. Ultimately, these laws not only went back to biblical precedents but were considered a Sinaitic tradition.[24]

As against these uncompromising prohibitions, the Talmudic law developed a most tolerant attitude toward intermarriage with proselytes. The Talmudic teachers went to great lengths to legalize marriage with Gentile converts, often resorting in the process to forced reinterpretations of biblical injunctions. Thus, for instance, the biblical exclusion of Ammonites and Moabites from joining the Jewish community is interpreted in the Mishna as relating only to males, while "their females are permitted at once." Despite the objections raised by some teachers to such liberalizations, the biblical prohibitions were declared inoperative early in the Tannaitic period.[25]

According to the Mishna which is the basis of all subsequent Jewish religious law, converts and freed slaves were allowed to marry Israelites, that is, Jews who were neither of priestly descent (*Kohens*) nor Levites.[26] In this terse legal decision no trace is left of the ancient biblical injunction against admitting converts from certain specified ethnic groups to marriage with Israelites. Some teachers wanted to extend this freedom of intermarriage given to converts even to priests,[27] but these and other such details are of no interest to us in the present context. Only an Israelite who had had sexual relations with a Gentile woman was forbidden to marry her after her conversion to Judaism. In some places even half-converted Gentiles (who were circumcised but not baptized) were allowed to marry Jewish girls (e.g., in Gabla). In any case, these discussions and laws prove that marriages between Jews and converts or freed slaves occurred or were planned often enough to make Talmudic teachers of several generations devote close attention to their legal aspects. The same conclusion can be reached from the frequent mention by name, or identification as a group, of proselytes in Talmudic writings.[28]

Often it is pointed out in Talmudic passages that certain well-known individuals were the descendants of proselytes which, of course, presupposes that their proselyte ancestor intermarried with Jews. In a few cases, specific mention is made of individuals who converted to Judaism and thereafter sought and received permission to marry a Jewess. One of these was a sage, Yehuda the Ammonite. His case is most instructive because it allows an insight into the exegetic method used by the Tannaim to overrule in effect a biblical prohibition. When Yehuda the Ammonite convert came to the court and asked for its ruling as to whether or not he was allowed to marry a Jewess, Rabban Gamaliel refused to give him his permission, quoting the biblical passage: "An Ammonite and a Moabite shall not enter into the assembly of the Lord even to the tenth generation." Whereupon Rabbi Yehoshua countered: "Do the Ammonites and Moabites still dwell in their place? Did not Sanherib king of Assyria come and mix up all the nations?" In other words, Rabbi Yehoshua's argument that the nations which constituted distinct entities in biblical days had in the meantime lost their ethnic identity prevailed and Yehuda the Ammonite was granted permission to marry into Israel. The same argument was used by Rabbi Akiba (second century A.D.) to allow an Egyptian convert to marry a Jewess. On the basis of these Tannaitic rulings, Maimonides a thousand years later declared the biblical law barring certain proselytes from marrying into the Jewish community obsolete.[29]

Faced with the actual frequency of Jewish-proselyte intermarriage in the large Jewish community of Alexandria, the Hellenistic Jewish philosopher Philo (c. 20 B.C.–c. A.D. 40) felt constrained to justify the practice by applying the well-known prophetic "light of the nations" argument. Intermarriages with outsiders, Philo argued, "create new kinships not a whit inferior to blood relationship" and thus help "spread the goodly plant" of Jewish faith.[30] As to the normative Jewish attitude to intermarriage with proselytes, it is characteristic that the Talmudic teachers were much more concerned about the results of marrying into the family of an uneducated Jew than about marrying proselytes. The rabbis taught, "Under no circumstances should one marry the daughter of a man of the common people because they are an abomination . . ." and Rabbi Meir said, "If one gives his daughter in marriage to a man of the common people, it is as if he would tie her up and set her before a lion. . . ."[31] No such emotionally colored warnings against intermarriage with proselytes are found in the Talmudic literature.

Intermarriage with unconverted Gentiles was, of course, a different matter altogether. In the early years of the Christian era, Jewish objections to such intermarriages became more severe and came to be extended to "keeping company" with a Gentile. Nevertheless, Jewish-Gentile marriages continued to occur, with both spouses often retaining their own religion. The royal Herodian family, although itself of proselyte Idumaean extraction, insisted on the conversion (including circumcision) of those with whom they intermarried. Josephus reports two cases in which planned marriages between Herodian princesses and foreign royalty came to naught because the suitors would not agree to conversion, and two other cases in which the foreign royal bridegrooms converted before marrying sisters of the Jewish King Agrippa II.[32]

In Talmudic times the view became popular among the sages that intermarriage with pagans was a desirable thing because through it pagan women were led to conversion to Judaism. Looking back at biblical history, these teachers praised those men who had married foreign women: Joseph, Moses, Joshua (who according to Talmudic legend married Rahab, the harlot of Jericho), and Boaz. Even King Solomon, who is censured in the Bible itself for having married many foreign women, is excused and praised by Rabbi Yose ben Ḥalafta, who holds that in so doing Solomon's purpose was to

101

convert all these women. In a rare reversal of the usual trend, the Talmudic rules governing intermarriage are more liberal than those Ezra tried to impose upon the Jews of Judah in the fifth century B.C.[33]

UNDER EARLY CHRISTIANITY

No sooner did Christianity attain a position of strength in the Roman world than it began to fight against Jewish-Christian intermarriage and extramarital sex relations. Both were sharply condemned by the Council of Elvira in Andalusia, Spain (about A.D. 300), which decreed that Christian girls must not be married to Jews or pagans and that parents who transgressed this prohibition would be excommunicated for five years.[34] Soon thereafter followed the Edict of Milan (A.D. 313), which granted toleration to all religions and before long led to the victory of Christianity in the Roman Empire. In A.D. 315 Constantine renewed the old pagan Roman legislation against seduction to the monotheistic faiths, but applied it only against Judaism, threatening with the death penalty both converts and those who won them over. Even intermarriage between Jews and Christians was made a capital offense, unless of course the former abandoned their faith. The same prohibition was repeated in 339 by the Emperor Constantius, and in 388 by Theodosius the Great.[35]

Soon after the establishment of Christianity as the official state religion, both Roman imperial codes and Church councils began to reiterate the prohibition of intermarriage between Jews and Christians under the threat of various penalties.[36] The very fact that these injunctions were repeated every few years shows that they frequently remained a dead letter, so that the authorities felt compelled to renew them again and again. The Codex Theodosianus (439) treats Jewish-Christian unions on a par with adultery and imposes severe penalties on the culprits. The Council of Chalcedon (451) repeats the same injunction and in addition prohibits feasting with Jews and even using the services of Jewish physicians. Alaric II's *Lex Romana Visigothorum* (506) repeats essentially the injunctions of the Theodosian Code, as do the Code of Justinian (533), and the Councils of Orléans (533), Clermont (535), Orléans (538), and Toledo (589 and 633).[37] The Third Council of Toledo (589), realizing the ineffectiveness of the severest penalties, merely demanded that the offspring of mixed Jewish-Christian marriages be raised in the Christian faith. This provision was renewed by Sisebut in the first year of his reign (612), together with other anti-Jewish laws, but, finding his decrees ineffective, within a year he ordered all the Jews of Spain to accept baptism.[38] The Roman Council of 743 forbade marriage between a Christian woman and a Jew, and at the end of the eighth century the Jews living under Lombard rule were again warned against intermarriage and the possession of Christian slaves. Late in the ninth century a council in southern Italy warned

Christians to watch over their womenfolk lest they commit adultery with Jews. The extent to which such laws remained ineffective is illustrated by the expulsion in 876 of the Jews from the French town of Sens, "apparently for having seen too much of the local nuns, who were expelled at the same time." [39]

Jews were frequently led to marrying Christians or having extramarital relations with them by the simple fact that it was primarily Jewish males who were adventurous enough to try their luck in countries uninhabited by Jews. Thus in France in the sixth century the Jewish population was not only small but consisted mostly of males who, in the circumstances, often had no choice but to seek sexual contacts or marriage partners among the Gentiles. [40]

The rulers of the Eastern Christian empire exhibited the same negative attitude toward mixed marriages between Christians and Jews. In sixth-century Byzantium such marriages were strictly forbidden, except if the Jewish partner first converted to Christianity. A Christian's conversion to Judaism, on the other hand, was punished by exile and confiscation of property. As time passed, the penalties became more severe, and by the ninth and tenth centuries intermarriage was equated with adultery and was subject to capital punishment. [41]

IN THE MUSLIM WORLD

In pre-Islamic Arabia, intermarriage between Jews and pagan Arabs was frequent. Some of the offspring of these mixed unions achieved fame and renown and thus historical data concerning them are extant. The famous Medinese poet and Jewish scholar, Ka'b ibn al-Ashrāf, a contemporary of Muḥammad, was of mixed pagan-Jewish descent. Ka'b himself was said to have been in the habit of demanding cohabitation from the wives of Muslims who had bought food from him and could not pay in cash. This, it was rumored, led Muḥammad to have him assassinated. On the other hand, the story is told of a Jew who was in charge of a prisoner of war, noticed his wife paying undue attention to the prisoner, and castrated the man in a fit of jealousy. One of the wives of Muḥammad, Ṣafiyya, was the daughter of the Jew Ḥuyyay ibn Akhṭab; one of his concubines—another Jewish girl, Rayḥana bint Sam'ūn. [42]

With the expansion of Islam, Jews intermarried not only with Arabs but also with members of the nations drawn into the Muslim orbit by the Arab conquests. A famous example of the latter occurred after the Arabs took Iraq, when the head of the Jewish community, the exilarch Bustanai, was given a Persian princess by the victorious Arabs as a reward for the important services he had rendered. Since the princess was a prisoner of war, she became technically Bustanai's slave, and should have been formally manu-

103

mitted by him before the marriage. Bustanai apparently failed to do this and consequently, after his death, his legitimate sons insisted that she and her children by Bustanai were still slaves. The rabbinical court, however, decided that the sons had to grant them letters of manumission and thereby legalize their status. Several generations later, the descendants of the Persian princess became exilarchs of the Jews.[43]

This, of course, was an exceptional case. In general, the Arab conquests reduced the Jews (as well as the Christians and Zoroastrians) to the status of *dhimmīs*—protected but second-class people, intermarriage with whom was legal only for Muslim men. Marriage between a Jew and a Muslim woman was disallowed. The Jewish religious authorities, for their part, did their best to discourage sexual relations between Jews and Muslims. They prescribed the penalty of flogging and shaving the hair for a Jewish woman who as much as put on cosmetics and visited a non-Jewish house of worship; and flogging, excommunication, exile, and fasting for a man found guilty of cohabitation with a Muslim woman. Despite all these efforts, Jewish women did become the mistresses or wives of Muslims, and Jewish men had sexual relations with Muslim women. Nor did any of the penalties stem the practice of Jewish-Muslim intermarriage, of which numerous instances are on record.[44]

The situation was similar between Christians and Jews in Muslim countries. In the Cairo Geniza there is a document concerning the love affair of a Christian physician and a Jewish girl. The story of Masrūr and Zayn al-Mawāṣif in the *Arabian Nights* tells of a rich Christian youth who falls in love with a mature Jewish woman of great beauty and superior intelligence; they convert to Islam and marry.[45]

An unusual case is recorded in the responsa of Asher ben Yeḥiel (1250–1327), the famous German Jewish codifier who spent the last decades of his life in Spain. This concerned a Jewish widow who had illicit relations with an Arab, gave him all her property, and bore him twins, a boy and a girl. The boy died, and the girl was taken by the Arabs to be bought up as a Muslim. The rabbi of the locality where this case occurred wrote to Asher in 1320 telling him of his fears lest this case become an example to be imitated by other Jewish women, and informing him that he intended to punish the woman by "disfiguring her face," which probably meant cutting off her nose. He concludes by asking Asher's opinion on this proposed punishment. Asher's reply is affirmative.[46]

MEDIEVAL EUROPE

In Medieval Europe the position of the Jews in general was much more difficult than in the "House of Islam." Bitter experience had taught the Jews in the countries of both Eastern and Western Christianity to be always apprehensive lest their womenfolk be molested, seduced, or raped by Gentiles. To prevent such occurrences, the Jewish communities resorted to the only measure they had at their disposal: the issuance of ordinances restricting the movements of their women and prohibiting practically all contact between them and Gentiles. The Christian authorities, on their part, outlawed not only Christian-Jewish sexual relations but also all kinds of social contact between members of the two religions, and backed up their injunctions with generally severe penalties imposed on both the Jewish and the Christian partners to the crime. However, the very frequency and repetitiousness of the promulgation of such laws are once again indications of their ineffectiveness. This is the only conclusion we can come to also from the great number of actual court cases in which persons were tried for violating these laws of segregation.

The Middle Ages and the Renaissance were periods of great moral laxity in Mediterranean Europe, a circumstance which could not fail to influence the Jewish communities. This—coupled with the close social relations between Jews and Gentiles in the Iberian Peninsula, Provence, and Renaissance Italy—resulted in a considerable loosening of morality in the Jewish communities, as well as in frequent marital and extramarital relations between Jews and Christians. We have, of course, no full picture of the frequency of sexual activity between Jews and Gentiles because we know only of those relatively few cases which led to criminal prosecution. True, quite a number of Jews were tried and condemned in Renaissance Venice and Florence, for example, for sexual intercourse with Christian women, including nuns; but the number of cases which remained undetected, or which were prosecuted but still left no traces in the extant documents, must have been several times greater.

Typically, throughout the period in question Jews and Gentiles considered it a lesser transgression if their own men married, or dallied with, women of the other faith than if their own women became involved with men of the other community. Consequently, legal provisions, too, punished guilty women more severely than men. Thus, while Christian public opinion sharply condemned sexual relations between Jews and Christian women, it did not consider it a serious crime at all if Christian men had such relations with Jewish women. In fact, popular literature, as Baron points out, "described seductions of Jewish girls by Christian suitors with considerable sympathy." Similarly, Jews in general objected more strenuously to Jewish women having relations with Christian men than to Jewish men having Christian mistresses or concubines.

Exceptions to these rules occurred only occasionally. For instance, an Italian Jewish conference held at Forli in 1418 condemned relations of Jewish men with Christian women, but did so because of the possibility of begetting children outside the faith. For a Jewish woman to have sexual relations with a Gentile man, on the other hand, was considered by the Jews as a capital offense, a position in which one can perhaps recognize a late echo of the ancient biblical and Middle Eastern views on female sexual honor. How frequently such cases occurred, we do not know; but in a few instances they not only became known but led to homicide. In 1272 Rabbi Meir of Rothenburg was asked about a Jewish woman who had had relations with a Gentile during her husband's absence, had given birth to a daughter whom she killed, and then made plans to convert to Christianity in order to escape punishment. In 1311 two Jewish brothers were accused of having killed their sister because she had relations with a Christian and became pregnant.[47]

Spain

In Spain, in both the Christian and the Muslim realms, the Jewish mores were profoundly influenced by the prevailing morality, which considered women in general and the women of the opposite religion in particular fair game for any sexual purpose. In this atmosphere the Jews frequently made use of the freedom afforded them by the absence of laws against marrying Christian women in the Muslim areas and Muslim women in the Christian parts. Extramarital cohabitation between Jews and members of the ruling religions in both the Christian and the Muslim domains in the peninsula was also frequent.

Spanish legislation intended to prevent these practices is characterized by a peculiar lack of consistency. Side by side with frequently reiterated capital punishment one finds occasional great leniency. However, even when laws imposed loss of life on fornicators, the extreme penalty was not often exacted. This can clearly be seen from the fact that the actual execution of a Jew because of a sexual crime was of the greatest rarity, while cases in which the culprit was allowed to get off with a slight punishment, or no punishment at all, occurred quite frequently. In thirteenth- and fourteenth-century Spain, as Baron remarks, "the few recorded accusations usually ended with the royal squashing of proceedings because of lack of evidence or personal favoritism." A case in point is that of Lupus Abnexeyl, who was prosecuted for a variety of crimes including illicit affairs with Christian women, visits to prostitutes, and procuring; all charges against him were dismissed in 1318 by royal decree. Moreover, in some Spanish ordinances the enforcement of such prohibitons was left to Jewish authorities, especially to the *berure averos* ("Supervisors of sin"), as in the 1377 decree of Pedro IV.[48]

While the laws providing the death penalty for Jewish-Christian sexual relations remained largely dead letters, the legal efforts to institute a complete separation between members of the two faiths continued. A law enacted in the fifteenth century ordered the Jews and the Moors to move, within eight days, to separate quarters surrounded by walls, and enjoined Christian women from visiting them at any time of day or night. A married woman who disobeyed this prohibition was to be fined for each entry; if she was an unmarried or a kept woman, she was to lose the clothes she had on; if a prostitute, she was to receive 100 lashes and be driven out of town. To prevent the possibility of carnal relations between Jews and nuns, the provincial council of Alcalá passed a resolution, echoed by the delegate of the archbishop of Toledo in 1436, to the effect that a Jewish (or Moorish) physician or carpenter should enter a convent only when accompanied by a Christian.[49]

These Christian efforts at preventing social and sexual relations between members of the two faiths were paralleled by Jewish enactments. Although the Jews had no power to punish Christian transgressors (except by denouncing them to the Christian authorities) and could not impose the death penalty even on Jewish culprits (except in the Middle Ages in Spain), their condemnation of cohabitation of Jews with Christians was equally decisive. The interdiction was incorporated into the great Code of Maimonides (1135–1204) and into subsequent Jewish legal compendia.[50]

However, it was a far cry from codified law to its actual observance in practice. Unable to stem what they considered a wave of immorality, the rabbis repeatedly bemoaned it. Baron remarks that Jewish "enactments to prevent illicit sex relationships among Jews, or between Jews and Gentiles, as well as the record of practices which produced the laws, would . . . fill a substantial volume," and that "the rabbis themselves had to admit that in Spain and in northern Africa there were 'a great many Jewish lawbreakers entertaining forbidden relationships with Gentile women.' "[51]

Rabbi Moses of Coucy, a highly respected French rabbinical authority, informs us that during his visit to Spain in 1236 he persuaded many Jews to send away their Christian and Muslim wives. However, despite Coucy's efforts, intercourse with Gentile women continued. Characteristically, in 1323 the statutes of the Jewish burial society in Huesca provided no greater punishment than expulsion from the society of a member who had intercourse with a Christian woman; which provision, incidentally, was confirmed by the Infante Alphonso who evidenced a similarly lenient attitude.[52]

A century later another rabbi exhorts his congregation not to allow their Gentile maidservants, "who are a snare to Israel," to dress in richly embroidered garments and thus incite immorality, and complains that "many children have been born to Jews by their non-Jewish maidservants."[53]

After Spanish pressure forced many Jews to convert officially to Christianity (while continuing in secret to adhere to their ancestral faith), the problem of mixed marriages assumed a new dimension. Many of the Marranos practiced endogamy for the simple reason that the presence of an "Old Christian," that is, a non-Marrano, husband or wife in the home would have made Jewish observances impossible. Especially in the early stages, until the beginning of the sixteenth century, the opinion of such Jewish leaders as the brothers Simon and Zemaḥ Duran (in the sixteenth century) or Joseph ibn Leb was that exogamous marriages were extremely rare among the Marranos. However, as time passed there was a relaxation, partly as a result of the growing ignorance of Jewish law.[54]

With the age-old Jewish proclivity to attributing catastrophes that befell the Jewish community to its own sins, fifteenth- and sixteenth-century rabbis singled out the moral laxity of their co-religionists as responsible for the major Spanish Jewish disasters. Abraham Zacuto (c. 1450–after 1510) states that he has heard a tradition according to which many Jews were killed during the 1391 wave of persecutions by their own sons, born to them by Christian women whom they had taken into their houses. These children were brought up in the Christian faith and joined the mob which attacked the Jews.[55] In the same vein, Solomon ibn Verga (fifteenth to sixteenth century) gives as one of the reasons for the catastrophic expulsion of the Jews from Spain in 1492 the frequent intercourse Jews had with Christian women.[56] Jewish communal leaders considered the moral conditions among the Spanish Jews so dismal that in several communities they felt constrained to set up special "morals committees" empowered to administer severe punishment to culprits.[57]

After their expulsion from Spain, the Spanish Jews carried their sexual mores to the countries in which they found refuge. The Jewish authorities reacted by prohibiting bridegrooms from visiting the houses of their future fathers-in-law, to prevent the possibility of intercourse between engaged couples. In the Netherlands a municipal council, enraged over the frequency of immoral relations between Jewish refugees from Portugal and the daughters of the land, passed a strict prohibition of all carnal intercourse between Jews and Christian women, including prostitutes.[58]

From Germany we hear of one Diego Teixera de Sampayo, a Marrano born in 1581 in Portugal, who settled in 1646 in Hamburg together with his Christian-born wife and two sons, one of whom was illegitimate. In the following year he returned openly to Judaism, had himself and his sons circumcised, and his wife, as well as another Christian woman from Antwerp, converted to Judaism.[59]

Italy

The situation in Italy closely duplicated the Spanish conditions. The penalty for Jewish-Christian sex relations vacillated here, too, from fines to death; and the laws seem to have been equally unable in both countries to stem the practice. A 1420 decree of Padua outlawed all such intercourse with severe penalties. Similar legislation was passed in Ferrara in 1464 and renewed in 1489 and 1598. In Milan, a decree of 1439 provided merely a fine of 100 lire, or, in case of insolvency, four months in prison; but a new decree in 1470 imposed the death penalty.[60] In 1473 Ercole I of the House of Este reduced the monetary fine for Jewish bankers apprehended in illicit sex relations with Christian women, but "later ordinances prohibited fornication even among Christians under the sanction of galley slavery and a large fine of 500 gold scudi. These sharp penalties were repeated in an ordinance of 1686, but they had to be reduced in 1715 to 50 scudi, five lashes, and the obligation to marry the lady. Since for Jewish paramours such marriage was illegal, the ordinance gave much leeway to judges by providing that 'the penalty shall consist of flogging, galley slavery, or even death.' " Jewish offenders occasionally managed to escape punishment if they converted to Christianity.[61]

In Mantua, the penalties imposed on Jews for cohabitation with Christian women changed rapidly from leniency to extreme severity. In 1522 Federico of Mantua decreed that the maximum penalty for this sin should be a fine of 25 gold scudi. However, in 1577 the penalty was raised to confiscation of property and beheading, with permission given to the judges to resort to inquisitorial methods of questioning in order to extract a confession from the accused. A short time thereafter the Jews were forbidden by decree to employ Christian women as servants. In subsequent decades, and throughout the seventeenth century, laws of this kind were issued frequently. Another indication of the low state of Jewish morality in Mantua, especially after the Jews were forced into a crowded ghetto in the seventeenth and eighteenth centuries, was the great number of illegitimate children.[62]

Still in the sixteenth century a fine legal point was discussed in a Mantuan court in connection with the question of what precisely should be the penalty for Jews who had sexual relations with Christian women. One jurist contended that such offenders ought to be sentenced to death. Another pointed out that there was no precedent in Mantua for the execution of a Jew for such a crime. Two other doctors of law suggested that the best penalty would be to cut off the culprit's testicles, "a most beautiful spectacle for a carnival. . . ."[63]

In the second half of the sixteenth century, many Italian cities adopted stringent measures to make all contact between Jews and Christians impossible, or at least extremely difficult. Interfaith dancing and music lessons were prohibited, and Christians were not allowed to make use of the services of Jewish marriage brokers. The penalties were most severe.[64] Alberto Bolognetti, in a dispatch to Rome, describes a case that occurred in Venice while he served as papal nuncio in that city (1578–81). Giovanni Ribiera, son of a Portuguese Christian merchant in Venice, married a noble Jewish woman who was a relative of the influential Giovanni Miches (i.e., João Miguez, better known as Don Joseph Nasi, duke of Naxos, c. 1520–79).

Young Ribiera's father, Gaspar, approved of the marriage and in writing promised 3,000 scudi to his daughter-in-law. Giovanni Ribiera moved to the ghetto, lived there with his wife in open and legitimate union, and promised her that as soon as he settled his affairs he would emigrate with her to Turkey to live there as a professing Jew. In the same dispatch Bolognetti also mentions that some Venetian Jews had been accused of having purchased Moorish children and converted them to Judaism. However, the defendants argued that the children in question were their own offspring by Moorish women, which seemed likely in view of the presence of quite a number of Moors in the Venetian ghetto.[65]

Christian-Jewish intrigues in sixteenth-century Italy occasionally had a truly Boccaccio-like flavor. In Reggio, in 1536, a Christian couple thought they had found a way of getting rich at one stroke—at the expense of the lady's Jewish paramour. The woman agreed to receive the wealthy Jew, who promised to bring her a gold belt. She then arranged that he be surprised, while with her, by her husband. The latter, in turn, obtained the help of the *podestà* and his two assistants. The husband and his three co-conspirators burst in on the frightened Jew, but allowed him to get away against a gift of 400 scudi. The postscript to the story is that the *podestà* was publicly punished for the conspiracy.[66]

In his bull *Hebraeorum gens sola* of February 26, 1569, Pope Pius V justifies his unprecedented step of banishing the Jews from the Church states in both Italy and France by advancing a whole array of accusations against them. Among these is the argument that the Jews were allegedly procuring "honest" Christian women for sinners of all kinds. In 1624–25, jurisdiction over the Roman Jews' sexual relations with Gentiles was transferred from the Inquisition to other ecclesiastical organs. In 1628, the Roman Jewish mistress of the son of the duke of Parma was burned.[67]

Even the death penalty was not able to counteract the influence of the lax sexual mores of the Renaissance upon the Jews of Italy. Perhaps most characteristic of the prevailing mentality among both Christians and Jews was the case of a Jew of Foligno who dared to go so far as to teach that it was not sinful for Christian women to cohabit with Jews. He was summoned before an ecclesiastic court, but was acquitted for lack of evidence.[68]

One can easily imagine the chagrin these conditions caused the Jewish moralists. As early as 1418 a conference of rabbis convened in Forli. After lengthy deliberations, in the course of which the frequency of sexual transgressions was duly bemoaned and execrated, it was decided to appoint special officers in each town and city with tasks and powers paralleling those of the "morals committees" set up in Jewish communities in Spain. Among the duties of these officers were to institute careful investigations and search out all offenders against morality.[69]

Other European Countries

In other countries, too, illicit sexual relations between Jews and Christians were considered a clear and present danger that prompted the authorities to take action or at least to issue stern warnings. In thirteenth-century England a Jew guilty of fornication with a Christian woman was merely fined (1256), and conditions were such that Pope Honorius IV in his 1286 bull, *Nimis in partibus,* addressed to the archbishops of Canterbury and York, felt constrained to complain that "Christians and Jews continue meeting in one another's houses. They spend their free time in feasting and banqueting together; hence there is much opportunity for mischief." [70]

In Switzerland conditions were similar. In 1254 Pope Innocent IV warned the bishop of Constance that "the Jews of your province and diocese" did not observe the decree of the Third Lateran Council of 1179, which enacted for all Western Christendom the general rule that Christians who lived with Jews should be excommunicated and that the Jews must wear a special badge. Hence, the pope notes, the Jews "may dare to commit the sin of damnable intercourse" with Christian women. Despite this papal admonishment, Christian girls in Constance and Zurich continued to have affairs with Jews. If caught, they were paraded through the street with Jewish conical hats on their heads, and then banished (1349, 1378). [71]

The situation was not much different in France. A letter found in the Cairo Geniza, but coming possibly from Anjou, presents a striking case of French-Jewish intermarriage in the eleventh century. Written by the congregation in behalf of a young widow, it recounts her tragic history: the daughter of a wealthy Christian family, she converted to Judaism, and was married in Narbonne to Rabbi David of the family of Rabbi Todros, who was head of the Jewish community. Six months later she learned that her family had instituted a search for her, whereupon she escaped to Anjou. There they lived for a number of years and had three children. Then came an attack on the Jewish community, during which her husband was killed in the synagogue. Two of his children, Jacob and three-year-old Justa, were taken captive and all his possessions were despoiled. The widow and her youngest child, a few months old, remained desolate and destitute. The extant fragment of the letter ends with a request for help, and asks the addressees to help the widow raise ransom money for her children. [72]

In the province of Poitou, to which the Jews returned in 1315, soon rumors began to spread to the effect that many local women had married Jews. In 1381 the provost of Paris himself, Hugues Aubriot, was denounced for alleged sexual relations with Jewesses. In 1404 a Jew of Burg in Savoy was fined 120 florins because, among other crimes, "he cohabited with many Christian women" which he was able to do on account of "the abundance of his finances." As late as the seventeenth century, a Christian

111

Frenchman by the name of Jean Allard had "kept a Jewess in his home in Paris and had several children by her; he was convicted of sodomy on account of this relation and burned together with his paramour, since 'coition with a Jewess is precisely the same as if a man should copulate with a dog.' " [73]

In German lands, too, although sex relations between Jews and Christians were outlawed, they nevertheless must have occurred much more frequently than is recorded in the sources. Occasionally the seduction of a Christian woman by a Jew was advanced as the reason for prohibiting the employment of Christian domestics in Jewish households. As elsewhere, love laughed at laws, and both Jewish and non-Jewish authors refer to love affairs between Christian men and Jewish women. Caesarius von Heisterbach (c. 1170–1240), for instance, mentions that "many Christian young men evinced special preference for beautiful Jewish girls." The German *Book of the Imperial Land and Vassals' Right,* popularly known as the *Schwabenspiegel* (c. 1275), states that "if a Christian fornicates with a Jewess, or a Jew with a Christian woman, they are both guilty of superharlotry ('*Überhure*')—they shall be placed one upon the other and burned to death. . . ." The death penalty was provided for the same offense also by the municipality of Iglau in Moravia in 1249, and in the Freising law book. On occasion the penalties imposed by the Church were much more moderate. Thus two councils held in 1267 in Vienna and Breslau, while sharply condemning Jewish-Christian sexual relations, demand only a fine of 10 marks for the Jewish male culprit, and public flagellation and banishment from the city for the Christian woman.

Data from Ratisbon in Bavaria provide some idea of the frequency of these transgressions. In the brief span of seven years (1460–67), no less than three members of the religiously most observant Ratisbon Jewish community were prosecuted by the state for sexual intercourse with Christian women, and at the same time several other Jewish men and Christian women were in jail awaiting trial. In general, in fifteenth- and sixteenth-century Germany relations between Jews and Christians were friendly in many places, and these circumstances not too infrequently led to sexual intercourse between members of the two religions. The prohibitions issued by the German authorities against this transgression were mostly very severe, but occasionally we find here, too, surprisingly mild penalties. Thus in the mid-sixteenth century a Jew, Isaac of Mantua, was punished in Augsburg only with a fine of 10 florins for the "capital crime" of intercourse with a Christian woman.

As to the rabbinical authorities, while they were unanimous in condemning illicit sexual relations between Jews and Christians, they did not discourage Jewish men from marrying proselyte women. Rabbi Judah ben Samuel HeHasid ("the Pious," d. 1217), the influential ethical writer and mystic whose Yeshiva in Regensburg became an important center of Jewish learning, taught that "if a Jew of good character marries a woman proselyte of good character, modesty, and charity, who gets along well with people, his children ought to be preferred to the offspring of a born Jewess who does not possess the same virtues, for the issue of [such] a proselyte are [likely to be] righteous and good persons." [74]

In Hungary, the adoption of Christianity by the pagan Magyars in the tenth century was soon followed by the emergence of concern about keeping the Jews down and separate from the Christian majority. It was felt that the Judaizing influences, discussed in our chapter on proselytism, had to be kept in check, and for this purpose the Council of Szabolcs in 1092 prohibited Jews from marrying Christians, owning Christian slaves, and so on. Illicit sexual relations between Jews and Christians nevertheless continued. One case has become known because it involved a Jew who was destined to play a significant role in Hungarian history. He was Shneur Zalman, who later became famous under the name Imre (Emerich) Fortunatus. About 1505, when he was already middle-aged, with a Jewish wife and two married sons, Fortunatus became entangled in an illicit extramarital relationship with a Christian woman from Buda. The affair became known; in order to escape the painful death which was the legal penalty for a Jew caught fornicating with a Christian woman, Fortunatus converted to Christianity, and married his lady love. Something of a financial genius, Fortunatus made a splendid career, which culminated in the position of state treasurer of Hungary. His financial machinations led temporarily to his downfall, and he spent some time in prison, but soon gained freedom, and managed to recover his fortune and position. He reached a ripe old age, and before his death repented and returned to Judaism. A few weeks after his death, Hungary fell to the Turks (1526). [75]

A similar picture emerges from Eastern Europe. In the latter part of the thirteenth century, an anonymous memorandum concerning the Jews of Poland states that they hire Christian women to nurse their children and force them to cohabit with them. The fifteenth-century Polish historian Jan Długos tells the story of Casimir the Great and his love affair with the Jewess Esterka, who became the mother of four children by the king. Two were sons who were raised as Christians; the other two were daughters whom she raised as Jews. [76]

On the Jewish side, strenuous efforts were made to prevent Jewish women from exposing themselves to the danger of being seduced or raped by Gentiles. Numerous communities enjoined Jewish business women from entering Gentile houses unless accompanied by their husbands or a male Jewish minor. The Lithuanian Jewish Council went even farther and in 1628 required that a Jewish woman trader be accompanied by two Jewish men, so that she should not be left alone in the Gentile house in case one of the men must leave it on a brief errand. In 1632 the same council prohibited Jewish couples from settling in villages, unless at least one other Jewish family lived there, or unless they employed a Jewish manservant, so that the woman should have a protector during her husband's absences. And in 1751 it outlawed entirely all peddling by Jewish women in Christian houses.[77] These increasingly strict precautions prevented Jews from settling precisely in places where they were most likely to be able to make a living—in villages where no other Jews lived and where their "Jewish" trades or businesses would have no competitor. There can be little doubt that bitter experiences forced the Jewish leadership to adopt these measures.

MODERN TIMES

Toward the end of the Middle Ages the position of the Jews in Europe worsened considerably, and consequently the number of intermarriages declined. By the seventeenth century in many places the social and religious distance between Christians and Jews had grown to such an extent that mixed marriages had become a practical impossibility. This remained the situation until the French Revolution, which transformed marriage from a religious to a civil act in which the adherence of the bride and groom to two different religions constituted no impediment. Civil marriage rapidly spread from France into other countries of Western, Northern, and Central Europe, as well as into the United States.

Simultaneously with this liberalization of the European view on mixed marriages, the spread of the Jewish Enlightenment and assimilation eroded the traditional resistance of the Jewish spiritual leaders to marriage with Gentiles. The French rabbis were more liberal in this respect than their German colleagues, as became evident in the deliberations of the Sanhedrin, or Jewish High Court, convened by Napoleon in 1807. The Sanhedrin was preceded by an Assembly of Jewish Notables (1806), to whom the French government submitted twelve questions including the following: "May a Jewess marry a Christian, or a Jew a Christian woman? Or does Jewish law order that Jews should only marry among themselves?" The answer given by the Assembly was in the affirmative, and was subsequently discussed in the Sanhedrin which, like the Sanhedrin of old, consisted of seventy-one members, two-thirds of whom were rabbis and one-third laymen. The rabbis represented Jewish congregations in France, Italy, Holland, and Germany. The opposition of the conservative German (Alsatian) rabbis was overruled, and the Sanhedrin confirmed that "marriages contracted between Israelites and Christians are binding, although they cannot be celebrated with religious forms."

In the course of the nineteenth century practically all Christian countries introduced civil marriage, and by the time of World War I mixed marriages were legal in every one of them except Russia and Russian Poland. In this case, law and practice went hand in hand, and from the second half of the nineteenth century on, the incidence of mixed Jewish-Gentile marriages increased rapidly. A few figures will have to suffice as illustrations. In the state of Prussia the intermarriage rate (i.e., the number of Jews who married non-Jews in relation to the total number of Jews who married in one year) grew from 4.79 per cent in 1875 to 21.63 in 1927. In Berlin it increased from 13.88 per cent in 1876 to 27.36 in 1927. In Hamburg it rose from 13.10 per cent in 1886 to 33.58 in 1928. In Hungary, from 2.90 per cent in 1895 to 12.46 in 1926. And in Trieste, from 14.30 per cent in 1887 to 56.10 in 1927.

If, instead of the annually marrying persons, the annually formed marriages are taken as the basis, the incidence of intermarriages appears much higher. Thus in Amsterdam in 1926 or 1927 as against every 100 marriages in which both spouses were Jews, there were 30.42 marriages in which only one of the partners was Jewish. In Breslau the corresponding percentage was 38.32; in Budapest, 39.44; in all Hungary, 28.46; in Berlin, 64.23; and in all Germany, 53.94.[78]

From the genetic point of view it is not the mixed marriages themselves that are important, but the number and religious affiliation of their offspring. It is therefore interesting to note that in the 1920's it was found that mixed couples had fewer children than all-Jewish couples, and that most of the children born to mixed couples were brought up as Christians. Nevertheless, Ruppin calculated that in Prussia the number of children born to mixed couples and brought up as Jews, plus the children born illegitimately to Jewish women from Christian men, constituted 4.05 per cent of all children born to Jewish mothers. On this basis he concluded that as a result of this process,

> we actually find among the Jews increasingly more "foreign types," that is, persons who differ in their physical traits from the mass of the Jews and are similar to the Christian population of their environment. The longer this process of penetration of foreign blood continues, the greater becomes the percentage of foreign types. If, in the course of one generation, annually 4 per cent foreign blood enters the Jewish community, then a few generations later there will be no more Jews left who are totally free of this intermixture.[79]

Today, almost two generations after Ruppin made these predictions, intermarriage between Jews and Gentiles continues. For the 1950's and 1960's statistical information is more abundant than it was in his day, although it is confined largely to the Western democracies. From the data it appears that there is some correlation between the size of the Jewish community and the percentage of Jews in the general population on the one hand, and the frequency of intermarriage on the other. The smaller the size of the Jewish community and the percentage of the Jews in the total population, the greater the incidence of Jewish-Gentile intermarriage. In the United States, where the Jews constitute about 2.5 per cent of the total population, of all Jewish persons who got married during the 1966–72 period, 31.7 per cent intermarried; in Indiana (23,300 Jews forming 0.5% of the population of the state), the corresponding figure for 1960–63 was 48.8 per cent; in Switzerland (20,000 Jews forming 0.37% of the population), 56.7 per cent.[80]

In all these figures mixed marriage is always taken to mean a marriage between two persons belonging to two different religions at the time of the wedding. Were one to add those unions in which the Gentile spouse converts to Judaism prior to the marriage, as we should if we are interested in the *genetic* consequences of intermarriage, the percentages would be considerably higher.

CONCLUSION

In concluding this rapid, admittedly incomplete review of Jewish-Gentile sexual relations and the resultant interbreeding, we can state in general terms that the data indicate an influx of non-Jewish genes into the Jewish groups from the earliest times to the present in most places and ages. Interbreeding must be considered one of the main factors making for the often observed similarity in physical type between Jews and non-Jews in every country except those where the Jews are relative newcomers.

From the genetic point of view two important questions arise out of this amply documented historical process of Jewish-Christian and Jewish-Muslim sexual relations. First, how frequent were they in relation to the total number of the Jewish populations in question? And second, what was the religion in which the offspring of these unions were brought up? For the first question, as we have seen, statistical information is available only from the late nineteenth century on. But data of a non-statistical nature lead one to conclude, as indeed Baron seems inclined to do,[81] that such "offenses" occurred quite frequently. If we take into consideration the fact that throughout the two millennia from about 200 B.C. to A.D. 1800 the total number of Jews rarely exceeded 2 million, and that they were dispersed in numerous small communities of frequently fewer than 100 persons each, one must conclude that the genetic effect of the sexual relations between Jews and Gentiles must indeed have been considerable.

The question of the religion in which the offspring of interreligious unions were brought up, or of the community into which they were absorbed, can also be answered only tentatively. If a Christian bride converts pre-nuptially to Judaism, the children of the couple are brought up as Jews. If she does not, the likelihood is that in more than 50 per cent of the cases the resulting offspring are not brought up in the Jewish faith. If a Christian man marries a Jewish woman and she undergoes pre-nuptial conversion to his faith, the children are brought up as Christians; that is, such marriages do not result in the introduction of Christian genes into the Jewish gene pool. If his Jewish bride retains her faith, the likelihood again is that in more than 50 per cent of the cases the children are not brought up as Jews.

In addition to mixed marriages, illegitimate unions of various types must also be considered in discussing Jewish-Gentile interbreeding and its genetic results. Wherever a higher prestige group lives in the proximity of a subordinate, weak, and underprivileged one, many males of the former are ready and able to take advantage sexually of the women of the latter, but they will rarely marry them. This was the relationship between Christians and Jews for many centuries. What did happen frequently was that Christian males interbred with Jewish women in the course of temporary alliances or casual encounters, including, especially in periods of acute persecution, rape. The offspring of such unions was in almost every case brought up within the Jewish community, as it had to be, unless the mother was willing to abandon her child which meant its certain death. On very rare occasions it happened that a Jewish woman who gave birth to a child fathered by a Gentile murdered it in order to prevent her shame from becoming public knowledge; or that the male members of her family killed the woman when they learned that she had become impregnated by a non-Jew.[82] Equally rare were the cases in which the child was forcibly taken away from the Jewish mother to be brought up in the religion of its father.

The general rule was that when an illegitimate child was fathered by a Gentile on a willing or unwilling Jewish woman, the mother had no choice but to bring it up, which meant to bring it up as a Jew. This raised the question of the status of the child, which had been hotly discussed in Talmudic times for several generations. The consensus finally crystallized that such an illegitimately conceived child was a Jew, and this is the ruling of the Jewish law codes, the last one of which, the *Shulḥan 'Arukh,* is still valid today.[83] The frequency with which illegitimate children fathered by Gentiles were born to Jewish women in the Middle Ages must have been a factor in the unquestioning application of this old Talmudic rule and in the relatively favorable treatment of illegitimate children in medieval Jewish law.[84]

In those cases in which interbreeding took place between a Jewish male and a Christian woman, the latter usually was, or had been previously, taken into the home of the Jewish man, as wife (with or without conversion to Judaism), concubine, or servant girl. Offspring resulting from such unions would—again with some exceptions—be brought up as Jews. In all these cases, therefore, the interbreeding between Jews and Christians resulted in the introduction of Christian genetic factors into the Jewish community.

Since, as emphasized above, the total number of the Jews throughout the period discussed was small, and in most localities in which Jews lived they numbered not more than a few families (in the midst of a many times larger Christian population), it follows that, even if only one or two mixed offspring were thus added to a Jewish community in every generation, the cumulative effect of this interbreeding was a considerable intermingling of the Jewish with Christian blood; or, to put it more accurately, a considerable addition of genes from the surrounding Christian population to the Jewish gene pool.

In considering the genetic results of Jewish-Gentile interbreeding one must also take into account the various negative or depletive factors which from time to time decimated, or even reduced to one-half or less, the Jewish population of a community or a whole country. One such factor was the conversion of Jews to Christianity or to Islam. In almost every age and place Jews suffered from the demographic effects of either forced or voluntary conversions to the religion of the majority in whose midst they lived. These conversions were a constant drain on the Jewish stock, as were the oft-recurring persecutions, massacres, pogroms, expulsions, which took their toll over and above the effects of epidemics and other catastrophes, and the generally high infant mortality. These losses were, to some extent, made up by the accrual and absorption of Gentile individuals (mostly women) into the Jewish population, and by the inclusion into the Jewish community of practically every child born to a Jewish woman irrespective of its paternity. The combined effect of these factors was that, despite the consistently very high Jewish fertility, the number of Jews in the world remained more or less constant from antiquity to the beginning of modern times. But the genetic material (or gene pool) of a by-and-large constant Jewish population at the end of this long period was very different from what it had been at its beginning.

CHAPTER V

Slavery and Concubinage

INTERBREEDING BETWEEN JEWS and Gentiles occurred frequently as a result of slavery, and especially its subvariety, known as concubinage.

Slavery was an integral part of the social structure of all but the simplest cultures from the earliest Sumerian and Egyptian times down to the nineteenth century. It was everywhere taken for granted, so much so that neither the Greek philosophers, the Hebrew prophets, nor Jesus of Nazareth uttered a word against it. Aristotle, as we have seen, held that nature made slaves, while Jesus refers to slavery for purposes of illustration [1] without ever criticizing it, as if totally unaware of the institution's violation of his own principles of love and brotherhood. Slavery survived all over the world until the nineteenth century, and in our own days, despite its official abolition everywhere, it continues to exist de facto in some places, notably the Arabian Peninsula and North Africa.

IN BIBLICAL AND TALMUDIC TIMES

Since the possession of Hebrew slaves by Hebrew masters in biblical times had no bearing on the question of Jewish race mixture, we shall not deal with it in the present context. As for non-Hebrew slaves, these were originally acquired as a result of warlike contact with other peoples in the course of the Israelites' settlement in Canaan. One early example is the voluntary fraudulent submission of the inhabitants of the city of Gibeon (about 6 miles northwest of Jerusalem) to Joshua. The Gibeonites, a Hivite people, were made "hewers of wood and drawers of water for the congregation and for the altar of the Lord," that is to say, they became temple slaves, and as

119

such were absorbed by the Israelites. The women and children of those ethnic groups which resisted and were defeated in battle were spared and made
slaves. The neighboring peoples for their part would capture Israelites, including children, and make them slaves. In the course of the strife between
Israel and Judah, the Israelites took captive even Judaite women and children, but, upon the admonishment of a prophet, did not enslave them as
they had planned but returned them to Judah.[2]

Biblical legislation sanctions the existing custom of purchasing slaves
from the nations that lived around the borders of Israel, and from the aliens
who lived within the country. It provides that such non-Israelite slaves had
to be circumcised, after which they were to be admitted to partaking of the
Passover meal. In practice, participation in this family feast meant the admission of the slave into the family circle. Like all members of the Israelite
family, slaves, too, had to rest on the Sabbath so as to be able to "become
refreshed." [3] The slaves, both male and female, thus became practicing
Israelites, and were received into the fold. By Mishnaic times (the first to
second centuries A.D.) the law forbade their master to sell them to a
Gentile, since this might lead them to a renunciation of the Jewish faith. If
the Jewish master disobeyed this injunction, the law court forced him to
redeem the slave and manumit him; or if the slave escaped from his Gentile
master, he automatically achieved the status of a freedman. However, the
same law prohibited a male slave from marrying an Israelite woman, or an
Israelite man from marrying a slave girl. Likewise, Mishnaic law prohibited
an Israelite who had had sexual relations with a slave girl from marrying her
after she attained freedom. The child of a slave woman fathered by an
Israelite, even by her master, was a slave.[4]

Manumission was frequent. According to the biblical law, if a master
inflicted bodily injury on his slave, by striking him and causing the loss of
an eye, or even a tooth, the slave went free. From Roman times, cases of
Jews manumitting their slaves are frequently recorded. A certain Rufina,
directress of a synagogue in Smyrna, had a tomb built for her freedmen. As
a number of inscriptions on the Bosporus and in Pontus show, the freeing of
slaves was considered a religious duty for Jews. Talmudic sources often
speak of freedmen and of freeing slaves, for which act a legal document was
drawn up.[5]

Mishnaic law makes provision for a slave to buy himself free or acquire
his own freedom in other ways. If the master gives a free woman in marriage to his slave, this act itself frees him, and the master is required to
manumit him formally. If, however, the master betroths his slave girl for
himself, this act in itself does not imply manumission, unless the master
said: "Be free through this betrothal document and betrothed to me." Rabbi
Joshua ben Levi quotes a popular Jerusalemite saying to the effect that if
one's daughter becomes nubile one should hurriedly marry her off even if it
means manumitting one's slave to make him her husband.[6]

The Talmud devotes detailed attention to the question of various bodily injuries which, if caused by a master to his slave, secure the release of the latter in accordance with the biblical law. One of the cases discussed is that of a physician who, while rendering obstetrical services to his slave girl, introduced his hand into her womb and inadvertently blinded the child; in such a case, the child becomes free.[7] Numerous other legal provisions in Talmudic literature concerning the manumission of slaves, including actual cases, show that their emancipation was a frequent practice.

While biblical law enjoins an Israelite from having sexual relations with another man's slave girl, numerous "case histories" in the Bible show that Israelites in fact had relations with, and children by, their own slave girls or slave girls owned by their wives. Thus Abraham had Ishmael by his wife Sarah's slave girl Hagar; Jacob had two sons each by his wives' handmaids Bilhah and Zilpah. A biblical law provides that a man can buy a Hebrew slave girl to serve as his or his son's concubine. The same rule may have applied to foreign-born slave girls as well.[8]

Biblical law imposes the death penalty on an Israelite who kills, or whose ox gores to death, another Israelite. If the person killed by an Israelite is a slave, the penalty is the same. But if an Israelite's ox causes the death of a slave, the owner of the ox must pay the owner of the slave 30 shekels of silver. The kidnapping of a free man is punished by death, and so is the stealing and selling of a man into slavery. While the law thus distinguishes to a limited extent between the penalty for causing death to a free man and a slave, there is at least one case recorded in the Bible in which the brutal abuse and murder of a slave-concubine by a group of hoodlums led to bloody revenge not only on the perpetrators of the crime but on an entire tribe of Israel.[9]

Throughout the biblical period we hear not a word of moral objection to concubinage. The use of slave girls for sexual purposes was taken for granted and, evidently, no opprobrium whatsoever attached to it. This attitude, however, underwent a change in Hellenistic times. In the pietistic view of some of the authors of the apocryphal books, female slaves appeared as sources of temptation to immorality. Thus Jesus (Jeshua) ben Sirach, a Palestinian Jew who wrote his Hebrew Book of Wisdom (or Ecclesiasticus) about 180 B.C., warns against looking at a strange woman and going near a slave girl.[10]

The issue of the union between a free man and his female slave presented special problems in many societies. Was such a child a legal offspring of its father, as one would assume it would be in a patrilineal society; or was it a slave like its mother? Among the biblical Israelites the answer to this question seems to have been far from unequivocal. Instances are recorded in the Bible in which the son of a slave-concubine ranked equal with the sons of the father by his free and legally married wives. The twelve sons of Jacob are a case in point. Eight of them were borne by his wives Leah

121

and Rachel, and four by the handmaids of the latter, Bilhah and Zilpah. Yet Jacob does not seem to have discriminated among them in any way, except that before his meeting with Esau, to which he looked forward with trepidation, he divided his family into three groups: the handmaids and their children foremost, Leah and her children next, and Rachel and her son Joseph last. While this reflects the difference in Jacob's emotional attachment to those three parts of his family, it does not imply a difference in status. In the blessing Jacob gave his sons on his deathbed he addressed them in this order: first the six sons of Leah, then the four sons of the two concubines, and lastly the two sons of Rachel. Immediately thereafter the text goes on: "All these are the twelve tribes of Israel"—evidently none of them ranked higher or lower than the others.[11]

Other biblical references, too, show that the son of a slave-concubine would inherit his father's property and blessing both in patriarchal times and later. The Israelite "judge" Gideon had many wives and many sons, and, in addition, a concubine (i.e., a slave woman) in Shechem who bore him Abimelech. A similar relationship existed between Jephthah and his half brothers, except that Jephthah's mother is described, not as the concubine of Jephthah's father, but as a "harlot" and "another woman." Both men eventually became leaders of their tribes and people.[12]

Nothing is said in the Bible about the conversion of alien slaves to the religion of their Hebrew masters; however, the circumcision of all the males, free or slave, whether "born in the house or bought with money of any foreigner," was an old Abrahamic tradition and considered the sign of the covenant between God and Abraham. Much later, when the Talmudic teachers discussed in detail the position of a non-Jewish slave owned by a Jew, the consensus crystallized that as soon as a non-Jewish slave was acquired by a Jew, he had to be baptized (i.e., immersed in water) and, if a male, circumcised. The baptism had to be performed at once; the circumcision could be postponed for a maximum of twelve months. Thereafter, if the slave refused to be circumcised, he had to be sold to a non-Jew.[13]

Once these rites were taken care of, the slaves, whether male or female, had to observe those rules of the Jewish law that were obligatory for women; but they were exempt from observing those positive commandments whose performance was tied to definite times. Thus, for example, a slave (like a Jewish woman) was not required to pray, to make the pilgrimage to Jerusalem, and so forth. On the other hand, all negative commandments had to be observed by slaves (as by women): not to work on the Sabbath and holy days, not to eat non-kosher food, to fast on the Day of Atonement. A slave, like a woman, could also make a religious vow and thus become a *nazir* (Nazarite).[14]

In the purification ritual required of a woman who had a spontaneous abortion, no distinction was made between a free and a slave woman. At the

122

time of manumission, both male and female slaves underwent a second submersion (baptism) and therewith not only acquired their freedom but also became fully proselytes. Because slavery under a Jewish master thus meant first partial and ultimately full observance of the Jewish law, Talmudic teachers considered the acquisition of non-Jewish slaves a meritorious act, which "brings them under the wings of the Shekhina." [15]

These laws were developed either in Palestine or in Babylonia, both places where the Jews constituted large, compact communities with considerable internal autonomy. In most periods no outside authority interfered with the ways in which they regulated their own lives, including the ritual demands they made on slaves they owned. In the Western Diaspora, and especially in Christian Rome, the situation was very different.

UNDER EARLY CHRISTIANITY

No sooner was Christianity established as the ruling religion of the Roman Empire than it embarked on a campaign against the Jews which, as time passed, became more and more intensified. Several regulations, aiming at the prevention of close social relations between Jews and Christians, were formalized by the Council of Chalcedon in 451.[16]

Among the legal strictures imposed upon Jews were provisions concerning their possession of Christian slaves. At first, laws were enacted which increased the number of those conditions under which it was legally justified to take away Christian slaves from their Jewish masters, with or without compensation. Finally, Jews were enjoined altogether from owning Christian slaves (Councils of Orléans, 538 and 541; Mâcon, 583; Toledo, 589; Clichy 626–27; Toledo, 633, Chalon-sur-Saône, c. 650; and Toledo, 656). One of the gravest crimes a Jewish slaveowner could commit in the eyes of the Church was to convert his Christian slave to Judaism. Even in the sixth century, when the mere ownership of Christian slaves by Jews was countenanced, such an attempt was a punishable offense. In 589 the Third Council of Toledo provided that if a Jewish owner circumcised his slave, the latter would be taken from him. Ten years later the very ownership of Christian slaves by Jews, still permitted by the Frankish monarchs Theodoric, Theodebert, and Brunichild, was vigorously protested by Pope Gregory I, whose interest in slaves is attested in both legend and history.[17]

The pope's reproach evidently went unheeded, for as soon as the Visigothic King Sisebut (r. 612–21) ascended the Spanish throne he felt constrained to renew the decisions of the Third Council of Toledo, and extended the prohibition even to the employment by Jews of Christian coloni and free domestic servants. The latter provision was evidently intended to prevent the possibility of such household help being attracted to the Judaism practiced by their socially superior employers. Before long, however, Sisebut had to allow three or four months of grace for the Jewish owners to dispose of their Christian slaves. When this, too, failed to be effective in many cases, he threatened with severe penalties those Christians who helped the Jews evade this law. Finally, still within a year of his accession, he resorted to the ultimate measure of issuing a decree forcing the Jews of Spain to convert to Christianity (613). The *Leges Visigothorum,* promulgated in 654, included a provision prohibiting Jews from acquiring a Christian slave either by purchase or by gift, under sanction of immediate emancipation of the slave in question. Moreover, if the Jewish owner dared to circumcise his slave, all his other property was to be confiscated.[18]

The Roman Council of 743 again forbade the sale of Christian slaves to Jews, and the Council of Meaux and Paris, 845–46, prohibited the Jews from converting their slaves to Judaism and exporting slaves to Muslim lands. Between 820 and 828 Agobard, archbishop of Lyon, argued in his anti-Jewish treatises and letters that it was the duty of a pagan slave purchased by a Jew to convert to Christianity (and thereby gain his freedom), despite the privilege the Jews of Lyon held from the emperor under which no one could convert their slaves to Christianity without the owner's permission. Agobard also fulminated against the Jewish owners whose slaves, under the influence of their masters, took to observing certain Jewish rituals. Late in the ninth century another Church Council was held in southern Italy and, among other things, prohibited the Jews from owning Christian slaves. At the Council of Rouen (1074) this prohibition was extended to Christian wet nurses. Such prohibitions recur several times in compilations of canonical laws made in the tenth century.[19]

In Germany, the prohibition of Jews acquiring and owning Christian slaves was repeated many times, evidently because it was often violated. In fact, numerous documents show that in the early centuries of the Middle Ages Jews actually possessed Christian slaves. Henry IV (1050–1106), king of Germany and head of the Holy Roman Empire, issued privileges to the Jews of his realm which guaranteed the right of Jewish slaveowners to possess slaves even in the event of their being baptized. A heavy fine was imposed on him who tried to lure any slave from his Jewish master by persuading him to accept Christianity.[20]

In Hungary, until the end of the eleventh century the Jews were permitted to own foreign (non-Hungarian) slaves and were debarred only from the ownership of Hungarian slaves. The diet of 1101–2 passed a series of laws (known as the Decrees of King Kálmán) which stated explicitly that the Jews were permitted to have their land worked by pagan slaves. However, at about the same time Kálmán (Coloman) issued a special Jew-law, whose first paragraph says: "From now on no Jew shall dare to purchase, sell, or keep in his service a Christian slave of any language or nation. He who transgresses this decree will be deprived of the Christian slave found in his possession.'' This meant that Jews who wished to continue having their land cultivated—which at the time could be done only by slave labor—had to hire slaves from others. The Council of Esztergom (1114) deprived the Jews of this possibility as well. It decreed that "the Jews should not dare to keep Christian slaves or slave women, whether as possession, or for sale, or as hirelings.'' Since by that time pagan slaves were totally unavailable, had these prohibitions been effective, it would have meant the end of Jewish agricultural activity in Hungary. In reality, however, Jews continued to own and cultivate large landed estates.

The Council of Szabolcs (1092) had passed a decree prohibiting Jews from purchasing Christian slaves and from marrying Christian women. The Hungarian Jewish historian Samuel Kohn interprets this law as referring to a situation in which Jews both bought Christian slave women and then used them as concubines, and intermarried with free Christian women. Despite this law, however, mixed marriages continued, as can be seen from the reaffirmation of the prohibition by Andreas II in 1233 when he rendered an oath to Bishop Jacobus, the delegate of Pope Gregory IX, and solemnly undertook to see to it that the Jews (and Saracens, i.e., Muslims) should wear a distinguishing badge; forbade them to buy or keep Christian slaves; and threatened those who lived either in legal or illegal marriage with Christians with the confiscation of all their property and being sold into eternal slavery to Christians.[21]

The situation was similar in the realm of Eastern Christianity. In Byzantium laws were passed, and periodically re-enacted down to the ninth and tenth centuries, making the circumcision of a Christian slave a capital crime. By the tenth century, regulations of this type had become standard all over Europe. These laws, however, could not always be enforced, and pious Christian monarchs had to resort to ransoming Christian slaves from Jewish traders: for doing precisely this, Bishop Adalbert (Wojtech) of Prague (in 997), and Queen Judith, wife of King Ladislas Herrmann (1079–1102), received the chroniclers' accolades. In general, in the High Middle Ages Jewish masters were able to, and actually did, exert considerable pressure on their slaves to convert to Judaism. This was in keeping with ancient Jewish religious law, and aimed, among other things, at enabling the master to make full use of his slave without incurring ritual difficulties. In a Jewish household a pagan slave was a constant source of actual or potential ritual pollution: for instance, he could not be allowed to handle food, and especially wine. Quite apart from these inconveniences, the presence of a pagan—an individual who did not acknowledge God—was inevitably an irritant to the pious. To all this was added another, equally old, view of Talmudic origin, which held that the very act of converting slaves to Judaism was a work of piety and a God-fearing deed. Toward the end of the Middle Ages, Jewish slave ownership in Christian lands became extremely rare.

125

Nevertheless, a case is recorded in 1462 of a Jew of Caltagirone, in Sicily, who was arrested for acquiring a Christian female slave.[22]

IN THE MUSLIM EAST

Even before the end of the Talmudic period (A.D. 500), the practice of slavery had spread to the Jewish Diasporas in the Middle East. In pre-Islamic Arabia the Jews, like the Arabs, had male and female slaves. The medieval Arab biographers of Muḥammad, Ibn Hishām and al-Wāqidī, say of the Medinese Jewish tribe Naḍīr that when it was expelled from the city of Muḥammad, its women rode on richly caparisoned camels, dressed in luxurious clothing, and its slave girls accompanied the procession with tambourines and other musical instruments. From this incidental intelligence we learn that the Jews of Medina kept slave girls, among them musicians, and that in general they were a rather well-to-do class in the city.

When the Zoroastrian Persians conquered Jerusalem (614), several thousand Christian captives were sold to the Jews of the city, who allegedly killed all those who refused to accept Judaism.[23]

Under Islam Jews could purchase and keep as slaves only pagans or Christians. Muslim law strictly forbade them to buy or own Muslim slaves. The Covenant of Omar contains the provision that it is forbidden to the *dhimmī* (the "protected" Jews, Christians, and Zoroastrians tolerated within the "House of Islam,") to buy slaves who were owned by Muslims.[24] The old Jewish legal provision that slaves purchased or owned by Jews must be converted to Judaism was paralleled by the Muslim law which made the conversion of their slaves to Islam a duty for all Muslim slaveowners. Many Jewish masters, however, neglected to convert their slaves to Judaism. Amram Gaon, who served as head (*"Gaon"*) of the Sura Academy in Iraq from 856 to 874, felt it necessary to deal with this problem. In one of his responsa he reminded Jewish slaveowners that it was forbidden for them to keep male or female slaves in their homes unless the slaves were willing to accept Judaism, that is, to observe some of the basic commandments as specified in the Talmud, and that within one year from the day a slave was purchased he must complete and formalize his conversion by being circumcised and baptized if a male, and baptized if a female.[25]

Another Gaonic responsum mentions that "there are places [in Muslim countries] where Jews are not allowed to own women slaves unless they are Christians, except when unknown [to the authorities] which is a dangerous thing. Some of them [the Christian slave women] are converted immediately, others after the passage of time. But still others, and they are in the majority, stall or refuse outright." [26] In the latter case, according to the Talmudic *halakha* referred to above, the slave had to be sold to a non-Jew.

Muslim law provided that if a slave owned by a Jew (or other *dhimmī*) converted to Islam he had to be freed immediately, or sold to a Muslim—because a Muslim could not be owned by a non-Muslim.[27]

No such easy way to get rid of a master was available for slaves owned by Muslims. This single circumstance led to a far-reaching difference in the treatment of slaves by Muslim and by Jewish masters. Nothing prevented a Muslim master from maltreating his slaves, if he wished; the slaves had no way out of their predicament. If, on the other hand, a Jewish master aroused the dissatisfaction of his slaves with the manner in which they were treated, the simple act of conversion to Islam took them out of the master's hand, and gave them liberty. Nor could pagan slaves be expected to hesitate to take this step because of loyalty to the Jewish religion. Thus, even if other historical data as to the humane treatment slaves received from their Jewish masters were lacking, one could take it for granted that the slaves in a Jewish household were treated on a par with members of the family. One could even say that as far as slaves owned by Jews were concerned, the continuation of their services in the house of their master was a matter of their own **voluntary decision. Documents found in the famous Cairo Geniza reveal** that slave girls were found in every well-to-do Jewish family as domestic help and nurses of children. Male slaves were rarer, and their duties consisted only of personal services for their masters. As to the Muslims, the rich among them owned hundreds of slaves. The viceroy al-Malik al-Afḍal (1094–1121) can be mentioned as an example: when he died, he left behind a harem of 800 concubines.[28]

As to the provenance of the slaves owned by Jews, they were mostly Nubians. Second came Europeans from Byzantium (*"Rūm"*), Greece, Italy, Slavic countries (referred to as "Canaanites"), and Frankish lands; and third Indians. Libyan, Sudanese, Abyssinian, Negro ("Zangai"), and Persian slaves are also mentioned. The slave girls acquired by Jews were frequently born in slavery (*"muwallada"*), or would be bought at the tender age of six years or so, in order to enable the master (or more frequently the mistress) to train and educate them and familiarize them with certain minimal rules of the Jewish religion. The Geniza material indicates that in Fatimid and Ayyubid times (909–1260) the Islamic injunction against conversion to any religion but Islam was largely disregarded, and thus slaves bought as pagans could be, and were, converted to Judaism. By the time such a converted slave-girl child reached puberty, she would, to all practical purposes, be like a Jewish girl, and her nubile charms often attracted the attentions of the master or a younger male member of his family. Although Jewish law regarded sexual intercourse with a slave girl as a serious sin, the atmosphere of the Muslim environment, in which a female slave was at the disposal of her master, could not fail to weaken whatever moral resistance the Jews felt they must put up to such temptations. In the eighth and ninth centuries, intimacy with female slaves reached such proportions among the

127

Jews in Muslim lands that the rabbis felt constrained to decree more and more prohibitions. In most cases such liaisons were kept *sub rosa* and left no historical traces. Occasionally they led to complaints or even litigation, and then records remained of them. Several responsa of the Geonim (the heads of the central Talmudic academies in Babylonia-Iraq) deal with such questions as how to proceed against a master who has had sexual relations with his slave girl. One of the legal decisions is that she must be taken away from him, sold, and the money distributed among the poor, while the master receives the traditional punishment of flogging, his head is shaved, and he is excommunicated for thirty days.[29]

Another Gaonic decision punishes a man who has illicit relations with his fellow man's slave girl by obliging him to buy her, liberate her, and marry her. In many cases the slave girl was a willingly consenting party, because she achieved a favored position, and the children she bore to her master were treated by him as his own. Such concubines were found in many houses. In the medieval Muslim social order of which the Jews were part, the men were much freer than the women to engage in extramarital sexual activity. Nevertheless the reverse, too, happened occasionally and is likewise reflected in the responsa literature. We hear of a woman of the *Kohen* (priestly) class who was caught with a slave, of children being born to women while their husbands were on extended trips, and the like. In any case, whether the non-Jewish partner in such extramarital affairs was the male or female, the resulting offspring were frequently brought up by the Jewish parent as Jews, which introduced non-Jewish genes into the Jewish gene pool.[30]

On one occasion, Maimonides was asked to decide a case in which a young unmarried Jew bought a beautiful slave girl and began to cohabit with her. After three months, his stepmother and her three daughters, who lived with him in what is described as a "big house," lodged a complaint against him with the Muslim authorities. The judge questioned the girl, who stated that she was a Jewish girl who had been captured and brought here. The judge thereupon dismissed the case, the girl returned home, and the young man renewed relations with her. The questioner asks Maimonides what to do, and how to prevent her staying in the house. Maimonides' answer is that the rabbinical court should try its best to remove the girl from the house; "or let him [the master] set her free and marry her, despite the *halakha* which prohibits a man from marrying a liberated slave girl with whom he has had sexual relations." He adds that he has in the past ruled in such cases that the master should liberate the slave girl and marry her, and has done so in order to enable those who repent to improve their moral condition. Despite such documented cases, a foremost student of the Cairo Geniza feels that the Jewish society in the eastern part of the Arab world differed markedly in this respect from the Jews of Spain, among whom concubinage seems to have been the order of the day.[31]

128

The Muslim law enjoining Jews from owning Muslim slaves was frequently circumvented. The situation prompted the Mameluk authorities in Egypt to include in their 1354 decree a strict injunction against *dhimmīs* buying Muslim male or female slaves, or such slaves as had been in the possession of Muslims, or had been brought up as Muslims. Also the conversion of a slave to Judaism and Christianity was forbidden. But even after the issuance of this decree the old practices continued. Muslim and pagan girl slaves in particular were bought and owned by Jews and used as concubines, to the great chagrin of the rabbinical leaders. In the responsa literature of the twelfth to sixteenth centuries, complaints about the presence of Jewish and non-Jewish slave girls in Jewish houses and the immorality occasioned by them are frequent. Rabbi David ben Solomon ibn Abi Zimra, who was for forty years chief rabbi of Cairo in the sixteenth century, refers repeatedly to these conditions in his voluminous responsa. He mentions that rich Jews used to have Negro, Abyssinian, and other slave-concubines, who often became pregnant and had children by their masters, or by their paramours, since the Abyssinian slave girls especially were much given to fornication, and would then attribute ensuing children to their masters. The slave girls, Abi Zimra complains, are a veritable "pagan plague" for the Jews. Then, "whenever they become displeased with their position, they convert to Islam, which happens every day," and thus gain their freedom.[32] While cohabitation between Jews and slave girls was common in the countries of the Muslim East, when the Spanish exiles and Marranos began to arrive in the Orient, the local rabbis observed with dismay that their sexual mores were even looser than those of the Egyptian and Syrian Jews. Concubinage was ripe among them and cases of adultery and fornication were not infrequent. Having for long posed as Christians in Spain, the Marranos were used to considerable sexual freedom with the Christian population, and after they settled in Egypt and Syria they continued to seek and to have intercourse with non-Jewish women and to beget children with them. Many of the Marranos, who were brought up without any Jewish education, did not even know that the Jewish law forbade cohabitation with slave girls. Those who knew would manumit their slave girls before commencing cohabitation with them, or did so after the girls became pregnant.

It is not surprising that under these conditions the looseness of the sex mores spilled over into other areas as well. Occasionally, both Jewish males and females became known to have committed adultery and fornication, Jewish men raped girls, and Jewish women bore children as a result of extramarital relations.[33]

As in Talmudic times, so under medieval Islam the Jews frequently manumitted their slaves, and they did so not only in order to be able to marry their concubines or to legitimize their children. Formal manumission had to be performed before a rabbinical court. It converted the slave into a person with all the religious duties of a Jew, and enabled him to marry a

129

Jewish wife. A special question arose in connection with the liberating of Negro slaves, but the majority of the Geonim considered them as eligible for manumission and proselytism as any other slave, and this became the established *halakha*. There are numerous documented cases showing that freed slave men actually married Jewish women, and that Jewish men married freed slave women.

Many of the masters took pains to make sure that the children of their manumitted slaves received a good Jewish education. The status of a child born to a Jewish master and his non-Jewish slave girl is discussed at length in Gaonic literature. Some of the Gaons held that such a child was a slave, others that it was free and a legitimate offspring of its father. As early as the mid-ninth century Natronai Gaon, head of the Sura Academy, issued a decision to the effect that a child of a Jewish master and his woman slave should be considered a legitimate offspring of its father: "It is like its father in every respect." [34] This ruling was actually followed in practice, as we know from a case discussed by Abi Zimra: A Jewish man bought a Muslim girl, and had her undergo Jewish baptism in order to be a suitable servant. He subsequently cohabited with her and she gave birth to a girl. Thereafter, the slave woman scandalized her master with her adulteries, and he sold her to a Muslim. But he kept the daughter she bore him, brought her up as his own child, and arranged a marriage between her and a Jew. [35]

IN MUSLIM AND CHRISTIAN SPAIN

In Spain the practice of concubinage was so widespread among the Jews in both the Muslim and the Christian parts of the peninsula that it led to the development of two distinct types of concubines. One was the "betrothed" concubine, who was referred to by the traditional biblical term for concubine, "*pilegesh*." In taking such a concubine, a man would go through the betrothal ("*qiddushin*") cememony, which is the first part of the traditional Jewish wedding, but not follow it up with the second part, the so-called *ḥuppa* (lit. "canopy") or nuptials, required according to Jewish law to complete the wedding ceremony and make the woman his legally wedded wife. Such a "betrothed concubine" had a certain acceptable status, whether her master was a bachelor or already had a wife. She was either a Jewish woman, or a freed and converted slave girl.

The other type of concubine was referred to by the rather romantic-sounding term "*ḥashuqa*" (lit. "desired one"), or paramour. She was a slave woman who was not betrothed to her master and thus did not enjoy even this semblance of legalized status. Her situation was similar to that of a concubine slave woman among the Muslims. She would, in most cases, live in the house of her master but had no legal claim whatsoever on him. To prevent a man from indulging in concubinage, a bridegroom would often be required to include in the marriage contract the undertaking that he would purchase neither a *pilegesh* nor a *ḥashuqa* without the consent of his wife.[36]

Despite this legalization of the *pilegesh* concubinage by the Jewish religious authorities, the sexual mores of the Spanish Jews remained unsatisfactory from the rabbis' point of view. A sampling of the responsa of three rabbis yields two cases of suspicion of Jewish women's infidelity with Gentiles, five of adultery and fornication between Gentiles and Jewish women, six of sexual relations between a Jewish master and a servant or slave woman, five of concubinage, and six of illegitimate children. In one case the Jewish court compelled a Toledo Jew, owner of a Moorish slave girl who served as his concubine, either to send her away or to free her and make her his wife. In another case, a Jewish master set free his Moorish concubine, converted her to Judaism, performed the betrothal ceremony, and continued to live with her. In the fourteenth century this custom of living with a concubine spread among the Jews of Spain to such an extent that ethical teachers felt constrained to deplore it repeatedly and to state that it would be less reprehensible to keep a mistress or to resort to polygyny.[37]

In vain did the great Maimonides try to prohibit concubinage; not only did the practice continue, but most contemporary and later rabbinical authorities—Abraham ben David (1120–1198), the famous French Talmudist of Posquières; the Kabbalistically inclined Nahmanides (1194—c. 1270) who served as rabbi of Gerona in Aragon; and others—accepted it. Acceptance, of course, did not mean approval. On the contrary, Jewish moralists repeatedly and vehemently attacked the practice, directing their wrath especially against those Jews who kept Christian concubines. Thus Rabbi Jona ben Abraham Gerondi (of Gerona, c. 1180–1263), a foremost rabbi and ethical author who spent the last part of his life in Toledo, warned his co-religionists that it was forbidden to keep a concubine without betrothal and nuptials, and in general cautioned them against fornication, cohabitation with slave girls, and the like. Incidentally, one of the great-grandmothers of Gerondi himself was a concubine, taken by his great-grandfather when his wife proved barren. Rabbi Solomon ben Abraham Adret (1235–1310), known as RaShbA, who was for fifty years rabbi of Barcelona, mentions and decries cases of married Jews who took concubines.[38] After the attack on the Jews of Toledo in 1280–81, Todros Abulafia, the influential astronomer and Kabbalist who lived in the city, emulated Ezra and expelled many non-Jewish women, concubines, and the like from the Jewish quarter. Under his influence the leaders of the community undertook to see to it that all the Jews of the city would either send away, or else marry, their slave girls. But, again as in the days of Ezra, those resolves were either not carried out or the measures taken were shortlived. Within a few years Moses de Leon, the author of the *Zohar* (the *Book of Splendor,* the holiest book of the Kabbala) again had reason to complain that the Jews cohabited with

131

foreign women, which for him was a most heinous sin because it disrupted the mystical union between God the King and his consort the Shekhina-Matronit.[39]

That conditions did not improve in the subsequent two centuries is attested by Solomon ibn Verga, author of the famous *Shevet Yehuda* (*Rod of Judah*), who lived first in Spain, and after the Spanish expulsion (1492), in Portugal (until 1497), then in Italy. Throughout the period in question, the responsa literature contains ample testimony to the continuing practice of concubinage, as well as to the birth of offspring from relations between Jews and their concubines and female slaves, and between Jews and prostitutes.[40]

Most of the slaves owned by Jews in Christian Spain were Moors, or less frequently of Tartar or pagan European origin, as was the case with the slaves owned by the Christian Spaniards. In 1488 Ferdinand II, surnamed the Catholic, king of Aragon, sent a gift of 100 Moorish slaves to Pope Innocent VIII who, in turn, presented them to his cardinals and other court notables. Of a rich Spanish Jewish financier, Simuel Abulafia, it is reported that he owned eighty male and female Moorish slaves. For a while the Christian authorities tolerated the practice of Jews acquiring Muslim Moorish slaves, but before long the Inquisition managed to find a legal basis for prosecuting Jews who had converted some of their Muslim slaves to Judaism. Since, as we have seen, Jewish religious law required that a master convert his slave to Judaism within a year of having acquired him or her, these inquisitorial measures made Jewish slave ownership impossible for those who wished to observe the Jewish law.[41]

The old Jewish custom and moral duty of manumission was frequently observed in Spain. Some slaves were set free upon their total adoption of Judaism. Others were rewarded for faithful services rendered. Occasionally it happened that a slave would resist conversion. A case is reported of a slave woman who had accumulated property of her own (as was possible according to Jewish law) and preferred to pay her master a substantial amount for her freedom rather than become a Jewess. When the Marranos emigrated to Turkey they would occasionally take along their slaves and concubines; upon arrival in the Muslim country, these slaves would also convert to Judaism and would be liberated.[42]

IN THE ASHKENAZI WORLD

The institution of the "betrothed concubine" could not become popular in Ashkenazi communities because Rabbenu Gershom ben Yehuda of Mainz had had polygyny banned by the synod he convened in the year 1000. A betrothed concubine was considered to be like a wife, which precluded married Ashkenazi men from entering into such a relationship with a woman. While no such legal obstacle existed if a married man wanted to acquire a non-betrothed concubine, no case of concubinage is mentioned in the responsa of Ashkenazi rabbis, which is an eloquent testimony to the difference in sexual morality between the Ashkenazim and their Sephardi brethren. Nevertheless, the suspicion that Jewish employers would sexually exploit Christian maid-servants continued to linger in the Christian mind. A Christian woman who accepted service in a Jewish house was consequently treated with contempt. An example of this attitude was the rejection of the testimony of a Christian woman in connection with a Blood Accusation in Winchester in 1192, because the fact that she had done service for Jews rendered her an "in-famous" person. In Provence—whose Jewish population, however, was of Sephardi origin—the old prohibition against employment of Christian ser-vants by Jews was reiterated in the Decree of 1294, and was abolished only in 1454 by King René. In Ratisbon, Germany, a compromise decree was issued in 1393 prohibiting Jews from employing Christian maidservants under the age of fifty; a transgressor against this law was punished in 1472.[43]

Despite the traditional absence of concubinage from the Ashkenazi world, one Ashkenazi rabbi of the eighteenth century, Rabbi Jacob Israel Emden (c.1697–1776) of Altona in Germany, found it necessary to declare the practice legal, because he felt such legalization would help combat sex-ual immorality. (We have seen that the opponents of concubinage used the same argument in their fight against it.) Emden enjoined the master to in-form his concubine that "the children she will have by him will be without blemish, like those of the pure blood of Israel." The latter provision was, of course, in accordance with old Jewish tradition; in Spain, children born to a master by his concubine, whether she was betrothed or not, were also con-sidered fully legitimate both in respect to succession to their father and to consanguinity as it affects incest.[44]

Emden's permission to keep concubines came too late as far as the Ashkenazi Jews were concerned. Even had the general circumstances and their own social and civic conditions been such as to enable them to pur-chase non-Christian slave girls, conversion to any other religion than Chris-tianity was strictly prohibited by the laws of the Christian countries, and for a Jew legalized concubinage was possible only with a slave woman who had converted to Judaism. More importantly, from the end of the eighteenth cen-tury on, slavery itself was gradually abolished in all Christian countries, which made the entire institution of concubinage obsolete.

Only a few words need be said about Jewish slave ownership in the New World. The first Jewish settlers in the newly discovered continent were Sephardi Jews, mostly Marranos, who hoped to find refuge in the Spanish and Portuguese territories of America from the Inquisition which hounded them at home. However, before long the Holy Office followed them across the Atlantic, and by the early sixteenth century was busily engaged in hunting down not only Christianized Indians who were suspected of having relapsed into their pagan ways, but also secret Jews and Judaizers, in the West Indies (from 1511 on), South America (1516), and Mexico (1571). When Brazil came under tolerant Dutch rule (*c.* 1620), many of the Marranos openly returned to Judaism and founded a Jewish congregation in Recife (Pernambuco). In 1654, however, the Portuguese re-established their rule, and the Jews had to flee again, some going to Holland, others to New Amsterdam (later New York), while still others joined their brethren in Surinam (Dutch Guiana), which had the oldest Jewish community in the Americas.

Much of the economy of the New World colonies was based on slavery, and the Jewish settlers, as could be expected, had their share of slaves. In 1668, of the 9 sugar plantations in Surinam, 6 belonged to Portuguese Jews whose fields were worked by 181 Negro slaves. In 1730, of the 400 sugar plantations, 115 were owned by Jews and worked by approximately 9,000 Negro slaves. Even if these Jewish slaveholders did not follow the old Jewish rule of converting their slaves to Judaism, it was inevitable that some Jewish religious customs should be adopted by the slaves, especially those who took care of domestic chores. Many Jewish traditions were known and retained among these house slaves after the abolition of slavery in 1853.

During the two centuries of Jewish slave ownership in Surinam, sexual relations between Jewish masters and Negro female slaves were quite common (as they were between Gentile masters and their slaves), resulting in the emergence of a sizable Mulatto population. Many of these persons of mixed descent became members of the Jewish community. The 1791 census of the Jewish community of Paramaribo in Surinam showed, next to 834 Sephardim and 477 Ashkenazim, 100 Mulattos; the latter, although slaves, were counted as Jews. Their descendants have remained faithful to Judaism even after emancipation, and are not infrequently encountered in the Caribbean area, wearing a Star of David, and, upon inquiry, proudly declaring, "I, too, am a Jew." Some of these West Indian and South American Negro Jews have moved to New York and joined the Jewish congregations in Harlem.[45]

In the twentieth century the last vestiges of concubinage were found in the Muslim world together with the remnants of slavery. Accordingly, the only report of concubinage among Jews in recent years also comes from a Muslim environment: the Mzab Valley in Algeria, in the northern part of the Sahara. Here slavery was still observed as a functioning institution in the 1950's by Lloyd Cabot Briggs, who remarks that Negro slave women "have occasionally left the mark of their race clearly stamped on the features of both Moslems and Jews of the Mzab who firmly maintain, often enough no doubt in full sincerity, that they surely have no negroid, far less Negro ancestors." Briggs surmises that "the usual process is for a Negro serving woman to bear a male child whose father is her white master, after which the half-breed son grows up around the house and one day has secret relations with his master's wife, who, in due course, produces a hybrid child which all the family assume to be the master's.'' In fact, 5.5 per cent of the Mzab Jews measured anthropometrically by Briggs ''showed faint but unmistakable traces of negroid admixture.'' Jewish-Arab sexual relations were also frequent in the Mzab. Well-to-do Jews often took Arab married women as mistresses, but, as Briggs remarks, the offspring of these unions were usually absorbed by the Arab community, for the women's husbands were generally thought to be the children's fathers.[46]

In conclusion we may quote the opinion of a student of medieval Jewish slavery concerning the effects of this institution on the Jews:

> Many if not all of the Judaized slaves were finally emancipated and were absorbed by the Jewish population. A reasonable guess would be that between the seventh and eleventh centuries Middle Eastern and North African Jewry doubled as a result of the proselyting of slaves. There is strong possibility that the institution of slavery had more far-reaching anthropological, sociological, and economic effects than is generally assumed.[47]

JUS PRIMAE NOCTIS

The *jus primae noctis* (''right of the first night''), that is, the claim of the overlord to deflower the virgins within his domain on their wedding night before the bridegrooms were allowed to approach them, is a widespread folkloristic motif found in Germany, France, Switzerland, Denmark, Scotland, Ireland, and India, as well as in Jewish folk tales.[48] As to whether or not feudal lords actually claimed the seignorial right of concubinage with their tenants' brides, Frazer's investigations led him to a negative conclusion. He felt that neither in England and Scotland nor on the Continent has this right ever existed, and that the *jus primae noctis* was a legend that arose out of a misunderstanding of quite another rule which originally bore this name. There was a Church requirement, enacted by the Fourth Council of Carthage in 398 A.D., that ''when the bridegroom and bride have received the benediction, let them remain that same night in a state of virginity out of reverence for the benediction.'' Subsequently, the Church granted dispensation to free.newly married couples from the obligation of complying with this ancient custom, and this was the original *jus primae noctis*.[49]

Frazer's negative conclusion notwithstanding, references contained in Jewish sources to the *jus primae noctis* give the impression that in Greek and Roman times some of the foreign overlords of the Jews of Palestine did, in fact, exercise the right of the first night on Jewish virgin brides.

Talmudic tradition dating at the latest from the fourth century A.D. has it that when the Romans conquered Jewish Palestine, they decreed that the

135

high officers of the Roman army (*"stratiotes"* or *"strategos"*) should deflower all Jewish brides. To prevent this from happening, the rabbis, in turn, ordered that the bridegroom should cohabit with his bride some time before the wedding while she was still in her father's house. Once she had lost her virginity, the Roman officers could no longer claim their right to be the first to sleep with her.

The Babylonian Talmud, too, mentions the decree forcing every Jewish virgin to submit first to an officer (here called *"hegemon"*) on her wedding night. The old Jewish custom was, we learn, that the weddings of virgins were celebrated on Wednesdays. However, since on Wednesdays the authorities were on the lookout for weddings, the custom developed of solemnizing the weddings one day earlier, on Tuesdays.[50]

In later Midrashic sources this story is elaborated and linked with the origin of the Maccabean uprising and the Feast of Hanukkah. According to a tenth-century Midrash for Hanukkah, the Maccabean revolt was triggered by the act of a Greek who brutally exercised the *jus primae noctis* on the beautiful daughter of Matityahu the Hasmonean, and did so provocatively in front of her bridegroom.[51]

In the commentary to *Megillat Ta'anith* we read:

> In what way did the kings of Greece persecute them? They placed *quaestores* (*"qastiraot"*) in their cities in order to violate the brides, and thereafter they [the brides] were married to their husbands. . . . Consequently, nobody wanted to marry because of the quaestors. So they arranged to celebrate the weddings in secret. . . . And Mattathias son of Johanan the high priest had a daughter, and when her time came to get married, and the quaestor came to defile her, they did not let him. And Mattathias and his sons became incensed and they prevailed over the Greek authority. . . .[52]

Although this story is clearly legendary, the memory of a historically exercised *jus primae noctis* may well be preserved in it.

On the basis of these and other references, it was suggested that the *jus primae noctis* was introduced into Roman Palestine by the praetor Lusius Quietus about A.D. 117.[53] However that may be, the legal measures reported in the Talmudic sources to counteract the *jus primae noctis* as demanded by the Romans seem to be related to an actual situation and not merely to a fable devoid of factual basis.

About the year 1,000, the Arab historian Abū Rayḥān Muḥammad ibn Aḥmad al-Bīrūnī repeats the Midrashic story about the origins of Hanukkah. It was the practice of King Antiochus, he reports, to have the Jewish brides brought to him and to deflower them before their bridegrooms were allowed to approach them. When the turn of the only daughter of an unnamed Jew came to be violated, the youngest of her brothers took her place, was led in to the king, and killed him. This act was followed by the Jewish revolt and their victory over the Greeks. The same story, with some variations, is repeated by Ismāʿīl b.ʿAlī al-Ayyūbī Abū ʾl-Fidāʾ (1273–1331).[54]

The *jus primae noctis* re-emerges in the nineteenth century in another part of the Middle East. The Jewish traveler Israel Joseph Benjamin, who from 1846 to 1855 visited many countries in search of Jewish communities, reports on the tyrannical chieftains of Kurdistan:

> A custom which reminds us of the old feudal barbarism of the Middle Ages is the so-called master's claims. When a young Israelite or Nestorian [i.e., Christian] wishes to marry, he must purchase his bride from the master to whom she belongs. . . . In addition, before the bride enters the house of her husband, she must serve the lust of her master which appears to be an old custom introduced among the Orientals.'' [55]

Subsequent research has shown that at least the first part of Benjamin's report is correct. Down to the middle of the twentieth century, the local Kurdish Agas (chieftains) claimed and enforced their right to grant or withhold permission for weddings planned by members of the Jewish communities of their villages. Occasionally, the Aga gave his consent only after he received a sum of money. In some villages the Aga would receive one-third of the bride price paid by the bridegroom to the father of the bride. Where the power of the Aga was great, he could even take the entire bride price for himself.[56]

In conclusion we must state that the Jewish references to the *jus primae noctis* are meager and do not constitute a sufficient basis for establishing the historicity of the custom. However, if Jewish brides anywhere were actually subjected to this *droit du seigneur,* the possibility of their impregnation was considerable. According to the Jewish laws of sexual purity, a husband is forbidden to approach his wife for full seven days after the cessation of her menstrual discharge.[57] Consequently, weddings were (and still are) celebrated in most cases precisely in the middle of the bride's monthly period, when she happens to be most likely to conceive. Thus, if the *jus primae noctis* was exercised—as all the references state—on the wedding night, it could well have resulted in the introduction of non-Jewish genes into the Jewish gene pool.

PART TWO

Psychological

CHAPTER VI

The Jewish Mind

EARLIER CHAPTERS HAVE pointed quite definitely toward a negative answer to the question whether or not the Jews constitute a race. Also the biological evidence, to be discussed in Part Three, indicates that genetically in most countries the Jews approximate the surrounding non-Jewish population, the more so the longer they have lived there. We must now ask whether this Jewish tendency to approach the non-Jewish majority can be observed in the psychological realm as well. The importance of this issue is obvious. Among other things it will throw some light on the oft-observed Jewish inclination to preserve a separate group identity with special religious, cultural, and social interests.

In this chapter we shall attempt to discuss the similarities and differences between the Jewish and non-Jewish mind in three major areas: 1. general intelligence; 2. special talents; 3. character traits. There is, of course, a considerable overlap among these three categories. Nonetheless, the division serves as a useful general guide to make this complex subject somewhat more manageable.*

In particular, we shall focus attention on the following questions:

1. Are there measurable differences in general intelligence between Jews and non-Jews? If so, what is the nature of these differences?

2. Are there differences in special talents or abilities between Jews and non-Jews? If so, what is the nature of these differences?

3. Are there differences in character traits between Jews and non-Jews? If so, what is the nature of these differences?

4. Having established that there are certain differences in general in-

141

---

*Since the appearance of the first edition of this book, Raphael Patai has published a six hundred page study entitled *The Jewish Mind* (New York: Charles Scribner's Sons, 1977).

telligence, special talents, and character traits between Jews and non-Jews, how do we explain them?

5. Are there differences in general intelligence, special talents, and character traits among the various Jewish ethnic groups? If so, what is the nature of these differences and how can they be explained?

THE PROBLEM OF COMPARATIVE INTELLIGENCE

Before presenting and evaluating the results of quantitative studies dealing with Jewish intelligence, we must briefly review the general issue of differences in intelligence among human groups. This is a question that has been debated, often with considerable heat, for a long time.

More than a century ago, John Stuart Mill, the great English economist, philosopher, and reformer, reached the conclusion that "attributing the diversities of conduct and character to inherent natural differences" was the most "vulgar mode of escaping from the considerations of the effect of social and moral influence upon the human mind." [1] Along similar lines many modern anthropologists and psychologists who have studied the interrelationship between race and intelligence have stressed, in the words of Franz Boas, that "the claim to biologically determined mental qualities of races is not tenable. Much less have we a right to speak of biologically determined superiority of one race over another." [2]

The same position was subsequently taken by the psychologist Otto Klineberg: "Every racial group contains individuals who are well endowed, others who are inferior, and still others in between." Moreover, as far as it is possible to judge, says Klineberg, "the range of capacities and the frequency of occurrence at various levels of inherited ability are about the same in all racial groups." [3]

Other scholars take a different point of view, based on the now widely accepted fact that human intelligence, as measured by intelligence tests, has a large genetic component. They argue that, just as there are genetic differences between races in many physical features, so there may be racial differences in intelligence. The well-known British statistician and student of races, G. M. Morant, states that

> there seems to be no reason why the general rules regarding variation within and between groups should not apply to mental, as well as to physical, characters. . . . It seems to be impossible to evade the conclusion that some racial differences in mental characters must be expected. Existing evidence may not be extensive and cogent enough to reveal them, but it must be inferred that some exist.

Subsequently in the same study Morant emphasizes that "the general inference is that there are racial differences in mentality, although clear demonstration of them—regarding particular characters and particular pairs of populations—is not available yet." [4]

More recently, the population geneticists Walter F. Bodmer and Luigi Cavalli-Sforza have pointed out that the intelligence quotient (I.Q.) is a complex characteristic which is influenced by many genes, each contributing on the average a small effect. In discussing possible genetic differences in I.Q. between whites and blacks, they state that

> there is no *a priori* reason why genes affecting I.Q., which differ in the gene pools of blacks and whites, should be such that on the average whites have significantly more genes increasing I.Q. than blacks do. On the contrary, one should expect, assuming no tendency for high-I.Q. genes to accumulate by selection in one race or the other, that the more polymorphic genes there are that affect I.Q. and that differ in frequency in blacks and whites, the less likely it is that there is an average genetic difference in I.Q. between the races. The same argument applies to the differences between any two racial groups.

Nonetheless these authors, whose ideas represent the mainstream of thought in modern genetics, "do not by any means exclude the possibility that there could be a genetic component in the mean difference in intelligence between races. We simply maintain that currently available data are inadequate to resolve this question." [5]

Is it true then that the questions posed at the beginning of this chapter cannot be answered? Not at all. However, one must keep in mind that human intelligence never manifests itself purely in its inherited form. It is always expressed as the end result of environmental influences which mold it even before birth and for many years thereafter. Even if we go along with Boas and Klineberg and hold that there are no racial differences in inherited ability, there may be considerable differences between one human group and another in their observable functioning intelligence which, as has often been pointed out, is the sum total of the combined effects of heredity and environment.

The issue can be illustrated by a simple example taken from the realm of physiology. Imagine a pair of identical twins, that is, two individuals who by definition have the same genetic equipment. Suppose one of them is held to a strict consistent régime of strenuous physical exercise, while the other is confined to a sedentary and totally inactive life. The first will develop powerful muscles and an athletic physique, while the second will become a puny weakling. They will differ considerably in girth, weight, and endurance. An observer seeing only the end result of this differential upbringing might conclude that the first twin was the child of powerful muscular parents, while the second would appear to be the offspring of physically underendowed progenitors. Yet in reality both have not only the same parents, but an identical assortment of genes. In this case it is the difference in environmental influence alone that resulted in a weakling in one case and an athlete in the other.

It happens, of course, that in the case of muscle power the effect of the environment (in this case exercise) is unmistakably evident, and one is led directly to the conclusion that both individuals must have been born with a genetic endowment for the same maximum potential in muscle power, and that whether or not they realized their potential depended on the circumstances of their lives, that is, on environmental factors. The same relationship between heredity and environment holds good for such physical features as height or weight, and even for such functional abilities as athletic achievement, manual dexterity, and the like.

When it comes to mental functioning, it is more difficult to demonstrate that this, too, is the result of a combination of hereditary and environmental factors. Again an imaginary example may help. Let us assume that Einstein had an identical twin. This second Einstein, of course, had the very same genetic equipment that enabled Albert Einstein to manifest his genius. But as soon as Albert's twin was born he was spirited away from the home of his German-Jewish middle-class intellectual parents and deposited in the Australian bush, where he was brought up as the son of an aborigine family. What would have become of this imaginary Einstein twin? Perhaps a talented hunter, a leader of the tribe, an improver of hunting weapons and techniques? One thing is certain: he would never have become a second Einstein, simply because he did not have the environmental influences to mold and stimulate him as they did Albert. Incidentally, studies on identical twins brought up separately are available and contain valuable information on the role of heredity *versus* environment.[6] The conclusion to which this example leads us is that observable and measurable mental functioning (just like physical functioning) depends on two sets of factors, one genetic and one environmental. As Eliot D. Chapple, following Sewall Wright, has pointed out,

the genes set the limit for the behavioral capabilities or potentialities of the organism. Whatever the effects of experience (of learning taken in the broadest sense), they must all necessarily occur within those limits which the genetic constitution provides. Environment, therefore, achieves its influences by modifying the expression of particular genes or their combinations in the phenotype.[7]

While these observations illuminate the mechanics of the bases of mental functioning, they are not particularly helpful in an attempt to sort out its genetic and environmental components. For the fact remains that each of these two sets of components comprises almost infinite possibilities of variation. When faced with the end result of their combined effect—the functioning individual intelligence—it is impossible to attribute any of its features decisively to one of the two sets of factors. In intelligence tests it has long been recognized that the scores are "due to the interaction of hereditary and environmental factors which cannot be disentangled," [8] and that the two factors "continuously interact in the most intricate manner." [9]

In order to be meaningful, intelligence tests must hold the environment as constant as possible. To illustrate what is meant by this, let us go back for a moment to the Einsteins. If, instead of Einstein's hypothetical twin being spirited away into the Australian bush, the child of an Australian aborigine couple had been placed in the Einstein household and brought up with Albert in identical circumstances, any disparities indicated by an intelligence test administered to the two boys would have had to be attributed to genetic differences alone. In imagining such a situation, one would have to postulate a fully identical environment for the two boys, to the exclusion even of such factors as the subliminal differential reactions of the Einstein parents to the different skin colors, facial features, and so on, of their two "sons." Factors such as these would make the execution of such an experiment virtually impossible.

Nevertheless, intelligence tests administered in a school with a socio-culturally homogeneous or closely similar student body can serve as approximative indicators of differences in genetic mental endowment among pupils. In other words, intelligence tests are valid methods of establishing the relative standing of an individual's intelligence among peers of identical or closely similar socio-cultural background. They become less and less valid as the cultural differences between the tested individuals increase.

But when it comes to establishing differences in intelligence, not between individuals from different cultural backgrounds but between human groups (i.e., "races"), each with its own culture, the task again defeats us, because so far it has not proved possible to design a test for "native," or innate, hereditary intelligence alone. All existing intelligence tests measure hereditary intelligence as realized through the influences of the environment. Different cultural environments realize or develop the hereditary intelligence potential in different ways and to different degrees—this is the factor that so far has made intercultural intelligence testing impossible.

JEWISH GENERAL INTELLIGENCE

Let us examine the nineteenth- and twentieth-century beliefs and findings on Jewish intelligence. Chauvinistically inclined Jews believe in, and often speak of, the mental superiority of the Jews as a group compared to any other human group. In support of their conviction, they point to the great concentration of Jews in academic, intellectual, artistic, and literary fields, and triumphantly clinch their argument by referring to the number of Jewish Nobel Prize winners which, in fact, is proportionately much higher than that of any other people (we shall present a factual analysis of this argument below). This Jewish pride in the superior Jewish intelligence has its distorted mirror image in the anti-Semitic view, which considers the Jews a menace to the world precisely because of the various superior capabilities it attributes to them, all couched, of course, in negative terms, such as shrewdness, business acumen, quick adaptability, ruthlessness, exploitativeness, and "astuteness which makes him master of the honest Aryan." In reading certain types of anti-Jewish literature one almost gets the impression that the anti-Semitic attitude to the Jew was an ambivalent one: he was hated because one could not help admiring, or at any rate envying, his superior intelligence.[10]

In some places, of course, the otherness of Jewish immigrants from remote countries was in itself sufficient to create the impression of inferiority. This was especially true in Victorian England during the heyday of rampant cultural evolutionism, which judged non-British cultures inferior to British to the degree to which they differed from it. Thus in 1884 Sir Francis Galton, to whose work we shall have occasion to refer below, wrote to the distinguished Swiss botanist Alphonse de Candolle: "It strikes me that the Jews are specialized for a parasitical existence upon other nations, and that there is need of evidence that they are capable of fulfilling the varied duties of a civilized nation by themselves." Forty years later, Galton's disciple and biographer, Karl Pearson, repeated, even more emphatically, the allegation that the Jewish immigrants into Britain "will develop into a parasitic race," and concluded that "taken *on the average,* and regarding both sexes, this alien Jewish population is somewhat inferior physically and mentally to the native population." [11]

As against such anti-Semitically motivated views one can find numerous Gentile scholars who gave unstinting recognition to Jewish intellectual aptitudes. To quote just one, Gustave Lagneau, a leader of the Parisian Anthropological Society and Academy of Medicine, stated in 1891:

> I recognize the superiority of the Jews from the point of view of certain demographic movements; likewise I recognize the great intellectual aptitudes of the Jews. But as against this, I am obliged to state the relative frequency among them of diabetes, nervous afflictions, and in particular mental illness.[12]

More objective appraisals of Jewish intelligence, in the form of intelligence tests administered to Jews and non-Jews, began to be published in the years preceding World War I.[13] In time, the tests became more and more refined and increasing attention was paid to the comparability of the subjects, that is, to keeping the background circumstances of the two groups tested as similar as possible. After World War I several dozens of such studies were carried out, most of them in the United States, others in England.

The question of ethnic background *versus* environment was raised as early as 1912 by J. and R. Weintraub, who administered the Binet-Simon tests to three groups of seventy-five children each in New York: 1. Mostly

146

native-born American children, some Jewish, all from wealthy families of the higher social strata (in the Horace Mann School); 2. Mostly native-born American children whose fathers were small businessmen and wage earners (in the Speyer School); and 3. Jewish, mostly Russian Jewish, children who had been inmates from four to ten years at the Hebrew Sheltering Orphan Asylum. In all cases the children of the Speyer School scored lowest in the test results, while the Horace Mann and the asylum children were always close together, with the latter ahead in many instances, particularly in language use, ability to reason, reading, sentence building, definitions, and so on.[14]

Following World War I a growing number of intelligence studies, mostly, it is true, on a small scale, were carried out in England and the United States comparing Jewish and non-Jewish children and students. In one larger British study, 1,894 children aged eight to fourteen, one-half of whom were Jewish, were given the Northumberland Standardized Tests. The results showed that the Jewish children were superior in intelligence, English, and arithmetic to non-Jewish children, whether the groups compared belonged to the upper, middle, or lower social level. The lower the social level, the greater was the difference evinced by the test scores. In fact, the Jewish children of the poorest socio-economic background were found to be practically equal to the general non-Jewish average. The difference between Jewish and non-Jewish boys was 11.8 in the I.Q., 12.1 in the arithmetic quotient, and 14.8 in the English quotient. Between the Jewish and non-Jewish girls, the three corresponding quotient differences were 9.2 in I.Q., 10.6 in arithmetic, and 11.1 in English. When the children were divided into four groups, it was found that in the top group ("very able and capable") there was about three times as high a percentage of Jewish as non-Jewish children, while in the lowest group ("dull and very dull") the percentage of Jewish children was consistently less than that of non-Jewish children.[15] In another study, Christian and Jewish children in London's East End were tested with similar results.[16] When English-speaking Irish Christian children were compared with Jewish children who had a language handicap, coming from non-English-speaking homes, the Jews still scored as high as the Irish.[17] Other studies carried out in England tend to confirm these findings.[18]

In the United States in 1926, V. T. Graham compared native American, Jewish, and Italian children in the Habit Clinic of the Massachusetts Division of Mental Hygiene and found that in both verbal and non-verbal tests the Jews scored higher than the Americans, while the Italians made a poor showing. The relationship proved to be the same even when all language factors were ruled out.[19] A comparison in 1929 between 296 Jewish and non-Jewish college students, who were given the Thorndike Intelligence Examination, the George Washington Social Intelligence Test, and the Laird

Personal Inventory B2, and also measured by college grades, showed that, when classified as to "ancestry" (i.e., English, Italian, etc.), Jewish college students were found to rank higher in college grades than the other groups. They were ahead also in general intelligence, although the difference here was not so great as in college achievement. There were no reliable differences in the Social Intelligence or the Laird Personal Inventory. When classified as to "religion," the Jewish students were again considerably ahead of both the Catholic and the Protestant groups in general intellectual as well as college achievement. They were slightly superior in social intelligence and somewhat less stable emotionally as measured by the Personal Inventory. These last differences, however, are not reliable.[20]

In 1936, M. Brill presented a critical analysis of studies comparing Jewish and non-Jewish general intelligence. He concluded that the Jewish children were found to be superior or at least equal in intelligence to non-Jewish children of similar socio-economic status and, in most cases, superior to the children of other foreign-born racial or national groups. Among the Jewish children, differences were found between groups coming from different countries in Europe. The Jewish college students were found to be definitely superior to the non-Jewish college students. The distributions of the general intelligence of Jewish children were found, as a rule, to be more homogeneous than those of non-Jews. The Jewish children compared favorably with non-Jewish, native white American children in frequency of high and low scores. As to the difference between Jewish and non-Jewish children in nonverbal intelligence, there were not sufficient data to warrant conclusions.[21]

Additional studies, carried out after the above survey was published, tend in general to confirm its conclusions. Only a very few studies do not show unequivocally the superiority of Jewish subjects when compared with non-Jewish subjects. One of them is a 1941 study of more than 300 Jewish and Gentile college students, which found only one significant difference between the two: the mean score of the Gentile men was reliably lower than that of the Gentile girls, Jewish men, and Jewish girls.[22]

Another study which did not find the Jewish subjects consistently superior was published in 1942. Catholic, Protestant, and Jewish new students at Washington Square College were compared. The 1935, 1936, and 1937 forms of the American Council of Psychological Examination were used. On the 1935 form, the Protestant scores averaged highest, with the Catholic means generally lowest. On two of the five test parts the Jewish subjects scored significantly above the combined Christian group. The elimination of all foreign-born, of those aged twenty-two years and three months or more, and of transfer students, decreased these differences somewhat. On the 1936 and 1937 forms, the results were mixed. That is, these results failed to confirm previous findings that Jewish students were superior to non-Jewish on intelligence tests.[23]

148

Similar results were found in a 1944 test; 323 second-generation Scandinavian children and 324 second-generation Jewish children in the kindergartens of Minneapolis public schools were given the 1916 revision of the Stanford-Binet Scale. Rigorous control of sex, age, and socio-economic status was exercised. A marked relationship was found between intelligence and socio-economic level, but no differences between the two cultural groups with other variables controlled. Differences appeared, however, on specific tests: Jewish children were superior on tests requiring distinguishing left from right, comprehension, naming coins, counting pennies, giving the date, and repeating four digits backwards. Scandinavian children were superior in drawing a square, copying a diamond, solving a test of patience, and solving the ball and field test.[24]

Apart from these three studies (and, perhaps, a few others which may have escaped our attention), the overwhelming majority of the studies in question agree in their finding that Jewish groups, when compared with similar non-Jewish groups, score higher on tests measuring general intelligence, and especially verbal intelligence. Note, however, that these results were all based on examination of Ashkenazi Jews only, so that they say nothing about the relative intelligence of Oriental or Sephardi Jewish populations. In fact, low intellectual performance of Oriental Jews has been reported in several studies, thereby confirming the diversity of Jewish populations (see below).

The explanation for the superior performance of Western Jews on intelligence tests must be sought both in historical factors which have operated on Jews for the last two thousand years and in present-day influences. But before examining these possible factors in detail, we must emphasize the difference between *genetic* and *environmental* effects on a population.

We have seen that populations are different genetically if they differ in gene frequencies. Any circumstance in the environment which results in changes in gene frequencies in subsequent generations is said to have a *genetic* effect. For example, a cold climate is believed to favor the development of a compact body and short extremities. Let us hypothesize a human population of diverse body proportions living in a geologic era of decreasing temperatures. The members of the population who are compactly built will fare the best in the cold weather and will be more likely to reproduce. Over many generations the frequency of a compact body build in the population will increase. If, after fifty generations, some members of the cold-adapted population are moved to a warmer climate, most of their children will still have a compact body build. Hence the cold climate has effected a genetic change in the population, consisting of an increase in the frequency of compact body build, which is passed on to succeeding generations even if the selection pressure is removed.

In contrast, let us recall Pavlov's famous experiment in which he cut off

149

the tails of mice to see if this change would be inherited. He found that the young of the tailless mice had normal-sized tails, and this continued to be true even after fifty generations of tail cutting. In order to continue producing tailless mice, Pavlov had to continue cutting off the tails *of each generation.* Pavlov's knife constituted a form of environmental "selection pressure" which was only temporary, since it did not produce any inherited changes in the population. This is what we refer to as an *environmental* effect.

It is easy to confuse genetic and environmental effects, since in both cases some factor in the environment results in a change in the population when compared to a similar population not influenced by this factor. The key difference between the two effects is that, in the former case, the resultant population differs genetically from its ancestors, whereas the latter produces only a temporary change which is reversible in the next generation if the causative factor in the environment is removed. A selective force with a purely environmental effect must be present continuously, generation after generation, if its effect is to continue.

Jewish history for the last two thousand years contains several elements which might explain the superior performance of twentieth-century Jews on I.Q. tests. It is important to differentiate those elements which had a genetic effect from those having only a temporary environmental effect. If actual genetic changes were involved, then the present-day descendants of the Jewish populations affected might be superior to their ancestors of two thousand years ago in terms of the inherited component of intelligence. On the other hand, if factors having a purely environmental effect were involved, then those same factors must still be acting on present-day Jews in order to influence their intellectual performance.

At least two historical processes have been suggested which, if in fact they occurred, would have resulted in increased "native intelligence" in Jews of the twentieth century as compared with their ancestors. One is their long history of persecution and oppression, which is too well documented and known to require recapitulation here. Living as they did as a persecuted, oppressed, or in the best of circumstances tolerated but disliked minority, in the midst of many different dominant majority populations, the Jews had to exercise their functioning intelligence to the utmost in order to survive, let alone to prosper. Just as in the Darwinian framework of "nature red in tooth and claw" only the strongest beasts of prey, the fastest gazelles, the longest-necked giraffes, the best camouflaged chameleons could survive, so in the inimical or unfriendly Christian and Muslim environments, only those Jews could survive who were equipped with sufficient intelligence to cope with the exigencies of their Diaspora life. This may have resulted in a societal selection which was no less cruel than the Darwinian natural selection.

Hypothetically, one can assume that what happened was that, as a result of this selective process, in the course of many generations the percentage of Jews who were more intelligent increased over the number of those Jews who were less intelligent. As Julius B. Maller put it in 1931, after surveying a number of studies: "It is reasonable to assume . . . that the trials and ordeals of the Jews throughout the centuries placing a premium on mental acumen in the struggle for survival operated as selective factors in raising the average intelligence of the Jews as a group." [25] There is of course no way of comparing the intelligence of modern Jews with that of Jews, say, at the time of the Roman exile, so that this sequence of events remains pure speculation.

A second possible cause of increased "native intelligence" among Jews through the centuries relates to their classical tradition, which valued learning above all other accomplishments. Throughout the Middle Ages and down to the nineteenth century, in all parts of the Diaspora Jews considered Talmudic scholarship the greatest of achievements. The appreciation of scholarship was inculcated into the children to such an extent that, generally speaking, all the boys who had the mental capacity endeavored to achieve— and many actually attained—scholarly status. Those who distinguished themselves among the many budding scholars obtained coveted positions as rabbis of Jewish communities, or as heads of Yeshivot (Talmudic academies), of which there was a surprisingly large number all over Europe. Scholarship thus meant status and prestige. But it also meant financially carefree living, because promising young rabbinical scholars were chosen by wealthy Jews to be their sons-in-law. Since the girls, although not given scholarly education, were also impressed from an early age with the surpassing value of Talmudic scholarship, a rich man's daughter felt it was a great distinction if her father married her off to a young scholar. A result of this system was that an outstanding young Talmudist had a better chance to marry early, to father more children, and to save more of them from the ravages of infant mortality than did a youth who showed no scholarly promise. Some modern sociologists and historians feel that this marriage preference, continued as it was throughout the centuries, must have contributed to a gradual increase in the proportion of intelligent individuals within the Jewish communities, and especially in the larger urban centers. [26] It is not, of course, possible to determine whether in fact this "sexual selection" resulted in a substantial increase in "native intelligence" among Jews.

Whether or not such historical factors resulted in an increased level of the genetic component of intelligence in Jews is a moot point. But there is no need to resort to them in order to explain the Jews' high intellectual performance; several factors with a purely environmental effect have also operated on the Jews historically and continue to do so today.

One important environmental factor which affects the intelligence is urban *versus* rural living. The difference between the stimulus effect of the two environments has been clearly demonstrated in studies which showed that among black schoolchildren of Southern rural origin who had lived for varying lengths of time in New York or other big cities in the North of the United States, there was a close relationship between the I.Q. test scores and the length of residence in the city: those who had lived in the city the longest obtained, on the average, the best scores; those who had arrived only recently from the South had the poorest scores. Studies of rural whites who had migrated to American cities, and of rural migrants in German cities, have shown similar results.[27] There is thus basis for assuming that these findings are of general validity and that life in an urban environment generally stimulates intelligence more than life in a rural setting. The process of rural-urban migration can, in itself, result in a considerable difference in the I.Q. scores between two parts of a genetically identical group, and this can be effected within a single generation. That such a change is not genetic will be disputed by no one; if a family moves back to the country, the I.Q. scores of its grandchildren are likely to be depressed and to be typical of rural rather than city dwellers.

The question of rural-urban population distribution bears directly and importantly on Jewish intelligence. The Jews have always evinced a marked preference for urban rather than rural living, whereas this was not the case with the Gentiles until quite recent times. In very general terms, it can be said that "whereas the populations of all countries prior to 1800 were overwhelmingly rural, the Jewish Diasporas were, ever since ancient times, overwhelmingly urban." [28] From the nineteenth century on, a tendency for urban concentration developed among the non-Jews, and, simultaneously, became more pronounced among the Jews.

There are, of course, no I.Q. tests from historical times which could substantiate the hypothesis that the highly urbanized Jews were more intelligent than the Gentiles whose majority lived in rural environments. But a reading of Jewish history renders such an assumption likely.[29]

By the early twentieth century, 91–93 per cent of all the Jews of Central Russia, Latvia, Bohemia, and Asian Russia lived in cities and towns; 80–87 per cent in Czechoslovakia, Carpatho-Ruthenia, Switzerland, and the whole of Soviet Russia; and 75–77 per cent in the Ukraine and Poland. The same trend resulted in the concentration of the Jews in the big cities of Egypt (90.7% in 1917), Morocco (73% in 1947), Algeria and Tunisia (56 to 65% in 1926–27).[30] One result of this situation was that the urban Jews themselves made a sharp distinction between their own kind and their country cousins; the latter were often regarded as ignorant and uncouth, and, because of their ignorance, unreliable in matters of religion and family purity. In the East European and, generally, Ashkenazi environment, the urban Jew prided himself on being a *"Talmid hokhem,"* that is, a scholar, which was possible only for somebody who had a *"Yiddisher kop"* or "Jewish head." The latter expression, incidentally, was the nearest equivalent in traditional Yiddish of our modern term "intelligence." Those uneducated in Jewish law and lore, most of whom were poor Jews who eked out a living in the villages, were contemptuously called *"amhoretz"* (from the Hebrew ʿ*am haʾaretz,* "ignoramus"), the greatest opprobrium applied to whom was "*Goyisher kop,*" or "Gentile head." Similarly, in Yemen, the Jews of the capital city of Ṣanʿa looked down upon those of their brethren who lived in the villages, and considered them not only ignoramuses, but descendants of Arab proselytes.

The environment can also, of course, influence the development of intelligence in a negative direction. Studies carried out among American black children, white canal-boat children in England, and American white children in the mountains of Kentucky and Virginia show that at an early age their I.Q. approximated average levels, but as they grew older it declined. These studies suggest that "an inferior environment exerts a cumulative negative influence [on the individual] as the years go by." [31]

From pre-World War II Poland comes a study which shows that environmental deprivation affects the Jews in the same way as it does blacks. The study was carried out in an anti-Semitic racist atmosphere and its conclusions must therefore be read with utmost caution. More than 10,000 "Aryan" and Jewish pupils were tested in several Polish towns. A high positive correlation was found between the intelligence level of the pupils in general and the size of the town. As to differences between the intelligence of the "Aryan" Polish and the Polish Jewish pupils, it was found that in the lower grades the Jewish pupils surpassed or equalled the Polish pupils, but in the higher grades the Polish pupils surpassed the Jewish ones in observation, perception, and imagination. In verbal memory the Jewish pupils were superior or equal to the Poles. The shadow of Hitler falls heavily across the pages of this study: the author concludes that the Jewish pupils have a deteriorating effect upon the Aryan pupils, and that the inferiority of the Jewish youth is due, not to cultural or environmental differences, but to an inherent difference in "psychophysical type" or psychic make-up. [32]

Assuming that the author's summary of the test scores is reliable, all one can legitimately conclude from them is that in the oppressively anti-Semitic atmosphere of the Polish small-town secondary schools much of the native mental endowment of the Jewish children became increasingly thwarted, as manifested in their deteriorating scores in the higher grades.

Probably the most important single factor responsible for the present-day intellectual achievement of Jews, and one which has a purely environmental effect, is the age-old Jewish tradition of learning. Jewish parents of almost any class or occupational level upheld, and still uphold, the ideal of study and intellectual achievement. This is for them both a matter of emotional commitment and a decision reached by logical deduction. Hence the average

Jewish parents did, and still do, everything they can to stimulate and advance the intellectual development of their child. They surround him from birth with an enriched environment, including nowadays the latest fads in educational toys and games, talk to him a lot, fondle him, and implant in his mind at a very early age the idea that he must excel in his studies, and ultimately become a rabbi, a doctor, a lawyer, a scientist, or some other type of intellectual giant. Needless to say, they will also do everything possible to send him to the best schools and to create in the home the best of circumstances conducive to doing all homework in the most satisfactory manner. In addition to all this, Jewish parents simply assume that their child will do well in school, which communicates itself to the child and thus becomes a self-fulfilling expectation. Moreover, among middle-class urban Jews today the interest of many children is being channeled into specific areas of learning at an exceedingly young age. Most Jewish homes have books and magazines around, which is yet another feature conducive to awakening the interest in reading in children long before they enter school. Statistical information is not available, but the clear impression is that childhood environments of this type are found more frequently in Jewish than in non-Jewish families. Thus, even if at birth the I.Q. of the Jewish child differs but little or not at all from that of the average non-Jewish child, as the years go by it reaches a higher level because the Jewish child grows up in an environment which is superior from the point of view of intelligence development.

Boris M. Levinson, who by 1957 had administered numerous intelligence tests to a great variety of groups of all ages, explained the higher I.Q. consistently found among Jewish children as compared with non-Jewish children in terms of socio-economic background, superior verbal ability of Jewish children because of cultural pressures, the book-centered culture of the Jewish home, and the motivation toward intellectual achievement imparted to Jewish children by the parents.[33]

Again, in a study of the effects of ethnic origin on giftedness, it is pointed out that the higher-than-expected giftedness among Jewish students found by several workers is linked to the high valuation of learning within traditional Jewish culture which, unlike other cultures, holds gifted individuals in high esteem.[34]

The importance of motivation toward intellectual achievement is confirmed by data which show that when such motivation is missing in the home and the larger socio-cultural environment, the intelligence level of the Jewish children (and adults) remains low. Such a situation is (or was) found among Middle Eastern Jews, both in their home countries and after their immigration to Israel.

Studies carried out in recent decades among European and Middle Eastern Jewish children in Israel indicate that differences in intelligence found between the two groups are due to environmental factors and not to genetic predisposition. In 1953, Dr. Gina Ortar reported the results of various intelligence tests administered in Israel to three groups of children aged six to sixteen: one Ashkenazi (i.e., European Jewish) group; one local Oriental Jewish (children of old immigrants in Israel) group; and a group of children of Oriental Jewish new immigrants. When members of each group whose general level of intelligence was identical were compared, the Ashkenazi children were found superior in command of language; the Oriental Jewish children were found superior in their command of numbers. No differences were found among the three groups in ability to make abstractions. However, it was found that social and cultural differences made for differences in mental level: among the Ashkenazim, who were of a higher socio-cultural background, there was a greater number of talented children than among the Oriental Jews. On the other hand, the qualitative differences were found to decrease as a result of education in Israeli schools: while abstract thinking ability was weaker in the new immigrant Oriental Jewish children, the children of Oriental Jewish oldtimers in Israel equalled in this respect the Ashkenazi children.[35]

These findings confirm that intelligence—including ways of thinking, command of language or of numbers, extent of talent, mental level, and abstract thinking are all influenced by the socio-cultural background.

The poor showing in intelligence tests and motor achievement of Yemenite Jewish children, who did not complete elementary school, was similarly explained as being due to environmental circumstances and not to "racial"-biological factors.[36]

Similar conclusions were reached by Reuben Feuerstein and M. Richelle, who compared Moroccan Jewish children from the *mellah*—the old Jewish quarter of Casablanca—with Swiss children. In various aspects of mental functioning, investigated by the authors and others whose work they quote, it was found that the ability of the North African children, who grew up in the deprived environment of the *mellah,* was in almost every case inferior to that of the Swiss children who served as a control group. The authors attribute the differences overwhelmingly to differences in the cultural environment in general, and the educational environment in particular. They found that, when the schools improve, performance also improves. They emphasize that the apparent backwardness in mental functioning which was found among the Moroccan Jewish children has no hereditary basis but is due only to early educational environmental influences.[37]

To sum up, on the basis of the historical and cultural influences on the Jews which have been discussed in this section, we can conclude first, that it is possible that long-term persecution combined with "sexual selection" of the brightest young scholars may have increased somewhat the level of the genetic component of intelligence in *some* Jewish populations. Secondly, that it is not necessary to resort to genetic explanations, as there are several factors with purely environmental effects as, for example, the emphasis on learning and the tendency toward urban living, which have operated historically, and continue to do so, to maximize the intellectual performance of Jews.

JEWS AND GENIUS

When speaking of group intelligence, there is an unavoidable temptation to discuss, along with the I.Q. averages, the upper limits of ability. Klineberg states that, "it has been suggested that the contributions of [a given human] group will depend not so much upon the ability of the majority, as upon its outstanding or exceptional individuals, those who are at the upper end of the distribution scale. Ethnic groups have therefore been compared in terms of the frequency of occurrence of men of 'genius.' " As we shall recall, one of those making such a suggestion was Morant. Klineberg himself, after remarking that to make such a comparison "is obviously a difficult and complicated task," criticizes this approach by pointing out that "there is no simple criterion by which we can recognize the man of genius," and that "the creations of genius build upon the achievements of an earlier day." A Beethoven could appear only within the context of European musical tradition, and Einstein had to be familiar with the achievements of modern physics. Therefore, the greatest hereditary genius growing up in a country in which these traditions and achievements are unknown cannot become a Beethoven or an Einstein. Klineberg also argues that "the upper limits of ability, as measured by intelligence tests, are reached by members of many different ethnic groups," and cites the case of a nine-year-old American Negro girl who scored 200 on an I.Q. test, a "very remarkable performance." [38]

Despite these doubts, students of intelligence long before Morant attempted to reach an estimate of group genius by a combination of qualitative and quantitative data. One of these was Sir Francis Galton, to whose anti-Semitism reference was made above. Applying statistical methods to the study of mental ability, Galton extracted a list of geniuses and men of eminence from British biographical dictionaries, and calculated the percentages represented by these men per million Englishmen. The results were incorporated in his well-known *Hereditary Genius,* published in 1869. Several years later, a Jewish statistician who was also a folklorist and historian of note, Joseph Jacobs (1854–1916), applied Galton's method to a study of Jewish genius and talent, and found that in Western Europe, where the Jews enjoyed the freedom of study and professional advancement, they produced percentage-wise more geniuses, men of eminence, and men of talent than the British. In Russia, on the other hand, where oppression prevented the

Jews from secular achievement, they did not contribute to the galaxy of Jewish ability. Jacobs also calculated that "the average Jew has 4 per cent more ability than the average Englishman." [39]

We cannot suppress serious reservations as to the reliability of the "Eminent Victorians" method used by Jacobs in showing differences between the average mental ability of Englishmen and Jews down to a 4 per cent accuracy. Nevertheless, the general approach developed by Galton should not be discarded offhand. We should rather consider whether an objective yardstick can be found for what is considered "genius"; whether each of the groups studied is a carrier of Western culture and is comparable in several other respects, and whether the differences found are statistically significant (i.e., of a much higher order of magnitude than the rather dubious 4 per cent). If the answer to all these questions is in the affirmative, we are justified in concluding that the differential results indicate something about differences in the mental functioning of the groups studied. What precisely they indicate should have become clear from what was said above about the hereditary and environmental components of intelligence. To recapitulate the conclusions as briefly as possible, a greater frequency of eminent minds in an ethnic group can be taken to indicate greater selective pressures—in the direction of a greater incidence of intelligence—to which the group was exposed in its past.

In the case of the Jews, such pressures in an extreme form were part of their history for the last two thousand years. The nature and intensity of the pressures may have differed from country to country and from period to period, but they were present in almost every place and age. The typical Jewish response to them consisted of attempts to overcome obstacles by using the head rather than the muscles, and of efforts to make ends meet by brain rather than brawn. In most countries, especially Christian Europe down to the onset of the nineteenth century, state and Church laws, city ordinances, and guilds' statutes excluded the Jews from most of those occupations which required manual labor or manual dexterity, such as agriculture and handicrafts. This meant that an inordinately high percentage of the Jewish breadwinners were forced into commerce and the money business in which, more than in other occupations, good judgment, shrewdness, and the quick grasp of connections and consequences—in a word, keen intelligence—made all the difference, not only between success and failure, but between surviving and perishing. Talmudic learning, too, became the key to livelihood for many (e.g., as rabbis or teachers), and thus supplied additional proof, if any was needed, that mental ability was a Jew's most valuable possession. As the Yiddish proverb put it: "Learning is the best merchandise."

In these circumstances it was inevitable that, as soon as Enlightenment and emancipation made it possible for them (from the nineteenth century on), Jews should flock into the academic professions, as well as into all fields of literary and artistic endeavor, in proportions many times higher than their percentage in the general, or even in the urban, population in every Western country. This development, in turn, led to the emergence of a large number of Jews who became outstanding enough in their chosen specialization to merit inclusion in the various *Who's Who* type of biographical publications in Europe and America (see below). This, very briefly and sketchily, is the story behind the findings made by Dr. Jacobs only one or two generations after the Jewish emancipation.

When Jacobs made his calculations, he had to select his eminent Jews from national and other biographies, which made it almost impossible to prevent subjective judgment from influencing his choice. Today, in the Nobel Prize, we have a presumably objective measure of international eminence in various fields of science and literature (although, regrettably, not in the other arts). By the time the first Nobel Prizes were awarded (1901), the emancipation of the Jews was an accomplished fact in all the countries of Europe—in America, the Jews did not have to be emancipated—although in East Europe the emancipatory laws were still far from having been carried out in practice. But it took several more years even in Western Europe before the Jews established themselves sufficiently in the secular sciences and in European literatures to reach Nobel Prize stature.

The first Nobel Prize to a Jew was awarded in 1905. By 1930, 20 of the total 153 prizes awarded to individuals, or 13 per cent, had gone to Jews (including 5 half-Jews and 4 who had left Judaism). From 1931 to 1972, no less than 18 per cent of the Nobel Prize winners were Jews. All in all, of the 406 prizes awarded to individuals from 1901 to 1972, 65 went to Jews, or 16 per cent of the total. These figures show two things: one, that intellectual performance of Nobel Prize caliber was found with greater frequency among Jews than among non-Jews; and two, that the frequency differential tended to increase after 1930. This differential was even more pronounced after World War II: in the thirty years from 1943 to 1972 Jews won forty-three Nobel Prizes, or more than twice as many as the twenty they had won in the thirty years from 1901 to 1930.

Back in 1886 Jacobs found that the Jews tended to gravitate toward a few specific fields. In philology and metaphysics there were proportionately nine times as many outstanding Jews as non-Jewish Europeans; in music, six times; in high finance, three and a half times; in medicine and the acting profession, 1.6 times.[40] Almost a century later, the Nobel Prize data throw additional light on this subject too. The general principle followed by the Nobel Prize committee is to award one prize annually in each of the same six fields. However, if the committee finds that in any of the fields no individual has made a contribution outstanding enough to deserve the prize, they can withhold it that year. On the other hand, if they find that two or more individuals have made outstanding contributions in one field, they can divide the prize among them. Over the years these variations have resulted in considerable differences in the number of prizes awarded in each of the six fields. Thus the number of prizes awarded in a field can be interpreted as an indication of the relative importance of that field. After all, it stands to reason that the number of people making outstanding contributions in a field is correlated to the total number of people working in that field, which in turn reflects the relative importance of that field in the general cultural configuration of the Western world. An interesting fact emerges: the greater the general Western preoccupation with a field, the greater the Jewish participation in it. Leaving out of consideration the field of economics, in which the first prize was awarded only in 1969, we find that the greatest number of prizes was awarded in Physiology and Medicine, and that in this field the percentage of Jews among the winners was the highest; next followed, in decreasing order of both total number of prizes and Jewish percentages, Physics, Chemistry, Literature, and Peace (see table).

Number and Percentage of Jews Among Nobel
Prize Winners, 1901–85

FIELD	TOTAL NUMBER	NUMBER OF JEWS	PERCENTAGE OF JEWS
Economics (1969–85)	23	6	26.1
Physiology and Medicine	139	35	35.2
Physics	124	25	20.2
Chemistry	102	13	12.7
Literature	82	9	11.0
Peace	70	6	8.6
Total	540	91	16.8

From these data one can conclude that those fields to which the non-Jewish environment devotes most of its attention exert the greatest attraction on the Jews, and vice versa; or that, "the greater the stimulus provided by the cultural atmosphere and attainments of the gentile environment in a given field, the higher the level of Jewish performance in that field." [41]

A similar conclusion is indicated by another correlation: the highest percentage of Jewish Nobel Prize winners is found in those countries in which the total number of prize winners is the greatest. [42]

These data seem to militate against the assumption made by earlier students of Jewish intelligence that the Jews have a special mental proclivity for excelling in certain selected fields (see below). [43] Instead, we are led to the conclusion that while there is undoubtedly a general Jewish inclination to intellectual activity, the special direction this activity takes depends on the intellectual preferences of the non-Jewish environment in which the Jews live.

It will be fascinating to watch the developments in Israel, where Jewish intellectual activity is not directed or influenced by a surrounding non-Jewish majority but will follow directions of its own choosing.

The proportion of Jews in the 1938 edition of the *Who's Who in America*—the only edition subjected so far to a statistical analysis comparing the number of Jews and non-Jews listed—presents an apparent contrast to the remarkable Jewish record in Nobel Prize awards. A count carried out by M. Smith and R. B. Moton found that 1 in 4,212 Jews in the United States was considered prominent enough to have his biography included, as against 1 in 4,140 persons in the total population of the country. The authors of the study point out that the Jews are largely urban and that persons born or living in cities have more chance of attaining eminence than those residing in rural communities. They consequently conclude that the Jewish contribution of prominent Americans is not as high as that of the population in general. In explanation they refer to discrimination, interest, opportunity, and tradition.[44] It seems to us that one more factor should be taken into consideration: the newness of the Jewish community in the United States. In 1938, only fourteen years after the introduction of restrictive immigration laws, most of the American Jews were first-generation immigrants (the number of Jews in the U.S. increased from 938,000 in 1897 to 4¼ million in 1927), whose children were still in high school or college, or at the very beginning of their careers.

The Jewish immigrants were for the most part secularly uneducated persons from East Europe, who had to struggle hard to make a living. Yet by 1938 this underprivileged immigrant ethnic group was represented in the *Who's Who* in the same proportion as the general population—quite an extraordinary feat. One wishes that a similar study would be carried out on the basis of the latest edition of the *Who's Who in America*: we can anticipate that it would show a relatively much higher proportion of Jews.[45]

SPECIAL TALENTS

In discussing the Jewish record of Nobel Prize winners, we briefly mentioned the fields in which Jews won the highest, next highest, and so on, percentages of Nobel Prizes. We then moved from the question of general intelligence to that of special talents. Probing now deeper into this subject let us, first of all, ask: Which are the fields of mental activity or ability in which the Jews manifest special talents?

In the nineteenth century it was fashionable to answer this question by making sweeping generalizations. In many cases these took the form of juxtaposing the abilities or historical achievements of the so-called Aryan peoples with those of the "Semites" in general or the Jews in particular. At that stage of essaying psychological portraits of the major races into which mankind was believed to be divided, it was taken for granted that the features discerned in, or allegedly characterizing, the human "races" were constants, manifesting themselves from the earliest periods of their history down to the present. Thus, talking of the Jews, conclusions derived from biblical passages were lumped indiscriminately together with observations made by nineteenth-century authors in contemporary Germany or France, without giving a thought to the possible changes that may have resulted from three thousand years of historical vicissitudes.

Reminiscent of the views of the sixteenth-century Spanish physician and author Juan Huarte, of whom more will be said below,[46] several nineteenth-century students of Aryan *versus* Semitic, or Christian European *versus* Jewish national characters were inclined to seek their origins in the natural environment. In particular, the great religious achievements of the Hebrews and Jews were attributed to the desert: monotheism, the great innovation of the biblical Hebrews in the field of religion, was said to be derived directly from the monotony of the desert with its harsh, rigorous, unmerciful conditions.[47]

An attempt to define in more concrete terms the Jewish specific talents (aside from the religious) was made as early as 1889 by Joseph Jacobs. In a pamphlet containing the outline for a book on *The Jewish Race: A Study in National Character*, which he never actually wrote, Jacobs asserts that the Jews "are naturally fitted by original stock for practical life" and are therefore eminent in those professions in which "theory touches practice," for example, law, medicine, mathematics, abstract thought, finance, chess, and philology. They have a special talent also for music, acting, business, literature, and politics. On the other hand, "want of communion with nature lessens their capacity for natural science." As to the genesis of these features, Jacobs explains that they are the result of Jewish "self-consciousness, travel, use of two languages [i.e., bilingualism], town life, education, commerce," and are also due to the Jews' "social isolation and their own traditions and customs." If the specific Jewish "moral, social and intellectual qualities" appear nowadays to be the product of a "hereditary pre-disposition toward certain habits and callings, these can only be regarded as secondary racial acquired hereditary tendencies which cannot be brought forward as proof of racial purity." [48]

While Jacobs was an indefatigable student of Jewish demography, the intuitive nature of his observations cannot be denied. His assertion, for instance, that the Jews have a lesser capacity for natural science was subsequently to be vitiated by the Nobel Prize records in which, as we have seen above, the Jews figure most prominently precisely in Physiology, Medicine, Physics, and Chemistry.

From the 1920's, the presentation of the Jewish (or "Semitic") national character in sweeping generalizations or in impressionistic terms and catch-

161

word capsules, as Jacobs had done, was gradually replaced by quantitative studies, which concentrated on a few selected traits that were investigated with the help of psychological tests.

One of the first to carry out and report on such tests comparing Jews and non-Jews was Dina Wolberg. She chose as her subjects 155 German and Lithuanian Jewish and non-Jewish elementary-school pupils aged 8.5 to 10.5, high-school pupils aged 15 to 18, and college students aged 20 to 27. The tests, designed to measure visual ability, consisted of recognizing figures, recognizing parts of a whole, putting together parts of a pattern, and reconstruction of a shape. In all these tests the non-Jewish subjects scored considerably higher than the Jewish, from which Miss Wolberg concluded that visual ability was more developed among the non-Jews than the Jews. The test results showed no difference between the non-Jewish and Jewish elementary-school pupils; in the high-school age group a difference appeared, and in the college age group it was pronounced. This increasing difference with increasing age led Miss Wolberg to hypothesize that the Jewish children were genetically "less disposed to visuality" than the non-Jewish children, and that, in addition, this lesser disposition was exposed to a smaller amount of environmental stimulus.[49]

While we may have our reservations concerning the explanations put forward by Miss Wolberg, her findings as to the lesser visual ability of the Jews seem to receive some confirmation from a recent study carried out by Gerald S. Lesser and colleagues in the 1960's (see below).

A related area in which Jewish children were found to achieve lower scores than Christian children is manual dexterity. A test carried out in East End elementary schools in London showed that while the Jewish children were intellectually superior to Christian children, in manual dexterity, as shown in handwriting, Jewish and Christian boys were nearly alike, while Christian girls were superior to Jewish girls.[50] Also Julius B. Maller found that Jewish children were less able in tests involving manual dexterity and the manipulation of objects.[51] In the comparison carried out in the early 1940's between 324 Jewish and 323 Scandinavian kindergarten children (all second generation) in Minneapolis public schools, Jewish children did not score high on tests involving manual dexterity.[52] In another comparison, this one between Jewish and Italian aged persons in New York, the Italians had significantly higher performance I.Q.'s than the Jews, while in verbal I.Q. the relationship was reversed.[53] Within the Jewish aged group itself, the verbal I.Q. was higher than the performance I.Q.[54] In a later study, which compared first-grade children from four cultural groups in New York City— Chinese, Jewish, Negro, and Puerto Rican—the Jewish children ranked significantly higher than all other ethnic groups in verbal ability, ranked first in numerical ability, but were outranked by the Chinese children in reasoning and space conceptualization.[55]

162

In a still more recent study of close to 3,000 Jewish, non-Jewish white, Negro, and Oriental twelfth-grade students in the United States, the Jewish students again ranked significantly higher than the others in verbal knowledge, somewhat higher in perceptual speed accuracy (visual-motor coordination under speeded condition), but were outranked by the Orientals in mathematics, by both Orientals and non-Jewish whites in English language (grammar and language usage) and in visual reasoning (spatial ability), and by all the three other groups in memory (short-term recall of verbal symbols).[56]

On the basis of these studies, it seems safe to conclude that Jews in general tend to register lower scores than non-Jews on tests measuring visual ability and manual dexterity, but higher scores than the non-Jews on tests measuring verbal intelligence or verbal knowledge.

An area in which the investigations of Jewish children and adults have resulted in surprisingly contradictory findings is arithmetic. To mention only a few examples, in an early (1927) study of the intelligence of Jewish college freshmen as compared with non-Jews, the Jewish students were found to be less successful in arithmetic and number completion tests than in tests involving language knowledge.[57] Similarly, in a recent test carried out in the United States, Jewish high-school seniors were found to be outranked, although not significantly, by Oriental high-school seniors.[58] As against this, in a 1965 study in New York City Jewish children outranked Chinese children in numerical ability, while the latter outranked them in reasoning and spatial relations.[59]

In view of these contradictory findings on Jewish numerical ability, it is interesting to note that in a comparative test carried out in Israel in 1953 among three groups of children—European Jewish children, Middle Eastern Jewish children born or raised in Israel, and new immigrant Middle Eastern Jewish children—it was found that the Middle Eastern Jewish children were superior to the European Jewish children in their command of numbers (in command of language, the relationship was reversed).[60]

It would thus seem that the almost proverbial Jewish mathematical ability ("Do you think I am an Einstein?") is not borne out by objective quantitative studies.

When it comes to specialized intellectual, artistic, and literary abilities, quantified information as to their prevalence among Jews relative to non-Jews is extremely meager. Even where data are available, they pertain as a rule to Jewish success in performance in the field in question, and not to the frequency and quality of Jewish talent in that field. Successful performance, however, as is only too well known, depends on quite a number of extraneous factors in addition to the presence and extent of talent. This is the great shortcoming of the approach which attempts to estimate Jewish talent on the basis of Nobel Prizes or biographies included in *Who's Who*. All we es-

tablish by such methods is the proportion of Jews among those who succeeded in achieving recognition in their chosen field of endeavor.

This question aside, the only specialized intellectual activity in which the
relative participation of Jews is numerically attested is music. Ever since
their emancipation, the Jews have had the reputation of possessing a special
talent for music. In recent decades, the proportion of Jews in various musical branches is several times as high as one would expect on a statistical
basis. The ratio of Jewish violin virtuosi is from 12 to 25 times expectancy;
and Jewish eminence in American musical life, for example, is beyond
question. In view of these data, it is most remarkable that tests which purport to measure basic capacities required for musical success (namely, the
Seashore musical tests, the Kwalwasser-Dykema tests, and the Drake musical memory tests) showed no significant differences between Jewish and
non-Jewish children aged ten to eleven, and, moreover, the direction of
whatever differences were found was inconsistent. From this it was concluded that the striking musical activity of adult Jews cannot be explained by
the existence of a special Jewish endowment, or talent, for music. What
seems to account for the intensive Jewish representation in music is a set of
extraneous factors, such as historical and social forces. Jews are attracted to
music because for the last two or three generations it has been a field comparatively less closed to them than other professions, and because Jews have
found in music a means of expression for other frustrated desires and ambitions.[61]

Another area in which Jews manifest special talents is acting. While no
quantitative study on Jewish participation in acting is available, an individual-psychological investigation of Jewish acting ability concluded that
an aptitude for mimicry and gestures developed among the Jews because of
the dangerous physical environment in which they had lived in the Middle
East. After their dispersion, these expressive traits became more accentuated
in response to the need to adjust to the inimical social environment in which
they were forced to live. To these factors were added the enforced development of the ability to observe closely human expressions and attitudes, sensitivity to the moods of others, and an ambition for achievement and recognition. All these constituted a syndrome of basic traits required for a
successful career on the stage.[62]

The Jews have also shown special abilities in the art of magic, or pres-
tidigitation,[63] and in recent decades have successfully penetrated a field entirely new for them: that of architecture.[64]

As far as literature is concerned, the lack of quantified studies of Jewish
participation in the major world literatures makes it impossible to present an
objective picture of Jewish talent in this primary area of intellectual activity.
It is, of course, well known that one of the outcomes of the Jewish Enlightenment was that many Jews gravitated toward various literary fields, and not

a few became outstanding in them. A statistical comparison of Jewish and non-Jewish writers in a large modern literature, such as the American, would show without doubt a considerably higher percentage of Jews than might be expected on the basis of their proportion in the population. However, any conclusion from this figure as to a greater Jewish than non-Jewish literary talent would be unwarranted, because (as already indicated above) successful achievement in literature, as in any other field, is the result of several factors in addition to the extent of talent.

How much the Jews have retained of what in antiquity must have been a special religious talent is open to question. To judge from the percentage of religious persons among the Jews, which quantitative studies have shown to be smaller than in the Christian majority in whose midst most Jews live, the inclination toward a religio-centered way of life has diminished since the European and Jewish Enlightenment more among Jews than among Christians. In the Muslim countries, where modernization has only very recently begun to make inroads into religious sentiment, the Jews seem to have retained a religious commitment as strong as that of the Muslims—until their mass emigration to Israel. If there is a Jewish religious awakening in the making in Israel, as some observers incline to believe, its clear manifestations still lie in the future.

In summing up this section we must state that concretely we know very little about special Jewish talents. Quantitative studies about Jewish *versus* non-Jewish participation in such specific fields as the artistic, literary, scientific, and legal are, with a very few exceptions, nonexistent. One cannot therefore enumerate with absolute certainty the areas in which Jews have proved themselves to be more talented than non-Jews.

CHARACTER TRAITS

Character traits belong to an area in which every observation is heavily value-laden. Despite all the efforts of the earlier moral relativists, such as Edward Westermarck, and the later cultural relativists, such as Melville J. Herskovits, even the most scholarly students of man find it almost impossible to divest themselves of an attitude of moral approbation or disapproval when dealing with human character traits. In fact, most of the expressions in any language describing character traits are emotionally charged. Inherent connotations, "good" or "bad," are practically always present whether one describes a person as generous or stingy, brave or cowardly, unselfish or selfish, merciful or cruel, full of love or hate, forgiving or vengeful.

In ninety nine cases out of a hundred, any description of the character traits of an individual or group is colored by subjectivity, depending on the general attitude of the observer to the subject of his inquiry. Observations about the Jewish character tend to cluster around the two extremes. Those who have an anti-Jewish bias never tire of adducing more and more findings to justify their preconceived opinion about the base qualities and sinister nature of the Jews. And those who admire the Jews continue with similar zeal to marshal data in support of their own foregone conclusion as to the superiority of the Jewish character. At both extremes one can find Jews as well as Gentiles, although obviously enough almost all Jews favor the positive end of the spectrum, while among Gentiles critical and negative views are more prevalent.

The earliest source containing pronouncements on the Jewish character is the Bible. In it, the Children of Israel, following their Exodus from Egypt, are described as a "stiff-necked people," quarrelsome, disobedient, and rebellious. Interestingly, the most appreciative portraiture of the Children of Israel in the pre-conquest period is put into the mouth of the non-Israelite seer, Balaam: "None has beheld iniquity in Jacob, neither has one seen perverseness in Israel. . . . Behold a people that riseth up as a lioness, and as a lion doth he lift himself up. . . ." The great Hebrew prophets and poets, several centuries later, have a long list of negative character traits which they attribute to the people of Israel and Judah.[65] In Talmudic literature, the other side of the Jewish character is emphasized; the Jews are described as "the merciful sons of merciful fathers," in which trait they imitate God.[66] The Greek and Roman authors, some of whose pronouncements on the Jews were quoted earlier, were on the whole anti-Jewish and had only derogatory statements to make about the Jews.

One of the first authors to derive the Jewish character from environmental influences was the sixteenth-century Spanish physician Juan Huarte de San Juan (d. 1592), considered the founder of modern psycho-technology and vocational guidance. He attributed the specific traits of the Jewish mind to the hot climate and infertile environment in which the Children of Israel lived, and to the limited diet (manna) on which they subsisted during the forty years of their wanderings in the desert following their Exodus from Egypt. Despite all subsequent experiences, including persecutions, subjection to slavery, and the like, says Huarte, the Jewish character remained as it was formed in that ancient period.[67]

The persistence of character traits formed in remote antiquity is a theme that recurs, two centuries after Huarte, in the writings of Isaac de Pinto (1715–87), the Sephardi economist, moralist, and Jewish apologist. Pinto held that the Spanish and Portuguese Jews—in contradistinction to the other Jews—were characterized by an "elevation of the mind" and other "distinctions," all of which were due to their descent from the nobility of the tribe of Judah. When the other Jews were taken into the Babylonian captivity—in 586 B.C.—"the chief families of Judah were sent to Spain" where the superior qualities of this Jewish elite were preserved for more than two thousand years.[68]

In more modern times, Joseph Jacobs in 1889 spoke of the Jewish character. He found that the Jewish personality was characterized by versatility, flexibility, enthusiasm, patience, stiff-neckedness, optimism, cheerfulness, *"Hutzpa"* (cheek), gracefulness, charitableness, tact, pity, worldliness, vulgarity, idealism, and rationalism. The Jews, Jacobs says, are sensitive to public opinion, have a historic sense, are cosmopolitan, play the role of intermediaries, have strong ethical conceptions and religious feelings. [69]

Some four decades later, the German Jewish sociologist and historian Fritz Kahn generalized: "The Jewish genius is not creative and contemplative like the Aryan; its geniality is not that of the brain, the eye, or the hand, but is the geniality of the heart. The Jewish genius is the genius of the soul. . . . Through the genius of the heart Israel has become the ethical mother of mankind." [70]

There have been many impressionistic generalizations about Jewish character traits but few quantified studies. Only from the 1930's on have a few such studies been published, all of them with American Jews, mostly college students, as their subjects.

In one of the earliest, the Benreuter Personal Inventory and the Heidbrecher introversion-inferiority questionnaire were administered to 114 Jewish and 113 non-Jewish American families (each consisting of two parents and a college student son or daughter). It was found that, compared to the non-Jewish families, the Jewish group was characterized by (1) gregariousness or a strong social dependence, (2) submissiveness, (3) drive and over-action, and (4) various anxiety states and symptoms of mood change; and that (5) the neurosis and inferiority scores of the Jewish group exceeded the mean of the non-Jewish group by about 60 per cent. [71]

About a decade later, another study of 490 Jewish and non-Jewish students found that the Jews were rated by their non-Jewish instructors higher in aggressiveness, and somewhat higher in alertness and enthusiasm. The results of a Bell Adjustment Inventory administered to the same group showed that the Jewish students, as compared with the non-Jewish, appeared on the average to be less religious, more liberal and radical, probably more gregarious, and slightly less stable emotionally, and to exhibit a greater percentage of aggressiveness, as well as a smaller percentage of timidity. [72]

Jewish aggressiveness is often expressed in a desire for superiority, which appears to be a contributing factor in a more intense motivation. Especially among Jews who had been living in ghettos and had become emancipated recently (in 1950 this category would still have included the majority of the Jews living in the United States and Europe), aggression seemed to be converted into a craving for superiority, which, a psychoanalyst found, had a childlike quality resembling sibling jealousy. Connected with this trait he found a curious self-centeredness, which tended to personalize every issue and often manifested itself in irrational behavior; also, "we

167

caught a glimpse of masochistic tendencies." [73] On a non-psychoanalytical plane, a study of the scholarly aptitude scores and first-semester grades of 6,774 freshmen at Northwestern University from 1925 to 1941 showed that when aptitude scores were held constant, the grade point averages of Jewish men definitely, and of Jewish women probably, were significantly higher than those of non-Jewish students. The author of this study emphasizes that the obtained differences between actual and expected grade point averages could be attributed neither to errors nor to irregularity in grading, and that, therefore, the findings are "compelling evidence" of the higher motivation of Jewish students. [74]

In a nationwide sample survey in which thematic apperceptive measures were administered to three religious groups, high motivation scores were most prevalent in Jewish men, less in Catholic, and least in Protestant men. [75] High motivation, then, seems to be a striking example of aggression deflected (or perhaps sublimated) into special efforts to achieve superiority.

Jewish youth is, of course, directed toward such special efforts also by the expectations of its parents. Parental expectations make Jewish boys find high-status occupations more attractive, and consequently they have actually a better chance in later life of occupying higher positions. [76] The connecting link between parental expectation and the actual achievement of high-status occupations as expected by the parents is working harder at college. A negative effect of this situation is that because of the extreme pressures toward academic overloading which result from the traditional Jewish emphasis on learning, Jewish religious youth suffers from an inevitable curtailment of social and recreational activities. To a higher degree than their non-Jewish counterparts, Jewish college students expect to enter scientific, literary, and social service careers, and to a lesser extent mechanical, computational, artistic, and musical vocations. [77]

On the basis of several previous studies, Nathan Hurwitz listed the following traits as characterizing American Jews: they subscribe to a democratic philosophy, have a worldly orientation, utilitarian attitude toward life, rationalistic and empirical approaches toward the environment, an emphasis on moderation, a high regard for literacy, strong family unity and solidarity, foresight, calculability, and flexibility. As to the sources of these specific Jewish traits and values, the same author believes they lie in four historical features: (a) religious tradition, (b) business ethic, (c) urban adaptation, and (d) minority group status. [78] It might be mentioned here in passing that the lower suicide rate among Jews may have something to do with these traits. [79]

To sum up, the few available quantified studies of American Jewish character indicate that, compared with non-Jews American Jews can be expected to be characterized by a greater prevalence of the following traits:

Gregariousness or strong social dependence
Solidarity, family unity

Submissiveness, but lesser timidity
Drive and over-action, aggressiveness
Achievement motivation, regard for literacy
Foresight, calculability, and flexibility
Tendency toward high-status occupations
Rationality, empiricism
Various anxiety states
Symptoms of mood change, lesser emotional stability
Neuroses
Inferiority feelings
Alertness
Enthusiasm

There can be no doubt that this list covers only some of the character traits in which American Jews differ quantitatively from American non-Jews. The available data are much too meager to allow even a preliminary attempt at outlining a character portrait of the American Jew. As to other Jewish groups, and especially those hailing from the Muslim countries of the Middle East now largely gathered in Israel, information is even more rudimentary.

The difficulties encountered in trying to measure intelligence appear quite minor when compared to the obstacles that have to be overcome in attempting to measure character.[80] For one thing, functional intelligence is, or can be considered, one-dimensional: an individual can have either more or less of it than the established group average—this is why it can be expressed in a single number, the Intelligence Quotient. Character, however, is multi-dimensional: it is composed of a large number of factors which may be present in varying intensities and in many different combinations. This means that character cannot be reduced to simple numerical terms such as the I.Q. The factors whose sum total is character are called "personality traits." Some of these traits are unique individual features found in one person only; others are shared by most, or many, members of a given human group. It is the latter which are significant in studying group character. These group membership determinants can be biologically derived, although in most cases they are the result of formative influences emanating from the environment. Just as the environment, and in the first place, the cultural milieu, influences human behavior, so it influences motivations which are at the root of behavior patterns.[81] As Chapple defined it, character is the "cultural transmutation" of the human temperament; "it is the structuring of emotional-interactional patterns within the accepted constraints of a particular society." [82]

The reference to "a particular society" leads us to the observation that it is *a priori* fallacious to make any statement on Jewish character in general, as was done by several of the authors quoted above. Even if their observations were based on some research, whatever validity they had was confined to one of the many Jewish ethnic groups, usually the one which inhabited the area in which they themselves lived and with which they were familiar. This, however, did not prevent them from making sweeping generalizations in the form of statements about the character of "the Jews," as if the latter were a uniform group.

Exactly the opposite, of course, is the case. Just as the Jews were genetically influenced by the Gentiles among whom they lived, so they developed personality traits which were, to a considerable extent, a response to the stimuli provided by their non-Jewish environment. There is, however, one significant difference between the two. In the physical realm, the genetic processes led the Jews everywhere in the direction of approximating to the Gentiles. In the realm of personality, the Jews approximated to the non-Jews in certain respects, while others of their character traits developed in reaction to the Gentile socio-cultural environment, and thus became markedly different from the non-Jewish norm or mode. Whichever of the two mechanisms prevailed, the Jews in every country developed a specific set of character traits which marked them off from other Jewish groups as much as the locally developed genetic traits.

We must now admit to our inability to give even a most tentative approximation of the biologically derived (or genetically determined) traits that may form part of the Jewish character. Our position here parallels our agnostic stand on the genetic aspect of Jewish intelligence as manifested in mental ability. This leaves the environmental influence on Jewish character to be considered. It seems to us that we can commit ourselves to a minimal statement to the effect that the Jews developed character traits (or, perhaps, a "modal personality") in response to the socio-cultural pressures to which they were exposed in the countries of the Diaspora for many centuries. In trying to illustrate this general thesis, we must fall back on a few impressionistic generalizations which today form part of the stereotyped view of certain Middle Eastern and Western Jewish communities current in Israel.

The Yemenite Jews are known in Israel as modest, undemanding, quiet, diligent people, peaceful, satisfied with their lot, yet capable, intelligent, hardworking, clean, and conscientious. It is not difficult to show that these characteristics developed in Yemen in the course of more than fifteen centuries of history in response to the extremely oppressive conditions in which the Jews lived there until their emigration in 1948 to the new State of Israel. The Yemenite Jews in Yemen were treated as the untouchables used to be in India. They had to defer to the Muslim Yemenites as soon as they stepped out of their ghetto, and often even within it. When a Jew encountered a Muslim in the street, he had to move aside humbly, often into the midst of the putrefying refuse that lay around everywhere in the alleys, lest his inadvertent touch render the Muslim impure. If a Yemenite Jew died and left small children behind, they were taken away by force from the surviving adult members of his family to be brought up as Muslims. Protestations, if they occurred at all, only brought more cruel oppression. Many Yemenite Jews made a living as silversmiths, producing beautiful filigree-work daggers, bracelets, jewels, and other objects for the Muslims. If a Muslim preferred not to pay for what the Jew made him, the Jew had no recourse but to keep his peace and hope for a better customer next time. These were some of the circumstances that imprinted the Yemenite Jews with the character traits for which they are still known in Israel more than a quarter of a century after the last of them had left Yemen. It must be understood, of course, that this retention of traditional character traits by second-generation Yemenite Jews in Israel, despite the entirely different circumstances in which they live, is not due to inheritance but to cultural conditioning by their parents.

The Moroccan Jews are notorious in Israel for their uncontrolled temperament, which can burst into violence at the slightest provocation. "Morocco—knife" is an oft-quoted saying in Israel. They are also reputed to be quarrelsome, self-righteous, never satisfied, overly demanding, and unreliable. These, too, are characteristics which developed among the Moroccan Jews in response to the environment in which they lived for many centuries. The general atmosphere in Morocco was one in which each of the two major population elements, the Arabs and the Berbers, held their own against the other by force of arms, or, at least, by the reputation of being ready, on a moment's notice, to reach for sword, dagger, or gun to defend themselves and what they considered their rights. Pronounced tribal factionalism within the Arab and the Berber sectors contributed its share to the conviction that the only way to maintain oneself against the inimical pressure of the outgroups was by frightening them off with a show of strength. In this situation the Jews, often located between Arabs and Berbers, learned that they, too, must resort to the same type of behavior or become ruthlessly victimized. When in the Late Middle Ages Sephardi refugees from Spain arrived in Morocco, their pride—itself a reflection of the Spanish *grandezza*—became a thorn in the side of the native Moroccan Jews and increased their traditional pugnaciousness. Superimposed on the local scene, the Sephardi presence added fuel to the flame of Moroccan Jewish readiness to brandish knives (symbol of self-assertion as well as masculinity) in defending themselves against real or imagined slights. Twenty-five years in Israel were certainly not enough to eradicate such patterns of behavior, which had become part of the Moroccan Jewish personality in the course of many generations.

Having alluded to the influence of the Spanish mentality on Sephardi Jews, let us add one or two other features to the picture of Spanish-Sephardi relations. Of all Jewish communities, the one which most emphatically held itself superior to other Jewish groups, refused to intermarry with them, to

171

pray with them in the same synagogue, or to be buried with them in the same cemetery was that of the Sephardi Jews. This pride can be explained only as a feature acquired by the Sephardi Jews from the Spaniards. Another Sephardi feature is reminiscent of the Spanish Catholic attitude: the extremely rigid control exercised by the *"maᶜamad,"* the heads of the Spanish-Jewish congregation, over the religious behavior of their members.[83]

Many other Jewish Diasporas, too, were influenced by character traits prevalent among their non-Jewish neighbors. The French Jews were impatient and had as much *esprit* as the French Christians. The German Jews were known for their meticulousness, precision, punctuality, and formality—all typically German features. The Hungarian Jews were patriotic in the extreme, a trait for which the Hungarian Christians were famous. The Kurdish Jews were rough and tough and disdainful of danger, traits well known among the Kurdish Muslims. These observations, of course, do not mean that the personality of the Jews in any given country was largely similar to that of the non-Jews, but merely that the Jews in many places assimilated some of the most pronounced character traits of their host peoples. Despite the similarities in certain personality traits and in the specific directions into which mental abilities were channeled (discussed earlier in this chapter), the fact remains that the Jews differed from the Gentiles in mind as well as body, as indicated by the quantitative studies quoted above.

CONCLUSION

In conclusion we can sum up our answers to the questions posed at the beginning of this chapter.

1. There are differences in general intelligence between Jews and non-Jews. These differences *are* measurable, that is, their existence and magnitude are shown by group studies carried out mostly among schoolchildren and college students, although occasionally also among adults and old people. The nature of the differences, as shown by most studies, is that the Jews are superior to comparable groups of non-Jews, especially in verbal intelligence. To formulate these findings more precisely, one can say that there is a higher percentage of individuals with a high general intelligence among Jews than non-Jews.

2. As to the existence of differences in specific talents or abilities between Jews an non-Jews, our answer here, too, is affirmative, but with a greater measure of uncertainty. The available information is very meager, but it indicates that there are several fields of endeavor which attract relatively more Jews than non-Jews. Especially in scholarly, intellectual, literary, and artistic pursuits, the Jews seem to be proportionately over-represented. Several studies presenting the Jewish contribution to civilization

along these lines are available,[84] although their statistical basis is either very weak or nonexistent. Whether this phenomenon is actual proof of special Jewish talent in the fields discussed, or the result of extraneous circumstances which impelled the Jews to concentrate in specific areas, remains open to question. In any case, the distribution of the Jewish community in any country along the occupational spectrum differs from that of the general population. At the same time, we must not lose sight of the important fact that the occupations engaged in by the Jews are correlated with, and depend on, the occupations found in the general population; they are a function of the general socio-cultural configuration in each country. Thus there are greater differences among various Jewish communities in specific abilities than between the Jews and non-Jews in any single country. Specific Jewish abilities appear everywhere as the product of the particular non-Jewish cultural environment, whose influences are filtered through the Jewish condition. To mention a few random examples, in the modern American cultural environment Jews have produced a disproportionately high number of doctors, lawyers, musicians, writers, comedians; in Yemen, they became silver filigree workers; in the Europe of the Middle Ages, moneylenders. In each of these fields the Jews displayed "special talents" in response to local conditions. But to say that "the Jews" have a special talent for becoming comedians, or silversmiths is patently absurd. Local circumstances everywhere led to specific Jewish responses, which in turn became fixed in many places as cultural traditions, often transmitted within families through many generations.

3. As far as character traits are concerned, it is most difficult to pinpoint differences between Jews and non-Jews. Character traits seem to be formed to a lesser extent by historical conditioning and to a greater extent by personal experiences in the immediate environment than either general intelligence or special talents. This means that one must expect to find a greater variability and a lesser permanence in character traits than in the other two aspects of the human mind discussed. It also means that it is even more nonsensical to speak of "the Jewish character" than it is to speak of "Jewish talents."

The variability and changeability of Jewish character traits have nowhere been demonstrated as impressively as in Israel. Differences in the ethnic character traits of the various Jewish communities and resultant clashes constitute, next to peace with the Arabs, the gravest problem of the young state. On a different plane, a tendency has been observed in certain circles in Israel to develop what has been termed a Spartan mentality—certainly an entirely new departure for a people long used to suffering in silent submission in many a country.

For lack of data it is not possible to determine the nature of the differences between Jewish and non-Jewish character traits. But one can say in general that the Jewish character approximates frequently that of the non-Jews in a given environment, while in other cases the Jewish character develops as a reaction to that of the non-Jewish majority and thus seems to be diametrically opposed to it. The pride of the Sephardi Jews is an example of the former, while the humility of the Yemenite Jews illustrates the latter.

4. The explanation of the differences between Jewish and non-Jewish intelligence, special talents, and character traits must be sought, not in the genetic area, but in environmental factors. There is no evidence for the assumption that Jews are genetically more intelligent than non-Jews, although Jewish history lends itself to the interpretation of a two-thousand-year-old mechanism for selective pressure militating against the survival of the less intelligent. But there is ample evidence that environmental factors influenced the Jews, *in every generation anew,* toward cultivating their intelligence to the utmost. The Jews were forced by the inimical Gentile world in which they lived to rely on their brains in order to survive. They gravitated, in every country and every period, toward the cities—an environment known to be more stimulating than the rural for the growth of intelligence. They inherited from antiquity a tradition that valued learning more than any other achievement. Despised and baited by the Gentiles, they had to develop a psychologically sustaining self-image of moral and intellectual superiority which became the ideal for every Jew to live up to. As soon as and wherever Enlightenment and emancipation liberated them from their physical and mental isolation, they translated the traditional ideal of the rabbinical scholar into the secular image of the Jewish doctor, lawyer, scientist, researcher. Hence, in every country in which the Jews enjoyed even a modicum of civil liberties, they gravitated into academic, intellectual, literary, and artistic professions. Another field of traditional Jewish specialization which has retained its attractiveness for Jews to the present day is commerce—buying and selling on all scales. In fine, the factor more responsible than any other for the differences between Jewish and non-Jewish intelligence, talent, and character is the cumulative effect of specific socio-cultural and historical experiences to which the Jews alone of all the peoples of the Western world have been exposed for the last two thousand years.

5. The foregoing explanation is supported by a consideration of the differences in general intelligence and special talents among various Jewish ethnic groups. Although the number of studies available on the subject is very meager, one can conclude from them that the socio-cultural environment was the decisive influence in both the level of general intelligence and the directions and extent of special talents found in each of the Ashkenazi and Oriental Jewish communities. When Jewish children of disparate ethnic backgrounds are placed into the same educational environment, these traditional differences diminish and tend to disappear. Specifically, what is considered by educators and educationally oriented psychologists as "backward-

174

ness'' shows improvement under the influence of an improved educational environment.

Lastly, an answer can be given to the question, Is the Jewish approximation to the non-Jewish majority population in physical features paralleled by a similar phenomenon in the psychological realm? The answer is a qualified Yes. They approximate to the Gentiles in psychological features as well, but at the same time they retain (or develop) certain differences which, in several cases at least, have been found to be statistically significant. The German Jew, when compared with a Yemenite Jew, impresses one as very much German. Yet when compared with a non-Jewish German, he appears as definitely Jewish. To put it differently, the differences between a German Christian and a Yemenite Muslim are certainly greater than those between a German Jew and a Yemenite Jew. The same observation can be made in comparing the Jews of any country to the non-Jews of the same country on the one hand, and to the Jews of any other country on the other.

As to the genesis of this specific Jewish pattern, one can only say that it is the combined result of two diametrically opposed forces: one of assimilation, that pulled the Jews in every country toward a psycho-cultural approximation to the non-Jewish majority; and an opposite force that impelled the Jews in every country to preserve as much as was feasible of their own traditional Jewish personality. How to strike a balance between these two forces, for the last two thousand years, has been the major problem confronting every Jewish community in the Diaspora. Only one more point should be added: the issue has nothing to do with the question of race.

CHAPTER VII

The Latest Libel:
The Jew as Racist

A N ESSENTIAL COMPONENT of the psychology of every human group—
with the exception of a totally isolated one which hypothetically
could exist—is its reaction to the treatment meted out to it by other
groups, the attitudes displayed toward it by those other groups, and, recip-
rocally, its own treatment of, and attitudes toward, other human groups. In
the case of the Jews, their interrelationships with other peoples supplied
especially significant features to their psyche because contact with the outside world has played a greater role in their history—even in its biblical
period—than in that of probably any other people in the world. For the
past two thousand years the Diaspora, the dispersion of small Jewish
groups among Gentile majorities, was the framework of Jewish existence,
which meant daily contact between most members of the Jewish community and the surrounding world, whether Christian or Muslim, and—of
necessity—a correspondingly intense preoccupation with the relationships
between it and the non-Jewish environment. Although the Jewish community as a whole was not devoid of psychological armature—the belief, as
the Bible says, that the Jews were "a kingdom of priests and a holy nation"
(Ex. 19:6) was a powerful sustaining force, as was until modern times the
high valuation of Jewish learning against the largely illiterate Gentile society—still the influence of the attitude of the Gentile environment toward
the Jews was an important factor one must reckon with in attempting a
psychological portrait of any Jewish community. For this reason, if for no
other, a few comments on the latest resurgence of anti-Jewish attitudes
that have taken the form of a libel accusing Zionism, Israel, and, by implication the Jews in general, of racism are in place in the psychological part
of the present book.

THE BLOOD LIBEL IN HISTORY

To be libeled has been a frequent experience for the Jews ever since they came in contact with other peoples. In antiquity, when those other peoples were polytheists, their chief accusation was that the Jews denied the existence of the gods. In ancient Greece, as we know from the trial and condemnation of Socrates, such a denial was a capital offense. As for Rome, we have seen that Seneca termed the Jews "this criminal nation" and that Tacitus accused them of making proselytes "despise the gods" (see p. 59). Although Tacitus's charge had at least some truth to it, for denying the existence of the gods could appear in Roman eyes as despising them, another contemporary accusation that the Jews observed an annual ritual during which they killed a Gentile adult or child and ate his flesh was completely the figment of malicious anti-Jewish imagination.

This calumny first appeared in the writings of Apion, a first century A.D. Alexandrian Greek rhetorician and anti-Jewish propagandist, who himself had a poor reputation among the serious Roman authors of the period, such as Pliny the Elder. Nevertheless, his anti-Jewish calumnies and fabrications were given credence, survived him and even the Roman Empire, and became a staple in the medieval Christian arsenal of anti-Jewish propaganda.

The infamous series of medieval blood libels against Jews began in Norwich, England, in 1144, and continued, with slight variations, down to the twentieth century, often serving as an excuse for massacring the Jews. Even after the European Enlightenment, in the nineteenth century alone, more than 48 cases were reported from Central and East Europe, Greece, Turkey, Russia, Syria, and Egypt. It is even harder to believe, but it is a sad fact that in our own "rational" century there were still many cases, several of which were dealt with in notorious trials. Although in both the nineteenth and the twentieth centuries Russia was the principal locale of blood libels, with the rise of Nazism in Germany the blood accusation was systematically exploited for anti-Jewish propaganda, and for stirring up brutal Jew-hatred. The May 1, 1934, issue of Julius Streicher's infamous newspaper *Der Stürmer* was designated "Ritual Murder Issue," and carried a front-page article titled "Jewish Plan of Murder against Non-Jewish Humanity Unmasked," with an illustration showing two Jews, drawn in the typical bestial fashion that was the hallmark of the paper, catching the blood of Christian children in a large platter.[1]

A late echo of this type of blood-libel could be heard in a statement made in 1972 by King Faysal of Saudi Arabia, in which he asserted that in 1970 he was present in Paris when the police found the bodies of five murdered children whose blood had been drained by Jews to mix it with the "bread" they eat on a certain holiday.[2]

177

On a different level as far as the tone is concerned, but perhaps even more damaging because of the prestigious forum in which they were presented, were the insidious allegations in the article "Ritual Murder" contained in the great German *Encyclopedia of German Superstition*, widely hailed as an exemplar of German scholarship and thoroughness. The article contains a long list of cases against Jews accused of having murdered non-Jews to use their blood for a great variety of ritual purposes, and then concludes with a call for "incontestable scholarly research that would make it possible to draw conclusions from *the several cases that have been proven correct* to others contained in the foregoing list and their factuality."[3] Reading the words in italics, one cannot help shuddering at such a "scholarly" willingness to support the worst Nazi calumnies against the Jews.

TWENTIETH CENTURY ANTI-SEMITISM

At the end of World War II it was almost inevitable that a world shaken by the revelations of the incredible inhumanity of National Socialist Germany and its satellites should pity the Jews who were the chief victims of Nazi racism. This meant that anti-Semitism in its traditional form, which consisted of hating, oppressing, persecuting, and killing Jews *qua* Jews, fell out of fashion, but it did not mean that the old antipathy to the Jews, inculcated throughout the centuries into both Christians and Muslims by their respective religious teachings, was suddenly wiped away. To the contrary: it continued to influence popular attitudes toward the Jews in many places and remained virulent especially in Russia and other Communist countries and in the Arab world.

In the U.S.S.R. anti-Semitism was first disguised as a campaign against "rootless cosmopolitans." But it soon led to the judicial murder of leading Jewish writers and artists, culminated in the so-called Doctors' Plot of 1953, and was clearly aimed at the total liquidation of Jewish cultural life. In Poland, a faithful follower of Russia, similar anti-Jewish policies, including ruthless anti-Semitic campaigns, resulted in a flightlike emigration of the few thousand Jews who survived the Nazi genocide of three million Polish Jews. Thus by 1970, after having been for many centuries the home of the largest and most Jewish of all Jewish communities, Poland became practically *Judenrein*. However, since anti-Semitism was associated with the defeated and discredited Third Reich and was officially frowned upon by the Soviet system, the Russians and, after them, the Poles and their other satellites introduced a new cover-term for their anti-Jewish stance: it was not anti-Semitism, but "anti-Zionism." Couched in the language of opposition to Zionism, anti-Semitism became, as Daniel Patrick Moynihan put it, "the preferred vehicle of the Soviet Union and its clients in international forums for political assault against the democratic nations—most obviously Israel, but ultimately all the West, and especially the United States."[4]

Those familiar with the conditions under which Jews have lived in Russia since the days of Stalin will not be surprised at the ability of the Soviets to find a few Russian Jews who could be persuaded, or coerced, to help in their campaign of defaming Zionism. In March 1970 considerable official publicity was given to a statement by a "group of Soviet citizens of Jewish nationality" claiming that "Zionism has always expressed the chauvinistic view and racist ravings of the Jewish bourgeoisie."[5] The Russian anti-Zionist position found a ready echo in the Arab world: in the United Nations and other international forums the Arab representatives became the most vociferous champions of combatting Zionism.

ARABS VERSUS ISRAEL

The Arab position on Israel is not a subject that falls within the purview of this book. But the circumstances in which the Arab states embraced the Zionism = racism idea and the manner in which they used it in their fight against Israel are part and parcel of the odious story of the latest anti-Jewish libel of the twentieth century. For some thirty years after the establishment of Israel, the Arab states, most of which gained independence about the same time as Israel, did not acquiesce in the existence of the small "Zionist entity" (as they referred to it) in their midst. Their leaders involved their people in no less than four wars against Israel, and in between those armed conflicts officially embraced a policy of "no recognition, no negotiations, and no peace" with Israel. The last of the Arab-Jewish wars, that of October 1973, known as the Yom Kippur War because it was launched by Egypt on that holiest day of the Jewish religious year, was crowned with initial Arab success mainly because Israel was caught by surprise. This produced in the Arabs a mood of self-confidence that persisted even after Israel gained the upper hand in the struggle and even after the Separation-of-Forces Agreements concluded in 1974 between Israel on the one side and Egypt and Syria on the other. Although Israel retained control of most of the Sinai Peninsula—that is, a sizable piece of formerly Egyptian territory—and of a mile-wide strip on the Golan heights that previously had been part of Syria ever since it gained independence in 1945, the Arabs continued to feel that they had proven themselves in confronting Israel.

In this state of mind, whatever its varied psychological and political roots among which the anti-Israel stance of the Soviet Union played an important role, the Arabs felt encouraged to use their oil-power as a weapon for strengthening their position in the world, and, for the first time

179

since the Middle Ages, to make their influence felt vis-à-vis the West. Having been unable either to defeat Israel on the battlefield, or to inflict on it appreciable economic damage with the commercial boycott they organized, the Arab states directed their efforts to the international political arena, there to bait and beat the young Jewish state and its ideological parent, Zionism.

After a period of mutual encouragement in intra-Arab conferences and competition for leadership in the anti-Israel cause, in August 1975 the Arab states brought their recommendation to censure Zionism before the Conference of Ministers for Foreign Affairs of nonaligned countries, held in Lima, Peru. In response to Arab prodding, that conference condemned Zionism as a threat to world peace and security, and called upon all countries to oppose its "racist and imperialist" ideology.[6] The Arab anti-Zionist effort also claimed the attention of United Nations-sponsored international forums. The International Women's Conferences, organized by the United Nations in Mexico City in 1975, and in Copenhagen in 1980, adopted resolutions condemning Zionism as one of the most serious obstacles to the emancipation of women. Among the countries whose delegations worked and voted for these resolutions were the Arab states in several of which the position of women—what with polygyny, repudiation, veiling, segregation, and the painful practices of clitoridectomy and infibulation—is still the subject of bitter complaints by their relatively few feminists, which complaints however, never reached the floor of the conferences.

RESOLVED: ZIONISM = RACISM

In the United Nations, the Arab states have consistently tried to oust Israel from its midst. When these efforts failed year after year, they presented resolutions to the United Nations Educational, Social, and Cultural Organization (UNESCO) and the United Nations Social, Humanitarian, and Cultural Committee condemning Zionism. These were adopted by an automatic majority of Arab, Third World, and Communist countries. The crowning achievement of this anti-Israel campaign came on November 10, 1975, when the General Assembly adopted a resolution defining Zionism as "a form of racism and racial discrimination." Seventy-two countries voted for the resolution, 35 against it, 32 abstained, and three were absent. The resolution states that "the racist regime in occupied Palestine and the racist regimes in Zimbabwe and South Africa have a common imperialist origin, forming a whole and having the same racist structure and being organically linked in their policy aimed at repression of the dignity and integrity of the human being." That is, the resolution condemned not only Zionism as "a form of racism" but also the State of Israel (which it refers to as "the racist regime in occupied Palestine").

Before the voting, Fayez A. Sayegh, the representative of Kuwait, himself a Palestinian Arab, argued that many Jews were also against Zionist policies, that Arabs had "reverence for Judaism" but opposed Zionism, and that "we reject the equation between anti-Zionism and anti-Semitism." After the vote, the chief American delegate, Daniel Patrick Moynihan, said: "The U. S. rises to declare before the General Assembly of the United Nations and before the world that it does not acknowledge, it will not abide by, it will never acquiesce in this infamous act." Kurt Waldheim, the Secretary General of the United Nations, issued a statement, carefully kept in guarded neutral tones, to the effect that it was necessary to make progress "in a search for a solution of the Middle East problems." Could it be that in saying this he remembered the Nazi "final solution" of population problems in which he himself played a minor role?

Although the resolution, like all the General Assembly decisions, had no immediate effect and was not binding on member countries, nor demanded any action of them, it had, from the Jewish point of view, an ominous ring. Only thirty years after the Jews were singled out by Nazi Germany for the most special of the special treatment it accorded to unwanted minorities, and were stamped by Hitlerite doctrine as an inferior, evil, and harmful race, now the world forum of the United Nations went on record condemning as racist Zionism, the one movement that united practically all the Jews who survived the holocaust, and the State of Israel, the small homeland that inspired and animated world Jewry.

Although the language of the resolution did not speak of Judaism, but of Zionism, as a form of racism, its purport was much wider than that, in view of the fact that long before 1975, Zionism or the support of Zionism and Israel had become the generally embraced position of the Jews all over the world. That this indeed was the case was exemplified by the programs and work of such major Jewish organizations as the expanded Jewish Agency (founded in 1929), the World Jewish Congress (founded in 1936), and the Conference of Presidents of Major American Jewish Organizations (founded in 1955).

JEWISH SUPPORT FOR ISRAEL

That a firm pro-Zionist and pro-Israel stance is not merely an organizational or political matter but a basic religious commitment was recently again evidenced by a study conducted in 1985 by rabbis Mark I. Winer and Sanford Seltzer for the Union of American Hebrew Congregations and published in 1987. The union, which is the organization of Reform Judaism in North America, and represents about one-third of all American Jews, was relatively late among the major American Jewish religious bodies to take a pro-Israel position. Before the adoption of its 1937 "Columbus Platform," Reform Judaism had considered anti-Zionism a mandate of its religious universalism. That platform, however, laid down the principle that it was the obligation of all Jewry to aid in the upbuilding of a Jewish homeland in Palestine, and since then the union has actively cooperated with other American and world Jewish organizations in support of the *yishuv*, and, since 1948, of Israel.

The 1985 study showed that in time the support of Israel had become much more than just a Jewish "obligation" as far as Reform Judaism was concerned: it had developed into a fundamental tenet. Responses to a questionnaire administered to twenty-one hundred top leaders of Reform Judaism who were delegates to the convention of the union, and to leaders of the National Federation of Temple Sisterhoods, indicated that "support of Israel was rated on a par with belief in God as one of the significant aspects of 'being a good Jew.' "[7] In the same spirit, at its 1987 convention the union adopted a resolution calling for a greater involvement of the union with Israel, and stated in its preamble: "We know that all Jews share in the destiny of the Jewish state and in the responsibility of maintaining her survival and security."[8]

A more telling proof of the Jewish psychological identification of Judaism as a religion and of a pro-Israel stance as an emotional commitment could hardly be imagined. If it is a Jewish conviction that the belief in God and the support of Israel are two equally significant aspects of being a good Jew, it is patently evident that to condemn Zionism and Israel as racist means nothing less than a like condemnation of Jews and Judaism. Moreover, because racism can characterize only a human group that believes itself to be racially superior (ghosts of the Nazi "super race"!), the equation Zionism = racism meant that the Jews were therewith again identified as a race, and, to wit, a race that considered itself superior to others, and maintained and exhibited hostile attitudes, discriminatory policies, and in general evil intentions against human groups it held racially inferior to itself.

In this manner the myth of the Jewish race was resuscitated in a particularly vicious form and given a new lease on life. In the past, the anti-Semitic racist theories maintained that the Jews constituted an inferior race, and, in their most virulent form as developed by Nazi Germany, drew therefrom the conclusion that the Jewish race must be exterminated. The new, United Nations-sanctioned racial theory implies that the Jews, constituting a race that itself embraces a racist position, must be opposed and fought, or at least, to borrow a famous Koranic expression, "brought low."

RACIAL ANTI-SEMITISM

For a student of the myth of the Jewish race it is of interest to probe the antecedents of the Russo-Arab allegation that Zionism and Israel, meaning the Jewish people, are racist. The fact is that neither the Soviets nor the Arabs were the inventors of this latest libel, although they gave it new and wide publicity. Its sources go back to nineteenth-century racial anti-Semitism (discussed briefly in the introduction to this book), which was, occasionally at least, directed against Muslims as much as against Jews. An early example is the position of D. Kimon, who in his French book *The Pathology of Islam and the Means to Destroy It*, published in Paris in the 1890's, condemns both "Israelitism" and "Islamism" in one breath, so to speak, and in very similar terms. He writes:

> Israelitism is a Semitism, that is to say a parasite, perfected, composed of one *single* [emphasis in the original] race, or rather of one kind, spread all over the world, acclimatized to all regions, speaking all languages, mixing with all peoples, without fear of intermingling or of being absorbed, disguising itself with the garb of all nations but forming together a vast army admirably organized by nature, by hereditary ability, and by the Hebrew religion . . . with its institutions of vice and immorality, of corruption and lies, and pursuing but one single goal: the disintegration of the civilized and toiling societies in order to dominate them, exploit them, and destroy them.
>
> Islamism is a Semitism or a bastard parasite. It is composed of several races or several kinds, very different from one another. . . . It absorbs, by violent practice, all the peoples which it encounters on its way . . . and enjoys, without working, the goods and labor of the neighbor.
>
> The Israelite . . . is an element of disintegration, of moral perturbation, of inextricable confusion, a fatal poison for sane reason, prudence and wisdom. It is the same with the Muslim. . . .[9]

Following this diatribe Kimon goes on to advise his readers on "How to combat the Semites victoriously."

It was in the tradition of this early wholesale condemnation of Jews and Muslims that two generations later the allegation was put forward that the Jews themselves—and in particular those who embraced the ideology of Zionism—were racists. Jean Baubérot, in his book *The Wrong of Existing: From the Jews to the Palestinians*,[10] first speaks in general terms of "the hostility toward the Arabs," which, "like the contempt toward the Jews . . . took a veritably racist turn in the nineteenth century" when "the Semitic race was considered inferior" and "both Jews and Arabs were victims of the same contempt." Then, however, he directs his barbs against Zionism in particular, which, he asserts, is responsible for developing a racist view in the Western world vis-à-vis the Arabs. He goes on to refer to the methods used by the "crypto-Zionism of the French press to develop and propagate anti-Arab racism." In the latter allegation he bases himself on findings published by the Mouvement contre le Racisme Anti-Arabe

(MRAA, Movement against Anti-Arab Racism), and gives examples to show that the press and individual authors present the Jews in a favorable, and the Arabs in an unfavorable, light.

Next Baubérot turns his attention to the racism that he alleges exists in Israel, not only toward the Arabs but also toward the Sephardi and Oriental Jews. In support of this thesis, he quotes the French-Jewish author Marc Hillel, who in his book *Israël en danger de paix* (Israel in Danger of Peace) characterizes the attitude of the Israelis of European extraction toward the Sephardim as "a form of racism," and asserts that the Jews of Morocco and Tunisia would return, if they could, to their old countries. (Let us interject right here that this statement is patently false. King Hasan of Morocco has, in recent years, issued invitations to the Jews who had left Morocco for France and Israel to return, promising them most favorable treatment, but his appeals fell on deaf ears.) Among Baubérot's other accusations are that "the fundamental laws of the Israelite state have as their aim to render the Arabs strangers in their fatherland," that "the Palestinians face taboos from the Jews," and that Zionism is a movement that "has sought to make the totality of the Jews subject to it . . ." and to enlist all Jews "actively as abettors of its anti-Arab racism and of its fight against the Palestinians. . . ."

Here we have it in a clear and explicit formulation: Zionism, the "Israelite state," and the Jews in general are racist and responsible for the spread of anti-Arab racism in the Western world. Let us turn to an examination of the ascertainable facts as against these allegations.

EARLY ISRAELI CULTURAL ETHNOCENTRISM

To begin with, a brief glance back into the 1940's. From our present-day perspective, with the racial issue one of the most controversial in the world's perception of Israel and Zionism, it is interesting and instructive to look back at the formative years of Israel when the newness of Jewish rule over an Arab population and of the large-scale immigration of Jews from Muslim countries created serious problems for the young Jewish state. Raphael Patai's book *Israel Between East and West*,[11] written in those years, is devoted mainly to these issues, but the concept of race is conspicuously absent from its 350 pages. The problem, as seen in those days, was *cultural* assimilation, of how to help the non-Western communities in Israel adopt the dominant Western-type culture of the *yishuv* (the Jewish community in mandatory Palestine), without depriving them of their traditional cultural heritage. The book reproached the cultural and political leadership of Israel with several shortcomings in this area, including cultural ethnocentrism vis-à-vis both the Arab and the Oriental Jewish communities, and the single-minded effort to assimilate them as rapidly and as totally as possible

184

to the dominant Western-Israeli culture. But in all this not a word was said about racism, in fact the very terms *race* and *racism* did not appear in the book. The focus was on cultural differences and cultural amalgamation—the racial issue simply did not exist. It became part of the "Palestine problem" only when it was artificially made a focal point by countries trying to use any and all means for the purpose of denigrating Zionism, Israel, and the Jews in the eyes of the world.

NEW MUTUAL ACCUSATIONS

As for Israel as it is today, it is an open society in which people are free to express opinions even if diametrically opposed to those held by the majority or by the government. Hence Israeli sociologists are able to, and do, take public opinion polls on any subject they wish. Thus much is known about all varieties and shadings of people's attitudes and positions on many issues, as well as about the percentages of individuals in the population holding unpopular or extreme opinions. Among these opinions there are inevitably those unfriendly to, or derogative of, the Arabs, and the public availability of these data enables those inimical to Israel to refer to them in their writings as "proofs" of the racist character of Zionism and the State of Israel.

One such publication is an anonymous French pamphlet titled *Zionism and Racism: A Question That Demands an Answer,*[12] published in Paris in 1971. It quotes extensively from a public opinion poll conducted in Israel in that year and, misinterpreting the true purport of that poll, concludes from its findings that they show the racist character of Zionism and Israel. Another is a French book by the North African Arab writer and vice president of the Canadian-Arab Federation, Abdelkader Benabdallah, titled *Israel and the Black Peoples: The Israeli–South African Racist Alliance,* in which the author "proves" the sinister similarities between the two countries, their cultural, political, ideological relations, and so forth.[13]

Among the other Arab authors and political leaders there are those who do not even bother with referring to actual or fictitious data, but are instead satisfied with reiterating the blanket assertion that Zionism is racism and must therefore be combated. An example can be found in the keynote address of Ahmad Hassan al-Bakr, president of Iraq, with which he opened an international symposium on Zionism in Baghdad in November 1976. The initiative for the symposium was taken by Baghdad University, and the participants were 300 Arab intellectuals who presented a total of 38 papers. President al-Bakr's address, delivered by Saddam Hussein, who at the time was vice-chairman of the Iraqi Revolution Command Council and not long thereafter replaced al-Bakr in the presidency, was published, still in 1976, in an English translation, as a pamphlet of 17 pages, titled *Zi-*

185

onist Racism Is Regressing, by the Iraqi Ministry of Information. The address does not present a single fact, but reiterates the assertion that Zionism is racism. One of these statements was considered so important by the publishers tht they put it in italics:

> *There is no experience like Zionism both in theory and in practice, which is more replete with the negative aspects of racism, or more dangerous as a menace to the Arab world peace and universal civilization.*

Glancing at history, President al-Bakr sees all the invasions of the Arab homeland as "racist": "The Arab homeland had witnessed waves of invasions, all of which were based on racism be they religious, national or both, in addition to the colonial wave." This places Zionist racism on a par with such other "racist" invaders of Arab lands as the Seljuk Turks, who conquered Iraq, Asia Minor, Syria, Lebanon, and Palestine in the eleventh century; the Mongols, who overran the Arab lands in the thirteenth century; the Ottoman Turks, who conquered the same area plus Arabia, Egypt, and North Africa from the fourteenth century on; and the European powers England, France, and Italy, who carved up the Arab provinces of the Ottoman Empire among themselves in the nineteenth and twentieth centuries.

Of interest is a reference President al-Bakr makes to an invitation extended by the Iraqi Revolution Command Council to the Iraqi Jews who had fled Iraq in 1950–51 and were airlifted to Israel to return to Iraq, and his designation of the non-Zionist "Arab Jews" and all other Jews as "victims of Zionism":

> Furthermore a decision was taken by the Revolutionary Command Council inviting back the Iraqi Jews who had left Iraq under Zionist pressure and intrigue. . . . That decision was an expression of the human and cultural motives which bind us to the history of our nation, and which not only differentiate between Zionism and Judaism, but view the Arab Jews in the first place, and all other Jews who are not committed to the Zionist ideology, as victims of Zionism.

We wish to add only one brief footnote to this statement. The 120,000 Jews who left Iraq for Israel in 1950–51 did so because they were persecuted, and none of them returned to Iraq either before or after the above invitation.

There would be no point in adding more examples of the propagandistic use to which some Arab authors and political leaders have put the allegation that Zionism and Israel are racist. Let us instead point out that it would be a grave mistake to think that all the Arab or Muslim writers who have dealt with racism, the Jews, Judaism, Zionism, and Israel have taken this position. An example showing the other side of the coin is Mohand Tazerout, who in his French book *Manifesto against Racism* uses a philosophical-psychological approach in discussing racism. Racism, he says, "is inseparable from the European colonization of the entire world," which is but a restrained way of saying that European colonialism was the source of racism. In his book he gives a balanced summation of Jewish religious teachings, and at its end he condemns racism as "a cancer of humanity" and "a parody of truth," without accusing the Jews in particular of being guilty of spreading this cancer.[14]

The Arab attacks on Israel, Zionism, and the Jews as racist have their opposite number in Jewish and Christian allegations that Arabs, Arabism, and Pan-Arabism are racist. One example of the literature produced by this side will suffice. In 1960 the French *Comité d'Action de Défense Democratique* published a pamphlet titled *Racism and Pan-Arabism: A Conspiracy against Human Liberties*, which asserts in its introduction that "anti-Semitism and anti-Zionism are but two faces of one and the same coin." The Introduction is followed by an article by Jacques Soustelle, the well-known French anthropologist, sociologist, and political leader, who broke with de Gaulle when he refused to force Algeria to remain in union with France. In his article Soustelle calls for a determined fight against racism whatever the political elements associated with it. This is followed by a paper by Shlomo Friedrich on "Pan-Arabism: A New Racist Menace?" which offers a sharp critique of Nasser's book *The Philosophy of the Revolution*, and terms it "a mere pale imitation of Hitler's *Mein Kampf*."[15] Thus both sides in the Arab-Jewish conflict have their pugnacious accusers, but even a cursory survey of the available literature shows that the percentage of Arab authors who accuse the Jews and Zionism of racism is higher than that of Jewish authors who level the same accusation against Arabs and Pan-Arabism.

WHAT THE POLLS SHOW

It is now time to turn to the actual findings concerning the position of the Jewish population of Israel on the Arabs. Although the 1975 United Nations resolution does not characterize the Israeli Jews as racist, but speaks of the country's "racist regime," in a true democracy such as Israel, where the "regime" is representative of the will of the people, the two necessarily coincide, so that the libel that Israel is a "racist regime" clearly implies also a condemnation of the people who elected that regime as racist.

The issue of racism in Israel, or, more precisely, the question of the Israeli Jews' attitudes toward and opinions about the Arabs, has constituted subjects of inquiry for both polls and individual concerned authors. Among important polls is the public opinion survey, already referred to, carried out in 1971 (that is, some four years before the United Nations resolution equating Zionism with racism and condemning the government of Israel as a "racist regime"). It was initiated by *Time* magazine jointly with the Louis Harris organization, and carried out with the help of the Public Opinion Research of Israel. The poll was administered to a "carefully selected sample" of 1,177 Israeli Jews and 128 Israeli Arabs, and its results were summarized in an article published in the April 12, 1971, issue of *Time*.

The findings were enlightening in several respects. They showed a wide range of differing opinions on issues such as the retention of all or most of the territories occupied by Israel in the Six-Day War of 1967 (only 21% of the Jews questioned were in favor), the annexation of East Jerusalem and the Golan Heights (93% and 88% respectively in favor), and more evenly divided opinions on the Arabs. On the latter, the results were as follows (in diminishing order of evincing an anti-Arab attitude): 84% of the Jews questioned said that they "would be bothered" if a friend or a relative were to marry an Arab; 74% if their children became close friends with Arabs; 54% if their children had an Arab teacher; 49% if an Arab moved next door; 26% if they had to work closely with an Arab; 23% if an Arab sat next to them in a restaurant; and 25% admitted that there exists in Israel a prejudice against the Arabs. On the issue of Arab refugees, 57% believed that they should be settled in Arab countries with Israel paying them compensation.

As to the character and personality of the Arabs, 53% believed that they were more lazy than the Jews; 74% that they were less intelligent than the Jews; 68% that the Arabs had a blind hate for Israel: 75% that the Arabs were more cruel than the Jews; 80% that they are not as courageous as the Jews; 66% that they were less honest than the Jews; and 67% believed that they were inferior to the Jews.

Before tackling the question of whether these responses show that the Jewish population in Israel is racist when it comes to the Arabs, we must point out that among the respondents the most biased against the Arabs were the Jews who had recently arrived in Israel from Asian and African Middle Eastern countries; less biased were the Europe-bred Ashkenazi Jews, and least biased the Israel-born "Sabras," native Jews. The explanation of this intra-Jewish variation in attitude toward the Arabs is not far to seek. The Jews who, before their immigration to Israel had experienced the strongly discriminatory treatment to which they were exposed in the Arab countries and in Iran, reacted to it with a psychologically founded anti-Arab bias that they retained after their settlement in Israel. The Jews who had come from Europe, where they had had no opportunity for firsthand acquaintance with Arabs, came next, while the Sabras, the young Israel-born generation, whose limited contact with Arabs was from a position of strength vis-à-vis members of the Arab minority, had the least negative attitude toward, and image of, the Arabs. Because, in the natural course of demographic development, the former two immigrant Jewish groups are destined to be replaced more and more by the third group, the native-born Israeli Jews, this means that whatever anti-Arab bias was manifested in the 1971 poll was bound to diminish with time, and, other things being equal, to approximate the 1971 level of opinions and attitudes found by the poll among the Sabras.

That the developments move in this direction was indicated by a poll conducted by Dr. Minna Tzemah̄ of the Dah̄af Institute under the auspices of the Van Leer Institute of Jerusalem. It was carried out in May 1987 and its results were summarized in the October 26, 1987, issue of the Tel Aviv daily *HaAretz*, which found it important enough to give it first page coverage. A questionnaire was administered to 612 Jewish high school students aged 15–18, probing their attitudes toward, and opinions of, the Israeli Arabs. One of the questions asked what they thought about the loyalty of the Arabs to the State of Israel. The response of one-third was that in their opinion most of the Israeli Arabs were loyal to the state. This response represented a marked increase compared with that of two years earlier, when only 13% of the respondents did not question the loyalty of the Arabs. Other responses, too, testified to an increasingly positive attitude to the Arabs: 30% believed that the Arabs have almost complete rights to the West Bank and Gaza; 40% was for granting the Arabs full civil rights; and about 50% believed that the rights of the Arabs should not be curtailed.

Now as to the question of whether the attitudes and opinions of the average Israeli as disclosed by the 1971 poll can, or must, be interpreted as racist. A considered response to this question is that what that poll shows is, at the utmost, the existence of a quasi-racist attitude on the part of a minority among the Jews of Israel. No less than 75% of the Jewish respondents were not aware, or did not admit, that there was prejudice against the Arabs in Israel; 77% had nothing against an Arab sitting next to him in a restaurant, and 74% had nothing against working closely with an Arab. These figures are significant in that they show that almost all the Israeli Jews had no objection to Arabs sharing with them places of work and relaxation. When it came to sharing living quarters, even there a bare majority (51%) thought that they would not be bothered by Arabs moving next door to them, which must be considered and evaluated in view of the fact that the traditional form of residential patterns in the Middle East, including Israel, has been for each origin group to tend to live in its own quarter —hence the Bokharan quarter in Jerusalem, the Yemenite quarters there and in Tel Aviv; the Armenian, Christian, Muslim, Jewish, and other quarters in the Old City of Jerusalem, and so forth. The poll did not ask the question, but had it asked the Yemenite Jews whether they would be bothered if a Moroccan Jew would move next door, there can be little doubt that the majority would have answered yes.

189

The same perspective must be applied to the responses to the questions about Arab teachers and Arab close friends of their children, and intermarriage with Arabs. Each ethnic group in Israel—and this holds good for Arabs as much as for Jews—wishes to preserve its ethnic identity, which wish is expressed most stringently by the endogamous marriage preferences. The Jews in Israel, as in other countries, know only too well that having Arab teachers and Arab friends will predispose their children to marrying Arabs, just as in Western countries having Christian teachers and Christian friends predisposes Jewish children to intermarrying with Christians. In fact, as things stand in the last quarter of the twentieth century, Jewish-Christian intermarriage rates are so high in the United States and other Western countries that they endanger the entire future existence of the Jewish communities, and the question "Will there be a Jewish people by the end of the twenty-first century?" is being heard more and more frequently.[16] Hence the objection of a sizeable majority (84%) of the Israeli Jewish respondents to Jewish-Arab intermarriage cannot be taken as a manifestation of a racist attitude, but must be interpreted as an expression of the feelings and awareness of most Israeli Jews that out-marriage constitutes a danger to the future existence of the Jewish people in Israel as it does in the Diaspora.

That the objection to marrying Arabs is not based on racial prejudice but on religious considerations is further evidenced by the fact that if the Arab partner in such a planned marriage converts to Judaism before the nuptials, the objections by the society, and of the Israeli rabbinate itself, are eliminated, just as a like step eliminates secular and rabbinical objections to marrying a Christian in the countries of the Diaspora. The making of a sharp distinction between marrying a non-Jew, strongly objected to, and marrying a convert to Judaism, approved and accepted, goes back to the Middle Ages, and beyond them to Talmudic times, as indicated in our chapter on "Intermarriage and Interbreeding." Hence the only legitimate conclusion from the results of the 1971 poll is *not* the one drawn by the pamphlet *Zionism and Racism*, that it evidences the racist nature of Israeli society, but that a major segment of the Jewish population of Israel is intent on preserving the future Jewishness of the state by opposing, on religious grounds, intermarriage with non-Jews, which in Israel means in most cases intermarriage with Muslim and Christian Arabs.

Incidentally, the 1971 poll also revealed some interesting facts about the Arab population of Israel. The sample of Arabs questioned was too small (only 128) to be truly representative, but it can at least be taken as indicative of what to expect should a larger sample be questioned. It showed, first of all, that only 54% of the Israeli Arabs felt discriminated against, which means that 46% not only did not feel discriminated against but were willing to make a statement to this effect—a substantial percentage considering the strong influence, bolstered by intra-Arab terrorism, wielded by the Palestine Liberation Organization (PLO) among the Israeli Arabs.

Perhaps even more significant is that only 49% of the Israeli Arabs stated that they would like the West Bank to become a Palestinian Arab state. Evidently this near-half of the Israeli Arab population was neither intimidated by Israeli rule to the extent of hiding their true feelings about a Palestinian Arab state nor apprehensive that by expressing its support of such a state it would jeopardize its position in Israel as Arab citizens of the Jewish state. As for the 51% of Israeli Arabs whose response was that they did not wish to see the West Bank become a Palestinian Arab state, their position indicates enough identification with Israel not to wish for the establishment of an Arab state on the West Bank, which, in all probability, would be dominated by the PLO or by pro-PLO elements inimical to Israel, and whose very existence would place them in a precarious, or at least ambiguous, position fraught with political and emotional conflicts. Were a Palestinian Arab state to come into existence, the Israeli Arabs would have to make difficult choices between the natural sympathy they would have for the political ambitions of their next of kin just across the nearby border and the equally natural desire to continue to enjoy without outside interference the safety, freedom, and higher standard of living that are theirs as citizens of Israel. We may perhaps be reading too much into this response of the 51% of Israeli Arab nay-sayers to an independent Arab state in the West Bank, but there can be little doubt that the explanation of this surprising figure must be sought in a pro-Israeli orientation.

One last item in the poll requires comment. The poll found that 88% of the Israeli Arabs questioned inclined to a return of all or some of the territories occupied by Israel since the 1967 war. This is a high percentage but not much higher than the 77% of Israeli Jews who gave the same response. That among the latter there are 23% who wish to retain all the territories held by Israel since that war should come as no surprise: security considerations alone are enough to prompt that percentage of Israeli Jews to oppose any return of land that would bring the menace of Arab attack back to the narrow—eight-mile wide—central waistline of pre-1967 Israel. But it is more than surprising that among the Israeli Arabs there were 12% who believed that Israel should not return any part of the occupied territories. This indicates that there is a small, but in the circumstances significant, percentage among the Israeli Arabs whose identification with Israel and its politics is so complete that they prefer the continuation of Israeli rule over territories in which other Arabs wish to establish their independent Palestinian state. The existence of these 12% is in itself eloquent testimony to the libelous nature of the allegation that Israel is an anti-Arab racist state.

191

The overwhelmingly anti-racist sentiments of the Jewish population of Israel found expression, among several other manifestations, in the International Conference of Teachers on the theme: "The Fight against Racism, Anti-Semitism, and the Violations of Human Rights." The conference took place in Tel Aviv on November 10–14, 1980, and its proceedings were published in Hebrew, English, French, German, and Spanish.[17] One of the main speakers was Leon Poliakoff, the well-known French-Jewish historian, whose multivolume study of the history of anti-Semitism is a classic in the field. Poliakoff's lecture was entitled "Is There a Scientific Basis to the Inferiority of Certain Peoples?" and, as could be expected from a scholar of his caliber, his answer was a resounding No! This large-scale conference of teachers, whose views have a decisive influence on those of the young generation and whose consensus was formulated in Poliakoff's lecture, was expressive of the prevalent opinion among Israeli Jews on questions of race and racism.

JEWS AGAINST ISRAEL

To complete the picture of the available evidence, we now must undertake the painful task of discussing, at least briefly, some of the few Jewish voices that have joined the Russo-Arab chorus accusing Zionism, Israel, and the Jews of racism. Jewry has had in every age its share of apostates, some of whom, to demonstrate that they had truly severed all ties to the people of their origin, became vociferous and vicious defamers of the Jewish people and the Jewish religion. These Jewish anti-Semites were in some respects more hurtful to Jewry and Judaism than the average Gentile anti-Semitic polemicist, because their Jewish background gave them a familiarity with Jewish customs, doctrines, and religious laws, and by presenting these, even if in a distorted manner, they were yet able to convey the impression of authoritativeness and credibility. This is why Jewish scholars have always felt impelled to devote more attention and energy to disproving false allegations made by renegade Jews than assertions proffered by the less knowledgeable Gentile antagonists. It is to this category of apostate Jewish anti-Semites that the few authors briefly discussed here belong, whether or not they took the step of formally seceding from Judaism, and even if they live in Israel and enjoy all the rights of Israeli citizenship.[18]

We can dispose summarily of a 1973 book of Ronald Segal, which takes a sharply anti-Israeli position and accuses Israel of racism. The quality of this author's proofs of his assertions can be judged from the following example: Segal equates the attitude of the government of Israel toward the Arabs with South African apartheid, and states that in Israel "Jewishness has been made an essentially biological phenomenon."[19] The fact, of course, is that in Israeli law Jewishness is a *religious* issue: any person, of whatever biological or racial background, who undergoes a formal religious conversion to Judaism counts as fully Jewish as a descendant of generations of rabbis.

Among Israeli writers who accuse Israel of racism is Israel Shahak, founder and president of the strongly leftist-oriented League for the Rights of Man and Citizen in Israel. In March 1974 Shahak was invited to testify before the Foreign Affairs Committee of the United States House of Representatives, and submitted a "declaration" in which he accused Israel of all kinds of racist crimes against the Arabs, and of establishing "racist colonies" in the territories Israel occupied in the 1967 war. Like some of his Arab counterparts, Shahak professes to distinguish between Zionism, which he condemns, and Judaism, which he upholds while actually knowing little about it. In his 1975 book *Le Racisme de l'Etat d'Israël* he writes that "devotion to Israel is at once immoral and opposed to the main current of Jewish tradition"[20]—which is patently false.

A less strident but still overly critical presentation of Israeli policies is in Pierre Paraf's book *Racism in the World*, which discusses racism in both the Arab countries and Israel. Paraf is a well-known French-Jewish author, editor, and broadcasting executive, and founder of the *Ligue International contre le Racisme et l'Antisémitisme*. In speaking of Israel, Paraf concentrates on the attitude of the Israeli government toward the Oriental Jews in the country and finds that it is a "social racism," the nonacceptance of atheism is a "religious racism," and the Law of Return (which gives all Jews the right to immigrate to Israel) is an "institutional racism."[21] Evidently, Paraf uses the term *racism* in a sense different from the generally accepted one; he speaks of "racism" when we would speak of "discrimination." His combination of "racism" with the adjectives "social," "religious," and "institutional" is, to say the least, difficult to follow. Let us have a closer look at only one of them, at what he terms "religious racism." What is the actual position of Israel vis-à-vis persons of the black race who profess Judaism? The Ethiopian Jews, known as Falashas, supply a test case.

THE CASE OF THE FALASHAS

The Falashas are as black as the other Ethiopians, and no appreciable physical differences exist between them and the Galla, Amhara, Tigre, etc., majority populations who are either Christians or Muslims (see pages 36, 235, 284). The Falashas themselves state that they do not differ in physiognomy from other Ethiopians.[22] The Falashas seem to be descendants of a segment of the indigenous Agau population that converted to Judaism under the influence of Jewish missionaries from either Egypt or Yemen in the early centuries of the common era. Their religion is based

193

solely on the Bible, besides which they are acquainted with a few Apocrypha, but the postbiblical, Talmudic, and rabbinic development of Judaism has been unknown to them.

As soon as a trickle of Falasha immigrants began to arrive in Israel there was considerable discussion among the rabbinical authorities as to whether they were to be regarded as Jews, and hence whether intermarriage between them and other Jews was halakhically permissible. In 1973 the Sephardi chief rabbi of Israel, R. Obadiah Yosef, with the concurrence of the Ashkenazi chief rabbi, R. Shlomoh Goren, ruled that "the Falashas are Jews, and it is our duty . . . to hasten their immigration to Israel." However, in view of the differences between the religious practices of the Falashas and those of halakhic Judaism, the rabbis decreed that, to remove all doubt as to their acceptance as Jews, the Falashas should undergo a formal act of ritual conversion to Judaism. One may be inclined to criticize this ruling as a *religious* interference with civil rights, but in all this the fact that the Falashas were black, that is, belonged to a different race, did not even arise. After the religio-legal question of the Falashas' Jewish identity was thus settled, the Israeli ministry of the interior recognized the rabbinical ruling as the law of the country, and thenceforth the Falashas were entitled to enter Israel as Jews and receive automatic Israeli citizenship under the 1950 Law of Return.

However, the Israeli government was not satisfied with this and went a significant step further: it went out of its way to bring the Falashas to Israel. After the Negus Haile Selassie was deposed in 1974, the Marxist regime that replaced him evinced an increasingly hostile attitude toward the Falashas. This situation, to which were added the effects of famine and war, and the belief that their community had no future in Ethiopia prompted many Falashas to flee the country to refugee camps in neighboring Sudan. From there the Israeli government organized an airlift, codenamed "Operation Moses," which, in the winter of 1984–85, brought close to 15,000 Falashas to Israel.[23]

When the news about the airlift leaked, both the Ethiopian and the Sudanese governments put obstacles in the way of its continuation, and it had to cease before it achieved its goal: the rescue of all Ethiopian Jews. Still, the Israeli government did not give up, and continued to press Ethiopia to permit the emigration of the remaining Falashas whose number was estimated at 15,000. In September 1987 Israeli Foreign Minister Shimon Peres met in New York with the Ethiopian Foreign Minister Berhanu Bayih, and again requested him to permit the emigration of the Falashas. The request was denied with the pretext that if the Jews were permitted to emigrate, non-Jewish Ethiopians would also ask to leave the country.[24] If the libel that Israel was a racist state had any truth in it, the government of Israel would certainly not have brought thousands of Falashas into the country, nor would it continue in its efforts to secure the release by Ethiopia of the remainder of this old black ethnic group whose religious beliefs and practices place it on the peripheries of Judaism.

One more comment before we leave the issue of racism in Israel. The Israeli Security Service Law of 1959 provides that all Jewish citizens of the state, whether male or female, upon reaching the age of eighteen, must undergo military training and service in the Israel Defense Forces. At the explicit request of the Druze community in Israel, this law was subsequently extended to its members. The Bedouins and members of the Christian Arab communities may volunteer for service. As for the non-Bedouin Muslim Arabs (who constitute the majority of the Israeli Arab population), they are neither conscipted nor accepted as volunteers. Some critics of Israel interpret this as a manifestation of racial discrimination; they argue that the very fact that the Arabs are excluded from the Israel Defense Forces proves that they are considered second-class citizens. In fact, the reasons behind the exclusion have nothing to do with racism. They are anchored in two considerations. One is a matter of security. In view of the close family ties most Israeli Arabs have with their kinfolk across the borders, Arab soldiers in the Israeli army could constitute a security risk. The other is a humanitarian consideration. It is believed that Arabs should not be placed in a situation in which, in the event of war, their military duty would demand that they fight other Arabs. Still, in 1987, for the first time, a report prepared by high-ranking Israeli politicians and military men was submitted to the government recommending that the defense establishment examine ways to encourage Arabs to volunteer for the Israel Defense Forces.[25]

THE JEWISH RESPONSE TO THE LIBEL OF RACISM

By the second half of 1987 the Zionism = racism libel seemed to have passed the peak of its credibility. On September 21 of that year the Parliament of Europe, meeting in Strasbourg, adopted a resolution with the overwhelming majority of 181 to 3, repudiating the twelve-year-old United Nations resolution that equated Zionism with racism and declaring that resolution "unacceptable." Note that the statement of the Parliament of Europe was initiated by a representative of the West German Bundestag, Otto von Hapsburg, who has been a champion of Jewish rights in the Soviet Union and who is none other than the former Crown Prince Otto, son of Charles IV, the last king-emperor of the Austro-Hungarian monarchy.

A month later (October 23, 1987) a "Sense-of-the-Senate Resolution," introduced by Senator Daniel Patrick Moynihan, was adopted urging the United States to have the United Nations General Assembly rescind its 1975 resolution equating Zionism with racism. At the time of this writing

(October, 1987), a similar resolution was pending in the House of Representatives.

Other public bodies, too, have taken a position against the 1975 United Nations resolution, and, it is hoped, the day is not too far when it will be repealed by the General Assembly itself. In the meantime, however, the allegation that Zionism equals racism, that Israel is a racist state, and that, by implication, the Jews and Judaism are racist has deeply wounded the Jews sensitized by their history to potentially dangerous libels.

The religiously based anti-Semitism the Jews had encountered for many centuries in both the Christian and the Muslim countries and its successor the racial anti-Semitism of the nineteenth and twentieth centuries have implanted into the Jewish psyche the awareness that the small and weak Jewish communities lived in the Diaspora amid a large, powerful, and hostile Gentile world. The European emancipation of the Jews during the nineteenth century alleviated the Jewish condition to varying degrees for a few decades, but even before they learned to breathe freely in a world that was opening up before them, the Nazi genocide visited upon them the greatest cataclysm of their long history. The defeat of Germany in World War II saved the rest of the Jews from extermination, and when two years later the nations of the world approved the establishment of Israel, Jews believed that at long last they would be allowed to take their rightful place in the family of nations as one of its many members, shouldering the same duties and enjoying the same rights as all the others.

But no. Less than three decades later the international forum of the United Nations, now consisting of more than twice as many members as in 1947 when it voted for the establishment of a Jewish state in Palestine, went on record with a most serious allegation against Israel and the global Jewish movement that had worked for its creation and continued to work for its support. The blow that the Zionism = racism resolution dealt the State of Israel and the Jewish people all over the world was psychological rather than political. Politically, Israel carried on as before, and the Jews of the Diaspora continued to give it their unstinting support. But psychologically, the November 10, 1975, resolution, which in effect condemned the Jewish people as a whole, resuscitated the old Jewish sense of isolation in the world. World Jewry saw with utter dismay that, within a generation after the Nazi genocide, most of the nations of the world still—or again—constituted an enemy camp intent on defaming and denigrating it and in effect came close to advocating this time its exclusion from the comity of nations and its relegation to pariah status.

The overt Jewish response to this latest libel of racism was, and has remained, indignation, defiance, and readiness to fight back. In Israel it took the form of a resurgence of the conviction that to assure its survival it must be militarily strong so as not to allow its enemies to imagine that they

196

could prevail in a renewed armed conflict. In the Diaspora, and especially in the United States, the general Jewish feeling was that world Jewry must do all in its power to fight the libel and to prove its spuriousness. Yet—and this is the psychologically most damaging effect—despite these positive action-oriented responses, the very fact that for the first time in history Zionism, Israel, and through them Judaism have officially been condemned by the highest international forum, produced symptoms of withdrawal, and reawakened in the Jewish psyche a sense of global isolation that, after the establishment of Israel, many fondly had believed had been a ghost laid once and for all. It will take much positive thinking and acting by the Jews and much felicitous use of the optimism and self-certainty implanted—whether by history or by providence—into their psyche before they will be able to overcome the psychological damage inflicted upon them by the Zionism = racism resolution.

CONCLUSION

To recapitulate, we can state most emphatically not only that the Zionism = racism resolution was a crude travesty—this has been stated since by many individuals and public bodies—but also that the Jews, having suffered more from racism than any other people, are by this one circumstance alone made incapable of being racist. Their historical experiences have immunized them against this infection, and their hallowed traditions have dinned into them for centuries that all men are descended from one single pair of God-created ancestors. Ancient Jewish religious sources teach explicitly, moreover, that God made all men descend from precisely one couple to preclude one human group looking down upon another because of descent.[26] Mankind, in the traditional Jewish view, is one large family, and if the Children of Israel were chosen by God, they were not chosen to constitute a superior race but a "kingdom of priests and a holy nation" (Ex. 19:6)—we do not mind quoting this biblical word a second time in this chapter—membership in which was, and has remained, open to any and all persons whatever their race, color, language, or ethnic background, if they are willing to accept Judaism. A proselyte, by the very act of conversion, becomes a spiritual son or daughter of Abraham (in fact, his or her official name becomes "X. son or daughter of Abraham"). It cannot be overemphasized that racism, as known in other parts of the world, is essentially foreign to Judaism, which for two millennia has considered, and still considers, religion the only criterion that differentiates between Jew and non-Jew. It is equally foreign to Israel, which has accepted the purely religious traditional definition of membership in the Jewish community. Jewish history abounds in examples of Gentiles having converted to Judaism and become teachers and spiritual leaders of the Jewish people. The

197

very fact that Judaism in every age has attracted many proselytes (see the overview given in chapter III) proves uncontrovertibly not only that the Jews are not a race but also that they are not racist.

PART THREE

Genetic

CHAPTER VIII

Morphological Traits

THE APPLICATION OF morphological traits to population studies began many years ago. Most of these studies, done a generation or more ago, remain incomplete. As C. L. Brace points out, "In much recent biological thinking there has been the feeling that morphological variation is difficult to appraise since the precise mode of inheritance is so poorly known, and the result has been the abandonment of morphology as a valid area for investigation by many recent students." Maps of the worldwide distribution of skin color, hair form, shape of nose, and so forth, have been drawn,[1] but the best data on Jewish populations still come from relatively old studies.

In 1911 Maurice Fishberg analyzed in detail the morphological characteristics of various Jewish groups.[2] In accordance with the prevailing anthropological thinking in the early twentieth century, Fishberg's approach to the question of the Jewish "race" was primarily typological. In a chapter entitled "Types of Jews," he described more than a dozen Jewish types in detail. He believed that each of the two main Jewish types, the Ashkenazi and the Sephardi, comprise several distinct subtypes. Among the Ashkenazim, the most common type is the Slavonic, followed by the Turanian, the North European or Teutonic, the Mongoloid, and the Negroid type. The Sephardi type is, according to Fishberg, far less heterogeneous, but nevertheless it comprises subtypes resembling the Spaniards, the Moors, the Italians, the French, the Arabs, the Berbers, the Kabyles, and so on.[3] Fishberg applies this typological approach to the Jews of dozens of countries. In these descriptions the phrase "very interesting type" crops up frequently, especially in describing Jewish groups that are markedly different from the more familiar East European Ashkenazi "type." Thus the Jews of the Algerian oasis of Mzab "are a very interesting type," while the Jewish cave dwellers of Tripoli are "the most interesting of the North African Jews," and "the most curious class of negro 'Jews' is said to have existed in Jamaica and Surinam."[4] We do not, however, denigrate the importance of Fishberg's pioneer study. Nobody else either before or after him has brought together so many detailed observations on the great variety of Jewish physical types, nor presented such a rich array of related material on Jewish proselytism, intermarriage, demography, pathology, social and economic conditions, education, occupations, criminality, political conditions, social disabilities, and even assimilation versus Zionism. Although subsequent advances in genetic studies have rendered Fishberg's conclusions largely obsolete, his 600-page book is an important historical document, and the morphological data he collected remain valuable.

In the following pages we will present a rapid survey of those Jewish morphological features on which sufficient data are available. Much of it is taken from Fishberg, whose material is supplemented whenever subsequent studies exist. We also add completely new observations on hand clasping and arm folding, on fingerprint patterns, and on dental morphology.

HEIGHT

Height is greatly influenced by environment; better living conditions, and in particular better nutrition and physical exercise, result in increased height, as has often been proved when comparing parents with their children. Nonetheless, height is primarily determined by heredity. No one doubts, for instance, that the difference in average height between the Nilotic and Pygmy populations in Africa is largely due to genetic factors.

Fishberg looked into the then common belief that Jews are shorter than non-Jews, and that this is a Jewish "racial" characteristic. He found, first of all, that the stature of Jews is far from homogeneous. In Poland and Lithuania, the Jews averaged about 161 cm. in height; in South and Little Russia, they were taller, about 163–166 cm.; and in England and the United States, they averaged 168–171 cm. (167 cm. = 5 feet 6 inches). Second, he found a close correlation between the heights of Jews and non-Jews in every locality. Thus, Jews in Poland averaged 161.3 cm. and non-Jews, 162.5 cm. in height. In Rumania, both the Jews and non-Jews were taller, the Jews averaging 165.4 cm. and the indigenous Ruthenians 167.3 cm. In North Africa, the Jews of Algeria, Morocco, and Tunisia were even taller, averaging 166.9 cm., just like the Moslem Kabyles, Arabs, Berbers, and others inhabiting the same countries. Fishberg concluded: "One thing is certain, the stature of the Jews varies with the stature of the non-Jewish population among which they live."

East European Jews, however, averaged 1 to 2 cm. less in height than East European non-Jews. Because he was fully aware that stature is greatly influenced by environment, Fishberg believed that the cause of this deficit might be the "poverty and privations in which they are generally employed, and the absence of agricultural laborers among them."[5]

In the Caucasus, the mean heights of six Jewish samples were 162.2 cm. to 164.4 cm., compared with 165.5 to 171.1 cm. for other Caucasian ethnic groups. If data based on the small Jewish samples are representative of the population, then Caucasian Jews are near the lower end of the range exhibited by the non-Jewish groups.[6]

In the Middle East, data on Jews are sparse. For a small sample of Iraqi Jews, Seltzer reports a mean height of 164.1 cm. Field found that the stature of Iraqi Jews, with a mean of 164.5 cm., was 3.84 cm. shorter than that of the Arabs, and 2.25 cm. shorter than that of the Marsh Arabs. The differences between Jews and other ethnic groups were smaller.

In northern Iraq, the Jews were taller—165.7 cm.; in Damascus, Syria —164.5–166.3 cm.; in Isfahan, Iran—164.9 cm.; in Egypt—174.4 cm. Jewish women were in all countries considerably shorter than Jewish men: in San'a, Yemen—145.7 cm.; in northern Iraq—150.9 cm.; in Iraq—151.1 cm.; in Sandur, Kurdistan—151.3 cm.; in Aleppo, Syria—152.1 cm. In all these places there were no significant differences in stature between Jewish and non-Jewish women. For non-Jews in the Middle East, Seltzer reports a mean height of 167.2 for Syria and 166.2 cm. for Armenia.[7] In contrast, two small samples of Samaritans had mean heights of 171.1 and 173.0 cm., making this semi-Jewish group the tallest population in the region. The Habbanite Jews, on the other hand, are very short, with a mean of 161.7 cm. for men and only 147.4 cm. for women.[8]

Among Jews living in the Sahara Desert, the mean height for males was 166.1 cm. The height of non-Jewish males of the Sahara ranged from a mean of 162.0 cm. for the Mzabites and 165.9 cm. for the Moors, to 174.2 cm. for the western Tuareg. The Jewish mean is thus well within that of non-Jewish tribes of the Sahara.[9]

These additional data confirm Fishberg's general conclusion: "In countries where the indigenous population is of tall stature, the Jews are of superior height; and, reversely, wherever the non-Jewish population is short of stature, the Jews are also deficient in this respect."[10]

Recently Kobyliansky and Livshits[11] calculated morphological distances based on previously published data on the length of various bones in the body (which is related to the person's height), the circumference of trunk and limbs (which is related to one's weight), and skinfold thickness (also related to weight), for Jewish and non-Jewish men from East Europe, Central Europe, South Europe, Middle East, and North Africa. The greater the number they calculated, the greater is the physical difference between two populations. Distances were calculated for pairs of populations. They found that the Jewish populations were much closer to each other than to non-Jewish groups. The morphological distance ranged from 0.228 (between Central and South European Jews) to 6.558 (between Central European Jews and North African non-Jews). The average calculated morphological distance between Jewish communities was 0.780, and between Jews and non-Jews 4.044. These differences are certainly remarkable and contrast with earlier studies on height in various populations. The authors conclude that there is a significant genetic contribution to the morphological traits they studied, and suggest a genetic similarity among the diverse Jewish populations.

Interpretation of these results is confounded by the well-known environmental contribution to morphological traits. For example, when 2400 healthy adult Israelis were measured in a recent study, the native Israelis were found to be significantly taller than were immigrants. This was true for both men and women. For example, the mean height of men born in Israel was 171.2 cm., compared with 167.4 cm. for men born in Asia and North Africa (Sephardi and Oriental Jews), and 168.8 cm. for those born in Europe, America, and South Africa (Ashkenazim).[12] These findings confirm the important contribution of environmental factors to height.

HAIR AND EYE COLOR

The predominant type of complexion of Jews today is dark: black and brown hair and eyes are in the majority. However, blond Jews are found almost everywhere. Fishberg summarized a set of investigations on hair and eye color in European and Asian Jews (see Table 8.1).

Among more than 4,000 Jews observed by Fishberg in New York, 10.4% of the males and 10.3% of the females had fair hair *and* blue eyes, and another 37% of males and 32.8% of females had fair hair *or* blue eyes ("mixed types"). Dark hair and dark eyes were found in 52.6% of Jewish males and 57% of Jewish females. Fishberg concluded that the "brunette type, which is considered characteristic of the Jews from time immemorial, is thus reduced to only 52% among the [male] European representatives of the race, while among Jewesses it is not much larger."[13]

Most of the blond Jews are found in countries where the general population has a considerable proportion of blonds, for example, in Germany and England. In Italy, where the Christian population is generally brunette, fewer than 5% of the Jews are blond; in Algeria, Bokhara, and the Caucasus, the percentages are even lower.

The modern blond Jews have been considered by some (for example, von Luschan) to be the descendants of the Amorites, who are said to have been blonds, and with whom the Hebrews extensively intermarried. How-

Frequency of Blond Hair and Blue Eyes Among Jewish Groups

COUNTRY	% FAIR HAIR	% BLUE EYES
England	25.5	41.2
Galicia	20.3	52.1
Bosnia	18.5	30.9
Little Russia	17.7	53.7
Rumania	14.7	51.3
Lithuania	14.1	37.8
South Russia	13.0	33.0
Baden, Germany	12.8	51.2
England (Sephardim)	11.9	33.2
United States	11.3	44.3
Hungary	17.9	50.7
Turkey	10.0	18.7
Poland	7.2	43.9
Italy	4.8	30.0
North Africa	5.2	16.9
Caucasus	2.0	15.7

SOURCE: Maurice Fishberg, *The Jews*, London: Walker Scott Publ. Co., and New York: Charles Scribner's Sons, 1911, pp. 64–65.

ever, Fishberg concludes that "all available data about the interrelation of stature, complexion and head-form point to a similarity between the Jews of Eastern Europe and the Gentile races among which they have lived for centuries."[14] That is, most blond Jews may be the result of intermixture with Slavic populations.

NOSE

Among 2,836 adult male Jews in New York City, Fishberg found that 57.3% had straight, or "Greek," noses; 22.1% had *retroussé*, or snub, noses; 14.2% had aquiline, or hooked, noses; and 6.4% had flat and broad noses. Among 1,284 Jewish women, 59.4% had straight noses, 13.9% snub, 12.7% hooked, and 14.0% flat and broad noses. Thus, the predominant type of nose among the Jews is straight; only 13–14% had hooked noses.

Observers in Russia, Austria, Hungary, and other countries, have also found a low proportion of hooked noses among Jews. Moreover, this kind of nose is also found among non-Jewish populations. It is found in more than 10% of Little Russians, more than 6% of Poles and Ruthenians of Galicia, and in 31% of the Germans in Bavaria. Bavarian Jews also have a higher proportion of hooked noses than Jews in other countries. The beaked nose, the tip of which makes a twist backward, is mostly found among the Bavarian Jews and is extremely rare among Jews in other countries. This form of nose is also very common among non-Jewish Caucasian tribes, and in Asia Minor, among Armenians, Georgians, Ossets, Lesghians, and Syrians. In the Mediterranean countries of Europe—Greece, Italy, France, Spain, and Portugal—the aquiline nose is more common than among East European Jews. The North American Indians also often have "Jewish" noses. In the words of Shapiro:

> Much has been made of the so-called Jewish nose as a distinguishing racial feature. Considering the origin of the Jews from a population identified as Mediterranean in its fundamental affiliation, and its early absorption of various local strains found in the Near East, it is not surprising that the convex nasal bridge and the depressed nasal tip be found among them. It is a common enough type of nasal development among these people and in that part of the Mediterranean. Moreover, these features are also to be found in varying degrees in some European populations as well.[15]

CEPHALIC INDEX

The cephalic index has long been the most popular component of racial studies. This index of head shape is obtained by measuring the maximum width of the head from a point over one ear to the opposite point over the other ear, then measuring the maximum length of the head from a point on the middle of the forehead between, or slightly above, the eyebrows to a point on the occiput (the back part of the head). The width is then divided by the length and the result multiplied by 100. Among the great majority of human adults the cephalic index ranges from 70 to 85. A human group whose mean cephalic index is less than 75 is considered long-headed, or dolichocephalic; if the mean index ranges between 75 and 80, the group is medium-headed, or mesocephalic; and if the mean index exceeds 80, it is broad-headed, or brachycephalic. When the pair of measurements is carried out on a skull rather than a living head, the result is called the *cranial index,* which is usually 1.5 to 2 points lower than the corresponding cephalic index.

Until the celebrated study of Franz Boas on *Changes in the Bodily Form of Immigrants and Their Descendants* (1911), the cephalic index was considered to be unaffected by environment. Boas, however, showed that the children of broad-headed East European immigrants to the United States had a lower cephalic index (were longer-headed) than their parents, while the children of long-headed Sicilian immigrants were more broad-headed than their parents.[16] Subsequent studies[17] have indicated that the length of the head increases with the height of the individual but its breadth does not. An increase in stature in a population of European origin, which may result from an improvement in diet, is usually accompanied by a decrease in cephalic index, for the head becomes longer without becoming broader. However, this phenomenon has not been found in long-headed populations of Mediterranean origin, nor in populations of East Asian origin. In fact, the growth in stature of Chinese born in the United States and of Japanese born in Hawaii has been reported to be associated with broadening of the skull.[18]

In confirmation of the influence of environment on cephalic index are the data of Kobyliansky on changes in the cephalic index in Israeli-born offspring of Jewish immigrants.[19] Significant differences were found between siblings born abroad and in Israel, in contrast with small differences in the cephalic index of unrelated persons born in Israel. The cephalic index of immigrants was similar to that of their country of origin, whereas the cephalic index changes in Israeli-born persons were closer to the "Mediterranean type" of mesocephaly.

Although the cephalic index may be of limited usefulness in studies of populations that have undergone major environmental changes, such as migration from Europe to America or to Israel, it remains valuable in stationary populations or in populations that undergo only limited movement and cultural-environmental change. On the basis of the measurements of more than 5,000 individuals in the Middle East, Ariëns Kappers concluded that the cephalic index has hereditary value. He also showed that the cephalic index of the Egyptians has remained unchanged for four to five thousand years.[20]

More recently, a study of more than 450 families in Czechoslovakia found that the cephalic index of an infant does not correlate at all closely to those of his parents as a pair, but that in half the cases the cephalic index of the child falls within 1% of that of one of the parents, and in 80% of cases within 3%. It is therefore hypothesized that the shape of the head is inherited in a unitary fashion, the child taking after one or the other parent. This study confirms that there is a strong genetic component in the determination of the cephalic index.[21]

Keeping in mind that the cephalic index is subject to environmental effects, we may look at the data on Jews and non-Jews of different countries. Considerable differences even within countries were found by different workers, so that often only the range of means found by various observers has been given.

The cephalic index data indicate considerable diversity among different Jewish populations. Jews from Habban in the Hadhramaut Valley of southern Yemen are extremely broad-headed.[22] Jews from Central and Eastern Europe, northern Italy, the Caucasus, Russia, and Kurdistan are broad-headed. Those from the Balkans, Cochin, Iran and Iraq, Egypt, and Morocco are medium-headed; and Jews from Yemen, the Barbary Coast, and the Mzab (Sahara) are long-headed.

Table 8.2 also indicates the relationship between the Jewish and non-Jewish cephalic indices. In those places where the Jews have lived for a long time, their cephalic index is much like that of the non-Jews; where they have lived for a shorter period, there are marked differences. For instance, in Morocco, where Jews and non-Jews have lived side by side for at least 1,500 years, the Jewish cephalic index ranges from 75 to 78.2, and that of the Moslems is approximately 74. The ranges of the Jewish and non-Jewish cephalic indices in Iraq are likewise very similar. In contrast, the cephalic index of the Sephardi Jews, whether they live in Turkey or the Balkans, is similar to that of the Spaniards, Portuguese, and North African Muslims among whom they lived until their expulsion in 1492, rather than to that of the Turks, Bosnians, and Greeks among whom they have lived for the last four centuries.

The dissimilarity of the cephalic index of Sephardi Jews in Turkey and the Balkans and that of the non-Jews among whom they have lived for over four hundred years indicates, incidentally, the stability of the cephalic index (in the absence of extensive intermarriage) and suggests that the migration from the Iberian Peninsula to the Balkans did not result in major environmental modification of the cephalic index.

In Eastern Europe, where Jews had lived for many centuries, Pearson found that the correlation between the cephalic index of Jews and Gentiles in the same area is .8365.[23] This very high correlation can probably be explained best by interbreeding, for which there is considerable evidence, although some environmental influence cannot be excluded.

Montagu prefers to deal with the percentage of various head shapes in a population rather than with a single figure giving the mean index. He reports that among London Ashkenazi Jews, 28.3% have long heads, 24.3% have moderately round heads (mesocephals), and 47.4% have round heads. Among South Russian Jews these figures are 1, 18, and 81%, respectively. For London Sephardi Jews the figures are 17, 49, and 34%, respectively. Galician and Lithuanian Jews yield a proportion of 85% broad heads and only 3.8% long heads. "These percentage distributions show that head shape or cephalic index, like all other characteristics, is very variable among the Jews as a whole, the head shape of the Jews in various countries varying substantially from one to another."[24]

This brief review shows that the cephalic index of Jews is highly variable, ranging from 72.0 in the Mzab Jews of Ghardaia in the Sahara, which is near the minimum for any living people, to over 87 in the Caucasus and the Habban region of southern Yemen. This conclusion, based on living populations, is also true of the remains of Jews who lived approximately two thousand years ago. At Lakhish (Tell Duweir), in southern Israel, 695 crania were found in a few moss tombs. It seems that about the year 700 B.C. a large proportion of the population perished as a result of a natural

Cephalic Index of Jews and Non-Jews

EUROPE	JEWS		NON-JEWS
Germany	80.8–88.6		79–84.1
Galicia	83.3–83.6		83.75
Hungary	82.45		83–85
North Italy	82.1	Italians	77–87
Poland	81.6–82.9		79.8–82
Western Russia	81.9–81.7		81–83
Lithuania	80.9–81.7		79.8–80.6
White Russia	80.3–81.7		83.2
Bosnia	80.1		85.3
England	80.0		77–79
Sephardim	78.1–79	Spaniards	77–79
Turkey (Sephardim)	76.0–77.1	Portuguese	76.4
		Turks	82.2–87.2
		Greeks	81.9–87.2

ASIA	JEWS		NON-JEWS
Georgia (Caucasus)	85.1–85.9		80.6–83.5
Bokhara	84.0		84.2
Turkestan	83.5		75.2–85.8
Crimea Karaites	82.4–85.6	Crimea Tartars	84.1–85.3
Kurdistan	79.7–93.9		78.5–89.5
Samaritans	77.6–78.1		
Iraq	76.6–81.1		74.7–82.5
Iran	76.6–81.1		73.5–78.4
(Iran		One study	87.2)
Yemen	73.4–76.7		76.0–83.2
Habbanites (southern Yemen)	males 87.32		
	females 91.70		
India (Cochin)	males 78.0		
	females 77.9		

NORTH AFRICA	JEWS	NON-JEWS
Egypt	77.5	72.2–75.9
Morocco	75–78.2	74.3–74.8
Barbary Coast	74	
Mzab (Sahara)	72	

211

catastrophe, perhaps pestilence or earthquake, and was hastily interred. A study of these skulls and the other skeletal remains led D. L. Risdon to conclude that "the population of the town in 700 B.C. was entirely, or almost entirely, of Egyptian origin . . . probably derived from Upper Egypt."[25] The difficulty with this conclusion is that, as far as is known from historical sources, the population of Lakhish in 700 B.C. was Judaean, that is, Jewish. In fact, by 700 B.C. Lakhish had been settled by Hebrews for several centuries.[26] The solution of the problem seems to lie in the assumption that the Hebrews of Lakhish in 700 B.C. were genetically very close to the Egyptians.

During the various expeditions to the Judaean Desert organized since 1955 by the Israel Department of Antiquities, the Israel Exploration Society, and the Hebrew University, a number of human skeletons have been found. A total of forty-nine skeletons from the period of Bar Kokhba (second century A.D.) were found by Aharoni in the "Cave of Horror" of Nahal Hever and in the Cave of Nahal Seelim, and by Yadin in the "Cave of Letters" of Nahal Hever. A second group of eighty-one skeletons found by Avigad and ten skeletons found by Yadin in the caves of Ein-Gedi probably also belong to a Jewish population living in the first or second century B.C.[27] A third group of nine skeletons found in the caves of Nahal Mishmar and one found in the "Cave of Horror" appear to date to the Chalcolithic period (ca. 4,000–3,000 B.C.) and are therefore too early to be of concern for us in the present context.[28]

Among the Judaean skulls, the group of the Bar Kokhba period probably represent the remains of Jewish families who took refuge in these caves during the war against the Romans (A.D. 133–35). This group comprises mainly brachycranic (broad-headed) and some dolichocranic (long-headed) individuals. The Ein-Gedi caves were probably used as a cemetery. The skulls found there showed a clear predominance of mesocranics (medium-headed), with a minority of brachycranics and dolichocranics.[29]

More recently, the remains of thirty-five individuals were found in three burial caves at Giv'at Ha-Mivtar, Jerusalem.[30] They are believed to have died approximately between 100 B.C. and A.D. 70. Nineteen skulls were sufficiently preserved to permit cranial measurements; eleven were long-headed (C.I. 65–74), three medium headed (C.I. 75–79), and four broad-headed (C.I. 80–95). In contrast with the predominantly broad-headed skulls found by Aharoni and Yadin, which dated from the period of Bar Kokhba, the Giv'at Ha-Mivtar skulls are predominantly long-headed, although the latter individuals lived only shortly before the Bar Kokhba period. This recent finding again supports the heterogeneity of ancient Jewish populations.

HAND CLASPING AND ARM FOLDING

Everyone has a preferred way of clasping the hands (left thumb over right or right over left) and folding the arms (left arm over right or right over left). These differences are believed to be inherited, but the contribution of environmental factors is uncertain. The frequencies of right-over-left hand clasping are around 50 to 55% in most Caucasian populations, whereas values of 60% and higher have been found in Negroes in Angola and Brazil and in Australian aborigines, New Guinea natives, and Filipinos.[31]

A sample of 172 Kurdish Jews in Israel had a frequency of right-over-left hand clasping of 50%; the frequency in a sample of 74 Yemenite Jews was significantly higher: 68%. A group of Samaritans had a frequency of 56.8%.[32] This value did not differ significantly by statistical tests from either the Kurdish or Yemenite Jews. The Yemenite Jews show a Negro-like pattern of hand clasping, and do in fact have some Negro admixture. The Kurdish Jews, in contrast, show a Caucasian pattern. The hand-clasping data suggest that the Kurdish and Yemenite Jews are very different.

The frequency of right-over-left arm folding was 44% in the Kurdish Jews, 47% in the Yemenite Jews, and 44% in the Samaritans. Unlike hand clasping, the frequency of arm folding shows no tendency to cluster according to geographical or ethnic groupings, and this trait is thus less useful as an anthropological marker.

FINGERPRINT PATTERNS

The whorls, loops, and arches of the fingerprint patterns, like most morphological traits, cannot yet be analyzed into exact genetic systems. However, because they are known to be inherited and are not subject to strong environmental selection, they are useful in anthropological studies.

L. Sachs and M. Bat-Miriam examined the fingerprint patterns of eight Jewish populations who came to Israel from Germany, Poland, Bulgaria, Turkey, Egypt, Morocco, Iraq, and Yemen, and of an unselected group of Israeli Arabs. For each population they examined the frequencies of whorls, loops, and arches on each of the ten fingers in five hundred males.[33]

There were striking similarities in the frequencies of whorls and loops in the eight Jewish groups. On the other hand, all the frequencies differed from those found among non-Jewish Englishmen, Portuguese, and Dutch.

The frequencies of whorls and loops can be combined to form a "pattern index," which is useful in comparing populations. It is obtained by adding the percentage of loops to twice the percentage of whorls and dividing by 10. The pattern index of the Jewish populations ranged from 13.30

213

for all the Jews from Bulgaria to 13.98 for those from Poland. The mean index for all the Jewish groups was 13.67. A previous study of Jewish men in Germany yielded a similar figure, 13.87. The pattern index of the Habbanites in Israel was 13.13,[34] which is not far from that of the Bulgarian Jews. A more recent analysis of dermatoglyphic patterns of Israeli males yielded very similar results—the pattern indices of men from Eastern Europe, Central Europe, Middle East, and North Africa were very close to one another, varying only from 13.39 to 14.40.[35]

In contrast with the Jewish index figures, non-Jews from Europe and North America have lower indices, ranging from 11.85 to 12.59. None of the Jewish populations, even those that have resided for long periods in these same countries, have such low indices. High indices are, however, found among some non-Jews from the eastern Mediterranean region such as Egyptian Copts and Israeli Arabs, the latter having a pattern index of 14.01. The value in Lebanese non-Jews is 14.3, and in Syrian Arabs it is even higher, 14.6. These results suggest that in this trait an East Mediterranean heritage has been preserved among European (Ashkenazi) Jews.[36]

In a recent study of fingerprint patterns of Israeli Jews of East European, Middle Eastern, North African, and Yemenite origin, dermatoglyphic genetic distance coefficients were calculated for pairs of Jewish populations and for pairs of Jewish and non-Jewish groups. The larger the coefficient found, the greater the genetic distance between the two populations being compared. The calculations for the non-Jewish groups were based on previously published data. Based on fingerprint patterns, the European, Middle Eastern, and African Jews were closely related to each other, but were very different from the Yemenite Jews. When the Jews were compared with non-Jewish populations, the Jewish patterns were most like those of non-Jews from the Caucasus mountain region of the U.S.S.R. For example, the dermatoglyphic distance coefficient for the Caucasus Russians and the Middle Eastern Jews was only 1.84, and the index for Caucasoids and North African Jews was 3.21, compared with an index of 11.50 for Eastern European Jews and Yemenite Jews, and an index of 11.8 for African blacks and East European whites. The index for Middle Eastern and North African Jews was 3.04, and for East European and North African Jews, 2.95.

Thus, according to the fingerprint pattern results, non-Jewish Russians from the Caucasus region are as close genetically to diverse Jewish populations as the Jewish groups are to one another. Both groups are very different from Yemenite Jews, African blacks, and Asian mongoloids.[37] The authors conclude that because their results are in agreement with gene frequency and skin color differences among the various populations, fingerprint patterns are a legitimate area for study of population distances. However, the inheritance of fingerprint patterns is so complex that in our opinion such studies are useful primarily to confirm results of population studies of traits that have a simpler mode of inheritance.

TOOTH MORPHOLOGY

A recent study compared the shapes of teeth of five Jewish and six non-Jewish populations.[38] Nine of the samples were living people, and two were skeletal remains. The contemporary Jews were from Eastern Europe, Habban, Kurdistan, and Morocco. A Jewish group of 124 skeletal remains, excavated on Mount Zion, Jerusalem, was estimated to be 3,000 years old. The contemporary non-Jews were Bedouins, Circassians (Moslems from the Caucasus now living in Israel), Druze, Samaritans, and a group from Northern Sudan now living in Wadi Halfa. A non-Jewish group of 96 skeletal remains was excavated on the east coast of Australia and dated at 1,000–2,000 years old. Each group comprised 70–228 individuals. Nineteen morphological variables were scored and a measure of distance between each pair of groups was calculated.

The authors conclude that, except for the Habbanite Jews, all the other Jewish groups were related, despite the fact that they came from a wide geographical area. In particular, the skeletal remains from Mount Zion showed greater affinity with three of the four living Jewish populations (except for the Habbanites) than with most of the non-Jewish groups. The Habbanites, in contrast, were very different from the other Jewish groups, from the Jewish skeletal group, and from all the non-Jewish groups, thereby again confirming the genetic uniqueness of this isolate. Another genetic isolate, the Samaritans, were also very different from all the Jewish and non-Jewish groups studied. The Druze, in contrast, were close to the Circassians, Bedouins, and all the Jewish groups except the Habbanites. They were particularly close to the Mount Zion remains and to the Eastern European Jews.

The data show, however, that the Bedouins, Circassians, and Druze are all closer to the European Jews than are the Kurdish Jews, Moroccan Jews, the Mount Zion remains, and, of course, the Habbanite Jews. Thus, it cannot be concluded that the various Jewish groups are more closely related to one another than to non-Jews. To gain perspective on the significance of the distances between pairs of Jewish and non-Jewish populations, it would be helpful to have a similar analysis of tooth morphology for modern European populations so that additional distances between Jewish and non-Jewish groups can be calculated.

CONCLUSIONS

In this chapter we have surveyed the height, hair and eye color, nose shape, cephalic index, hand clasping and arm folding, fingerprint patterns, and tooth morphology of the Jews. Each of the first four features shows such variability among the Jews and such correspondences between the Jewish and non-Jewish values in each locality that they refute the hypothesis of Jewish racial unity. In fact, the ranges found among the Jews for these traits are generally as broad as the corresponding ranges among the non-Jewish majority populations among whom the Jews have lived after their dispersion from Palestine. On the basis of these four features alone, one would have to conclude that the Jews are about as unlikely to constitute a single human race as would be a group composed of Russians, Germans, Italians, Spaniards, Moroccans, Iraqis, Persians, people from the Caucasus, and Yemenites.

The hand-clasping findings support this conclusion for two well-established groups of Middle Eastern Jews, the Kurds and Yemenites, who had no contact with each other for centuries and consequently diverged in their gene pools. The results of fingerprint analysis, however, reveal some relatedness among such widely separated Jewish groups as those from Germany, Turkey, Morocco, and Yemen. The pattern found in all these groups is suggestive of a Mediterranean origin. The picture that emerges is of a group of people who originated in the Mediterranean region and subsequently have diversified greatly in their genetic make-up. Only in fingerprint patterns, a trait believed to be minimally influenced by the environment, can we still see remnants of the Mediterranean gene pool in European Jews. As for tooth morphology, which is probably somewhat affected by environmental factors, additional population studies are needed to draw conclusions about how closely related are the various Jewish populations examined.

216

CHAPTER IX

Looking Jewish

"Thou must know that we people of Persia are
skilled in physiognomy; I saw the woman to be
rosy-cheeked, blue-eyed and tall-statured . . . and I
knew she was a Jewess."[1]

From "The Story of the Weaver Who Became a
Leech"

—*The Arabian Nights*

T HE PREVIOUS CHAPTER presented evidence that the Jews do not have a
monopoly on a particular type of hair and eye color or nose shape,
and that they are heterogeneous with respect to these traits. Yet in Western
countries outside the Mediterranean area many Jews can be readily identified as such by the man in the street, apparently on the basis of physical
appearance. How can this paradox be resolved?

On-sight identification of Jews seems to have two components, physical and cultural. Carl C. Seltzer, in his 1939 paper, "The Jew—His Racial
Status," states his view that most Jews can be identified by their physical
features:

> No matter what racial blends the various groups of Jewish people are com-
> posed of, virtually all possess a small remnant of Mediterranean and Iranian
> Plateau blood. In some Jewish people these strains are stronger than in others.
> The physical expression of the Iranian Plateau element in a dominant nasality
> [which Seltzer describes as a strongly dominant, beaklike nose with a thick
> and depressed tip and incurved nostrils]. . . . It is certainly a feature which
> aids in making the Jews physically distinctive. The Mediterranean strain is
> expressed in part by a certain thickness and eversion of the lips, together with
> a strong tendency towards very wavy and curly hair; and probably by promi-
> nent, widely open and large-lidded eyes. . . . In the majority of cases, they
> seem to be distinctive enough to aid in the separation of Jew and Gentile, es-
> pecially when these characteristics are found associated with certain extra-
> verted social and psychological features.[2]

But the earlier findings of Fishberg on the frequency of hair and eye color
and shape of nose appear to cast doubt on Seltzer's assertion that the majority of Jews can be identified on the basis solely of the physical features

217

he describes. Seltzer himself invokes social and psychological features to aid in the identification; the importance of these will be discussed later.

Juan Comas seems to hew closer to empirical reality when he writes:

How it is that in fact some Jews can almost infallibly be identified as such at first glance? The probable explanation is that the Jews in question are those who retain certain ancestral Jewish characteristics: aquiline nose, pale skin in combination with dark eyes and hair. Nevertheless, we fail to notice and identify a much larger number of Jews who have taken on the traits of the people among whom they live and pass unnoticed.[3]

Similarly, Harry L. Shapiro stresses that

in some of the northwestern and eastern countries of Europe . . . one might expect . . . that Jewish settlers . . . would display obvious differences, springing from their diverse racial components, and some overlap where certain strains were common. Although centuries, even millennia, of contact have established an unknown but appreciable amount of gene flow between Jewish colonies and the surrounding population, as the corresponding gene frequencies suggest, these initial differences have not been completely eliminated. Jewish populations in these areas still retain some elements of genetic difference, while they have departed from the standards of the original population from which they were derived.[4]

The consensus among these analysts of the question of "looking Jewish" is that *most* Jews are *somewhat* different from the non-Jews of European stock and that *some* Jews have retained sufficient Mediterranean features to enable identification in non-Mediterranean settings. In subsequent chapters we shall look more closely at the extent of genetic differences between Jews and neighboring non-Jews, to see whether there is any basis for the view that despite their extensive interbreeding with surrounding peoples throughout their history most European Jews have retained a "core" of Mediterranean genes, which links them genetically with Jews in other parts of the world. Meanwhile, let us remark that the physical features in question, as Seltzer has emphasized, are not exclusively Jewish but are shared by non-Jewish Mediterranean populations. However, in countries like Germany or Poland the only sizable population element that exhibited them to any marked extent was the Jewish, and hence a Mediterranean-looking individual was "recognized" as a Jew. (Similarly, in the same countries, an Indian-looking individual was "recognized" as a Gypsy.) Even if only a small proportion of the Jews had Mediterranean features, it sufficed to confirm a stereotype.

Moving down from Central Europe to the Mediterranean basin, we find ourselves in an area where the similarity in physical features between Jews and non-Jews is much greater. In fact, their physical features alone would not make Jews recognizable among Spaniards, Italians, Greeks, Turks, Arabs, and other North Africans. This is the world area to which the Jews are indigenous, in which whatever interbreeding occurred between them and non-Jews took place mostly with other Mediterraneans, or with peoples who had the same physical features as themselves.

The same is true in lands to the east and south of the Mediterranean basin. It is unusual to find any physical difference between the Iranians, the Afghans, the Yemenites, the Hadhramis, the Indians, the Ethiopians, and the Jews who live among them. Yet it is (or was) just as easy to recognize the Jews in these countries as it is (or was) in Germany or in Northeastern Europe. However, as Shapiro pointed out, the basis on which Jews are recognized in these regions is cultural rather than biological.[5]

The observation that the differences between Jews and non-Jews in any country are cultural or social rather than genetic is not a new one. On January 27, 1883, Ernest Renan, the famous French Orientalist, delivered a lecture entitled *Le judaisme comme race et comme religion (Judaism as a Race and as a Religion)* in which, among other things, he touched upon the question of why and how the Jews can be recognized. That they *can* be recognized, and easily at that, was taken for granted by Renan, as it was by others who observed Jews shortly after their emancipation and at an early stage of their assimilation of the social and cultural values of the societies in whose midst they lived. There are several Jewish types, says Renan, which can be recognized not because of their race but because of certain Jewish peculiarities that are a result of having been subjected for centuries to ghetto life. The Jews resemble one another because of their costume and customs, because of facial expression but not facial features, because of bodily posture but not bodily form, and because of the psychology of a religious (but not racial) minority.[6]

Of all the factors enumerated by Renan, facial expression soon became most popular as the alleged sign by which Jews can be recognized.

In the early 1900's, several observers reiterated that Jews differ from non-Jews, not in physical features, but in their specific facial expression. Facial expression, or "mimic function," it was held, can make even disparate racial types appear similar, and it is by this, not by physical traits, that the Jews (or many Jews) can be recognized.[7] One expert physiognomist even went so far as to suggest that the typical "Jewish nose" was the hereditary product of a habitual expression of indignation.[8]

Fishberg assembled much relevant material on the Jewish facial expression, which various students attributed to ghetto life, social ostracism, ceaseless suffering, the stamp of occupations. He himself shared their views, and quoted Emerson's *English Traits:* "Every religious sect has its physiognomy. The Methodists have acquired a face, the Quakers a face, the nuns a face."[9] Although there is no general agreement as to what precisely constitutes the Jewish facial expression, some of the characteristics most often mentioned are worry, anxiety, fear, pain, melancholy, irrita-

219

tion, and nervousness, much of which emanates from the eyes and brows. A surprising number of late-nineteenth- and early-twentieth-century ethnologists used the phrase "look like Jews" when describing the most varied peoples (including Japanese, Indonesians, North and South American Indians, Papuans, Kaffirs, Afghans, Baluchis, and Hindus) among whom they observed individuals with a facial expression that somehow reminded them of Jews they knew back home.[10]

In those places where Jews wore a distinctive garb, this feature alone made them stand out. Until the nineteenth century, most Jews in most countries had their own traditional clothing and head covering, which meant that they were instantly recognized by the clothes they wore. In the same places Jewish men usually wore their hair and beard in a distinctive style (shaved head, long sidelocks, and long beard), which again made their identification as Jews almost automatic. In the countries of the Middle East this remained the case everywhere—with the exception of the thin modernized upper- and middle-class Jewish sectors in the biggest cities, such as Baghdad and Cairo—until the large mass exodus following the establishment of the State of Israel in 1948.

Among Ashkenazi Jews, clothing and hair style varied from country to country. In Russia, until the Bolshevik revolution of 1917 the situation was like that in the Middle East: most Jews, except the well-to-do in the big cities, had their own clothing and hair style and could easily be recognized on the basis of these features alone. After the revolution, the Jews began to dress and wear their hair and beard in the same fashion as the non-Jews, so that their outward appearance no longer advertised their being Jewish. In Poland, the same process was not yet completed by the time the Nazi genocide destroyed almost the entire Polish Jewish community. As one went from Poland westward, say, in 1939, one found fewer and fewer Jews in each locality who had retained their traditional appearance. Today in every Western country where Jews live, only a small, religiously most observant minority retains the traditional Jewish clothing, hair, and beard style.

Yet another cultural trait that in the past made the identification of many Jews possible was their speech. Until the end of the eighteenth century, Yiddish was the mother tongue of most Ashkenazi Jews and their knowledge of the languages of the countries in which they lived was rudimentary. The mother tongue in general colors the pronunciation of every other language learned by a speaker. Sensitive ears could detect traces of the peculiar Jewish speech in German, Polish, Russian, Rumanian, Hungarian, French, or English as late as the mid-nineteenth century. A parallel phenomenon could be observed in the countries of the Middle East where the Jews spoke Judaeo-Arabic, Judaeo-Persian, and so on, which differed not only in containing some Hebrew words, but also in the pronunciation of Arabic or Persian from the way in which these languages were spoken by Moslems. However slight the actual phonetic differences, they assumed great significance when they fell upon anti-Semitic ears, were interpreted as indication of Jewish inability to speak correctly, and were considered manifestations of Jewish inferiority that evoked disgust and revulsion.

As early as 1714, the German anti-Semitic author Johann Jakob Schudt remarked that the peculiar accent of the Jews reveals them as soon as they open their mouths.[11] And the well-known German Africanist Gerhard Rohlfs (1831–96), speaking of the Jews of North Africa, says, "Nothing is more ridiculous than to hear a Jew twangle (*schminzeln*) in Arabic . . . or Berber . . . the Jew twangles in general in all languages." Making himself even more explicit, he remarks that "we know that the Jew in Germany can always be recognized by the dissonance of his speech. The same is the case with the Jews in all European countries."[12]

The anti-Semitism of Richard Wagner led him from a criticism of Jewish music to that of Jewish speech:

> It is in particular the purely sensuous manifestation of the Jewish speech that revolts us. Culture was unsuccessful in eradicating the peculiar stubbornness of the Jewish nature with respect to the characteristics of the Semitic manner of expression despite two thousand years of intercourse with European nations. One's ear perceives especially the hissing, shrill-sounding, buzzing and grunting tonal expression of the Jewish way of speech as thoroughly foreign and unpleasant. In addition, the arbitrary twisting of words and phrase constructions, which is totally uncharacteristic of our national language, gives this tonal expression the character of a completely insufferable confused babbling in listening to which our attention involuntarily dwells more on this revolting *how* of the Jewish speech than on the *what* contained in it.[13]

The German anthropologist Richard Andree, who, as we have seen, believed in the "unchangeability of the Jewish type," was convinced of the indelibility of the peculiarly Jewish pronunciation of every language spoken by Jews. The Jewish way of speaking was called *mauscheln* in German, and Andree subscribed to the tenet that *mauscheln* was a Jewish racial characteristic that was as unlikely to disappear as their physical type. Even the majority of the cultured Jews, he held, retained this peculiar lisping enunciation, which struck the German ear as most unpleasant.[14]

Twenty years later, the British anthropologist Augustus Henry Keane (1833–1912) suggested that the Jewish inability to learn European languages properly, even after having dwelt for hundreds of years amid Europeans, should be given priority as an important subject of study.[15]

No refutation of these views is necessary. But as a matter of curiosity it might be mentioned that even before the nineteenth century drew to a close some of the greatest actors and actresses on the stages of London, Paris, Berlin, Vienna, and Budapest, who delighted and captivated highly critical audiences not only with their acting but also with their diction, were Jews.

In summary, in the past Jews could most frequently be recognized, not by their physical traits, but by such culturally determined features as facial expression, costume, and language. One could add bodily posture, customs, mannerisms, and other behavioral traits; but these, though culturally determined and thus part of Jewish ethnicity, would lead us into more difficult terrain that is better left unexplored in the present context.

We might, however, quote the conclusions reached independently in this century by two leading authors, one an American and the other a Mexican. In 1945 Ashley Montagu stated:

> There undoubtedly exists a certain quality of looking Jewish, but this quality is not due so much to any inherited characters of the persons in questions, as to certain culturally acquired habits of expression, facial, vocal, muscular, and mental. Such habits do to a very impressive extent influence the appearance of the individual and determine the impression which he makes upon others. . . . It is possible to distinguish many Jews from members of other cultural groups for the same reason that it is possible to distinguish Englishmen from such groups, or Americans, Frenchmen, Italians, and Germans. . . . Members of one cultural group do not readily fit into the pattern of another.[16]

In 1961 Juan Comas expressed himself in a similar vein:

> The fact that some Jews can be identified as such on sight is due less to inherited physical traits than to the conditioning of emotional and other reactions productive of distinctive facial expressions and corporal attitudes, mannerisms, intonation and tendencies of temperament and character, by Jewish custom and the treatment inflicted on Jews by non-Jews.[17]

In the late 1980's the important facet of the issue of "looking Jewish" is that it is a rapidly disappearing phenomenon. In the United States, where the largest concentration of Jews currently lives, the number of those who still retain any of the Jewish characteristics listed is fast diminishing. Jewish, like non-Jewish, youth is caught up in changing fashions of hair and beard style, speech mannerisms and garb, behavioral patterns and attitudes; in many cases only the demonstrative wearing of Jewish insignia, such as a *chai* or *mezuza* dangling on a chain between bra-less breasts, or a small *yarmulke* attached with hairpins to the back of a mane falling to the shoulders, gives away the girl's or boy's Jewish identity.

In Israel, the phenomenon of "looking Jewish" is also on its way out but for entirely different reasons. Except for the small, self-isolated, ultraorthodox group of the Neture Karta ("Guardians of the City") in the Mea Sh'arim quarter of Jerusalem, one will search in vain among the young generation for any remnants of that facial expression of worry, anxiety, fear, pain, melancholy, or irritation that has long been considered typically Jewish. The experience of living in their own country, of being the dominant majority and thus masters of their own fate for the first time in almost two thousand years has wrought a most remarkable transformation. The heirs of those earlier ethnologists who had found people or tribes "looking Jewish" in all parts of the world now come to Israel and find that the young Israelis do not "look Jewish" at all. It is as yet too early to say how they do or will look. But whatever the emerging Israeli look will be, one thing is certain: it will bear little if any relation to what in the past was so often, and with such remarkable unanimity, described as "looking Jewish."

CHAPTER X

Criteria for the Classification of Races

THE TRADITIONAL CRITERIA for classifying races have been easily observable morphological traits: height, weight, skin color, shape of the nose, facial form, shape of head, hair color and texture, eye color and shape, and so on. However, many of these traits may be affected by the environment (for instance, by diet or by exposure to sunlight) or by cultural practices (for instance, binding a baby's head to a board); moreover, they have a complex mode of inheritance that is poorly understood. Although quantitative measurements of these traits may be made, it is difficult to separate the genetic and environmental contributions to the phenotype, the external appearance, and it is impossible to translate these measurements into gene frequencies. Single phenotypic features are usually the combined results of many genes that cannot be identified individually. For example, the African blacks and the Oceanic Negroids are both dark-skinned and have similar hair form. Yet their blood groups, which are inherited in a simple and well-understood fashion, differ in their gene frequencies; these differences suggest that these populations are not closely related.[1]

Morphological indices used to be another favorite tool of anthropological studies. Hundreds of thousands of men, women, and children were subjected to careful and detailed measurement of height, breadth, weight, head, face, nose, eye, skin type, and hair color and consistency. However, the use of these measurements, too, has its drawbacks. The value for race studies of some measurements (for example, head length and breadth) is diminished because they are influenced by other factors such as the individual's height. On the other hand, ratios of these measurements (such as

224

the cephalic index) have been found to be more useful. One problem with the use of such indices is that the measurements on which they are based may be inherited separately. That is, the index is not inherited as a single factor, but may represent the chance outcome of several different complicated genetic factors at work.

Because of the complex inheritance and environmental components of the traditional morphological traits used to study races, anthropologists have recently turned to studies of variations in blood groups and other biochemical traits whose inheritance is simple. As Ashley Montagu put it,

> what must be studied are the frequencies with which such genes occur in different groups or populations. . . . The morphological characters which anthropologists have relied upon for the "racial" classifications have been very few indeed, involving a minute fraction of the great number of genes which it would actually be necessary to consider in attempting to make any real—that is genetically analytic—classification of mankind.[2]

Since these words were written, the frequencies of a total of perhaps sixty genes have been measured in some human groups. Although only a very small proportion of the total genes of man, they are all we have to work with at the present time.

Genetic traits whose inheritance is simple can also be affected by the environment, so that not all of them are equally suitable for population studies. The environment can affect genetic traits in two ways. In one sense, the genes determine the range of possibilities for an individual's final make-up, whereas the environment determines the actual realization of this genetic potential. This is the way one must understand the actual attainment by an individual of his height, weight, muscle power, manual dexterity, or intelligence. An example is the disease phenylketonuria (PKU), caused by an inherited deficiency of one chemical in the body. A child who eats a normal diet is likely to be mentally retarded, but can grow up with normal intelligence if his diet is modified in early childhood. In the latter case, the change in the environment (diet) produces a change in the *phenotype*, or final appearance; the individual's *genotype*, or genetic make-up, remains unchanged.

In another sense, however, the environment is an extremely important cause of genetic changes in populations. To understand this, let us assume that a certain gene is present in a population in two alternative forms (alleles), one of which is "normal" and the other harmful (for example, it may cause a disease). If mating occurs at random in the population, and if every person has an equal chance of leaving offspring, the proportion of the two alleles will not change from one generation to the next. However, if the possessors of the harmful gene are less fertile than the possessors of the normal gene, they will have proportionately fewer children in each generation. Gradually, the relative frequencies of the two alleles will change. The

225

process by which gene frequencies change as a result of differential reproduction was termed by Darwin *natural selection*. The effect of natural selection on any gene depends on the particular environment. Advances in technology and medicine have greatly reduced the effectiveness of selection against some harmful genes. For example, in early hunting and gathering societies, individuals with poor vision were obviously at a disadvantage and thus tended to die out; today, thanks to eyeglasses, most people with poor vision can function as well as those with excellent sight; moreover, industrial society permits a wide range of occupations. Consequently, natural selection against genes causing poor vision has undoubtedly decreased since prehistoric times. Genes whose frequencies have changed substantially in the past millennium as a result of strong natural selection are not very useful in studies of the origins of today's racial groupings.

Another factor that can result in a change in gene frequencies is *mutation*, a sudden random change in the genetic material that is inherited. Because the genetic material (DNA) is complex and usually performs its function well, most random changes in its structure are harmful to its function; hence most mutations are harmful. Bacterial studies (in which billions of individual bacteria can be easily examined) have shown that most types of mutations occur repeatedly, though at low frequencies. Extending these results to man, we can assume that the genes for a lethal condition that are eliminated by natural selection are replenished in the population by rare but repeated mutations, occurring perhaps in 1 in 100,000 individuals. When the frequency of the harmful gene in the population is stable, the number of genes eliminated by natural selection is just balanced by those replenished by mutation.

A gene mutation producing a disease that is lethal in childhood is an extreme example. Much more common, and more difficult to unravel, is a situation in which the fertility of the possessor of a certain genotype is only slightly reduced, or in which selection acts against only a small proportion of the possessors of a certain genotype. In the past, for example, certain communicable childhood diseases may have affected individuals of one ABO blood type more frequently than those of another blood type, resulting in proportionately more deaths among the affected blood types. That is, these diseases would have constituted a form of natural selection against certain blood types. However, because modern medicine has largely eradicated these diseases, we no longer have any way of studying their possible interaction with the blood groups.

A third factor that can change the gene frequencies of a population is simply interbreeding with neighboring populations. In this way new genes can be introduced into a population or the frequencies of genes already present can be altered. We have already seen how important a factor various forms of interbreeding have been in the history of Jewish populations.

226

In small populations, a fourth factor can cause gene frequencies to change. In such populations, the frequency of a particular gene may increase or decrease simply because of chance fluctuations. A person who happens to carry the particular gene may have more children than his neighbors, or he may have none. In a large population, the genetic contribution of any one individual to the next generation is relatively unimportant. But in a community of only thirty or forty families, the frequency of a gene in the next generation may be significantly altered because some people happen to pass on the gene and others do not. Such accidental fluctuations in gene frequencies that occur in small populations are called *genetic drift*. These chance fluctuations are more likely to occur in a small population that is reproductively isolated, that is, does not have a significant gene flow from other populations.

An example analogous to genetic drift is described by L. C. Dunn. In small communities, family names may spread or become extinct simply because of a run of luck in a family in the proportion of sons and daughters. If the name is transmitted through males only, a family with many sons would have its name spread in a small community, whereas the name of one with no sons would disappear. As a result, the name of an ancestor who lived a few generations ago could be common in one village and absent in the neighboring one. In large cities such fluctuations would not be noticeable, but small populations may diverge from one another by such accidents.[3]

In subsequent chapters we shall see that some Jewish groups (the Habbanites, the Karaites) and one semi-Jewish group (the Samaritans) possess gene frequencies that differ greatly from other Middle Eastern populations. Each group consists of a few persons who for centuries have maintained an extremely high rate of inbreeding with very little intermarriage with other populations. In this type of situation genetic drift can be an important factor in gene frequency changes. In fact, genetic drift is usually regarded as at least part of the explanation for the unusual genetic traits found.

A special example of genetic drift is the phenomenon termed *founder effect*. The founders of a small group, for example, the original settlers of a village, may by chance carry some genes more or less commonly than the population from which they came. As a result, these genes will have a higher or lower frequency among their descendants than in the parent population. This will be especially true if the small population is isolated. Thus, the frequency of a certain allele may be 30% in the parent population, but by chance it may be only 15% in the settlers of the new village, or only half as frequent.

For rare genes, even more dramatic differences between the parent and new populations may result from chance events. Suppose that a rare gene, present in the parent population in only 1 in 1,000 people, happens to be

227

present in 1 of the 50 people who founded a new isolated village. The gene may be eliminated as a result of genetic drift. But if it is passed on, two hundred years later this village may still have approximately the same freuqency of the gene as when the village is founded, that is, 1 to 50. This frequency would be twenty times as great as in the parent population, and nothing in the environment of the village could explain why the frequency is so high. The only plausible explanation would be the founder effect. Founder effect and genetic drift have been used to explain the atypical frequencies of some genes among reproductively isolated populations whose historical migration pattern is known, such as the Amish in the United States.

To be useful in population studies, genetic traits must not be subject to too much modification by the environment; they must be relatively stable in time (that is, not subject to a great deal of natural selection); and they must not mutate frequently. In addition, the traits should be well-defined, so that different observers classifying a population by using the trait would get the same results. Finally, the mode of inheritance of the trait should be well understood. Several blood proteins that occur in more than one chemical form fulfill these criteria. Biochemical traits have the additional advantage that their possessor is usually unaware of them. Consequently, his choice of marriage partner is independent of the alternative form of blood protein he or she happens to have. In contrast, it is well known that marriages are often not random as far as anthropometric features such as height or skin color are concerned, and this complicates attempts to untangle genetic from environmental components.

Because of the paucity of data based on traits determined by single genes, it would be a mistake to rely exclusively on such data. The few dozen traits that have been extensively studied are not a random, and hence representative, sample of the 10,000 to 50,000 genes which each human being possesses.[4] Furthermore, for most blood groups and other serological traits the natural selective factors that have operated on them over the centuries are unknown. This means that similarities in gene frequencies between different populations may reflect similar natural selection processes at work as well as a common origin. One can get around this problem by comparing many different simple traits, on the assumption that populations that have similar frequencies of many genes are likely to be genuinely related; this will be done for the Jews in later sections. One can also examine some of the older anthropometric measurements, keeping in mind the drawbacks discussed above.

CHAPTER XI

Jewish Inbreeding and Its Effects

I N EARLIER CHAPTERS, the effects of Jewish-Gentile interbreeding were discussed within the framework of a rapid historical survey of proselytism, intermarriage, slavery and concubinage, and forms of illegitimate sexual relations. We concluded that the Jewish physical type in every country tended to resemble that of the Gentiles. This in itself made for a considerable dissimilarity among Jewish communities domiciled for centuries in countries inhabited by genetically diverse majority populations.

Another factor contributing to the genetic variety among Jewish communities is inbreeding. Inbreeding, especially cousin marriage, is an ancestral tradition among the Jews, going back to the Abrahamic family more than 3,500 years ago.[1] With the dispersion of the Jews in Asia, Africa, and Europe, the old custom of cousin marriage underwent modifications influenced by the marriage customs of the Gentile environment. In Christian Europe, where inbreeding was not practiced among the Gentiles, its incidence among the Jews diminished, although even there it did not disappear altogether. In the Muslim Middle East, where inbreeding, especially patrilateral parallel cousin marriage (marriage between the children of two brothers), was in vogue among the general population, cousin marriage and other varieties of close endogamous unions remained the preferred forms of marriage among the Jews. In several parts of the Middle East, among both Moslems and Jews, every young man who had a father's brother's daughter of approximately suitable age married her as a matter of course; if no such first cousin was available, a more distant relative was chosen.[2] Father Ayrout, a lifelong student of the Egyptian fallahin, estimated that 80% of all the marriages contracted by fellahin take place between first cousins; and Fredrik Barth, in his study of southern Kurdistan, found that in tribal villages 57% of all marriages were cousin marriages, with an additional 14% between close relatives, making a total of 71% of in-family endogamy.[3]

As to the Jews, some statistics on the extent of inbreeding within various communities are available from Israel. One survey of the relationships between parents of newborn infants was carried out in 1955–57, another in 1969–70.[4] In both, information on the parents' background was obtained by interviewing the mothers shortly after delivery. In the earlier study, a total of 4,734 Ashkenazi couples had an incidence of 1.4% of first-cousin marriage, and 1.06% of the marriages were between more distantly related individuals. The incidence of first-cousin marriage between non-Ashkenazim (6,690) was 8.8%, and an additional 6.0% of marriages were between more distantly related spouses. Thus, a total of 14.6% of marriages between non-Ashkenazim were consanguineous, as compared with only 2.5% of Ashkenazim.

The highest frequencies of consanguineous marriages were found among Jews from Iraq (28.7%) and Iran (26.3%). High rates were also found among couples from Yemen (18.3%), Aden (17.8%), Tunisia (13.4%), and among Oriental Jews from the U.S.S.R. (6.9%). Marriages between relatives occurred in 7–10.7% of couples from Egypt, Syria, Lebanon, and Turkey. These figures do not make a distinction between Kurdish Jews from Turkey, Iraq, and Iran, and Jews from other parts of these three countries. This is regrettable, for is it known from other sources that inbreeding is particularly high in Kurdistan, among both Jews and non-Jews.

In the second study, the incidence of first-cousin marriage among 1,242 Ashkenazim was 0.3%; the incidence of marriage between more distantly related people was 1.0%. Among 1,916 non-Ashkenazim, the incidence of first-cousin marriage was 6.2%, and that of more distantly related marriages 8.1%. As in the earlier study, Jews from Iraq and Iran had the highest rates of inbreeding, and Sephardi Jews had lower rates, which were, however, still considerably higher than the rates of inbreeding among European Jews (1.5%).

Among the Habbanite Jews in Israel, 56% of marriages are between first cousins. Thus, this group is ideal for revealing new recessive mutations. The Samaritans also have a very high rate of inbreeding: 43% of marriages are between first cousins, 13.7% between first cousins once removed, and 19.6% between second cousins. In only 19.6% of marriages are the spouses not related. The small size and genetic isolation (caused by the custom of close endogamy) among the Habbanite and Samaritan groups can be expected to favor genetic drift resulting in gene frequencies that may differ greatly from surrounding populations.[5]

As these data indicate, different Jewish populations have widely differing degrees of inbreeding, which should be kept in mind in any discussion of the incidence of inherited diseases in these groups.

A frequent lay view is that inbreeding results in sickly or degenerate offspring. The fact is that inherited diseases affect an individual only if he inherits one recessive allele for the disease in question from each of his parents. If he inherits only one such allele he will not be afflicted by the disease, although he, in turn, can pass on the gene to his children. Inbreeding can indeed result in an increased incidence of recessive conditions. If a person's parents are related, the chances that he inherits a copy of the same gene from each parent are obviously greater than if his parents are unrelated. If the presence of two harmful genes is necessary for the disease to appear, an inbred population will have a *higher incidence of the disease* than a population with random mating, even though the *frequency of the harmful gene* in the two populations is the same. This increased incidence of recessive diseases as a result of inbreeding explains why marriages between relatives are considered unwise.

On the other hand, in the long run, inbreeding tends to reduce the frequency of harmful genes. In a randomly mating population most of the harmful genes are "hidden" in heterozygotes, that is, individuals who inherited only one copy of them from one parent. These individuals will reproduce the harmful genes. In an inbreeding population, however, relatively more of the harmful genes are found in homozygotes, who inherited two copies of them (one from each parent), and who consequently are severely ill and do not reproduce. This results in a more rapid decrease of the harmful gene in the inbred than in the randomly mating population. After many generations of inbreeding, the frequency of the harmful gene will stabilize at a lower level in the inbred population. Because of the possibility of new mutations, it may not be totally eliminated despite strong selection against the gene.

It follows that if an ethnic group that has previously had a high rate of inbreeding now increases its rate of outbreeding (as is happening among Kurdish and other Oriental Jewish communities in Israel), the frequency of homozygotes for any rare recessive condition will rapidly fall. That is, the incidence of diseases caused by the presence of two recessive genes in the same person will decrease. However, the harmful genes will now increasingly be hidden in heterozygotes in whom they have fewer ill effects and will no longer be eliminated as rapidly from the population; in consequence, their frequency will gradually rise. Ultimately, there will be a new genetic equilibrium with a higher frequency of the harmful recessive gene.

For a rare recessive disease that may have resulted from only a single mutation hundreds of years ago (this has been postulated by some for the Tay-Sachs disease), it is assumed that elimination of the genes by the death

231

of affected individuals is not compensated for by new mutations. In such a situation, the frequency of the harmful genes will gradually decrease and they will ultimately disappear. In an inbred population, the harmful gene will disappear more rapidly than in a randomly mating population, for the inbred population has relatively more affected individuals.

A final conclusion can be drawn from these considerations. Inbreeding as it has been practiced by Middle Eastern Jewish communities for centuries contributed considerably to a diversification of the Jewish physical type. It is partly as a result of inbreeding that several distinct Yemenite Jewish physical types exist, although the Yemenite Jews in general closely resemble the Yemenite Moslems. The same holds good for Moroccan Jews, Kurdish Jews, Persian Jews, and so forth. If one adds to this phenomenon the relative isolation of the Yemenite, Moroccan, Kurdish, and Persian Jews from one another, and the inevitable interbreeding that occurred between the Jews and Muslims in each country, one has isolated the main factors responsible for the great and readily apparent physical diversity of the Middle Eastern Jews.

CHAPTER XII

The "Jewish" Blood; ABO

T HE GENETIC TRAIT for which the most data have been collected is the ABO blood groups. The blood group to which an individual belongs depends on which of three major genes, A, B, and O, he or she possesses. The frequencies of these genes have been designated p, q, and r, respectively. Extensive tables have been compiled of these gene frequencies for different populations.[1] The available data pertaining to Jews, together with parallel data for non-Jews, are shown in Table 1 in the Appendix. Because the data were collected over many years by different workers, there are naturally questions about the validity of comparing results of different studies. A recent study helps to allay these concerns. In 1979 Bonné-Tamir and coworkers[2] examined the ABO blood groups of German, Polish, and Russian Jews living in Israel and compared their results with those obtained 15 years earlier on a different and much larger sample by another researcher. The results were strikingly similar in the three populations. For example, among German Jews the percentages of the p gene were 25.5% and 26.7%; q, 14.4% and 13.3%; and r, 60.1% and 60.0%. It seems legitimate, therefore, to proceed with comparisons among the various studies.

The ABO data reveal a great diversity among the different groups of Jews. Statistical comparisons of ABO frequencies in Jews from different areas show highly significant differences between Yugoslavian Jews and Dutch Jews, Sephardi Jews and Dutch Jews, Moroccan Jews and Dutch Jews, Ashkenazi Jews and North African Jews, Ashkenazi Jews and Cochin Jews, Ashkenazi Jews and Iranian Jews, Oriental Jews and Polish Jews, Ukrainian Jews and Karaites from Lithuania and the Ukraine, and Russian Jews and Georgian Jews.

Among the Jews in Asia, the ABO gene frequencies are very heterogeneous. Jews from Bukhara, Iran, Iraq, and Kurdistan have both high p and high q values, and therefore low r values, as do the non-Jewish populations of these areas. Much higher r values are found in other groups of Asian Jews, including the Habbanite, Yemenite, and Cochin Jews, and among the Samaritans.

The Habbanites are a group of Jews from the town of Habban and some five neighboring villages in the Hadhramaut Valley (today part of Southern Yemen) who immigrated to Israel around 1950. The Habbanites had highly significant differences in ABO frequencies when compared with every other Jewish group tested. The q value among the Habbanite Jews is much higher than in the Yemenite Jews, who lived for many centuries some 200 miles to the west of Habban; it is also higher than that among any of the Saudi Arabian groups studied.[3] A high rate of inbreeding (56% of marriages are between first cousins) may help to explain why the ABO frequencies of the Habbanites have diverged from those of the neighboring Yemenite Jews.[4] The ABO frequencies of the Habbanites are like those of the Jebeliya, a Bedouin tribe living in the South Sinai. Another South Sinai Bedouin tribe, the Towara, have quite different ABO frequencies.[5]

The Samaritans in Israel have a frequency of gene r which is nearly the highest in the Middle East, exceeded only by the Arabs in western Saudi Arabia. The frequency of gene q in the Samaritans, on the other hand, is relatively low when compared with most Asiatic and Eastern populations.

The differences in ABO gene frequencies between Samaritans and all other Jewish groups tested are highly significant. The differences between North African and Sephardi Jews and between Yugoslavian and Ashkenazi Jews are smaller but still significant. In contrast, Jews from the Balkan countries and from Central Europe do not differ greatly in their ABO frequencies.

The ABO frequencies of Yemenite Jews differ greatly from those of other Jewish populations. Highly significant differences were found between their frequencies and those of Jews from Lebanon, Kurdistan, Iraq, and Habban. On the other hand, the ABO frequencies of the Yemenite Jews closely resemble those of Yemenite Arabs, suggesting extensive genetic admixture between Yemenite Jews and Arabs.

The frequencies for Ashkenazi Jews in Israel do not differ significantly from those for Jews in Austria, Poland, the Ukraine, and the United States, which is what one would expect in view of the recent migration of Ashkenazi Jews from Europe and America to Israel.

ABO typing of 55 ancient skeletons, unearthed at Jerusalem and Ein Gedi, revealed a very different distribution of ABO types from those of current Middle Eastern populations.[6] The gene frequencies of these remains were estimated to be $p = .52$, $q = .37$, and $r = .11$. Among these Israelite inhabitants of Palestine who lived 1600–2,000 years ago, the frequencies of p and q were significantly greater, and that of r much smaller, than in any living population. Egyptian mummies have also yielded a high frequency of the q allele and an extremely low frequency of r. These findings indicate that the ABO blood group system may have undergone significant change in the past 2,000 years.

The above survey shows great heterogeneity in ABO gene frequencies among the Jews; it is also revealing to compare Jews and non-Jews within the same area. Among the Falashas of Ethiopia, Jews who are probably descended from an indigenous population that converted to Judaism centuries ago, ABO frequencies resemble other peoples of Ethiopia. The "Black Jews" of Cochin in southern India have a higher q than p. This is true both of those tested in India and of immigrants tested in Israel, although the absolute values differed considerably. Although Cochin (non-Jewish) Indians have a higher p than q, the reverse is true of many Indian populations. The blood group findings support the impression given by the dark skin color of the Black Jews in suggesting a considerable proportion of indigenous Indian ancestry.

The unusually high frequencies of gene q found in the Habbanite and Yemenite Jews in southern Arabia are also present in the Saudi and Yemenite Arabs and the Towara Bedouins of the South Sinai, indicating a genetic similarity between the Jews and non-Jews of this general region.

Dutch Jews, who have the lowest known q frequency of any Jewish community, have p and q frequencies almost identical to those of Dutch non-Jews. This can only be explained by assuming that Dutch Jews have acquired many non-Jewish genes by interbreeding.

In the Middle East, Iranian Jews and non-Jews have barely significant differences in their ABO frequencies, Lebanese Jews and Muslims do not differ significantly, and Syrian Jews and Arabs are also very similar. Iraqi and Kurdish Jews do differ significantly from the corresponding Arab populations, mostly because both Jewish groups have higher frequencies of gene p than do other Middle Eastern Arabs and Jews. However, in general, these findings suggest genetic similarities between the Jews and non-Jews of the same regions, probably because of interbreeding coupled with environmental effects acting in the same way over a long time on both Jews and non-Jews.

Some information is available on the ABO frequencies of Jews and non-Jews within small areas in Europe. To permit visual comparisons of the Jewish and non-Jewish frequencies, these will be shown in diagrams in a three-coordinate system devised for this purpose. In most of these diagrams the solid-line triangle represents the Jewish gene frequencies in a given locality, and the broken-line triangle shows the non-Jewish frequencies in the same locality (see diagrams in the Appendix). In other diagrams, the gene frequencies of two Jewish groups are compared. In Rumania, for example, the Jews and non-Jews in the city of Maramures have very similar frequencies, as do Jews and non-Jews in the city of Jassy; in contrast, the frequencies of Jews from Maramures differ considerably from those of Jews from Jassy. Jews have lived for many generations in both Maramures and Jassy; considerable interbreeding must have taken place between Jews and non-Jews in each city.

In Germany, Jews and non-Jews are again very similar. So are Jews and Arabs in Aleppo, Syria; Jews and non-Jews in Lithuania; Jews and non-Jews in Kharkov, Ukraine; and Jews and non-Jews in Amsterdam, Holland. Jews in Amsterdam differ much more from Jews in Rumania than from non-Jews in Amsterdam.

The differences in ABO frequencies observed between Dutch Jews and non-Jews would be expected to occur 80% of the time by chance alone. That is, these populations are very similar. The differences between Kharkov Jews and Kharkov non-Jews, Hungarian Jews and Hungarian non-Jews, Lithuanian Jews and Lithuanian non-Jews, Aleppo Jews and Aleppo Arabs, Moscow Jews and Moscow non-Jews, German Jews and German non-Jews, Iranian Jews and Iranian non-Jews, Jassy Jews and Jassy non-Jews, and Maramures Jews and Maramures non-Jews were all not significant. Oran Jews and non-Jews and Rabat Jews and Moroccan Arabs had significant, but not highly significant, differences between their ABO blood group genes. In contrast, there were highly significant differences in ABO gene frequencies between Maramures Jews and Jassy Jews, Rabat Jews and Rabat Muslims, Jassy non-Jews and Maramures non-Jews, and Rabat Muslims and Moroccan Arabs.

In recent years, many genetic loci have been found to have more than the number of alleles that were originally known to exist. Such is the case for the ABO locus; blood type A is now known to consist of two subtypes, termed A_1 and A_2, determined by alleles called p_1 and p_2, respectively. In the newer studies, which separate out p_1 and p_2, these alleles add up to the frequency of gene p in the older studies. The sum of all 4 alleles—p_1, p_2, q, and r—must of course total 100. Representative data for Jewish and non-Jewish populations are presented in Table 2.

In most populations of the world, the p_1 allele is much more common than is p_2. The Samaritans, who are unusual in their very high gene r frequency, are also unusual in their p_1 and p_2 frequencies. In contrast with most populations, the frequency of p_1 in the Samaritans, 3.87%, is significantly lower than the frequency of p_2, 7.6%. This unusual pattern (the high frequency of gene r and the predominance of the A2 subtype) attests to the strictly endogamous marriage patterns of the Samaritans, which have persisted to the present day. A recent survey showed that 43% of marriages are between first cousins.[7]

The Samaritans are not unique in their high frequency of gene p_2. The Karaites, a Jewish sect which originated in Iraq in the eighth century A.D. and later migrated to Egypt and Eastern Europe, have unique ABO gene frequencies. Karaite Jews from Iraq have a much greater frequency of p_2, 18.3%, than of p_1, 4.3%.[8] Karaites from Egypt also have an excess of p_2, but the frequencies of both p_1 and p_2 are unusually low—3.5% and 3.7%, respectively. Both Karaite communities have a higher r gene frequency, 34.5%, than any other Jewish or non-Jewish community examined. The unusual ABO distribution of the Karaites is further evidence for the uniqueness of this genetic isolate.

With respect to the ABO blood group data, Jews of any given area tend to resemble the non-Jews of that area, whereas Jews from different parts of the world are very heterogeneous. The same is not true when the frequencies of another important blood group, Rh, are examined, as will be seen in the next chapter. A. E. Mourant[9] has stated that the resemblance among ABO frequencies of Jews and non-Jews may be "deceptive and accidental," and attributes more importance to the Rh data. Clearly there is disagreement over the findings of greater similarity among diverse Jewish groups for some blood groups than for others, but there can be no disagreement about the fact that the ABO data confirm the heterogeneity of different Jewish populations.

237

CHAPTER XIII

The "Jewish" Blood: Other Blood Groups

ALTHOUGH NO OTHER blood group has been studied as extensively as ABO, comparison is now possible between Jewish and non-Jewish populations for the MN, Rhesus (Rh), Kell, Kidd, and Duffy blood groups.[1] In the MN system, two antigens, M and N, are determined by two allelic genes that can combine to form three blood groups, M, MN, and N. A person with two genes for M is of blood type M; if he has one gene for M and one for N, his blood type is MN; and if he has two genes for N, his blood type is N. The MN system is inherited independently of the ABO system.

Representative MN gene frequencies are summarized in Table 3 in the Appendix. Whereas Australian aborigines have a very low frequency of M and high N, and Eskimos have a very high M and low N, European populations in general have approximately equal frequencies of both genes, with a slight excess of gene M. Ashkenazi Jews, Moroccan Jews, other North African Jews, and Sephardim all have similar frequencies of M and N, averaging about 55% M, as do non-Jews in Europe and North Africa. In Asia, Jews from Baghdad, Cochin, Kurdistan, and Iran have somewhat higher frequencies of M, about 60%; this is also found in non-Jewish Indians and Iranians. Yemenite Jews have a considerably higher frequency of M, about 75%; nearly identical frequencies are found in Yemenite Arabs. In Saudi Arabia, Sunni townsmen of the Najd (central) and western provinces have a frequency of M of about 75%, and Saudi Arabian Bedouins have a frequency of about 78%. An equally high frequency, 78.5%, is found in the Habbanite Jews, who immigrated to Israel from southwestern Saudi Arabia. Totally different are the Samaritans, whose M frequency is only approximately 40%.

Significant differences in MN frequencies are found only between Samaritans and all other Jewish groups, between Yemenite Jews and other Jewish groups except Habbanites, and between Habbanites and other Jews except Yemenite Jews. One study showed an extremely high frequency of gene M, 98.1%, among Karaites from Iraq. Karaites from Lithuania did not have this high frequency; therefore, further data on Karaite populations are required before conclusions can be drawn.

These results corroborate the ABO data in showing (1) that Jews are at least as diverse as non-Jews in their MN frequencies; (2) that Yemenite Jews and Habbanites are different from other Middle eastern Jews but resemble the indigenous non-Jewish populations; (3) that the Samaritans and Iraqi Karaites have very unusual MN values; and (4) that the Jews of any given area tend to resemble the non-Jews of the same area.

The Rh groups were discovered in 1940 by Landsteiner and Weiner, who found that antibodies formed in rabbits and guinea pigs injected with the blood of the rhesus monkey agglutinated not only the monkey red cells but also the red cells of about 85% of white people in New York. The factor present in 85% of the people, who were called Rh-positive, was inherited as a dominant trait. Within a few years it became obvious that the Rh groups were more complex than seemed at first. Besides the original anti-Rh antiserum, human blood may or may not react to each of several other anti-Rh antisera. The Rh system may be thought of as consisting of three very closely linked genes called C, D, and E. Each of these genes has two or more alleles, for example, C and c, D and d, E and e. Each parent will pass on a combination of alleles at the several sites or loci, such as cDe or CDe. With only two alleles at each of the three sites, eight combinations of alleles, or haplotypes, are possible, of which four are common: CDe, cDE, cDe, and cde. Persons who carry two small d's (for example, cde and cde or Cde and cdE) are Rh-negative. Only the d genes are of clinical importance, for only these are responsible for the Rh-positive "blue babies" born to Rh-negative mothers. However, the various combinations are of interest because their frequencies differ among different populations.

The cDe chromosome combination, for example, is called the "African chromosome," since it attains frequencies of 45–90% in Africans, compared to only 2–3% among European populations (see Table 4 in the appendix). The CDe haplotype is called the "Mediterranean chromosome" because its frequency is higher in this area: 53% in Ferrara, Italy; 52% in Madrid, Spain; and 46% in Egypt, compared with 43% in England, 44% in Germany, 41% in Poland, 41% in Sweden, 39% among Basques, and about 10% in South African Bantus. High frequencies of the CDe chromosome are, however, also characteristic of Asiatic populations: 63.7% among Indians in Calcutta, about 70% in Chinese tested in New York City, and 60–68% among Japanese tested in the United States.

Low frequencies of cDE and cde, compared with European populations, are also considered Mediterranean features.

Among white populations, the cDE haplotype is called the "North European chromosome," as it is more common in Northern and Eastern Europe than in the Mediterranean.

Several researchers have tested the Rh blood types of Jews in Israel whose origins were in Europe, Asia, and Africa. Among the Ashkenazi Jews, the frequencies of the "Mediterranean chromosome," CDe, were generally higher than the corresponding non-Jewish frequencies. Thus, for example, Austrian Jews had a CDe frequency of 49.2%, compared with 47.3% for Austrian non-Jews; German Jews, 48.2%, versus 43.9% for German non-Jews; Polish Jews, 50.5%, versus 41.4% for Polish non-Jews. These relatively high values were close to the levels encountered in other Jewish communities living in the Mediterranean region. For example, the frequencies of CDe in Moroccan and Tunisian Jews were 48–53% and 51–56%, respectively. However, the Ashkenazi Jews had a higher frequency of the "North European chromosome," cDE (11.10–14.4%), than did these other Mediterranean Jewish populations (6.3–9.2% in Morocco and 6.6% in Tunisia). The frequency of cDE among Libyan Jews was even lower, 2.3%. According to Mourant, this is what would be expected in a Mediterranean population that has acquired a considerable local component during residence in Central and Northern Europe.[2] However, the origin of the "North European chromosome" is in question, as its frequency is also high in Egyptians (14%), Chinese (20%), Japanese (27–30%), Alaskan Eskimos (40%), Brazilian Indians (47–49%), New York blacks (18%), Argentine whites (15%), Italians in Naples (10–15%), and some Spaniards (8–14.5%). It is also of interest that Egyptian Jews had a significantly higher frequency of the North European chromosome, 12.3%, than did other African Jewish populations. However, Egyptian Jews had a frequency similar to Egyptian Arabs (13.7%).

The frequency of the Rh-negative chromosome, cde, in Ashkenazi Jews was 25%–36%, which is higher than the frequencies in most Oriental Jewish communities but still somewhat lower than in non-Jewish European populations (36.5% in Austria, 37.8% in Germany, 37.5% in Poland). Not surprisingly, among European Jews the frequency of the Rh-negative phenotype (the combination cde/cde) is lower than the percentage found among European non-Jews; 9.4% among European Jews in one study versus 12–16% in non-Jews.

The frequency of the "African chromosome," cDe, is generally lower in the Ashkenazim (4.6–9.4%) than in Sephardi (7.6–10.8%), Moroccan (7.9–9.4%), Tunisian (8.3–8.5%), and Tripolitanian Jews (9.5%), as might be expected. Nonetheless, the frequency in the Ashkenazim is significantly higher than the 2-3% found among European non-Jews, suggesting some African admixture.*

Among Sephardi Jews from the Balkan countries, the frequency of the Mediterranean chromosome, CDe, is similar to that in Ashkenazi and North African Jews. The frequency of the Rh-negative chromosome, cde, is lower than that of CDe. Although various studies showed some spread in the cde frequencies, ranging from 25.6% to 34.5%, the range was similar to that of Ashkenazi Jews and tended to be lower than non-Jews from Spain (35.7%) and Greece (35.4%). The frequency of the "African chromosome," cDe, among Sephardi Jews ranged from 7.6% to 10.8%, values comparable to those encountered in Moroccan and Tunisian Jews (9.4% and 8.5%, respectively). According to Mourant, this component was presumably acquired by the Sephardi Jews mainly in Egypt and elsewhere in North Africa, but some may have come through Spain, where elevated cDe frequencies are found in several regions, especially in Galicia and northwest Spain. Margolis *et al.* consider the latter possibility more likely, as there are no historical indications to suggest the permeation of considerable North African elements in Sephardi Jews.[4]

Among Jews from North Africa, the Rh frequencies resemble those of Sephardi Jews. Although some studies have shown higher frequencies of the "Mediterranean chromosome," CDe, among Moroccan and Tunisian Jews, other studies show lower frequencies resembling those of the Sephardi and Ashkenazi Jews. The "North European chromosome," cDE, is significantly less frequent among most North African Jewish populations than among Sephardi and Ashkenazi Jews, which is not surprising. The relatively high frequency of the "African chromosome" in Moroccan and Tunisian Jews may indicate an African influx. In contrast, Rh frequencies among Libyan Jews indicate no evidence of African genes. The frequency of cDe, the "African chromosome," 6%, is similar to other Caucasian populations and is significantly lower than the 11% found in non-Jewish Libyans.

Non-Jewish North African populations show a much higher frequency of the "African chromosome," a comparable frequency of the "Mediterranean chromosome," 46.5%, and a lower frequency of the Rh-negative chromosome than the frequencies in African Jews. Egyptian Arabs, for example, have a frequency of the "African chromosome," cDe, of 23.9%,

---

*Ottensooser *et al.* (1963) do not believe that this is the correct explanation. The penetration of the "African chromosome" in Sephardi Jews, they believe, "could be associated to a long process of mixing after dispersal throughout the Mediterranean basin, having probably absorbed a considerable Arabic component in Spain and North Africa. However, this explanation fails to apply to the high cDe frequencies of Ashkenazim who, since the first centuries of the Christian era, remained in Central and Eastern Europe without contact with cDe-rich people. It seems likely that the ancient Palestine Jews had . . . a high cDe frequency" and also a low frequency of Rh-negatives.[3]

241

"Mediterranean chromosome," CDe of 46.5%, and the Rh-negative chromosome, cde, of 15.4%. The comparable values among Algerian Arabs are 29.2%, 33.1%, and 30.4%, respectively. Among Moroccan Arabs, the figures are 24–35%, 22–31%, and 33%, respectively. One study of Libyan non-Jews, interestingly, revealed a very low frequency of the African chromosome, 11%, compared with other North African non-Jewish populations.

Among Oriental Jews in Israel, the frequency of the "African chromosome" is lower than in other Jewish populations, ranging from 2.6 to 6% in Iranians, 3.7–4.7% in Iraqis, and 6.4–7.5% in Jews from Yemen. An unspecified sample of Oriental Jews had a cde frequency of 5.7%. Among 4 isolates studied in Israel, the frequencies of the cde chromosome were exceedingly variable, ranging from a low of 2.8–6.2% in the Cochin Jews, 5.6% in the Samaritans, and up to a strikingly high value of 29.3% among the Habbanites. This high frequency is most likely due to genetic drift coupled with extensive inbreeding in this isolate. Karaite Jews from Iraq had a very high frequency of the "African chromosome," 20.9%, a finding also consistent with their high rate of inbreeding.

Frequencies of the "Mediterranean chromosome" among Oriental Jews tend to be higher than among other Jewish populations. High frequencies of the "Mediterranean chromosome" were found among Jews from Iran, and this is considered by Mourant to be a mark of Asiatic as much as of Mediterranean origin. The frequency of the "North European chromosome," cDE, ranges from 7.9% among Yemenite Jews to highs of 15.8% in Baghdad (Iraq) and 17.9–20.27% among Kurdish Jews. Mourant considers the high frequency of cDE to be a feature of the Middle East generally, as well as of Northern and Eastern Europe. Similarly high frequencies of this chromosome are also found among non-Jewish populations of the area.

Frequencies of the Rh-negative chromosome in different Jewish populations are variable. Among Ashkenazi Jews the frequencies of the Rh-negative chromosome tend to be lower than among European non-Jews. For example, the frequencies for Germany were 37.8% for non-Jews and 29.5% for Jews; and for Austria, 36.5% among non-Jews and 24.8% among Jews. Jews from the Middle East had even lower values, and again they were lower than the corresponding non-Jews. Thus, non-Jews from Baghdad, Iraq, had a frequency of 28.6%, compared with 19.8% for Baghdad Jews; non-Jews from Iran, 32–39%, versus 20.9–22.7% for Jews from Iran. In North Africa, the cde frequencies are variable among both Jews and non-Jews.

As might be expected, unusual Rh frequencies are found in the genetic isolates. The Black Jews of Cochin have a lower frequency of CDe, the "Mediterranean chromosome," than Iranian, Kurdish, and Yemenite Jews —41.5% in one study, 47.1% in another—and a strikingly high frequency of the Rh-negative, cde, chromosome, 40–44%, the highest in any Jewish population except for the Samaritans, whose cde frequency is even higher, 42.9%. Like the Cochin Jews, the Samaritans also have a relatively low frequency of the Mediterranean chromosome. However, the Samaritans and Cochin Jews have very different frequencies of the MN genes. As for the ABO system, both have high frequencies of the O gene, but the Samaritans have an unusually low frequency of the B gene and the Cochin Jews do not. It is likely that the unusual frequencies in the two isolates arose independently as a result of inbreeding. In contrast with a similarity in ABO frequencies, the Samaritans and the Saudi Arabian tribes do not share a close affinity in their Rh frequencies.[5]

The Habbanite Jews differ from other Middle Eastern Jews in having an exceptionally low frequency of the cDE chromosome, only 1.2%, and an exceptionally high frequency of the "African chromosome," cDe, 29.3%. In contrast with the great similarity found in the ABO frequencies, the Rh frequencies of the Habbanites show no resemblance to those of the South Sinai Jebeliya, nor to another South Sinai tribe, the Towara.[6]

Jews show a greater uniformity in their Rh gene frequencies than in ABO and MN frequencies. They have high frequencies of the "Mediterranean chromosome," CDe, relatively high frequencies of the "African chromosome," CDe, and lower frequencies of cde than non-Jewish Europeans. These traits, which differentiate them from non-Jewish European populations, have been found in Ashkenazi Jews tested in Israel, South America, and Canada. According to Mourant, "Jews from Europe, even if scarcely distinguishable from their former European non-Jewish neighbors by their ABO groups, show by their Rh groups that physically they are more nearly related to their Mediterranean ancestors than to these European neighbors."[7]

How can it be explained that the ABO and Rh blood groups, which reside in the same individuals, yield different conclusions? The factors responsible for these differences include (a) the likelihood that the ABO blood groups are subject to greater environmental selection than the Rh groups, and that consequently their frequency changes more rapidly with time; and (b) the association of high frequencies of certain Rh chromosomes with certain geographical areas. Factor (a) obscures the ancient history of a people, so that only fairly recent events can be detected. Thus, the ABO data tell us that in the past several hundred years much interbreeding has occurred between Jews and the surrounding people, wherever they lived. The relatively greater stability of the Rh system, together with factor (b), implies that the relatively high frequency of the "Mediterranean chromosome" in European Jews reflects their Mediterranean origin, and the slightly increased frequency of the "African chromosome" in these same Jews indicates some African admixture.

243

We do not believe it is valid to conclude, as Mourant did, that the Rh findings are more revealing of the true relationships of the Jews than are the ABO and MN findings. Instead, what these data show are that most Jews have at least one distant ancestor of Mediterranean stock, and a highly variable assortment of other ancestry. The Mediterranean ancestry may represent a major, or only a very minor proportion of the total genetic endowment of any particular Jewish group; it by no means indicates uniformity in the genetic make-up of all Jews. By examining other blood characteristics and different traits, we may be able to shed more light on the question of whether the Jews are more closely related to their Mediterranean ancestors or to their comparatively recent neighbors.

Kell, Duffy, and Kidd are the names of three other blood groups useful in population studies. Each of these systems has at least two alleles found in different proportions among different populations. Blood samples from 10,000 Jews in Israel, originating from 20 counties, were typed for the Kell, Duffy, and Kidd systems.[8]

The Kell blood group comprises two alleles, K and k; k is by far more common in all populations tested. The frequency of K varied from 0% to 12.3% in the Jewish populations tested (see Table 5 in the Appendix). Among European Jews the frequencies were uniform, between 5.3% and 8.3%, and were higher than among the corresponding European non-Jews. For Russian and Rumanian populations, however, the K frequencies were similar among Jews and non-Jews. The frequencies of gene K among Ashkenazi Jews were generally higher than among Sephardi, Asian, and African Jews.

Sephardi Jews had K frequencies that were like those of non-Jews of the area. Among Turkish Jews, for example, the value was 4.8%, similar to the 5.3% among non-Jewish Turks.

Middle Eastern Jews generally had K frequencies lower than in Ashkenazi Jews and similar to those of Middle Eastern non-Jews. Iranian Jews had an unusually high frequency of allele K, 12.3%, an unexplained finding. Jews from Iraq, in contrast, had a frequency of 6.1–6.2%; those from Lebanon and Syria had a frequency of 3.5%, similar to the 3% frequency found in non-Jewish Druze in Lebanon. Bedouin tribes in the Sinai peninsula also have elevated frequencies of the K allele.

Unusual K frequencies were found, as might be expected, among the Jewish genetic isolates. The Karaites of Iraq had a high K frequency, 9.5%. In contrast, the K allele was totally absent among Cochin Jews. In non-Jewish southern Indian populations the K antigen is found in 1–7% of the people. The K allele frequency was low, 0.43%, in a large sample of Habbanite Jews. It was also low, 1.7–3.8%, in Jews from other areas in Yemen. Such a low frequency was also found among Arabs in Palestine, whereas Arabs from South Yemen had a higher frequency.

244

The Kell blood groups show about as much variation among different Jewish populations as among the corresponding Gentile groups, with unusual distributions in the genetic isolates. The frequencies in Ashkenazi Jews are a little higher than among European non-Jews but also higher than among other Jewish populations, and therefore cannot be used as evidence for the Mediterranean origin of the Ashkenazi Jews.

The next blood group, Duffy, comprises three alleles, Fy^a, Fy^b, and Fy. The first two alleles are found in nearly equal frequencies in many populations; Fy is found primarily in Africa. The Fy allele is absent from non-Jewish European and United States whites, but has a frequency of 6.3% among Central European Jews and 2.5% among Jews from Eastern Europe (see Table 7 in the Appendix). Its frequency is 21.9% among Sephardi Jews from Bulgaria, Yugoslavia, and Turkey. These relatively high Fy frequencies have been used as evidence for the common origin of the Jews.

The Fy^a allele has frequencies of approximately 42–45% in most Ashkenazi, Sephardi, and Asian Jewish populations (see Tables 6 and 7 in the Appendix). The frequency is somewhat lower in African Jewish populations, which may be accounted for by an increased frequency of the "African allele," Fy. Non-Jewish North Africans, however, have a lower frequency of Fy^a, and therefore most likely a higher frequency of Fy, than do Jewish North Africans, suggesting a greater extent of interbreeding with other Africans by the non-Jews than by the North African Jews.

Yemenite Jews have a particularly low frequency of Fy^a, approximately 22%, and a correspondingly greater frequency of Fy, 59–76%. The low Fy^a frequency among Habbanite Jews resembles that of other Yemenite Jews. Arabs in Yemen have an equally low frequency of Fy^a, 10.5%, and a correspondingly high frequency of Fy, 76.9%. In contrast, among Indian Cochin Jews, the Fy^a allele frequency of 68% is the highest observed in Jewish communities. Among non-Jews in southern India frequencies of 40% to 71% were observed and in other areas of India and Southeast Asia Fy^a has an even higher frequency, up to 100%.

The Kidd blood group has two alleles, found in approximately equal frequencies in most populations. The frequencies of the Jk^a allele are uniform in most Jewish populations, 52–70% among Ashkenazim, 52–59% among Sephardim, 39–62% among Jews of the Middle East, and 40–56% in Jews from North Africa (see Table 8 in the Appendix). Similar figures are found in the adjacent non-Jewish populations. Among Cochin Jews, the 40% frequency of the Jk^a allele is among the lowest observed in Jewish communities, again confirming the uniqueness of this isolate. In European non-Jewish populations, Jk^a frequencies are near 50%, whereas they are about 75% in African populations tested and very low, about 30%, in Chinese.

245

In summary, the Rh and Duffy blood groups reveal evidence of the common Mediterranean origin of the Jews; the ABO blood group frequencies show significant differences among different Jewish populations and similarities with neighboring non-Jews; the MN and Kell data show at least as much diversity among different Jewish populations as among non-Jewish groups; and the Kidd gene frequencies are too uniform to yield definitive conclusions. Studies of each of these genes support the uniqueness of several Jewish genetic isolates now residing in Israel.

CHAPTER XIV

Serum and Red Cell Proteins

INTRODUCTION

B ESIDES THE MANY blood types found in the red cells, blood can yield other information of value to population genetics. The red blood cells contain several enzymes that may exist in more than one form. Each form is determined by a different allele, and the frequency of each allele can differ from population to population. The variant structure of each enzyme usually does not affect its activity, so that each form is as "good" as any other. The differences are detectable only by special laboratory tests. There are now data on the frequency of the genes for different forms of the red cell enzymes phosphoglucomutase (PGM_1), red cell adenosine deaminase (ADA), acid phosphatase (AP), adenylate kinase (AK), glutamic-pyruvic transaminase (GPT), phosphoglycolate phosphatase, esterase D, erythrocyte glyoxalate 1 (GLO), and glucose 6-phosphate dehydrogenase (G6PD). Since variants of G6PD are rare among white populations, they will not be discussed further. Besides structural variation in the G6PD molecule, a deficiency of the enzyme is very common in some populations, and this will be discussed in a separate chapter.

Blood plasma or serum (the fluid part of the blood) also contains several proteins that can exist in more than one chemical form. These include haptoglobins (Hp), the Gm and Inv genes of immunoglobulins, transferrins (Tf), group-specific component (Gc), serum pseudocholinesterase (PCE), the HLA system, and ceruloplasmin. Not all are equally useful for population studies.

Tf occurs in at least three forms, but two of them are very rare. All of 900 Israeli Jews tested had only the most common gene of this series, TfC.[1] The rarer form, or allele, TfB, was found among the Habbanite Jews, but only at a frequency of 0.25%.[2] Variation in ceruloplasmin, a copper-containing protein, has not been found in Jews.

HAPTOGLOBIN (Hp)

Haptoglobins are proteins that bind hemoglobin from aged and broken-down red blood cells. Two alternative forms of the gene (alleles), Hp^1 and Hp^2, determine different haptoglobin molecules, which can be distinguished from each other by their different electric charges. A summary of gene Hp^1 frequencies is presented in Table 9 in the Appendix. Because frequencies of Hp^1 and Hp^2 must add up to 100%, it is not necessary to list the frequencies of gene Hp^2 as well.

Haptoglobin frequencies are similar throughout the European Continent, ranging from 35% to 43% for gene Hp^1 in most areas. In most of Asia, however, gene Hp^1 frequencies are appreciably lower (9–28%). In Africa, on the other hand, gene Hp^1 frequencies of up to 90% are found.[3] Two studies of haptoglobin frequencies among Ashkenazi Jews from east Europe found Hp^1 frequencies of 29% and 34%;[4] the weighted average is 30%. Ashkenazi Jews have a significantly lower frequency of gene Hp^1 than do East European non-Jews. The difference between Polish Jews and Polish non-Jews was also significant.

The Hp^1 frequencies of the Ashkenazi Jews are like those of Oriental Jews. Goldschmidt and colleagues find it "surprising" that the Ashkenazim are like Oriental Jews in this respect, because the Ashkenazim are set apart from the Oriental Jews by characteristics such as ABO gene frequencies and physical appearance, which they share with the Gentile populations of Central and Western Europe.[5]

Both Jews and non-Jews in the Middle East and North Africa have generally lower gene Hp^1 frequencies than do non-Jews of Europe. However, rather high frequencies are found among certain Arab groups. A small sample of Israeli Arabs (75) had a frequency of Hp^1 of 36%. A more substantial sample (198) of South Sinai Towara Bedouins had the very high frequency of 42.9%.[6] The frequency among Arabs of the Hadhramaut region in southern Yemen is 46%. In Iran, the only country in which gene Hp^1 frequencies for both Jews and non-Jews are available, the frequencies are similar (29–30% and 28%, respectively).[7]

The Hp^1 frequency of a small sample (44) of Sephardi Jews from Bulgaria, Greece, Italy, and Yugoslavia, 38%, is in good agreement with the frequencies in other Mediterranean and European countries.

Among Cochin Jews from India, the frequency of the Hp[1] allele was only 18.2%, which is lower than that observed in any other Jewish group but is similar to that observed in Indian populations.[8]

The Habbanite Jews have a lower frequency of gene Hp[1], 21.4%, than do other Middle Eastern Jews.[9] The Samaritans, in contrast, have a high frequency, which is well within the range of the European frequencies.[10]

Only tentative conclusions can be drawn from the scanty data available on haptoglobin frequencies. European Jews tend to show somewhat lower frequencies of gene Hp[1] than European non-Jews, and their frequencies resemble those in Oriental and North African Jews. Although the gene Hp[1] frequency of all Oriental Jews is slightly lower on the whole than that of Ashkenazim, this difference is not statistically significant. This finding may resemble the data for Rh frequencies, in which the European Jews also were like the Mediterranean peoples. There are not sufficient haptoglobin data yet for non-Jewish Middle Eastern and North African countries with which to compare the Jews of those areas.

According to Fried, "it may well remain impossible to decide whether the haptoglobin frequencies of Ashkenazic Jews reflect their early origin from the Near East or their later convergence toward their Slavic neighbors."[11]

THE IMMUNOGLOBULIN GENES: Gm and Inv

Immunoglobulins are proteins in the blood that function as antibodies, helping to fight infection. Immunoglobulins have a complex structure, consisting of two short protein chains, termed light chains, and two longer ones, called heavy chains. There are several different light chains and heavy chains, each coded by a different gene. The genes for the different heavy chains are closely linked on the same chromosome, whereas the genes for the light chains are on a different chromosome. Some of the genes have multiple alleles, so that an endless variety of antibody structure is possible.

The gene for one of the heavy chains, IgG, is at a locus called Gm which has more than 20 different forms or haplotypes. Each reacts with a different set of numbered chemicals in a laboratory test. For each person, the Gm phenotype is a combination of the two haplotypes that he inherited from his parents. For example, a person who inherits a Gm haplotype 1,2,3,4,5,6 from the mother and 1,3,5,7,10,15 from the father will have a Gm phenotype 1,2,3,4,5,6,7,10,15. Because of the variability in different populations, this gene locus is proving to be very useful in genetic studies. The gene for one of the light chains, kappa, is at a locus called Inv, which has 3 different alleles. This gene, too, is now being studied in different populations.

Steinberg and Bonné-Tamir[12] tested serum samples from Libyan and Ashkenazi Jews and from Armenians, all living in Israel, for their Gm phenotypes. From their results they calculated the frequencies of six haplotypes for each population. The results are summarized in Table 10 in the Appendix. Haplotype 1 is uniquely Caucasian. Haplotypes 2 and 3 are predominantly Caucasian, but also occur with high frequencies among Mongoloids. Haplotype 4 is essentially African, and its presence in the Libyan Jews and the Armenians most likely indicates African admixture. Haplotype 5 occurs among the Bushmen in Africa and among Mongoloids, and haplotype 6 is primarily Mongoloid, so that its presence among Ashkenazi Jews suggests Mongoloid admixture. However, this haplotype was not found among Ashkenazi Jews living in the northern United States or in Toronto, Canada,[13] so the significance of this finding is unclear.

The haplotype frequencies among the Libyan Jews differed markedly from those among the Ashkenazi Jews, but were similar to those of some non-Jewish populations tested earlier in Lebanon and Egypt. Like the Libyan Jews, the latter groups had a relatively low frequency of haplotype 1, a relatively high frequency of haplotype 2, and considerable African admixture. Steinberg and Bonné-Tamir conclude that the data for the Gm system indicate similarity between the Libyan Jews and the non-Jewish populations in the area.

Among Cochin Jews[14], the frequency of haplotype 2 is greater than of haplotype 1. In a survey of the world literature, the only other Caucasian populations in which this is true are those from southern India and Sri Lanka. The striking similarities in haplotype frequencies of the Cochin Jews and these other Indian populations led Steinberg and coworkers to conclude that a very large proportion of the genome of the black Cochin Jewish population is derived from Indian admixture. The Cochin Jews had some unusual haplotypes, including a variant of haplotype 3 in which there is no reaction to reagent 26; this variant was present at the relatively high frequency of 8.6%.

A large-scale study of immunoglobulin types was reported recently by Stevenson and coworkers for Jews living in the United States and Israel.[15] The calculated Gm haplotype frequencies are summarized in Table 10. The researchers concluded there is less heterogeneity within Jewish populations from Europe, Middle East, and North Africa than in corresponding non-Jewish populations living in the same regions. Nonetheless, the Gm haplotype frequencies for each Jewish population were "not often significantly different from adjacent populations," according to Stevenson and coworkers.

Thus, the recent immunoglobulin studies once again suggest a common Jewish gene pool but provide ample evidence for gene flow from neighboring non-Jewish populations.

For Inv, the other polymorphic immunoglobulin gene investigated, not enough data are yet available. Of the 3 Inv alleles, the Inv[1] allele is more frequent among blacks than whites. A study in Israel found that Libyan Jews have a significantly higher frequency of Inv[1] (12%) than do Ashkenazi Jews (4.7%). Among Armenian non-Jews, the frequency was 7.3%.[16] Cochin Jews had an Inv[1] frequency of 3.7%.[17] The frequencies of Inv[1] were unusually low among Middle Eastern Jews—0.3% in Iranians and 0.6% among Kurdish Jews.[18] A recent publication summarized the data available on Inv[1] frequencies.[19] Although the different Jewish populations differed significantly from one another—3.7% for European, 6.2% for Sephardi, 4.9% for Asian, and 8.1% for North African Jews—in each case the Jewish frequencies were significantly lower than for the corresponding non-Jewish groups: 7.1% for European, 15.7% for Sephardi, 31.4% for Asian, and 27.8% for African non-Jews. The Jewish values were more homogenous than the non-Jewish Inv[1] frequencies. Thus, although data for this gene locus are still very sparse, what is available does support a closer relationship among Jewish populations than between the Jews and corresponding non-Jews.

GROUP-SPECIFIC COMPONENT (Gc)

The group-specific component (Gc) of plasma is a protein found in two forms, the frequencies of which differ in different populations. Two alleles, Gc[1] and Gc[2], are responsible for the two forms, and combinations of the two alleles result in three patterns when the proteins are subjected to electrophoresis, a process that separates substances by their electric charge. The three patterns are found in persons whose genetic make-up (genotype) is Gc[1]/Gc[1], Gc[1]/Gc[2], and Gc[2]/Gc[2], respectively.

The Gc[2] allele is everywhere the rare of the two (see Table 11 in the Appendix). Its frequency ranges from 19 to 33% in European, Chinese, and Japanese populations, from 9.8 to 35.8% among East Indian populations, and from 5 to 10% among blacks.[20] In a study of the Gc types of different Jewish populations in Israel,[21] the frequencies of gene Gc[2] varied from 19.0% among Kurdish Jews to 33.8% in Ashkenazi Jews. The frequency of gene Gc[2], 26%, in a small sample of Israeli Arabs, was within this range. The gene Gc[2] frequency of the Ashkenazi Jews is high compared with that of most European populations. However, a large sample of Polish non-Jews had the same frequency of gene Gc[2], 33.7%, and a large sample of Germans from Berlin also had a high frequency, 31.3%. (Other studies of Gc frequencies in German populations have yielded a wide spread, going as low as 22.2% in a sample from southwest Germany.) The frequency of Gc[2] in Ashkenazi Jews, many of whom came from Poland and Germany, is thus not greater than the frequencies in non-Jews from Poland and some parts of Germany.

251

Although Yemenite and Kurdish Jews had somewhat lower frequencies of Gc^2 than did Jews from Iran, Iraq, and North Africa, the differences were not significant. Nor were there significant differences between any of the Asian Jewish groups and the Ashkenazi Jews. However, the average frequency of all the non-Ashkenazi Jews is compared with that of the Ashkenazi Jews, the difference in frequency between them is significant.

A large sample of Iranians yielded the very high Gc^2 frequency of 35.4%, which is close to the highest ever reported.[22] Other Middle Eastern populations must be studied before it can be determined whether these results are typical for the Middle East or have some other explanation.

The frequency of Gc^2 in the Samaritans is similar to that of other Middle Eastern Jewish populations.[23]

SERUM PSEUDOCHOLINESTERASE (PCE)

Serum pseudocholinesterase is an enzyme that comes in at least five different forms, determined by at least five different genes. Four of the genes, known as the usual, atypical, silent, and flouride-resistant genes, are allelic and function at the same locus, called the E_1 locus; the fifth gene functions at a different gene locus, called E_2.

Caucasian populations have a frequency of the atypical allele at locus E_1, or E_1^a, of more than 1%. The gene appears to be absent from some Oriental populations, Thais, Koreans, Eskimos, and Nigerians, and is very low (0.5%) in American blacks. Within white populations, the differences in E_1^a frequency are not great enough to be of use in population studies.[24] However, a recent survey of pseudocholinesterase variants among Jewish populations in Israel revealed a higher frequency of E_1^a in Iraqi and Iranian Jews than in any other population previously studied: 7.5% and 4.7%, respectively[25] (see Table 12 in the Appendix for other frequencies). These two communities differed significantly from all the other groups. A relatively high frequency of this gene was also observed among Jewish subjects from the Balkans and Turkey (2.6%), and this group differed significantly from the Ashkenazi Jews and from the Jews from North Africa. However, the frequency was only slightly higher than the frequencies of E_1^a observed among some non-Jewish populations of the area, 1.8% for Greece and 2.1% for Italy. Some of the Jews in Turkey originally came from Iraq and Iran, and their presence may have contributed to the increased frequency of the E_1^a allele in this group.

At present it is impossible to decide whether the high frequency of gene E_1^a in Iraqi and Iranian Jews is a result of genetic drift or represents the outcome of positive selection because of some unknown advantage of carriers of this gene in the region of Iraq and Iran. The non-Jewish populations of this region have not yet been studied. Only one small sample of Iranians has been examined, and it showed a relatively low frequency.

RED CELL ACID PHOSPHATASE (AP)

Red cell acid phosphatase (AP) is an enzyme found in three forms, A, B, and C, determined by three alleles, p^a, p^b, and p^c, respectively. Pairwise combinations of the three alleles can result in six phenotypes, which can be detected in the laboratory by the different electric charge of each enzyme form. The frequencies of these three alleles in several populations are listed in Table 13 in the Appendix. The data for this table and for the three following come primarily from a 1972 review[26] and a more recent investigation of several polymorphisms in Israeli Jews.[27]

In European populations, the frequency of allele p^b lies between 57 and 67%. The frequency of gene p^c, 3–9%, is higher than in other parts of the world. Gene p^c is generally absent in African and Oriental populations. In the Middle East, the frequency of gene p^b tends to be higher than in Europe, and the frequency of p^a lower. The frequency of p^b in Bulgaria, 79.9%, is clearly more characteristic of the Middle East than of Europe.

Several Jewish populations, including the Ashkenazim, have a frequency of gene p^b exceeding 70%, which is far above the North European level and is more typical of Mediterranean populations.

Yemenite Jews have a very high frequency of gene p^b, 84%. The Habbanite Jews have a frequency of 95.2%, which is among the highest ever recorded. In these high frequencies, the Habbanite and Yemenite Jews resemble both African peoples and other Middle Eastern non-Jewish populations, including the Hadhramaut Arabs (frequency of gene p^a = 13%, and therefore the frequency of p^b is probably around 85%), the South Sinai Towara Bedouins, and the Jebeliya Bedouins. The resemblance between Habbanite Jews and Jebeliya Bedouins is reminiscent of their similarity in ABO frequencies. The similarity in gene p^b frequency between the Yemenite Jews and Towara Bedouins recalls their similar ABO frequencies.

The lowest frequencies of gene p^b among Jews, 61–67%, is in the Middle Eastern Jews and in the samples from Iran, Iraq, and Kurdistan, and is in close agreement with the non-Jews from Iran and Kurdistan, who have frequencies of 62–66%.

PHOSPHOGLUCOMUTASE (PGM₁)

Three separate genes are involved in the synthesis of the red blood cell enzyme phosphoglucomutase (PGM). At the PGM_1 gene locus, several alleles are known, but all except two, PGM_1^1 and PGM_1^2, are rare. Each of

253 of

these two alleles specifies an enzyme of slightly different structure. Among non-Jews, the frequency of the PGM_1^2 allele is about 21–22% in Central Europe, 22–24% in Spain, and higher in the Mediterranean countries— 29.6% in Italy and 30% in Cyprus (see Table 14 in the Appendix for a complete listing). In Bulgaria, however, a very low frequency of gene PGM_1^2 was found, 16.5%.[28] Higher values are found in the Middle East, often exceeding 30%: in Turkey (32.3%), Kurdistan (34%), and among Israeli Arabs (30.0%).

The Jewish populations tested showed a similar distribution (see Table 14 in the Appendix), with a lower value of PGM_1^2 among the Ashkenazim than among Iraqi and Yemenite Jews. North African Jews had a frequency very much like that of other Middle Eastern Jews. Some samples of Ashkenazi Jews had a PGM^2 frequency somewhat higher than among European non-Jews, but other samples did not. The Ashkenazi Jews differed significantly from the other Jewish groups and from the Israeli Arabs. The differences between the Iraqi, Yemenite, and North African Jews were not significant, nor did these groups differ significantly from the Israeli Arabs.

Several non-Jewish Middle Eastern populations, however, have very different frequencies of the PGM genes. The South Sinai Towara and Jebeliya have unusually low PGM_1^2 frequencies, especially the Towara (15%).[29] Arabs in the Hadhramaut region of southern Yemen also have a very low frequency of gene PGM_1^2 (17%). Besides the alleles PGM_1^1 and PGM_1^2, the Jebeliya also have 1.05% of a third allele, PGM_1, usually found only in Africans.

The Habbanite Jews have a frequency of PGM_1^2 of 57.6%, the highest yet reported. No other Middle Eastern or African population shows a frequency anywhere near so high. Genetic drift and a high degree of inbreeding most likely account for this unusual frequency. Among the Cochin Jews of India, the frequency of 36.2% is higher than in any other Jewish group except the Habbanites, and might also be explained by genetic isolation. No data are available for surrounding native Indian populations with which to compare the Cochin Jews. The Samaritan isolate, in contrast, had an unusually low frequency of PGM^2, 16%.

ADENOSINE DEAMINASE (ADA)

Adenosine deaminase is another red cell enzyme; it occurs in two chemical forms, determined by two alleles, ADA^1 and ADA^2. Among non-Jews, the frequency of the ADA^2 gene is 4–7% in Central Europe, rising to about 9% in Southern Europe and even higher in the Middle East (see Table 15 in the Appendix). Among Japanese the frequency is much lower (3.2%), and the gene is rare in most black populations. It was absent from a group of American Indians.

In a sample of Ashkenazi Jews, the frequency of gene ADA^2, 10.6%, was significantly higher than that of Western Europe and comparable to frequencies in Southern Europe. However, most of the Ashkenazim originated from Eastern Europe.[30] In non-Jews from Bulgaria the frequency of the ADA^2 gene was 13.8%, the highest thus far recorded in Europe.[31] Non-Jews from Poland and Czechoslovakia had lower frequencies of ADA^2, 6.0% and 4.3%, respectively.[32] Thus, the elevated frequency of ADA^2 in Ashkenazi Jews compared with European non-Jews supports the Mediterranean origin of the Jews.

Jews from Iraq and Yemen had frequencies of gene ADA^2 of 14.9% and 13.5%, respectively, which are higher than in Ashkenazi Jews and may or may not be higher than in other Middle Eastern populations; only two samples have been examined for ADA frequencies—Kurds from Iran, whose ADA^2 frequency was 11.8%, and Israeli Arabs, with 11.2%. The frequency in a sample of North African Jews was comparable to those in Ashkenazi Jews and other Mediterranean non-Jewish groups. Significant differences were found between the ADA frequencies of Iraqi and North African Jews, Iraqi and Ashkenazi Jews, and Yemenite and North African Jews.[33] Cochin Jews from India had a rather low frequency of ADA^2, 6.2%.[34]

ADENYLATE KINASE (AK)

This enzyme, found in the red blood cells, comes in two chemical forms, determined by two different alleles at one gene locus. One of these alleles, Ak^2, has not been observed in American Indians and is rare among blacks. Its frequency is highly variable in Asian populations but very uniform in whites. As shown in Table 16 in the Appendix, the frequencies of the alleles in the Middle East are very much like the values in Europe. Jews as well as non-Jews from these regions average about 3–5% of Ak^2. North African Jews have similar values.[35] There were no significant differences among any of the Jewish groups nor between the Jews and the Israeli Arabs. No data are available for North African Arabs. In Ethiopia the frequency of gene Ak^2 is lower, 1.32%. The Ak^2 allele was absent from a sample of 71 Karaite Jews from Iraq, but was present at an unusually high frequency, 13.8%, among Cochin Jews from India. Non-Jewish Indians also had relatively high rates of this allele, 8.7–11.1%.

RED CELL GLUTAMIC-PYRUVIC-TRANSAMINASE (GPT)

This red blood cell enzyme occurs in two common chemical forms, determined by two different alleles, Gpt^1 and Gpt^2. Four other rare alleles have also been described. The results of the few population studies thus far

255

done demonstrate significant differences in gene frequencies, suggesting that this system may be a useful genetic marker in human population studies (see Table 17 in the Appendix). German non-Jews had frequencies of the Gpt^2 allele of 46–47%, Greeks 43.4%, Spaniards 49%, and Turks 46%. These values are all much higher than the frequencies found in African populations, which range from 12.8% in Mozambique to 25.9% in the Congo. The highest value was found in the Philippines, where the frequency of Gpt^2 was 69.3%.[36]

Five population groups in Israel differed significantly in the frequencies of Gpt^2.[37] The frequency in Ashkenazi Jews, 40%, is close to that in German non-Jews. Yemenite Jews and North African Jews had considerably lower values than did Ashkenazi Jews, Iraqi Jews, and Israeli Arabs. Although the low values in the Yemenite and North African Jews might suggest gene flow from African populations, other studies do not support this conclusion. The sickle hemoglobin gene, which is common in African populations, is completely absent in these Jewish groups. As shown in chapter XIII, the frequency of the Rh cDe chromosome (the "African chromosome") is not significantly higher among the Yemenites or North African Jews than among other Jewish or Near Eastern populations. In the Gc system, blacks have usually lower Gc^2 gene frequencies than Europeans. The Gc^2 gene frequencies among North African Jews and Yemenites are close to those found in Europe. In the adenylate kinase polymorphic system, the AK^2 allele, which is rare in populations of African origin, is found among the Yemenites and North African Jews in frequencies within the range characteristic for most European or Near Eastern populations. In the adenosine deaminase polymorphic system, the ADA^2 gene is absent or rare among blacks, whereas it is common among North African and Yemenite Jews. In the absence of evidence for a marked flow of black genes into the North African and Yemenite Jewish populations, the low frequency of the Gpt^2 gene in these populations may be connected with some unidentified selective factor operating in Asia and southwestern Arabia.[38]

PHOSPHOGLYCOLATE PHOSPHATASE (PGP)

Phosphoglycolate phosphatase (PGP) is an enzyme found in red blood cells. Of the three alleles found at the PGP genetic locus, PGP^1 is by far the most common. Among 1,385 Jews in Israel[39] originating from Yemen, Algeria and Tunisia, Libya, Iraq, Turkey, Morocco, Europe, Egypt, the Balkans, and Iran, significant differences were found in the frequencies of genes PGP^2 and PGP^3. The frequency of PGP^2 ranged from 1.85% among Yemenite Jews to a high of 6.88% in Iranian Jews. Highly significant differences were also observed in the frequencies of gene PGP^3, which ranged from a low of 0.62% in the Iranian Jews and 0.93% in the Yemenite Jews to a high of 5.47% in Moroccan Jews. In Ashkenazi Jews, the frequencies of PGP^1, PGP^2, and PGP^3 were 94.9%, 4.12%, and 0.98%, respectively. The only information currently available on non-Jews is a study in Europeans, who had a PGP^1 frequency of 82% and PGP^2 of 12.9%. It appears that the Ashkenazi Jews resemble most other Jewish communities and differ significantly from European non-Jews in their PGP frequencies. However, more data will be needed before any firm conclusions can be drawn.

ESTERASE D

Another red cell enzyme, esterase D, has at least two forms. Two allelic genes, EsD^1 and EsD^2 determine three common phenotypes. Significant differences in gene frequencies exist in various populations. Table 18 in the Appendix compares the frequencies of EsD^2 found among 1,429 Israelis[40] with earlier studies on non-Jews.[41] The EsD^2 gene frequencies varied from 10.0% among the Ashkenazi Jews to 21.2% in the Yemenite Jews. The differences between the Ashkenazi Jews and the Yemenite Jews were statistically significant, as were the differences between the Ashkenazi and the Iraqi Jews. The EsD^2 frequency of Ashkenazi Jews was very similar to that of European non-Jews. This frequency was also like that of North African Jews, but this similarity may be coincidental, as African non-Jews also have a low frequency. Yemenite Jews and Israeli Arabs were also similar, and had high frequencies approaching those of South Asiatic populations.

There are not many data yet on this new red cell polymorphism, but so far the esterase D gene locus appears to be another of those that show significant differences between Jewish populations and similarities to neighboring non-Jewish peoples.

ERYTHROCYTE GLYOXALATE I (GLO)

Another red cell enzyme that exhibits polymorphism is erythrocyte glyoxalate I, which is determined by a pair of of alleles at an autosomal locus. Table 19 in the Appendix, based on the findings of Golan and coworkers,[42] who have done many of the recent studies on red cell polymorphisms, lists the frequencies of gene GLO^1 in several populations. The GLO^1 gene frequencies varied from 22.9% among the Iranian Jews to 39.6% in the Egyptian Jews. Iranian Jews differ significantly from those from Yemen (GLO^1 = 33.2%), Turkey (33.4%), North Africa (31.7%), and Egypt (39.7%). The Jews from Egypt differed significantly from the Ashkenazi and Iraqi Jews and from Israeli Arabs.

European non-Jews had a significantly higher frequency of GLO^1, (43–45%) than did the Ashkenazi Jews (30%), whose frequency was similar

257

to that of most non-Ashkenazi Jews. As for the ADA and haptoglobin polymorphisms, the Ashkenazi Jews resembled other Jewish populations more than they did the non-Jews among whom they had lived. It would be of interest to have information on the GLO genes in other Mediterranean non-Jewish populations to whom the Jews can be compared.

RED CELL GLUTATHIONE PEROXIDASE (GSH-Px)

Two alleles, GSH-Px^L and GSH-Px^H, code for high and low activity of this red cell enzyme. In non-Jewish Americans, the frequency of the allele for low activity was 18.1%; in contrast, the frequency among Jewish Americans was much higher, 55.6%.[43] A study of the glutathione peroxidase activity in blood samples from Israeli Jews found no significant differences in the frequency of gene GSH-Px^L among Ashkenazi Jews or those from the Balkans, Iraq, Turkey, Iran, Yemen, and North Africa. All had high frequencies in the range of 43–56%, in confirmation of the earlier results.[44] Before any conclusions can be drawn, more studies on non-Jewish populations are necessary.

THE HLA SYSTEM

Recently, a new genetic marker, termed HLA, has been introduced into population studies. There are several HLA genes, each of which has several alleles. Each produces a protein called an antigen, found on the surface of most tissues. The importance of this antigen system is that for organ transplantation to succeed, the HLA antigens of the donor and recipient must be as similar as possible. Because of the several different HLA genes and the multiple alleles at each gene locus, there are many different combinations of HLA proteins. This diversity makes the HLA system very useful in population studies.

Two of the genes comprising the HLA system, HLA-A and HLA-B, have been studied extensively by Bonné-Tamir and her colleagues.[45] Just as with the Rh system, in which each person inherits one C, one D, and one E gene from each parent, in the HLA system each person inherits from each parent one of the many alleles in the HLA-A locus and one of the many in the B locus. A particular combination of HLA-A and HLA-B alleles is called a haplotype, and each person inherits one HLA haplotype from each parent. Bonné-Tamir's group determined the frequencies of each of 9 HLA-A alleles and each of 16 HLA-B alleles in 20 populations. The Jewish populations included those from Yemen, Armenia, Libya, Morocco, Iraq, Cochin, Germany, Poland, Russia, and Rumania. The non-Jews comprised Arabs, Lebanese, black Africans, Turks, Indians, Germans, Poles, Russians, and European Caucasians. Based on the allele frequencies of both the A and B loci, the authors calculated genetic distances between pairs of Jewish and non-Jewish populations. The reader is referred to chapter XVIII for an explanation of genetic distances and how they are calculated. Briefly, the larger the calculated number, the farther apart genetically are the two populations being compared.

For the HLA-A locus (see Table 20 in the Appendix), the most common allele in most of the populations was A2, whose frequency in non-Jews ranged from 12.3% among black Africans to 28.9% in Poles. A2 was also the most frequent allele among most Jewish populations, but its frequency was consistently lower than among the non-Jews. Among Polish Jews, the frequency of this allele was only 14.4%. The frequency for German non-Jews was 26%, compared with only 19% for German Jews. Cochin Jews had a frequency of the A2 allele of 10.3%, compared with 16.8% for non-Jewish Indians. Yemenite Jews, Armenians, and Cochin Jews differed from all other populations in that the most common allele in both populations was A9; its frequency was 30.7% in the Yemenite Jews, 19.1% in the Armenians, and 17.9% among Cochin Jews. (It should be noted, however, that a more recent study of HLA frequencies in Cochin Jews[46] obtained a very different frequency of the A9 allele—only 4.2%, which is the lowest of any population thus far studied. Clearly, additional studies in this population are necessary to resolve this discrepancy.) In other populations, the frequency of this allele was similar—14.1% in Iraqi Jews, 14.2% in German Jews, 14.5% in Polish and in Russian Jews, 17.7% among non-Jewish Poles, 15.6% among Germans, and 17.9% among Lebanese.

At the HLA-B locus (see Table 21 in the Appendix), the European non-Jewish populations have distinctly higher frequencies of alleles B7, B8, and B12 than do the Ashkenazi Jewish populations. For example, the frequency of B12 is 4.8% among German Jews, 7.8% among Polish Jews, and 5.7% among Russian Jews. In contrast, the frequencies for non-Jews are 12.2% for Germans, 13.8% for Poles, and 8.7% for Russians. Ashkenazi Jews have significantly elevated frequencies of HLA-B14 compared with European non-Jews and with non-Ashkenazi Jews. Non-Ashkenazi Jews have higher frequencies of HLA-B12 than do Ashkenazi Jews: 18.8% among Yemenite Jews, 13.1% in Libyan Jews, 12.9% in Moroccan Jews and 10.2% among Iraqi Jews. The most striking distinctions are in the Bw35 allele, which is significantly more common in Jewish than in non-Jewish populations. Its frequency in Russian Jews was 19.1%, compared with 10% in Russian non-Jews; 20.8% in German Jews, versus 8% in German non-Jews; 9.1% in Yemenite Jews, versus 5% in Arabs; 22.7% in Iraqi Jews, versus 15.2% in Turks.

Cochin Jews had an HLA-B pattern unique among Jewish populations. Their frequency of B7, 11%, was higher than any other Jewish population,

259

and was higher than most non-Jewish populations, including European, Middle Eastern, and North African. Their B7 frequency, however, was like that of non-Jewish Indians, 10%. Cochin Jews also had a higher frequency of allele Bw17, 15%, than did any other Jewish population. Other Jewish populations had Bw17 frequencies that ranged from 1.8% to 10%. Among non-Jews, only black Africans had a Bw17 frequency that was higher than that of the Cochin Jews, 18.1%.

Genetic distances were calculated between populations, based on the HLA gene frequencies. The average genetic distance between widely separated populations, such as black Africans and European Caucasians, was 40. The distance among non-Jewish Middle Eastern populations (Arabs, Armenians, Turks, and Lebanese) was 8.7; among Ashkenazi Jews (Polish, Russian, Rumanian, and German), it was 3.8. Thus, Ashkenazi Jews are very homogenous. The genetic distance between Ashkenazi Jews and Libyan Jews was 14; Moroccan Jews, 17; Iraqi Jews, 23; Yemenite Jews, 23; and Cochin Jews, 25. Surprisingly, the genetic distance between Ashkenazi Jews and East European non-Jews was equally high, 22; Armenians, 14; and Turks, 17.

The authors conclude that there is considerable heterogeneity among Jewish communities with respect to HLA, that Ashkenazi Jews show substantial differences in HLA frequencies for many centuries, and that the HLA data suggest clear elements of a common origin for the diverse Jewish populations.

CONCLUSIONS

We have reviewed the population data for the genetics of several different polymorphic proteins found either in the red blood cells or the blood plasma. One of these genes, that responsible for the formation of the enzyme adenylate kinase (AK), may not be helpful in population studies because most white populations have similar frequencies. The transferrin polymorphism is also not useful, as only one allele, TfC, has been found in Jewish populations. Phosphoglycolate phosphatase (PGP) is a new enzyme polymorphism that shows significant differences in gene frequencies among different Jewish populations; not enough information is available for non-Jewish groups to draw any significant conclusions at this time.

The frequency of the atypical pseudocholinesterase E_1^a gene is also fairly uniform among white populations, which would limit its usefulness in population studies. However, the interesting finding of unusually elevated frequencies among Iraqi and Iranian Jews shows that for this gene there are significant differences among different Jewish populations. Until information on the frequency of gene E_1^a in Iraqi and Iranian non-Jews is available, the cause of the high frequency among the Jews of this region will remain unclear.

For several genes, population surveys revealed significant differences between different Jewish populations. In some cases, the frequencies in Ashkenazi Jews resembled those in European non-Jews; in other cases, the frequencies in Ashkenazim tended more toward Mediterranean values. Yet other genes showed no major differences among different Jewish populations.

For four genes, Gc (group-specific component), PGM_1 (phosphoglucomutase), Gpt (glutamic-pyruvic transaminase), and ADA (adenosine deaminase), the frequency in Ashkenazi Jews differed significantly from those of Middle Eastern and North African Jews. The frequencies of the Gc, Gpt, and PGM genes in Ashkenazi Jews were similar to those of European non-Jews; the Gc and PGM frequencies of non-Ashkenazi Jews were similar to those of Israeli Arabs. For these three genes, different Jewish populations are heterogeneous and, where information is available, tend to resemble the surrounding non-Jewish populations more closely than they do one another. These conclusions are like those reached from analysis of the ABO gene frequencies.

The esterase D locus belongs with other genes that show significant differences between Jewish populations and similarities to neighboring non-Jewish peoples. More data are needed, however.

For the immunoglobulin Gm locus, Jews of any given region resembled their neighbors, but there was less diversity among the Jews than the non-Jews. At the immunoglobulin Inv locus, different Jewish populations differed significantly from one another, but in each case the Jewish frequencies were significantly lower than the corresponding non-Jewish frequencies and the Jewish values were more homogeneous than the non-Jewish.

The frequency distribution of seven other polymorphic genes yield clues as to the origin of the Jews. In these cases, the frequencies in Ashkenazi Jews differ from those of European non-Jews and tend to resemble those of Mediterranean populations. The haptoglobin frequencies were similar in all the major Jewish populations tested. The acid phosphatase allele p^b, which is typical of Mediterranean populations, was significantly more common in Ashkenazi Jews than in European non-Jews. The frequencies of adenosine deaminase ADA^2 also differed in various Jewish groups, but Ashkenazi Jews had an elevated frequency more typical of the middle East. Ashkenazi Jews had a significantly lower frequency of erythrocyte glyoxalate I (GLO) than did European non-Jews and tended to resemble non-Ashkenazi Jews. All Jewish groups tested had similar frequencies of red cell glutathione peroxidase $GSH-Px^L$, but sparse information is available on non-Jewish populations. In the HLA system, Jewish groups were very diverse, but there were also significant differences between Ashkenazim and European non-Jews. These findings suggest a Med-

261

iterranean origin for European Jews, in agreement with the conclusions drawn from the Rh gene frequencies and fingerprint patterns in Jewish populations.

Thus, all the traits examined so far—morphological traits, blood group genes, and red blood cell and serum proteins—show, on the one hand, an extensive admixture of different non-Jewish populations with the Jews, resulting in great heterogeneity among different Jewish groups; and, on the other hand, evidence for a common Mediterranean ancestry for these diverse Jewish groups.

The data also document very clearly the unusual genetic characteristics of the Karaites, Habbanites, Cochin Jews, and Samaritans, small groups in which genetic drift and inbreeding have played an important part in determining present-day gene frequencies.

1 England: blue eyes, brown hair.
2-3 Holland: 2. blue eyes, blond hair. 3. blue eyes, light brown hair.
4-6 Belgium: 4. blue eyes, blond hair. 5. blue eyes, light brown hair. 6. green
  eyes, black hair.
7-9 France: 7. green eyes, black hair. 8. brown eyes, brown hair. 9. brown-
  green eyes, black hair.

10. 11. 12.

13. 14. 15.

16. 17. 18.

10-15 Germany: 10. green eyes, light brown hair. 11. brown eyes, brown hair. 12. brown eyes, brown hair. 13. brown eyes, brown hair. 14. brown eyes, brown hair. 15. blue eyes, black hair.

16-18 Austria: 16. brown eyes, brown hair. 17. green eyes, brown hair. 18. green eyes, brown hair.

264

19-21 Czechoslovakia: 19. blue eyes, brown hair. 20. blue eyes, light brown hair. 21. brown eyes, blond hair.

22-25c Hungary: 22. grey eyes, brown hair. 23. grey eyes, brown hair. 24. brown eyes, brown hair. 25a-c. light blue eyes, light blond hair.

265

26-29 Rumania: 26. green eyes, blond hair. 27. brown eyes, black hair. 28. blue eyes, light brown hair. 29. blue eyes, light blond hair.

30 Lithuania: green eyes, brown hair.

31 Latvia: blue eyes, dark brown hair.

32a-c Poland: brown eyes, brown hair.

266

33-35 Poland: 33. blue eyes, blond hair. 34. greenish-brown eyes, black hair. 35. brown eyes, brown hair.

36-41 Russia: 36. green eyes, blond hair. 37. green eyes, light brown hair. 38. brown eyes, brown hair. 39. grey eyes, brown hair. 40. blue eyes, light brown hair. 41. brown eyes, black hair.

42-46 Bulgaria: 42. brown eyes, black hair. 43. greenish-blue eyes, light brown hair. 44. brown eyes, brown hair. 45. information not available. 46. information not available.

47 Yugoslavia: green eyes, light brown hair.

48 Italy: brown eyes, black hair.

49-50 Greece: 49. brown eyes, brown-black hair. 50. green eyes, light brown hair.

51.	52a	52b
53a	53b	53c
54.	55.	56.

51-52b Turkey: 51. brown eyes, black hair. 52a-b. blue eyes, blond hair.
53a-55 Morocco: 53a-c. brown eyes, black hair. 54. brown eyes, light brown
hair. 55. brown eyes, black hair.
56 Algeria: brown eyes, black hair.

57-59 Tunisia: 57. black eyes, black hair. 58. dark brown eyes, black hair. 59. brown eyes, brown hair.

60-62 Libya: 60. brown eyes, brown hair. 61. information not available. 62. information not available.

63-65 Egypt: 63. brown eyes, black hair. 64. brown eyes, brown hair. 65. black eyes, black hair.

66-69 Egypt: 66. brown eyes, brown hair. 67. brown eyes, brown hair. 68. brown eyes, black hair. 69. brown eyes, brown hair.

70-71 Habban (Hadhramaut).

72a-c Yemen.

73 Lebanon: brown eyes, black hair.
74-75 Syria: 74. green eyes, brown hair. 75. green eyes, brown hair.
76-81 Iraq: 76. brown eyes, black hair. 77. brown eyes, brown hair. 78. brown eyes, brown hair. 79. black eyes, black hair. 80. brown eyes, black hair. 81. brown eyes, brown hair.

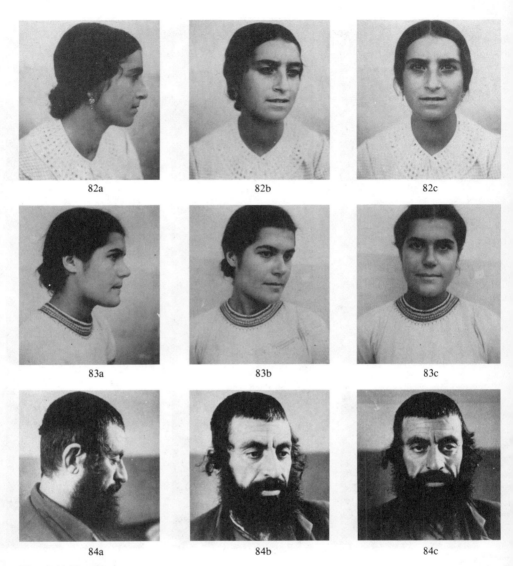

82a   82b   82c

83a   83b   83c

84a   84b   84c

82a-84c Kurdistan.

85a   85b   85c

86a   86b   86c

87a   87b   87c

85a-87c Kurdistan.

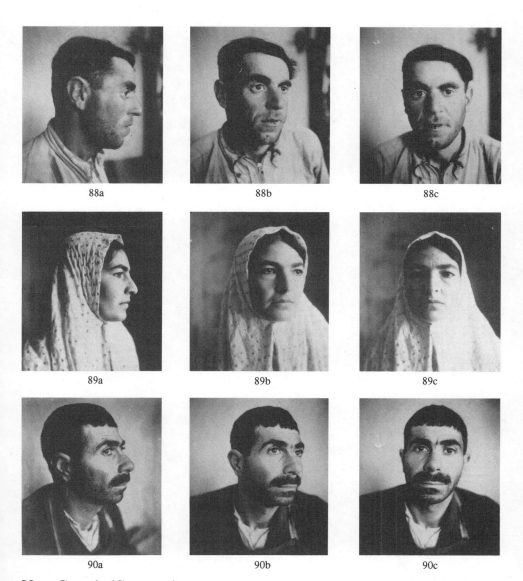

88a 88b 88c

89a 89b 89c

90a 90b 90c

88a-c Georgia (Caucasus).
89a-90c Iran.

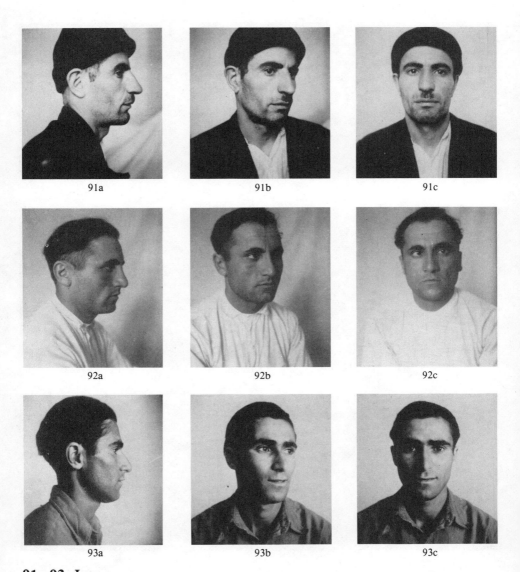

91a 91b 91c

92a 92b 92c

93a 93b 93c

91a-93c Iran.

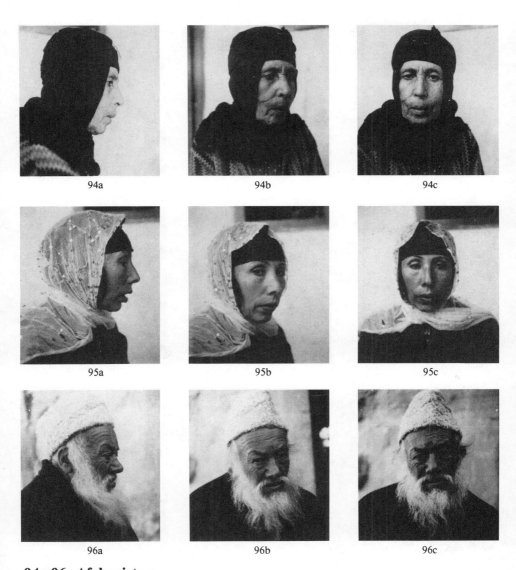

94a   94b   94c

95a   95b   95c

96a   96b   96c

94a-96c Afghanistan.

97a 97b 97c

98a 98b 98c

99. 100. 101.

97a-c Bukhara.
98a-c Turkestan.
99-101 India.

CHAPTER XV

Glucose-6-Phosphate Dehydrogenase Deficiency

G LUCOSE-6-PHOSPHATE dehydrogenase (G6PD) is an enzyme that plays a role in the metabolism of cells, especially red blood cells. An inherited deficiency of G6PD usually does no harm and is apparent only in laboratory tests. However, under particular circumstances, the red blood cells of an affected person hemolyze, or break up, and he develops a severe anemia. This can happen when he eats broad beans (*Vicia fava*) or takes an antimalarial drug such as quinine or primaquine.

The gene for G6PD deficiency is located on the X chromosome (one of the sex chromosomes), close to the two genes for color blindness and to the gene for hemophilia A. The gene is passed from father to daughter to son and from mother to son to daughter. A male needs only one defective gene to be susceptible to hemolytic anemia. Although some females carrying only one gene for G6PD deficiency are susceptible to the disease, two genes are generally required for susceptibility in women. Because the chances of getting two defective genes (one from each parent) are considerably less than the chance of getting only one, more men than women are affected. All the frequencies in this chapter refer only to males; the frequency of affected males when a condition is X-linked is the same as the gene frequency.

G6PD deficiency occurs in less than 10% of American black males and in about 30% of African black males. It is generally rarer in whites, but occurs in several populations in the Mediterranean area, including Sicily, Sardinia, Italy, Yugoslavia, Greece, Cyprus, Turkey, Lebanon, Israel, Egypt, Saudi Arabia, and Kuwait, as well as in Iran (see Table 22 in the Appendix). G6PD deficiency has also been found in India and Southeast Asia.[1]

The enzyme G6PD occurs in two forms, A and B, in healthy black subjects. The two types, which can be separated by laboratory tests, result from the action of two allelic genes on the X chromosome. Because males inherit only one gene for G6PD, they can have only one or the other form, whereas heterozygous black females may have both forms. Blacks who are deficient in G6PD usually have the A form. In contrast, among Mediterranean populations, only the B form is found in both healthy and G6PD-deficient persons. The Mediterranean (B) type of G6PD deficiency is a more serious illness than is the disease among blacks. The disease among Jews is the typical Mediterranean variety.

Individuals with G6PD deficiency appear to be less susceptible than others to falciparum malaria (the most serious form of malaria, caused by the protozoan *Plasmodium falciparum*), either because the malaria parasite requires a normal blood cell to multiply or because the anopheles mosquito, which injects the protozoan into the bloodstream, prefers to bite normal individuals.[2] There is a convincing correlation in various populations throughout the world between the frequency of G6PD deficiency and malaria; the enzyme defect is very common in many malarious areas. G6PD deficiency thus plays a role like that of the sickle cell trait, which also provides protection against malaria. However, the sickle cell trait is mostly confined to blacks in Africa or of African extraction.

The distribution of G6PD deficiency has been studied in the various communities is Israel in both adults[3] and newborns.[4] In Ashkenazi Jews the frequency was very low, 0.4%; the enzyme-deficient subjects had come to Israel from Russia, Poland, or Germany. Among 944 male newborns with Ashkenazi parents the frequency was 1.8%.

Among Sephardi Jews in Greece and Bulgaria, the frequency of G6PD deficiency (0.7–2.0%) was much like that of Spanish non-Jews (0.74%) and lower than that of Greek non-Jews (4.8–32.4%). After the Spanish expulsion in 1492, many Spanish Jews went to the Balkan countries, and their descendants retained frequencies of G6PD deficiency characteristic of Spain. The higher frequency among Turkish Jews (1.7–4.3%) might possibly reflect the inclusion of a few Kurdish Jews from eastern Turkey, with their much higher frequency; the origin of the sample of Turkish Jews is not specified.

Among Oriental Jews, G6PD deficiency was much more common than among Ashkenazi and Sephardi Jews; those from Yemen and Aden had a frequency of 5.3–5.4%; from Iran, 15.1% (and 13.5%); from Iraq, 24–25.3%; and from Kurdistan, 50–58.2%. The Kurdish Jews had the highest frequency of this trait ever recorded for any population. However, even this community was not homogeneous. Along the northern Iraqi border (Zakho, Dahok, Sandor, Amadia), the frequency of G6PD deficiency among Jewish males reached 70%, whereas in other parts of Kurdistan (farther south in Iraq and in western Iran), the frequency was only 35%. In a more recent study, the frequency of G6PD deficiency among Kurdish males varied from 68% among those who came from Iraq and 57% among those from Turkey (Jazirah, Diyarbakir, Cermik, Urfa, and others) to 25% among a small sample (20) originating from Iran. The frequency in the total sample of 344 males was 61.6%.[5]

Among the non-Jews of Kurdistan, the incidence of G6PD deficiency among adult males in Diyarbakir in southwest Turkey was 1.9%. West of Turkish Kurdistan, in Tarsus and Adana along the Turkish-Syrian border, the frequency of G6PD deficiency was 11.4%. Tarsus and Adana are in a highly malarial region. In other parts of Turkey outside Turkish Kurdistan, lower frequencies were found: 0.5% in Ankara in central Turkey, and 0% in Rize in northeast Turkey. In Cyprus, the frequency was found to be 3.5%. These frequencies are like those in Jews from the non-Kurdish regions of Turkey.

The rugged mountainous area in central Kurdistan, mainly along the Turkish-Iraqi border, appears to constitute the region of the highest concentration of G6PD deficiency in the world. The low frequency in non-Jews in Diyarbakir is unexplained. Ten of eleven Jews from Diyarbakir and Cermik (a town very near Diyarbakir) were G6PD-deficient. There may be a real difference between Jews and non-Jews in this small area. On the other hand, the findings in Tarsus and Adana may be more typical. Central Kurdistan is well known for the great isolation of the people in almost every village, so that genetic drift can bring about considerable differences in gene frequencies between one locality and another. To determine whether the low incidence of G6PD deficiency in non-Jews from Diyarbakir is typical of Kurdish non-Jews in general, more towns and villages would have to be sampled.

The meager serologic studies do not support the possibility that random genetic drift has resulted in large genetic differences between Jews and non-Jews in Kurdistan, but they do not argue against it. The ABO frequencies of Jewish and non-Jewish Kurds do not differ greatly. The frequencies of red cell acid phosphatase and adenylate kinase are also similar for Jews and non-Jews in Kurdistan.

Local differences in G6PD deficiency frequencies are also found among Iraqi and Iranian Jews. Those coming from Kurdish (western) Iran and Kurdish (northern) Iraq have much more G6PD deficiency than do Jews from Baghdad or central Iran. Iraqi Jews from Baghdad have a frequency of 24.5%, in contrast to 52% for those from Mosul, Erbil, and Murkuk (in Iraqi Kurdistan). Similarly, Jews from central Iran have a frequency of 10.8%, compared with 44% for Jewish males from western Iran. Among Jews from western Iran, including Kurdistan, 20.6% of men were G6PD deficient, compared with 16.7% of men from southern Iran and only 6.7%

of those from central Iran.[6] Muslim males from Iran had a frequency of 9.8%,[7] similar to that in Jews from central Iran.

In Baghdad, favism (hemolytic anemia caused by eating the broad bean *Vicia fava*) is considered mainly a disease of the Jewish minority.[8] In the seventeenth and eighteenth centuries, two severe epidemics of cholera and plague decimated the Jewish and Arab populations of Baghdad. Many of the surviving Jews emigrated to other countries. The recovery of the Jewish community of Baghdad began only around the mid-eighteenth century, when many Jewish immigrants from other countries settled there. These Jews came mainly from Iran, but also from Kurdistan and various parts of the Ottoman Empire. Only 1.9% of Sephardi Jews from western Turkey are G6PD deficient, 0.7% of those from Greece and Bulgaria, and 2.2% from other Balkan countries. However, the frequency in Jews in Iran is higher (15%) and in Kurdistan, as we have seen, even more so (58%). The migration of Jews from other countries might therefore explain the differences in the occurrence of favism reported in Baghdad between Jews and Arabs.

G6PD deficiency was common (28%) in Jews from the Caucasus (a mountainous region between the Black and Caspian Seas, north of Iran and Turkey). This contrasted with a total absence of the defect in male Muslim Circassians. However, the Circassians are relative newcomers to the Caucasus; they came in the middle of the nineteenth century from European Russia because of religious persecution, and apparently have retained the characteristic European absence of G6PD deficiency. Although the samples on which these frequencies are based were small (25 Jews and 57 Circassians), they do suggest that G6PD deficiency is much more prevalent in the Jews than non-Jews from the same area. A study of larger samples would indicate whether these frequencies are in fact representative of the Jews and non-Jews of this region. A comparison of other gene frequencies in these groups should help determine whether they indeed are very different genetically, or whether the difference is restricted to this one gene alone and is due to environmental effects and/or genetic drift. Although no information is available on blood group gene frequencies in Circassians, the mean ABO gene frequencies of Jews and non-Jews from Georgia, which is in the Caucasus region, show major differences supporting the possibility that Jews and non-Jews in the Caucasus differ genetically. However, the indigenous populations of Georgia also vary highly in their ABO gene frequencies, suggesting that Georgian non-Jews are in fact genetically heterogeneous groups.

Not a single male with G6PD deficiency was found among sixty-nine Samaritans who live in Israel near Tel Aviv.[9] This is particularly interesting because, before moving to Israel, these people had lived for about 2,700 years in the Nablus area, a highly malarious region. Because there is usually a good correlation between the presence of malaria in a region and a high frequency of G6PD deficiency, the Samaritans might be expected to have a high frequency of G6PD.

None of forty Iraqi Karaite males tested in Israel had the enzyme deficiency.[10] Its absence in Karaites and Samaritans reflects the genetic difference between these groups and the Jews. The Karaite sect, an offshoot of Judaism, was founded in Iraq about A.D. 760. The Karaites might therefore be expected to show genetic affinities with Jews from Iraq. However, in contrast with the 25% frequency of G6PD among Iraqi Jews, no case of G6PD deficiency was found in 250 Egyptian Karaites. Therefore Goldschmidt concludes that "if they are derived from Mesopotamian Jews, they have since moved pretty far away from them."[11] The Egyptian Karaites differed also from Egyptian Arabs, among whom they have lived for more than a thousand years; G6PD deficiency is very common among Egyptian Arabs. Thus the difference between the Karaites and the Baghdad Jews cannot be ascribed to gene flow between the Karaites and Egyptians. The differences between Karaites and Baghdad Jews and between Karaites and Egyptian Arabs are also reflected in differences in ABO gene frequencies between these groups.

Arabs and Druze tested in Israel both had an average frequency of G6PD deficiency of 4.4%, similar to the frequency of 6.3% found in Jews from Syria and Lebanon. Only 11 out of 760 Arab and Druze newborns had G6PD deficiency, a frequency of 1.45%.[12] Other Arabs in the Middle East had enzyme deficiency rates of 15% for adults in Saudi Arabia, 3.1% for Lebanese, 9.8% for Iranians, and 20.4% for adults in Kuwait. A small sample of Arabs from neighboring Iraq living in Kuwait had a frequency of about 30%. Iraqi Arabs living in Kuwait are mostly new arrivals from Iraq, lured to Kuwait by the oil boom of the past 25 years. Their frequency of G6PD deficiency is like that of Jews from Baghdad.

The incidence of G6PD deficiency among Habbanite males was only 1.4%, which is low compared to the 5% frequency among Yemenites.[13] Among Cochin Jews from India, 3.2% of men were G6PD deficient in one study[14] and 10.3% in another.

Jews from North Africa have a generally low frequency of G6PD deficiency. None was found in Jews from the island of Jerba, 0.5% in Jews from Morocco, 0.9% in Jews from Libya, Algeria, and Tunisia, and 3.8% in Jews from Egypt. In Egyptian Arabs, mostly Moslems, enzyme deficiency was more frequent in the rural districts (29.7%) than in the metropolitan cities (15.8%).[15] The genetic make-up of the metropolitan cities is mixed. Some of the populations are descendants of immigrants from Europe, where G6PD deficiency is uncommon. The incidence of malaria is also lower in the cities than in rural areas. Because almost all the Egyptian Jews who migrated to Israel came from the metropolitan areas, this might explain their low frequency compared with Egyptian Arabs. However, G6PD deficiency in the Egyptian Jews is still significantly less common than in Egyptian Arabs from the metropolitan areas, indicating a possible genetic difference between these groups. A higher proportion of Egyptian Jews are of European, particularly Spanish, extraction, and may have retained a measure of the low Spanish frequency of G6PD deficiency.

No case of enzyme deficiency was detected among the Falashas, a group of Jews who live in northern Ethiopia. This group seems to represent an indigenous population that converted to Judaism centuries ago. No cases of enzyme deficiency were found among 1,000 Ethiopians belonging to six different tribes.

Because malaria exerts strong selection pressure on G6PD deficiency, much greater differences in frequency are found for this gene than for some others, even within a small part of the world. The important effect of the environment (malaria) makes it more difficult to draw conclusions from the distribution of this gene than from other genes that have been fairly stable over the centuries.

Nonetheless, certain general trends are evident. The frequency of G6PD deficiency in Jews ranges from 0% among the Falashas of Ethiopia and the Karaites to 70% among Kurdish Jews living along the northern Iraqi border. Thus the Jews are extremely heterogeneous with respect to this gene, in fact as heterogeneous as the non-Jewish population of the world. Furthermore, the absence of the enzyme deficiency in the Falashas parallels its absence in other Ethiopians; the low frequency in Ashkenazi Jews resembles its rarity in Europeans in general; Jews from Syria and Lebanon are like Israeli Arabs; and Sephardi Jews of Greece and Bulgaria closely resemble those of Spain from where they migrated. No studies of G6PD deficiency have yet been reported on Kurdish non-Jews, but it is likely that they will also show high frequencies. Although some discrepancies exist (Jews from the Caucasus versus Circassians, Egyptian Jews versus Egyptian Arabs, and possibly Baghdad Jews versus Baghdad Arabs), the results of this brief survey support the notion that the Jews are a heterogeneous people, who tend to resemble the populations among which they live more closely than they resemble Jews from other parts of the world.

CHAPTER XVI

PTC Taste Sensitivity

P HENYLTHIOCARBAMIDE (PTC) IS a substance which tastes bitter to most people. However, some people can taste only concentrated solutions of PTC. The ability to taste PTC is inherited as a simple dominant gene. To determine whether a person is a "taster" or a "nontaster," he tastes a series of PTC solutions of increasing concentration. The first solution that tastes bitter to him is called his *concentration threshold*. When the thresholds of many people are plotted, a bimodal distribution results; the trough can be taken as the point that separates tasters from nontasters. The analysis is complicated by the fact that women in general are more sensitive to PTC than men, and therefore can taste more dilute solutions.

The incidence of nontasters (those who are homozygous for the nontasting allele) differs in different populations. In Africa, only 2.3% of Bantus are nontasters, as are 13.7% of Nigerians. Japanese and Chinese have low proportions of nontasters (2–10%). In Europe, the incidence of nontasters is higher, ranging from 24 to 35%. In the Middle East, 27.5% of Kurdish non-Jews are nontasters (see Table 23 in the Appendix).[1]

In a study of various Jewish groups in Israel, the frequency of nontasters among Ashkenazi Jews (20.7%) was like that of Sephardim from the Balkans (21.7%).[2] These frequencies were close to that of Polish Jews living in Brazil,[3] but were much higher than the 9.5% found in Ashkenazi Jews living in Israel.[4] Among North African Jews, the frequency of nontasters was significantly higher among females than males. In consequence, the frequency of nontasters among females from Europe, North Africa, Near East, and Yemen was almost identical, while among the males significant differences were observed. Among Habbanite Jews, the frequency of nontasters among males is 19.4%, and among females 20.1% (mean 19.8%).[5] These values do not differ from that found for Yemenite Jews.

The frequency of nontasters in the Jewish Cochin community (31.7%) is like that of Hindus (about 33%), and significantly greater than that of Kurdish, North African, Iraqi, Ashkenazi, and Sephardi Jews.[6] These findings are in agreement with the many other gene frequencies, for which the Cochin Jews also differ from other Jewish communities.

The highest frequency of nontasters, 41.4%, was observed among the Jews of the island of Jerba off the Tunisian coast. This finding suggests that the Jews of Jerba differ from all other North African Jewish communities, in which a significantly lower frequency of nontasters was observed (15.0%). The blood group data support this conclusion: Jews from Algeria, Tripolitania, Morocco, and Tunisia have a homogeneous ABO gene frequency distribution, whereas a small sample of Jerba Jews had much higher O and lower A gene frequencies. However, among the Jews of Jerba there is a preponderance of *Kohens*, and consequently they may not have been a random sample of the Jewish community even at the time they settled on Jerba (see the founder effect in chapter X).

The lowest frequency of PTC nontasters was found among the Samaritans in Israel (6.4%). Their uniqueness in this respect parallels the findings in the ABO system and Hp genes.[7]

Comparisons of Jewish and non-Jewish frequencies of PTC nontasters are impossible in many areas of the world, because data on non-Jews are lacking. In the Middle East, only a group of Kurds has been tested.[8] Their frequency (27.5%) is significantly higher than that of Kurdish Jews, which may reflect relatively little intermarriage between the two groups. The high incidence of cousin marriages among the Kurdish Jews supports this conclusion. The frequencies of PTC nontasters among non-Jews in Central and Western Europe are uniformly higher than those of Ashkenazi and Sephardi Jews, but no Eastern European populations have been tested. Nonetheless, it appears that relatively fewer European Jews than non-Jews are nontasters. Because Oriental Jews have even lower frequencies of nontasters, the depressed values in European Jews may reflect an element of Mediterranean ancestry. However, until more Eastern European and Oriental non-Jewish groups are tested, this remains only a guess. Meanwhile, it is apparent that Jews are not uniform in their ability to taste PTC.

CHAPTER XVII

Color Blindness

T HERE ARE TWO types of red-green color vision defects. *Deutan* anomalies are caused by defects or lack of the green-sensitive pigment in the eye, and *protan* abnormalities are due to defects or deficiency of a red-sensitive pigment. Synthesis of the two pigments is governed by several genes on the X chromosome, which are tightly linked to one another, and to the gene for glucose-6-phosphate-dehydrogenase deficiency. Each locus has at least two abnormal alleles besides the normal allele. One causes a severe defect, or "——opia" (deuteranopia and protanopia) and the other a mild defect, or "——anomaly" (deuteranomaly and protanomaly).

Because females have two X chromosomes and males only one, any abnormal recessive gene located on one female X chromosome is likely to be at least partly "masked" by the presence of a normal allele on the other chromosome. In males, on the other hand, the defective gene is always expressed. This is why sex-linked defects, such as color blindness and glucose-6-phosphate deficiency, are more common in males than females. The frequency of an X-linked allele is the same as the proportion of affected males; frequencies of X-linked genes are usually measured in males. The following discussion of the frequency of color blindness refers only to males unless otherwise specified.

Until recently it was uncertain whether the protan and deutan types of color blindness were due to alleles at one or more than one gene locus. For this reason, the frequencies of all red-green defects have often been lumped together, and one figure for the total frequency of red-green color blindness has been given. One must realize that this figure is the sum of at least four different defective alleles at two loci. Thus similarities in the total frequen-

287

cies do not necessarily indicate similarities at each locus (see Table 24 in the Appendix).

In European countries, the total frequencies of red-green color blindness are about 7–10%. In two samples of Ashkenazi Jews the frequencies were 8.0% and 9.1%, which lie within the European range. The frequency in a sample of Polish Jews studied in Israel was 8.7%, and in two samples of Russian Jews, 7.7% and 8.1%.[1]

A detailed study in Sardinia showed marked heterogeneity between villages, with frequencies ranging from 1.3% to 12.5%.[2] Different regions in Greece showed a range of 6.4–8.7%.

In Sephardi Jews, the incidence of color blindness was 5.5%. This low frequency, compared with that of European Jews, is also characteristic of Jews of Asia and North Africa. The frequency in Yemenite Jews is particularly low—3.8% and 4.7% in two samples. Iraqi Jews had frequencies of 3.9–6.1%, and Iranian Jews, 5.7–6.3. None of 28 male Karaite Jews from Hit, Iraq, were color-blind.[3] North African Jews had similarly low frequencies, ranging from 3.7% in Tunisians to 6.0% and 7.0% in two samples from Morocco. Egyptian Jews had a frequency of 7.4%.[4]

Among non-Jews of this region, similarly low frequencies were found in Egypt (5.0%), Turkey (5.3%), and Iran (4.5%). However, other studies of Middle Eastern Arabs have yielded higher frequencies, 10.0% among the Druze in Israel and 12.0% in Israeli Arabs. The high "European" frequency among the Druze is interesting, because this community is believed to have absorbed some of the Crusaders settling in Palestine.

Among Kurdish Moslems in Iran, 8.1% were color blind, as were a similar percentage of Kurdish Jews. However, there were proportionally more deuteranomalous males among the Kurdish Jews (4.3%) than among the Kurdish Muslims (0.9%). In addition, 3.0% of the Muslims, but none of the Jews, had severe nonclassifiable color defects. These differences, coupled with the significant differences in ability to taste PTC found between Kurdish Jews and Muslims (see chapter XVI), suggest that there has been little interbreeding between these two groups.[5]

Because the overall frequency of color blindness is the sum of two separate gene loci, by examining the ratio of protan to deutan defects in populations with similar total frequencies, we should obtain some idea of whether the frequencies at each locus are also similar. Seven samples of European non-Jewish populations had a mean protan/deutan ratio of 0.37. A similar value, 0.39, was reported for European Jews. Thus, not only are the total frequencies of these two groups similar, but the frequencies of color blindness at each of the two loci are also close. In contrast, Jews from Yemen and Aden had an unusually low protan/deutan ratio, 0.18, whereas the ratio in Iraqi Jews, 0.50, was considerably higher. In Moroccan Jews the ratio was even higher, 1.00, and Iranian Jews had the unusually high protan/deutan ratio of 2.00.[6] Thus, the different Middle Eastern Jewish populations show considerable diversity in the frequencies of the two genes for color blindness.

In the Samaritan isolate in Israel, the frequency of color blindness was extremely high, 27.7%. All affected men had deutan defects. Both of these findings are very unusual and confirm the genetic distinctiveness of this group.[7]

The Habbanite isolate, in contrast, is characterized by a virtual absence of color blindness. Only two color-blind males were found, and both mothers of these males came from the town of Beida and were not Habbanites.[8] Among the Cochin Jews of India, color blindness is also extremely uncommon; only one protanop male was found among 113 males examined in Israel, a frequency of 0.9%.[9] This is the lowest frequency in any Jewish population except the Habbanites.

This brief review shows that Jews are heterogeneous with respect to the incidence of color blindness, which is lower among Sephardi, North African, and Asian Jews than among Ashkenazim. The extremes are found in two relatively isolated groups, the Habbanites (0%) and the Samaritans (27.7%). The Jewish frequencies generally reflect the local non-Jewish frequencies of color blindness, but a great deal of variation in the non-Jewish frequencies prevents a firmer conclusion.

CHAPTER XVIII

Genetic Distance between Jewish and Non-Jewish Groups

WITH COMPUTER ASSISTANCE, it is possible to combine the differences in gene frequencies between any two populations in such a way as to come up with a single overall measure of the genetic difference between the two, based on all the gene frequencies available for them. Such a measure is called *genetic distance*. The formulas we have used for calculating genetic distance are technical and therefore relegated to the Appendix (p. 333). The first step in reaching such a formula is to calculate the individual genetic distance between two populations separately for each gene locus (for example, ABO or color blindness). After individual genetic distances have been computed for each locus, the distances are combined to give the average, genetic distance between the two populations. The reliability of this figure increases with the number of loci on which it is based, so that a genetic distance based on ten gene loci is more trustworthy than a distance based on only three loci. In the latter case, an anomaly at any one gene locus can greatly influence the final result.

The average genetic distance between the two populations is usually expressed by a number between 0 and 1, but we will convert this scale to between 0 and 100 for easier reading. Two populations with a genetic distance of 0 would be identical in all their gene frequencies. However, it is extremely unlikely that such a value would ever be obtained; even if two samples of the same population were compared, they would differ because of sampling errors. Two populations with a genetic distance of 100 would be totally different in every gene frequency. That is, at every gene locus examined, one population would have a frequency of 100% and the other a frequency of 0%. Such populations do not exist; real populations that are extremely different rarely have a genetic distance much greater than 30.

The results of the genetic distance computations are presented in the Appendix in Tables 25–27, which give the genetic distance between pairs of populations on a scale of 0 to 100 and the number of loci from which each distance was computed. The maximum number of loci on which a distance could be based was 15. The possible loci are the blood groups ABO, MN, RH, Kell, Duffy, and P; the serum protein loci haptoglobin (Hp), group-specific component (Gc), adenosine deaminase (ADA), adenylate kinase (AK), atypical pseudocholinesterase (PCE), phosphoglucomutase (PGM), and alkaline phosphatase (AP); and the loci for the ability to taste PTC, and for color blindness. In fact, in no case was information available for all fifteen loci; the number of loci on which the distance was based is given for each pair of populations. The frequencies from which the distances were computed were obtained from the sources listed in the relevant chapters. Although another major genetic system, the HLA system, is now available, we have chosen not to recalculate all the genetic distances originally derived for the earlier edition of this book. Instead, the reader is referred to the section on HLA for discussion of genetic distances that incorporate this system. We do not believe that addition of this one new system would significantly alter the conclusions.

Table 25 lists the genetic distance between pairs of non-Jewish populations, arranged in order of decreasing distance. This does not intend to be an exhaustive list, but merely a representative sample. The most dissimilar pair of populations are the American blacks and the Chinese, who have a genetic distance of 33.3. Also extremely dissimilar, with a genetic distance of about 20, are American whites and Bantus, American whites and Chinese, and Eskimos and Nigerians. At the other end of the scale, the populations that are the closest genetically are the American whites and English (genetic distance = 2.3), English and Dutch (2.4), Danish and Swedish (2.4), and Danish and German (3.0). More different genetically are the French and English (genetic distance 4.0), Spanish and English (4.5), and French and Americans (4.5). Looking at the populations we know to be dissimilar genetically, we find that their genetic distances are even greater: 6.4 for Greek and English, 7.3 for Norwegians and Sicilians, 10.1 for American blacks and Bantus, and 14.8 for English and Egyptians. From these figures we may conclude very generally that population pairs that have a genetic distance between 5 and 10 are moderately similar; and those with a distance greater than 10 are dissimilar.

Table 26 lists the genetic distance between pairs of Jewish populations. In this table, the Ashkenazim, Habbanites, and Samaritans are each compared with several other Jewish groups. The Jewish group separated by the largest genetic distance from the Ashkenazim is that of Habbanites. The value of 20.9 shows that the Habbanites and the Ashkenazim are genetically very dissimilar, about as dissimilar as the American whites and Chinese. The Habbanites are also genetically different from the Sephardi Jews (genetic distance = 17.6) and from North African Jews (17.0), as well as from the Samaritans (21.7). As we have seen, extensive inbreeding and reproductive isolation in the Habbanite population have resulted in gene frequencies that sometimes differ greatly from those of any other Jewish (or non-Jewish) population.

Next to the Habbanites, the greatest distance from Ashkenazi Jews is shown by the semi-Jewish Samaritans (genetic distance = 13.0) when compared with all Ashkenazim and 17.4 when compared with German Jews. The Samaritans are equally distant genetically from Oriental Jews (16.6) and Habbanite Jews (21.7). As with the Habbanite Jews, extensive inbreeding and genetic drift have resulted in unusual gene frequencies in the Samaritans.

The genetic distance between Ashkenazi Jews and Oriental (Middle Eastern) Jews is generally in the range of 7.2 (Iranian Jews) and 9.4 (Kurdish Jews). That is, Ashkenazi Jews are more different genetically from Middle Eastern Jews than Germans or English are from Greeks, and at least as different as Norwegians and Sicilians.

Distances were also computed between Ashkenazim in general and individual European Jewish populations for which sufficient information was available. For most genes the frequencies for Ashkenazi Jews were calculated on the basis of samples that consisted of a mixture of European Jews who had migrated recently to Israel. The results of the genetic distance computations show, as expected, that these "Ashkenazi Jews" are more closely related to individual European Jewish populations than to Sephardi or Middle Eastern Jews. The genetic distance between "Ashkenazim" and Polish Jews is exceedingly low (1.4), which leads us to suppose that many of the Ashkenazi Jews sampled in Israel were of Polish extraction. The distances between Ashkenazi Jews and Rumanian (2.4) and Russian Jews (2.2) are also very small. The genetic distance between Ashkenazi Jews and German Jews (5.0) is larger, suggesting that German Jews contributed relatively less to the Ashkenazi groups sampled in Israel.

Table 27 lists some values for genetic distance between pairs of Jewish and non-Jewish populations inhabiting the same regions. To be able to operate with a sufficient number of loci, it was necessary to lump together some populations; thus we obtained a "North African" non-Jewish group, a "Balkan" non-Jewish group, and "East European" Jewish and non-Jewish groups. The greatest difference is shown between Habbanite Jews and surrounding Arabs; this may be explained by the high degree of inbreeding and genetic isolation of the Habbanites. North African Jews are relatively distant from North African non-Jews combined and from Egyptians (Egyptian Jews have a larger European admixture than non-Jews). Sephardi Jews are moderately different from Balkan non-Jews, undoubtedly a consequence of their Spanish origin. Equally different are the Jews and non-Jews of Kurdistan, who lived in small towns in relative isolation and practiced extensive inbreeding.

For the remaining population pairs, the genetic distance between Ashkenazi Jews and European non-Jews ranges between 3.7 and 5.6, the smaller distances being found in comparisons with East European populations and the larger ones in comparisons with Western European populations. This is in agreement with the previous supposition that the Ashkenazi Jews sampled in Israel for recent gene frequency studies comprise primarily Eastern European Jews.

The smallest genetic distance found between a European Jewish and non-Jewish population (slightly under 4 between Eastern European Jews and non-Jews) is still larger than that between the most closely related pairs of non-Jewish populations for which a genetic distance was calculated (Danish and Swedish, Americans and English). This finding can be explained on the basis of the conclusion—reached independently from an analysis of morphological data, on the one hand, and blood group and serum protein data, on the other—that European Jews still retain some element of the Mediterranean gene pool contributed by their Mediterranean ancestors. However, it should be noted that the genetic distance between East European Jews and East European non-Jews, or even between Ashkenazi Jews and English non-Jews, is considerably smaller than the distance between Ashkenazi Jews, on the one hand, and Iranian, Iraqi, Kurdish, Oriental, Yemenite, or Habbanite Jews, on the other.

Thus, the results of genetic distance computations provide a quantitative confirmation of the major conclusions we reached in earlier chapters after examining individual gene frequencies and morphological traits. These conclusions were: (1) Jewish groups from different parts of the world are very different genetically; (2) Jews of a certain area tend to resemble the surrounding non-Jews more than they resemble Jews from other parts of the world; and (3) European Jews have a residue of non-European (Mediterranean) genes.

Based on the gene frequencies found in Ashkenazi Jews for six different blood groups and the HLA A and B loci, Bonné-Tamir and coworkers calculated genetic distances between European Jewish populations and between European Jews and non-Jews.[1] They found a 3- to 5-fold greater average genetic distance between Ashkenazi Jews and European non-Jews (10 + 0.3) than within the Ashkenazi populations (2 + 0.8) or within non-Jewish Europeans (3 + 0.5) and concluded that "not much admixture has taken place between Ashkenazi Jews and their Gentile neighbors during the last 700 years." This conclusion is refuted by the historical evidence. Moreover, it is not surprising to have statistical support for the homogeneity of Ashkenazi Jews, a finding that is supported historically. What is of

293

more interest is that genetic distances between Ashkenazim and other Jewish populations are at least as great as those between Ashkenazim and European non-Jews, implying significant heterogeneity among different Jewish populations.

Other researchers have also recently calculated genetic distances between different Jewish populations and between Jews and non-Jews. Their calculations were based either on their own data or on previously published numbers. For example, Roychoudhury[2] determined in 1982 that Yemenite Jews were more closely related to Israeli Arabs than to Iranian Jews, Ashkenazi Jews, or North African Jews. Iranian Jews were closer to Iranian non-Jews than to the other Jewish groups. Ashkenazi Jews were closer to European non-Jews than to other non-Jewish groups or to Iranian or Yemenite Jews. However, he found a close affinity between Ashkenazi Jews and North African Jews, who are of Sephardi origin. His results therefore confirm both the genetic links of Jews to the indigenous non-Jewish populations among whom they live, and also the unique genetic relatedness of different Jewish populations, which can be explained by their common Middle Eastern origin. Thus, these results are compatible with our conclusions.

The disagreement among different workers about the extent of admixture between Jewish and non-Jewish populations is compounded by our ignorance of the gene frequencies of the ancestral Jews. Using plausible assumptions, some workers have attempted to calculate the most likely original frequencies and have drawn conclusions from their results about the relatedness of present-day populations. For example, based on current frequencies in 12 Jewish populations, Carmelli and Cavalli-Sforza estimated the original gene frequencies of four blood groups, and attempted to estimate the extent of genetic drift and migration since the time of the original Jews.[3] They concluded that most Jewish populations retain evidence of their Middle Eastern origin but have undergone substantial genetic drift because of their small size. They also concluded that, except for Ashkenazi Jews, most Jewish populations did not interbreed significantly with neighboring peoples. Their conclusions, however, are clearly speculative. For Ashkenazi Jews, the same authors estimate a total admixture of 40%, supporting the conclusion of extensive interbreeding with neighboring European populations.[4]

CHAPTER XIX

"Jewish" Diseases

INTRODUCTION

T HE OCCURRENCE OF particular diseases can be used as a genetic marker for particular ethnic groups. Several rare diseases of clearly genetic origin differ in incidence between Jews and non-Jews. In the United States, a child born with Tay-Sachs disease or with familial dysautonomia, to name just two, is very likely to be Jewish or to have at least one Jewish ancestor. The occurrence of such diseases predominantly in Jews has been presented as evidence that Jews are genetically distinct from non-Jews.

Such a conclusion, while persuasive at first glance, is not necessarily valid. The use of rare genes in population studies lends itself poorly to statistical analysis, for the genes in question are found in only a small proportion of the population. In addition, when the gene causing the rare disease is recessive, so that the disease is apparent only in individuals who carry two such genes, it may be difficult to determine how much of a relatively high incidence of the disease in any one population is due to the effects of inbreeding and how much is the result of a relatively high gene frequency in the population.

Even when a disease is very common in the population, the causes of the phenomenon may still be uncertain. Is the rare gene uniformly distributed over the entire population, or is it restricted to persons from a particular geographical area? If the latter, it is possible that genetic drift or the founder effect (see chapter X) have produced an exceptionally high frequency of the rare gene in a particular village or area. In such a situation, the high gene frequency tells us only that the people of the particular village or area differ genetically from other members of the population being studied; it tells us nothing about the population as a whole.

With these problems in mind, we can examine the incidence of several inherited diseases in Jewish populations. Since the publication of the previous edition of this book, dozens of genetic diseases have been found to be more prevalent or less prevalent in particular Jewish populations compared with other Jews and with non-Jews. This chapter cannot provide an exhaustive accounting of these diseases. A good recent text that deals extensively with such diseases is *Genetic Disorders among the Jewish People*, by Richard M. Goodman.[1]

The use in population studies of commonly occurring inherited diseases does not involve the problems found in the study of rare genes. The frequencies of genes for common diseases can be used in the same way as the frequencies of blood group and other similar genes. In this chapter we will also look at the distribution among Jews of a common inherited disease of the red blood cells, thalassemia, which occurs predominantly in the Mediterranean area.

Many common diseases—diabetes, cancer, heart disease, and even alcoholism, for example—have a genetic component in their causation. Some families tend to suffer from one or another of these diseases more than other families. Because the incidence of these diseases differs in different populations, they are useful in population studies. However, the role of environment is important in all of these common diseases, although the genetic contribution to them is poorly understood. Hence, when we are comparing different populations, the effects of diet and other environmental factors must be considered before any differences in the incidence of common diseases can be attributed to heredity.

The point is shown nicely in a study of the incidence of kidney stones (nephrolithiasis) in Israel.[2] A survey carried out in 1957–58 in the central and northern parts of Israel showed an incidence of kidney stones of 11.8%, twelve times as high as in the United States. Kidney stones occurred more frequently in the hotter regions than in the cooler. In Afikim, in the hot Jordan Valley, the frequency was 34.1%, compared with only 1.6% in Maoz Zion in the cool Judaean mountains. The disease was more prevalent among immigrants from Europe (27%) than among those from the Middle East and North Africa (7.9%). In a single settlement with a mixed population, Afikim, 60% of European Jews had kidney stones, but only 8.7% of Middle Eastern and North African Jews.

Inadequate fluid intake was the reason for the high incidence of kidney stones in the hotter regions. A person who drank too little water produced a small volume of highly concentrated urine, which was conducive to stone formation. The ethnic differences could be explained by drinking habits: the immigrants from the Middle East and North Africa were accustomed to drinking much more liquid than immigrants from the cooler European climate. Educating the immigrants to drink more fluids resulted in a significant reduction in the incidence of kidney stones.

Thus, the difference in the incidence of kidney stones between European and Oriental Jews was due to nothing more complex than differences in the amount of water they drank, and was unrelated to differences in their genetic background.

INHERITED DISEASES WITH UNUSUAL FREQUENCY IN ASHKENAZI JEWS

This section will describe the population genetics of several diseases whose inheritance pattern is well established and which are more or less common among the Ashkenazi Jews than other Jewish populations and non-Jews. Each of these diseases occurs as a result of a mutation in a single gene. Most of the diseases are rare. Several of the rare inherited diseases which are *more* common in Jews than non-Jews in the United States are in fact common only in Ashkenazi Jews. They are as rare in non-Ashkenazi Jews as in non-Jews. These diseases include familial dysautonomia, Tay-Sachs disease, Gaucher's disease, Niemann-Pick disease, Bloom's syndrome, and essential pentosuria. It is of interest that most of these diseases affect the nervous system. Another rare disease, phenylketonuria, is *less* common in Ashkenazi Jews than in non-Ashkenazi Jews and non-Jews.

1. Tay-Sachs Disease

Tay-Sachs disease (TSD) is a recessively inherited disease in which the absence of hexosaminidase A, an enzyme involved in fat metabolism, results in the accumulation of fatty substances (sphingolipids) in the brain. The affected infants gradually deteriorate neurologically and mentally and usually die by the age of three or four. Prenatal diagnosis of this disease is possible so that the birth of affected infants can be prevented. Heterozygous carriers can also be detected by means of a blood test.

Although the disease was once thought to be confined exclusively to Jews, many non-Jewish cases have been reported. About one-third of the cases in the United States are in non-Jews. Nonetheless, the disease is much more prevalent in Jews than non-Jews.

In the United States the incidence of TSD in Jewish infants is 12–23 per 100,000, which corresponds to a gene frequency of 1.1–1.5%. Among Ashkenazi Jewish communities in the United States, Canada, South Africa, and Israel about 1 in 30 people is a carrier.[3] Most of the ancestors of the Jewish TSD cases in the United States came from Poland, Lithuania, and Russia. The incidence among non-Jews in the United States is 0.17–0.26 per 100,000, about 100 times less than in Jews, and the gene frequency is about 10 times less.[4] About 1 in 300 non-Jewish Americans is a carrier.

In Israel the incidence of TSD is 20 per 100,000 Ashkenazi Jews, corresponding to a gene frequency of 1.4%. Among Jews originating from all other communities, it was only about 2.6 per 100,000. Only 2 cases among approximately 77,000 births were found, corresponding to a disease frequency of 2.6 per 100,000.[5] However, among 250 Moroccan-born Jews in Israel, 4 were carriers,[6] suggesting that Moroccan Jews may have a high frequency of this gene. One of the Moroccan carriers had a slightly different form of the enzyme hexosaminidase A, which may indicate that the disease in Moroccan Jews stems from a mutation different from that found in Ashkenazim.

Myrianthopoulos and Aronson point out that the "birth incidence of Tay-Sachs disease among the Sephardi and Oriental communities of the Middle East and North Africa appears to be even lower than that found in non-Jewish Europeans and Americans." These authors believe that genetic drift cannot be the predominant factor responsible for the elevation of the TSD gene frequency among the Ashkenazim:

> Genetic drift could be held partly accountable for the rise of the Tay-Sachs gene at a very high frequency if it could be shown that the Jewish isolates of Europe, especially of northeastern Poland and the surrounding areas, were composed of very small marriageable populations without social contact with neighboring communities. There is sufficient historical commentary, however, to indicate a fertile intercommunication between these religious-cultural communities. . . . The grandparents and great-grandparents of children with Tay-Sachs disease, at least as far back as 1850, were sufficiently mobile to choose marriage partners in centers beyond their own immediate communities. . . . We can find no evidence for circumstances which theoretically might favor drift, such as migration of small groups, famine, disease, or war, affecting all or a large number of these Jewish communities simultaneously.[7]

They propose another explanation—what is called *heterozygote advantage*. According to this hypothesis, Jewish heterozygotes for TSD that is, individuals who inherited the Tay-Sachs gene from one parent only, were more fertile than unaffected individuals and thus contributed relatively more children carrying the mutant gene to the next generation. (It must be assumed that at least one maternal grandparent and one paternal grandparent of an affected child is a heterozygote.) A comparison of the number and survival of offspring of the grandparents provided some support for this hypothesis. The heterozygous parents may have been more fertile because they were more resistant to typhoid fever or to tuberculosis than were individuals without any TSD genes. The mechanism for such resistance is unknown.[8]

298

Myrianthopoulus and Aronson argue that there is no evidence that small groups lived in genetic isolation in the nineteenth century. Proponents of the importance of founder effect do not contest this; instead, they argue that the relevant genetic isolation took place much earlier. Thus Chase and McKusick say that

> migration of Jews to eastern Europe, especially Lithuania, 6 and 7 centuries ago . . . probably took place in small bands which may have been semi-nomadic for many years before reestablishing permanent settlements. . . . The gene [for Tay-Sachs disease] may have originated prior to the formation of these communities. It is suspected on linguistic grounds that the Jewish communities in Poland and Lithuania stemmed from earlier isolates in the Rhineland. One isolate, in which the Tay-Sachs disease might have originated, could have contributed to several communities at the later stage. A disproportionate contribution from a founder carrying the TSD gene would manifest itself only much later in history, when Jews from different Polish-Lithuanian-Russian isolates might marry in the United States and give birth to a TSD infant. . . . The presently high incidence of affected infants is but a transient phenomenon due to the chance encounter of recessive genes whose frequency has reached a high level partly as a consequence of diminished inbreeding.[9]

Another proponent of founder effect, Frank B. Livingstone, did computer simulations of small populations carrying harmful genes and calculated the frequencies of these genes after several generations during which the originally small population expanded in size. He concluded that, mathematically, a high frequency of the Tay-Sachs gene in the fourteenth- and fifteenth-century Eastern Jewish population, followed by expansion of the population size and then very slow elimination of the gene, could in fact explain the present frequency of the Tay-Sachs gene in East European Jews. He also believes that the historical record is compatible with these conclusions:

> The Tay-Sachs gene attains its highest frequencies in the Jewish populations of Southern Lithuania and Northeast Poland, which were founded in the 12th century after the Crusades led to the persecution of the Jews in Germany. Although the Jewish settlements in Lithuania were founded by refugees from the west, they preceded by two or three centuries the Jewish settlements in Mazovia to the west in Poland. Thus, these colonies were isolated for some time and were actually expanding to the west into Northern Poland when the Jews were expelled from Lithuania in 1495. Most moved to adjacent territories but then moved back to Lithuania in 1503. Hence, the population history of these Jewish groups seems to be one of expansion from a few founders. In any case, by the time of the flowering of Eastern Jewish culture in the Sixteenth Century, the population was very large and continued to expand up to the Twentieth Century.[10]

Although Chase and McKusick speak of "the gene" for Tay-Sachs disease having originated in a specific Jewish community, as if this mutation occurred only once, it is clear that repeated mutations of this gene have oc-

299

curred throughout history. Otherwise one would have to postulate that the 1 out of 380 American non-Jews who carry the TSD gene have a Jewish ancestor, an unlikely possibility. Support for the concept of different mutations is presented in a recent study of Ashkenazi Jewish and non-Jewish French Canadians with TSD.[11] A population of non-Jewish French Canadians in eastern Quebec have a frequency of TSD as high as in Ashkenazi Jews, and the study was done to determine whether these two groups have the same mutation. DNA probes were used to directly analyze the structure of the gene coding for the abnormal hexosaminidase A enzyme in 2 Jewish and 2 non-Jewish patients with TSD. The TSD gene in the two Ashkenazi Jewish patients showed a different abnormality from the gene in the affected Canadians, indicating that 2 different mutations were involved. More patients must be studied to determine whether the mutations in these two populations are identical, but is clear that the TSD gene in the non-Jewish patients does not have the same origin as the gene in the Jews.

It seems clear that mutations for TSD are repeatedly occurring and that these replenish the pool of TSD genes lost by deaths of children with the disease. As for the cause of the particularly high frequency of the TSD gene in Ashkenazi Jews, the limited geographic origin of Jewish carriers of the gene favors the founder effect. A reproductive advantage of heterozygotes for the TSD gene may also have been operating to maintain a high frequency of this gene. These two basic mechanisms—founder effect plus genetic drift versus heterozygote advantage—are still being debated by geneticists today.

To further complicate the picture, at the same gene locus for Tay-Sachs disease there are additional alleles that cause a milder form of the disease. Several adults with a form of Tay-Sachs disease have been described who carry one of these alleles. It is estimated that 1 in 1200 American Jews are carriers of a variant allele of TSD.[12] All 17 adults found in Israel who had a form of Tay Sachs Disease were Ashkenazim.[13] Both the American and Israeli studies indicate that the variant alleles, like the classic Tay Sachs disease gene, is more common in Ashkenazi Jews than in other peoples. Because the original mutation to each variant allele was a separate event from the original mutation to the classic TSD gene, the finding that more than one abnormal Tay-Sachs gene is particularly common among Ashkenazi Jews weakens the founder effect/genetic drift argument and favors some type of heterozygous advantage for carriers of these abnormal genes.

2. Gaucher's Disease

Gaucher's disease may be the most prevalent Jewish genetic disease. As in Tay-Sachs disease, fatty substances (sphingolipids) accumulate in the body. In Gaucher's disease, the cause is absence of the enzyme glucocerebrosidase, a lack of which causes the body to store abnormal quantities of lipids in the liver, spleen, and bone marrow. The victims develop a massively enlarged spleen, liver enlargement, anemia, and bone and joint inflammation. Unlike Tay-Sachs disease, Gaucher's disease is not fatal. Heterozygote carriers can be detected by a blood test or skin biopsy. Prenatal diagnosis is also possible, so that the birth of an affected child can be prevented.

There are three forms of the disease. Type 1, the chronic adult form, is the most prevalent; it has increased incidence in Ashkenazi Jews but is also found in black, Hispanic, and other ethnic groups. Type 2, which begins in infancy and causes death by age 2, is rare. Type 3 occurs primarily in Swedish individuals of Norrbottnian descent.[14] Each type is inherited as an autosomal recessive trait. The responsible gene has been localized to the long arm of chromosome 1.

The incidence of Type 1 Gaucher's disease among Ashkenazi Jews in Israel is approximately 1:2,500, the same as Tay-Sachs disease; the gene frequency was estimated at 0.02.[15] The disease is rare among non-Jews. Most Jewish cases of Gaucher's disease in the United States can be traced to the northeastern provinces of Poland and the Baltic states. The similarity in the backgrounds of Jews with this disease and Tay-Sachs disease can, according to Myrianthopoulos and Aronson, be explained on the ground that both are subject to the same unknown selective force.[16]

3. Niemann-Pick Disease

Niemann-Pick disease is a lethal autosomal recessive disorder closely related to Gaucher disease. In Niemann-Pick disease, a fatty substance termed sphingomyelin accumulates in the body. Beginning in infancy, muscular and intellectual functions rapidly deteriorate and the child usually dies before age 4. Prenatal diagnosis is possible, and heterozygote carriers can also be detected.

About two-thirds of affected infants have Ashkenazi Jewish parents. Like Gaucher disease, Niemann-Pick disease occurs primarily in Jews whose ancestors came from the northeastern provinces of Poland and the Baltic states. Among Ashkenazi Jews, about 1 in 100–140 are carriers.[17]

4. Hunter Disease and the other Mucopolysaccharidoses

The mucopolysaccharidoses, or glycogen storage diseases, are a group of inherited diseases in which starchy substances accumulate in the tissues. Each results from the deficiency of a different enzyme needed in the breakdown of the starchy substances. Each disease is inherited in an autosomal recessive pattern, except for mucopolysaccharidosis type II, or Hunter disease, which is transmitted as an X-linked recessive. In this type of inheritance, transmission is from mother to son, and only males are affected.

Hunter disease is a fatal disorder characterized by short stature, coarse facial features, stiff joints, progressive deafness, and death at a young age. Its incidence in Caucasian populations is approximately 1:150,000 live births. However, the estimated incidence, 1:67,500, among Jews in Israel is significantly higher.[18] The disease was found in Ashkenazim as well as in Oriental and Sephardi Jews. Several explanations have been suggested for the elevated frequency of Hunter disease, including genetic drift. However, families of Ashkenazi patients had a significant excess of affected males and carrier females, suggesting prenatal selection favoring the X chromosome carrying the Hunter gene among Ashkenazi Jews. The data on non-Ashkenazi families are incomplete.[19]

In contrast with Hunter disease, Hurler disease (mucopolysaccharidosis type I) is less common among Israeli Jews than in other Caucasian populations.[20]

5. Familial Dysautonomia

Familial dysautonomia is a rare, recessively inherited disease in which many of the automatic processes of the body do not function properly. The victim has difficulty swallowing, extreme fluctuations in temperature, intermittent high blood pressure, episodes of vomiting, skin blotching, excessive sweating, a dryness of the eye that may result in ulceration of the cornea, and markedly diminished pain sensation. Taste buds are absent from the tongue, and skeletal abnormalities are often present. The disease is often fatal during childhood. Among 210 cases found in the United States, all but one of the parents were Jewish or had Jewish ancestry. All were of Ashkenazi stock, most of whom traced their ancestry to an area of Eastern Europe comprising central and southern Poland, Galicia, the western Ukraine, northeastern Rumania, and to a lesser extent Lithuania. The disease incidence in North American Jews is 5–10 per 100,000, corresponding to a gene frequency of 1% at the most.[21]

In Israel, twenty-three cases were found, all in Ashkenazi Jews originating from Eastern Europe. The incidence of the disease was estimated at 8.3 per 100,000, corresponding to a gene frequency of 0.91%. Not a single case has been found so far among Sephardi and Middle Eastern Jews, although they comprise over 50% of the population in Israel.[22]

Mutations causing dysautonomia may have occurred at least as far back in history as the thirteenth century, when the Jews began migrating from the Rhineland and other parts of Central Europe to Eastern Europe. After their migration into Poland and Russia, they lived in small groups that were relatively isolated. Random genetic drift may have operated in some of these small groups to increase the frequency of this gene.

6. Bloom's Syndrome

Bloom's syndrome is a rare genetic disease, probably inherited as an autosomal recessive. Affected persons have stunted growth, rarely reaching a height of 5 feet. In addition, there is a reddening of portions of the face, which is made worse by exposure to the sun. Life expectancy is considerably shortened, and there is a high likelihood of developing cancers. Of twenty-seven affected individuals in North America, fifteen had Jewish ancestry. The Jewish families were all of Eastern European origin, coming from the Ukraine and neighboring Eastern European regions. This area is farther south than the area from which the ancestors of Jews with Tay-Sachs disease originated.[23] Considering the small percentage of Jews in the total population of North America (about 2.7%), it is obvious that this disease is many times more frequent in Jews than non-Jews.

In Israel, all 8 affected persons came from Ashkenazi families. The frequency of the Bloom's syndrome gene in Ashkenazim was estimated to be .0042, yielding a heterozygote frequency of at least 1 in 120. Analysis of each family confirmed an autosomal recessive mode of inheritance. Among Jews, Bloom's syndrome appears limited to Ashkenazim.[24] In fact, most affected Jewish families in Israel trace their origin to the same small area in Eastern Europe from which affected patients in the United States originated.

7. PTA (Factor XI) Deficiency

A deficiency of one of the clotting factors, plasma thromboplastin antecedent, or factor XI, is common among Ashkenazi Jews. Affected persons have excessive bleeding after dental extraction or other minor surgery. It is inherited as an autosomal trait. In Israel, 33 of 34 affected individuals were of Ashkenazi background.[25] Their families had come from Poland, U.S.S.R., Czechoslovakia, Hungary, and Rumania. If the mutation for this disorder had a single origin, its wide distribution makes it likely that it occurred historically at an earlier time than did the Tay-Sachs mutation.

8. Nonclassical steroid 21-hydroxylase deficiency

This autosomal recessive endocrine disorder is surprisingly common among various populations and especially in Ashkenazi Jews. It causes enlargement of the adrenal gland and, in women, increased hairiness. The prevalence of the disease was 3.7% (1:27) of Ashkenazi Jews sampled in Israel, Europe, and the United States, corresponding to a gene frequency of .191. The gene is much more common in Ashkenazim than is the gene for Tay-Sachs disease. Non-Ashkenazi Jews have not yet been studied. The prevalence of the disease was 1.9% in Spanish people, 1.6% among Yugoslavs, and 0.3% in Italians. Nonclassical 21-hydroxylase deficiency is probably the most frequent autosomal recessive genetic disorder in man.[26]

The gene for nonclassical 21-hydroxylase deficiency is closely linked to the HLA locus on the short arm of chromosome 6. HLA typing was carried out on the patients and a highly significant increase in the frequency of HLA B-14 was found among the patients in each ethnic group except Yugoslavs, when compared with ethnically matched controls. The highest gene frequency for B14, 69.6%, was found in the Ashkenazi Jewish patients. The HLA allele B14 was increased among Ashkenazi Jews but not among Sephardi and Oriental Jews. Another HLA allele, B35, was significantly decreased in all ethnic patient groups with nonclassical 21-hydroxylase deficiency except Yugoslavs.[27] The mutation in Yugoslav patients may have had an independent origin from that found in Ashkenazim, Italians, and Hispanics.

9. Torsion dystonia

Torsion dystonia is a movement disorder characterized by irregular involuntary movements and abnormal posture. The disease is inherited, but the pattern of inheritance is not yet clear. Torsion dystonia has a high prevalence among Ashkenazi Jews. Among 42 patients in Israel, the prevalence among Jews of European origin was 22 per million, compared with only 1.5 per million for Jews of African or Asian origin. The disease was particularly common among Jews of East European origin, where it had a prevalence of 25.8 per million.[28] The authors postulate an autosomal dominant mode of inheritance.

10. Essential Pentosuria

Essential pentosuria is not strictly a disease, for affected individuals are healthy; it is rather a physiological condition, a rare inherited error of metabolism. Affected persons excrete the sugar L-xyloketose in their urine, and may be thought erroneously to have diabetes. The condition is almost completely confined to Jews, except for one Arab family from Lebanon in whom it was found.

Between 1956 and 1961, eighteen Jews with pentosuria were discovered in Israel. All were Ashkenazim from Central Europe (Poland, Russia, Rumania, and Czechoslovakia). The prevalence of pentosuria among Ashkenazim was estimated at 1 in 5,000, which corresponds to a gene frequency of about 1.4%, assuming that affected persons are homozygous for a recessive autosomal gene.[29]

11. Phenylketonuria

Phenylketonuria (PKU) is a recessively inherited disease in which an enzyme needed for the breakdown of the amino acid phenylalanine, an important constituent of all proteins is lacking. Most patients are severely retarded mentally. This, however, can be prevented by feeding the infant a special diet low in phenylalanine. Detecting the disease during the newborn period is thus important.

In the United States, the frequency of PKU is 1 in 10,920. A few years ago PKU was thought to be extremely rare among Jews, as only one Jewish case was reported until 1959. Improved detecting methods have permitted wide-scale screening in Israel, where fifty-four cases were found between 1960 and 1968. Except for one Arab child, all the cases were in Middle Eastern Jewish families who had immigrated to Israel from Turkey, Iraq, Iran, Afghanistan, Yemen, Aden, and North Africa. None were found among Ashkenazi (European) Jews, although this group constitutes about 50% of the Jewish population in Israel.[30]

Since 1964, all newborns in Israel have been screened for PKU. Among 45 cases found through 1976, not a single one was among offspring of Ashkenazi Jews. The disease frequency among the non-Ashkenazi communities was 1 in 9,000, which is like that in the United States.[31] PKU was found in Jews from North Africa, Iran, Iraq, Yemen, Afghanistan, and Turkey, and also among Arabs. There was a high degree of consanguinity in most of the affected families.

The absence of cases among the Ashkenazi Jews in Israel agrees with the rarity of PKU among Jews in Western countries. A. Szeinberg suggests that the very high frequency of consanguineous marriages in some Middle Eastern Jewish groups may explain the differences between them and the Ashkenazim. As already explained, a high rate of inbreeding results in an increased incidence of rare recessive diseases, although the gene frequency may be unchanged. Szeinberg suggests that the frequency of the PKU gene may be similar in Ashkenazi and Middle Eastern Jews, but that among the latter the consanguineous marriage pattern results in more individuals homozygous for the PKU gene. However, since American Gentiles do not have a high incidence of inbreeding, the similar incidence of PKU among them and Middle Eastern Jews suggests that the frequency of the PKU gene is lower in the Middle Eastern Jews than in Americans. Szeinberg's hypothesis therefore implies that all Jews have a lower frequency of the PKU gene than non-Jews, but does not explain why.

A more reasonable hypothesis is presented by Chase and McKusick, who accept that Ashkenazi Jews in fact have a lower frequency of the PKU gene than Middle Eastern Jews. They suggest that this low frequency may represent a negative founder effect. That is, the original founders of some small European Jewish settlements centuries ago happened to have a relatively low frequency of the PKU gene, as did their descendants who migrated to the United States and Israel.[32]

INHERITED DISEASES WITH UNUSUAL FREQUENCY IN ORIENTAL AND SEPHARDI JEWS

In contrast with the diseases just described, other inherited diseases are found primarily in Oriental (Middle Eastern) or in Sephardi Jews. These include the Dubin-Johnson syndrome, familial Mediterranean fever, peroxidase and phospholipid deficiency in the granulocytes, and familial neutropenia. Another disease, cystic fibrosis of the pancreas, is only about one-third as frequent in non-Ashkenazim as in Ashkenazi Jews and non-Jews. Only a few diseases of Oriental and Sephardi Jews will be covered in this section. However, dozens of uncommon recessively inherited syndromes have been discovered in these groups. For a listing, the reader is referred to Goodman's text.[33] A recessive disease requires inheritance of the abnormal gene from both parents; the chances of this happening are greater if the parents are closely related. The frequent discovery of such syndromes is undoubtedly due at least in part to the high incidence of consanguinity in these populations. Another part of the explanation for the long list of unusual diseases among Jews is that Israelis are being studied more intensively than are most peoples. It is likely that other unusual diseases would be discovered in any other group of people were they to be equally examined.

1. The Dubin-Johnson Syndrome

The Dubin-Johnson syndrome is an inherited liver disease, in which the patient has chronic or intermittent jaundice and in which a dark pigment is deposited within liver cells. Some patients also have a mild bleeding tendency. The condition may begin as early as infancy or as late as middle age. Although some patients have abdominal pain and an enlarged liver, many have no symptoms and appear healthy.[34] Many cases have been described throughout the world; the disease is not limited to only one or a few ethnic groups. However, in Israel, the Dubin-Johnson syndrome is particularly prevalent in Jews from Iran. Of 101 patients, 64 came from Iran, 9 from Iraq, 9 from Morocco, 8 were Sephardim, 7 were Ashkenazim, 1 came from Afghanistan, and 3 were Israeli Arabs. These patients represented 59 unrelated families, of whom 34 were from Iran. These 34 families originated from at least 12 widely dispersed localities all over Iran. Three of the Iranian and 1 of the 6 Iraqi kindreds originated from the Kurdish regions of these two countries.[35]

The minimum incidence of the Dubin-Johnson syndrome among Iranian Jews was estimated to be 1 in 1,300, among the highest, if not the highest, in the world. The incidence is much lower in the other Jewish communities.

The study of a large number of families with the Dubin-Johnson syndrome led to the conclusion that this condition is inherited in an autosomal recessive manner. This contradicts an earlier view that it is dominantly inherited.[36]

The distribution of the Dubin-Johnson syndrome indicates a clear genetic difference between Iranian and other Jews.

2. Familial Mediterranean Fever

Familial Mediterranean fever (FMF) is an autosomal recessive disease characterized by attacks of fever and pain in the abdomen, chest, or joints. The attacks usually begin in childhood or adolescence and then continue irregularly throughout life. About one-third of patients with FMF also have amyloidosis, an accumulation in the body of amyloid, a complex starchy protein, which eventually leads to kidney failure and death. Most affected Jews in Israel (455 out of 470 cases) are of Sephardi and Middle Eastern origin. Among the Ashkenazi patients, five were from Rumania, four from Poland, and one from Germany. Five Israeli Arabs had the disease. The incidence of FMF in Middle Eastern and Sephardi Jews is 1 in 2,000, representing a gene frequency of 2.2%.[37]

Of 347 cases reported in the medical literature, 58% were in Jews, almost exclusively Sephardi Jews, 27% were in Armenians, and 10% in Arabs. All but one of the Arabs were from the Middle East. Of the 6% non-Jews, 17 out of 22 were from the Mediterranean basin.[38]

As with the Dubin-Johnson syndrome, the incidence of FMF among non-Ashkenazi Jews greatly exceeds its incidence in Ashkenazim, thus attesting to the genetic heterogeneity of various Jewish groups. Moreover, 37% of 156 Sephardi patients from North Africa had amyloidosis, compared with 21% of 98 Jews from Iran and only 1 out of 14 Ashkenazi Jews (7%). This variation in the incidence of amyloidosis suggests that FMF in North African Jews and FMF in Ashkenazi Jews may be different recessive disorders.[39]

3. Peroxidase and Phospholipid Deficiency in Eosinophilic Granulocytes

In 1968 a new type of congenital anomaly was reported in a Yemenite Jewish brother and sister. The enzyme peroxidase and the fatty substance phospholipid were absent from one type of white blood cell. The lack of these substances did not seem to do the affected subjects any harm. The condition is inherited as an autosomal recessive.

In a large-scale survey of almost 65,000 people in Israel[40], 88 had the same defect in their white blood cells. Most (44) were Jews of Yemenite origin, representing a frequency of affected individuals of 3.9 per 1,000; for 26 affected North African Jews, an incidence of 2.5 per 1,000. The incidence in Iraqi-Iranian Jews was 1.7 per 1,000. Three cases were found among almost 34,000 Ashkenazi Jews, an extremely low incidence of 0.8 per 1,000. No cases were found among Sephardi Jews from the Balkans. There were two cases among 1,182 Arabs surveyed, an incidence of 1.7 per 1,000. The incidence of this defect among other non-Jewish ethnic groups is not known. It is clear, however, that the frequency of this abnormal gene differs greatly among the different Jewish groups.

4. Familial Neutropenia

Familial neutropenia is a benign, asymptomatic condition in which there is a decreased concentration of one type of white blood cell in the blood. It is inherited in an autosomal dominant fashion; that is, a person has the abnormality even if he carries only one gene for it. Familial neutropenia in Israel affects primarily Jews of Yemenite origin. A study of 780 Yemenite Jewish patients in one hospital in Israel found that familial neutropenia was present in at least 2% of them.[41] Another study of 200 healthy Yemenite Jews found that 37.5% had the anomaly.[42]

The uneven distribution of familial neutropenia among Jews is another example of their genetic heterogeneity.

5. Cystic Fibrosis of the Pancreas

Cystic fibrosis is one of the most common lethal genetic diseases in the United States. The gene responsible for this recessively inherited disease has been mapped to chromosome 7 and can be detected prenatally in the fetus of parents who already have one affected child. Cystic fibrosis affects the pancreas, sweat glands, and other glands in the body, so that they produce abnormal secretions; the disease is usually diagnosed by finding abnormal amounts of salt in the sweat.

308

The disease occurs only in whites. Its incidence in Ohio is approximately 1 in 3,700, or 0.27 per 1,000. In Switzerland, cystic fibrosis occurs in 0.7 per 1,000 births; in Sweden, in 0.13 per 1,000.[43]

The incidence of cystic fibrosis among Ashkenazim in Israel is approximately 0.2 per 1,000, a value like that found in Ohio. The incidence of cystic fibrosis was approximately three times lower among non-Ashkenazim.[44] A second study in Israel confirmed that cystic fibrosis is as common among Ashkenazi and Arab populations as it is in Europeans, but is only about half as frequent in Sephardi Jews.[45] These differences once more indicate genetic variations among different Jewish groups.

6. Down Syndrome

Down syndrome, formerly called mongolism, is a genetic disorder caused by the presence of an excess chromosome 21 in all body cells. This results in characteristic facial features, mental retardation, and other congenital malformations. Approximately one-third of cases are inherited; the remainder are sporadic, caused by abnormal behavior of the reproductive cells at the time of conception. The incidence of the sporadic cases rises with increasing maternal age; approximately 1% of babies born to mothers aged 45 will have Down syndrome. It is primarily to detect this disease that amniocentesis is recommended for all pregnant women older than 35.

In Jerusalem mothers born in North Africa or Asia had twice the likelihood of giving birth to a child with Down syndrome than did mothers born in Europe or the United States.[46] The results were corrected for possible age differences in the mothers. The North African mothers were mainly from Morocco, and those from Asia had been born in Iraq, Iran, Turkey, and Yemen. The rate of Down syndrome births among the mothers from Africa and Asia is among the highest found in the world. There were no significant differences among mothers of European, American, North African, and Asian descent born in Israel, suggesting that the differences among the foreign-born mothers may have been due to nongenetic factors. Support for this suggestion comes from the finding that Orthodox families were significantly overrepresented among Down syndrome children in Jerusalem.[47] The authors hypothesized that the increased number of pregnancies in Orthodox mothers might be related to their higher risk of having children with Down syndrome. The explanation for the increased incidence of Down syndrome is still uncertain.

7. Cystinuria

Cystinuria is a rare autosomally inherited disease. Because the amino acid cystine cannot be transported properly within the kidney, it accumulates and causes kidney stones to form. There are several forms of this disease, each due to a different abnormal gene at the same gene locus. Type I cystinuria is completely recessive—the heterozygote appears normal. Heterozygotes for types II and III excrete increased amounts of cystine in the urine, but do not form stones. Most people who are homozygous for cystinuria have the type I gene. However, among cystinuric Jews from Libya, most were found to be of type II or III.[48] The incidence of homozygous cystinuria has been estimated at 1:20,000 for England and 1:100,000 for Sweden. For Libyan Jews, the frequency is much higher, about 1:2,500.[49] Other Jewish populations do not have an increased frequency of cystinuria.

8. Thalassemia

Thalassemia is a group of disorders of hemoglobin synthesis in which there is a decreased production of one of the two protein globin chains that are part of the hemoglobin molecule. In *alpha*-thalassemia there is an abnormality in synthesis of the *alpha* chain. Each human chromosome-16 normally has two α-globin genes, so that a normal person has 4 functional α genes. Absence of all 4 genes (--/--) is fatal; the person with only 1 functional α gene (α-/--) has "hemoglobin H disease" and severe anemia; the person with 2 functioning α genes (α-/α-) or (αα/--) has "thalassemia trait," and the person with 3 functioning α genes (αα/α-) is clinically healthy and is called a "silent carrier." Lack of one or more of the α genes occurs through actual loss of genetic material (termed a *deletion*) rather than through a point mutation.

In *beta*-thalassemia, production of the *beta* chain is decreased (β⁺-thalassemia) or absent (β⁰-thalassemia). In either case, an anemia results. In the homozygote, the anemia may be severe enough to cause death at a young age. Heterozygotes have a milder anemia and are considered to have "β-thalassemia trait."

Thalassemia is considered primarily a Mediterranean disease. The frequency of thalassemia trait in Greece ranges from 3.3% in Macedonia and Thrace to 14% in the Ionian Islands. Of 500 Greek newborns, 0.3% had the α-thalassemia trait.[50] In Cyprus, 26% of those examined had the thalassemia trait.[51] In Spain, 1.2% of people in Madrid and 1.7% in Huelva are carriers of the β-thalassemia trait.[52] The frequency of thalassemia trait in the Po Delta in Italy and in Sicily ranges from 7 to 15%. The α-thalassemia trait was found in 0.1% of 1,200 Italian newborns and 4% of more than 1,000 Chinese newborns.[53]

The frequencies of *alpha* and *beta* thalassemias among the Jews is highly variable (see Table 26 in the Appendix). In Israel, β-thalassemia is common among Oriental Jews, particularly immigrants from Kurdistan, and among the local Arab population. Because of the high incidence of consanguinity in these groups, homozygous β-thalassemia is relatively common. In one study, the β-thalassemia trait was absent in Israeli Jews from Europe and the United States, rare in Jews from Yemen, and present in 2% of Jews from Iran and 18% of Jews from Kurdistan.[54] Other estimates of β-thalassemia trait in Kurdish Jews range from 12% to 20%.[55] Thus, among Israeli Jews, β-thalassemia seems almost restricted to those from Kurdistan. The frequency of the β-thalassemia genes in Kurdish Jews is approximately four times than the α-thalassemia gene in this population.

In contrast to β-thalassemia, α-thalassemia is found in several Jewish communities, primarily among Kurdish, Iraqi, and Yemenite Jews. Approximately 1 out of 80 Kurdish Jews are affected. Jews from Yemen and Iraq have an extremely high incidence of the α-thalassemia trait. It was found in 17% of 181 Yemenite Jewish newborns and 11% of 105 Iraqi Jewish newborns.[56] Such frequencies are remarkably high compared with those described in other populations. Although α-thalassemia trait is rare among non-Mediterranean Europeans, it was recently found in several members of an Ashkenazi Jewish family of Polish origin. In addition, a young Hungarian Jewish man had α-thalassemia trait (α-/α-) and an elderly German Jewish man was a silent carrier (αα/α-).[57] The most likely explanation for these findings is that one or more independent deletions in the α-globin genes occurred in these families.

These findings show that the Jews are extremely heterogeneous with respect to the frequency of the genes for α- and β- thalassemia. As with non-Jews, thalassemia is uncommon in Jews of European background and more common in Mediterranean Jews.

9. Cerebrotendinous xanthomatosis (CTX)

Cerebrotendinous xanthomatosis (CTX) is a rare, autosomal recessive lipid storage disease. A fatty substance called cholestanol accumulates in body tissues, causing neurological problems and fatty tumors. Although only 50 cases have been reported worldwide, 6 of them were in Sephardi Jews from Morocco living in Israel. The estimated gene frequency among Moroccan Jews is 1:108, with a carrier frequency of 1:54.[58]

10. Metachromatic leukodystrophy (MLD)

Metachromatic leukodystrophy (MLD) is an autosomal recessive disorder in which absence of a particular enzyme in the body causes accumulation of substances in the brain that cause neurological deterioration. In the infantile form of this disease, the first symptoms begin in infancy, and there is progressive muscular and mental decline and early death. No ethnic group exhibits an increased incidence of this disease, except for the Habbanite Jews in Israel, who have an incidence of the infantile form of MLD of 1 per 75 births. This contrasts with the incidence in Sweden of approximately 1 per 40,000.[59] Seventeen percent of the Habbanite community were carriers, putting this population at unusually high risk for this lethal disease. This finding is another example of the unique genetic structure of the Habbanites, whose genetic isolation and extensive inbreeding have been previously described.

11. Werdnig-Hoffman disease (Spinal muscular atrophy)

Werdnig-Hoffman disease is an autosomal recessive disorder in which atrophy of nerve cells in the spinal cord causes atrophy of muscles and then death, usually by age 2–4 years. In the Egyptian Karaite community in Israel, 4 unrelated cases were found among 1600 people, an unusually high incidence, which corresponds to a gene frequency of .05. About 1 in 10 persons in this community is therefore a carrier. The Karaite community was a religious and reproductive isolate for over ten centuries; thus, genetic drift is the most likely explanation for the unusual frequency of this gene.[60]

COMMON DISEASES WITH A GENETIC COMPONENT

Although cancer, heart disease, diabetes, and alcoholism are greatly influenced by the environment, the fact that they have a genetic component makes it worthwhile to examine their occurrence in different populations. It has been reported that Jews in general have a high incidence of diabetes and a low incidence of certain types of cancer and of alcoholism. Just as with the rare inherited diseases, more detailed studies have shown that a high or low incidence of diabetes or cancer is characteristic of certain groups of Jews rather than of Jews in general.

1. Cancer

Cancer is a collective term for a large group of diseases characterized by uncontrolled growth of certain cells in the body. Some cancers are caused primarily by environmental factors. For example, lung cancer is much more likely in a heavy cigarette smoker than in a nonsmoker, and skin cancer is more common in the Southwest of the United States than in other parts of the country because of the increased sun exposure. Other cancers have a well-known genetic component. For example, a woman whose mother and sister have breast cancer has a high risk of contracting the same disease herself. In different population groups, differing frequencies of particular cancers can be due to different genetic backgrounds, different environments, or a combination. It is often not easy to separate these out.

A 1971 study of cancer mortality rates in New York showed that Jews had different mortality risks than non-Jews for several sites of cancer. Both foreign-born and American-born Jewish males had a relatively low risk of cancer of the mouth, pharynx, and prostate. Foreign-born Jewish males and females had a relatively higher risk of cancer of the esophagus. The high risk did not persist among their native-born children, suggesting that primarily environmental factors such as diet or smoking may have been responsible. Foreign-born Jews of both sexes also had a higher risk for cancer of the stomach, and moderately higher risk for cancer of the colon. Jewish women had relatively higher risks for cancer of the pancreas, lung, breast (native-born Jewish women only), and ovary, and for leukemia and lymphomas. Jewish men also had a higher risk of leukemia and lymphomas, but not as high as Jewish women.[61]

In Israel, a form of leukemia called chronic lymphocytic leukemia (CLL) occurs more frequently in Ashkenazim than in Asian and African Jews. It is particularly common in immigrants from Poland and Rumania. The disease appeared at a significantly younger age in patients born in Asia and Africa than in those from Europe. Males predominated among the European-born patients; females predominated among the Asian- and African-born people. The authors speculate that genetic differences between these two ethnic groups may explain the different patterns of disease.[62]

Another study analyzed more than 31,000 cases of cancer listed in the Israel Cancer Register between 1960 and 1966.[63] The incidence of cancer in Jews born in the following countries and areas was compared: Turkey, Iraq, Yemen, Iran, Northwest Africa (Algeria and Tunisia), Libya, Egypt, Greece and Bulgaria, East Europe, "other Europe" (Central Europe), and Israel. The annual incidence for all cancers was higher in Jews from Europe and America than in those from Asia and Africa. The annual incidence of all cancers for all ages, per 100,000 population, ranged from 170.9 for males and 152.6 for females from Asia, and 193.2 for males and 156.2 for females from Africa, to a high of 242.8 for males and 269.0 for females from Europe and America. The average incidence for all Jews of all ages was 213.9 for males and 221.7 for females. Rates among non-Jews in Israel were lower than for any Jewish group: 144.10 for males and 81.1 for females.

Despite their relatively low incidence of all cancers, Yemenite and Iranian Jews had a particularly high rate of esophageal cancer: 8.1 per 100,000 population aged forty-four to seventy-four for men and 11.7 per 100,000 for women from Yemen, and 12.3 and 26.6 for men and women, respec-

313

tively, from Iran. In comparison, the rates for men and women from all of Europe and America were 6.3 and 4.9, respectively, and the average rates for all Israel for men and women 6.1 and 5.0 per 100,000, respectively.

Almost all groups had a high rate of stomach cancer (average for all Jews of all ages, 27.0 per 100,000 for males and 16.4 for females). Stomach cancer was most prevalent among Jews from Europe and America, and was particularly low among Jews from Iraq (12.5 for males and 5.2 for females) and Yemen (12.3 for males and 13.4 for females). Cancer of the large intestine was less prevalent than stomach cancer. There was a marked difference in the rates for both males and females between Jews from all European countries and those from other countries, with the exception of Turkey. The rates for Europe and America averaged 22.7 for males and 24.1 for females; those for Jews from Turkey were 18.6 for males and 16.3 for females; the rates for Jews from other Asian countries ranged from 4.8 to 9.1 for males and from 7.4 to 12.1 for females. Jews from Africa averaged 8.0 for males and 8.24 for females. Thus, North African and Asian Jews have a lower incidence of colon cancer than do Ashkenazi Jews. This is still true in Israel, where a recent study found that the incidence of cancer of the colon among European and American-born Jews is 2.5 times that among Jews born in Asia and Africa.[64]

The incidence of lung cancer was highest in Jewish males from Greece, Bulgaria, and Turkey in the age group 35–64, and outstandingly low in Yemenite males and females in the same age group. The sex ratio for lung cancer differs widely among Jews from different areas. Lung cancer figures are influenced by smoking practices, which differ in Jews from different regions. A 1982 study of 17-year old Israelis reported, for example, that 13% of girls and 18.6% of boys whose fathers were born in Europe smoked, compared with 29.8% of girls and 47.7% of boys whose fathers had come from North Africa. The corresponding figures for children of Asian-born fathers were 14% of girls and 30.8% of boys. If these smoking patterns persist into adulthood, one might expect lung cancer figures to follow.[65]

Breast cancer is the most frequent type of cancer in Jewish women in Israel. However, the rates varied widely; they were much higher in Jewish women from Europe and America (63.6 per 100,000) than in those from Asia (26.6) and Africa (27.0). Jewish women from Yemen had a particularly low incidence of breast cancer (11.6), and those from Central Europe had a particularly high rate (76.9). Jews from Turkey and Egypt had higher rates of breast cancer than did Jews from other Asian and African countries, and in this respect resembled the European Jewish women.

A recent study compared the incidence of breast cancer in Jewish women in Israel in the period 1960–72 with the period 1972–76. In all age groups and populations, the incidence increased between 1960 and 1976. It is of interest that the increase was greatest among the Jewish women from

314

Asia and Africa, the groups with the lowest initial rates. In these women, the incidence of breast cancer rose from 22.2 per 100,000 in 1960–66 to 34.1 in 1972–76. At the same time, the incidence in women from Europe or the United States rose from 55.5 to 61.9. Thus, there was a narrowing of the differences between the various Jewish population groups.[66] This narrowing suggests that environmental factors in Israel are at least in part responsible for the increase in breast cancer; changes in diet and childbearing practices are two possible factors.

In the 1971 study, cancer of the ovary was generally higher in Jewish women from Europe (average, 15.2 for all ages) than in those from Asia (4.9) and Africa (4.0). However, Turkish Jews had an unusually high incidence (15.8).[67] Among 107 patients with ovarian cancer studied more recently in Tel Aviv, significant differences were found between Ashkenazi and Afro-Asian women. Ovarian cancer was found more frequently than expected in the Ashkenazi women and less frequently in the Afro-Asian women, compared with their percentages in the total city population. Although less common in the Afro-Asian women, ovarian cancer was diagnosed significantly earlier and survival was shorter than in the Ashkenazi women.[68]

From 1960 to 1976, the average incidence of ovarian cancer in Israel was 15–19 per 100,000 women. The disease was 3–5 times more prevalent in women of European/American origin than in those of Asian/African descent.[69] In New York City, ovarian cancer deaths were significantly more common among Jewish women (presumably Ashkenazi) than non-Jews, and among whites than blacks.[70]

Other types of cancer also had different rates among Jews from different areas. Prostate cancer was particularly low among Jewish men from Yemen. Cancer of the nervous system was uncommon in Jews from Yemen and northwest Africa, and common in Jews from East Europe and Central Africa. Intestinal lymphoma was significantly more common in North African and Yemenite Jews than in European Jews, and was similar in Israeli Arabs and immigrants from North Africa.[71]

Cancer of the cervix of the uterus has traditionally been considered so uncommon in Jewish women that routine screening by means of Papanicolaou (Pap) smears was not even introduced in Israel until 1978. There are several well-known predisposing factors in the development of cervical cancer. These include younger age at first coitus, earlier and more frequent sexual intercourse with more than one sexual partner, more pregnancies, and younger age at first pregnancy. Infection of the cervix by Herpes simplex virus may also predispose to cervical cancer, and it is possible that the reason that multiple partners are a risk factor for cervical cancer is that they increase the likelihood of Herpes infection.

315

In New York City non-Jewish whites had a much higher incidence of cancer of the cervix (15.0 per 100,000) than did the Jews (4.1 per 100,000). Blacks in New York City had an even higher incidence (49.6) than did non-Jewish whites. In contrast, cancer of the remainder (the body) of the uterus was slightly more frequent among Jews (15.6) than among non-Jewish whites (13.1), whereas the incidence among blacks was even lower (10.0 per 100,000 population).[72]

Jewish women in Israel had almost the same rate of cervical cancer (4.8) as did the Jewish women in New York. In both groups, the peak incidence of cervical cancer occurred almost fifteen years after the menopause, whereas the peak incidence among non-Jewish white women coincided with the menopause. In Israel, Jewish women of Ashkenazi background had the same low rate of cervical cancer (4.7) as did Jews of Sephardi and Oriental background (4.9). In contrast, the Ashkenazi women had higher rates of ovarian, uterine body, and breast cancer than did other Jews.[73]

In agreement with other studies, cervical cancer was less common in Jews (5.4 per 100,000 for all Jewish women of all ages) than in non-Jews. However, the average rate for African Jews (10.9) was higher than for those from Asia (4.3) and Europe (4.2), and Yemenite Jews had an unusually low incidence of cervical cancer (1.5). The incidence of cervical cancer in Jews from Northwest Africa (11.9) approaches that of non-Jewish whites in New York (15.0).[74]

With the introduction of routine pap smears in Israel, it is now possible to identify cervical cancers at an earlier stage, when it is easier to treat. These earlier lesions are termed cervical intraepithelial neoplasia (CIN). Among 2,150 Israeli women who had routine pap smears, the incidence of CIN was 3.2% among Israeli-born women, 1.8% among European and American born, and 0.5% among Asian-African born women. The incidence was much lower among Israeli-born non-Jews (Moslems, Christians, and Druze), who had an incidence of CIN of only 0.2%.[75] Different results were reported in 1985 by Baram and others, who found abnormal pap smears (CIN and milder lesions) in 2.5% of Eastern and Sephardi women and only 1.1% of Ashkenazi women.[76] Of Israeli women aged 20–29 who had routine pap smears, 7.5% had CIN lesions, not far from the rates found during the first mass screening programs in San Diego, California.[77] The high incidence of cervical lesions among a population that has in the past been characterized by a very low risk of cervical cancer is possibly due to an increase in sexual permissiveness in Israel in the past 25 years. Indeed, the women with abnormal pap smears were younger and more sexually active than control women, they had more pregnancies and more sexual partners, and fewer of them considered themselves religiously observant.

Although CIN lesions are considered precursors of cervical cancer, successful treatment of the lesion at this stage prevents the development of cervical cancer. Thus, the incidence of cervical cancer in Israel might be expected to remain the same or even to drop in the coming years if pap screening becomes widely used. The incidence of cervical cancer has in fact remained stable: it was 4.5 per 100,000 women in 1965–68, and 4.65 in 1977–80.[78] If sexual permissiveness continues and pap smears are not routinely obtained, one might expect the incidence of cervical cancer to increase. As for heart disease (see below), a significant alteration in life-style may result in a rising disease risk, which may blur the genetic differences in risk among different Jewish populations in Israel.

Cancer of the uterine body has a distribution different from that of cancer of the cervix. The incidence in the 1971 study was almost double that of cervical cancer (9.8 per 100,000); it was most prevalent among Jewish women from Central Europe (18.3) and least common in Jews from Northwest Africa (3.5) and from Asia (3.85 in Jews from Iran). Jews from Egypt had an incidence of 12.8, like that of Jews from Europe (11.8).

This survey shows that Jews from different areas differ in their rates of particular cancers. These differences are likely to be a combination of hereditary and environmental factors, with the environment differing in importance for different cancers.

2. Heart disease and Blood Lipid Levels

Coronary heart disease is a leading cause of illness and death in Western countries. Coronary heart disease may first appear as sudden death, chest pain (angina), or a heart attack (myocardial infarction). The cause is usually partial or complete obstruction of one or more of the coronary arteries, the main blood vessels that supply food and oxygen to the heart muscle. Starting at a young age, a person's coronary arteries become progressively narrower because of the depositing of cholesterol-containing material on the arteries' inner walls. The higher the blood cholesterol level, the more rapidly the blood vessels are likely to become narrowed and the younger the age at which a person is likely to experience symptoms of coronary artery disease. This is why there is currently a great emphasis among physicians to encourage people to lower cholesterol levels. Often a change in diet is sufficient, but at times drug treatment may be necessary.

An elevated cholesterol level is not the only factor that increases a person's risk of heart disease. The other major factors are diabetes, smoking, elevated blood pressure (hypertension), and a family history of heart disease. All except family history are amenable to intervention. In other words, diabetes, high blood pressure, and elevated cholesterol can all be treated by diet alone or by a combination of diet and drugs, and smoking

317

can be stopped. Smoking is the only factor with a strictly environmental causation, and a person's family history is by definition strictly a genetic factor. The other three—high blood pressure, elevated cholesterol levels, and diabetes—all have both environmental and genetic components. Their genetic components are amenable to analysis for different population groups.

The incidence of heart attacks (acute myocardial infarction, AMI) in Israel varies for different population groups. In a nationwide study reported in 1975, the annual incidence of first attacks was 0.9 per 1,000 (1.3 in men and 0.5 in women).[79] Among men, the incidence varied from a high of 1.6 among European-born men to a low of 0.5 for African-born men. The rates for Israeli-born and Asian men were 1.2 and 0.7, respectively. European-born men had approximately three times the incidence of heart attacks as the African and Asian-born men. The relatively high rate for Israeli-born men implies a considerable effect of the environment on the risk of heart attacks.

Similar results were found in an earlier survey of 842 consecutive autopsies observed in males and females thirty years of age and older. Among 568 autopsies of Ashkenazim, about 20% had evidence of acute myocardial infarction, compared with only 8% of 274 non-Ashkenazim. There was a single case of acute myocardial infarction as the cause of death in the non-Ashkenazi group before the age of fifty, whereas among the Ashkenazim 10% of those who died under age fifty had died of acute myocardial infarction. Despite the differences in life-style among the various ethnic groups, the findings on heart disease in Ashkenazi and non-Ashkenazi Jews suggest "that there may still be a residue of genuine genetic variance among them."[80]

Yemenite Jews have an unusually low prevalence of coronary heart disease. The Israeli Ischemic Heart Project collected extensive data on 10,000 middle-aged men, including 380 Yemenites who had been in Israel an average of 25 years. There were 3 cases of definite coronary heart disease in this group over a 5-year follow-up period, a rate that was eightfold less than for European-born Jews.[81]

Although serum cholesterol levels are significantly influenced by diet, there is also a clear genetic component. In most persons there are probably several genes influencing cholesterol levels. In some persons an elevated cholesterol level is due to a single dominant gene, which causes moderately elevated levels in heterozygotes and severely elevated levels in homozygotes. One might expect a direct correlation in different populations between serum cholesterol levels and incidence of heart attacks, and this is indeed observed. In the Israeli Ischemic Heart Disease Study reported in 1979, the average total cholesterol level for more than 6,500 adult males aged over 40 was 208 mg/dl. Significant differences were observed among men from different regions of birth, ranging from a high of 216 mg/dl for men from Eastern and Central Europe, 208 for men from Southeast Europe, 210 for Israel, 202 for the Middle East, and down to 193 mg/dl for men from North Africa. Among men who died of a myocardial infarction during the study period, the rate of MI deaths increased steadily with increasing baseline total cholesterol levels, thus confirming the role of elevated cholesterol level as a risk factor for heart disease.[82] The differences in cholesterol levels observed in this study are in agreement with the difference in incidence of heart attacks among the different population groups. The highest incidence of heart attacks is observed in European-born Israelis, the same group that has the highest cholesterol levels.

These results have been confirmed in other studies. For example, the Jerusalem Lipid Research Clinic Prevalence Study measured cholesterol levels of almost 7,000 middle-aged Jerusalem residents and found a mean total cholesterol level of 191.7 mg/dl among men born in North Africa, 194.8 for Asia, 200.5 for Europe, and 206.1 mg/dl for men born in Israel. Again, the North African-born Jews had the lowest levels and the European-born Jews the highest.[83]

In an attempt to sort out genetic from environmental factors, plasma cholesterol levels were measured in 17-year-old Jerusalem offspring of Jews from 19 countries of birth. Although cholesterol levels, as expected, were generally lower in the teenagers than in older people, there were significant differences among the four main groups classified according to father's country of origin. The mean cholesterol level for the entire group of more than 3,600 boys was 133.8 mg/dl, with individual average values of 126.9 for North Africa, 132.7 for Asia, 137.1 for Israel, and 137.40 mg/dl for Europe. The North African and Asian groups differed significantly from the Israeli and European groups, which were like each other. A breakdown of individual paternal countries of origin showed a wide range of mean cholesterol levels, from a low of 126.2 mg/dl for Morocco and 127.0 for Yemen, to a high of 143.0 for Austria and Switzerland and 140.7 for the United States and Canada.[84]

Because most of the young people in this study were born in Israel, the results suggest a genetic component to the differences in cholesterol level. Interestingly, though, when adult Israeli-born Jerusalem residents were divided into region of origin of their fathers, there were no significant differences in total cholesterol levels, which ranged from 200.7 mg/dl for men with Asian-born fathers, to 209.2 mg/dl for those with European-born fathers.[85] It is likely that over the years, the diet and life-style of the Israeli-born Israelis has elevated their cholesterol levels and obliterated any genetic differences among them. Not surprisingly, mortality rates for cardiovascular disease have risen rapidly among Asian and North African Jews living in Israel, and differences between them and European-born Israelis are narrowing.

We can conclude that although known genetic factors influence serum cholesterol levels and undoubtedly account for part of the differences among Jews of different countries of origin, there are also strong environmental influences, which in the melting pot of Israel are minimizing the differences. We can expect that over the next 20 or 30 years the average cholesterol levels and coronary artery disease mortality rates will continue to converge among Israeli-born Jews of different backgrounds.

3. Diabetes

Diabetes is a common disease in which there is a relative or absolute lack of insulin, a hormone produced by the pancreas, which is necessary for the metabolism of sugar by the body. There are two basic types of diabetes—insulin-dependent (IDDM), or juvenile, diabetes, in which the patient requires daily insulin injections, and non-insulin-dependent diabetes (NIDDM), which can often be treated by diet alone or by diet and oral medication. NIDDM is much more common than IDDM, and is often found in overweight elderly persons. Genetic factors are important in both types of diabetes. Most researchers believe that multifactorial inheritance is involved rather than a single gene.

It has often been stated that the Jewish people are especially disposed toward diabetes. In different parts of the world, the percentage of diabetics in the total population varied from 0.26 in Iceland, 0.73 in Jamaica, and 1.5 in Mecklenburg, Germany, to 2.0 in Australia and 3.2 in New York. The prevalence of diabetes in Ashkenazi Jews in Israel is 2.5%, which is not as high as among non-Jews in New York. The prevalence of diabetes among non-Ashkenazi Jews is even lower.[86] These data do not justify the conclusion that the Jews in general are more prone to diabetes than other ethnic groups.

In Israel, the prevalence of diabetes in 1958–59 was 1% (or 10 per 1,000) among more than 4,000 Sephardi immigrants from the Mediterranean region and 2.5% (or 25 per 1,000) among more than 4,000 Ashkenazi immigrants from the Western countries. There were almost no cases of diabetes among 5,000 Yemenite newcomers to Israel and none among approximately 1,000 Kurdish newcomers; in contrast, 2.9% of 751 Yemenite and almost 600 Kurdish old settlers who had lived in Israel for more than twenty-five years had diabetes, an incidence even higher than in Ashkenazi Jews.[87] Environment (and primarily food-consumption patterns) clearly has a pronounced effect on the prevalence of diabetes. The main dietary change in the Yemenite old settlers compared with the new arrivals was an increased intake of sugar; this factor may be responsible for the increased prevalence of diabetes. Another group of Yemenites surveyed 25 years after their arrival in Israel had a markedly increased incidence of diabetes, especially among overweight persons.[88] This finding confirms the importance of environmental factors in the onset of diabetes.

In a five-year prospective study of 10,000 adult Israeli male government workers between 1963 and 1968, significant differences were found in the incidence of diabetes according to the area of birth. The prevalence per 1,000 population ranged from a high of 62 for men born in Israel, to 60 for those born in North Africa, and 57 for men born in Asia, to lower rates of 42 for Southeastern Europe, 40 for Eastern Europe, and 38 for Central Europe.[89] In contrast with the earlier study, this survey found lower rates of diabetes in Ashkenazi than in Oriental and Sephardi Jews. Goodman[90] offers various explanations for this discrepancy, such as the possibility that the government workers sampled in the second survey were not an equivalent population sample to the earlier study. The rates among second-generation Israelis are even higher than among first-generation Israelis, suggesting that environmental factors are masking genetic differences among the children of immigrants from different regions.

Yet a third study was reported in 1984. Among almost 5,000 residents of Jerusalem more than 15 years old, the prevalence of diabetes was 5.8% (58 per 1,000) among men and 4.6% among women. The prevalence was higher in those born in North Africa (9.4% of men and 6.1% of women) than in those born in Israel (5.3% of men), Asia (4.9% of men), and Europe (4.6% of men). Although the prevalence of diabetes in North African-born men was almost twice that in European-born males, no differences in mean body weight was evident between these two groups.[91] Thus the difference cannot be explained by obesity and is more likely to reflect genetic differences among the various Jewish groups.

Israeli children surveyed in 1963 had a crude prevalence of diabetes of 0.16 per 1,000 (which is low compared with the prevalence in the United States). The prevalence was lowest among children born in Asia and Africa, and among Israel-born children whose fathers were born in Africa and Asia.

In 1968 another survey found a 70% increase in the prevalence of diabetes in children compared with the earlier study. The prevalence was again higher among children born in Europe and America than among those born in Asia and Africa. The Israel-born children of Israel-born families seemed to have a prevalence midway between the highest and lowest frequencies.[92]

These two surveys of juvenile diabetes show that its incidence is increasing in Israel and that children of parents born in Asia and Africa are less often affected than children of parents born in Europe and America. Thus, although the Western environment is clearly having an adverse effect on the incidence of diabetes, genetic differences among these populations are likely to account for the remaining differences in incidence of this disease.

4. Alcoholism

Alcoholism is a disease that is primarily environmental in origin but for which there is a clear-cut genetic component. Studies of identical twins as well as studies of children of alcoholics who have been brought up by adoptive parents support the presence of genetic factors in the development of alcoholism. Although not all studies concur, in most twin studies identical twins (who share 100% of their genes) are significantly more concordant for alcoholism than are fraternal twins (who share 50% of their genes) despite the similar environment.[93] Whereas the prevalence of alcoholism in the American population is about 10%, there is a 25% likelihood that a man will become alcoholic if one parent is affected with this disease, and a striking 50% likelihood if both parents are affected. Even when the child of alcoholics is adopted into a non-alcoholic home, his risk for alcoholism is much increased.[94] Alcoholics' children who have been adopted have a fourfold greater risk of alcoholism than do non-alcoholics' children who have been adopted.[95]

In a comparison of the per capita alcohol consumption in 27 countries, Israel was ranked last (2.18 liters of absolute alcohol in 1974), while the United States ranked 13th (8.36 liters in 1978); Portugal ranked first, with 17.4 liters in 1974.[96] The mortality rate from cirrhosis of the liver, an alcohol-related disease, was also *much* lower among Jews—8.20 per 100,000 men in Israel in 1971, versus 22.52 in the United States and 48.04 in France.[97]

Jews in most countries have a low prevalence of alcoholism. There has been much speculation on the reasons for this. In *The Natural Mind*,[98] Andrew Weil poses a similar question about Amazonian Indians, who regularly use hallucinogenic drugs but have no problem with drug abuse or chemical dependency. He lists several cultural factors that he believes answer this question: (1) The Indians prefer natural drugs (peyote, coca) to the highly purified chemicals (mescaline and cocaine, respectively); (2) the use of drugs is highly ritualized, with the drugs being taken only in certain ways for certain purposes; (3) the drug is used only for positive reasons, *not* to escape from boredom or anxiety.

It is interesting that the traditional Jewish use of wine fulfills each of these criteria: The beverage consumed is natural wine, not distilled liquor; it is used in well-defined rituals in which a benediction, with the mention of the name of God, is recited over the wine during important religious ceremonies such as weddings, bar mitzvahs, and the Sabbath welcome, and to celebrate annual holy days. Its purpose is purely religious-ritual, and never to induce intoxication or even hilarity. Weil also notes that the Amazon Indians recognize the drive of children to experiment with drugs, so they administer them to children under supervision. Jewish children are

322

similarly given a little wine early and under supervision, beginning with the taste of wine the infant boy is given at circumcision.

Mark Keller, in his article, "The Great Jewish Drink Mystery,"[99] concludes that Jewish culture, dominantly influenced by the religion, evokes attitudes that inhibit drinking to intoxication, even while it encourages frequent but controlled drinking. He also suggests that Jews may possess genetic traits that protect them from alcoholism. Stated another way, the frequency of the genes promoting alcoholism may be lower among Jews than among Italians or Irish. One cannot investigate this hypothesis at present, however, because not enough is known about the genetics of alcoholism.

If Jewish religious beliefs are the explanation for the low incidence of alcoholism in Jews, one might expect Orthodox Jews to be less likely to become alcoholics than non-Orthodox Jews. This is indeed what the statistics show. One might also expect an increasing problem with alcoholism in recent years in countries such as the United States where Jews have drifted away from Orthodoxy. Of nine studies conducted between 1970 and 1983 on alcoholism in American Jews,[100] only four used sound sampling techniques; each of these concluded that alcoholism continues to be a rarity in the American Jewish community. Thus, even among secular Jews social and perhaps genetic influences maintain a low rate of alcoholism.

One explanation has been proposed by Snyder,[101] who suggests that even among non-Orthodox Jews, sobriety is considered a Jewish virtue and drunkenness a Gentile vice. Jewish sobriety is considered part of Jewish identity, a distinguishing feature of the "in-group" Jews from the frequent alcohol excess of the "out-group" Gentiles. The definition of alcoholism as non-Jewish may, unfortunately, make it more difficult for the Jewish alcoholic to seek treatment.

Patai[102] believes that the answer lies in the "domination of the Jew by his religious tradition." Jewish religion encouraged Jews to drink frequently in moderation but made it a sin to become intoxicated. There were similar rules regarding sex and eating. Jews did not have a special relationship with alcohol; instead, they behaved toward alcohol, as they did toward food and sex, as their religion dictated.

The preceding discussion relates to American Jews, who are primarily Ashkenazim. Among Israelis, only 3–5% of drinkers drank more than two drinks per day, contrasted with 33% of American drinkers, who reported consuming 3 or more drinks on an average drinking day.[103] A study of alcoholism among Jews in Israel confirmed that Ashkenazi Jews have a low incidence of drinking problems, but found that Sephardi and Oriental Jews have a greater extent of alcoholism.[104] Several different sampling methods were used to include diverse socioeconomic levels and to avoid bias due to possible selective use of alcoholism treatment facilities by different population groups.

323

Oriental Jews from Morocco, India, and Yemen were highly overrepresented among alcoholics; Sephardi Jews from Bulgaria and Greece and Oriental Jews from Algeria, Tunisia, and Turkey were also overrepresented, whereas European Jews were underrepresented. Because the overall pattern of subgroup variation in alcoholism does not correlate neatly with known genetic differences among the subgroups, the differences in drinking patterns might be explained by a sociocultural rather than a genetic interpretation. Each of the subgroups that had a high incidence of alcoholism had experienced severe cultural stress and/or economic disadvantage upon immigrating to Israel and might therefore be more vulnerable to alcoholism. However, Moroccan and Yemenite Jews had a higher incidence of alcoholism even in their native countries, so that their relatively high rates in Israel cannot be entirely explained by environmental influences in their new home. In support of Snyder's "in-group–out-group" hypothesis, it is of interest that both Yemen and Morocco are Moslem countries where drinking is severely sanctioned. Jewish sobriety would therefore not distinguish the Jewish minority from the Moslem majority, who have a very low rate of alcoholism.

It is unclear, therefore, if there are any genetic differences between Jews and non-Jews with regard to alcoholism. What is clear, however, is that the incidence of alcoholism is low in Ashkenazi Jews (even among secular Ashkenazim) and higher in various subgroups of Oriental and Sephardi Jews. A genetic contribution remains a possibility, but cultural and socioeconomic factors may suffice to explain these patterns.

OTHER DISEASES BELIEVED TO BE MORE COMMON IN JEWS

1. Inflammatory bowel disease (Crohn's disease and ulcerative colitis)

Crohn's disease and ulcerative colitis, collectively termed inflammatory bowel disease, are chronic relapsing diseases of the gastrointestinal tract that cause diarrhea, bleeding, cramps, and frequently require surgery. Both tend to strike young adults, and both have been reported to be more common in Jews than in non-Jews in several countries. The cause of these diseases is not known.

In the Jewish population of Tel Aviv, ulcerative colitis was less frequent than in Rochester (Minnesota), Oxford (England), and Copenhagen (Denmark).[105] The annual incidence in Tel Aviv was 3.66 per 100,000 population and the prevalence was 37.4 per 100,000. The rates varied for different countries of origin. Jews from Asia had a prevalence of 24.1, those from Africa had 29.5, and those from Europe and America had 51.5. The authors suggested that a key variable is a rural versus urban population and that the earlier studies may have been comparing the primarily urban Jewish population with a disproportionately rural Gentile group. Ulcerative colitis may be primarily an environmental disease related to the urban life-style.

In all populations studied, Crohn's disease increased in incidence for several decades, peaking in the late 1970's. Among Ashkenazi Jews, the incidence of Crohn's disease varied from none in Aberdeen and Uppsala, 1.6 per 100,000 in Tel Aviv, 2.2 in Basel, 2.8 in Cape Town, 7.2 in Baltimore, to 24 in Malmö. For comparison, the rate for other whites in Baltimore was 2.5 and in Malmö 4.8 per 100,000.[106] Both Crohn's disease and ulcerative colitis were rare in several nonindustrialized populations and their incidence rose with migration to an urban environment. The authors suggest that environmental factors are important causes of both these diseases.

Because the incidence of Crohn's disease increases with age, it is important to adjust prevalence figures for the age of the population. When this was done for the Jewish population in Beer Sheva, Israel, the prevalence rates for Crohn's disease were 15.8 per 100,000 for Jews born in Europe and the United States, 12.5 for Jews born in Africa and Asia, and 9.7 for those born in Israel. This study showed that Crohn's disease is not as uncommon in Oriental and Sephardi Jews as previously thought.[107]

Although these studies do show marked differences in prevalence rates among different Jewish populations, they generally support the view that in urban populations, inflammatory bowel disease is more common among Jews than non-Jews. The cause of this disease is still not known, but a genetic component is likely.

CONCLUSIONS

When certain diseases appear to be more or less common in Jews than non-Jews, closer inspection usually reveals that the high or low incidence of the disease is in fact a feature of only one group of Jews. The group may consist of Middle Eastern Jews, Sephardi Jews, or even Ashkenazi Jews originating from a small area in Eastern Europe. None of the diseases described is characteristic of Jews in general. It is particularly striking that no one disease (with the partial exception of familial Mediterranean fever in the Sephardi community) can be observed throughout either the Oriental or Sephardi community. As Goodman[108] points out, when one speaks of genetic diseases in Oriental or Sephardi Jewry, it is essential to define the community precisely, for each community has its own specific genetic disorders.

325

Thus, the distribution of particular diseases cannot be used to differentiate Jews in general from non-Jews, although the discovery of a particular disease in an American might suggest an Eastern European Jewish background (for example, familial dysautonomia or Tay-Sachs disease), a Yemenite Jewish background (peroxidase and phospho-lipid deficiency in eosinophilic granulocytes), or a non-Jewish background (phenylketonuria or cervical cancer).

The evidence in this chapter also shows that Jews are heterogeneous in the distribution of both rare and common diseases with a genetic component.

CHAPTER XX

Conclusions to Part III

I N PART III we compared Jewish and non-Jewish populations of the world with respect to several morphological traits, gene frequencies of various blood groups and other blood proteins, the occurrence of glucose-6-phosphate dehydrogenase (G6PD) deficiency, the ability to taste the bitter chemical phenylthiocarbamide (PTC), the incidence of color blindness, and the occurrence of various diseases and causes of death. A reasonably consistent picture emerges from these studies.

In their height, hair and eye color, and shape of nose are concerned, Jews are not uniform. Only half of European Jews have dark hair and dark eyes, classically considered to be "Jewish" features. In contrast, Jews originating from countries where dark hair and eyes were the norm also had predominantly dark hair and eyes. Aquiline, or hooked, nose, another traditional "Jewish" feature, was found in only approximately 14% of Jews in New York City. This type of nose is common among some non-Jewish populations, for example, Germans in Bavaria, and among various Mediterranean groups. Different Jewish groups differed widely in their cephalic index; in the countries where Jews had resided for centuries, the Jewish cephalic index values resembled those of the non-Jews among whom they live. In the frequencies of the two different patterns of hand clasping (left-over-right and right-over-left), the Yemenite Jews were significantly different from Kurdish Jews, with the former showing a blacklike frequency. This feature, along with several other morphological traits, shows that even within the Middle East, Jewish populations, isolated from one another for centuries, are very dissimilar and evidence differing gene influxes from other populations.

Fingerprint patterns were similar among all Jewish groups analyzed and were suggestive of a Mediterranean origin. Fingerprint patterns are believed to be very resistant to environmental change, and may therefore reveal remnants of a common gene pool in a population that has subsequently undergone much change in other characteristics.

The pattern suggested by the morphological data is confirmed and extended by blood group and blood protein studies. The frequencies of the ABO blood group genes in Jews of any given area tend to resemble those of the non-Jews of that area, whereas Jews from different parts of the world vary widely in their ABO frequencies. Similar results are obtained with the MN blood group genes. The Rh genes, in contrast, show a greater uniformity in frequency among all Jews, with relatively high frequencies of the "Mediterranean" and "African" chromosomes, again suggesting an element of Mediterranean ancestry.

Among genes controlling the production of blood proteins, one (atypical/pseudocholinesterase) was very common in Iranian and Iraqi Jews, but not in other Jews. Jewish frequencies of three genes (GC, PGM_1, and ADA) were like their non-Jewish neighbors, and different from other Jewish groups. All Jews had uniform frequencies of other genes (adenylate kinase, haptoglobin, acid phosphatase, and some of the HLA alleles), which were like the respective frequencies in Mediterranean non-Jewish populations. These latter genes again give evidence of a Mediterranean origin for European Jews. For various reasons, their frequencies were probably less subject to environmental selection pressure and consequently have remained more stable over the centuries than have the frequencies of the Gc, PGM_1, and ADA genes.

Bonné-Tamir and coworkers compared the genetic blood markers of Libyan and Moroccan Jews and observed significant differences between these two populations at many genetic loci, concluding that geographical proximity does not guarantee genetic relatedness. The Moroccan Jews had high B and lower A frequencies in the ABO system. They concluded that the different Jewish communities must have maintained a high degree of isolation even in the same geographical area.

The gene for glucose-6-phosphate dehydrogenase (G6PD) deficiency, which is subject to strong environmental selection in malarial regions because of the resistance to malaria it confers, varied greatly among Jews and non-Jews in different parts of the world. The Jews were more diverse in this respect than non-Jews, with exceptionally high frequencies of the gene for G6PD deficiency being found among Jews in some areas of Kurdistan.

Jewish populations were also very diverse in the frequency of the gene causing inability to taste the bitter chemical PTC.

The frequencies of color blindness in Jews were like those in non-Jews, tending to be lower among Sephardi, North African, and Asian Jews than among Ashkenazim.

In the section on "Jewish" diseases, we showed that rare diseases considered characteristically Jewish are in fact characteristic only of Jews originating from small areas of the world. No diseases are characteristic of all Jews. Conversely, phenylketonuria (PKU), once thought to be extremely rare in Jews, is rare only among Ashkenazi Jews, and occurs among non-European Jews with frequencies like those in non-Jews.

Although less commonly known in the United States, where the Jewish population is predominantly of European background, another group of diseases is unusually common among non-Ashkenazi Jews. The Dubin-Johnson syndrome, for example, is very common among Iranian Jews. The inherited disease thalassemia, common among Mediterranean populations, has a highly variable distribution among Jews, being most prevalent, as expected, among Middle Eastern Jews and absent in Jews of European origin. Kurdish Jews have an unusually high frequency of one of the two forms of the disease, β thalassemia. Finally, the incidence of common diseases with a genetic component—cancer, diabetes, and heart disease—also varies among different Jewish groups.

These genetic studies indicate that the Jews of the world are a very diverse lot. On the other hand, the frequencies of some traits, namely, fingerprint patterns, Rh genes, and genes for the blood proteins haptoglobin and red cell acid phosphatase (AP), indicate an element of Mediterranean ancestry common to all Jewish groups. After consideration of these data, some workers have concluded that the contribution of non-Jews to the Jewish gene pool has been small[1] or else that the direction of gene flow has been largely from Jewish to non-Jewish populations.[2] These workers do not, however, take account of the historical data, according to which the Jews originated in the Mediterranean Basin and migrated therefrom, subsequently undergoing extensive interbreeding with the peoples among whom they lived. It is, then, not surprising to find some Mediterranean features among Jews. But these features do not provide justification for concluding that the Jews are a single race, for in many other ways they are at least as different from one another as are any other white populations.

The genetic studies also point out some unusual features of certain Jewish groups that set them apart genetically from other Jews. The Karaite sect, for example, originated among the Jews of Iraq about A.D. 760 and subsequently migrated to Egypt and Eastern Europe. Iraqi Karaites lived in Hit, Iraq, from the tenth century A.D. until approximately 1950, when most of the remaining families moved to Israel and began extensive interbreeding with Egyptian Karaites. Iraqi Karaites have unusual ABO gene frequencies, with low A and high B values, which differentiate them from all other Jews as well as from Egyptians and Europeans, and indicate a common origin for the Egyptian and Crimean branches of the sect. Another distinctive feature of Karaites is that the frequency of allele A_2 was extremely high, .183, whereas that for A_1 was unusually low. At the Rh locus, the frequency of the "African chromosome," cDe, was very high, as was the frequency of cde. The M allele had an extremely high frequency, 0.98. Of the blood protein polymorphisms, the most striking observation was the complete lack of the acid phosphatase allele p^a; the adenylate kinase allele AK^2 was also absent. The Egyptian and Iraqi Karaites are further differentiated from Iraqi Jews and from Egyptian Arabs by a total absence of G6PD deficiency, in contrast with its common occurrence in Egyptians and in Iraqi Jews. These unusual findings are most likely due to the strong influence of isolation and genetic drift among the small Karaite communities.

The Samaritans, a semi-Jewish sect living in Israel who have practiced close inbreeding for the past two thousand years, have a unique genetic position among other Middle Eastern peoples. The Samaritan community has the highest frequency of the ABO gene O in the Middle East, and a higher frequency of the ABO gene A_2 than A_1, an unusual finding. They also have a complete absence of G6PD deficiency, in contrast with its high frequencies in neighboring populations. The frequency of PTC nontasters among them is low, and the incidence of color blindness exceptionally high. The frequency of the haptoglobin gene Hp^1 is also high, and the frequency of the blood group P gene P is unusually low. Genetic drift has apparently had a major effect among the Samaritans, causing some of their gene frequencies to diverge greatly from those of their neighbors.

The Habbanite Jews have developed an equally unique combination of gene frequencies, again as a result of genetic drift. This group, which migrated to Israel from southern Yemen in the 1940's, had for centuries maintained a high rate of inbreeding. The Habbanites have a much higher frequency of the ABO gene B than adjacent populations; it is very much higher than among the Yemenite Jews, their nearest Jewish neighbors. In addition, this population is one of the few known groups with more ABO A_2 than A_1 genes. In the Rh system, the Habbanites have an unusually low frequency of the Mediterranean chromosome, cDE, and a frequency of the Rh negative chromosome, cde, which among them is near the low end of the range of the Middle Eastern values. The Kell gene K, which has a frequency of 10% or more in Arabs, is almost absent in the Habbanites. The frequency of the haptoglobin gene Hp^1 is among the lowest recorded. In the phosphoglucomutase system, the allele PGM_1^1 has the lowest frequency in the Habbanites ever reported. In the acid phosphatase system, the frequency of the p^b allele in the Habbanites is one of the highest ever found.

The "Black Jews" of Cochin, India, whose Jewish ancestors may have originally settled there as early as the second century A.D., are another group with genetic characteristics that clearly differentiate them from other

Jews. Besides obvious morphological differences (dark skin color), they have a frequency of PTC nontasters higher than all other Jews (except those of the Tunisian island of Jerba) and like that of some Hindu tribes. They also have an unusual ABO gene distribution, with an excess of gene B over A. This feature is also found in many parts of India. The high frequencies of the Duffy Fy^a and adenylate kinase AK^2 frequencies were not observed in other Jewish populations but are like those observed in southern Indian populations. JK^a and haptoglobin Hp^1 frequencies are the lowest observed in Jewish population groups. Researchers of this population agree that the Cochin Jews bear little biochemical genetic resemblance to any other Jewish population and that there has been extensive infiltration of Indian genes into this community.

The existence of these genetically isolated Jewish communities is further proof of the genetic diversity of the Jews of the world.

The Yemenite Jews have gene frequencies for many loci that differ from other Jewish populations, but which show a close relationship to Yemenite Arabs.[3] Those from the southern part of Yemen have a higher frequency of African marker genes than do those in the north. The Habbanite Jews also have a high frequency of African genes. The Kurdish Jews from Iran and northwestern Iraq show a moderate genetic resemblance to the indigenous Kurds of Iran, while those from southeastern Iraq differ considerably.[3] The Kurdish Jews differ markedly in their blood-group frequencies from the Yemenite Jews and are nearer to the non-Jewish Kurds than to either the Yemenite Jews or the Arabs of Arabia. Ashkenazi Jews show a resemblance at multiple gene loci to European non-Jews. All of these results support genetic admixture between Jews and adjacent non-Jewish populations.

Since the publication in 1975 of the first edition of this book, many researchers both in Israel and abroad have continued their intensive study of Jewish populations. New genetic polymorphisms, such as the HLA system, have been investigated, and new techniques such as direct analysis of DNA—the genetic material—are being used. For example, Bonné-Tamir and her coworkers[4] are comparing variations in human mitochondrial DNA in different populations in Israel; results based on the small samples thus far studied show the presence of polymorphisms, which will be useful in population genetics.

Some of the leaders in the field have erroneously taken our conclusion that Jews of any given area tend to resemble the non-Jews of that area as a denial that there is a core of genetic identity among all Jews, arising from their common Mediterranean origin. Casting themselves in opposition to our supposed position on the genetics of the Jews, they have then used the results of their own studies to "prove" us wrong by demonstrating that for certain genes there is greater similarity among most Jews than between Jews and non-Jews.

The result has been the establishment of two camps, one in agreement with our conclusions, the other in opposition. For example, Mourant *et al.* in 1978 concluded that "each major Jewish community as a whole bears some resemblance to the indigenous peoples of the regions where it first developed;[5] Morton *et al.* in 1982 reported a high level of admixture between Jews and non-Jews[6]; and Chakraborty and Weiss, who calculated genetic distances for four Jewish and four non-Jewish populations, concluded that the Jewish populations were genetically closer to their neighboring non-Jewish populations.[7] On the other hand, Kobyliansky and co-workers reported in 1982 that most Jewish populations are genetically closer to each other than to non-Jewish populations.[8] Karlin and associates reached similar conclusions.[9]

To us, artificially establishing a dichotomy between the position that Jews resemble their neighboring non-Jews and the position that they are genetically related among themselves makes about as much sense as did the heredity versus environment issue that was so hotly debated in the medical and anthropological literature for so many years. We now realize that both genetics and environment make important contributions to most traits in man, but that one may be relatively more important than the other for individual traits. Similarly, the sum of the data on Jewish populations shows us both that they are genetically related to the non-Jewish peoples among whom they have lived and that they have a common Jewish gene pool. This is exactly what one would expect of a people who had a common origin and then spread out and interbred with other peoples.

We do not agree with A. Szeinberg who, on the basis of the data on blood protein polymorphisms, concluded that the influx of foreign genes into the Jewish gene pool was not significant.[10] Where different Jewish groups have similar frequencies for a particular gene, he cites this finding as evidence to support his hypothesis. When differences are found among different Jewish populations, he attributes these to the existence of local selective forces that induced changes in the gene frequencies. Section I of this book shows convincingly that, judging from the historical record, there was a significant influx of non-Jewish genes into the Jewish gene pool over the centuries.

The sum of the genetic data is therefore consistent with the hypothesis, confirmed by historical study, that the Jews originated as a small group, which then became genetically diverse through extensive interbreeding and through subjection to genetic selection pressure, which differed in their differing environments. Evidence of their common gene pool is seen in the persistence of characteristic frequencies of several genes not subject to significant selection pressure, such as the HLA system. Other genes, however, and the variability of genetic disease frequencies among the different groups attest to the divergent genetic forces that have acted on the different Jewish populations.

Diagrams and Tables
Notes
Glossary
Index

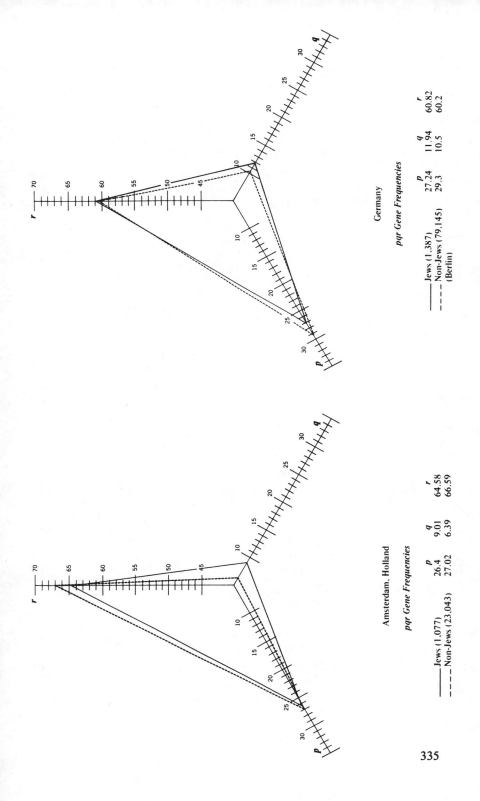

Amsterdam, Holland

pqr Gene Frequencies

	p	*q*	*r*
Jews (1,077)	26.4	9.01	64.58
Non-Jews (23,043)	27.02	6.39	66.59

Germany

pqr Gene Frequencies

	p	*q*	*r*
Jews (1,387)	27.24	11.94	60.82
Non-Jews (79,145)	29.3	10.5	60.2
(Berlin)			

335

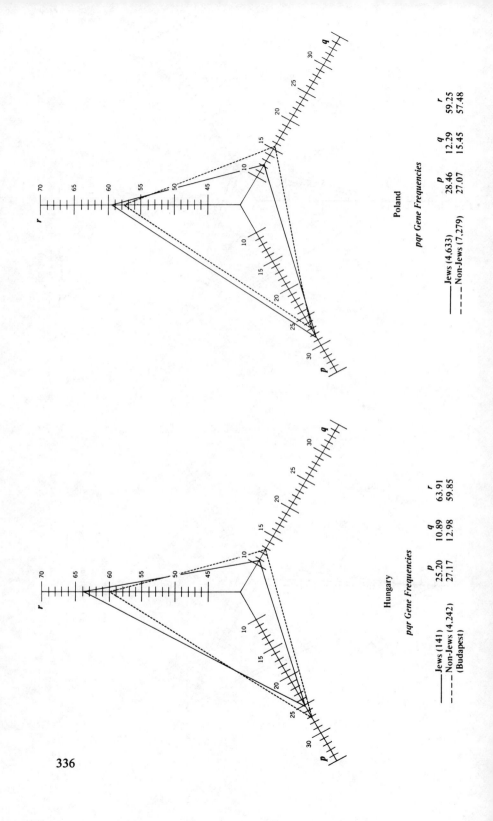

Hungary

pqr Gene Frequencies

	p	*q*	*r*
—— Jews (141)	25.20	10.89	63.91
- - - Non-Jews (4,242) (Budapest)	27.17	12.98	59.85

Poland

pqr Gene Frequencies

	p	*q*	*r*
—— Jews (4,633)	28.46	12.29	59.25
- - - Non-Jews (7,279)	27.07	15.45	57.48

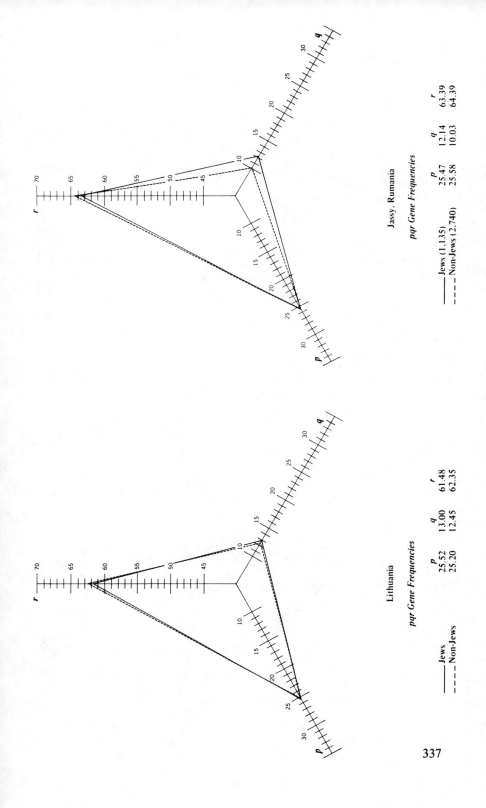

Lithuania

pqr Gene Frequencies

	p	q	r
Jews	25.52	13.00	61.48
Non-Jews	25.20	12.45	62.35

——— Jews
– – – Non-Jews

Jassy, Rumania

pqr Gene Frequencies

	p	q	r
Jews (1,135)	25.47	12.14	63.39
Non-Jews (2,740)	25.58	10.03	64.39

——— Jews (1,135)
– – – Non-Jews (2,740)

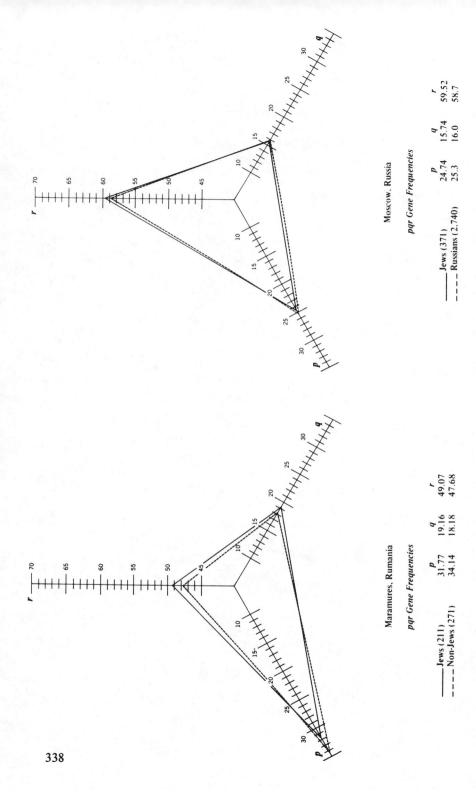

Maramures, Rumania

pqr Gene Frequencies

	p	*q*	*r*
Jews (211)	31.77	19.16	49.07
Non-Jews (271)	34.14	18.18	47.68

Moscow, Russia

pqr Gene Frequencies

	p	*q*	*r*
Jews (371)	24.74	15.74	59.52
Russians (2.740)	25.3	16.0	58.7

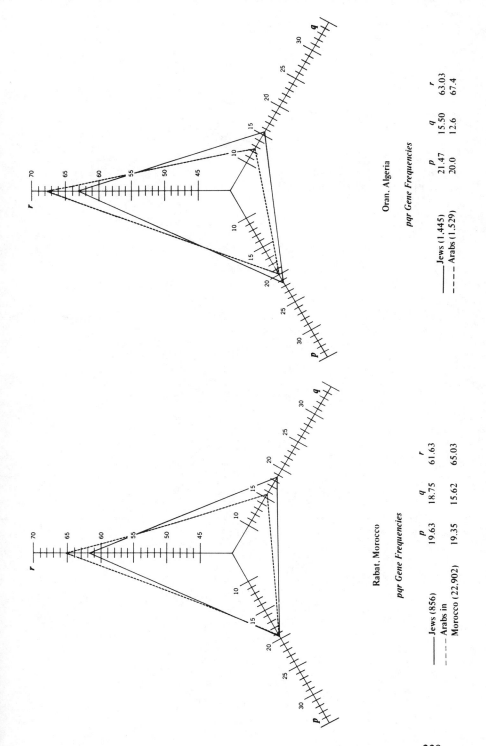

Rabat, Morocco

pqr Gene Frequencies

	p	*q*	*r*
Jews (856)	19.63	18.75	61.63
Arabs in Morocco (22.902)	19.35	15.62	65.03

Oran, Algeria

pqr Gene Frequencies

	p	*q*	*r*
Jews (1,445)	21.47	15.50	63.03
Arabs (1.529)	20.0	12.6	67.4

339

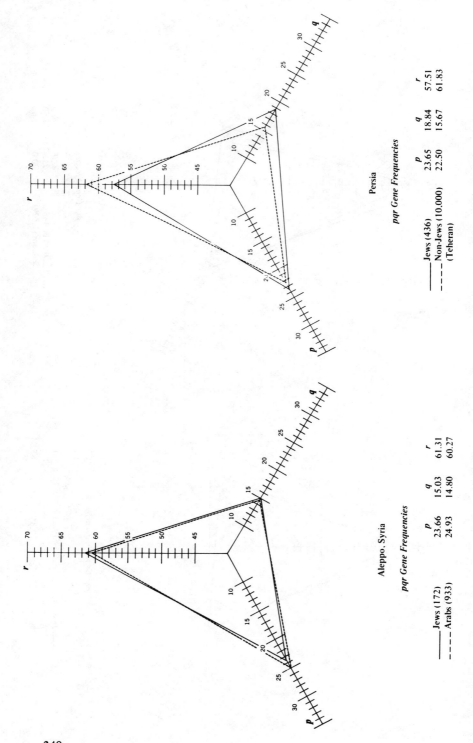

Aleppo, Syria

pqr Gene Frequencies

	p	*q*	*r*
—— Jews (172)	23.66	15.03	61.31
- - - - Arabs (933)	24.93	14.80	60.27

Persia

pqr Gene Frequencies

	p	*q*	*r*
—— Jews (436)	23.65	18.84	57.51
- - - Non-Jews (10,000)	22.50	15.67	61.83
(Teheran)			

340

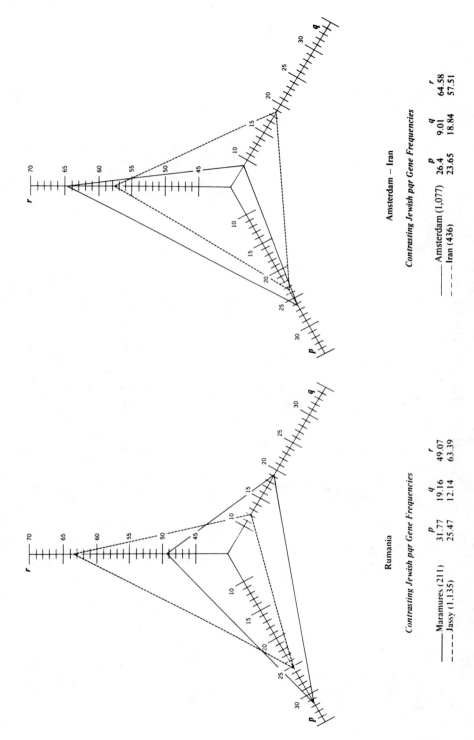

Rumania

Contrasting Jewish pqr Gene Frequencies

	p	q	r
——— Maramures (211)	31.77	19.16	49.07
– – – Jassy (1,135)	25.47	12.14	63.39

Amsterdam – Iran

Contrasting Jewish pqr Gene Frequencies

	p	q	r
——— Amsterdam (1,077)	26.4	9.01	64.58
– – – Iran (436)	23.65	18.84	57.51

Table 1. ABO Frequencies (in percentages)

Europe	Jews				Non-Jews				
	No.	p	q	r	No.	p	q	r	
Ashkenazim									
Unspec. I	2,662	27.2	12.6	60.2					
In Israel	946	27.43	10.89	61.68					
Unspec. II	1,500	27.87	13.39	58.74					
E. Europe	5,271	28.04	13.15	58.81					
Manitoba	140	28.53	11.45	60.02					
In Israel	349	24.91	10.61	64.48					
Brooklyn	500	26.44	12.05	61.51					
Ohio	523	27.01	10.61	62.38					
In Israel	465	26.57	11.53	61.90					
Austria									
In Israel	361	24.20	12.24	63.56	8,790	28.05	9.76	62.09	
Austria	187	34.33	8.99	56.69					
Czechoslovakia									
I	144	33.09	14.55	52.36	2,085	34.01	16.52	48.87	Prague
II	535	24.64	16.19	59.17	2,429	28.55	13.74	57.71	Bratislava
Bratislava—Israel	239	25.30	11.97	62.73	5,957	25.5	15.0	59.5	
Czechoslovakia	380	24.35	10.97	64.67					
Average	918	26.06	14.80	59.14	17,754	29.58	14.76	55.66	
Germany									
In Israel	1,387	27.24	11.94	60.82	20,000	28.53	9.27	62.20	Soldiers
Berlin	230	26.56	8.63	64.81	79,145	29.3	10.5	60.2	Berlin
Germany	514	26.50	13.13	60.37					
	101	25.6	14.4	60.1					
Average	1,617	27.14	11.46	61.40	179,244	28.24	8.93	62.83	

Table 1. ABO Frequencies (Continued)

Europe (Continued)	Jews					Non-Jews			
	No.	p	q	r	No.	p	q	r
Hungary								
In Israel	141	25.20	10.89	63.91	19,953	29.64	14.40	55.96
Unspecified	483	28.77	12.12	59.11				
Hungary	273	27.73	11.37	60.90				
Lithuania								
In Israel	535	25.52	13.00	61.48	5,028	24.02	13.24	62.74
Netherlands								
I	705	25.2	9.5	65.3				
II	142	27.10	7.63	65.27				
Amsterdam	1,077	26.4	9.01	64.50				
Average	1,924	25.90	6.20	67.90	492,925	26.57	6.10	67.33
Poland								
I	818	28.92	13.64	57.44				
II (In Israel)	4,633	28.46	12.29	59.25				
Poland	1,310	28.57	13.49	57.94				
	223	27.7	13.0	59.3				
Average	5,451	28.53	12.48	58.99	12,384	27.31	14.81	57.88
Rumania								
Maramures	211	31.77	19.16	49.07	271	34.14	18.18	47.68
Yasi	1,135	25.47	12.14	62.39	2,740	25.58	10.03	64.39
Wallachia					1,278	27.67	13.67	58.66
Bucharest	2,266	32.31	14.48	53.25	2,593	27.25	12.42	60.33
Unspecified	329	29.07	12.10	58.83	1,031	28.12	13.65	58.23
Rumania	1,233	29.59	11.96	59.35				
Average	3,941	29.96	13.84	56.20	78,359	30.22	12.97	56.81

343

Table 1. ABO Frequencies (Continued)

Europe (Continued)	Jews				Non-Jews				
	No.	p	q	r	No.	p	q	r	
Russia									
Leningrad	104	27.99	14.55	57.46	1,700	28.79	17.60	53.61	Soldiers
Leningrad					1,000	24.82	16.50	58.68	Ukraine
Moscow	371	24.74	15.74	59.52	2,200	26.0	16.2	57.8	Russia
Moscow					2,740	25.3	16.0	58.7	Russia
White Russia	116	26.54	18.70	54.76	1,448	24.7	13.8	61.5	Russia
White Russia	297	29.82	13.71	56.47	131	28.34	12.59	59.09	Ukraine
White Russia Average	764	28.75	13.21	58.04	1,994	24.77	13.42	61.81	Russ. & Ukr.
Russia	576	27.99	13.36	58.65					Russia
Russia	133	27.8	13.2	58.9					Russia
Russia									
Irkutsk, Siberia	217	28.82	14.68	56.50					
Average	2,582	23.84	13.66	62.50	24,869	24.55	17.76	57.69	
Ukraine									
Kharkov I	108	29.4	19.3	51.3	2,075	27.3	16.2	56.5	Soldiers
Kharkov II	243	27.0	11.2	61.8	310	24.08	13.65	62.27	Ukraine
					808	27.98	17.36	54.66	Russia
					822	25.81	16.39	57.80	Russia
Kherson	322	25.72	13.27	61.01	665	25.04	15.09	59.87	Russia
Dnetropetrovsk	114	31.63	17.53	50.84	312	29.52	18.30	52.18	Ukraine
Odessa I	1,475	27.78	11.52	60.70	2,120	23.7	15.9	60.4	Russ. & Ukr.
Odessa II	529	33.31	9.87	56.82	264	26.40	16.28	57.32	Russia
					513	27.16	16.14	56.70	Russia
Average	3,174	28.70	12.43	58.87	10,492	26.52	15.62	57.86	

344

Table 1. ABO Frequencies (Continued)

Europe (Continued)	Jews				Non-Jews				
	No.	p	q	r	No.	p	q	r	
Karaites									
Lith. & Ukraine		16.43	20.23	63.34					
Troki, Lithua.		9.50	23.30	67.20					
Vilna		12.87	21.83	65.30					
Egypt	250	7.2	34.5	57.7					
Krimchaks									
Ukraine		27.16	25.93	46.91					
United States						28.29	7.49	64.22	
Sephardim									
Yugoslavia	500	21.39	15.36	63.25	20,000	29.25	12.42	58.33	Belgrade
Radevina, Serbs					691	24.07	12.03	63.90	
Serbs					6,863	28.82	13.77	57.41	
Croats	105	28.11	15.75	56.14	2,060	28.13	12.91	58.96	
Average					58,632	28.59	12.70	58.71	
Sephardim									
I	1,107	22.7	15.4	61.9					
II	158	19.5	16.4	64.1					
From Balkans only mainly Turkey & Bulgaria (In Israel)	200	32.15	13.68	54.17					
Bulgaria	283	33.92	15.34	50.74					

Table 1. ABO Frequencies (Continued)

Sephardim (Continued)	Jews				Non-Jews				
	No.	p	q	r	No.	p	q	r	
Spain									
Catalonia					6,428	29.20	6.12	64.68	
					11,628	28.6	5.0	66.4	
Italy									
North & Central					11,227	27.5	7.6	64.9	
South					220	22.01	9.07	68.92	
Portugal					9,830	30.73	6.11	63.16	
Greece									
I					10,000	25.34	10.45	64.21	
II					6,378	24.27	9.26	66.47	
Athens					21,635	24.80	9.37	65.83	
Asia									
Georgia									
Tbilisi	1,983	30.58	17.36	52.06					
					1,791	20.93	4.09	74.98	Svani
					1,549	19.54	12.46	68.00	Osetini
					512	19.01	13.22	67.77	Lezgini
					707	19.30	3.32	77.38	Azerbaijan
					134	23.75	13.64	62.61	Georg, East
					245	18.12	7.39	74.49	Georg, West
					1,838	17.41	5.86	76.73	Guribi
					2,916	20.89	6.88	72.33	Imeretini

Table 1. ABO Frequencies (Continued)

Asia (Continued)	Jews				Non-Jews				
	No.	p	q	r	No.	p	q	r	
Georgia									
Tbilisi (continued)					1,274	28.01	11.11	60.88	Kakhetinitsi
					4,268	27.34	9.02	63.64	Kartatintsi
					20,425	22.71	8.43	68.86	Average For all Caucasus pops.
India									
Cochin	106	5.34	8.39	86.27					
	120	10.1	12.4	77.5					
Cochin (In Israel)	275	10.12	16.83	73.05	132	15.94	9.06	75.00	
Cochin	441	11.57	14.32	74.11	493	19.00	14.39	66.61	
Bombay (Bene/Israel)	200	17.30	20.03	62.07					
Iran									
I	436	23.65	18.84	57.51					
II (In Israel)	200	26.37	18.59	55.04	565	23.8	14.4	61.8	Yazd, Central Iran
III (In Tbilisi)	132	33.03	17.20	49.77	307	20.09	24.06	55.85	
IV	116	37.0	22.4	44.5					
	154	24.38	17.84	57.78					
Average	768	25.87	18.50	55.63	14,285	22.65	16.03	61.32	
Iraq									
Baghdad I	210	30.24	20.80	48.96		21.45	19.49	59.06	Baghdad Muslims
Baghdad II	215	30.66	19.59	49.75					
Baghdad/Israel	162	30.09	20.60	49.31	493	21.15	18.98	59.87	Iraq Arabs
Average	587	30.35	20.29	49.36	1,673	21.24	17.39	61.73	
	1,147	30.19	21.72	48.09					
Iraq. Karaites	72	22.5	34.6	42.9					

Table 1. ABO Frequencies (Continued)

Asia (Continued)	Jews					Non-Jews			
	No.	p	q	r		No.	p	q	r
Kurdistan									
Hills	129	32.02	16.76	51.22	Iraq	1,500	25.29	18.73	55.98
In Israel I	147	31.03	14.08	54.89	Azerbaijan	157	26.49	14.46	59.05
In Israel II	250	36.00	14.04	49.96	Persia	148	21.58	14.18	64.24
In Israel III		32.0	16.8	51.2	Average	1,904	24.81	17.80	57.39
Lebanon									
Beirut	181	29.92	20.13	49.95	Muslims	1,777	26.30	15.31	58.39
					Christians	2,091	29.12	10.38	60.50
Saudi Arabia					Central		14.37	12.12	73.50
					East		12.01	14.99	73.00
					SW		11.42	4.12	84.46
					Bedouin	178	17.19	10.36	72.45
					Total	1,384	13.44	12.37	74.19
S. Sinai Towara						202	16.48	9.36	74.16
S. Sinai Jebeliya						95	12.35	26.03	61.62
Habban	595	14.93	21.34	63.73					
Samaritans									
Israel	132	11.47	6.27	82.26					
		15.55	7.59	76.86					
Nablus, Beirut	83	21.2	7.7	71.1					

Table 1. ABO Frequencies (Continued)

Asia (Continued)	Jews				Non-Jews				
	No.	p	q	r	No.	p	q	r	
Syria									
Aleppo	172	23.66	15.03	61.31	933	24.93	14.80	60.27	Arabs
Aleppo & Damas.	104	22.06	16.72	60.69					
Christians					2,091	28.7	9.8	61.4	
Moslems					1,777	26.0	14.9	59.1	
Druzes					229	27.1	15.2	57.6	
Jews	181	28.2	18.2	53.5					
Syria and Lebanon	204	25.72	14.57	59.71					
Turkey									
Mersin	297	29.84				28.55	14.97	56.47	Turks
Mersin						30.54	8.88	60.58	Eti-Turks
Turks in Georgia					300	27.86	20.93	51.21	
Central Asia									
Samarkand	616	20.82	21.65	57.53	237	20.64	22.56	56.80	Persians
Samarkand	514	23.9	24.7	53.8	500	21.40	31.28	57.32	
Bukhara I	153	31.64	24.41	43.95	2,192	26.49	18.46	55.05	Turkomans
Bukhara II	1,000	24.14	19.83	56.03	994	25.10	17.48	57.42	Uzbekistan
Bukhara III		27.74	20.62	51.64					
in Israel	121	21.47	22.54	55.99	228	23.65	21.91	54.46	Uzbekistan
Average	1,274	24.74	20.62	54.64	1,172	25.50	26.94	47.56	Kazakhstan
Yemen I	1,000	15.14	9.42	75.44	269	17.53	6.73	75.74	
In Israel	500	18.50	9.11	72.39					
In Israel	200	19.06	8.90	72.04					
In Israel	104	26.60	6.47	66.92					
Average	1,902	17.37	9.51	73.12					
	374	19.54							

Table 1. ABO Frequencies (Continued)

	Jews				Non-Jews				
	No.	*p*	*q*	*r*	*No.*	*p*	*q*	*r*	
Asia (Continued)									
Armenia									
Turkey	297	29.84	16.29	53.87	3,080	34.7	12.3	53.0	
Africa									
Algeria									
Oran I	1,445	21.47	15.50	63.03	300	23.96	12.50	63.54	
Oran II	205	19.17	18.57	62.26	1,529	20.0	12.6	67.4	
					1,829	20.65	12.60	66.75	Average
Egypt I	536	25.11	17.23	25.23	144	24.4	21.5	54.1	
Egypt II					130	32.0	22.5	45.5	
Egypt Karaites	250	7.2	34.5	57.7					
Ethiopia									
Falashas		24.	10.	66.	400	15.57	16.81	65.52	Unspec.
					808	15.54	9.64	74.82	Unspec.
					104	22.74	15.61	64.26	Amharas
					878	19.23	16.51	64.26	Soldiers
Libya	100	22.67	16.42	60.91		20.44	11.65	67.91	Unspec.
		30.16	16.40	53.44					
Tripolitania	200	21.09	16.45	62.46					

Table 1. ABO Frequencies (Continued)

Africa (Continued)	Jews				Non-Jews				
	No.	p	q	r	No.	p	q	r	
Morocco									
I	642	24.59	14.72	60.69	1,057	20.51	13.52	65.97	Women
II	730	24.70	14.55	60.75	527	24.47	14.22	61.31	Arabs
in Israel I	220	23.87	15.69	60.44	22,902	19.35	15.62	65.03	Arabs
in Israel II	160	23.07	14.74	62.19	4,947	25.3	11.7	63.0	Berbers
in Israel III	856	20.48	17.74	61.78	8,282	19.27	8.97	71.76	Berbers
Rabat		19.62	18.75	61.63	1,863	19.42	11.22	69.36	Rabat
Average	2,697	22.66	16.44	60.90	51,417	19.56	12.91	67.53	Average
	426	17.99	20.85	61.17	256	6.46	4.40	89.14	Ait Haddidu Berbers
Tunisia									
I	200	24.33	14.85	60.82	543	23.31	11.73	65.06	Moslems
In Israel	200	21.15	15.91	62.94	500	21.08	11.20	67.72	
Average	400	22.79	15.43	61.78					
	99	26.57	15.19	58.24					
Jerba									
"Sephardim" from N. Africa, Bulgaria, and Greece	252	22.93	14.67	62.40	148	26.03	9.21	64.76	Berbers
					400	20.81	9.13	70.06	Unspec.
North Africa		22.15	15.95	61.90					
Sahara Desert									
Northern Haratin					202	32.6	24.8	44.5	
Southern Haratin					267	26.7	21.6	53.8	

Table 1. ABO Frequencies (Continued)

Africa (Continued)	*Jews*				*Non-Jews*			
	No.	*p*	*q*	*r*	*No.*	*p*	*q*	*r*
Sahara Desert (Continued)								
Teda					140	13.5	6.8	80.2
Ajjer Tuareg					89	8.8	7.1	84.1
Ahaggar Tuareg					73	20.0	5.3	74.9
Moors					260	15.8	15.4	67.4
Zenata					212	15.3	13.1	72.4
Fezzanese					592	18.0	13.1	68.9
Chaamba					312	19.1	18.3	63.5

(Sources listed in note 1 to chapter XII. The "Jewish" Blood: ABO.)

Table 2. P_1, P_2, Q, and R Frequencies in Selected Populations

Jews

Europe:	No.	P_1	P_2	q	r
Ashkenazim					
Austria	187	25.14	10.23	8.99	56.69
Czechoslovakia	380	18.52	5.83	10.97	64.57
Germany	514	20.26	6.24	13.13	60.37
	101	20.4	5.1	14.4	60.1
Hungary	273	20.80	6.93	11.37	60.90
Poland	1,310	22.73	5.84	13.49	57.94
	223	20.8	6.9	13.0	59.3
Rumania	1,233	22.43	7.16	11.96	59.35
Russia	576	21.78	6.21	13.36	58.65
	133	20.9	6.9	13.2	58.9
Sephardim					
Yugoslavia	105	22.84	5.27	15.75	56.14
Bulgaria	283	28.75	5.17	15.34	50.74
Turkey	297	23.87	5.97	16.29	53.87
Asia					
India, Cochin	120	9.2	0.9	12.4	77.5
India, Bene Israel	200	16.09	1.21	20.03	62.67
Iran	154	17.01	7.37	17.84	57.78
Iran, Kurdish	94	22.63	5.66	21.39	50.32
Iraq	1,147	27.41	2.78	21.72	48.09
Iraq	188	29.4	4.7	18.4	47.5
Karaites, Iraq	72	4.3	18.3	34.6	42.9

Non-Jews

	No.	P_1	P_2	q	r
Europe					
Germany	100,000	19.77	6.83	7.95	65.45
Hungary	1,324	23.39	7.63	14.59	54.37
Poland	2,000	21.84	4.85	16.73	56.38
Italy, Rome	2,000	17.79	6.80	8.89	66.52
Spain	859	24.72	4.79	6.60	63.89
Spain, Basques	113	16.45	13.18	3.59	66.78
Yugoslavia	10,038	22.00	4.60	11.99	61.41
Yugoslavia, Gypsies	350	20.75	12.49	8.46	58.30
Asia					
U.S.S.R., Georgia	359	20.18	2.66	7.23	69.93
Turkey	108	21.77	6.77	14.94	56.52
Iran	348	15.07	2.92	17.08	64.93
Iran, Kurds	127	15.36	7.76	16.66	60.22
Iraq	99	16.47	3.06	18.26	62.21
Saudia Arabia, Shia	465	8.45	3.60	14.98	72.97
Yemen, Aden, Arabs	110	10.07	6.26	7.52	76.15
India, Kerala	190	11.48	2.43	15.44	70.65
Africa					
Libya	6,000	20.36	3.28	12.96	63.40
Morocco	300	13.07	3.94	11.13	71.86

Table 2. P_1, P_2, Q, and R Frequencies in Selected Populations (Continued)

Asia (Continued)	No.	Jews P_1	P_2	q	r
Iraq, Kurdish	50	10.61	1.12	25.17	63.10
Lebanon & Syria	204	21.52	4.20	14.57	59.71
Yemen	374	11.63	7.91	5.64	74.83
Karaites, Egypt	250	3.5	3.7	34.5	57.7
Aden (Yemen)	127	13.99	10.22	13.06	62.73
Africa					
Algeria	1,445	18.29	3.18	15.50	63.03
Egypt	536	19.58	5.53	17.23	57.69
Ethiopia, Falasha	152	18.10	6.27	10.06	65.67
Libya	100	28.03	2.12	16.40	53.45
	148	31.62	3.55	10.32	54.51
Morocco	426	15.72	2.27	20.85	61.18
	191	16.69	2.50	21.50	59.31

Source: See note 1, chapter XII, The "Jewish" Blood: ABO.

Table 3. Frequencies of MN Allele M

Jews

	Number	M (in %)
Europe		
Ashkenazim		55.53
		63.5
		52.0
Austria	187	58.0
Czechoslovakia	377	61.1
Germany	513	54.0
		57.1
Hungary	271	55.0
Poland	1,305	55.4
Rumania	1,221	57.2
Russia	577	59.0
Sephardim		50.0
Bulgaria	283	55.1
Turkey	297	56.7
Yugoslavia	105	55.7
Asia		
Aden	127	72.8
Baghdad		60.0
Kurdistan	120	52.9
		66.4
Iran	152	59.2
	147	56.9
		50.0
Iraq	1,142	56.3
	188	57.2

Non-Jews

	Number	M (in %)
Europe		
Austria	240	54.79
Czechoslovakia	4,038	53.79
Poland	3,100	59.65
Hungary	15,000	56.77
Romania	366	62.57
Russia, Caucasus	641	59.05
Bulgaria	1,000	55.45
Yugoslavia	410	56.71
Asia		
Turkey	1,266	56.91
Iran, Teheran	256	63.48
Iraq, Baghdad	387	60.47
Lebanon, Druze	203	53.69
Syria, Bedouins	304	74.51
Yemen		74.78
Saudi Arabia, Sunni		69.06
India, Calcutta	1,123	56.90
India, Bombay	200	59.00

355

Table 3. Frequencies of MN Allele M (Continued)

	Jews		Non-Jews	
Asia (Continued)	Number	M(in %)	Number	M(in %)
Iraq-Karaites	72	98.1		
(Karaites, Lithuania)	51	69.6		
Lebanon & Syria	203	54.7		
Yemen	500	75.6		
	104	75.5		
	374	79.0		
Habbanites	553	78.5		
Samaritans	131	40.1		
		39.8		
Cochin, India	275	60.0		
	120	65.0		
Africa			*Africa*	
Morocco	220	55.9	Algeria	316	50.16
	423	63.1	Egypt, Cairo	502	52.29
	196	63.0	Libya	700	48.57
Tunisia	200	55.5	Morocco, Berbers	178	17.98
	98	58.2	Morocco, Arabs	135	53.33
Egypt	534	58.2	Tunisia	532	51.03
Libya	99	64.6		
	148	57.4		

Source: See note 1, chapter XIII, The "Jewish" Blood: Other Blood Groups.

Table 4. Rh Gene Frequencies (in percentages)

Population	"Med." CDe	"N. Eur." cDE	"Afr." cDe	cde	other
European Jews					
Ashkenazim	52.23	11.10	5.25	30.64	0.78
Canada	45.10	12.68	4.63	36.01	1.58
Austria	53.44	11.46	5.43	26.33	2.64
Czechoslovakia	49.25	14.42	9.45	24.80	2.08
Germany	51.35	13.19	7.88	25.73	1.85
Hungary	48.16	12.34	8.06	29.48	1.96
Poland	52.11	13.17	4.92	28.22	1.58
Rumania	50.55	12.80	5.67	29.38	1.60
Russia	51.90	12.71	7.36	26.51	1.52
	50.42	12.60	7.89	28.64	0.45
Sephardim	49.0	6.53	8.87	34.47	1.13
Bulgaria	50.00	13.64	7.65	26.43	2.28
Turkey	52.20	9.47	10.12	25.59	2.62
Yugoslavia	45.79	12.93	10.77	28.21	2.3
European Non-Jews					
Austria	47.29	13.31	2.36	36.47	0.57
Poland	41.43	15.97	1.38	37.50	4.02
England	43.07	13.65	2.83	38.85	1.60
Germany	43.90	13.71	2.57	37.80	2.02
Greece	45.11	7.31	5.64	35.41	6.52
Italy, Ferrara	52.70	11.45	2.61	25.44	7.80
Spain (Madrid)	51.67	9.11	3.32	35.74	0.55
Spain (Aragon)	44.07	10.48	3.18	37.11	5.16

Table 4. Rh Gene Frequencies (Continued)

Population	"Med." CDe	"N. Eur." cDE	"Afr." cDe	cde	other
European Non-Jews (Continued)					
Trieste	46.89	9.13	1.79	36.64	5.55
Yugoslavia	42.65	13.79	4.02	37.42	2.12
Asian Jews					
U.S.S.R. (Bukhara)	42.2	9.1	12.2	33.7	2.8
U.S.S.R. (Georgia)	55.8	18.9	0	24.0	1.3
Iraq, Baghdad	53.5	15.8	4.1	19.8	6.8
Iraq	52.03	16.43	3.74	25.02	2.78
Iraq	55.42	15.07	4.68	19.75	5.08
Iraq, Karaites	22.9	3.5	20.9	52.7	0
Iran	60.5	10.9	6.0	22.7	0
Iran	56.69	16.66	2.61	22.18	1.86
Iran	51.3	21.9	4.1	20.9	1.8
Yemen	56.1	7.9	6.4	28.2	1.4
Kurdistan	45.55	10.44	7.47	32.63	3.91
Kurdistan	37.24	20.27	15.75	21.51	6.23
Syria & Lebanon	53.0	17.9	5.2	15.0	8.9
Syria & Lebanon	48.46	11.74	7.06	28.54	4.2
Oriental Jews	46.75	9.26	5.76	37.25	0.97
India, Cochin	41.5	5.0	6.2	44.4	2.9
India, Cochin	47.1	9.1	2.8	40.2	0.8
Habbanites	41.34	1.17	29.32	23.61	4.56
Samaritans	42.81	8.71	5.62	42.86	0

Table 4. Rh Gene Frequencies (Continued)

Population	"Med." CDe	"N. Eur." cDE	"Afr." cDe	cde	other
Asian Non-Jews					
Iraq (Baghdad)	43.74	15.18	9.77	28.60	2.91
Iran	41.5	11.10	4.43	39.31	3.60
	42.1	5.2	10.7	32.3	9.6
Lebanon, Druze	52.19	10.13	5.66	32.02	0
Lebanon, Sunni,	51.62	10.52	9.39	27.40	1.07
Saudi Arabia (all)	41.69	14.22	12.03	24.37	7.69
Bedouin	40.38	16.57	13.86	27.99	1.20
Sunni	42.47	11.24	13.24	28.79	4.46
S. Sinai Towara	26.07	9.01	10.19	52.43	2.30
S. Sinai Jebeliya	48.09	17.13	1.31	32.03	1.45
India, Calcutta	63.76	1.64	4.60	32.03	2.12
India, Kerala	77.57	8.20	3.24	0	10.99
North African Jews					
Egypt	49.90	12.31	6.55	27.06	4.18
Libya	51.69	2.32	4.08	40.06	1.85
	49.38	4.73	6.01	37.23	2.65
Morocco	53.40	6.34	9.45	30.80	0
	48.42	9.25	7.89	31.67	2.77
	55.53	9.62	10.51	22.47	1.87
Tripolitania	43.0	7.8	9.5	36.4	3.3
Tunisia	56.09	6.58	8.47	28.45	0.41
	51.32	6.63	8.26	32.05	1.74

Table 4. Rh Gene Frequencies (Continued)

Population	"Med." CDe	"N. Eur." cDE	"Afr." cDe	cde	other
North African Non-Jews					
Algeria, Arab tribe	21.57	7.61	48.40	21.39	1.03
Algeria, Arab tribe	55.89	6.77	14.51	22.83	0
Algeria, Arabs	33.09	5.69	29.19	30.44	1.59
Egyptian Arabs	46.48	13.70	23.89	15.37	0.53
Libya	41.2	13.3	11.0	32.9	1.60
Morocco, Arabs	22.51	7.33	35.55	33.61	0
Morocco, Arabs	31.34	11.82	23.71	33.13	0
Tunisia	39.99	11.38	15.05	32.20	1.38

Source: See note 1, chapter XIII, The "Jewish" Blood: Other Blood Groups.

Table 5. Frequency of Kell Allele K

Jews

Population	Number	K Frequency (%)
European		
Ashkenazim		
Austria	187	6.07
Czechoslovakia	378	8.14
Germany	513	7.49
	93	7.25
Hungary	271	8.28
Poland	1,304	6.46
Rumania	1,227	6.92
Russia	577	5.34
East European	171	4.09
Sephardim		
Bulgaria	283	3.05
Turkey	297	4.83
Yugoslavia	105	5.89
Asian		
U.S.S.R., Georgia	134	4.3
U.S.S.R., Bukhara	113	7.7
Iran	152	12.27
Iran	159	13.2
Iraq	1,146	6.21
Iraq	188	6.12
Karaites, Iraq	72	9.48

Non-Jews

Population	Number	K Frequency (%)
European		
Austria	1,303	4.23
Czechoslovakia	418	5.03
Germany	10,000	3.93
Germany	3,000	3.96
Hungary	835	5.29
Hungary	400	3.56
Poland	1,000	5.82
Poland	6,000	5.15
Romania	200	6.19
Russia, Moscow	5,617	4.16
Russia, Ukraine	392	4.59
Greece	479	5.03
	382	3.46
Italy, Florence	4,521	3.09
Italy, Verona	374	5.07
Spain	97	5.29
Asian		
Turkey	116	5.31
Iran	302	3.20
Iran, Kurds	127	5.67
Jordan, Druze	53	2.87
Lebanon, Druze	151	3.03
Saudi Arabia, Bedouin	175	10.56
Saudi Arabia, Shi'ite	465	3.17

Table 5. Frequency of Kell Allele K (Continued)

Population	Jews Number	K Frequency (%)	Population	Non-Jews Number	K Frequency (%)
Asian (Continued)			*Asian (Continued)*		
Lebanon & Syria	203	3.51	Afghanistan	118	1.69
Middle East	124	5.24	Palestine, Arabs	88	1.70
Aden, Yemen	127	3.20	S. Yemen, Arabs	236	5.08
Yemen	374	2.03	India, South	100	0
	117	3.85	India, Bombay	100	0
	202	1.75			
Habban	580	0.43			
India, Cochin	120	0.00			
			African		
African			Algeria	223	1.58
Egypt, Sudan	533	4.31	Algeria	291	2.26
Libya	99	5.72	Tunisia	47	6.60
	148	3.09			
Morocco	423	6.35			
	196	7.15			
Tunisia	98	2.58			
Tunisia, Djerba	27	0.00			
North Africa	109	5.96			

Source: See note 1, chapter XIII, The "Jewish" Blood: Other Blood Groups.

Table 6. Frequency of Duffy Allele Fyᵃ

	Jews			Non-Jews	
Population	Number	Frequency of Fyᵃ	Population	Number	Frequency of Fyᵃ
European			*European*		
Ashkenazim			Austria	113	38.32
Austria	187	45.28	Czechoslovakia	539	51.65
Czechoslovakia	378	42.04	Czechoslovakia	600	38.90
Germany	512	41.87	Poland	1,244	42.24
Hungary	271	43.67	Hungary	835	39.07
Poland	1,305	44.50	U.S.S.R., Moscow	1,445	49.53
Rumania	1,226	42.88			
Russia	577	44.77	Italy	500	42.38
			Spain	97	39.93
Sephardim			Turkey	116	42.76
Bulgaria	283	42.37	Spain, Basques	116	25.15
Turkey	297	41.68			
Yugoslavia	105	53.20			
			Asian		
Asian			U.S.S.R., Armenians	418	43.38
U.S.S.R., Georgia	134	53.1	Iran	78	37.98
U.S.S.R., Bukhara	113	48.6	Iran	348	43.02
Aden	127	33.01	Iran, Kurds	127	45.30
Iran	152	47.43	Iraq, Assyrians	99	75.38
	158	39.4	Jordan, Druze	68	44.43
Iran, Kurdish	106	53.42	Lebanon, Shi'iah	75	29.76
Iraq	1,146	42.87	Saudi Arabia, Bedouins	175	26.31
	188	47.87	Saudi Arabia, Shi'iah	465	4.51
	184	48.10			

Table 6. Frequency of Duffy Allele Fy^a (Continued)

Population	Jews Number	Frequency of Fy^a	Population	Non-Jews Number	Frequency of Fy^a
Asian (Continued)			*Asian (Continued)*		
Iraq, Karaites	72	51.41	Saudi Arabi, Sunni	173	15.34
Lebanon & Syria	203	41.70	India, Bombay	196	45.6
Yemen	374	23.65			
	92	21.98			
	168	21.82			
India, Cochin	118	67.1			
Samaritans	128	46.97			
Habban (Yemen)	496	25.11			
Samaritans	124	46.37			
African			*African*		
Egypt	533	35.75	Algeria	82	19.61
Libya	99	40.54	Algeria	149	17.66
	148	44.60	Morocco	256	25.78
Morocco	423	35.68	Libya	165	39.0
	191	29.06			
Tunisia	98	36.11			

Table 7. Duffy Gene Frequencies

Population	Jews No.	Fy^a	Fy^b	Fy^c	Population	Non-Jews No.	Fy^a	Fy^b	Fy^c
Central Europe	110	41.68	51.98	6.30	Europe & U.S. whites		00		
Eastern Europe	160	50.60	46.94	2.46	Iran, Kurds	77	51.50	31.75	16.75
S. Europe (Bulgaria, Yugoslavia, Turkey)	129	39.68	38.40	21.91	Yemen, Arabs	236	10.47	12.62	76.91
Middle East	118	35.43	53.72	10.83	Egypt, Towara Bedouins	200	16.89	35.94	37.17
Iran, Kurdish	94	50.16	34.64	15.20	Egypt, Jebeliya Bedouins	95	23.86	16.62	59.52
Iraq, Kurdish	27	40.4	37.4	22.1	Ethiopia	174	22.79	21.33	55.88
Yemen	75	16.57	6.84	76.6	Sudan	97	12.71	8.65	78.65
Yemen	117	19.27	21.94	58.79	Uganda	236	1.06	1.92	97.02
Yemen, Habbanites	496	25.11	16.70	58.19					
North Africa (Morocco)	105	37.56	46.71	15.73					

Source: See note 1, chapter XIII, The "Jewish" Blood: Other Blood Groups.

Table 8. Frequency of Kidd Allele Jk^a

	Jews			Non-Jews	
Population	Number	Jk*a* Frequency (%)	Population	Number	Jk*a* Frequency (%)
European			**European**		
Ashkenazim			Austria	557	51.89
Austria	187	65.70	Germany	1,010	50.50
Czechoslovakia	376	60.05	Poland	395	42.19
Germany	511	62.72	U.S.S.R., Moscow	728	55.37
Hungary	271	61.58			
Poland	1,305	59.60	Italy	300	51.70
Rumania	1,226	56.03			
Russia	577	60.73			
Sephardim					
Bulgaria	283	59.25			
Turkey	297	52.15			
Yugoslavia	105	58.60			
Asian			**Asian**		
U.S.S.R., Bukhara	113	70.5	Palestine Arabs	89	57.60
U.S.S.R., Georgia	134	52.2	U.S.S.R., Caucasus	159	43.36
Aden	127	62.35	Yemen	218	53.07
Iran	152	62.83			
Iraq	1,145	56.87			
	186	39.09			
Lebanon & Syria	203	55.06			
Yemen	373	55.46			
Cochin	118	40.1			

Table 8. Frequency of Kidd Allele Jk^a (Continued)

Population	Jews Number	Jk^a Frequency (%)	Population	Non-Jews Number	Jk^a Frequency (%)
African			*African*		
Egypt	533	56.25	Egypt, Towara Bedouins	162	47.88
Libya	99	52.86	Egypt, Jebeliya Bedouins	63	32.15
	148	38.49			
Morocco	423	54.91			
	188	40.30			
Tunisia	98	46.55			

Source: See note 1, chapter XIII, The "Jewish" Blood: Other Blood Groups.

Table 9. Frequencies of Haptoglobin Allele HP[1]

Jews

Population	Number	Hp[1]	Source Reference*
Ashkenazim	499	.29	44
Ashkenazim	170	.34	76
Poland	181	.28	44
Poland	105	.376	61
Poland	214	.320	15
German	101	.320	15
Russian	131	.298	15
Sephardim (Bulgaria, Greece, Italy, Yugosl.)	44	.375	44
U.S.S.R., Bukhara	113	.277	62
U.S.S.R., Georgia	134	.394	62
Near East (Turkey, Syria, Lebanon, Egypt)	48	.26	44
Oriental (N. Afr, Iraq, Kurdistan, Iran, Yemen)	345	.26	44
Yemen	41	.25	44
Kurdistan	42	.25	44
Kurdistan	113	.36	76
Iraq	79	.25	44
Iraq	118	.29	76
Iraq	160	.258	17
Iraq, Karaites	69	.283	45
Iraq, NW, Kurdish	50	.343	95

Non-Jews

Population	Number	Hp[1]	Source Reference*
Austria	714	.378	53
Czechoslovakia	1,320	.387	35
Czechoslovakia	981	.370	57
Czechoslovakia	662	.409	49
Poland	3,809	.38	36
Hungary	10,000	.363	78
Northern Germany	224	.351	83
U.S.S.R., Caucasus	141	.350	99
Yugoslavia	75	.332	33
Yugoslavia	459	.37	36
Bulgaria	136	.379	100
Turkey	299	.313	30
Greece	1,311	.35	36
Italy	285	.37	84
Southern Italy	877	.36	36
Spain	2,763	.40	36
Iran Moslem	429	.28	36
Iran Zoroastrian	145	.19	36
Iran Qashqai	117	.33	36
Israeli Moslems	69	.265	44
S. Yemen	254	.450	64
Egypt, Towara Bedouins	198	.429	14
Egypt, Jebeliya Bedouins	95	.210	14

Table 9. Frequencies of Haptoglobin Allele HP[1] (Continued)

	Jews				Non-Jews			
Population	Number	Hp[1]	Source Reference*	Population	Number	Hp[1]	Source Reference*
Iraq, SE, Kurdish	106	.270	34	India, Calcutta	456	.162	71
Kurdistan	113	.365	76	India, Bombay	200	.185	7
Kurdistan	96	.308	34	Liberia	356	.70	72
Iran	91	.30	76				
Iran	158	.304	27				
Iran	101	.29	34				
Habbanites	589	.214	17				
Yemen	202	.332	11				
Samaritans	125	.396	12				
North Africa	119	.28	44				
North Africa	104	.29	76				
Libya	148	.240	16				
Morocco	191	.283	18				
India, Cochin	118	.18	26				

* The numbers in these columns in Tables 9–17 refer to the numbered list of sources which follow Table 28.

369

Table 10. Frequencies of Selected Gm Haplotypes

Haplotype 1 = 3, 5, 10, 11, 13, 14, 26
Haplotype 2 = 1, 17, 21, 26
Haplotype 3 = 1, 2, 17, 21, 26
Haplotype 4 = 1, 5, 10, 11, 13, 14, 17, 26
Haplotype 5 = 1, 10, 11, 13, 15, 16, 17
Haplotype 6 = 1, 3, 5, 10, 11, 13, 14, 16

Haplotype	Armenian	Jews Libyan	Ashkenazi
1	.687	.563	.730
2	.242	.332	.164
3	.040	.051	.058
4	.008	.023	.015
6	.000	.000	.021

Population	No.	Haplotype 1	2	3
Ashkenazi Jews	248	.798	.138	.046
	507	.758	.179	.049
	237	.730	.164	.058
Czechoslovakia	41	.854	.108	.026
U.S.S.R.	167	.808	.131	.031
Germany	119	.777	.188	.03
Hungary	54	.824	.148	.009
Poland	292	.801	.143	.034
Rumania	124	.863	.096	.029

Table 10. Frequencies of Selected Gm Haplotypes (Continued)

| Population | No. | Haplotype | | |
		1	2	3
Ashkenazi Jews (Continued)				
Mixed	442	.803	.147	.034
Armenians	64	.687	.242	.040
Sephardi				
Turkey	48	.708	.187	.062
Egypt	31	.800	.120	.018
Asia (Oriental)				
U.S.S.R., Georgia	134	.773	.118	.038
U.S.S.R., Bukhara	113	.699	.193	.052
Iraq	160	.756	.149	.016
Iran	167	.766	.137	.030
Iran	89	.798	.135	.040
Yemen	42	.575	.272	.039
Iraq, Karaites	60	.767	.233	
Cochin Jews	223	.269	.313	.236
North Africa				
Morocco	269	.738	.178	.018
Tunisia	42	.702	.208	.024

371

Table 10. Frequencies of Selected Gm Haplotypes (Continued)

Summary of Jews and Non-Jews (Source Reference 45)

Population	No.	1	2	3
European Jews	1,372	.810	.142	.030
Non-Jews	1,369	.761	.155	.061
Sephardi Jews	79	.765	.154	.034
Non-Jews	69	.630	.192	.022
Asian Jews	295	.744	.157	.027
Non-Jews	1,548	.710	.166	.019
North African Jews	313	.724	.190	.023
Non-Jews	378	.612	.232	.041

Table 11. Frequencies of Group-Specific Component Allele GC^2

Jews				Non-Jews			
Population	No.	Gc^2	Source Reference	Population	No.	Gc^2	Source Reference
Ashkenazim	99	.338	25	N. Germany	224	.250	83
				SW Germany	958	.247	4
Yemen	49	.194	25	Germany (Berlin)	1,068	.313	63
Kurdistan	42	.190	25	Germany (Berlin)	247	.277	98
Iraq	85	.241	25	SW Germany	747	.222	100
Iran	49	.245	25	Austria	1,000	.279	46
Samaritans	125	.204	12	Poland	1,930	.337	54
North Africa	64	.297	25	Bulgaria	138	.232	100
				Yugoslavia	108	.298	33
				Iran	1,531	.354	5
				Israeli Arabs	48	.260	25

Table 12. Frequencies of Atypical Pseudocholinesterase Allele E_1a

Jews				Non-Jews			
Population	Number	E_1a(%)	Source Reference	Population	Number	E_1a(%)	Source Reference
Ashkenazim	4,196	1.74	90	Germany	952	1.6	1
Balkan & Turkey	674	2.82	90	Germany	137	7.3	68
				Czechoslovakia	312	1.44	1
Iran	159	7.55	90	Portugal	179	1.7	53
Iraq	1,057	4.7	90	Italy	382	2.09	104
Yemen	459	1.9	90	Yugoslavia	94	2.7	33
Lebanon & Syria	203	1.72	90	Yugoslavia, Adriatic	95	1.6	33
				Greece	360	1.81	104
North Africa	1,106	1.45	90	Iran, Arabs	36	1.39	104
Morocco	51	0.98	53	Israel, Arabs	110	9.1	90
				Lebanon & Syria, Kurds	162	6.1	97

Table 13. Red Cell Acid Phosphatase Gene Frequencies

	Jews						Non-Jews				
Population	Number	p^a	p^b	p^c	Source Reference	Population	Number	p^a	p^b	p^c	Source Reference
Europe						*Europe*					
Ashkenazim	479	.25	.72	.03	43	North Germany	210	.36	.50	.04	83
Germany	92	.29	.69	.02	15	Western Germany	3,714	.34	.59	.06	79
Germany	101	.27	.70	.03	15	Germany, Berlin	1,188	.36	.58	.06	73
Poland	214	.28	.67	.07	15	Austria	410	.37	.57	.06	9
Russia	131	.27	.69	.04	15	Czechoslovakia	300	.32	.61	.06	81
East Europe	104	.26	.73	.01	55	Czechoslovakia	307	.36	.58	.06	48
Central Europe	106	.24	.74	.02	55	Poland	1,064	.32	.58	.10	106
Southern Europe	123	.22	.74	.02	55	Spain, Madrid	190	.32	.62	.05	38
						Spain, Andalusia	213	.40	.58	.02	38
						Spain, Galicia	253	.30	.67	.04	38
						Bulgaria	119	.16	.80	.04	3
						Italy (Rome)	417	.26	.66	.08	66
Asia						*Asia*					
Habbanites	314	.02	.95	.03	17	Turkey	274	.29	.68	.03	51
Iraq	82	.34	.64	.02	43	Egypt, Towara	199	.13	.86	.00	14
Iraq	188	.31	.66	.03	17	Egypt, Jebeliya	93	.06	.94	.00	14
Iraq, Karaites	72	.00	.96	.04	45						
Iraq, Kurds, NW	61	.41	.55	.04	95						
Iraq, Kurds, SE	50	.33	.67	.00	95						
Iran, Kurds	107	.37	.59	.04	95						
Iran	49	.37	.61	.02	43						
Iran	157	.34	.63	.03	27						
Kurdistan			.63		43						

Table 13. Red Cell Acid Phosphatase Gene Frequencies (Continued)

| | Jews | | | | | | Non-Jews | | | | |
Population	Number	p^a	p^b	p^c	Source Reference	Population	Number	p^a	p^b	p^c	Source Reference
Asia (Continued)											
India, Cochin	120	.21	.79	.00	26						
Yemen	37	.15	.84	.01	43						
Yemen	88	.20	.72	.07	95						
Yemen	199	.14	.81	.05	11						
Samaritans	37	.07	.93	.00	12						
Africa						**Africa**					
North Africa	137	.22	.75	.03	43	Libyans	165	.14	.85	.01	16
Libya	148	.26	.72	.02	16						
Morocco	196	.22	.73	.04	18						

376

Table 14. Frequencies of Phosphoglucomutase Allele PGM_1^2

	Jews				Non-Jews		
Population	Number	PGM_1^2	Source Reference	Population	Number	PGM_1^2	Source Reference
European				**European**			
Ashkenazim	185	.208	92	Germany, North	224	.228	83
Germany	101	.327	15	Germany (Berlin)	492	.22	80
Poland	214	.291	15	Germany, West	2,357	.226	103
Russia	131	.216	15	Germany, North	4,403	.217	21
East Europe	163	.285	55	Austria	220	.209	47
Central Europe	109	.257	55	Czechoslovakia	320	.219	48
South Europe	129	.283	55				
				Spain (Madrid)	213	.244	38
				Spain (Andalusia)	219	.228	38
				Spain (Galicia)	233	.202	38
				Bulgaria	127	.165	3
				Greece	88	.307	50
				Italy	385	.296	82
Asian				**Asian**			
Middle East	120	.283	55	Cyprus (Turkish)	243	.300	50
Iraq	186	.320	92	Kurdistan	167	.339	97
Iraq, Karaites	70	.293	45	Iran, Kurds	77	.221	59
Iraq, Kurdish, N.W.	61	.164	95	Iran, Kurds	106	.316	59
Iraq, Kurdish, S.E.	50	.300	95	Israeli Arabs	203	.300	92
Iran, Kurdish	106	.226	95	Iran	127	.315	32
Iran, Kurdish	94	.245	37	Lebanon & Syria	167	.332	97
Iran	161	.283	27	S. Yemen Arabs	255	.214	64
Habbanites	297	.576	17	S. Sinai Towara	200	.150	14

Table 14. Frequencies of Phosphoglucomutase Allele PGM_1^2 (Continued)

Jews

Population	Number	PGM_1^2	Source Reference
Asian (Continued)			
Habbanites	222	.570	70
Samaritans	37	.162	12
Yemen	115	.317	55
Yemen	192	.271	92
India, Cochin	120	.362	26
African			
North Africa	107	.318	55
North Africa	183	.303	92
Libya	148	.211	16
Morocco	196	.398	18

Non-Jews

Population	Number	PGM_1^2	Source Reference
Asian (Continued)			
S. Sinai Jebeliya	95	.232	14

Table 15. Frequencies of Adenosine Deaminase Allele ADA²

Jews

Population	Number	ADA²	Source Reference
Ashkenazim	434	.106	91
U.S.S.R., Bukhara	113	.094	62
U.S.S.R., Georgia	134	.105	62
Iran	160	.134	27
Iraq	188	.152	17
Iraq	291	.149	91
Yemen	219	.135	91
India, Cochin	120	.062	26
North Africa	204	.091	91
Morocco	196	.105	18

Non-Jews

Population	Number	ADA²	Source Reference
Austria	250	.062	105
Germany, North	212	.042	83
Germany, Hamburg	1,070	.055	21
Germany, Berlin	302	.076	93
Germany, Stuttgart	435	.062	85
Czechoslovakia	360	.043	89
Poland	609	.060	89
Spain	187	.075	23
Spain, Madrid	160	.034	38
Spain, Andalusia	218	.057	38
Spain, Galicia	234	.049	38
Bulgaria	138	.138	3
Italy, Rome	320	.089	82
Greece	314	.090	29
Turkey	198	.083	23
Iran, Kurds	182	.118	96
Israeli Arabs	138	.112	90

Table 16. Frequencies of Adenylate Kinase Allele Ak²

Jews

Population	Number	Ak²	Source Reference
European			
Ashkenazim	191	.055	92
Germany	101	.089	15
Poland	214	.042	15
Russia	131	.064	15
East Europe	160	.059	55
Central Europe	111	.090	55
Southern Europe	129	.039	55
Middle Eastern			
Middle East	121	.058	55
U.S.S.R., Bukhara	114	.059	62
U.S.S.R., Georgia	134	.034	62
Iraq	139	.047	77
Iraq	190	.029	92
Iraq	188	.035	17
Iraq, Karaites	71	.00	45
Kurdistan	105	.052	92
Iran	160	.031	27
Yemenite	116	.030	55
Yemen	193	.036	92
Yemen	76	.053	37
India, Cochin	120	.138	26

Non-Jews

Population	Number	Ak²	Source Reference
European			
N. Germany	224	.015	83
N. Germany (Hamb.)	2,370	.0338	21
Austria	407	.034	70
Spain	187	.043	23
Spain (Madrid)	203	.039	38
Spain (Andalusia)	218	.048	38
Spain (Galicia)	249	.022	38
Italy (Rome)	841	.037	67
Turkey	274	.042	51
Asia			
Israeli Arabs	202	.025	92
Arabs (Palestine)	86	.035	94
Kurds, Lebanon & Syria	154	.039	97
Kurds, Iran & Iraq	182	.069	95
Iran (Moslems)	322	.050	20
S. Sinai Towara	201	.025	14
S. Sinai Jebeliya	95	.037	14
S. Yemen, Arabs	255	.023	64
India, North	271	.087	28
India, South, Madras	122	.098	93
India, South, Bombay	296	.111	10

Table 16. Frequencies of Adenylate Kinase Allele Ak[2] (Continued)

Jews

Population	Number	Ak[2]	Source Reference
North African			
North Africa	106	.038	55
North Africa	188	.056	92
Libya	148	.024	16
Morocco	196	.031	18

Table 17. Frequencies of Glutamic-Pyruvic Transaminase Allele GPT[2]

Jews

Population	Number	Gpt[2](%)	Source Reference
Ashkenazim	196	40.0	58
Iraq	192	41.1	58
Yemen	190	27.4	58
North Africa	193	32.9	58

Non-Jews

Population	Number	Gpt[2](%)	Source Reference
Germany (Hamburg)	2,023	47.0	22
Germany (Berlin)		31.2	75
SW Germany	304	46.0	66
Spain	184	49.	23
Italy	205	45	23
Greece	98	43.4	24
Turkey	213	46	23
Israeli Arabs	208	41.3	58
Kenya		14.3	24
Congo		25.9	24

Table 18. Frequencies of Esterase D Allele EsD^2

Population	Jews			Population	Non-Jews	
	Number	EsD^2			Number	EsD^2
Ashkenazim	235	.100		European		
				Germany	867	.098
				Great Britain	2,210	.108–.117
Iranian	70	.129			399	.113
Turkish	138	.131				
Balkan	113	.137		Italy	500	.147
Iraqi	213	.178				
Yemenite	156	.212		Israeli Arabs	221	.206
Egyptian	57	.132		Cameroons	92	.055
				Papua	155	.065
				India	278	.227
				Japan	1,066	.342

Source: See notes 40 and 41, chapter XIV, Serum and Red Cell Proteins.

Table 19. Frequencies of Erythrocyte Glyoxalate 1 Allele GLO[1]

| | Jews | | | Non-Jews | |
Population	Number	GLO[1]	Population	Number	GLO[1]
Ashkenazi	191	.301	England	296	.44
			Germany	655	.427
Balkan	145	.310	Holland	757	.454
Turkey	151	.334	Israeli Arabs	205	.295
Yemen	134	.332			
Iran	85	.229	Gambia	506	.28
Iraq	203	.271			
Egypt	63	.396			
North Africa	202	.317			

Source: See note 42, chapter XIV, Serum and Red Cell Proteins.

Table 20. Frequencies of Selected HLA-A Alleles in Jews and Non-Jews

Population	A1	A2	A9	A10	A11	AW19	AW24
Germans	.144	.260	.091	.059	.063	.105	
German Jews	.162	.190	.142	.120	.055	.153	
Poles	.153	.289	.177	.065	.053	.049	
Polish Jews	.144	.144	.145	.135	.065	.197	
Russians	.165	.276	.109	.118	.096	.077	
Russian Jews	.140	.180	.145	.138	.067	.163	
Rumanian Jews	.132	.200	.150	.128	.039	.150	
U.S.S.R., Georgia Jews	.190	.118					
U.S.S.R., Bukhara Jews	.118	.174					
Indians	.111	.168	.000	.000	.137	.000	.149
Cochin Jews	.090	.111	.042	.000	.093	.032	.142
Cochin Jews	.107	.103	.179	.053	.093	.158	
Arabs	.160	.200	.100	.060	.070	.160	
Lebanese	.117	.179	.179	.034	.084	.175	
Turks	.101	.249	.168	.107	.081	.126	
Black Africans	.047	.123	.110	.067	.003	.364	
Armenian Jews	.061	.170	.191	.051	.100	.118	
Yemenite Jews	.128	.170	.307	.024	.023	.186	
Libyan Jews	.152	.161	.138	.089	.110	.123	
Moroccan Jews	.245	.159	.112	.100	.011	.147	
Iraqi Jews	.186	.095	.141	.060	.079	.185	

Source: See notes 8 and 45, chapter XIV, Serum and Red Cell Proteins.

Table 21. Frequencies of Selected HLA-B Alleles in Jews and Non-Jews

Population	B7	B8	B12	B14	BW17	BW35	B blank
Germans	.152	.100	.122	.071	.039	.080	.057
German Jews	.048	.055	.048	.108	.090	.208	.069
Poles	.149	.107	.138	.028	.047	.070	
Polish Jews	.043	.031	.078	.123	.100	.191	.071
Russians	.127	.061	.087	.020	.024	.100	.076
Russian Jews	.042	.038	.057	.106	.077	.191	.054
Rumanian Jews	.024	.044	.062	.136	.075	.175	.038
U.S.S.R., Georgian, Jews	.042		.033	.000		.300	
U.S.S.R., Bukhara, Jews	.124		.105	.032		.140	
Indians	.103	.030	.126	.000	.082	.061	.149
Cochin Jews (B)	.108	.062	.136	.083	.161	.133	.060
Cochin Jews (C)	.111	.069	.137	.074	.148	.140	.024
Arabs	.030	.040	.050	.030	.040	.050	.260
Lebanese	.034	.020	.050	.048	.053	.234	.231
Turks	.030	.043	.078	.022	.040	.152	.126
Black Africans	.094	.038	.083	.044	.181	.068	.314
Armenian Jews	.050	.033	.063	.050	.051	.022	.146
Yemenite Jews	.027	.018	.188	.079	.053	.091	.062
Libyan Jews	.012	.067	.131	.029	.040	.140	.088
Moroccan Jews	.076	.046	.129	.046	.018	.115	.073
Iraqi Jews	.091	.008	.102	.008	.020	.227	.076

Source: See notes 8 and 45, chapter XIV, Serum and Red Cell Proteins.

Table 22. G6PD Deficiency Frequencies in Males

	Jews Number	Jews Percentage		Non-Jews Number	Non-Jews Percentage
Europe			**Europe**		
Ashkenazim (Russia, Poland, Germany)	819	0.37	Scotland	404	0
Ashkenazim	944	1.8	Italy, Ferrara	2,437	1.60
Sephardim: Turkey	256	1.9	Italia, Sardinia		6–30.1
Sephardim: Turkey	234	4.3	Spain, Valencia	504	0.20
Sephardim: Greece & Bulgaria	152	0.66			
Sephardim: Greece & Bulgaria	98	2.0	**Middle East**		
			Turkey, Ankara	1,000	0.50
Asia			Arabs	758	1.45
Kurdistan	196	58.2	Iran	77	6.5
Central		70.0	Iran	107	2.9
South		35.0	Iraq	46	11.4
Kurdistan			Kuwait	211	18.96
Iraqi	234	68.0			
Turkish	42	57.0	**Asia**		
Turkish	167	35.9	India, New Delhi	362	2.7
Persian	20	25.0	India, Kerala	1,372	1.31
Iranian and Iraqi	196	58.2			
Iraq	902	24.8	**Africa**		
Iraq	188	31.1	Algeria	1,397	3.15
Iraq	108	31.1			
Iraq	332	25.3			
Iran	557	15.1			
Iran	138	12.3			
Iran	89	13.5			
Iran	108	12.0			

Table 22. G6PD Deficiency Frequencies in Males (Continued)

	Jews	
	Number	Percentage
Asia (Continued)		
Caucasus	25	28.0
Georgia, U.S.S.R.	80	7.5
Georgia, U.S.S.R.	134	6.0
Bukhara, U.S.S.R.	113	2.2
Afghanistan	29	10.3
Cochin	58	10.3
Cochin	63	3.1
Yemen & Aden	415	5.3
Yemen	313	5.4
Bokhara	46	0
Syria and Lebanon	80	6.3
Syria and Lebanon	23	0
India (B'nai Israel)	102	2.0
India and Pakistan	201	4.5
Samaritans	69	0
North Africa		
Egypt	112	3.8
North Africa	1,786	1.62
Morocco	180	0.5
Algeria and Tunisia	112	0.89
Falashas	298	0
Egyptian Karaites	250	0
	18	0

387

Table 23. PTC Frequencies

Jews

Europe	Sample Size	Percentage of Nontasters
Ashkenazim		
Jews from Poland, W. Russia, Lithuania, Rumania, Hungary, Czechoslovakia	440	20.7
Poland	962	21.5
Bratislava		9.5
Sephardim from the Balkans	101	21.7
Asia		
Samaritans	125	6.4
Kurdish Jews from Iran	129	13.9
Iraq and Iran	336	16.1
Yemen	261	18.0
Cochin (India)	41	31.7
Africa		
Morocco, Tunisia, and Tripolitania	340	15.0
Jerba (Tunisia)	41	41.4

Non-Jews

Europe	Sample Size	Percentage of Nontasters
Hungary	436	32.2
England	952	34.1
England	835	27.5
Norway	266	30.5
Portugal	454	24.0
Spain (NE)	306	24.8
Asia		
Kurds from Iran	346	27.5
Africa		
Nigerians	184	13.7
Bantu	86	2.3

(Sources listed in the notes to chapter XVI, PTC Taste Sensitivity.)

Table 24. Frequencies of Color Blindness

Population	Jews Number	Percent	Population	Non-Jews Number	Percent
Europe			*Europe*		
Ashkenazim	1,604	8.0	Switzerland	2,000	7.95
Ashkenazim	778	9.1	Switzerland	1,000	9.0
Poland	252	8.7	Germany	1,000	7.55
Russia	117	7.7	Belgium	1,243	8.0
Russia	260	5.5	France	1,243	8.6
			Czechoslovakia	955	10.5
Sephardim	253	5.5	Russia	1,343	9.3
			Sardinia	1,990	1.3–12.5
			Greece	1,348	6.4–8.7
Asia			*Asia*		
Turkey	272	5.9	Turkey	473	5.3
Kurdistan (Iran)	508	5.7	Kurdistan (Iran)	504	8.13
Iran	352	5.7	Iran	949	4.5
Iran	206	6.3	Druze	337	10.0
Iraq	2,142	3.9	Israel Arabs	713	10.5
Iraq	245	6.1			
Samaritans	65	27.7			
Habbanites	297	0			
Cochin, India	113	0.9			
Yemen and Aden	115	4.7			
Yemen and Aden	1,128	3.8			

Table 24. Frequencies of Color Blindness (Continued)

Population	Jews Number	Percent	Population	Non-Jews Number	Percent
Africa			*Africa*		
Egypt	162	7.4	Egypt		5.0
N. Africa	618	6.2			
Morocco	184	6.0			
Morocco	226	7.0			
Tunisia	56	3.6			

Source: Mostly from Kalmus *et al.*, François *et al.*, and Adam; see note 1 to chapter XVII, Color Blindness.

Formula Used to Calculate Genetic Distance

The formula used for calculating individual genetic distance is a modified version of the formula used by Cavalli-Sforza, *et al.* * The present formula is:

$$D_i \text{ (individual distance)} = \sqrt{1 - \sum_{a=1}^{M} \sqrt{P_{a1} P_{a2}}} \times 100$$

Where p_{a1} is the frequency of allele a in population 1, p_{a2} is the frequency of the same allele in population 2, and the results are summed over all the alleles. M represents the total number of alleles, which ranges from 2 for the MN and PTC genes to 8 for the Rh gene locus.

The formula for computing the average distance between two populations is:

$$\text{average distance} = \frac{\sqrt{\sum_{i=1}^{N} D_i^2}}{\sqrt{N}} \times 100$$

where D_i is the individual genetic distance between the two populations at a given gene locus i, and the squares of this distance are summed over all loci. N is the total number of loci.

---

* L.L. Cavalli-Sforza, L.A. Zonta, F. Nuzzo, L. Bernini, W. W. W. DeJong, P. Meera Khan, A. K. Ray, L.N. Went, M. Siniscalco, L.E. Nijenhuis, E. van Loghem, and G. Modiano, "Studies on African Pygmies. I. A Pilot Investigation of Babinga Pygmies in the Central African Republic (With an Analysis of Genetic Distances)", *American Journal of Human Genetics*, 1969, 21:252.

Table 25. Genetic Distances Between Non-Jewish Groups

Population A	Population B	Distance	Number of Loci
U.S. Negroes	Chinese	33.3	8
Eskimos	Nigerians	20.5	7
U.S. Whites	Chinese	20.3	10
U.S. Whites	Bantu	20.1	8
Egyptian	English	14.8	5
U.S. Negroes	Bantu	10.1	6
Norwegians	Sicilians	7.3	4
English	Greek	6.4	8
German	Greek	6.3	7
Austrian	French	6.3	8
U.S. Whites	Italian	6.0	11
Danish	Italian	5.4	6
English	Spanish	4.5	7
U.S. Whites	French	4.4	8
Swiss	Yugoslavian	4.1	4
English	French	4.0	8
Danish	German	3.0	8
Danish	Swedish	2.4	6
English	Dutch	2.4	7
U.S. Whites	English	2.3	13

Table 26. Genetic Distances Between Jewish Groups

| | Ashkenazim | | Habbanite | | Samaritan | |
	Distance	No. of loci	Distance	No. of loci	Distance	No. of loci
Habbanite	20.9	5			21.7	6
Samaritan	13.0	7	21.7	6		
Kurdish	9.4	8				
Iraqi	8.1	11				
Oriental	7.9	11			16.6	9
Yemenite	7.9	11				
Moroccan	7.9	3				
Iranian	7.2	8				
Sephardim	6.8	7	17.6	4		
North African	5.2	10	17.0	5		
German	5.0	3			17.4	3
Rumanian	2.4	3				
Russian	2.2	3				
Polish	1.4	4				
East European	1.2	4				

393

Table 27. Genetic Distances Between Jews and Non-Jews

Jewish Group	Non-Jewish Group	Distance	Number of Loci
Habbani	Hadhramaut Arabs	20.4	4
Habbani	Saudi Arab. (West)	15.0	6
North African	North African	11.1	4
North African	Egyptian Arabs	9.8	5
Iranian	Iranian	9.7	6
Kurdistani	Kurdistani	6.6	4
Sephardi	Balkan	6.6	6
Ashkenazi	Austrian	5.6	7
Ashkenazi	English	5.5	11
Ashkenazi	U.S. White	5.5	10
Ashkenazi	German	4.9	9
Ashkenazi	East European	4.8	10
East European	East European	3.9	4
Czech	East European	3.7	3
Yemenite	Yemenite	2.6	2

Table 28. Frequency of Thalassemia Trait (i.e., frequency of heterozygotes)

Population	α-Thalassemia		β-Thalassemia		Total or Unspecified	
	Sample Size	Percent	Sample Size	Percent	Sample Size	Percent
Greece	500	0.3				
Peloponnese						6.3
Central Greece & Euboea						7.3
Thessaly						11.5
Ionian Islands						14.0
Macedonia & Thrace						3.3
Greece					1,600	7.4
Italy (Po Delta)	1,200	0.1				7– 15
Sicily						7– 15
Spain						1.7
Huelva					527	1.7
Madrid					6,610	1.2
Cyprus					478	26.0
Yugoslavia				7		
Turkey (Etiturks)			60	7		
North African Jews				"rare"	150	0.0
Yemenite Jews	181	17.0		2		
Iraqi Jews	105	11.0		12		
Kurdish Jews	70	4.3		18		25.0
				20		
U.S. Negroes	900	2.1				
British	500	0.0				
Chinese	1,112	4.0				

Source References for Tables 9-17

1. Altland, K.; Bucher, R.; Kim, T. W.; Busch, H.; Brockelmann, C.; and Goedde, H. W. "Population genetic studies on pseudocholinesterase polymorphism in Germany, Czechoslovakia, Finland, and among Lapps." *Humangenetik*, 1969, 8:158-61.

2. Ananthakrishnan, R., and Kirk, R. L. "The distribution of some serum protein and enzyme group systems in two endogamous groups in S. India." *Indian J. Med. Res.*, 1969, 57:1011-17.

3. Ananthakrishnan, R.; Walter, H.; and Tsacheva, T. "Red cell enzyme polymorphisms in Bulgaria." *Humangenetik*, 1972, 15:186-90.

4. Baitsch, H., and Ritter, H. "Untersuchungen zur Genetik der Serumproteine: Der Gc-Faktor nach Hirschfield und seine Allehaufigkeit in Sudwestdeutschland." *Blut*, 1963, 9:278.

5. Bajatzadeh, M., and Walter, H. "Investigation on the distribution of blood and serum groups in Iran." *Hum. Biol.*, 1969, 41:401-15.

6. Barker, R. F., and Hopkinson, D. A. "Genetic polymorphism of human phosphoglycolate phosphatase (PGP). *Human Genet.*" (London), 1978, 42:143-51.

7. Baxi, A. J.; Parikh, N. P.; and Jhala, H. I. "Haptoglobin and transferrin types in three Gujarati speaking groups." *Indian J. Med. Res.*, 1969, 57:2087-91.

8. Beutler, E., and Matsumoto, F. "Ethnic variations in red cell glutathione peroxidase activity." *Blood*, 1975, 46:103-10.

9. Bhasin, M. K., and Fuhrmann, W. "Geographic and ethnic distribution of some red cell enzymes." *Humangenetik*, 1972, 14:204-23.

10. Blake, N. M.; Kirk, R. L.; and Baxi, A. J. "The distribution of some enzyme group systems among Marathis and Gujaratis in Bombay." *Hum. Hered.*, 1970, 20:409-16.

11. Bodmer, J.; Bonné, B.; Bodmer, W.; Black, S.; Ben-David, A.; and Ashbel, S. "Study of the HLA system in a Yemenite Jewish population in Israel." In Dausset, J., and Colombani, J. (eds.), *Histocompatibility Testing 1972*. Baltimore: Williams and Wilkins, 1972, pp. 20-26.

12. Bonné, B. "Genes and phenotypes in the Samaritan isolate." *Amer. J. Phys. Anthropal.*, 1966, 24:1-20.

13. Bonné, B.; Ashbel, S.; Modai, M.; Godber, M. J.; Mourant, A. E.; Tills, D.; and Woodhead, B. G. "The Habbanite isolate. 1. Genetic markers in the blood." *Hum. Hered.*, 1970, 20:609-22.

14. Bonné, B.; Godber, M.; Ashbel, S.; Mourant, A. E.; and Tills, D. "South-Sinai Bedouin. A preliminary report on their inherited blood factors." *Am. J. Phys. Anthropol.*, 1971, 34:397-408.

15. Bonné-Tamir, B.; Ashbel, S.; and Kenett, R. "Genetic markers: Benign and normal traits of Ashkenazi Jews." In Goodman, R. M., and Motul-

sky, A. G. (eds.), *Genetic Disorders among Ashkenazi Jews.* New York: Raven Press, 1979.

16. Bonné-Tamir, B.; Ashbel, S.; and Modai, J. "Genetic markers in Libyan Jews." *Human Genet.*, 1977, 37:319–28.

17. Bonné-Tamir, B.; Ashbel, S.; and Bar-Shani, S. "Ethnic communities in Israel: The genetic blood markers of the Babylonian Jews." *Am. J. Phys. Anthropol.*, 1978, 49:457–64.

18. ———. "Ethnic communities in Israel: The genetic blood markers of the Moroccan Jews." *Am. J. Phys. Anthropol.*, 1978, 49:465–72.

19. Bonné-Tamir, B.; Bodmer, J. G.; Bodmer, W. F.; Pickbourne, P.; Brautbar, C.; Gazit, E.; Nevo, S.; and Zamir, R. "HLA polymorphism in Israel. 9. An overall comparative analysis." *Tissue Antigens*, 1978, 11:235–50.

20. Bowman, J. E., and Ronaghy, H. "Hemoglobin glucose-6-phosphate dehydrogenase, phosphogluconate dehydrogenase and adenylate kinase polymorphism in Moslems in Iran." *Amer. J. Phys. Anthropol.*, 1967, 27:119.

21. Brinkmann, B.; Hoppe H. H.; Hennig, W.; and Koops, E. "Red cell enzyme polymorphism in a northern German population." *Human Hered.*, 1971, 21:278–88.

22. Brinkmann, B.; Krukenberg, P.; Brinkmann, M.; and Hoppe, H. H. "Gene frequencies of soluble glutamic-pyruvic transaminase in a northern German population." *Humangenetik*, 1972, 16:355–56.

23. Brinkmann, B.; Reiter, J.; and Kruger, O. "Genhäufigkeiten einiger Enzympolymorphismen in Mittelmeerländern." *Humangenetik*, 1973, 20:141–46.

24. Chen, S. H.; Giblett, E. R.; Anderson, J. E. J.; and Fossum, B. L. G. "Genetics of glutamic-pyruvic transaminase: Its inheritance, common and rare variants, population distribution, and differences in catalytic activity." *Ann Hum. Genet.*, 1972, 35:401–9.

25. Cleve, H.; Ramot, B.; and Bearn, A. G. "Distribution of the serum group-specific components in Israel." *Nature* (London), 1962, 195:861–67.

26. Cohen, T.; Levene, C.; Yodfat, Y.; Fidel, J.; Friedlander, Y.; Steinberg, A. G.; and Brautbar, C. "Genetic studies on Cochin Jews in Israel: 1. Population data, blood groups, isoenzymes, and HLA determinants." *Am. J. Med. Genet.*, 1980, 6:61–73.

27. Cohen, T.; Simhai, B.; Steinberg, A. G.; and Levene, C. "Genetic polymorphisms among Iranian Jews in Israel." *Am J. Med. Genet.*, 1981, 8:181–90.

28. Das, S. R.; Mukherjee, B. N.; Das, S. K.; Blake, N. M.; and Kirk, R. L. "The distribution of some enzyme group systems among Bengalis." *Indian J. Med. Res.*, 1970, 58:866–75.

29. Detter, J. C.; Stamatoyannopoulos, G.; Giblett, E. R.; and Motulsky, A. G. "Adenosine deaminase. Racial distribution and report of a new phenotype." *J. Med. Genet.*, 1970, 7:356–57.

30. Erdem, S.; Aksoy, M.; and Cetingil, A. I. "Distribution of haptoglobin types in Turkish people." *Nature* (London), 1969, 210:315–16.

31. Farhud, D. D.; Ananthakrishnan, R.; Walter, H.; and Loser, J. "Electrophoretic investigation of some red cell enzymes in Iran." *Human Hered.*, 1973, 23:263–66.

32. Farhud, D. D.; and Walter, H. "Hp subtypes in Iranians." *Human Hered.*, 1972, 22:184–89.

33. Fraser, G. R.; Grunwald, P.; Kitchin, F. D.; and Steinberg, A. G. "Serum polymorphism in Yugoslavia," *Human Hered.*, 1969, 19:57–64.

34. Fried, K.; Bloch, H.; Sutton, E.; Neel, J. V.; Bayani-Sioson, P.; and Duvdevani, P. "Haptoglobins and transferrins." In Goldschmidt, E. (ed.), *The Genetics of Migrant and Isolate Populations.* Baltimore: Williams and Wilkins Company, 1963.

35. Galikova, J.; Vilimova, M.; Ferak, V.; and Mayerova, A. "Haptoglobin types in Gypsies from Slovakia (Czechoslovakia)." *Human Hered.*, 1969, 19:480–85.

36. Giblett, E. *Genetic Markers in Human Blood.* Oxford and Edinburgh: Blackwell, 1969.

37. Godber, M. J.; Kopec, A. C.; Mourant, A. E.; Tills, D.; and Lehmann, E. E. "Biological studies of Yemenite and Kurdish Jews in Israel and other groups in south-west Asia. ix. The hereditary blood factors of the Yemenite and Kurdish Jews." *Phil. Trans.*, 1973, 266:169–84.

38. Goedde, H. W.; Hirth, L.; Benkmann, GH. G.; Pellicer, A.; Pellicer, T.; Stahn, M.; and Singh, S. "Population genetic studies of red cell enzyme polymorphisms in four Spanish populations." *Human Hered.*, 1972, 22:552–60.

39. Golan, R. T.; Ben-Ezzer, J.; and Szeinberg, A. "Esterase D polymorphism in several population groups in Israel." *Human Hered.*, 1977, 27:298–304.

40. ———. "Erythrocyte glyoxalase I polymorphism in several population groups in Israel." *Human Hered.*, 1979, 29:57–60.

41. ———. "Red cell glutathione peroxidase in various Jewish ethnic groups in Israel." *Human Hered.*, 1980, 30:136–41.

42. ———. "Phosphoglycolate phosphatase in several population groups in Israel." *Human Hered.*, 1981, 31:89–92.

43. Goldschmidt, E. "Summary and conclusions." In E. Goldschmidt (ed.), *Genetics of Isolate and Migrant Populations.* New York: Williams and Wilkins, 1963.

44. Goldschmidt, E.; Bayani-Sioson, P.; Sutton, H. E.; Fried, K.; Sandor, A.; and Block, N. "Haptoglobin frequencies in Jewish communities." *Ann Human Genet.* (London), 1962, 26:39–45.

45. Goldschmidt, E.; Fried, K.; Steinberg, A. G.; and Cohen, T. "The Karaite community of Iraq in Israel: A genetic study." *Am. J. Hum. Genet.*, 1976, 28:243–52.

46. Herbich, J. "Häufigkeit der Gc-Gruppen der Bevölkerung von Wien und Umgebung: Brauchbarkeit dieses Systems in der forensischen Serologie." *Wien. Klin. Wschr.*, 1963, 75:803.

47. Herbich, J., and Pesendorfer, F. "Anwendung des Enzymsystems der Erythrozytenphosphoglukomutase bei der Vaterschaftsbegutachtung." *Wien. Klin. Wschr.*, 1969, 38:661–67.

48. Herzog, P., and Bohatova, U. "Zur Populationsgenetik der sauren Phosphatase der Erythrozyten (EC:3.1.3.1): Phänotypen—und Allelhaufigkeiten in der CSSR." *Humangenetik*, 1969, 7:183.

49. Herzog, P.; Bohatová, J.; and Blochová, K. "Serum proteins with affinity for hemoglobin. II. Haptoglobin types of the population of Prague." *Fal. Biologica*, 1963, 9:265.

50. Hopkinson, D. A., and Harris, H. "Rare phosphoglucomutase phenotypes." *Ann. Hum. Genet.*, 1966, 30:167–81.

51. Hummel, K.; Pulverer, G.; Schaal, K. P.; and Weidtmann, V. "Häufigkeit der Sichttypen in den Erbsystemen Haptoglobin, Gc, saure Erythrocytenphosphatase, Phosphoglucomutase und Adenylatkinase sowie den Erbeigenschaften Gm (1), Gm (2) und Inv(1) bei Deutschen (aus dem Raum Freidberg i. Br. und Koln) und bein Turken." *Humangenetik*. 1970, 8:330–33.

52. Jarosch, K., and Grims, H. "Statistischer Vergleich der Gm^a -Frequenz bei Mutter und Kind nach der Geburt und im ersten Lebensjahr." *Wien. med. Wschr.*, 1962, 112:622–23.

53. Kattamis, C.; Zannos-Mariolia, L.; Franco, A. P.; Liddell, J.; Lehmann, H.; and Davis, D. "Frequency of atypical pseudocholinesterase in British and Mediterranean populations." *Nature* (London), 1962, 196:599–660.

54. Kobiela, J.; Marek, Z.; and Turowska, B. "The Gc serum groups in populations of Cracow (Poland)." *Vox Sang.*, 1964, 9:634.

55. Kobyliansky, E.; Mic'le, S.; Goldschmidt-Nathan, M.; Arensburg, B.; and Nathan, H. "Phosphoglucomutase, adenylate kinase and acid phosphatase polymorphism in some Jewish populations in Israel." *Acta Anthropogenetica*, 1980, 4:29–36.

56. Kompf, J. "Population genetics of soluble glutamic-pyruvic transaminase (EC 2.6.1.2): Gene frequencies in southwestern Germany." *Humangenetik*, 1971, 14:76.

57. Kout, M., and Baitsch, H. 'Haptoglobínové sérové skupiny." *Bratislavske Lekarske Listy*. 1962, 42:134.

58. Lahav, M., and Szeinberg, A. "Red-cell glutamic-pyruvic transaminase polymorphisms in several population groups in Israel." *Human Hered.*, 1972, 22:533–38.

59. Lehmann, H.; Ala, F.; Hedeyat, S.; Montazemi, K.; Nejad, H. K.; Lightman, S.; Kopec, A. C.; Mourant, A. E.; Teesdale, P.; and Tills, D. "Biological studies of Yemenite and Kurdish Jews in Israel and other groups in south-west Asia. xi. The hereditary blood factors of the Kurds of Iran." *Phil. Trans.*, 1973, 266:195–205.

60. Lendrink-van Itallie, M. I.; Peeton, F.; and Nijenhuis, L. E. "The distribution of Gc types in the Netherlands." *Vox Sang.*, 1965, 10:349.

61. Levene, C.; Medalie, H. J.; and Cohen, T. "Haptoglobin and Gc in Polish and Iraq Jews." Pers. comm. to A. E. Mourant, in Mourant, A. E.; Kopec, A. C.; and Domaniewska-Sobczak, K., *The Genetics of the Jews.* London: Oxford University Press, 1978.

62. Levine, C.; Steinberg, A. G.; Friedlander, Y.; Brautbar, C.; and Cohen, T. "Genetic polymorphisms among Bukharan and Georgian Jews in Israel." *Am. J. Med. Genet.*, 1984, 19:623–41.

63. Marek, Z.; Bundschuh, G.; Kerde, C.; and Geserick, G. "Untersuchungen über die Anwendbarkeit der menschlichen Gc-Komponenten in der forensischen Serologie." *Arztl. Lab.*, 1963, 9:228.

64. Marengo-Rowe, A. J.; Aviet, K.; Godber, M. J.; Kopec, A. C.; Mourant, A. E.; Tills, D.; and Woodhead, B. J. "The inherited blood factors of the inhabitants of Southern Arabia." *Ann. Human Biol.*, 1974, 1:311–26.

65. Mayr, W. R., and Pausch, V. "Die Adenylkinasegruppen. Verteilung in Wien und die Anwendung in der Paternitatsserologie." *Ärztl. Lab.*, 1970, 16:53–54.

66. Modiano, G.; Filippi, G.; Brunelli, F.; Frattaroli, W.; and Siniscalco, M. "Study on red cell acid phosphatases in Sardinia and Rome. Absence of correlation with past malarial morbidity." *Acta Genet.* (Basel), 1967, 17:17–28.

67. Modiano, G.; Scozzari, R.; Gigliani, F.; and Santolamozza, C. "Gene frequencies of adenylate kinase polymorphism in the Roman population." *Humangenetik*, 1969, 8:253–54.

68. Mourant, A. E.; Kopec, A. C.; and Domaniewska-Sobczak, K. *The Distribution of the Human Blood Groups and Other Polymorphisms.* London: Oxford University Press, 1976.

69. ———. *The Genetics of the Jews.* London: Oxford University Press, 1978.

70. Mourant, A. E., and Tills, D. "Phosphoglucomutase frequencies in Habbanite Jews and Icelanders." *Nature* (London), 1967, 214:810.

71. Mukherjee, B. N., and Das, S. K. "The haptoglobin and transferrin types in West Bengal and a case of haptoglobin 'Johnson'." *Human Hered.*, 1970, 20:209–214.

72. Neel, J. V.; Robinson, A. R.; Zuelzer, W. W.; Livingstone, F. B.; and Sutton, H. E. "The frequency of the A_2 and fetal hemoglobin fractions in the natives of Liberia and adjacent regions, with data on haptoglobin and transferrin types. *Am. J. Hum. Genet.*, 1961, 13:262.

73. Radam, G., and Strauch, H. "Populationsgenetik der sauren Erythrocytenphosphatase." *Humangenetik*, 1966, 2:378–80.

74. ———. "Beitrag zur Populationsgenetik der Adenosindesaminase." *Humangenetik*. 1971, 12:173–74.

75. ———. "Daten zur Populationsgenetik der Glutamat-Pyruvat-Transaminase." *Dtsch. Gesundh.-Wes.*, 1972, 27:267–71.

76. Ramot, B.; Duvdevani-Zikert, P.; and Kende, G. "Haptoglobin and transferrin types in Israel." *Ann. Hum. Genet.*, 1967, 31:237–45.

77. Rapley, S.; Robson, E. G.; Harris, H.; and Maynard-Smith, S. "Data on the incidence, segregation, and linkage relations of the adenylate kinase (AK) polymorphism." *Ann. Hum. Genet.*, 1967, 31, 237–45.

78. Rex-Kiss, B., and Szabo, L. "Results of Haptoglobin types investigation in Hungary." *Humangenetik*, 1971, 13:78–80.

79. Ritter, H.; Wendt, G. G.; Zilch, I.; Kompf, J.; Cramer, H.; and Kirchberg, G. "Genetic and linkage analysis for the acid phosphatase of the erythrocytes." *Humangenetik*, 1971, 13:353–55.

80. Rittner, C.; Morath, D.; Klotz, K.; and Allen, F. H., Jr. "Some population and family data on the inheritance of red cell phosphoglucomutase." *Human Hered.*, 1969, 19:674–77.

81. Salák, J., and Palousova, Z. "On the phenotype distribution of red cell acid phosphatase in Czechoslovakia: The district of Ceské Budéjovice." *Humangenetik*, 1971, 13:247–49.

82. Scozzari, R.; Santolamozza, C.; and Arapalla, E. "Studies on the red cell adenosine deaminase polymorphism in Rome." *Humangenetik*, 1970, 8:364–68.

83. Seth, S., and Berndt, H. "Distribution of enzyme groups and serum proteins in a North German population." *Humangenetik*, 1973, 20:147–50.

84. Shim, B. S., and Bearn, A. G. "The distribution of Haptoglobin subtypes in various populations, including subtype patterns in some nonhuman primates." *Am. J. Hum. Genet.*, 1964, 16:477–82.

85. Sonnenborn, H. H., and Renninger, W. "Genfrequenzuntersuchungen der Adenosindesaminase-Isoenzyme mit einer neuen Technik." *Humangenetik*, 1970, 10:188–90.

86. Steinberg, A. G., and Bonné-Tamir, B. "Gm and Inv (Km) Allotypes among Libyan and Ashkenazi Jews, and Armenians living in Israel." *Human Genet.*, 1980, 55:391–95.

87. Steinberg, A. G.; Levene, C.; Yodfat, Y.; Fidel, J.; Brautbar, C.; and Cohen, T. "Genetic studies on Cochin Jews in Israel: 2. Gm and Inv data—polymorphism for Gm[3] and Gm[1,17,21] without Gm(26)." *Am. J. Med. Genet.* 1980, 6:75–81.

88. Stevenson, J. C.; Schanfield, M. S.; and Sandler, S. G. "Immunoglobulin allotypes in Jewish populations living in Israel and the United States." *Am. J. Phys. Anthropol.*, 1985, 67:195–207.

89. Szeinberg, A. "Polymorphic evidence for a Mediterranean origin of the Ashkenazi community." In Goodman, R. M., and Motulsky, A. G. (eds.), *Genetic Diseases among Ashkenazi Jews.* New York: Raven Press, 1979, p. 84.

90. Szeinberg, A.; Pipano, S.; Assa, M.; Medalie, J. H.; and Newfeld, H. N. "High frequency of atypical pseudocholinesterase gene among Iraqi and Iranian Jews." *Clinical Genet.*, 1972, 3:123–27.

91. Szeinberg, A.; Pipano, S.; Rozansky, Z.; and Rabia, N. "Frequency of red cell adenosine deaminase phenotypes in several population groups in Israel." *Human Hered.*, 1971, 21:357–61.

92. Szeinberg, A., and Tomashevsky-Tamir, S. "Red cell adenylate kinase and phosphoglucomutase polymorphisms in several population groups in Israel." *Human Hered.*, 1971, 21:289–96.

93. Tariverdian, G., and Ritter, H. "Population genetics of adenosine deaminase (EC:3.5.4.4): Gene frequencies in southwestern Germany." *Humangenetik*, 1969, 7:179.

94. Tills, D.; van den Branden, J. L.; Clements, V. R.; and Mourant, A. E. "The world distribution of electrophoretic variants of the red cell enzyme adenylate kinase (ATP:AMP phosphotransferase) EC 2.7.4.3." *Human Hered.*, 1970, 20:517–22, and ibid., 1971, 21:302–4 (corrected tables).

95. Tills, D.; Warlow, A.; Mourant, A. E.; Kopec, A. C.; Edholm, O. G.; and Garrard, G. "The blood groups and other hereditary blood factors of Yemenite and Kurdish Jews." *Ann. Human Biol.*, 1977, 4:259–74.

96. Van den Branden, J. L.; Clements, V. R.; Mourant, A. E.; and Tills, D. "The distribution in human populations of genetic variants of adenosine deaminase." *Human Hered.*, 1971, 21:60–62.

97. Vergnes, H., and Gherardi, M. "Les enzymotypes erythrocytaires et sériques dans un groupe de Kurdes." *Ann. Genet.*, 1971, 14:199.

98. Vogt, A.; Prokop, O.; and Schlesinger, D. "Die Vererbung der Serumgruppe Gc." *Blut.* 1963, 9:345.

99. Voronov, A. A. "Ethnogéographie des types généraux du haptoglobine de protéine sérique." *Soviet Ethnogr.*, 1968, 2:68–86 (in Russian).

100. Walter H.; Ananthakrishnan, R.; and Tsacheva, L. "Serum protein groups in Bulgaria." *Human Hered.*, 1972, 22:529–32.

101. Walter, H., and Bajatzadeh, M. "Studies on the distribution of the human red cell acid phosphatase polymorphism in Iranians and other populations." *Acta Genet.* (Basel), 1968, 18:421–28.

102. Welch, S., and Lee, J. "The population distribution of genetic variants of human esterase D." *Humangenetik*, 1974, 24:329–31.

103. Wendt, G. G.; Ritter, H.; Zilch, I.; Tariverdian, G.; Utermann, G.; Kindermann, I.; and Kirchberg, G. "Genetics and linkage analysis on phosphoglucomutase." *Humangenetik*, 1971, 13:350–52.

104. Whittaker, M. "Frequency of atypical pseudocholinesterase in groups of individuals of different ethnographical origin." *Acta Genet.* (Basel), 1968, 18:567–72.

105. Wust, H. "The red cell adenosine deaminase (ADA) polymorphism in Vienna." *Vox Sang.*, 1968, 15:304–5.

106. Wyslouchowa, B. "Red cell acid phosphatase types in Poland. Population and genetic studies." *Human Hered.*, 1970, 20:199.

107. Zaidman, J. L.; Leiba, H.; Scharf, S.; and Steinman, I. "Red cell glucose-6-phosphate dehydrogenase deficiency in ethnic groups in Israel." *Clin. Genet.*, 1976, 9:131–33.

Notes

Abbreviations

B.—Babylonian Talmud (completed *c*. A.D. 500)
M.—Mishna (completed *c*. A.D. 200)
T.—Tosefta (completed *c*. A.D. 200)
Y.—(Yerushalmi) Jerusalem or Palestinian Talmud
(completed *c*. A.D. 425)

Preface to the First Edition

1. Three years after the publication of Fishberg's books, Karl Kautsky (1854–1938), the well-known German-Jewish socialist leader and writer, published a booklet, *Rasse und Judentum* (Stuttgart: J. H. W. Dietz, 1914, 94 pp.; 2nd ed., *ibid.*, 1921, 108 pp.), which appeared in 1926 in an English translation as *Are the Jews a Race?* (New York: International Publishers). In it Kautsky discusses general race theories, races of animals and man, assimilation, anti-Semitism, Zionism, etc., and also recapitulates in 14 pages Fishberg's argument about the physical characteristics and mental qualities of the Jews, without adding anything new to it. Hence it was felt that the above statement to the effect that Fishberg's book was the only one published heretofore in English was justified.

Introduction

1. M. F. Ashley Montagu, *Man's Most Dangerous Myth: The Fallacy of Race*, 2nd ed., New York: Columbia University Press, 1945, p. 253.

2. S. L. Washburn, "The Study of Race," *American Anthropologist*, June, 1963, 65:528.

3. Genesis 4:21–22.

4. Aristotle, *Politics*, II:14, Loeb Classical Library edition, p. 23.

5. Al-Mas'ūdī, *Murūj adh-dhahab*, I, 164 f.; Ibn Khaldūn, *The Muqaddimah*, translated and edited by Franz Rosenthal, New York: Pantheon Books, 1958, I:174–76.

6. Gottfried Wilhelm von Leibniz, *Otium Hanoveriana sive Miscellanea*, p. 37, as quoted by Montagu, *op. cit.*, pp. 17–18.

7. Harry L. Shapiro, "Race Mixture," in *Race and Science*, New York: Columbia University Press, 1961, p. 352.

8. Cf. sources as quoted by Ashley Montagu, "Race: The History of an Idea," in Ruth Miller and Paul J. Dolan (eds.), *Race Awareness*, New York, London, Toronto: Oxford University Press, 1971, pp. 187–88.

9. Montagu, *op. cit.*, p. 18.

10. Christian Lassen, *Indische Altertumskunde*, 2nd ed., 4 vols., Leipzig: L. A. Kittler, 1867, I:494 ff. The first edition was published in 1844–61. My translation from the German, R. P.

11. Joseph Arthur comte de Gobineau, *Essai sur l'inégalité des races humaines*, Paris: Librairie de Firmin Didot Frères, 4 vols., 1853–55.

12. Ernest Renan, *Etudes d'histoire religieuse,* 5th ed., Paris: Michel Lévy Frères, 1862, pp. 85, 87, 89. My translation from the French, R. P. Cf. also Renan's lecture, "The Jews as a Race and as a Religion," delivered on January 27, 1883, and quoted in ch. VIII, "Looking Jewish."

13. Houston Stewart Chamberlain, *Die Grundlagen des neunzehnten Jahrhunderts,* Munich: F. Bruckmann, 1899.

14. The Nazi racial doctrines are presented and subjected to scholarly criticism in Karl Saller, *Die Rassenlehre des Nationalsozialismus in Wissenschaft und Propaganda,* Darmstadt: Progress-Verlag, 1961. Cf. also Max Weinreich, *Hitler's Professors: The Part of Scholarship in Germany's Crimes Against the Jewish People,* New York: Yiddish Scientific Institute (YIVO), 1946, pp. 27–36: "Racial Science."

15. My (R. P.) combined free translation of the German and Hungarian originals, which read as follows: "Was der Jude glaubt is einerlei—in der Rasse liegt die Schweinerei" (lit.: "What the Jew believes makes no difference—in the race lies the piggishness") and "A zsidóban a baj—nem a vallás hanem a faj" (lit.: "In the Jew the trouble—Is not the religion but the race").

16. Joshua Trachtenberg, *The Devil and the Jews: The Medieval Conception of the Jew and Its Relation to Modern Antisemitism,* New Haven: Yale University Press, 1943, pp. 6, 44–50, 116–17, 149, 226 n. 2, 227–28 n. 18, 247 n. 26.

17. Salo W. Baron, *A Social and Religious History of the Jews,* New York: Columbia University Press, and Philadelphia: The Jewish Publication Society of America, 1952–69, vol. XI, p. 352 n. 18, and vol. V, p. 297 n. 9. We shall frequently have occasion to refer to this invaluable 14-volume study, which will be abbreviated as "Baron" with vol. and page numbers.

18. Johann Jakob Schudt, *Jüdische Merckwürdigkeiten,* Frankfort and Leipzig: S. T. Hocker, 1714–18, part II, p. 369. My translation from the German, R. P. Cf. also Israel Lévi, "Le Juif de la légende," *Revue des Etudes Juives,* xx:249–52.

19. Washburn, op. cit., p. 522.

20. Carleton S. Coon, *The Races of Europe,* New York: Macmillan, 1939. By 1962, however, Coon modified his position and classified the living peoples of the world into five "basically geographical groups: the Caucasoid, Mongoloid, Australoid, Congoid, and Capoid," which he also termed "subspecies." Cf. his *The Origin of Races,* New York: Alfred A. Knopf, 1962, pp. 3–4.

21. L. C. Dunn and Theodosius Dobzhansky, *Heredity, Race and Society,* New York: New American Library, 1952.

22. L. L. Cavalli-Sforza and Walter F. Bodmer, *The Genetics of Human Populations,* San Francisco: W. H. Freeman & Co., 1971.

23. N. A. Barnicot, "Taxonomy and Variation in Modern Man," in Ashley Montagu (ed.), *The Concept of Race,* New York: The Free Press, 1964, pp. 180–227.

24. Washburn, *op. cit.,* p. 527.

25. Carl Vogt, *Vorlesungen über den Menschen,* Giessen: J. Ricker, 1863, II:238.

26. Maurice Fishberg, *The Jews: A Study in Race and Environment,* London: Walter Scott Publ. Co. and New York: Charles Scribner's Sons, 1911, p. 110.

PART I
I. Four Views on the Jewish Race

1. Saller, *op. cit.; idem,* "Die biologisch motivierte Judenfeindschaft," in Karl Thieme (ed.), *Judenfeindschaft: Darstellung und Analysen,* Frankfort on Main: Fischer Bücherei, 1963, pp. 180–208, 298–99.

2. See Erwin Baur, Eugen Fischer, and Fritz Lenz, *Menschliche Erblehre und Rassenhygiene,* Munich: J. F. Lehmann, 1936, pp. 748 ff.

3. *The Anthropological Treatises of Johann Friedrich Blumenbach,* London: Published for the Anthropological Society by Longman, Green, 1865, pp. 98–99, 122, 234. Translation of the 1795 edition of *De generis humani varietate nativa.*

4. Josiah Clark Nott and George R. Glidden, *Types of Mankind,* Philadelphia: Lippincott, Grambo & Co., 1854, pp. 116–18, 141. Four years earlier, Nott outlined the same ideas in an article, "The Physical History of the Jewish Race," in *Southern Quarterly,* 1850.

5. Paul Broca, "Des phenomènes d'hybridité dans le genre humain," *Journal de Physiologie de l'Homme et des Animaux,* 1859, 2:601–25; 1860, 3:392–439; translated into English by C. Carter Blake, London: Anthropological Society, 1864, pp. 61–71, as quoted in Earl W. Count (ed.), *This Is Race,* New York: Henry Schuman, 1950, p. 69.

6. Friedrich Anton Heller von Hellwald, in *Ausland* (a weekly), 1872, pp. 901 ff., 957 ff., as quoted in *The Jewish Encyclopaedia,* 1901, I:642, s.v. "Anti-Semitism"; cf. also *idem, Culturgeschichte in ihrer natürlichen Entwicklung,* Augsburg: Lampert & Co., 1875, p. 503.

7. Paul Topinard, *L'Anthropologie,* Paris: C. Reinwald, 1876, pp. 402, 413. My translation from the French, R. P.

8. Richard Andree, *Zur Volkskunde der Juden,* Bielefeld and Leipzig: Velhagen & Klasing 1881, pp. 24, 39. My translation from the German, R. P.

9. Joseph Jacobs, "On the Racial Characteristics of Modern Jews," *Journal of the Anthropological Institute,* London, 1885, vol. 15, reprint, p. 31. Cf. also Jacobs's articles "Anthropology," in *The Jewish Encyclopedia,* 1901, I:619 ff., and "Purity of Race," X:283 f.

10. Georg Buschan, "Einfluss der Rasse auf die Form und Häufigkeit pathologischer Veränderungen," *Globus,* 1895, vol. 67.

11. Madison Grant, *The Passing of the Great Race,* 3rd ed., New York: Charles Scribner's Sons, 1920, p. 18 (first ed. 1916); Baur, Fisher, Lenz, *op. cit.,* p. 293.

12. A. D. Elkind, *The Jews: A Comparative Anthropological Study, Especially of the Polish Jews* (in Russian), Moscow: Publ. of the Imperial Society for Ancient History and Ethnography, 1903, vol. 104; reviewed by Weinberg in *Arch. f. Rass. u. Ges. Biol.,* 1904, 1:915 f.

13. Ignacy Maurycy Judt, *Die Juden als Rasse,* Berlin: Jüdischer Verlag, 1903, pp. 203, 209, 233. Original Polish edition published in Warsaw, 1902.

14. Ignaz Zollschan, *Das Rassenproblem,* 4th ed., Wien and Berlin: R. Löwit, 1920, pp. 45–46, 55. My translation from the German, R. P.

15. Vogt, *op. cit.,* II:239. My translation from the German, R. P.

16. *Ibid.,* p. 238.

17. Gustave Lagneau, *Bulletin de la Société d'Anthropologie de Paris,* 1861, 2:389–90, 412, 416–20. Cf. also Lagneau's remarks, *ibid.,* 1865, 6:516. Subsequently, Lagneau spoke of an "ethnic duality" among the Jews, cf. *Bulletin de l'Académie de Médecine,* 1891, 26:291, *idem, Bulletin de la Société d'Anthropologie,* 1891, p. 540.

18. *Op. cit.,* 1865, 6:515.

19. Augustin Weisbach, *Körpermessungen verschiedener Menschenrassen,* Berlin: Wiegandt, Hempel, and Parey, 1878, pp. 214, 224 (*Zeitschrift für Ethnologie,* 1877, vol. 9 supplement).

20. Józef Majer and Izydor Kopernicki, *Charakterystyka fizyczna ludności Galicyjskiej,* Cracow: Sprawozdań Komisyi Antropologicznej, 1876, vol. 1; Ludwig Stieda, "Ein Beitrag zur Anthropologie der Juden," *Archiv für Anthropologie,* Braunschweig, 1883, vol. 14, 61–71.

21. Bernhard Blechman, *Ein Beitrag zur Anthropologie der Juden,* Dorpat: W. Just's, 1882; J. Kollman and Kahnt, "Schädel and Skeletreste aus einem Judenfriedhof des xiii. und xiv. Jahrhunderts zu Basel," *Verhandlungen der Naturforsch. Gesellschaft in Basel,* 1885, vol. 7.

22. Constantin Ikow, "Neue Beiträge zur Anthropologie der Juden," *Archiv für Anthropologie,* Braunschweig, 1884, vol. 15, 4:379–89.

23. Abel Hovelacque and Georges Hervé, *Précis d'anthropologie,* Paris: Adrien Delahaye et Emile Lecrosnier, 1887, pp. 548–50; cf. Georges Hervé's comments in *Bulletin de la Société d'Anthropologie de Paris,* 1891, pp. 542–43. My translation from the French, R. P.

24. John Beddoe, *The Anthropological History of Europe, Being the Rhind Lectures for 1891,* 1893 (first published in the *Scottish Review* in 1892–93), as reprinted in Count, *op. cit.,* p. 168.

25. Friedrich Maurer, *Völkerkunde, Bibel und Christentum,* Leipzig, 1905, as cited by Fishberg, *The Jews,* p. 106; Joseph Deniker, *The Races of Man,* London: Walter Scott Publ. Co. and New York: Charles Scribner's Sons, 1900, pp. 423–25.

26. Maurice Muret, *L'Esprit juif,* Paris: Perrin, 1901, pp. 21–22. My translation from the French, R. P.

27. S. Weissenberg, "Das jüdische Rassenproblem," *Zeitschrift für Demographie und Statistik der Juden,* Berlin, 1905, 1, 5:4–8.

28. Ferdinand Wagenseil, "Beiträge zur physichen Anthropologie der sefardischen Juden und zur jüdischen Rassenfrage," *Zeitschrift für Morphologie und Anthropologie,* Stuttgart, 1922, 23, 1:149; Max Wolfgang Hauschild, "Die kleinasiatischen Völker und ihre Beziehungen zu den Juden," *Zeitschrift für Ethnologie,* Braunschweig, 1920–21, 52–53:524.

29. Hans F. K. Günther, *Rassenkunde des jüdischen Volkes,* 2nd ed., Munich: J. F. Lehmann, 1930, pp. 191, 198 ff.

30. Erwin Baur, Eugen Fischer, and Fritz Lenz, *Grundriss der menschlichen Erblichkeitslehre und Rassenhygiene,* 2nd ed., Munich: J. F. Lehmann, 1923, I:148. My translation from the German, R. P.

31. Sigmund Feist, *Stammeskunde der Juden,* Leipzig: J. C. Hinrich, 1925, pp. 179–81.

32. Yulii Davidovich Brutzkus, *Les groupes sanguins parmi les populations juives,* Paris: Collection "Race et Racisme," no. 3, 1937.

33. *Idem,* "The Anthropology of the Jewish People," in *The Jewish People: Past and Present,* New York: Jewish Encyclopedic Handbooks, 1946, I:25.

34. Carleton S. Coon, "Have the Jews a Racial Identity?" in Isacque Graeber and Stuart Henderson Britt (eds.), *Jews in a Gentile World,* New York: Macmillan, 1942, pp. 30–33, 35, 37.

35. Mme Clémence Royer, "Discussion sur la race juive," *Bulletin de la Société d'Anthropologie de Paris,* 1891, p. 546.

36. Felix von Luschan, *Korrespondenzblatt der deutschen anthropologischen Gesellschaft,* 1892, nos. 9 and 10. Cf. also *idem,* "Zur physischen Anthropologie der Juden," *Zeitschrift für Demographie und Statistik der Juden,* Berlin, 1905, 1,1:1–4.

37. Fritz Kahn, *Die Juden als Rasse und Kulturvolk,* 3rd ed., Berlin: Welt-Verlag, 1922, pp. 137, 141, 159, 161–62.

38. Arthur Ruppin, *Soziologie der Juden,* Berlin: Jüdischer Verlag, 1930, vol. I, pp. 29–36.

39. Jan Czekanowski, "Die anthropologische Struktur von Europa im Lichte polnischer Untersuchungsergebnisse," *Anthropologischer Anzeiger,* 1939, 16:81–100, as reprinted in English translation in Count, *op. cit.,* pp. 600–1.

40. François-Maximilien Mission, *A New Voyage to Italy. . . ,* 4th ed., London: R. Bonwicke, 1714, II:139. Original French edition published in 1691.

41. Georges Louis LeClerc, comte de Buffon, *Histoire naturelle,* new ed., Paris: De l'Imprimerie Royale, 1799, vol. 20, p. 230. My translation from the French, R. P.

42. Samuel Stanhope Smith, *Essay on the Causes of the Variety of Complexion and Figure in the Human Species,* new ed. by Winthrop Jordan, Cambridge, Mass.: Harvard University Press, 1965, p. 42.

43. James Cowles Pritchard (Prichard), *The Natural History of Man,* 2nd ed., London: H. Ballière, 1845, p. 145. First edition published in London, 1843.

44. Cf. Rudolf Virchow's report in *Verhandlungen der Berliner Gesellschaft für Anthropologie und Urgeschichte,* 1876, pp. 16–18; and his "Gesamtbericht," in *Archiv für Anthropologie,* 1886, 16:275–475.

45. Data presented by Fishberg, *op. cit.,* pp. 62–65. On Palestine, cf. F. Schiff, "Anthropologische Untersuchungen an jüdischen Kindern in Jerusalem," *Archiv für Anthropologie,* 1914, p. 348, who reports that among Ashkenazi children in Jerusalem 40 per cent had blond hair and 30 per cent blue eyes, while among Sephardi children 10 per cent had blond hair and even fewer had blue eyes.

46. Ernest Renan, *Le Judaisme comme race et comme religion.* Conférence faite au Cercle Saint-Simon, le 27 Janvier 1883. Paris: Calmann Lévy, 1883, pp. 25, 28.

47. Friedrich Ratzel, *History of Mankind,* London: Macmillan, 1898, Vol. III, p. 548. Original German edition published in Leipzig: Bibliographisches Institut, 1885–87.

48. Carl H. Hahn, *Aus dem Caucasus,* Leipzig: Duncker und Humblot, 1892, pp. 181 ff.

49. William Z. Ripley, "The Racial Geography of Europe: A Sociological Study. Supplement: The Jews," *Appleton's Popular Science Monthly,* New York, vol. 54, nos. 2 and 3, Dec., 1898 and Jan. 1899, pp. 163–75 and 338–51, and especially pp. 340, 343, 345, 349, 351. Ripley's paper received much attention in Europe after its German summary was printed in *Globus,* Braunschweig, July 8, 1899, vol. 36, no. 2, pp. 21–27.

50. Fishberg, *op. cit.,* pp. 108–18, 120, 125–26, 128, 131, 133–34, 138, 142–46, 148–49.

51. Karl Kautsky, *Raise und Judentum,* Stuttgart: J. H. W. Dietz, 1914. The quotations in the text are from the English translation, *Are the Jews a Race?* New York: International Publishers, 1926, pp. 108, 118, 119.

52. Felix von Luschan, comments to the lecture by M. W. Hauschild quoted in n. 28, *Zeitschrift für Ethnologie,* 1920–21, 52–53:526–27.

53. Franz Boas, "Are the Jews a Race?" *The World of Tomorrow,* Jan. 1923, as reprinted in his *Race and Democratic Society,* New York: Augustin, 1945, pp. 39–41; cf. also p. 49.

54. Roland B. Dixon, *The Racial History of Man,* New York: Charles Scribner's Sons, 1923, pp. 164, 167.

55. Eugene Pittard, *Race and History,* New York: Alfred A. Knopf, 1926, pp. 350–51. The French original, *Les races et l'histoire,* was published in Paris: *La Renaissance du livre,* 1924, in the series *L'Evolution de l'humanité.*

56. Ernest A. Houton, "Methods of Racial Analysis," *Science,* Washington, D.C., 1926, pp. 75–81.

57. Julian S. Huxley and A. C. Haddon, *We Europeans,* New York: Harper, 1936, p. 73.

58. Louis L. Snyder, *Race: A History of Modern Ethnic Theories,* New York and Toronto: Longman, Green, 1939, pp. 304, 307.

59. Carl C. Seltzer, "The Jew—His Racial Status," *Harvard Medical Alumni Bulletin,* April 1939, p. 11, as reprinted in Count, *op. cit.,* p. 618.

60. Melville Jacobs, in Graeber and Britt, *op. cit.,* pp. 53–54.

61. Ellsworth Huntington, *Mainsprings of Civilization,* New York: J. Wiley, 1945, pp. 102, 155, 166.

62. Alfred L. Kroeber, *Anthropology,* New York: Harcourt, Brace, 1948, p. 144. Cf. the 1923 edition of this book, p. 57.

63. M. F. Ashley Montagu, *Statement on Race,* New York: Schuman, 1951, pp. 63–64. The same argument is further elaborated in Montagu's *Man's Most Dangerous Myth,* pp. 244–64.

II. An Excursus into Statistics

1. Cf. *The Itinerary of Benjamin of Tudela,* ed. by Marcus Nathan Adler, New York: Feldheim, no date (reprint of the London, 1907, edition).

2. Sources in Baron III:100.

3. F. Cantera Burgos, "Christian Spain," in Cecil Roth (ed.), *The World History of the Jewish People,* vol. XI, *The Dark Ages,* New Brunswick: Rutgers University Press, 1966, p. 379; Baron X:146, 155, XII:21–24, 48, 119, 256 n. 20.

4. Baron XI:7, 244 nn. 2. 3. 245 n.3. According to Cecil Roth in *Cambridge Medieval History,* VII (1964):648 n.1, the number of Jews in medieval England (1290) was 16,511. Cf. also *Jewish Encyclopedia,* V:174, s.v. England.

5. S. Schwarzfuchs, "France Under the Early Capets," in Roth, *The World History,* XI:153, 155.

6. Baron X:64, 86; XII:8–10, 246 n. 5, 247 nn. 7, 8.

7. Baron X:231, 264, 271–72, XII:16–17, 250 n. 13, 253 n. 16.

8. François-Maximilien Misson, *Nouveau Voyage d'Italie,* La Haye: Henri van Bulderer, 1691, II:95; Baron X:263; XII:18, XIV:62, 67, 101, 144–45.

9. Baron XII:19, 254 n. 16; XIV:73–74, 90–92, 97, 144–45.

10. Baron X:278, 280; XII:25.

11. Baron XII:12–15, 248–49 nn. 9, 10; Blumenkranz in Roth, *The World History,* XI:164.

12. Baron XII:249 n. 12; XIII:255; XIV:186, 200, 201, 206, 212–13, 233.

13. Baron XIV:191, 195, 268.

14. Baron XIV:199, 206, 269.

15. Samuel Kohn, *A zsidók története Magyaroszágon,* Budapest: Athenaeum, 1884, pp. 394–95; Baron XIV:171.

16. Baron XIV:269.

17. Arthur Ruppin, "The Jewish Population of the World," in *The Jewish People: Past*

and Present, New York: Jewish Encyclopedic Handbooks, 1946, vol. I, p. 350; *Encyclopaedia Judaica,* XIII:724, 731, 735, s.v. Poland.

    18. Ruppin, *Soziologie der Juden,* I:81.

III. Proselytism

    1. A recent treatment of Jewish proselytism through the ages is David Max Eichhorn (ed.), *Conversion to Judaism: A History and Analysis,* New York: Ktav Publ. House, 1965, which contains studies by the editor and Albert S. Goldstein, Sidney B. Hoenig, David J. Seligson, Abraham Shusterman, B. J. Bamberger, A. N. Franzblau, and Samuel Teitelbaum. Of the earlier rich literature on Jewish proselytism, the following may be mentioned: Bernard J. Bamberger, *Proselytism in the Talmudic Period,* 2nd. ed., New York: Ktav, 1968; William G. Braude, *Jewish Proselyting in the First Five Centuries of the Common Era,* Providence, R.I.: Brown University, 1940; Ben Zion Wacholder, "Cases of Proselytizing in the Tosafist Responsa," *Jewish Quarterly Review,* 1961, LI:288–315; Uriel Rapaport, *Jewish Religious Propaganda and Proselytism in the Periof of the Second Commonwealth* (in Hebrew with English summary), Jerusalem: Hebrew University, 1965 (a Ph.D. thesis).

    2. Emil Schürer, *Geschichte des jüdischen Volkes im Zeitalter Jesu Christi,* 4th ed., Leipzig: Hinrich, 1901–11, III:162, 164–65, 173–74, 176–77; cf. also p. 3. Emphases in the original. My translation from the German, R. P.

    3. Cf., e.g., Wilhelm Bousset, *Die Religion des Judentums,* Berlin: Reuther und Reinhard, 1903, p. 78; Michael Guttmann, *Das Judentum und seine Umwelt,* Berlin: Philo Verlag, 1927, pp. 66, 73; Baron I:178; cf. *ibid.,* pp. 172–77.

    4. Ruppin, *Soziologie der Juden,* I:69; E. E. Urbach in *Entziqlopedia 'Ivrit,* s.v. *Gēr.*

    5. Ben Zion Wacholder, "The Halakah and the Proselyting of Slaves During the Gaonic Era," *Historia Judaica,* 1956, XVIII:2, p. 106; cf. end of our ch. V. Slavery and Concubinage.

    6. Baron XIII:6–7, 15.

    7. Maimonides, *Responsa* (in Hebrew), ed. Alfred Freimann, Jerusalem: Meqitze Nirdamim, 1934, pp. 40–41, no. 42; cf. also pp. 335–37, no. 369.

    8. Baḥya ben Asher, *Kad haQemaḥ,* Warsaw, 1878, pp. 44–45, s.v. Ger. On the evaluation of proselytes in medieval Spain, cf. Fritz Baer, *A History of the Jews in Christian Spain,* Philadelphia: Jewish Publication Society of America, 1961–66, I:181 f., 415 ff. n. 79; II:10 ff. nn. 19–20; Wacholder, *Jewish Quarterly Review,* 1961, pp. 288–315; Baron XIII:15.

    9. Num. 15:14–16.

    10. Ex. 12:48–49; Lev. 19:33–34.

    11. Deut. 23:4–7; Gen. 34:14–17.

    12. Ex. 12:48; Lev. 24:10; Num. 11:4. Joshua 9; 1Chron. 22.2; 2Chron. 2:16–17; 8:7–8; cf. 1Ki. 5:29; 9:20–21. 1Sam. 27:10, 30:29; Ju.4:11, 17. Jer. 35; 1Chron. 2:55. Cf. *Entziqlopedia Miqrait,* Jerusalem: Mossad Bialik, 1955 ff., III:861–63, s.v. Y'raḥm'el.

    13. James Hastings (ed.), *Dictionary of the Bible,* rev. ed. by Frederick C. Grant and H. H. Rowley, New York: Charles Scribner's Sons, 1963, p. 548, s.v. Kenizzites.

    14. The problem is investigated by Bernard J. Bamberger, "Fear and Love of God in the Old Testament," *Hebrew Union College Annual,* 1929, VI:39 ff. Cf. also *Entziql. Miq.,* III:768–70.

    15. Ps. 115:9–11; 118:2–4. Mal. 3:16.

    16. 2Ki. 17.

    17. Ezra 4:1–2; Neh. 10:29–30.

    18. Esther 8:17.

    19. Judith 14:10; M. Yeb. 8:3; M. Yad. 4:4.

    20. Deut. 23:8–9. Josephus Flavius, *Ant.* XIII:8–10; 11:3; XIV:15:2; *idem, War,* IV:4:4; Schürer, *op. cit.,* I:256 ff., 265 n. 12, 275–76, 708 ff.; Guttmann, *op cit.,* p. 74.

    21. Josephus, *Ant.* XIII:15:4; XIV:4:4; 5:3; *War* I:7:7; Schürer, *op cit.,* I:286.

    22. Schürer, *op. cit.,* III:151–62; Bamberger, *Proselytism,* pp. 16–20.

    23. Strabo, as quoted by Josephus, *Ant.* XIV:72 (115). Baron I:180 and 375 n. 16 maintains that Strabo speaks here about the situation in 85 B.C.

410

24. Acts 13:16, 26; 16:1–3, 14–15; 10:2, 22; 13:43, 50; 17:4, 17; 18:7. Cf. Philo, *De monarchia*, 51–53; Galatians 5:3; Juvenal, *Satir*. XIV:96–106; Mekhilta Mishpatim 18; Guttmann, *op. cit.*, pp. 70 ff.; Urbach, in *Entziql*. *'Ivrit*, s.v. *Gēr*.

25. Philo, *Vita Mos*. II:4:20.

26. St. Augustine, *De civitate dei*, VI:11; Tacitus, *Hist*. V:5; *Annals* II:85; Dio Cassius, 67, 14, and 68; as quoted by Heinrich Graetz, "Die jüdischen Proselyten im Römerreiche unter den Kaisern Domitian, Nerva, Trajan und Hadrian," *Jahresbericht*, Breslau, 1884, pp. 3–6; cf. Schürer, *op. cit.*, III:167–68.

27. Juvenal, *Satir*. XIV:31–33, 96–106; Plutarch, *Problem.*, 4:5; Josephus, *Ant.*, Introd. 2; *idem*, *Cont. Ap.* 2:41; Graetz, *op. cit.*, pp. 21, 24–25; Israel Lévi, "Le proselytisme juif," *Revue des Etudes Juives*, 1905, 50:1–9; 1906, 51:29–31; Guttmann, *op. cit.*, pp. 72–73. On Epaphroditus, cf. Schürer, *op. cit.*, I:80, 89; cf. also *ibid.*, III:164–67, 172–73, 529–45, and the rich Greek and Roman material bearing on Judaism and Jewish proselytism analyzed on pp. 158–88.

28. Josephus, *Ant.*, XIV:7:2; XVIII:3:5; XX:2–4; *War* II:19:2; 20:2; IV:9:11; V:2:2; 3:3; 4:2; 6:1; VI:6:3,4; VII:3:3; *Cont. Ap.*, II:39. Also numerous Talmudic references deal with the royal family of Adiabene and its conversion: M. Nazir 3:6; M. Yoma 3:10; etc.; cf. Jacob Neusner, *A History of the Jews in Babylonia*, Leiden: Brill, 1965, vol. I, pp. 62–63.

29. Urbach, in *Entziql*. *'Ivrit*, s.v. *Gēr*.

30. Baron I:283–84.

31. The material relating to this important subject has been gathered and analyzed by Bamberger, *Proselytism*. Cf. also Guttmann, *op. cit.*, pp. 43–114.

32. M. Qid. 4:7; B. Qid. 73b; Maimonides, *Mishne Torah*, Issure Biah, 19:11; and the later codices; cf. Guttmann, *op. cit.*, pp. 79–80; Urbach, *op. cit.*

33. B. Yeb. 24b; analyzed by Guttmann, *op. cit.*, p. 77; cf. also Y. Qid. IV:1, 65b; B. Yeb. 47a; B. 'Arakhin 29a.

34. B. Pes. 87b; Y. Bik. 64a; B. Shevu'ot 39a. Cf. also the relevant legends in Tanhuma Lekh L'kha 6; Midrash Tehillim, ed. Buber, 146:8, p. 536.

35. Baron I:174–75.

36. B. Qid. 73a; B. 'Av. Zar. 64a.

37. Neusner, *op. cit.*, I:14.

38. Josephus, *Ant.*, XV:9:3 (317). For literature on the Jews in pre-Islamic Arabia, cf. Baron III:257–58 n. 79. Cf. also H. Z. Hirschberg, *Yisrael ba'Arav (Israel in Arabia)*, Tel Aviv: Mossad Bialik, 1946, pp. 46, 51–52.

39. Baron III:69–70; sources, *ibid.*, p. 260 n. 85.

40. Hirschberg, *op. cit.*, pp. 60, 71–74, 168; cf. *Enc. of Islam*, new ed., III (1971):223, s.v. Hārith b. Ka'b.

41. Hirschberg, *op. cit.*, pp. 100–7; cf. *Enc. of Ilsam* II(1965):243–45, where, however, different dates are given. Cf. also Baron III:67.

42. Hirschberg, *op. cit.*, pp. 111, 168; Jacob Sapir, *Even Sapir*, Lyck: M'kize Nirdamim, 1866, p. 100b. Ibn al-Kalbī, *Aṣnām*, 10, as quoted in the *Enc. of Islam*, III (1971):123, s.v. Hamdān; *ibid.*, p. 573, s.v. Djudhām; *ibid.*, p. 223, s.v. Ḥārith b. Ka'b.

43. Cf. Al-Yakūbī, *Hist.*, ed. M. Th. Houtsma, Lugd. Bat., 1883, I:298; *Kitāb al-Aghānī*, ed Maḥmūd al-Sāsī, Miṣr, 1322–23 H., VIII:139; H. Lammens, *Le Caliphate de Yazid I*, Beyrouth, 1921, p. 279, as quoted by Hirschberg, *op. cit.*, p. 126. Cf. *Enc. of Islam.*, I(1960):771, s.v. Aws.

44. *Enc. of Islam*, old ed., s.v. Medina, and new ed. I(1960):771, s.v. Aws; cf. also Hirschberg, *op. cit.*, pp. 111, 121, 122, 168.

45. Hirschberg, *op cit.*, pp. 135, 166–67; cf. Baron III:65.

46. Hirschberg, in *Zion*, X:94f.; Yosef Braslavsky, in *Zion* I:148–84; Baron, III:65, 257 n. 79. On the *jus primae noctis*, see pp. 135 ff.

47. Hirschberg, *Yisrael ba'Arav*, pp. 168, 172–73, 188.

48. Baron III:63 ff.; Hirschberg, *Yisrael ba'Arav*, 119–22, 166–68.

49. Baron I:176, and numerous studies quoted on pp. 374–75 n. 13.

50. Tertullian, *Adv. Judaeos* 13., cf. 8; II:634–38 (673–78), 616 (655): *Apolog*. 21; I:392 (449/50), 400 (394); cf. also *Adv. Marcionem* 3, 23; II:353–55 (382–83): Hirschberg, *Toldot*

411

NOTES

haYᵉhudim b'Afriqa haTz'fonit (*A History of the Jews in North Africa*), Jerusalem:Mossad Bialik, 1965, I:25–26, 29, 48.

51. St. Augustine, *Epistl.*, 196,1,4; 33, 891–92, 897–99; cf. Hirschberg, *Toldot*, I:53; Commodianus, *Instructiones* I,24, 37; *Patrologiae Series Latina* 5, 219, 229, as quoted by Hirschberg, *Toldot*, p. 54.

52. Cf. R. Patai, *Golden River to Golden Road: Society, Culture and Change in the Middle East*, 3rd ed., Philadelphia: University of Pennsylvania Press, 1969, p. 237; Hirschberg, *Toldot*, I:61–62.

53. Hirschberg, *Toldot*, I:106–8; II:9–36.

54. Fattal, *Non-Musulmans en pays d'Islam*, pp. 165–68; as quoted by S. Goitein, *A Mediterranean Society*, Berkeley and Los Angeles: University of California Press, 1971, vol. II, p. 592, n. 22.

55. Baron III:87, 89–90.

56. Hirschberg, *Toldot*, I:140, and sources, p. 360 n. 122; cf. also p. 337 n. 41; Urbach, in *Entziqlopedia 'Ivrit*, s.v. *Gēr*.

57. Goitein, *op. cit.*, II:305–7.

58. B. Blumenkranz, "The Roman Church and the Jews," in Roth (ed.), *The World History*, IX:86–87; S. Schwarzfuchs, "France and Germany under the Carolingians," *ibid.*, p. 140.

59. Maimonides, *Responsa*, II:548–50, 725–28; as quoted by Goitein, *op. cit.*, II:304.

60. Goitein, *op. cit.*, II:305.

61. *Ibid.*, II:309–10.

62. *Ibid.*, II:304, 306–8.

63. Baron III:157, and sources, p. 306 n. 41.

64. Z'vulun Qoret and Tzippora Kagan, in *Maḥanayim*, Tel Aviv, 1964, 92:122–29, 158.

65. Cf. Erich Brauer, *Die Ethnologie der jemenitischen Juden*, Heidelberg: Carl Winter, 1934, pp. 51–59; S. Tchortkower, in *Przeglad Antropologiczny*, Poznan, 1938, vol. 12, no. 4; as quoted by Hirschberg, *Yisrael ba'Arav*, p. 309 n. 53. Cf. R. Patai, *Israel Between East and West*, 2nd ed., Westport, Conn.: Greenwood Publ. Corp., 1970, p. 365; and *idem, Tents of Jacob: The Diaspora Yesterday and Today*, Englewood Cliffs, N.J.: Prentice-Hall, 1971, pp. 220–26.

66. Cf. Charles M. Doughty, *Travels in Arabia Deserta*, London. Jonathan Cape, 1936, vol. I, pp. 170, 362, 435, 600, 641; vol. II, pp. 92, 98, 146, 174; Patai, *Tents of Jacob*, pp. 220–26.

67. Patai, *Israel Between East and West*, p. 343.

68. Hugo von Kutschera, *Die Chazaren: Historische Studie*, 2nd ed., Vienna: Adolf Holzhausen, 1910; Alexandre Baschmakoff, "Une Solution Nouvelle du Problème des Khazars," *Mercure de France*, 1931, 229:39–73; *idem, Litterae Orientales*, 58:4–6; W. W. Ginzburg, "The Anthropological Materials on the Origin of the Khazar Khaganate" (in Russian), in *Sbornik* of the Moscow Museum for Anthropology and Ethnography, XIII:309–416; as quoted by Baron III:324–25 n. 30.

69. D. M. Dunlop, *The History of the Jewish Khazars*, New York: Schocken Books, 1967, pp. ix, 11, 34, 41–87, 175–77. On the Jews in Khiva, cf. Itzhak Ben-Zvi, *The Exiled and the Redeemed*, Philadelphia: Jewish Publication Society of America, 1957, pp. 247–48; Baron III: 196 ff.

70. Dunlop, *op. cit.*, pp. 144, 148, 155, 237–44, 247, 261.

71. Kutschera, *op. cit.*, pp. 13–17, quoting Carl Vogt, *Vorlesungen über den Menschen*. Cf. also Abraham N. Poliak, *Khazaria* (in Hebrew), 2nd ed., Tel Aviv: Mossad Bialik-Massada, 1943–44, Introduction, and esp. pp. 255–70; Dunlop, *op. cit.*, p. 261.

72. William E. D. Allen, *History of the Georgian People*, London: K. Paul, Trench, Trubner & Co., 1932, p. 323, citing William Z. Ripley, *The Races of Europe*, New York: D. Appleton, 1899; Dunlop, *op. cit.*, p. 262.

73. Alexander A. Vasiliev, *The Goths in the Crimea*, Cambridge, Mass.: The Medieval Academy of America, 1936, p. 100; Kutschera, *op. cit.*, p. 175; Brutzkus, in *Enc. Judaica*, Berlin, s.v. Chasaren; Dunlop, *op. cit.*, pp. 197–198, 262; *idem*, "The Khazars," in Roth (ed.), *The World History of the Jewish People*, XI:325–56; Baron III:206, 211–12, 329 nn. 41, 43, 332 n. 50.

412

74. Ruppin, *Soziologie der Juden*, I:34–35.

75. Ben-Zvi, *op. cit.*, pp. 155, 156, 301–2, 315; Dunlop, *op. cit.*, pp. 164, 194, 249 n. 70; Baron III:208, 329 n. 43.

76. Blumenkranz, *op. cit.*, pp. 76, 84, 87–88, 172–73; Baron III:46.

77. Blumenkranz, *op. cit.*, p. 86.

78. *Ibid.*, pp. 88, 165; C. Roth, *op. cit.*, p. 112; Baron III:189–90, 298, 320; A. Scheiber, "Fragment from the Chronicle of 'Obadyah, the Norman Proselyte," in *Acta Orientalia Hungarica*, 1954, IV:271–96.

79. Blumenkranz, *op. cit.*, pp. 165, 172–73; Baron V:114.

80. Blumenkranz, *op. cit.*, p. 88; Baron IX:24.

81. Baron X:134; XIII:14–16, 29.

82. Baron XIII:100, 124–25, 149–50.

83. Baron XIII:53–54, 85.

84. Simon Dubnow, *Weltgeschichte des jüdischen Volkes*, Berlin: Jüdischer Verlag, 1927, vol. VI, pp. 411–12; Cecil Roth, *History of the Marranos*, Philadelphia: Jewish Publication Society of America, 1932, pp. 150–51.

85. Roth, *op. cit.*, pp. 146–48.

86. *Ibid.*, pp. 152–55.

87. *Ibid.*, pp. 155–57.

88. *The Jewish Encyclopedia*, s.v. Silva, Francisco Maldonaldo de.

89. *Encyclopaedia Judaica*, s.v. Silva, Rodrigo Mendez (Jacob) da.

90. *The Jewish Encyclopedia* and *Encyclopaedia Judaica*, s.v. Silva, Antonio José da.

91. M. Banuelos, "Antropologia Actual: Valladolid," *Revista financiera del Banco de Viscaya*, Bilboa, no. 79, pp. 182–86, as quoted by Baron X:208.

92. Baron XIII:104, 164–65; XIV:64, 126, 136.

93. Baron X:72, 74; Dubnow, *op. cit.*, V:17, 49.

94. Baron XII:9–10.

95. Eichhorn, *Conversion*, pp. 116–17.

96. Baron X:103; XI:84.

97. *Encyclopaedia Judaica* XV:1346–47.

98. Dubnow, *op. cit.*, 1928, VII:416–18.

99. *The Jewish Encyclopedia*, I:600–1, s.v. Anglo-Israelism.

100. *Enc. Jud.*, VII:795–96.

101. *The Jewish Encyclopedia*, XI:607–9, s.v. Sweden; Eichhorn, *Conversion*, p. 122.

102. Baron XIII:214, 223.

103. Dubnow, *op. cit.*, V:202; Baron XIII:223, 226; Eichhorn, *Conversion*, 115, 121–22; *Enc. Jud.*, XIII:1188–89.

104. Kohn, *A zsidók története Magyarországon*, pp. 123–24. My translation from the Hungarian, R. P.

105. *Ibid.*, pp. 10–11, 357–59; Acsády Ignácz, "Áttérések a multban," *IMIT Évkönyv*, Budapest, 1905, pp. 76–77; Alexander Scheiber, "Hungary," in Roth (ed.), *The World History of the Jewish People*, XI:314, 317; *idem*, "Juden und Christen in Ungarn bis 1526," in Karl Heinrich Rengstorf and Siegfried von Korzfleisch (eds.), *Kirche und Synagoge*, Stuttgart: Ernst Klatt Verlag, vol. II, 1971, p. 564; *idem*, *Monumenta Hungariae Judaica*, Budapest, 1965, VIII:170, no. 190; Sh'lomo Ashkenazi, "Proselyte Women in Israel" (in Hebrew), in *Mahanayim*, Tel Aviv, 1964, no. 92, p. 118; *Enc. Jud.*, XIII:1188. On the Sabbatarians, see: Samuel Kohn, *A szombatosok: tötenetük, dogmatikájuk és irodalmuk*, Budapest: Athenaeum, 1889; *Magyar Zsidó Lexikon*, Budapest, 1929, s.v. Szombatosok; George Balázs, "Az erdélyi szombatosok 1941 tavaszán," in *Libanon*, Budapest, 1941, VI:18–22; *Enc. Jud.*, XV:139–40; and Dr. Alexander Scheiber, private communication Budapest, March 25, 1973.

106. Dubnow, *op. cit.*, VI:298–99; VII:119–20; Baron X:44; XIII:223; *The Jewish Encyclopedia*, X:147, s.v. Potocki; *Enc. Jud.*, XIII:713–14, 934–35; XIV:376.

107. Dubnow, *op. cit.*, 1927, V:475–76; VII:246–47; IX:181–84; *Enc. Jud.*, X:400–1; Baron, *The Russian Jew Under Tsars and Soviets*, New York: Macmillan, 1964, pp. 8, 353 n.

IV. Intermarriage and Interbreeding

1. There exists a very rich literature on Jewish-Gentile intermarriage. The earlier literature, mostly in German, was utilized by Arthur Ruppin in his *Soziologie der Juden*, I:205–31. The later literature, mostly in English, can easily be located by reference to the *Encyclopaedia Judaica*.

2. B. 'Av. Zar. 36b; B. Qid. 68b; B. Yeb. 45a–b. Maimonides, *Yad haḤazaqa* (or *Mishne Tora*), Issure Bi'a 12:1–2; Joseph Caro, *Shulhan 'Arukh, Even ha'Ezer*, 16:1.

3. Gen. 16, esp. v. 15; 25:1–2, 5; 26:34–35; cf. 27:46; 28:1–2; 29:31–33; 30:4–13, 17–24; 35:16–18, 23–26.

4. Gen. 38:2, 12; 46:20.

5. *Entziql. Miq.* V (1968):860.

6. Ex. 2:21; 18:2; Num. 12:1; Lev. 24:10–12; Ex. 12:38; cf. Num. 11:4; Deut. 26:5; Gen. 20:12; Eze. 16:3.

7. Num. 31:9, 18, 35, 40, 47; Deut. 21:10–13. Deut. 20:14; Gen. 34:29.

8. Deut. 7:1–4; 23:4.

9. 2Sam. 3:3; 1Ki.11:1; 16:31. Ruth 1:4; 2Sam. 11:3; 1Ki. 7:13–14; 1Chron. 2:17; 2Chron. 24:26; Jud. 14:1–2, 15; 16:1, 4 ff.; Ruth 1:4; 2:1; 4:10; Deut. 25:5–10; Ruth 4:21–22. Gen. 38:29.

10. Jud. 1; 4:2; 10:12; cf. Josh. 12:9–24.

11. Jud. 2:11, 13; 3:1–6.

12. Amos 9:7; Jer. 47:4.

13. 2Sam. 11:3, 13; 2Sam. 5:11; 6:20, 22; 8:2–4, 18; 15:18; 18:21–22, 31–32. Cf. *Entziql. Miq.* II (1954):398–400; IV (1962):332–34.

14. 1Chron. 27:30–31; 1Chron. 5:10.

15. Eze. 16:2–3.

16. Eze. 44:6–8; 1Ki. 9:20–21; Zech. 14:21; Ezra 2:43, 58–59, 64–65; 8:20; Neh. 7:46, 62, 65–67. Cf. *Entziql. Miq.* V (1968):985.

17. Louis Finkelstein, *The Pharisees*, Philadelphia: The Jewish Publication Society of America, 1938, vol. II, pp. 491, 554–57.

18. Ezra 8:1–21; 9:1–2; 10:10–17; Neh. 13:1–3, 23–24.

19. Ezra 10:18–44; Neh. 13:24.

20. Neh. 13:23, 28, 30; Mal. 2:11; cf. *Entziql. Miq.* V:819, 1031.

21. Salo W. Baron, *The Jewish Community*, Philadelphia: The Jewish Publication Society of America, 1942, vol. I, p. 70.

22. Finkelstein, *op. cit.*, II:561.

23. 1Macc. 1:15; Tob. 4:12; 6:15; Jub. 30:7–10, 13; Test. of Levi 14:6.

24. M. Meg. 4:9; B. Meg. 25a; B. Sanh. 82a; B. 'Av. Zar. 36b; M. Sanh. 9:6; Num. 25:6–8; B. Ber. 58a; B. 'Er. 19a; B. Sanh. 82a.

25. Deut. 23:4 ff.; M. Yeb. 8:3. Cf. Bamberger, *Proselytism*, pp. 77, 78.

26. M. Qid. 4:1.

27. Cf. Bamberger, *op. cit.*, p. 79.

28. M. Yeb. 2:8; B. Yeb. 46a. Cf. Bamberger, *op. cit.*, pp. 221–66.

29. Deut. 23:4; M. Yad. 4:4; T. Qid. 5:5; Maimonides, *Yad haḤazaqa*, Issure Bi'a 12:25.

30. Isa. 42:6; 49:6; Philo, *De Spec. Leg.* III:4:25; 5:29.

31. B. Pes. 49b.

32. Acts 10:28; 16:1; 1Cor. 7:12–13; Tacitus, *Hist.* V:5; Josephus, *Ant.* XIV:7:6; XVIII:3:5; XX:7:1 and 3; cf. Schürer, *op. cit.*, I:589, 591; Bamberger, *op. cit.*, p. 21.

33. Guttmann, *op. cit.*, p. 79.

34. Simon Dubnow, *Weltgeschichte des jüdischen Volkes*, Berlin: Jüdischer Verlag, 1926, IV:56; cf. Baron, *op. cit.*, I:225.

35. Cecil Roth, *The History of the Jews of Italy*, Philadelphia: The Jewish Publication Society of America, 1946, p. 31; Baron XI:78.

36. Baron II:401 n. 24; III:36–37.

37. Cecil Roth in *Cambridge Medieval History*, VII (1964):633; Baron II:401 n. 24; III:36–37, 50.

38. Baron III:36–38.

39. Roth, *op. cit.*, p. 41; Blumenkranz in Roth (ed.), *The World History of the Jewish People*, XI:76, 78; S. Schwarzfuchs, *op. cit.*, p. 146.

40. Baron III:50.

41. *Op. cit.*, 10, 189.

42. H. Z. Hirschberg, *Yisrael ba'Arav*, Tel Aviv: Mossad Bialik, 1946, pp. 168, 181, 199, 251, 318 n. 66; cf. Baron III:72.

43. *The Jewish Encyclopedia* III:330–31; Baron III:89, 144; *idem, The Jewish Community* I:177.

44. Goitein, *A Mediterranean Society*, II:277, 301; Baron III:143, 299 n. 25, 300 n.26. However, al-Jāḥiẓ (ninth century) states that the Jews did not intermarry, cf. Joshua Finkel, "A Risāla of al-Jāḥiẓ," *Journal of the American Oriental Society*, 1927, XLVII:328.

45. Goitein, *op. cit.*, II:301–2.

46. Asher ben Yeḥiel, *Responsa* (in Hebrew), Jerusalem: n.p., 1965, 18:13, p. 42; cf. also Louis M. Epstein, *Sex Laws and Customs in Judaism*, New York: Bloch Publ. Co., 1948, p. 173.

47. Baron XI:82–85.

48. Baron X:125, 127, 128, 175; XI:78, 81, 85; XIII:21–22.

49. Baron X:184; XI:80; *idem, The Jewish Community*, II:312.

50. Maimonides, *Yad haḤazaqa*, Issure Bi'a 12:2; Caro, *Shulhan 'Arukh, Even Ha'Ezer*, 16.

51. Baron, *The Jewish Community*, II:311; H. J. Zimmels, *Die Marranen*, pp. 61 ff. Cf. also a list of cases in Abraham A. Neuman, *Jews in Spain*, Philadelphia: The Jewish Publication Society of America, 1944, vol. II, p. 278 n. 22, which shows that Jewish women violated these laws as frequently as Jewish men. An interesting case from eleventh-century Barcelona is described by F. Cantera Burgos, "Christian Spain," in Roth (ed.), *The World History of the Jewish People*, XI:378.

52. Cf. R. Moses of Coucy, *Sepher Mitzwot Gadol*, Prohibitions no. 113, Commandments no. 3, Venice, 1547, pp. 39d, 96c f.; cf. Heinrich Graetz, *Geschichte*, VII:58; Neuman, *op. cit.*, II:11; H. J. Zimmels, *Ashkenazim and Sephardim*, London: Oxford University Press, 1958, p. 255; Baron XI:81–82.

53. An anonymous responsum in R. Judah b. Asher, *Zikhron Yehuda*, no. 91; cf. also *Tzeda LaDerekh* II:4,§6, p. 112b; V:6, pp. 119a f., as quoted by Zimmels, *Ashkenazim and Sephardim*, p. 256.

54. Baron XIII (1969):150 and 386 n. 93, quoting Simon and Zemaḥ Duran, *Yakhin uBo'az* II:3, p. 68c f.; Yoseph ben Moshe di Trani, *Teshuvot on Even Ha'Ezer*, no. xviii, Lvov, 1861, p. 62d, 63c; and other sources.

55. Abraham Zacuto, *Sepher HaYuhasin*, ed. Filipowski, London, 1857, p. 225a, as quoted by Zimmels, *Die Marranen*, p. 63 n. 3, and *idem, Ashkenazim and Sephardim*, p. 257.

56. Solomon ibn Verga, *Shevet Yehuda*, no. 63, ed. Warsaw, 1928, p. 133 f., as quoted by Zimmels, *Die Marranen*, p. 63, and *idem, Ashkenazim and Sephardim*, p. 257.

57. Neuman, *Jews in Spain*, II:278 n. 22; Zimmels, *Die Marranen*, pp. 60–62, 64–66.

58. Zimmels, *Die Marranen*, p. 69.

59. Baron XIV (1969):283–84.

60. Baron X:291–92; XI:79, 86.

61. Baron XIV:123, 126.

62. Shlomo Simonsohn, *Toldot HaYehudim b'Duksut Mantova*, Tel Aviv: Tel Aviv University and Ben Zvi Institute, 1962, vol. I, pp. 82, 84; vol. II, p. 395.

63. *Op. cit.*, I:84.

64. Baron XI:79; XIV:122.

65. Baron XIV:133.

66. Baron XIV:123.

67. Baron XIV:48, 63.

68. Baron XI:128.

69. Baron XI:8; *idem, The Jewish Community*, II:313.

70. Baron XI:80, 186.

71. Baron X:5; XI:80; *idem, The Jewish Community*, I:225; III:54.

72. Jacob Mann, *Texts and Studies in Jewish History and Literature*, 2nd ed., New York: Ktav Publ. House, 1972, vol. I, pp. 31–33.
73. Baron X:82; XI:80, 82, 85.
74. Baron III:133–34; XI:80, 82, 85, 186; XIV:212; *idem, The Jewish Community*, II:313; III:205 n. 25; Zimmels, *Die Marranen*, p. 64.
75. Baron III:212; Kohn, *A zsidók története Magyarországon*, pp. 271 ff., 387 ff. Cf. A. Scheiber in Roth (ed.), *The World History of the Jewish People*, XI:317.
76. Baron X:34, 44.
77. Baron, *The Jewish Community*, II:314 and sources, III:205 n. 27.
78. Ruppin, *Die Soziologie der Juden*, I:211–13. Earlier treatments of Jewish-Christian intermarriage are found in Kautsky, *Rasse und Judentum*, pp. 153–56 of the English translation, and Ignaz Zollschan, *Das Rassenproblem*, 3rd ed., Vienna: W. Braumüller, 1912, pp. 477–91.
79. Ruppin, *Soziologie*, 1:230. My translation from the German, R. P.
80. *Encyclopaedia Judaica*, 1971, XII:165–66; National Jewish Population Study of the Council of Jewish Federations and Welfare Funds conducted in 1971–73.
81. Baron XI:81, 84.
82. Baron XI:83.
83. B. Yeb. 23a, 45a; Maimonides, *Yad haḤazaqa*, Issure Bi'a 15:3; *Shulḥan 'Arukh, Even ha'Ezer*, 4:19.
84. Baron, *The Jewish Community*, II:314–15; cf. also *The Jewish Encyclopedia*, VI:560.

V. Slavery and Concubinage

1. Mark 12:2, 4; Matthew 24:45; John 8:35; etc.
2. Josh. 9:3–27; Num. 31:15–18, 26–47; Deut. 20:14; 21:10–14; 2Ki. 5:2; 2Chron. 28:8–15.
3. Lev. 25:44–46; Gen. 17:27; Ex. 12:44; 20:10; 23:13; Cf. *Entziql. Miq.* VI:1–14, s.v. Eved, 'Avdut.
4. M. Git. 4:6 and Bertinoro *ad loc.;* B. Git. 42a. M. Git. 4:5. M. Yeb. 2:8; however, cf. Y. Ket. 25c top.
5. Ex. 21:26–27. Cf. *Revue des Etudes Juives*, VII:161–66; Levy, *Jahrbuch für Geschichte der Juden*, II:223; *Jewish Encyclopedia*, XI:407–8.
6. M. Git. 1:3. B. Git. 40a. B. Pes. 113a.
7. Ex. 21:26–27; B. Qid. 24b.
8. Lev. 19:20–22; Gen. 16:5. Gen. 30:3–13; Ex. 27:7–11.
9. Ex. 21:12, 14, 20, 28–32; Ex. 21:16; Jud. 19:1–30.
10. Ben Sir. 41:21.
11. Gen. 33:2; Gen. 49:1–28.
12. Gen. 16:1 ff.; 21:13; Jud. 8:30–31, Jud. 11:1–2.
13. Gen. 17:9–14, 23–27; B. Yeb. 48a–b.
14. B. Hag. 4a; M. Hag. 1:1; M. Naz. 1: B. Naz. 61a.
15. M. Ker. 1:3; B. Ker. 7b; B. Yeb. 45b–46a, 47b; Y. 'Av. Zar. 1:1,39b mid.
16. Cecil Roth in *Cambridge Medieval History*, VII (1964):633.
17. Blumenkranz, *op. cit.*, pp. 70–71, 76; Baron III:32, 36, 51.
18. Baron III: 36, 38.
19. Blumenkranz, *op. cit.*, pp. 76–79, 137–39.
20. Otto Stobbe, *Die Juden in Deutschland während des Mittelalters*, Braunschweig: Schwetschke, 1866, p. 172; as quoted by Eli Strauss (Ashtor), *Toldot haY'hudim b'Mitzrayim w'Suriya (History of the Jews in Egypt and Syria)*, Jerusalem: Mossad haRav Kook, 1951, vol. II, p. 234; Blumenkranz, *op. cit.*, p. 171.
21. Kohn, *A zsidók története Magyarországon*, pp. 70, 72, 74, 76–79, 86–87, 370. My translation of the laws quoted, R. P.
22. Blumenkranz, *op. cit.*, p. 86; Baron XII:36, 189, 212, 219.
23. Ibn Hishām, *Das Leben Muhammeds*, ed. F. Wüstenfeld, Göttingen, 1858, p. 653; Julius Wellhausen, *Muhammed in Medina, d. i. Vaqidi's Kitab al-Maghazi*, Berlin, 1882, p. 165; as quoted by Hirschberg, *Yisrael ba'Arav*, p. 200; Baron III:22, and sources, p. 238 n. 24.

24. Strauss (Ashtor), *op. cit.*, II:234.

25. Hirschberg, *Toldot haY'hudim b'Afriqa haTz'fonit* (*History of the Jews in North Africa*), Jerusalem: Mossad Bialik, 1965, vol. II, p. 134; Goitein, *A Mediterranean Society*, I:136.

26. A. Harkavy (ed.), *T'shuvot haG'onim*, Berlin, 1888, no. 431; as quoted by Ben Zion Wacholder, "The Halakah and the Proselyting of Slaves During the Gaonic Era," *Historia Judaica*, 1956, XVIII:2, p. 94.

27. Strauss, *op. cit.*, II:235; Goitein, *op. cit.*, I:142.

28. Goitein, *op. cit.*, I:134–35, 143–45, 147; II:349.

29. *Ibid.*, I:135–39, 144–45; Hirschberg, *Toldot*, I:134–35; Epstein, *Sex Laws and Customs in Judaism*, p. 176.

30. Hirschberg, *Toldot*, I:139–40, 359–60 n. 121; Israel Abrahams, *Jewish Life in the Middle Ages*, Philadelphia: Jewish Publication Society of America, 1958, p. 95.

31. Maimonides, *Responsa*, ed. A. Freimann, Jerusalem: Mekitze Nirdamim, 1934, p. 151, no. 154; Goitein, *op. cit.* I:135.

32. Rabbi David ben Solomon ibn Abi Zimra, *Responsa*, part I, nos. 195, 196; part IV, no. 1360; as quoted by Strauss, *op. cit.*, II:236, 342, 525–26; cf. Zimmels, *Die Marranen*, pp. 69–70.

33. Abi Zimra, *Responsa*, part I, nos. 48, 188, 409; part II, no. 743; part III, nos. 443, 520, 961; part IV, nos. 1157, 1220, 1348; part VII, no. 4, 10, etc.; as quoted by Strauss, *op. cit.*, II:342, 525–26; and by Zimmels, *Die Marranen*, pp. 68 ff., and *Ashkenazim and Sephardim*, p. 257.

34. Goitein, *op. cit.*, I:134, 145–46; Wacholder, *op. cit.*, p. 102; Hirschberg, *Toldot*, I:134–35; B. M. Lewin, *Otzar haG'onim*, Jerusalem, 1936, VII:38–39. There is an extensive literature on slavery among the Jews in Muslim countries, part of which is listed in Hirschberg, *Toldot*, I:358–59.

35. Abi Zimra, *Responsa*, Sudylkow: Isaac Madpis, 1836, part III, no. 520.

36. Thus in Egypt, cf. Strauss, *op. cit.*, II:342. The two types of concubines are mentioned, e.g., by Isaac ben Sheshet (1326–1408), the famous Spanish halakhist who from 1391 was rabbi in Algiers; cf. Isaac ben Sheshet Barfat (known as RiBaSh), *Responsa*, ed. Israel Hayim Daiches, Jerusalem, 1968, no. 395, p. 245; cf. also Eliezer Ben Yehuda, *A Complete Dictionary of Ancient and Modern Hebrew*, s.v. ḥashuqa; Louis M. Epstein, "The Institution of Concubinage Among the Jews," *Proceedings of the American Academy for Jewish Research*, VI (1935):184–86; Neuman, *The Jews in Spain*, II:39, 287; Zimmels, *Die Marranen*, pp. 68 f., and *Ashkenazim and Sephardim*, p. 254.

37. Neuman, *op. cit.*, II:39–41, 278 n. 22, 287.

38. Cf. sources quoted by Epstein, "Concubinage," p. 183, and Zimmels, *Ashkenazim and Sephardim*, p. 258. Cf. also Yitzhaq (Fritz) Baer, *Toldot ha Y'hudim biS'farad haNotzrit* (*History of the Jews in Christian Spain*), Tel Aviv: 'Am 'Oved, 1945, vol. I, pp. 167, 169–72; A. T. Shrock, *Rabbi Jonah ben Abraham of Gerona*, London: Edward Goldstone, 1948, pp. 19–20.

39. Cf. *Zohar* I:93; II:3b, 48b; III:46; as quoted by Baer, *op. cit.*, I:169–72. On the Shekhina-Matronit, cf. R. Patai, *The Hebrew Goddess*, New York: Ktav Publ. House, 1967, pp. 137 ff., 186 ff.

40. Cf. Solomon ibn Verga, *Shevet Y'huda*, ed. Wiener, p. 95; Baron IX:128; XI:81; Zimmels, *Die Marranen*, p. 60.

41. Zimmels, *Die Marranen*, pp. 67–70; Baron XII:35–36; XIII:15–16.

42. Zimmels, *Die Marranen*, pp. 60, 69–70; Baron XIII:15.

43. Baron XI:86–87.

44. Epstein, "Concubinage," pp. 186–88, quoting Adret, *Responsa* II:363, IV:315; and Jacob Israel Emden, *Sh'elot Ya'vetz* II:15; Zimmels, *Ashkenazim and Sephardim*, pp. 253, 258; Baron XII:35–36.

45. J. D. Oppenheim, "Jewish Customs Among the Surinam (Dutch Guiana) Population," *Edoth: A Quarterly for Folklore and Ethnology*, Jerusalem, 1947–48, III:1–2, pp. lxv–lxvii; David Max Eichhorn, *Conversion to Judaism*, New York: Ktav Publ. House, 1965, pp. 123–24.

46. Lloyd Cabot Briggs, *Tribes of the Sahara*, Cambridge, Mass.: Harvard University

Press, 1960, pp. 91, 103; and *The Living Races of the Sahara Desert,* Cambridge, Mass.: Peabody Museum, 1958, pp. 73–74, 174.

47. Wacholder, "the Halakah, etc.," p. 106.

48. Stith Thompson, *Motif Index of Folk Literature,* rev. ed., T 161, and literature *ibid.;* Sir James George Frazer, *Folk-Lore in the Old Testament,* London: Macmillan, 1919, vol. I, pp. 481–534. Cf. also an earlier but still very valuable critical study on the subject by Karl Schmidt. *Jus primae noctis: Eine geschichtliche Untersuchung,* Freiburg I. M.: Herder, 1881, esp. pp. 163–76, 311.

49. Frazer, *op. cit.,* I:495–97, 530.

50. Y. Ket. 25c; B. Ket. 3b.

51. Adolph Jellinek, *Bet haMidrash,* reprint, Jerusalem: Bamberger & Wahrman, 1938, vol. I, p. 137.

52. Megillat Ta'anith, ch. 6, Amsterdam, 1711, p. 26a; Warsaw, 1874, pp. 23–24. My translation from the Hebrew, R. P. Cf. also Rashi *ad* Gen. 6:2.

53. Krauss, *Revue des Etudes Juives,* 30:24–42, 204–19. His argument was, however, refuted by Lévi, *ibid.,* pp. 220–31. Cf. also Louis M. Epstein, *Sex Laws and Customs in Judaism,* p. 157.

54. Abū Rayḥān Muḥammad ibn Aḥmad al-Bīrūnī, *Chronology of Ancient Nations, an English version . . . ,* translated and edited by C. E. Sachau, London: Oriental Translation Fund, 1879, ch. 14 (dealing with the feasts and fast days of the Jews), pp. 271–72, Arabic text, p. 278; *Abulfedae historia anteislamica,* Latin translation by H. O. Fleischer, Leipzig, 1831, pp. 161, 163. According to other Arab historians, the tyrannical king was not Greek but Jewish, cf. al-Moqaddasi, *Descriptio imperii moslemici,* ed. de Goeje, Leiden: Brill, 1877, III:179; Ibn al-Athir, *Chronicon,* ed. C. J. Tornberg, Lugduni Batavorum, 1886, I:492; Jacuts *Geographisches Wörterbuch,* ed. Fr. Wüstenfeld, Leipzig, 1886–73, IV:462; as quoted by Hisrchberg, *Yisrael ba'Arav,* pp. 123–24.

55. Israel Joseph Benjamin, *Acht Jahre in Asien und Africa von 1846 bis 1855,* Hanover: Selbstverlag des Verfassers, 1858, p. 97. My translation from the German, R. P.

56. Erich Brauer, *The Jews of Kurdistan* (in Hebrew), translated, edited, and completed by R. Patai, Jerusalem: Palestine Institute for Folklore and Ethnology, 1947, pp. 100, 186.

57. Solomon Ganzfried, *Code of Jewish Law* (*Kitzur Schulchan Aruch*), translated by Hyman E. Goldin, New York: Hebrew Publishing Co., 1927, ch. CLIII, p. 21, and ch. CLVII, p. 31.

PART II

VI. The Jewish Mind

1. John Stuart Mill, as quoted by Otto Klineberg, "Race and Psychology," in *Race and Science* (a UNESCO Publication), New York: Columbia University Press, 1971, p. 452.

2. Franz Boas, "Racial Purity," *Asia,* 1940, 40:234.

3. Klineberg, *op. cit.*

4. G. M. Morant, "The Significance of Racial Differences," in *Race and Science,* pp. 336–37, 340.

5. Walter F. Bodmer and Luigi Luca Cavalli-Sforza, "Intelligence and Race," *Scientific American,* 1970, 223:19–29.

6. Cf., for example, Curt Stern, *Human Genetics,* 2nd ed., San Francisco and London: W. H. Freeman, 1960, pp. 591–98, and the earlier literature listed there on pp. 607–8.

7. Eliot D. Chapple, *Culture and Biological Man,* New York: Holt, Rinehart and Winston, 1970, p. 136.

8. Klineberg, *op. cit.,* p. 431.

9. Marie Jahoda, "Race Relations and Mental Health," in *Race and Science,* p. 457.

10. Henry H. Goddard, director of the Psychological Clinic of Ohio State University, for example, takes it for granted that the basic motivation of the persecution of the Jews throughout history was jealousy; cf. his Introduction to Irma Loeb Cohen, *Intelligence of Jews Compared with Non-Jews,* Columbus, Ohio: The Ohio University Press, 1927, p. vi.

11. Francis Galton and Karl Pearson are quoted in Thomas Weaver (ed.), *To See Our-*

selves: Anthropology and Modern Social Issues, Glenview, Ill.: Scott, Foresman and Co., 1973, pp. 211–212.

12. Gustave Lagneau, *Bulletin de l'Académie de Médecine*, Paris, 1891, 26:300–1.

13. One of the earliest such studies was that of J. K. Van Denberg, "Causes of Elimination of Students in Public Schools in New York City," Teachers College Contributions to Education, no. 47, New York, 1911, 38 pp.

14. J. and R. Weintraub, "The Influences of Environment on Mental Ability as Shown by the Binet-Simon Tests," *Journal of Educational Psychology*, 1912, 3:577–83.

15. M. Davis and A. G. Hughes, "An Investigation Into Comparative Intelligence and Attainments of Jewish and Non-Jewish Children," *British Journal of Psychology*, 1927, 18:134–36; A. G. Hughes, "Jews and Gentiles," *Eugenics Review*, 1928, 20:89–94.

16. W. H. Winch, "Christian and Jewish Children of East End Elementary Schools," *British Journal of Psychology*, 20, part 3, Jan. 1930, p. 261.

17. Robert M. Yerkes and J. Foster, *A Point Scale for Measuring Mental Ability*, rev. ed., Baltimore: Warwick and York, 1923.

18. Karl Pearson and M. Moul, "The Problem of Alien Immigration into Great Britain," *Annals of Eugenics*, 1925, 1:125; A. G. Hughes, "Jews and Gentiles," *Eugenics Review*, 1928, 20:89–94; J. Rumyaneck, "The Comparative Psychology of Jews and Non-Jews," *British Journal of Psychology*, 1930–31, 21:404–24.

19. V. T. Graham, "The Intelligence of Italian and Jewish Children in the Habit Clinic of the Massachusetts Division of Mental Hygiene," *Journal of Abnormal and Social Psychology*, 1926, 20:371–76; Jewish as compared to Italian children were found to be superior in reading also by E. W. McElwee, "Differences in Reading Attainment of Italian and Jewish Children," *Journal of Applied Psychology*, 1935, 19:730–32.

20. H. E. Garrett, "Jews and Others: Some Group Differences in Personality, Intelligence, and College Achievement," *The Personnel Journal*, 1929, 7:341–48.

21. Moshe Brill, "Studies of Jewish and Non-Jewish Intelligence," *Journal of Educational Psychology*, May 1936, 27:331–52.

22. O. C. Held, "A Comparative Study of the Performance of Jewish and Gentile College Students on the American Council Psychological Examination," *Journal of Social Psychology*, 1941, 13:407–11.

23. A. M. Shuey, "Differences in Performance of Jewish and non-Jewish Students on the American Council Psychological Examination," *Journal of Social Psychology*, 1942, 15:221–43.

24. F. Brown, "A Comparative Study of the Intelligence of Jewish and Scandinavian Kindergarten Children," *Journal of Genetic Psychology*, 1944, 64:67–92. Cf. also *idem*, "A Comparative Study of the Intelligence of Jewish and Scandinavian Kindergarten Children," *Psychological Bulletin*, 1941, 38:595–96 (abstract).

25. Julius B. Maller, "Studies in the Intelligence of Young Jews," *Jewish Education*, 1931, vol. 3, no. 1, Jan.–March, pp. 10–11 (offprint).

26. Lajos Frigyes, *A zsidók természetrajza*, Budapest: Zsidó Szemle, 1920, p. 47; Günther, *Rassenkunde des jüdischen Volkes*, p. 202; Ruppin, *Soziologie der Juden*, I:55–56.

27. Klineberg, *op. cit.*, pp. 435–36.

28. Raphael Patai, *Tents of Jacob: The Diaspora Yesterday and Today*, Englewood Cliffs, N.J.: Prentice-Hall, 1971, pp. 91 ff.

29. *Ibid.*, p. 93.

30. *Ibid.*, pp. 95–97.

31. Carl Frankenstein, "Development of Intelligence Among Poor Children" (in Hebrew), *Megamot*, 1957, 8:153–70.

32. L. Jaxa-Bykowski, "Investigations of the Intellectual Level of Aryan and Jewish Pupils in Polish Secondary Schools" (in German), *Zeitschrift für Pädagogische Psychologie*, 1935, 36:38–40; *idem*, "The Intellectual Level of Polish and Jewish Youth in Our Secondary Schools" (in Polish), *Psychometrja*, 1935, 2:3–27.

33. Boris M. Levinson, "The Intelligence of Applicants for Admission to Jewish Day Schools," *Jewish Social Studies*, 1957, 19:129–40.

34. M. Adler, "A Study of the Effects of Ethnic Origin on Giftedness," *Gifted Child Quarterly*, 1963, 7 (3):98–101. Higher average I.Q. figures among Jewish than non-Jewish

children were found also in a series of tests administered to 2,453 children in 31 Jewish religious schools in New York, cf. N. Nardi, "The Intelligence of Jewish Children" (in Hebrew), *HaHinukh*, 1947–48, 21:257–70.

35. Gina Ortar, "Comparative Analysis of the Jewish Communities as to Structure of Intelligence" (in Hebrew), *Megamot*, 1953, vol. 4, no. 2, pp. 107–22.

36. Sh. Bakaliar-Alon, "Features of the Personality of Yemenite Youth" (in Hebrew), *HaHinukh*, 1948–49, 22:300–23.

37. Reuben Feuerstein and M. Richelle, *Children of the Mellah: The Cultural Backwardness of Moroccan Children and Its Meaning for Education* (in Hebrew), Jerusalem: Department for the Immigration of Youth and Children of the Jewish Agency and the Henrietta Szold Institute for Child and Youth Welfare, 1963, pp. 93, 232–33.

38. Klineberg, *op. cit.*, p. 442.

39. Cf. Joseph Jacobs, *Studies in Jewish Statistics, Social, Vital, and Anthropometric*, London: D. Nutt, 1891, Appendix B, "The Comparative Distribution of Jewish Ability" (a paper read before the Anthropological Institute on Nov. 10, 1886), pp. xlvii, li.

40. *Ibid.*, pp. liii–liv.

41. Patai, *Tents of Jacob*, p. 165.

42. Cf. the discussion of this subject, *ibid.*, pp. 164–66.

43. Some of the earlier literature on the subject is quoted in Ruppin, *Soziologie* 1:60–63. For a recent criticism of the assertions and denials of national, subnational, regional, or class differences of major magnitudes, cf. James A. Schellenberg, *An Introduction to Social Psychology*, New York: Random House, 1970, p. 292.

44. M. Smith and R. B. Moton, "Jewish Production of American Leaders," *Scientific Monthly*, 1942, 55:144–50.

45. A preliminary count, carried out by R. and Daphne Patai, of the obviously "Jewish" names beginning with A and E included in the 1972–73 edition of *Who's Who in America*, gave the following results: of the biographies included under A, 5% were those of Jews, while of those listed under E, 6.5% were Jewish. When taken together, the letters A and E yielded 5.6% Jewish biographies. Since in 1972 the Jews represented only 2.7% of the population of the United States, their percentage among outstanding Americans was more than twice the expected rate. In mentioning these figures we are fully aware that they are merely very rough approximations, since it is a practical impossibility to spot all the Jews listed in *Who's Who in America*. In all probability, the actual percentages are higher than stated.

46. Juan Huarte, *Examen de ingenios para las ciencias*, Pamplona, 1575, pp. 409 ff., as quoted by Werner Sombart, *Die Juden und das Wirtschaftsleben*, Leipzig: Dunker und Humblot, 1911, p. 419.

47. Cf., e.g., Renan, *Etudes d'histoire religieuse*, pp. 85–87; and Muret, *L'Esprit juif*, pp. 42–43, 50–51.

48. Joseph Jacobs, *The Jewish Race: A Study in National Character*. Plan of a projected work. London: Privately printed, 1889, pp. 12–21; *idem, Studies in Jewish Statistics*, p. iii.

49. Dina Wolberg, *Zur differential Psychologie der Juden: EXperimentelle Untersuchungen an Schülern und Studenten*. Jenaer Beiträge zur Jugend- und Erziehungspsychologie, no. 5, Langensalza: Julius Beltz, 1927, pp. 28–32.

50. Winch, "Christian and Jewish Children in East End Elementary Schools," pp. 261–73.

51. Maller, "Studies in the Intelligence of Young Jews," p. 10.

52. Brown, "A Comparative Study of the Intelligence of Jewish and Scandinavian Kindergarten Children."

53. Boris M. Levinson, "A Research Note on Subcultural Differences in WAIS Between Aged Italians and Jews," *Journal of Gerontology*, 1960, 15:197–98.

54. *Idem*, "jewish Subculture and WAIS Performance Among Jewish Aged," *Journal of Genetic Psychology*, 1962, 100:55–68.

55. Gerald S. Lesser, Gordon Fifer, and Donald H. Clark, *Mental Abilities of Children from Different Social-Class and Cultural Groups*. Monographs of the Society for Research in Child Development, vol. 30, no. 4. Chicago: University of Chicago Press, 1965, pp. 60–61.

56. Margaret E. Backman, "Patterns of Mental Abilities: Ethnic, Socioeconomic, and Sex Differences," *American Education Research Journal*, 1972, 9:1–12.

57. Irma Loeb Cohen, *The Intelligence of Jews as Compared With Non-Jews*, Columbus, Ohio: The Ohio State University Press, 1927, p. 37.

58. Backman, *op. cit.*

59. Lesser *et al., op. cit.,* p. 61.

60. Ortar, "Comparative Analysis of the Jewish Communities," pp. 107–22.

61. K. Sward, "Jewish Musicality in America," *Journal of Applied Psychology,* 1933, 17:675–712; Moshe Brill, "Comparative Psychological Studies of Jews and Non-Jews and Their Implication for Jewish Education," *Jewish Education,* 1936, 8:75–76. An Adlerian individual-psychological explanation (compensation for a Jewish racial tendency for defective hearing) of Jewish musicality is given by H. Rosenthal, "Die Musikalität der Juden," *Internationale Zeitschrift für Individual-Psychologie,* 1931, 9:122–31.

62. Cf. H. Rosenthal, "Die schauspielerische Begabung bei den Juden," *loc. cit.,* 1930, 8:325–32.

63. G. Dammann, *Die Juden in der Zauberkunst (Jews in the Art of Magic),* Berlin-Grunewald: Gunther Dammann, 1933. Contains the biographies of twenty-three outstanding Jewish magicians in the past two centuries.

64. Paul Goodman and Percival Goodman, "Jews in Modern Architecture," *Commentary,* 1957, vol. 24, no. 1, pp. 28–35.

65. Ex. 17:2–7; Num. 20:10, 13, etc.; Ps. 78:8, etc.; Num. 23:21, 24; Isa. 1; 30:1; 45:9; Jer. 5:23; Ps. 78:8.

66. B. Yeb. 79a; B. Shab. 133b.

67. Huarte, *op. cit.*

68. Isaac de Pinto, *Apologie pour la Nation Juive, ou Réflexions Critiques,* Amsterdam, 1762, as quoted by Zimmels, *Ashkenazim and Sephardim,* p. 51.

69. Jacobs, *op. cit.,* pp. 12–21.

70. Fritz Kahn, *Die Juden als Rasse und Kulturvolk,* 3rd ed., Berlin: Welt-Verlag, 1922, pp. 208–9.

71. K. Sward and M. B. Friedman, "Jewish Temperament," *Journal of Applied Psychology,* 1935, 19:70–84; Sward, "Patterns of Jewish Temperament," pp. 410–25. Related to point (4) above is the finding made ten years earlier to the effect that "the Jews" have an inferiority complex, cf. A. A. Roback, "Have the Jews an Inferiority Complex?" *B'nai B'rith Magazine,* 1925, 39:339 ff.

72. A. M. Shuey, "Personality Traits of Jewish and Non-Jewish Students," *Archives of Psychology,* New York, 1944, no. 290, p. 38.

73. Anton Lourié, "The Jews As a Psychological Type," *American Imago,* 1949, 6:119–55.

74. Edward L. Clark, "Motivation of Jewish Students," *Journal of Social Psychology,* 1949, 29:113–17.

75. J. Veroff, Sheila Feld, and Gerald Gurin, "Achievement Motivation and Religious Background," *American Sociological Review,* 1962, 27 (2):205–17.

76. Fred L. Strodtbeck, Margaret R. McDonald, and Bernard C. Rosen, "Evaluation of Occupations: A Reflection of Jewish and Italian Mobility Differences," *American Sociological Review,* 1959, 22:546–53.

77. Boris M. Levinson, "The Problems of Jewish Religious Youth," *Genetic Psychology Monographs,* 1959 (Nov.), 60:309–48; *idem,* "The Vocational Interests of Yeshiva College Freshmen," *Journal of Genetic Psychology,* 1961, 99:235–44.

78. Nathan Hurwitz, "Sources of Middle Class Values of American Jews," *Social Forces,* 1958, 37 (2), Dec., pp. 117–23.

79. Israel S. Draplin, "Aspects of Suicide in Israel," *Israel Annals of Psychiatry and Related Disciplines,* 1965, 3(1), April, pp. 35–50.

80. On these difficulties, cf. Gabriel Ward Lasker, *Physical Anthropology,* New York: Holt, Rinehart and Winston, 1973, pp. 358–61.

81. Clyde Kluckhohn and Henry A. Murray (eds.), *Personality in Nature, Society, and Culture,* New York: Alfred A. Knopf, 1967, p. 58.

82. Chapple, *op. cit.,* p. 72.

83. Patai, *Tents of Jacob,* pp. 279–85.

84. Cf. Joseph Jacobs, *Jewish Contributions to Civilization,* Philadelphia: The Jewish Publication Society of America, 1920; Abraham A. Roback, *Jewish Influence on Modern Thought,* Cambridge, Mass.: Sci-Art Publishers, and New York: The Jewish Forum Publ. Co., 1929; Cecil Roth, *The Jewish Contribution to Cvilization,* London: Macmillan, 1938; new ed., Ox-

ford: East and West Library, 1943; Dagobert D. Runes (ed.), *the Hebrew Impact on West-ern Civilization*, New York: Philosophical Library, 1951.

VII. The Latest Libel: The Jew as Racist

1. Reprinted in *Encyclopaedia Judaica* (Jerusalem, 1972), 4:1127, s.v. "Blood Libel."
2. Raphael Patai, *The Seed of Abraham: Jews and Arabs in Contact and Conflict*, Salt Lake City: University of Utah Press, 1986, and New York: Scribner's, 1987, p. 293.
3. *Handwörterbuch des deutschen Aberglaubens*, vol. 7, 1935–36, p. 734. Emphasis added.
4. Daniel Patrick Moynihan, "Introduction," to Jacques Givet, *The Anti-Zionist Complex*, Englewood, N.J.:SBS Publishing, 1982, p. ix.
5. *Loc. cit.*, quoting Bernard Lewis.
6. The *New York Times*, August 26, 1975, p. 26; Nov. 11, 1975, pp. 1, 16.
7. As reported in the *New York Times*, Nov. 1, 1987, part 1, p. 31.
8. Jewish Telegraphic Agency *Daily News Bulletin*, Nov. 4, 1987, p. 4.
9. D. Kimon, *La pathologie de l'Islam et les moyens de la détruire*, Paris, 1897 (2nd ed.), pp. 111–12.
10. Jean Baubérot, *Le tort d'exister: Des Juifs aux Palestiniens*, 33-Saint-Médard-en-Jalles près Bordeaux: Ducros éditeur, 1970, pp. 34, 124, 127, 141, 160, 171, 214.
11. Raphael Patai, *Israel Between East and West: A Study in Human Relations*, Phila-delphia: The Jewish Publication Society of America, 1953; 2nd enlarged edition, West-port, Conn.: Greenwood Publ. Corp., 1970.
12. *Sionisme et Racisme (une question qui demande réponse)*, Paris: Eurabia, n.d., 31 pages.
13. Abdelkader Benabdallah, *Israel et les Peuples Noirs; l'Alliance Raciste Israel-Sud-Africaine*, Montreal: Les Editions Canada-Monde Arabe, 1979.
14. Mohand Tazerout, *Manifeste contre le racisme*, Rodez, France: Edition Subervie, 1963, pp. 7, 137–43, 207–27.
15. *Racisme et Panarabisme: Une conspiration contre les libertés humaines*, Paris: Comité d'Action de Défense Démocratique, 1960, pp. 3, 11.
16. Cf., e.g., Jeremy Fish, "The Decline of World Jewry," in *Israel Scene*, Sept.–Oct. 1987, p. 28.
17. Published in Tel Aviv, by Otzar haMore, April 1982.
18. Cf. Jacques Givet's book quoted in note 4, which was originally published in French, Paris: Librairie Plon, 1979, and discusses in some detail the phenomenon of Jew-ish anti-Zionism and anti-Israelism.
19. Ronald Segal, *Whose Jerusalem? The Conflicts of Israel*, London: Jonathan Cape, 1973, pp. 13, 14.
20. Israel Shahak, *Le Racisme de l'Etat d'Israël*, Paris: Editions Guy Authier, 1975, pp. 92 and passim. Cf. also the discussion of anti-Zionism as a modern form of anti-Semitism in the Arab world by Eliyahu Biletzky, in his Hebrew book *Ha'Alila—Tziyonut = Giz'anut* (The Libel: Zionism = Racism), Tel Aviv: Alef Bet, 1978, pp. 71–80.
21. Pierre Paraf, *Le Racisme dans le Monde* (Racism in the World), Paris, 1964; re-printed Paris: Petit Bibliothèque Payot, 1981, pp. 130–35.
22. Cf. Wolf Leslau, *Falasha Anthology*, New Haven: Yale University Press, 1951, p. xii.
23. Cf. Tudor Parfitt, *Operation Moses*, London: Weidenfeld and Nicolson, 1985.
24. Jewish Telegraphic Agency (JTA) Daily News Bulletin of Oct. 23, 1987, p. 4.
25. Jewish Telegraphic Agency (JTA) Daily News Bulletin of Oct. 26, 1987, p. 2.
26. Tosefta Sanhedrin 8:4.

PART III
VIII. Morphological Traits

1. C. L. Brace, "A Nonracial Approach toward Understanding of Human Diversity," in F. M. Ashley Montagu (ed.), *The Concept of Race*, New York: Macmillan, 1964.

2. M. Fishberg, *The Jews: A Study of Race and Environment*, London: Walter Scott Publ. Co. and New York: Charles Scriber's Sons, 1911, pp. 21 ff.

3. *Ibid.*, pp. 90–120.

4. *Ibid.*, p. 145, 149.

5. *Ibid.*, p. 44.

6. C. Seltzer, *The Racial Characteristics of Syrians and Armenians*, Cambridge Mass.: Harvard University Press, 1936; Henry Field, *Ancient and Modern Man in Southwest Asia*, Coral Gables, Florida: University of Miami Press, 1956, pp. 249–50.

7. Seltzer, *op. cit.*, Field, *op. cit.*, pp. 266–72, 317–18.

8. B. Bonné, S. Ashbel, G. Berlin, and B. Sela, "The Habbanite Isolate III. Anthropometrics, Taste Sensitivity, and Color Vision," *Human Heredity*, 1972, 22:430–44.

9. L. Cabot Briggs, *The Living Races of the Sahara Desert*, Cambridge, Mass.: Peabody Museum, 1958.

10. Fishberg, *op. cit.*, p. 39.

11. E. Kobyliansky and G. Livshits, "A Morphological Approach to the Problem of the Biological Similarity of Jewish and non-Jewish Populations," *Annals of Human Biology*, 1985, 12:203–212.

12. M. B. Tartakovsky, R. S. Carel, and Y. Luz, "A Comparison of Body Height of the Israeli-born and Immigrants to Israel," *Human Heredity*, 1983, 33:73–78.

13. Fishberg, *op. cit.*, p. 66.

14. *Ibid.*, p. 76.

15. H. L. Shapiro, "The Jewish People: A Biological History," in *Race and Science: Scientific Analysis from UNESCO*, New York: Columbia University Press, 1961, p. 171.

16. F. Boas, *Abstracts of the Report on Changes in Bodily Form of Descendants of Immigrants*, Washington, D.C.: The Immigration Commission, Government Printing Office, 1911.

17. F. S. Hulse, *The Human Species*, New York: Random House, 1971, p. 426.

18. *Ibid.*, p. 427.

19. E. Kobyliansky, "Changes in Cephalic Morphology of Israelis due to Migration," *Journal of Human Evolution*, 1983, 12:779–86.

20. C. U. Ariens Kappers and L. W. Parr, *An Introduction to the Anthropology of the Near East*, Amsterdam: N. V. Noord-Hollandsche Uitgeversmaatschappij, 1934, pp. 5–6, 172.

21. B. Sekla and F. Soukup, "Inheritance of the Cephalic Index," *American Journal of Physical Anthropology*, 1969, 30:137–40.

22. Bonné, *et al., loc. cit.*

23. K. Pearson, "On Jewish-Gentile Relationships," *Biometrika*, London, 1936, 28:32–33.

24. M. F. Ashley Montagu, *Man's Most Dangerous Myth: The Fallacy of Race*, New York: Columbia University Press, 1945, pp. 225–26.

25. D. L. Risdon, "A Study of the Cranial and Other Human Remains from Palestine Excavated at Tell Duweir (Lachish)," *Biometrika*, London, 1961, 31:161.

26. *Entziqlopedia Miqrait*, Jerusalem: Mossad Bialik, 1962, vol. III, pp. 504–23, s. v. Lakhish.

27. H. Nathan and G. Haas, in E. Goldschmidt (ed.), *Genetics of Migrant and Isolate Populations*, New York: The Williams and Wilkins Co., 1963, p. 284.

28. H. Nathan, "The Skeletons of the Nahal Mishmar Caves," *Israel Exploration Journal*, 1961, 11:1–69.

29. *Ibid.*, p. 68.

30. N. Haas, "Anthropological Observations on the Skeletal Remains from Giv'at ha-Mivtar," *Israel Exploration Journal*, 1970, 20:38–59.

31. J. A. Lourie, "Hand Clasping and Arm Folding among Middle Eastern Jews in Israel," *Human Biology*, 1972, 44:329–34.

32. B. Bonné, S. Ashbel, and A. Tal, "The Habbanite Isolate, ii. Digital and Palmar Dermatoglyphics," *Human Heredity*, 1971, 21:478–92.

33. L. Sachs and M. Bat-Miriam, "The Genetics of Jewish Populations. I. Finger Print Patterns in Jewish Populations in Israel," *American Journal of Human Genetics*, 1957, 9:117–26.

34. Bonné, *et al.*, "The Habbanite Isolate," ii.

35. E. Kobyliansky, S. Micle, B. Arensburg, and H. Nathan, "Finger Dermatoglyphic Characteristics in Israeli Males," *Z. Morph. Anthropologie*, 1979, 70:75–81.

36. Sachs and Bat-Miriam, *op. cit.*

37. S. Micle and E. Kobyliansky, "Dermatoglyphic Distances Between Israeli Jewish Population Groups of Different Geographic Extraction," *Human Biology*, 1985, 47:97–111.

38. J. A. Sofaer, P. Smith, and E. Kaye, "Affinities Between Contemporary and Skeletal Jewish and Non-Jewish Groups Based on Tooth Morphology," *American Journal of Physical Anthropology*, 1986, 70:265–75.

IX. Looking Jewish

1. In the Arabic text of the *Thousand and One Nights*, the passage is corrupt; cf. Richard F. Burton, *Supplemental Nights to the Book of the Thousand and One nights*, London, privately printed by the Boston Club, n.d., vol. 1, p. 197 and n. 2.

2. C. C. Seltzer, "The Jew—His Racial Status," in E. W. Count (ed.), *This Is Race*, New York: Henry Schuman, pp. 608–18.

3. J. Comas, "Racial Myths," in *Race and Science*, New York: Columbia University Press, 1961, p. 38.

4. H. L. Shapiro, "The Jewish People: A Biological History," in *Race and Science*, pp. 171–72.

5. *Op. cit.*, p. 171.

6. E. Renan, *Le judaisme comme race et comme religion*. Lecture given to the Cercle Saint-Simon on Jan. 27, 1883. Paris: Calmann Lévy, 1883, pp. 25, 26, 28.

7. Cf. C. L. Schleich, "Judaische Rassenkopfe," *Ost und West* (a Jewish periodical), Berlin, 1906, p. 229; L. F. Clauss, *Von Seele und Antlitz der Rassen und Völker*, Munich: T. F. Lehmann, 1929, p. 84; both as quoted by Arthur Ruppin, *Soziologie der Juden*, Berlin: Jüdischer Verlag, 1930, vol. 1, pp. 52–53.

8. R. B. Bean, "On the Nose of the Jews and the Quadratus Labii Superioris Muscle," *American Anthropologist*, 1913, 15:106–8.

9. Fishberg, *op. cit.*, p. 166.

10. *Ibid.*, pp. 162–78.

11. Schudt, *Jüdische Merckwürdigkeiten*. Frankfurt and Leipzig: S. T. Hocker, 1714–18, part II.

12. G. Rohlfs, as quoted by Fishberg, *op. cit.*, p. 77; K. Kautsky, *Rasse und Judentum*, Stuttgart: J. H. W. Dietz, 1914, p. 45.

13. R. Wagner, *Das Judenthum in der Musik*, Leipzig; J. J. Weber, 1969, p. 15. Originally written in 1850 and published in the *Neue Zeitschrift für Musik*. My translation from the German [R. P.]. The English translation by Edwin Evans, *Judaism in Music*, New York: Charles Scribner's Sons, 1910, p. 13, is much too free for our present purposes.

14. R. Andree, *Zur Volkskunde der Juden*, Bielefeld and Leipzig: Velhagen & Klasing, 1881, pp. 116–18.

15. A. H. Keane, *Ethnology*, Cambridge: University Press, 1901, p. 194; as quoted by Fishberg, *op. cit.*, p. 389.

16. Montagu, *op. cit.*, pp. 230–32.

17. Comas, *op. cit.*, p. 34.

X. Criteria for the Classification of Races

1. N. A. Barnicot, "Taxonomy and Variation in Modern Man," in M. F. Ashley Montagu (ed.), *The Concept of Race*, New York: The Free Press, 1964, pp. 180–227.

2. Montagu, *Man's Most Dangerous Myth*, p. 35.

3. L. C. Dunn, "Race and Biology," in *Race and Science* (UNESCO publication), New York: Columbia University Press, 1961, pp. 283–84.

4. C. Stern, *Principles of Human Genetics*, San Francisco and New York: W. H. Freeman and Co., 1960, p. 29.

XI. Jewish Inbreeding and Its Effects

1. R. Patai, *Sex and Family in the Bible and the Middle East*, New York: Doubleday, 1959, pp. 23–31.

2. _____. *Society, Culture, and Change in the Middle East*, Philadelphia: University of Pennsylvania Press, 1971, pp. 138–43.

3. H. Ayrout, S.M., *Fellahs d'Egypte*, Cairo: Editions du Sphynx, 1952, p. 143. The 80% estimate is omitted from the English edition of this book, *The Egyptian Peasant*, Boston: Beacon Press, 1963, p. 118; F. Barth, *Principles of Social Organization in Southern Kurdistan*, Oslo: Brødrene Jørgensen, 1953, p. 68; *idem*, *Nomads of South Persia*, Boston: Little, Brown & Co., 1961, p. 65.

4. E. Goldschmidt and T. Cohen, "Inter-ethnic Mixture Among the Communities of Israel," *Cold Spring Harbor Symposium of Quantitative Biology*, 1964, 28:115–20; J. Tsafrir and I. Halbrecht, "Consanguinity and Marriage Systems in the Jewish Community in Israel," *Annals of Human Genetics*, 1972, 35:343–47.

5. B. Bonné, "The Samaritans: A Demographic Study," *American Journal of Human Genetics*, 1966, 18:61–89.

XII. The "Jewish" Blood: ABQ

1. A. E. Mourant, *The Distribution of the Human Blood Groups*, Springfield, Ill.: Charles C. Thomas, 1954; *idem*, "The Blood Groups of the Jews," *Jewish Journal of Sociology*, 1959, 1:155–75; E. Margolis, J. Gurevich, and D. Hermoni, "Blood Groups in Sephardic Jews," *American Journal of Physical Anthropology*, 18:197–99; A. E. Mourant, A. C. Kopec, and K. Domanievska-Sobrozak, *The Distribution of the Human Blood Groups and Other Polymorphisms*, London: Oxford University Press, 1976; T. Cohen, C. Levene, Y. Yodfat, J. Fidel, Y. Friedlander, A. G. Steinberg, and C. Brautbar, "Genetic Studies on Cochin Jews in Israel: 1. Population Data, Blood Groups, Isoenzymes, and HLA Determinants," *American Journal of Medical Genetics*, 1980, 6:61–73, E. Goldschmidt, K. Fried, A. G. Steinberg, and T. Cohen, "The Karaite Community of Iraq in Israel: A Genetic Study," *American Journal of Human Genetics*, 1976, 28:243–52; C. Levene, H. Medalie, Y. Friedlander, and T. Cohen, "The Distribution of ABO, MNSs, Rhesus, Kell, Duffy, and Kidd Blood Groups of Jews Originating from 20 Countries," *Israel Journal of Medical Sciences*, 1984, 20:509–18; B. Bonné-Tamir, S. Ashbel, and R. Kenett, "Genetic Markers: Benign and Normal Traits of Ashkenazi Jews," in R. M. Goodman and A. G. Motulsky (eds.), *Genetic Diseases Among Ashkenazi Jews*, New York: Raven Press, 1979.

2. Bonné-Tamir, Ashbel, and Kenett, *op. cit.*

3. G. Maranjian, E. W. Ikin, A. E. Mourant, and H. Lehmann, "The Blood Groups and Haemoglobins of the Saudi Arabians," *Human Biology*, 1966, 38:394–420.

4. B. Bonné, S. Ashbel, M. Modai, M. J. Godber, A. E. Mourant, D. Tills, and B. G. Woodhead, "The Habbanite Isolate. I Genetic Markers in the Blood," *Human Heredity*, 1970, 20:609–22.

5. B. Bonné, M. Godber, S. Ashbel, A. E. Mourant, and D. Tills, "South Sinai Bedouin: A Preliminary Report on Their Inherited Blood Factors," *American Journal of Physical Anthropology*, 1971, 34:397–408.

6. S. Micle, E. Kobilyansky, M. Nathan, B. Arensburg, and H. Nathan, "ABO-typing of Ancient Skeletons from Israel," *American Journal of Physical Anthropology*, 1977, 47:89–92.

7. B. Bonné, "Genes and Phenotypes in the Samaritan Isolate," *American Journal of Physical Anthropology*, 1966, 24:1–20; *idem*. "The Samaritans: A Demographic Study," *American Journal of Human Genetics*, 1966, 18:61–89.

8. E. Goldschmidt, K. Fried, A. G. Steinberg, and T. Cohen, "The Karaite Community of Iraq in Israel: A Genetic Study," *American Journal of Human Genetics*, 1976, 28:243–52.

9. See note 1.

XIII. The "Jewish" Blood: Other Blood Groups

1. Mourant, *The Distribution of the Human Blood Groups; idem*, "The Blood Groups of the Jews," *Jewish Journal of Sociology*, 1959, 1:155–75; Mourant, A. C. Kopec, and K. Domanievska-Sobrozak, *The Distribution of the Human Blood Groups and Other Polymorphisms*; Mourant, Kopec, and Domanievska-Sobrozak, *The Genetics of the Jews*, London: Oxford University Press, 1978; B. Bonné, "Genes and Phenotypes in the Samaritan Isolate,"; Bonné, *et al.*, "The Habbanite Isolate. I. Genetic Markers in the Blood"; B. Bonné, *et al.*, "South Sinai Beduin: A Preliminary Report on Their Inherited Blood Factors"; J. Gurevitch, E. Hasson, E. Margolis, and C. Poliakoff, "Blood Groups in Jews from Cochin, India," *Annals of Human Genetics*, 1955, 19:254–56; *idem*, "Blood Groups in Jews from Tripolitania," *Annals of Human Genetics*, 1955, 19:260–61; *idem*, "Blood Groups in Persian Jews: A Comparative Study with Other Oriental Jewish Communities," *Annals of Eugenics*, 1956, 21:135–38; J. Gurevitch and E. Margolis, "Blood Groups in Jews from Iraq," *Annals of Human Genetics*, 1955, 19:257–59; G. Maranjian, E. W. Ikin, A. E. Mourant, and H. Lehman, "The Blood Groups and Haemoglobins of the Saudi Arabians, *Human Biology*, 1966, 38:394–420; E. Margolis, J. Gurevitch, and E. Hasson, "Blood Groups in Jews from Morocco and Tunisia," *Annals of Human Genetics*, 157, 22:65–68; E. Margolis, J. Gurevitch, and D. Hermoni, "Blood Groups in Ashkenazi Jews," *American Journal of Physical Anthropology*, 1960a, 18:201–4; E. Margolis, J. Gurevitch, and D. Hermoni, "Blood Groups in Sephardic Jews," *American Journal of Physical Anthropology*, 1960b, 18:197–99; F. Ottensooser, N. Leon, and P. H. Saldanha, "Blood Groups of a Population of Ashkenazi Jews in Brazil," *American Journal of Physical Anthropology*, 1963, 21:41–48; E. Sunderland and H. M. Smith, "The Blood Groups of the Shi'a in Yazd, Central Iran," *Human Biology*, 1966, 38:50–59; C. Levene, J. H. Medalie, Y. Friedlander, and T. Cohen, "The Distribution of ABO, MNSs, Rhesus, Kell, Duffy, and Kidd Blood Groups of Jews Originating from 20 Countries," *Israel Journal of Medical Sciences*, 1984, 29:509–18; T. Cohen, C. Levene, Y. Yodfat, J. Fidel, Y. Friedlander, A. G. Steinberg, and C. Brautbar, "Genetic Studies on Cochin Jews in Israel: 1. Population Data, Blood Groups, Isoenzymes, and HLA Determinants," *American Journal of Medical Genetics*, 1980, 6:61–73.

E. Goldschmidt, K. Fried, A. G. Steinberg, and T. Cohen, "The Karaite Community of Iraq in Israel: A Genetic Study," *American Journal of Human Genetics*, 1976, 28:243–52; B. Bonné-Tamir, S. Ashbel, and R. Kenett, "Genetic Markers: Benign and Normal Traits of Ashkenazi Jews," in R. M. Goodman and A. G. Motulsky, (eds.), *Genetic Disorders Among Ashkenazi Jews*, 1979, Raven Press, New York; B. Bonné-Tamir, S. Ashbel, and J. Modai, "Genetic Markers in Libyan Jews," *Human Genetics*, 1977, 37:319–28; B. Bonné-Tamir, S. Ashbel, and S. Bar-Shani, "Ethnic Communities in Israel: The Genetic Blood Markers of the Babylonian Jews," *American Journal of Physical Anthropology*, 1978, 49:457–64; B. Bonné-Tamir, S. Ashbel, and S. Bar-Shani, "Ethnic Communities in Israel: The Genetic Blood Markers of the Moroccan Jews," *American Journal of Physical Anthropology*, 1978, 49:457–64; T. Cohen, B. Simhai, A. G. Steinberg, and C. Levene, "Genetic Polymorphisms Among Iranian Jews in Israel," *American Journal of Medical Genetics*, 1981, 8:181–90.

2. Mourant, 1954, *op. cit.*
3. Ottensooser, *et al., op. cit.*
4. Margolis, *et al.*, 1960b, *op. cit.*
5. B. Bonné, "Genes and Phenotypes in the Samaritan Isolate."
6. Bonné, *et al.*, 1970, *op. cit.*
7. Mourant, 1959, *op. cit.*
8. Levine, *et al.*, 1984, *op. cit.*

XIV. Serum and Red Cell Proteins

1. E. Goldschmidt, P. Bayani-Sioson, H. E. Sutton, K. Fried, A. Sandor, and N.

Block, "Haptoglobin Frequencies in Jewish Communities," *Annals of Human Genetics*, 1962, 26:39–45.

2. Bonné, *et al.*, "The Habbanite Isolate. I. Genetic Markers in the Blood."

3. E. Giblett, *Genetic Markers in Human Blood*, Oxford and Edinburgh: Blackwell, 1969.

4. B. Ramot, P. Duvdevani-Zikert, and G. Kende, "Haptoglobin and Transferrin Types in Israel," *Annals of Human Genetics*, London, 1962, 25:257–71; Goldschmidt *et al.*, 1962, *op. cit.*

5. Goldschmidt, *et al.*, 1962, *op. cit.*

6. Bonné, *et al.*, South Sinai Beduin: A Preliminary Report on Their Inherited Blood Factors."

7. Ramot, *et al., op. cit.*; Goldschmidt, *et al.*, 1962, *op. cit.*; M. Bajatzadeh and H. Walter, "Investigation on the Distribution of Blood and Serum Groups in Iran," *Human Biology*, 1969, 41:401–15.

8. T. Cohen, C. Levene, Y. Yodfat, J. Fidel, Y. Friedlander, A. G. Steinberg, and C. Brautbar, "Genetic Studies in Cochin Jews in Israel: 1. Population Data, Blood Groups, Isoenzymes, and HLA Determinants," *American Journal of Medical Genetics*, 1980, 6:61–73.

9. Bonné, *et al.*, 1970, *op. cit.*

10. Bonné, "Genes and Phenotypes in the Samaritan Isolate."

11. K. Fried, H. Block, E. Sutton, J. V. Neel, P. Bayani-Sioson, B. Ramot, and P. Duvdevani, "Haptoglobins and Transferrins," in E. Goldschmidt (ed.), *Genetics of Migrant and Isolate Populations*, New York: Williams and Wilkins Co., 1963.

12. A. G. Steinberg and B. Bonné-Tamir, "Gm and Inv [Km] Allotypes among Libyan and Ashkenazi Jews, and Armenians Living in Israel," *Human Genetics*, 1980, 55:391–95.

13. J. C. Stevenson, M. S. Schanfield, and S. G. Sandler, "Immunoglobulin Allotypes in Jewish Populations Living in Israel and the United States," *American Journal of Physical Anthropology*, 1985, 67:195–207.

14. A. G. Steinberg, C. Levene, Y. Yodfat, J. Fidel, C. Brautbar, and T. Cohen, "Genetic Studies on Cochin Jews in Israel. 2. Gm and Inv Data—Polymorphism for GM^3 and for GM^{1,17,21} Without GM (26)," *American Journal of Medical Genetics*, 1980, 6:75–81.

15. See note 13.

16. See note 13.

17. See note 14.

18. T. Cohen, B. Simhai, A. G. Steinberg, and C. Levene, "Genetic Polymorphisms Among Iranian Jews in Israel," *American Journal of Medical Genetics*, 1981, 8:181–90.

19. See note 13.

20. H. E. Schultze and J. F. Heremans, *Molecular Biology of Human Proteins. Vol. 1. Nature and Metabolism of Extracellular Proteins*, Amsterdam, London, and New York: Elsevier Publishing Company, 1966.

21. H. Cleve, B. Ramot, and A. G. Bearn, "Distribution of the Serum Group-Specific Components in Israel," *Nature*, London, 1962, 195:86–87.

22. Bajatzadeh and Walter, *op. cit.*

23. Bonné, "Genes and Phenotypes," 1966, *op. cit.*

24. M. Whittaker, "Frequency of Atypical Pseudocholinesterase in Groups in Individuals of Different Ethnographical Origin," *Acta Genetica*, Basel, 1968, 18:567–72.

25. A. Szeinberg, S. Pipano, M. Assa, J. H. Medalie, and H. N. Newfield, "High Frequency of Atypical Pseudocholinesterase Gene among Iraqi and Iranian Jews," *Clinical Genetics*, 1972, 3:123–27.

26. M. K. Bhasin and W. Fuhrmann, "Geographic and Ethnic Distribution of Some Red Cell Enzymes," *Humangenetik*, 1972, 14:204–13.

27. E. Kobyliansky, E. Micl'e, M. Goldschmidt-Nathan, B. Arensburg, and H. Nathan, "Phosphoglucomutase, Adenylate Kinase, and Acid Phosphatase Polymorphism in Some Jewish Populations of Israel," *Acta Anthropogenetica*, 1980, 4:29–36.

28. R. Ananthakrishnan, H. Walter, and T. Tsacheva, "Red Cell Enzyme Polymorphisms in Bulgaria," *Humangenetik*, 1972, 15:186–90.

29. Bonné, *et al.*, 1971, *op. cit.*

30. A. Szeinberg, S. Pipano, Z. Rozansky, and N. Rabia, "Frequency of Red Cell Adenosine Deaminase Phenotypes in Several Population Groups in Israel," *Human Heredity*, 1971, 21:357–61.

31. Ananthakrishnan, *et al.*, *op. cit.*

32. A. Szeinberg, "Polymorphic Evidence for a Mediterranean Origin of the Ashkenazi Community," in R. M. Goodman and A. G. Motulsky (eds.), *Genetic Diseases Among Ashkenazi Jews*, 1979, Raven Press, New York.

33. Szeinberg, *et al.*, *op. cit.*

34. See note 8.

35. A. Szeinberg and S. Tomashevsky-Tamir, "Red Cell Adenylate Kinase and Phosphoglucomutase Polymorphisms in Several Population Groups in Israel," *Human Heredity*, 1971, 21:289–96. See also note 23.

36. S. H. Chen and E. R. Giblett, "Polymorphism of Soluble Glutamic-Pyruvic Transaminase: A New Genetic Marker in Man," *Science*, 1971, 173:148.

37. M. Lahav and A. Szeinberg, "Red Cell Glutamic-Pyruvic Transaminase Polymorphism in Several Population Groups in Israel," *Human Heredity*, 1972, 22:533–38.

38. See note 37.

39. R. Golan, J. Ben-Ezzer, and A. Szeinberg, "Phosphoglycolate Phosphatase in Several Population Groups in Israel," *Human Heredity*, 1981, 31:89–92.

40. R. Golan, J. Ben-Ezzer, and A. Szeinberg, "Esterase D Polymorphism in Several Population Groups in Israel," *Human Heredity*, 1977, 27:298–304.

41. S. Welch and J. Lee, "The Population Distribution of Genetic Variants of Human Esterase D," *Humangenetik*, 1974, 24:329–31.

42. R. Golan, J. Ben-Ezzer, and A. Szeinberg, "Erythrocyte Glyoxalate I Polymorphism in Several Population Groups in Israel," *Human Heredity*, 1979, 57–60.

43. E. Beutler and F. Matsumoto, "Ethnic Variation in Red Cell Glutathione Peroxidase Activity," *Blood*, 1975, 46:103–10.

44. R. Golan, J. Ben-Ezzer, and A. Szeinberg, "Red Cell Glutathione Peroxidase in Various Jewish Ethnic Groups in Israel," *Human Heredity*, 1980, 30:136–41.

45. B. Bonné-Tamir, J. G. Bodmer, W. F. Bodmer, P. Pickbourne, C. Brautbar, E. Gazit, S. Nevo, and R. Zamir, "HLA Polymorphism in Israel. 9. An Overall Comparative Analysis," *Tissue Antigens*, 1978, 11:235–50.

46. See note 30.

XV. Glucose-6-Phosphate Dehydrogenase Deficiency

1. A. C. Allison, B. A. Askonas, N. A. Barnicot, B. S. Blumberg, and C. Krimbas, "Deficiency of Glucose-6-Phosphate Dehydrogenase in Greek Populations," *Annals of Human Genetics*, London, 1963, 26:237–41; E. Giblett, *Genetic Markers in Human Blood*, Philadelphia: F. A. Davis Co., 1969, pp. 444–82; A. H. Ragab, O. S. el-Alfi, and M. A. Abboud, "Incidence of Glucose-6-Phosphate Deficiency in Egypt," *American Journal of Human Genetics*, 1966, 18:21–25; B. Say, P. Ozand, I Berkel, and N. Cevik, "Erythrocyte G6PD Deficiency in Turkey," *Acta Paediatrica Scandinavica*, 1965, 54:319; Y. Shaker, A. Onsi, and R. Aziz, "The Frequency of Glucose-6-Phosphate Dehydrogenase Deficiency in the Newborn and Adults in Kuwait," *American Journal of Human Genetics*, 1966, 18:609–12; D. G. Walker and J. E. Bowman, "Glutathione Stability of the Erythrocytes in Iranians," *Nature*, London, 1959, 184:1325; C. Levene, A. G. Steinberg, Y. Friedlander, C. Brautbar, and T. Cohen, "Genetic Polymorphisms among Bukharan and Georgian Jews in Israel," *American Journal of Medical Genetics*, 1984, 19:623–41; T. Cohen, C. Levene, Y. Yodfat, J. Fidel, Y. Friedlander, A. G. Steinberg, and C. Brautbar, "Genetic Studies on Cochin Jews in Israel: 1. Population Data, Blood Groups, Isoenzymes, and HLA Determinants," *American Journal of Medical Genetics*, 1980, 6:61–73; J. L. Zaidman, H. Leiba, S. Scharf and I. Steinman, "Red Cell Glucose-6-Phosphate Dehydrogenase Deficiency in Ethnic Groups in Israel," *Clinical Genetics*, 1976, 9:131–33.

428

2. C. Sheba, "Environmental versus Ethnic Factors Determining the Frequency of G6PD Deficiency," in E. Goldschmidt (ed.), *Genetics of Migrant and Isolate Populations,* pp. 100–106.

3. C. Sheba, A. Szeinberg, B. Ramot, A. Adam, and I. Ashkenazi, "Epidemiologic Surveys of Deleterious Genes in Different Population Groups in Israel," *American Journal of Public Health,* 1962, 52:1101–6.

4. J. L. Zaidman, H. Leiba, S. Scharf, and I. Steinman, "Red Cell Glucose-6-Phosphate Dehydrogenase Deficiency in Ethnic Groups in Israel," *Clinical Genetics,* 1976, 9:131–33.

5. T. Cohen, "Genetic Markers in Migrants to Israel," *Israel Journal of Medical Science,* 1971, 7:1509–14.

6. T. Cohen, B. Simhai, A. G. Steinberg, and C. Levene, "Genetic Polymorphisms Among Iranian Jews in Israel," *American Journal of Medical Genetics,* 1981, 8:181–90.

7. Walker and Bowman, *op. cit.*

8. Sheba, *op. cit.*, p. 101.

9. Bonné, "Genes and Phenotypes in the Samaritan Isolate."

10. E. Goldschmidt, K. Fried, A. G. Steinberg, and T. Cohen, "The Karaite Community of Iraq in Israel: A Genetic Study," *American Journal of Human Genetics,* 1976, 28:243–52.

11. E. Goldschmidt, "Summary and Conclusions," in *Genetics of Migrant and Isolate Populations,* p. 204.

12. See note 4.

13. Bonné, *et al.,* "The Habbanite Isolate. 1. Genetic Markers in the Blood."

14. T. Cohen, C. Levene, Y. Yodfat, J. Fidel, Y. Friedlander, A. G. Steinberg, and C. Brautbar, "Genetic Studies on Cochin Jews in Israel: 1. Population Data, Blood Groups, Isoenzymes, and HLA Determinants," *American Journal of Medical Genetics,* 1980, 6:61–73.

15. Ragab, *et al., op. cit.*

XVI. PTC Taste Sensitivity

1. A. E. Allison, "Ability to Taste Phenylthiocarbamide Among Alaskan Eskimos and Other Populations," *Human Biology,* 1959, 31:352–58.

2. C. Sheba, I. Ashkenazi, and A. Szeinberg, "Taste Sensitivity to Phenylthiourea Among the Jewish Population Groups in Israel," *American Journal of Human Genetics,* 1961, 14:44–51.

3. Sandanha and Becak, 1959, reported by Sheba, *op. cit.*

4. N. Brand, "Taste Sensitivity and Endemic Goitre in Israel," *Annals of Human Genetics,* 1963, 26:321.

5. Bonné, "The Habbanite Isolate. III. Anthropometrics, Taste Sensitivity, and Color Vision."

6. Sheba, *et al., op. cit.*

7. Bonné, "Genes and Phenotypes in the Samaritan Isolate."

8. S. L. Lightman, D. L. Carr-Locke, and H. G. Pickles, "The Frequency of PTC Tasters and Males Defective in Color Vision in a Kurdish Population in Iran," *American Journal of Human Genetics,* 1970, 22:665–69.

XVII. Color Blindness

1. J. François, G. Verriest, V. Mortier, and R. Vanderdonck, "De la fréquence des dyschromatopsies congenitales chez l'homme," *Annales Oculistes,* Paris, 1957, 190:5–16; A. Adam, D. Doron, and R. Modan, "Frequencies of Protan and Deutan Alleles in Some Israel Communities and a Note on the Selection-Relaxation Hypothesis," *American Journal of Physical Anthropology,* 1967, 26:297–306; R. H. Post, "Population Differences in Red and Green Color Vision Deficiency: A Review, and a Query on Selection Relaxation, *Eugenics Quarterly,* 1962, 9:131–46; H. Kalmus, A. Amir, O. Levine, E. Barak, and E. Goldschmidt, "The Frequency of Inherited Defects of Color Vision in Some Israeli

Populations," *Annals of Human Genetics*, 1961, 25:51; H. Kalmus, A. Amir, O. Levine, E. Barak, E. Goldschmidt, and A. Adam, "Color Blindness," in Goldschmidt (ed.), *Genetics of Migrant and Isolate Populations*, pp. 280–81.

2. M. Siniscalco, "Linkage Data for G6PD Deficiency in Sardinian Villages," in Goldschmidt (ed.), *Genetics of Migrant and Isolate Populations*, pp. 106–14.

3. E. Goldschmidt, K. Fried, A. G. Steinberg, and T. Cohen, "The Karaite Community of Iraq in Israel: A Genetic Study," *American Journal of Human Genetics*, 1976, 28:243–52.

4. Adam, *et al., op. cit.*

5. Lightman, Carr-Locke, and Pickles, *op. cit.*

6. Post, *op. cit.*; Adam, *et al., op. cit.*

7. Bonné, "Genes and Phenotypes in the Samaritan Isolate."

8. Bonné, *et al.*, "The Habbanite Isolate. III. Anthropometrics, Taste Sensitivity, and Color Vision."

9. T. Cohen, C. Levene, Y. Yodfat, J. Fidel, Y. Friedlander. A. G. Steinberg, and C. Brautbar, "Genetic Studies on Cochin Jews in Israel: 1. Population Data, Blood Groups, Isoenzymes, and HLA Determinants," *American Journal of Medical Genetics*, 1980, 6:61–73.

XVIII. Genetic Distance between Jewish and Non-Jewish Groups

1. B. Bonné-Tamir, S. Ashbel, and R. Kenett, 1979, "Genetic Markers: Benign and Normal Traits of Ashkenazi Jews," in R. M. Goodman and A. G. Motulsky (eds.), *Genetic Diseases of Ashkenazi Jews*, New York: Raven Press.

2. A. K. Roychoudhury, "Genetic Distance between Jews and non-Jews of Four Regions," *Human Heredity*, 1982, 32:259–63.

3. D. Carmelli and L. L. Cavalli-Sforza, "The Genetic Origin of the Jews: A Multivariate Approach," *Human Biology*, 1979, 51:41–61.

4. L. L. Cavalli-Sforza and D. Carmelli, "The Ashkenazi Gene Pool: Interpretations," in R. M. Goodman and A. G. Motulsky (eds.), *Genetic Diseases Among Ashkenazi Jews*, New York: Raven Press, 1979, p. 101.

XIX. "Jewish" Diseases

1. Richard M. Goodman, *Genetic Disorders Among the Jewish People*, Baltimore: Johns Hopkins University Press, 1979.

2. A. de Vrties, M. Frank, O. Sperling, U. A. Liberman, and A. Atsmon, "Nephrolithiasis in a Subtropical Climate," *Proceedings of the 9th International Congress of Life Assurance Medicine*, Tel Aviv, 1968, pp. 132–42.

3. See note 1.

4. E. Goldschmidt, R. Lenz, and S. Merin, "Tay-Sachs Disease," in Goldschmidt (ed.), *Genetics of Migrant and Isolate Populations*, pp. 290–91; P. J. Kozinn, H Wiener, and P. Cohen, "Infantile Amaurotic Family Idiocy: A Genetic Approach," *Journal of Pediatrics*, 1957, 5:58–64.

5. Goldschmidt, *et al.*, 1963, *op. cit.*

6. J. Vecht, G. Bach, M. Zeigler, and M. Segal, "Tay-Sachs Disease Among Moroccan Jews," *Israel Journal of Medical Science*, 1983, 19:67–68.

7. N. C. Myrianthopoulos and S. M. Aronson, "Population Dynamics of Tay-Sachs Disease. I. Reproductive Fitness and Selection," *American Journal of Human Genetics*, 1966, 18:313–26.

8. N. C. Myrianthopoulos, A. F. Naylor, and S. M. Aronson, "Founder Effect in Tay-Sachs Disease Unlikely," *American Journal of Human Genetics*, 1972, 24:341–42.

9. G. A. Chase and V. A. McKusick, "Founder Effect in Tay-Sachs Disease," *American Journal of Human Genetics*, 1972, 24:339–40.

10. F. B. Livingstone, "The Founder Effect and Deleterious Genes," *American Journal of Physical Anthropology*, 1969, 30:55–60.

11. R. Myerowitz and N. D. Hogikyan, "Different Mutations in Ashkenazi Jewish and Non-Jewish French Canadians with Tay-Sachs Disease," *Science*, 1986, 232:1646–48.

12. D. A. Greenberg and M. M. Kaback, "Estimation of the Frequency of Hexosaminidase A Variant Alleles in the American Jewish Population," *American Journal of Human Genetics*, 1982, 34:444–51.

13. R. Navon and A. Adam, "Frequency of Hexosaminidase A Variant Alleles Among Ashkenazi Jews and Prenatal Diagnosis of G_{M2} Gangliosidosis," *American Journal of Human Genetics*, 1985, 37(s):1031–32.

14. D. Fabro, R. J. Desnick, and G. A. Grabowski, "Gaucher Disease: Genetic Heterogeneity Within and Among the Subtypes Detected by Immunoblotting," *American Journal of Human Genetics*, 1987, 40: 015–031.

15. K. Fried, "Population Study of Chronic Gaucher's Disease," *Israel Journal of Medical Science*, 1973, 9:1396–98.

16. Myrianthopoulos and Aronson, *op. cit.*

17. D. Fredrickson, "Sphingomyelin Lipidosis: Niemann-Pick Disease." In J. B. Stanbury, J. B. Wyngaarden, and D. S. Frederickson (eds.), *The Metabolic Basis of Inherited Disease*, 2nd ed., New York: McGraw-Hill, 1966.

18. T. Schaap and G. Bach, "Incidence of Mucopolysaccharidoses in Israel: Is Hunter Disease a "Jewish Disease"?" *Human Genetics*, 1980, 56:221–23.

19. J. Zlotogora, T. Schaap, M. Zeigler, and G. Bach, "Hunter Syndrome Among Ashkenazi Jews in Israel: Evidence for Prenatal Selection Favoring the Hunter Allele," *Human Genetics*, 1985, 71:329–32.

20. See note 17.

21. P. W. Brunt and V. A. McKusick, "Familial Dysautonomia: A Report of Genetic and Clinical Studies, with a Review of the Literature," *Medicine*, 1970, 49:343–71.

22. S. W. Moses, Y. Rotem, N. Jagoda, N. Talmor, F. Eichhorn, and S. Levine, "A Clinical, Genetic, and Biochemical Study of Familial Dysautonomia in Israel," *Israel Journal of Medical Science*, 1967, 358–71.

23. J. German, "Bloom's Syndrome. I. Genetic and Clinical Observations in the first 27 Patients," *American Journal of Human Genetics*, 1969, 21:11–17.

24. J. German, D. Bloom, E. Passarge, K. Fried, R. M. Goodman, I. Katzenellenbogen, Z. Laron, C. Legum, S. Levin, and J. Wahrman, "Bloom's Syndrome. VI. The Disorder in Israel and an Estimation of the Gene Frequency in the Ashkenazim," *American Journal of Human Genetics*, 1979, 29:553–62.

25. U. Seligsohn, "High Gene Frequency of Factor XI (PTA) Deficiency in Ashkenazi Jews," *Blood*, 1978, 51:1223–28.

26. P. W. Speiser, B. Dupont, P. Rubinstein, A. Piazza, A. Kastelan, and M. I. New, "High Frequency of Nonclassical Steroid 21-hydroxylase Deficiency," *American Journal of Human Genetics*, 1985, 37:650–67.

27. *Ibid.*

28. A. D. Korczyn, E. Kahana, N. Zilber, M. Streifler, R. Carasso, and M. Alter, "Torsion Dystonia in Israel," *Annals of Neurology*, 1980, 9:387–91.

29. O. Mizrahi and I. Ser, "Essential Pentosuria," in Goldschmidt (ed.), *Genetics of Migrant and Isolate Populations*, p. 300.

30. A. Szeinberg, "Biochemical Genetics and Prevention of Harmful Reactions to Drugs and Nutrition Products," in *Proceedings of the 9th International Congress of Life Assurance Medicine*, 1969, pp. 178–86; A. Szeinberg, B. E. Cohen, H. Boichis, S. Pollack, E. Bodonyi, N. Hirschorn, and R. Bar-Or, "Phenylketonuria Among Jews," in Goldschmidt (ed.), *Genetics of Migrant and Isolate Populations*, pp. 296–97.

31. B. E. Cohen, A. Szeinberg, Y. Levine, I. Peled, S. Pollack, M. Crispin, and M. Normand, "Phenylketonuria (PKU) in Israel," *Monograph on Human Genetics*, 1978, 9:95–101.

32. G. A. Chase and V. A. McKusick, "Founder Effect in Tay-Sachs Disease," *American Journal of Human Genetics*, 1972, 24:339–40.

33. See note 1.

34. U. Seligsohn, M. Shani, B. Ramot, A. Adam, and C. Sheba, "Dubin-Johnson Syndrome in Israel II. Association with Factor VII Deficiency," *Quarterly Journal of Medicine*, 1970, 34:569–84.

431

35. M. Shani, U. Seligsohn, E. Cilon, C. Sheba, and A. Adam, "Dubin-Johnson Syndrome in Israel. I. Clinical, Laboratory, and Genetic Aspects of 101 Cases," *Quarterly Journal of Medicine*, 1970, 34:569–84.

36. *Ibid.*

37. H. Heller, J. Gafni, and E. Sohar, "Familial Mediterranean Fever—A Disease Predominant in People of Mediterranean Stock," *Proceedings of the 9th International Congress of Life Assurance Medicine*, 1968, pp. 124–31.

38. *Ibid.*

39. M. Pras, N. Bronshpigel, D. Zemer, and J. Gafni, "Variable Incidence of Amyloidosis in Familial Mediterranean Fever Among Different Ethnic Groups," *Johns Hopkins Medical Journal*, 1982, 150:22–26.

40. B. Presentey and H. Joshua, "Peroxidase and Phospholipid Deficiency in Human Eosinophilic Granulocytes—A Marker in Population Genetics," *Experientia*, 1982, 38:628–29.

41. M. Feinaro and W. J. Alkan, "Familial Neutropenia in Jews of Yemenite Origin," *Proceedings of the 9th International Congress on Life Assurance Medicine*, 1968, pp. 172–77.

42. A. Shoenfeld, A. Weinberger, R. Avishar, R. Zamir, E. Gazit, H. Joshua, and J. Pinkhas, "Familial Leukopenia among Yemenite Jews," *Israel Journal of Medical Science*, 1978, 14:1271–74.

43. A. G. Steinberg, "Dependence of the Phenotype on Environment and Heredity," in Goldschmidt (ed.), *Genetics of Migrant and Isolate Populations*, pp. 133–43.

44. S. Levin, "Fibrocystic Disease of the Pancreas," in Goldschmidt (ed.), *ibid.*, pp. 294–95.

45. D. Katznelson and M. Ben-Yishay, "Cystic Fibrosis in Israel: Clinical and Genetic Aspects," *Israel Journal of Medical Science*, 1978, 14:204–11.

46. E. B. Hook and S. Harlap. "Differences in Maternal Age-Specific Rates of Down Syndrome Between Jews of European Origin and of North African or Asian Origin," *Teratology*, 1979, 20:243–48.

47. T. Sharav, "High-Risk Population for Down Syndrome: Orthodox Jews in Jerusalem," *American Journal of Mental Deficiency*, 1985, 89:559–61.

48. A. Weinberger, O. Sperling, M. Rabinovitz, S. Brosh, A. Adam, and A. De Vries, "Rarity of Cystinuria Type I Among Cystinuric Jews of Libyan Origin," *Israel Journal of Medical Science*, 1975, 11:1217.

49. ———. "High Frequency of Cystinuria among Jews of Libyan Origin," *Human Heredity*, 1974, 24:568–72.

50. D. J. Weatherall, "The Thalassemias," *Progress in Medical Genetics*, 1967, 5:8–51.

51. C. C. Plato, D. L. Rucknagel, and H. Gershowitz, "Studies on the Distribution of Glucose-6-Phosphate Dehydrogenase Deficiency, Thalassemia, and Other Genetics in Coastal and Mountain Villages of Cyprus," *American Journal of Human Genetics*, 1964, 16:267–82.

52. A. Pellicer, "Studies on Thalassemia, Glucose-6-Phosphate Dehydrogense Deficiency, and Sickle Cell Trait in the Province of Huelva (Spain)," *American Journal of Human Genetics*, 1969, 21:109.

53. Weatherall, 1967, *op. cit.*, p. 32.

54. C. Sheba, "Gene Frequencies in Jews," *The Lancet*, London, June 6, 1970, 2:1230–31.

55. A. Horowitz, T. Cohen, G. Goldschmidt, and C. Levene, "Thalassemia Types among Kurdish Jews in Israel," *British Journal of Haematology*, London, 1966, 12:555–68.

56. R. Zaizov and Y. Matoth, "α-Thalassemia in Yemenite and Iraqi Jews," *Israel Journal of Medical Science*, 1972, 8:11–17.

57. G. B. Sancar, D. B. Rausher, R. M. Baine, O. Platica, M. M. Cedeno, I. Nawabi, and R. F. Rieder, "Alpha-thalassemia in Ashkenazi Jews," *Annals of Internal Medicine*, 1983, 98:933–36.

58. V. M. Berginer and D. Abeliovich, "Genetics of Cerebrotendinous Xanthomatosis (CTX): An Autosomal Recessive Trait with High Gene Frequency in Sephardim of Moroccan Origin," *American Journal of Medical Genetics*, 1981, 10:151–57.

59. J. Zlotogora, G. Bach, Y. Barak, and E. Elian, "Metachromatic Leukodystrophy in the Habbanite Jew: High Frequency in a Genetic Isolate and Screening for Heterozygotes, *American Journal of Human Genetics*, 1980, 32:663–69.

60. K. Fried and G. Mundel, "High Incidence of Spinal Muscular Atrophy Type I (Werdnig-Hoffman Disease) in the Karaite Community in Israel," *Clinical Genetics*, 1977, 12:250–51.

61. W. Haenszel, "Cancer Mortality among U. S. Jews," *Israel Journal of Medical Science*, 1971, 7:1437–43.

62. A. Bartal, Z. Bentwich, N. Manny, and G. Izak, "Ethnical and Clinical Aspects of Chronic Lymphocytic Leukemia in Israel," *Acta Haematologica*, 1978, 60:161–71.

63. R. Steinitz and C. Costin, "Cancer in Jewish Immigrants," *Israel Journal of Medical Science*, 1971, 7:1414–26.

64. L. Bat, A. Pines, E. Ron, Y. Rosenblum, Y. Niv, and E. Shemesh, "Colorectal Adenomatous Polyps and Carcinoma in Ashkenazi and Non-Ashkenazi Jews in Israel," *Cancer*, 1986, 58:1167–71.

65. S.-T. Halfon, J. D. Kark, M. Baras, Y. Friedlander, and S. Eisenberg, "Smoking, Lipids, and Lipoproteins in Jerusalem 17-year-olds," *Israel Journal of Medical Science*, 1982, 18:1150–57.

66. L. Katz, R. Steinitz, and T. Sela, "Epidemiological Review of Breast Cancer in Israel," *Israel Journal of Medical Science*, 1981, 17:810–15.

67. See note 55.

68. S. Chaitchik, I. G. Ron, A. Baram, and M. Inbar, "Population Differences in Ovarian Cancer in Israel," *Gynaecologic Oncology*, 1985, 21:155–60.

69. S. Mor-Josef, S. O. Antby, and J. G. Schenker, "Trends in the Incidence of Ovarian Cancer in a Heterogenic Population (1960–1976)," *Gynaecolic Oncology*, 1985, 21:289–93.

70. S. Soichet, "Ethnic-related Incidence of Ovarian Carcinoma in New York City," *Israel Journal of Medical Science*, 1978, 14:363–69.

71. B. Ramot and E. E. Lash, "The Variable Expressivity of Malignant Lymphoma in the Israel Population," *Proceedings of the 9th International Congress of Life Assurance Medicine*, 1968, pp. 164–66.

72. J. Casper, "Epidemiology of Cancer of Uterine Cervix in Jewish Women," *Proceedings of the 9th International Congress of Life Assurance Medicine*, 1968, pp. 192–99.

73. *Loc. cit.*

74. Steinitz and Costin, *op. cit.*

75. H. Z. Suprun, J. Schwartz, and H. Spira, "Cervical Intraepithelial Neoplasia and Associated Condylomatous Lesions. A Preliminary Report on 4,764 Women from Northern Israel," *Acta Cytologica*, 1985, 29:334–40.

76. A. Baram, A. Galon, and A. Schachter, "Premalignant Lesions and Microinvasive Carcinoma of the Cervix in Jewish Women: An Epidemiological Study, *British Journal of Obstetrics and Gynecology*, 1985, 92:4–8.

77. A. Schachter and E. Avraham, "Changing Trends of Cervical Neoplasia in Israeli Jews," *The Lancet*, 1984, 2:1150.

78. J. Menczer, M. Modan, and L. Katz, "Cervical Carcinoma in Jewish Women," *The Lancet*, 1983, 1:875.

79. M. Shani, S. Schor, and B. Modan, "Some Epidemiologic Aspects of Acute Myocardial Infarction in Israel," *Chest*, 1975, 68:214–17.

80. H. Ungar, A. Laufer, and Z. Ben-Ishay, "Atherosclerosis and Myocardial Infarction in Various Jewish Groups in Israel," in Goldschmidt (ed.), *Genetics of Migrant and Isolate Populations*, pp. 120–27.

81. H. N. Newfeld, "Coronary Heart Disease—Genetic Aspects," *Circulation*, 1981, 64, Suppl 4:1–3.

82. U. Goldbourt and J. H. Medalie, "High Density Lipoprotein Cholesterol and Incidence of Coronary Heart Disease—The Israel Ischemic Heart Disease Study," *American Journal of Epidemiology*, 1979, 109:296–308.

83. S.-T. Halfon, B. M. Rifkind, S. Harlap, N. A. Kaufmann, M. Baras, P. E. Slater, G. Halperin, S. Eisenberg, A. M. Davies, and Y. Stein, "Plasma Lipids and Lipoproteins

in Adult Jews of Different Origins: The Jerusalem Lipid Research Clinic Prevalence Study," *Israel Journal of Medical Science*, 1982, 18:1113–20.

84. S.-T. Halfon, S. Eisenberg, M. Baras, A. M. Davies, G. Halperin, and Y. Stein, "Plasma Cholesterol, Triglyceride and High-density Lipoprotein-Cholesterol Levels in 17-year-old Jerusalem Offspring of Jews from 19 Countries of Birth," *Israel Journal of Medical Science*, 1982. 18:1121–29.

85. See note 83.

86. A. M. Cohen, "Lessons from Diabetes in Yemenites," *Israel Journal of Medical Science*, 1971, 7:1554–61.

87. *Loc. cit.*

88. A. M. Cohen, J. Fidel, B. Cohen, A. Furst, and S. Eisenberg, "Diabetes, Blood Lipids, Lipoproteins, and Change of Environment: Restudy of the 'New Immigrant Yemenites' in Israel," *Metabolism*, 1979. 28:716–28.

89. J. H. Medalie, C. Papier, J. B. Herman, *et al.*, "Diabetes Mellitus Among 10,000 Adult Men I. Five-year Incidence and Associated Variables," *Israel Journal of Medical Science*, 1974, 10:681–97.

90. See note 1.

91. M. Donchin, J. D. Kark, J. H. Abramson, L. Epstein, and C. Hopp, "Prevalence of Diabetes Among Ethnic Groups in Jerusalem: The Kiryat Hayovel Community Health Study," *Israel Journal of Medical Science*, 1984, 20:578–83.

92. T. Cohen, "Juvenile Diabetes in Israel," *Israel Journal of Medical Science*, 1971, 7:1558–61.

93. Z. Hrubec and G. S. Omenn, "Evidence of Genetic Predisposition to Alcoholic Cirrhosis and Psychosis: Twin Concordances for Alcoholism and Its Biological End Points by Zygosity among Male Veterans," *Alcoholism, Clinical, and Experimental Research*, 1981, 5:207–14.

94. D. W. Goodwin, "Alcoholism and Genetics: The Sins of the Fathers," *Archives of General Psychiatry*, 1985, 42:171–74.

95. D. W. Goodwin, F. Schulsinger, N. Moller, *et al.*, "Drinking Problems in Adopted and Nonadopted Sons of Alcoholics," *Archives of General Psychiatry*, 1974, 31:164–69.

96. M. M. Hyman, M. A. Zimmerman, C. Gurioli, and A. Helrich, *Drinkers, Drinking, and Alcohol-related Mortality and Hospitalizations*, New Brunswick, N.J.: Rutgers Center of Alcohol Studies, 1980.

97. L. Masse, J. M. Juillan, and A. Chisloup, "Trends in Mortality from Cirrhosis of the Liver, 1950–1971," *World Health Statistical Report*, 1976, 29:40–67.

98. A. Weil, *The Natural Mind*, Boston: Houghton Mifflin Company, 1972.

99. M. Keller, "The Great Jewish Drink Mystery," *British Journal of Addiction*, 1970, 64:287–96.

100. S. Bainwol and C. F Gressard, "The Incidence of Jewish Alcoholism: A Review of the Literature," *Journal of Drug Education*, 1985, 15:217–24.

101. C. R. Snyder, "Culture and Jewish Sobriety: The Ingroup-Outgroup Factor," in *Society, Culture, and Drinking Patterns (I)*, D. J. Pittman and C. R. Snyder (eds.), Carbondale, Illinois: Southern Illinois University Press, 1962.

102. R. Patai, *The Jewish Mind*, New York: Charles Scribner's Sons, 1977.

103. D. B. Kandel and M. Sudit, "Drinking Practices among Urban Adults in Israel: A Cross-cultural Comparison," *Journal of Studies on Alcohol*, 1982, 43:1–16.

104. C. R. Snyder, P. Palgi, P. Eldar, and B. Elian, "Alcoholism among the Jews in Israel: A Pilot Study. I. Research Rationale and a Look at the Ethnic Factor," *Journal of Studies of Alcohol*, 1982, 43:623–54.

105. T. Gilat, J. Ribak, Y. Benaroya, Z. Zemishlany, and I. Weissman, "Ulcerative Colitis in the Jewish Population of Tel Aviv Jafo. I. Epidemiology," *Gastroenterology*, 1974, 66:335–42.

106. T. Gilat and P. Rozen, "Epidemiology of Crohn's Disease and Ulcerative Colitis: Etiologic Implications," *Israel Journal of Medical Science*, 1979, 15:305–8.

107. J. Krawiecz, H. S. Odes, P. Lasry, P. Krugliak, and S. Weitzman, "Aspects of the Epidemiology of Crohn's Disease in the Jewish Population in Beer Sheva, Israel," *Israel Journal of Medical Science*, 1984, 20:16–21.

108. R. M. Goodman, "A Perspective on Genetic Diseases among the Jewish People," in R. M. Goodman and A. G. Motulsky (eds.), *Genetic Diseases Among Ashkenazi Jews*, New York: Raven Press, 1969, p. 10.

XX. Conclusions to Part III

1. A. Szeinberg, "Investigation of Genetic Polymorphic Traits in Jews," *Israel Journal of Medical Science*, 1973, 9:1171–80.

2. B. Bonné-Tamir, M. J. Johnson, A. Natali, D. C. Wallace, and L. L. Cavalli-Sforza, "Human Mitochondrial DNA Types in Two Israeli Populations—A Comparative Study at the DNA Level," *American Journal of Human Genetics*, 1986, 38:341–51.

3. D. Tills, A. Warlow, A. E. Mourant, A. C. Kopec, O. G. Edholm, and G. Garrard, "The Blood Groups and Other Hereditary Factors of Yemenite and Kurdish Jews," *Annals of Human Biology*, 1977, 4:259–74.

4. S. Karlin, *et al., American Journal of Human Genetics*, 1979, 31:341.

5. A. E. Mourant, A. C. Kopec, and K. Domaniewska-Sobczak, *The Genetics of the Jews*, 1978, Oxford: Oxford University Press.

6. N. E. Morton, R. Kenett, S. A. Yee, and R. Lew, "Bioassay of Kinship in Populations of Middle Eastern Origin and Controls," *Current Anthropology*, 1982, 23:157–62.

7. R. Chakraborty and K. M. Weiss, "Comments to N. E. Morton *et al.* Paper," *Current Anthropology*, 1982, 23:163–64.

8. E. Kobyliansky and G. Livshits, "Genetic Composition of Jewish Populations: Diversity and Inbreeding," *Annals of Human Biology*, 1983, 10:453–64.

9. S. Karlin, R. Kenett, and B. Bonné-Tamir, "Analysis of Biochemical Genetic Data on Jewish Populations. II. Results and Interpretations of Heterogeneity Indices and Distance Measures with Respect to Standards," *American Journal of Human Genetics*, 1979, 31:341–65.

10. A. Szeinberg, in *Genetic Diseases Among Ashkenazic Jews*, R. M. Goodman and A. G. Motulsky (eds.), New York: Raven Press, 1979, pp. 79–81.

Index